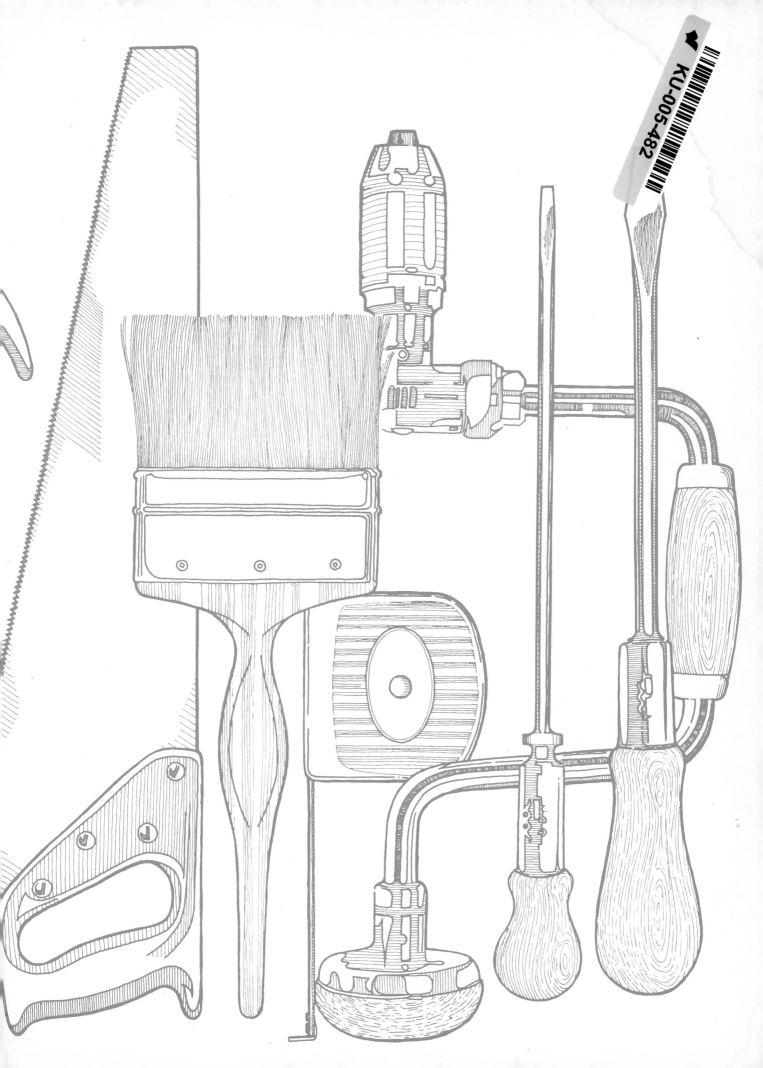

Golden Homes
Do-it-Yourself
COMPENDIUM

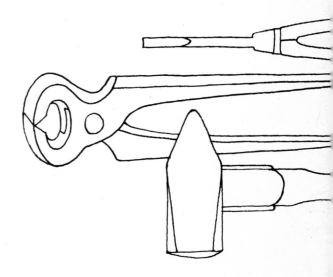

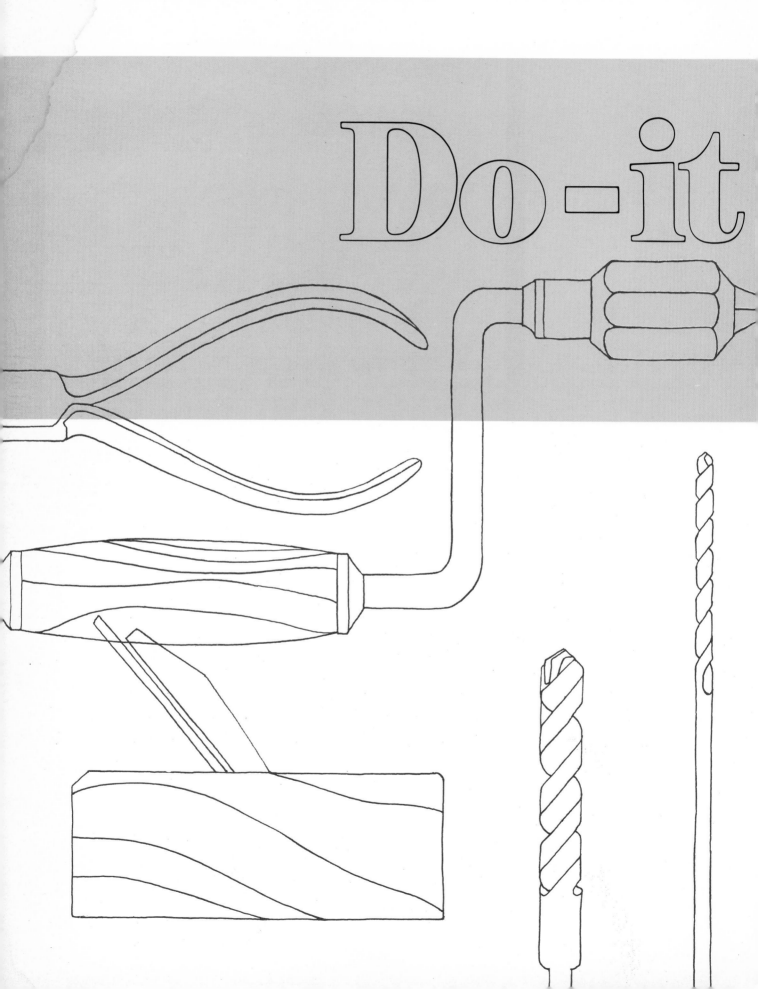

Do-it

Golden Homes Do-It-Yourself COMPENDIUM

Marshall Cavendish

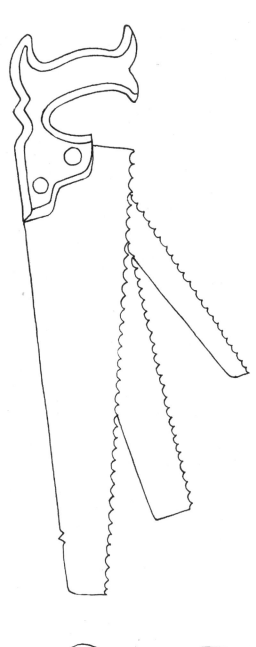

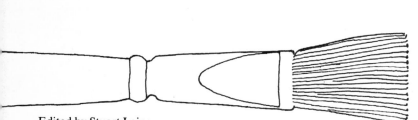

Edited by Stuart Laing

Published by Marshall Cavendish Books Limited,
58 Old Compton Street,
London W1V 5PA

First printing 1978
Second printing 1980
Third printing 1983

Printed and bound by L.E.G.O., Vicenza, Italy

ISBN 0 85685 493 X

Introduction

More and more people are now making the effort to maintain, furnish and decorate their homes, either from necessity or for their own pleasure. In both cases this book can provide you with the necessary information, advice and practical help and, after all, good advice is worth its weight in gold.

Improving and decorating your house can cost a lot of money; it is important to know which costs can be cut and which should not be. Lots of improvements, for instance, are subsidised by your local council.

The book goes through the reader's home, from hall via living room to kitchen, bathroom, bedrooms and up to the attic. Advice is given about each room with basic suggestions, alternatives, choice possibilities and practical solutions. The demands which the modern kitchen must satisfy are treated in various structural ways, and close attention is paid to the most important living areas – the sitting and living rooms. What are the various things you can do with a bathroom, loft or attic?

The *Golden Homes Do It Yourself Compendium* includes almost anything that you can do yourself. Lots of colour photographs show constructions in various stages, and the clear diagrams are invaluable aids to what is possible inside and outside the home.

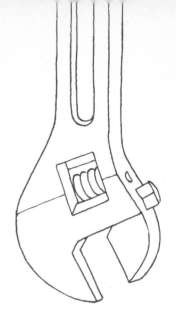

Contents

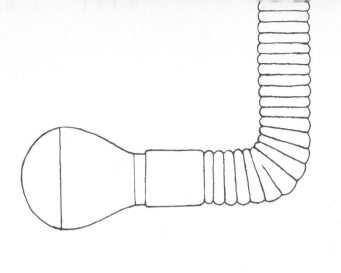
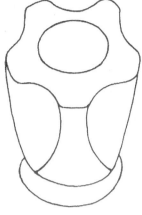
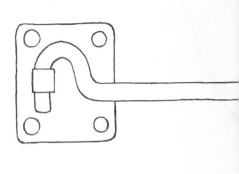

Halls that invite

The first impression anyone gets of your home is the hall. So ideally it should be bright, warm, welcoming, uncluttered, and draughtproof. But the one so many of us end up with is a dimly-lit corridor stacked with muddy shoes and prams or bicycles. Even the most unpromising hall can be considerably improved and brought up to the same decorative standard as the rest of the house.

Although it is really part of the exterior of the house, the front door is nevertheless an important part of any hall. The colour chosen for the outside should team not only with the colour of the external walls, but also with the colour of the hall.

House numbers of a decent size make identification from car or cab that much easier. Brass and chrome reflect brightly in headlights but need regular polishing while black numerals, though less reflective, need little maintenance.

Other door furniture is just as important. A well-designed set of knob, letterbox, and knocker, whether made of brass in an old design, or more modern anodised aluminium, adds importance to any door. One of the easiest mistakes to make is choosing a letterbox that is too narrow, so that wide envelopes have to be bent or crushed when inserted.

Burglar- and draught-proofing

Even more important to most of us than design considerations is the safety of our property. A good mortise deadlock, therefore, is vital. The kind of lock that is opened merely by inserting a key and giving it a half-turn to pull back the lever can be too easily opened with a piece of mica or thin plastic by anyone so inclined.

A front door is also one of the most likely places for cold air to enter the house. It has been estimated that the cracks and chinks round the average front door add up to an opening of 690 sq mm (27 sq in). If a wind of only ten miles an hour is blowing, this will let through about 1,224 m (2000 cu ft) of cold air an hour. Obviously, then, draught-

proofing this particular door is one of the most worthwhile household jobs you can do.

An inner, or secondary front door (where this is possible) is a structural alteration that improves the comfort of a house out of all proportion to its cost. As well as making an even more efficient job of the draught-stripping which you should treat the front door to, it performs a function similar to that of double glazing. The 'sandwich' of air between the two doors blocks off noise, and also helps to cut down on any condensation. Warmth from your heating system is kept inside the house more efficiently, and the area between the doors can serve as a handy little vestibule where people can hang their coats and hats, leave umbrellas, and wipe their feet before entering the rest of the house.

For the sake of your decoration have a door-stop or rubber buffer fixed to the appropriate skirting board. If an inner door is glazed, a cross bar at some point will help make it more visible to children.

If installing an inner door is impossible or just undesirable, a thick, heavy curtain can be used provided it does not block the source of light. Even this will cut down on heat loss and help to prevent draughts.

Flooring materials

Flooring must be tough, especially in halls, staircases and living rooms, where there is more traffic than anywhere else in the house. Another point to note, particularly relevant in a small area, is that the hall and staircase should be floored in the same material, or, if this is not possible, at least in the same colour to give a sense of continuity. And when you are considering what colour to use, remember that some colours or patterns are more likely to conceal dirt than others.

Right: *The hallway is one area of any house where you can afford to experiment with strong colours.*

In a flat anywhere above ground level most of the dirt will have been walked off on the communal stairs. This means if you are choosing a carpet for a town house hall, pick one of the darker colours if it is to be plain, or one with discreet patterns, perhaps in two tones of the same colour, or in two neutrals, like a grey and dark beige mix. Tight little geometric shapes, which might include floral designs, or elegant stripes, look a lot better on stairs than splashy abstracts or wreaths of flowers. In a country house, where dirt is less likely to be a problem than in a city, or in an upstairs flat, lighter colours are possible, though it is still worth remembering that these floors are always the ones that will get the hardest wear in the house.

In any case, whatever the colour or pattern of the carpet chosen, the quality should definitely be heavy duty. Wool carpets have a

grading system, so that you know exactly where you are. But there is no such system for carpets made of synthetic fibre. Your best safeguard here is to go to a reputable store and tell them exactly where you plan to use the carpet.

Sisal makes an excellent hall flooring, not only because of its toughness, but also because its tweedy flecked look is also dirt-concealing. If, as often happens, you have had to buy the stair carpet 'with the house' as part of the fixtures and fittings, covering the hall with matching sisal achieves a unified look. And it is a lot cheaper than lashing out on a matching carpet. Sisal is, however, unsuitable for stairs, because of its slipperiness.

Linoleum or vinyl can also be used for the hall floor and they should be heavy-duty grade. As with carpets, plain colourings or

unobtrusive patterns look best in narrow or small halls. But in a wider or bigger room all sorts of elegant effects can be achieved with tiles laid in formal patterns, as banding or bordering, or sometimes simply with one random dark tile here and there. In the halls of country houses, natural materials like flag-stones or quarry tiles look good.

If wood or cork is used for a hall floor, it must be very carefully sealed if dirt and grime are not to penetrate. This usually means annual resealing. Wooden stairs can have great charm (particularly in the country) and it is a lot cheaper to strip and seal the wood of your stairs than it is to buy carpeting. But wooden stairs are noisy and, if the house has more than two floors, may look a bit bleak. Carpeted stairs are softer and safer, especially if there are young children about.

Whatever flooring you choose try to have a

Left: Warm-toned elegance for this inviting hallway. Furniture and ornaments are kept to a minimum but are striking and harmonious.

Above: This doorway is given importance through its two tones and framing archway.

'well' for the doormat by the front door. This prevents the mat skidding under anyone and looks far neater.

Durable wall finishes

Like the floor, the walls of a hall have to stand up to knocks, bangs, and dirt. Decorating a hall and staircase is expensive if done professionally and, for the do-it-yourselfer, can be more difficult and time-consuming than any other room in the house. So it is worth picking a finish that will stand up to a lot of wear.

Wall fabrics, such as hessian, are good-looking, long-lasting, and do a good job of hiding or holding together defective plaster-work. When you use hard, shiny flooring like tiles, wall fabrics add a welcome softness of texture. Unfortunately, hessians are expensive, but some of them can be painted over when they are dirty.

The 'poor man's alternative' is a scrubbable vinyl. These have improved enormously in recent years, and one or two ranges now simulate anything from silk to Japanese grass-cloth almost undetectably. They are also available in a wide range of patterns, but on the whole these tend to look less attractive than the plainer ones.

Wallpaper in a hall can get easily torn, and emulsion paint in a pale colour often seems too unemphatic. One advantage of using gloss paint is that it can be washed over.

Like other rooms which you pass through quickly, halls can be decorated in stronger, brighter colours and tones than those which you would pick for a room where you might spend several hours at a stretch. Many halls are in themselves gloomy because of the lack of natural daylight. But again, warm colours help counteract this impression. In a north-facing (cold) hall, especially, colours like tomato red, orange or yellow give a cheerful look. These colours also look quite attractive under artificial lighting.

Sometimes, a hall may have distinctive architectural features; in such a case, unobtrusive colouring should be used to allow elegance to speak for itself. However, painting a pretty cornice white, against a deeper wall or ceiling colour, will give this its due emphasis. It is always best, where possible, to continue the hall colouring up the stairs. But if there is a natural break in the form of an arch or architrave, then the wall finish can be changed.

Lighting

A blaze of golden lamplight always looks welcoming on a cold night, but good strong

Right: A mini-cloakroom for a lobby. A few essential outdoor clothes can be curtained off for convenience, and keep the hall looking tidy.

lighting in halls is important for other reasons. Inadvertent accidents caused by stumbling over misplaced toys can be avoided and if your stairs end up in a very small hall it helps prevent any member of the family from crashing headlong down the stairs into the door.

A hall is one of the few rooms where overhead lighting is best, partly because of the wider throw of light it will give, and partly because there is no danger of it being knocked down, or cutting into wall space. Several over-head lights work far better than one, because their beams will interplay attractively. Down-lighters with focussing lampholders are particularly effective here.

For the stairs, the important thing is that both treads *and* risers are clearly defined. Over-head lighting alone will give a 'flat' look, and this may prove deceptively dangerous, especially to old people.

Storage

Priority storage for the hall is somewhere to house hats, coats and boots. Almost as important is storage space for larger items like bicycles or prams. If there is a lot of space available, the hall can also be used for storing general clutter like fishing rods, suitcases, sewing machines, and so forth.

In a long narrow hall, there is often little room for even minimal storage. In this case, coat and hat hooks will have to do. If you have an inner door, site them within this vestibule. Sometimes, with this sort of hall, there is a half-landing which can act as an auxiliary hall. You might try to have a cupboard for outdoor clothing here.

A useful extra in such a cupboard is a small, low-watt electric heater to dry off damp garments. It is best sited at floor level, because heat rises, and should be adequately safeguarded in case a piece of clothing falls on it. The hot-pipe type of radiator is even safer, and can serve the same purpose.

Where possible, a pram shed outside the house makes the best home for baby carriages and bicycles. It has the added advantage that no wheel dirt is brought into the house.

In many houses, there is sufficient space under the stairs to make a good-size cupboard. Sometimes this is even large enough to make into a mini-room such as a little sewing corner complete with machine, worktable and sewing drawers for instance, or a tiny study with desk, telephone, pinboard and filing wall, or even a shower.

In most halls, a safe rule is to keep accessories as unobtrusive as possible. A hall is, after all, a place of passage. It is also primarily a place for taking off outer clothing and for expansive gestures of welcome, so that anything delicate or fragile that can be knocked over easily, in all probability, *will* be knocked down.

The most important accessories are often a mirror, somewhere to stack letters, some kind of shelf or drawer fitment for keys, scissors, string, dog leads or any other vaguely communal property. If possible, try to provide a place to sit—especially important if the telephone is in the hall. The hall is also a good place for any wall collection, from prints to exotic tapestries.

A mirror in the hall can be a good deal more than something for a last-minute check on face or hair. To double the width of a narrow hall, use mirror all down one side, or mirror panels between louvres or pillars. A huge old mirror has more or less the same effect.

A table for letters can be something as simple as a shelf above a radiator. But before installing the radiator, with or without its overshelf, check that it is not too near the front door. Remember you might want to allow a pram through. A shelf above a storage radiator can sometimes be extended into a longer wall fitment, with narrow cupboards flanking the radiator itself so that it appears built-in.

One section of these cupboards could be kept to a lower level and the top covered with a cushion pad, so that it can be used as seating. Alternatively, narrow bench or pew type seating is often possible. A good-looking settee may be expensive, but other narrow seating can often be bought—or made—cheaply, then painted, stained or lacquered to match the decor.

Halls and landings are excellent places to hang collections of prints or pictures—and the halls, like cloakrooms, are often the place for anything that is 'amusing' rather than simply expensive. Again, a good strong colour or fabric background will enhance anything from a collection of Victorian cigarette cards to a shell collage. A wide hall can double as a library, taking a whole wall-ful of books.

Left: A light and bright treatment for a spacious hall. The flooring and colour scheme flow from hall to living room, creating a sense of continuity, and the plants enhance the decor.

Dealing with problem halls

Some halls have ceilings that are too high. You can install a false (lowered) ceiling which means that you will then be able to safely recess the down-lighters. Or you can paint the ceiling in dark or receding colours and focus a few spotlights downwards from high on the walls, so that the ceiling 'disappears' altogether.

Other halls may be too long and narrow. Try extending the floor colouring up a few inches on the walls on each side, using a different or lighter tone above. Or use mirror down one wall with, perhaps, a bamboo or leafy paper opposite.

Some halls have all the charm and character of a shoebox! You could add interest by panelling the back of the front door or painting a bullseye or dragon on it. You could also put in a hardboard arch just before the stairs start to give an elegant 'Georgian' effect.

Yet other halls have too many doors, and this could mean draughts. If you can, block up one or two and paint or paper over them. Occasionally, a cupboard and alcove or shelves can be fitted within the door archi-trave. These can be made especially attractive by fitting them with concealed lighting.

Some halls are simply too small. One drastic solution is to get rid of the hall and have a larger living room instead, with the stairs rising out of it, and a secondary, inner door cutting off the noise and cold from outside. In most two-storeyed houses, removing the existing living room wall is a massive knocking-through job. But in homes where this wall is not supporting a wall immediately above it, the idea is worth serious thought.

Below: A cool and unfussy modern hallway. Notice the open-fronted storage unit by the door to hold the telephone, directories and so on, and the recessed lighting for subtle effect.

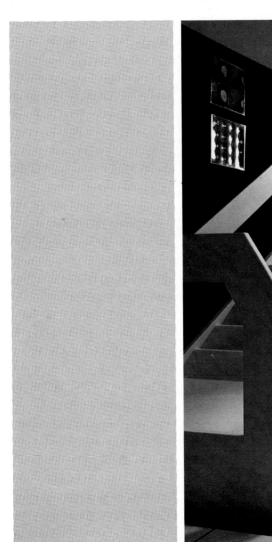

Easy-build streamlined staircase

Simple and stylish, an open-riser staircase will add a note of distinction to your home. With the right techniques you can build yourself an attractive and streamlined staircase.

The building of an open-riser staircase is a major construction job which has to be carried out accurately to achieve a good result, as well as to conform to any building regulations that apply in your case. It is a long and heavy job, and you may need assistance at certain stages.

There are two basic designs for open-risers. The most common one is where the steps, or *treads*, are supported at their ends by *strings*, timber pieces that run the whole length of the staircase. Housings are cut into the strings to accommodate the treads. In the second design the treads are supported from underneath by means of long timber pieces called *spines*.

For either design a power saw is virtually a necessity and for the first design a power-driven router, to cut the housings in the strings that take the ends of the treads, is a great advantage. An alternative method of cutting the housings is, however, given below. An electric orbital sander will considerably simplify the job of finishing the staircase.

Hardwood is the ideal timber for the staircase, 250mm × 40mm (10in × 1½in) being a size that will give solid construction. Softwood can be used, but unless it is an unusually strong type such as parana pine or British Columbian pine, the size should be increased slightly. For example, if common redwood or whitewood is used, a size of 250mm × 50mm (10in × 2in) is more suitable. These sizes apply to strings or spines and treads alike, unless the treads are unusually wide.

Technical terms

You will need to understand a few technical terms when planning your staircase (see Fig. 1).

Going is the horizontal distance between the front edge of one tread and the front edge of the next.

Right: An attractive and solid open-riser, its timber used perfectly to match the rest of the room. Here the treads are fixed to the strings with metal angle brackets.

Rise is the vertical distance between the face on one tread and the face of the next.

The pitch line is an imaginary line drawn through the top facing edge of each tread. This indicates the angle at which the staircase slopes.

Construction requirements

In Britain, all new constructions must conform to the requirements laid down in the Building Regulations. In the case of open-risers, the requirements are complicated but the basic ones are that:
each step must be level,
all steps must be of a similar rise,
the going of each step must be the same,
each step must overlap the next, on a plan view, by 16mm (⅝in) as shown in Fig. 1.

In addition to these basic items there are more complex requirements.

Sufficient headroom must be provided. Measured vertically from the pitch line, the clearance must be at least 2m (6ft 6in) to the ceiling. Measured at right angles to the pitch line, the clearance must be at least 1.5m (5ft) to the ceiling.

All staircases must be enclosed on both sides either by two walls or a wall on one side and a baluster on the other or balusters on both sides. A baluster or railing, this must be at least 840mm (33in) high, measured vertically from the pitch line. At landings the minimum height is 900mm (35in).

Fig.1. *A cross-section through part of an open-riser. In Britain each tread must overlap the one below it by at least 16mm (⅝in).*

Fig.2. *A triangular hardboard or plywood template is used to mark out the positions of the treads on the strings of an open-riser.*

In Britain, the Building Regulations also dictate the sizes of the rise and the going. There are two sets of regulations applying to private open-riser staircases, i.e. those in domestic use and 'common' open-risers—those used in public buildings. Be sure to consult the correct set. For private open-riser the minimum going is 220mm (8.7in) and the maximum rise is also 220mm (8.7in).

In addition, your staircase must conform to a certain formula. The sum of the going of a step plus twice its rise should not be less than 550mm (22in) and not more than 700mm (27.6in).

The pitch of the staircase will also dictate the rise and going you use. Private open-risers must not have a pitch of more than 42° to the horizontal. Therefore you cannot work to the maximum rise of 220mm (8.7in) and the minimum going of 220mm (8.7in) as this will give you too steep a pitch.

It is illegal in Britain to have an open-riser staircase leading to an attic unless there is some alternative means of leaving the attic, such as an external fire escape.

There is no simple formula for planning open-riser stairs. Take all the considerations given above into account when making your dimensional drawing for presentation to your local planning officer. He will tell you whether or not your planned staircase meets all the requirements.

Measuring the stairway

If your open-riser is to replace an ordinary staircase you may be able to use the same dimensions for the new construction as were used for the old. For example, the rise of the old staircase may be suitable to allow you to position the new treads in the same place as the old. You cannot, of course, simply remove the riser from an ordinary staircase to give you an open-riser staircase. This would make the whole structure come loose and fall apart.

If the dimensions do not conform, or the staircase is a new feature, then the first step is to measure the overall length of the stairway.

To do this, measure accurately the distance between the floors that the open-riser is to connect. You must make sure that you allow for any slope on the floor, or your height measurement will be out. Make a scaled and dimensioned drawing showing these two levels. Take the maximum permitted rise

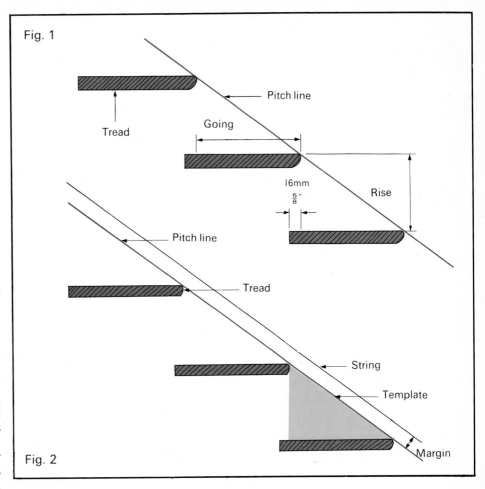

Fig. 1

Tread

Pitch line

Going

16mm
⅝"

Rise

Pitch line

Tread

String

Template

Margin

Fig. 2

between one step and another and divide this into the overall rise—the distance between the two floor levels. This will give you the minimum number of treads you can use. From this, you can calculate the minimum overall going of the staircase—the horizontal distance between one end of the staircase and the other.

Once the overall rise and going have been calculated check that the headroom this construction will allow conforms to the regulations. To do this, first mark on the lower floor the position of the bottom of the planned staircase. From this point, to the edge of the upper floor level, stretch a length of string, fixed at the ends with nails. Measure the headroom from this string, both vertically from it and at right angles to it. Use a steel tape rule to do this.

If the headroom is too tight, reduce the overall going if you can. If there is plenty of headroom, you may wish to increase the size of the treads or decrease the rise between each of them to, ideally, about 190mm (7½in). This will make the staircase easier to ascend and descend.

Having made these calculations, check that they conform to the formula for private open-risers given earlier. For example, if the overall rise is 2.20m (79in) the number of rises will be ten, with an individual rise of

220mm (7 16/16 in). If the overall going is 2.50m (80½in) this will give you ten goings at 250mm (9⅘in.) individual going. Twice the individual rise is 440mm (17¼in). This, plus one individual going adds up to 690mm (27⅛in). This figure is more than 550mm (21⅜in) and less than 700mm (27½in) so this particular design conforms to the requirements.

The final step in ensuring that the staircase conforms to the British Building Regulations is to check the pitch of the staircase. It must not exceed 42°. You can do this simply by laying a chain-store protractor on your scale drawing.

Design considerations

There are two basic designs of open-riser staircases. In the first the ends of the treads are housed in channels cut in the strings, or long timber side supports. In the second the treads are supported from underneath by means of spines. Triangular blocks of wood are fixed to the top edge of the spines so that the treads are horizontal. The use of strings gives better fixing for the handrails and balusters—but this is not an insurmountable problem if you want spines.

If you design your staircase with spines, you must use more than one spine. If only one spine is used, the treads would create excessive leverage on the spine if you put your

15

weight on one end of them.

Setting out the tread supports

In both types of staircase, the angles for making out the supports to show the positions of the treads have to be determined. This is done by using *similar triangles*. A similar triangle is one that has the same angles as another triangle but is larger or smaller than it.

In this case, the distance between the treads is estimated by drawing a similar triangle to that formed by the planned pitch of the staircase, the floor and a vertical line to the floor from the upper floor (the one to which the staircase will run). The two sides of the triangle that meet at right angles should be as long as the planned rise and going of the individual treads.

Make a template, sometimes known as a pitch board in this context, to match these sizes. This can be cut from hardboard or plywood.

If strings are used to support the treads the next step is to mark the distance you require between the top edge of the treads and the top of the strings. This distance is known as the *margin*. Mark it lightly with a marking gauge, or with a pencil and a strip of wood cut to the width of the margin. Along this line mark off distances that equal the longest side of the triangular template you have cut.

Then lay the template along the marked line between the stepped off points, with the longest side against the line. Draw a line on the string along the bottom edge of the template. This will indicate where the top edge of the tread will come (see Fig. 2).

Then mark on the strings the cross-section of the treads. Use a piece of the material you intend to use for the treads as a template. Mark out this section tight—the timber will be cleaned up later and it is desirable that the treads should fit tightly into the strings.

If spines are to be used to support the treads, step off the length of the longest side of the triangular template on the top edge of the spines. Do this with the planks laid together and their faces butting. Square lines through these marked points. This will indicate where the top edge of the triangular support blocks should meet the spines.

The triangular template can also be used to mark the angle at which the support pieces, either strings or spines, meet the floor. Lay the template on the pieces at the correct point with the longest side parallel to the top edge of the support piece. The side that indicates the going on the template gives the required angle for the line where the support piece meets the floor. The side that indicates the rise on the template gives the angle for a vertical end to the support pieces, for example for the mortise-and-tenon joint used

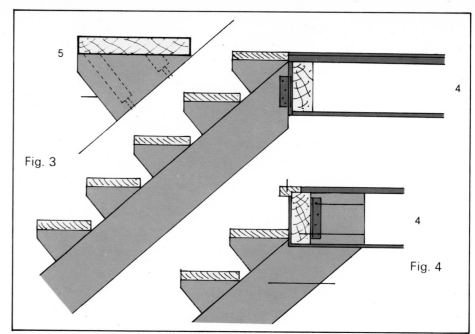

Fig. 3

Fig. 4

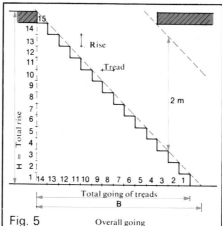

Fig. 5   Overall going

where a string is inserted into a newel post.

Housing the treads in the strings

The next step, if the treads are to be supported by strings, is to cut the housing joints on the inside face of the strings. The housings should be a minimum of 13mm (½in) deep. You can cut them with a power router and a jig, if you have one, and it will save you a lot of time.

If you do not have such a tool, you can cut the housings by drilling a series of holes within the areas marked out for the treads. These holes can be cut with an electric drill or a handbrace and bit. In either case it is advisable to use a depth stop to keep all the holes an even depth and avoid the necessity of having to even up the housings later.

A depth stop can be a piece of wood with a hole drilled in it that fits around the bit the required distance from the tip. Stop the wood from moving up the drill with a piece of adhesive tape. Alternatively, a proprietary type of stop that bolts onto the bit can be used.

Fig. 3. *String or spine fitted to the front of the trimmer joist.*

Fig. 4. *The string or spine fixed behind the trimmer using a piece of angle-plate.*

Fig. 5. *Staircase measurements showing the headroom measured vertically and at right angles to the pitch line, the total length of the going as well as the total length of the treads.*

Drill the holes so that their edges are almost touching. Remove the waste with a chisel and mallet. Carefully shape the front of the tread section to a rounded shape with the chisel; the fronts of the treads should be rounded off to save your shins.

The treads can now be cut to length. Each tread should be fitted individually to a particular housing. Number the ends of each tread and each housing so that there is no possibility of mixing up the pieces. The treads and housings can be marked as No.1 left, No.1 right, No.2 left, No.2 right and so on.

Assembly of the staircase

When you have cut the housings and numbered them the strings and treads can now be fitted together as a unit. You may need some assistance to do this, because of the weight of the strings. You will also need two low stools or saw horses and some sash cramps.

Lay one string on the stools or saw horses with the face with the housings uppermost. Position the treads in the housings as numbered. Lay the other string on top of the tread ends with the housings downwards. Align the treads with their housings, then apply glue to the upper ends of the treads. Knock the upper string onto the tread ends. Cramp the

Figs.6 to 8. Three ways by which strings can be jointed to the newel post and the newel post fixed to the floor.

Fig.6. Here the newel post is let in below a timber floor and the strings are double mortise-and tenoned to the newel post. Timber dowel pins strengthen the joint.

Fig.7. In a concrete floor the newel post is fixed with a galvanised mild steel dowel.

Fig.8. Here the string is let in below a timber floor and butts against blocking or a joist. The string and banister rail are housed into the newel post and dowel pinned.

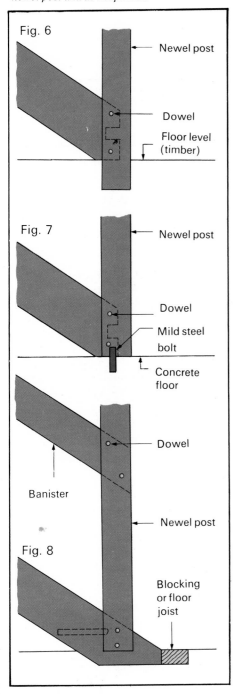

assembly. When the adhesive has dried, turn the assembly over and knock the other string off the treads. Apply adhesive to the ends and knock the string back down onto the treads. Then cramp the assembly up again.

The next step is to screw the treads to the strings. To achieve a good finish you can either use brass screws and cups or you can use ordinary steel screws counterbored below the surface of the strings. The cylindrical gap between the screw head and the surface of the string can be filled with plugs cut with a plug-cutter. These are glued and tapped into the countersunk holes and arranged so that the grain matches that on the string. Any part of the plugs that protrudes can be cleaned off with a smoothing plane when the glue is dry.

Once the assembly is complete, the strings can be cut to the size required. At the top, the strings are fixed to a timber *trimmer*—a piece of wood slightly heavier than the floor joists, and which will normally be in place already on the upper floor. The angled end of the top of the strings butts against the side of the trimmer and is screwed in position. At their bottom end, the strings should be left a little overlength for the time being.

At the bottom, the strings are fixed to newel posts. There are several methods of fixing these to each other and of fixing the newel post to the floor. Figs. 6-8 illustrate these. In the first, the strings are double-mortised into the newel post and a timber dowel pushed through the tenon and the newel post. In the case of a timber floor the newel post can be set into the floorboards so that its bottom end rests on the concrete underlayer of the floor. There should be a damp course between post and concrete. The

second method involves the same joint between the strings and the newel post, but the newel post is fixed to the floor by means of a mild steel dowel. This method is only suitable if the floor is concrete. In the third method, the strings and handrail are housed into the newel post. These are then screwed together. In this construction, the newel post ends at floor level but the strings are inset below the floorboards with their ends butting a floor joist, or a specially inserted timber block between the joists if these run the wrong way.

Supporting treads with spines

This construction method involves supporting the treads from underneath by means of spines. The setting out of the spines was described earlier.

The treads, in this type of design, are supported by triangular wooden blocks whose size depends on the going and rise of the treads. Their shape is similar to the triangular template cut earlier. The blocks are housed in a 13mm × 13mm ($\frac{1}{2}$in × $\frac{1}{2}$in) groove cut along the centre of the top edge of the spines. Cut a tongue on the bottom side of each block (the wastage caused by this means that the blocks will have to be cut out slightly larger than your template). Glue the blocks into the groove so that their top edges are in line with the stepped-off pencil marks made earlier with the template. Screw the treads to the blocks with brass screws and cups, or fix them with timber dowels.

The fixing of this design of staircase to the floor and trimmer is the same as that for a staircase constructed with strings, except that the spines are not attached to a newel post.

Stair repairs

Staircases are strong things. They are almost impossible to break in normal use, they do not generally suffer from rot, and as a rule the worst that can happen to them is that the handrail comes loose or some of the steps start to creak. Here is how to deal with both these faults, and some others.

Staircases are not difficult to repair. But it is essential first to know how they are constructed, because nearly every part of a staircase supports, and is supported by, some other part. And if you remove the wrong part you may easily bring the whole structure crashing down.

All wooden staircases are fairly alike in construction, but there are three main types.

The *closed-string staircase* (Fig.1) is the cheapest type, easier to make and repair and generally found in newer houses. The *cut-string staircase* (Fig.2) is better-looking but more complicated and expensive to build. It would typically be found in a house built before the first world war. The *open-riser* staircase is built like a step-ladder, with treads but no risers. It is most commonly found in open-plan architecture.

The closed-string staircase

The main load-bearing components of a closed-string staircase are the *strings* or *stringers*, pair of straight-sided pieces of wood running up each side of the staircase. The

treads and risers (horizontal and vertical parts of the steps) are fastened into the strings by housing joints.

Most staircases run along a wall, and have one *wall string*, which is solidly fastened to the wall and is about 29mm (1⅛in) thick, and one *outer string*, which has to be stronger and so is about 35mm (1⅜in) thick. The outer string is held in place by being inserted into the vertical *newel posts*, one at each end of each string, by a set of large angle mortise-and-tenon joints. The newel posts are bolted strongly to the floor joists.

Some staircases are completely free-stand-ing and have 'outer' strings on both sides. Others have a wall on both sides and two wall strings. But in both cases, the rest of the con-struction is completely normal.

There are two main methods of treads and riser construction. They can be tongued-and-grooved together, in which case it is impos-sible to remove one tread without dismant-ling the entire staircase. Or they can be screwed together, in which case it might just be possible to remove and replace one tread from below—though it would involve chisel-ling out the rear of the housing and a lot of other arduous work. The screwed construc-

Above: This entrance hall and staircase have been thoughtfully decorated in matching carpet and paint to make a welcoming and cosy atmosphere.

tion is not as strong as the tongued-and-grooved method.

The joint between each tread and the riser below it is reinforced by a triangular glue block with 76mm (3in) long screws passed through it. These blocks are, of course, used only in the inside angles on the *underside* of the step. If they were used on the top they

Fig.1. A closed-string staircase, seen from below to expose the structure.

Fig.2. A cut-string staircase, exploded to show its intricate joints.

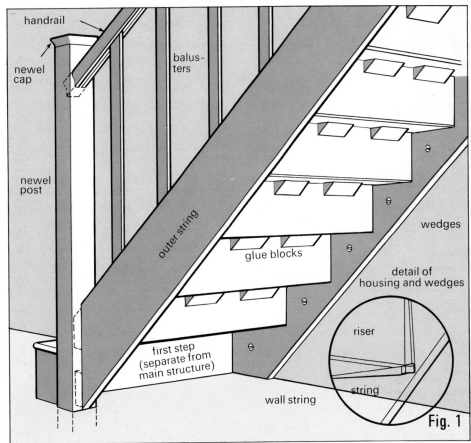

handrail

newel cap

balus-ters

newel post

outer string

glue blocks

wedges

detail of housing and wedges

riser

string

first step (separate from main structure)

wall string

Fig. 1

would get in the way of your feet.

The method by which the treads and risers are held firmly to the strings is found only in stair construction. They are jammed into their housings by narrow wedges driven *along* the groove of each housing, so that they are held firmly against the upper side of the housing (see Fig.1). The lower side of the housing, against which the wedge rests, is cut at a slant to accommodate it. The purpose of this wedging is to jam each tread and riser so firmly in place that it cannot rock or creak. If a stair creaks, it is generally a sign that the wedges have come loose under it.

The bottom step of a flight of stairs generally projects beyond the newel post. It is normally a completely separate unit from the rest of the stairs, and can be levered off without much difficulty if, for example, you want to repair the floorboards near it.

Vertical *balusters* are set in mortises in the top of the outer string to support the *handrail*. The tops of the balusters are sometimes inserted in mortises under the handrail, sometimes nailed or fastened by brackets into a groove cut all along the underside of the rail. The ends of the handrail are strongly fastened to the newel posts, generally by a mortise-and-tenon joint unless the hand rail is a curved decorative one of the type found in many old houses.

If there is a handrail on the wall side of the stairs, it is generally just fastened to the wall on brackets, and plays no part in the construction of the stairs. Sometimes there is a newel post fastened to the wall at the bottom to match the one on the outer string. It is just decorative, however, and can be removed if necessary. Removing the real, outer newel post would deprive the outer string of its support and might easily cause the whole flight to collapse.

The cut-string staircase

In a cut-string staircase, the wall string is the same as that of a closed-string staircase. The outer string, on the other hand, is completely different. It is cut away to the profile of the treads and risers (see Fig.2). The treads rest on it, instead of being housed into it. They are finished with decorative end mouldings that project a short way beyond the string, which gives the outer side of the staircase a very elegant appearance. The risers are mitred into the strings so that no end grain shows.

The balusters are not mortised into the

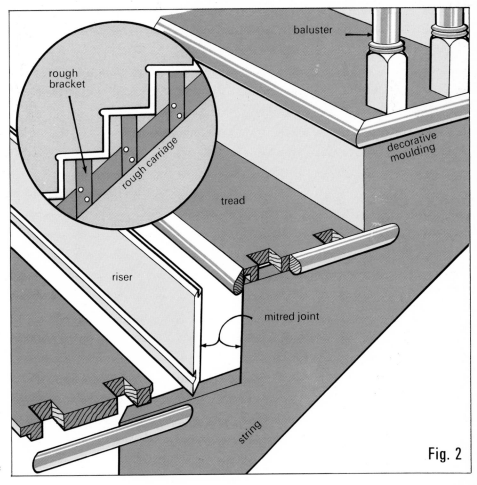

rough bracket

baluster

rough carriage

decorative moulding

tread

riser

mitred joint

string

Fig. 2

Above: An old cut-string staircase painted in contrasting colours to make the ornamentation stand out.

strings, because the tops of the strings are not exposed. Instead, they are inserted in cutouts in the outside ends of the treads, so that their outer sides are flush with the ends of the treads. The outside of the assembly is covered by the decorative end moulding of the tread, giving the cutout the effect of a mortise.

Since the outer string is largely cut away, it is not nearly as strong as a closed outer string. For this reason, there is a strong additional support called a *rough carriage* running down the centre of the flight. It consists of a heavy piece of timber, probably 100mm × 50mm (4in × 2in), just touching the bottom corner of each step where tread and riser are joined. As an extra support for the treads, timber blocks called *rough brackets* are screwed to the rough carriage, and reach up from it to the underside of each tread. The word 'rough' is used because the assembly is not seen, and does not need to be finished to the same standard as the rest of the staircase.

Fig. 3. *A method of securing the front edge of a tread by fixing a batten or moulding under it after first levering the tread and batten back into place.*

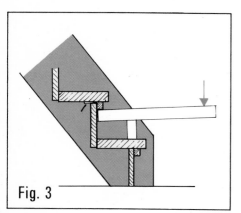

Fig. 3

Obviously, this type of staircase is much more complicated than a closed-string one. The cutting to shape of the outer string, the mitred joints of string and riser, the decorative mouldings on the treads and the rough carriage all take extra work. This explains why a cut-string staircase is seldom found in a modern house.

Repairs

As you may already have gathered, major structural repairs or alterations to a staircase are out of the province of the amateur handyman, and should only be done by a professional. Furthermore, in most countries (including Britain) planning permission is required for all work on the load-bearing parts of a staircase, other than extremely minor renovations.

This does not mean that you cannot substantially improve the appearance of a tatty old staircase. But it does outlaw some projects—for example removing the risers to create a modern-looking 'open tread' staircase. People quite often attempt to do this, but since the risers contribute to the strength of the stairs, removing them is a recipe for disaster.

Squeaky or loose treads

Treads often squeak when they are stepped on, and it is not a sign that they are about to collapse. But when the problem gets worse, and they can actually be felt to move under your feet, it is time to do something about it.

The cause of the problem is nearly always loose wedges. The glue blocks may be loose as well. Both have to be reached from underneath, however, and this may cause difficulties.

Where stairs run above a cellar or a hall cupboard, the underside is exposed and easy to reach. But where the lower side of the stairs can be seen from one of the inhabited parts of the house, it is generally covered with lath and plaster. This must be removed to repair the stairs—a really messy job that covers everyone and everything with plaster dust and the filth of ages from inside the staircase.

One consolation for having to perform this unpleasant task is that you can replace the plaster with plasterboard, painted chipboard or tongued-and-grooved boarding. Next time

Fig. 4. *A round newel post can be boxed in by means of a thick plywood 'yoke'.*

Fig. 5. *Four methods of repairing worn treads. The rounded front or nosing is cut off and a new batten fitted. The hollow is then filled with hard proprietary filler.*

the stairs need attention, it will be quite simple to remove this covering.

Cover everything with dust sheets and rip out the old plaster with a club hammer and bolster. It is a good idea to wear a motorcyclist's crash helmet and goggles, and a handkerchief tied round your nose and mouth.

When the dust has settled, look over the underneath and find all the loose wedges. Remove them one at a time and glue them back. If they are shrunken, warped or broken,

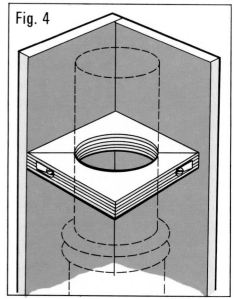

Fig. 4

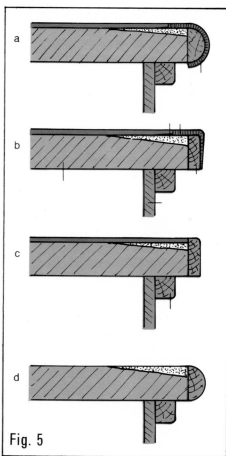

a

b

c

d

Fig. 5

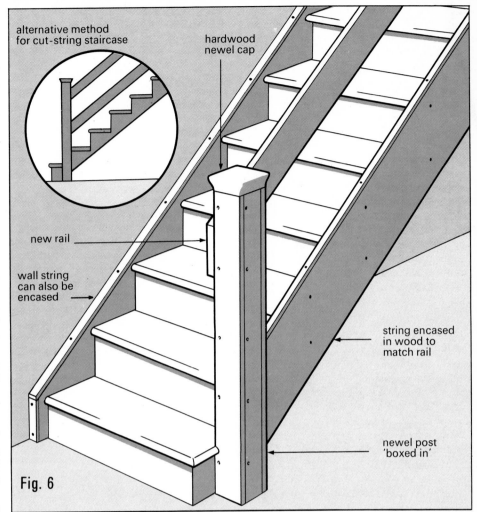

alternative method for cut-string staircase

hardwood newel cap

new rail

wall string can also be encased

string encased in wood to match rail

newel post 'boxed in'

Fig. 6

cut new ones, taking care to copy the slope of the original wedge exactly. Reglue any loose glue blocks and tighten their screws. Make sure that all surfaces you glue together are clean and dry. If you find a cracked tread, strengthen it with a metal angle bracket screwed to the tread and nearest riser.

Newel posts are very firmly fixed and seldom need attention. If they do come loose, take up the floorboards and inspect the way the posts are fastened to the joists. It should be possible to reinforce the joints with wood blocks or steel angle brackets screwed into the corners.

Sometimes the mortise-and-tenon joint between the outer string and the newel post becomes loose, loosening all the treads and risers with it. You can't take it apart, so the only thing to do is to brace it with 32mm (1¼in) square wood blocks glued and screwed into the inside corners. Knocking shallow wedges into the gap might work, but it might also split the newel post if it is not strong.

Replacing the handrail

The only structurally important parts of the handrail and baluster assembly are the newel posts. These should never be removed or weakened, but the rest of the structure is easy to repair or alter.

A few years ago people used to dislike the ornamental balusters of old houses, and board them up with hardboard or plywood to create the effect of a solid wall. This type of balustrade may or may not be to your taste, but it does have the disadvantage of making the stairs dark, and thus dangerous, unless they are well lit from above.

Today, most people appreciate old balustrades with turned balusters, but if they are in very bad condition, there is no alternative but to take them out and replace them. You might be able to get some more of the same type from a demolition contractor. Otherwise, there is a type of replacement that you can easily make yourself (see Fig.6). It looks like a 'ranch-style' fence and goes well with most modern furniture, but is not suitable for curved stairs.

The construction differs slightly for closed-string stairs (where you will probably want a single rail with the outer string finished to match) and cut-string stairs (where two rails will look better).

The first step is to remove the old handrail and balusters, and, in the case of a cut-string staircase, to fill the holes where the balusters fitted. This will present a problem only if the treads are finished in polished wood, which you might have some trouble matching. Glue

in small square blocks and plane them flat.

Next, box in the newel posts to give them a square section (unless they are square already). Use solid timber, or you will have trouble hiding the edge. Most newel posts have a square base, to which the timber can simply be screwed, but at the top you may have to make a 'yoke' out of thick plywood (see Fig.4) to provide something to screw the timber to.

If the newel post is too tall, saw the top off. Otherwise, put a square block in the top of the 'box' and pin it in place from the sides. You can screw a polished hardwood cap to the top of the posts if you like.

To box in the outer string of a closed-string staircase, first remove all projections such as electric cables. Then cover the outside of the string with the thinnest timber you can find in the necessary width—or you could use veneered plywood. Cover the inside with a strip of the same material scribed to the shape of the steps. This is a boring job but not difficult. The strips need only be pinned in place, since they are not carrying a load. Finally, cover the top of the string with a strip to hide the mortises. This strip must be solid wood, because the edges will show. If you have used veneered ply for the sides, the top should be

in the same material as the veneer; the idea is to create the appearance of a solid string matching the rails.

Finish the new balustrade with a rail or rails made of solid 150mm × 25mm (6in × 1in) boards screwed to the inside (wall side) of the newel posts. Allow plenty of extra length when buying them, because the ends will be cut at a slant.

Of course, there are many other designs for replacement handrails. One that is *not* recommended is replacing it with a rope. If you stumble and fall against it, it gives outwards and downwards and you tend to go over it head first.

Worn nosings

A *nosing* is the rounded front part of a tread. On uncarpeted stairs, the nosing wears away, particularly in the middle. Replacing the tread entirely is very difficult and not worth the trouble. A better idea is to cut away the nosing and patch the tread with new wood. Do not cut the wood right back to the riser, or you will weaken the joint there, particularly if it is a tongued-and-grooved joint.

The best tool to use for cutting away the old nosing is a spokeshave. Cut a flat surface, glue a wood strip to it (hardwood is best) and cut the strip to shape with the same tool when the glue is dry.

A worn bottom step can be replaced entirely if it is the separate, non-structural kind. But be careful to make the new step exactly the height and width of the old one. If it is different, it will alter the *going* (slope) of the stairs at the bottom, which might make people trip up at the unexpected change.

Finishes

If your stairs are structurally sound but covered in tired old paint, you can transform them simply by stripping off the paint. Scrape off a paint sample and see what kind of wood there is underneath. If it is hardwood, as old stairs often are, you are in luck. Unless it has been stained, which you can discover only by scraping a piece clean, it will look magnificent if it is wax-polished. Even an ordinary soft-wood staircase will look very good if carefully cleaned and given three coats of polyurethane varnish.

The intricate mouldings of an old staircase are best cleaned with chemical paint stripper (open all windows first!) and a combination shavehook. The treads, risers and strings can be finished with an orbital sander (or less well with a disc sander) when you have removed most of the paint. The rails and balusters must be hand-sanded.

If you have a really ornate staircase, and you aren't frightened of over-decoration, you might even bring out the relief on the mouldings with contrasting paints on the highlights.

Tailoring living rooms to fit your family

Planning a living-dining area is easy. Once you have fitted the dining table into the most obvious nook, and bunged in the sofa opposite the television set, everything else just clicks into place. But planning a *better* living-dining area—the one that looks a little better, works a little better, is a little more comfortable and accommodating—is a difficult job indeed. You need talent, concentration, or luck, or a combination of all three.

The first problem is, that unlike the kitchen, the function of which is reasonably constant, the living-dining area in the average house is playing quite different roles at different times of the day. Whether one room or two, it has to be coffee parlour, study, hobbies room, reading room, television 'cinema', music room, writing room and, when you are entertaining, restaurant. And some of these functions are quite incompatible.

The second problem is that what suits well now may be hopeless in, say, five years' time, when today's toddler has become a seven-year-old addict of television's noisier programmes. Or a studious 10-year-old has become a rumbustious teenager whose army of friends descends without warning.

It is impossible to design living and dining areas so that they will function perfectly for all time, regardless of family changes. In most cases, the family starts off as just a newly-married couple. It increases in numbers as children are born, and in physical size as the children grow up and develop wider interests. It contracts as the children leave home, but may increase again when, for example, an ageing relative, unable to live alone, becomes a resident member instead of an occasional visitor.

Since the range of a family's activities changes even more markedly than its numbers the best you can do, then, is to plan for the family as it is now and make some assessment of likely changes, at least to the time when the present furnishings have outlived their usefulness. This, if you have a houseful of growing children, will probably be sooner rather than later!

But regardless of the numbers or activities for which it is trying to cater, some things are quite fundamental to a successful living area:

1, The room itself must be of reasonable size if you are to avoid that 'shut in a telephone box' feeling. In many homes, separate living and dining rooms can be combined into a 'through room' which somehow always manages to look greater than the sum of its parts. In others, a tiny dining room can be combined into a 'through room' which somehow always manages to look greater than the sum of its parts. In others, a tiny dining room can be combined with the kitchen

to give a greater feeling of spaciousness in both.

Even if you cannot alter the physical dimensions of a small living room, you can often install a picture window to the back garden increasing the apparent dimensions by an amazing extent. (Be careful of picture windows to the street, however; if the room is close to the street, or below road level, you may find yourself self-consciously living in a 'goldfish bowl'.) And if there is positively no other way, you can make a small room look bigger by a careful choice of furniture. Choose as few pieces as possible, maximising space and minimising clutter; choose low items rather than tall; and try to keep the tops 'in line'—occasional tables the same height as seats, for example, and cupboard units the same height as armchair backs.

It follows that you should try to avoid making small rooms even smaller by partitioning them into little boxes, unless—and the difference is crucial—you can see over, or through, the partitions.

2, It must have a focal point because, without something to look at, it is difficult to relax and do absolutely nothing. There are times when even conversation is harder work than you feel like undertaking for the moment—and looking at another person without trying to converse is almost impossible.

Once, the hearth was the centre of family life; the word 'hearth' itself still conjures up pictures of warmth and companionship and hospitality. Now the hearth—or at least the open fire—is yielding place in British houses to central heating. In its place, the television set has become the focal point of most living rooms, as a glance at the seating arrangements will tell.

This is all very well, except that for perhaps half the time that the set is switched on at least one person is enduring, rather than enjoying the programme. (Quick check: In your family, how often does one person leave the room, try to read—go to bed, even—while others are watching a favourite programme?) And when it is switched off, the cold stare of a blank television screen is anything but inviting.

This is why some families retain an open fire, even with central heating, for nothing more than its *visual* warmth and the soothing movement of its flickering flames. There are plenty of alternatives: fish in a tank; birds in a cage (or outside in the garden, but still visible through a picture window); flowers; people or traffic passing by; a favourite col-

The versatility of a small living area is increased by a simple folding screen which acts as an effective sound barrier.

lection—of pictures, posters, pottery, ship models, or anything else you fancy.

3, It must look comfortable. Comfort is more than a physical thing; however much padding you provide for the bones and muscles, you cannot relax properly if distracting or irritating surroundings have your mind 'on edge'. (As one example, few people look less relaxed than the girl who demonstrates mattresses by 'sleeping' in furniture exhibitions or shop windows; in her place, would *you* feel at ease?) So a living area must not just be comfortable, but look comfortable too.

This is a point to bear in mind when buying, particularly, armchairs and sofas. It is an extremely personal, individual matter, but if a unit looks too cold and 'stiff' to you, remember that it will probably make your room look the same.

Floor covering can also help create a cosy atmosphere. If carpet seems impractical because the family eats in the living room, you might tile the floor of the dining area, and lay deep-pile carpet at the sitting end of the room. It will create a warm effect and help separate the two areas visually.

With these basic points in mind, you can begin to tailor your room(s) to suit your own family, whose needs are quite different from others'. The first thing is to list them, beginning with joint activities, and perhaps under these headings:

Eating

Some families take all meals formally, some eat in the kitchen or by the fireside or television. Either way, obviously, you need seats and some sort of dining surface, even if only a tray. But these can be suitable for other purposes and, if so, this will make better use of the space. If you seldom use a

conventional dining table and chairs, why have them? You may be better off with fold-away or multi-purpose furniture.

Relaxing, conversing, watching television

The main requirement here is comfortable seating. Armchairs offer maximum comfort, but are bulky; they should be kept to a minimum if space is limited. Sofas or settees are a little less comfortable, but make better use of the space and can be used for the occasional nap. (A sofa which is not long enough for sleeping is a bad buy; it can fulfil only one of the two—or more—uses for which it is intended.) Some chairs are essential, however, because the seating arrangement must be flexible enough for two people to talk in comfort, yet be capable of being moved so that the whole family can watch television or join in a general conversation. Chairs that can be pushed together to form a sofa are practical and versatile. Try not to acquire furniture that is too heavy, or rearranging it for changing daily needs will be a major undertaking.

Low tables are very useful. Have plenty, and space them about among the seats; when you are comfortable you do not want to keep getting out of your chair to reach an ashtray or pour another cup of coffee. Modern box-shaped tables also provide extra storage.

Storage facilities will probably be needed for books, magazines, records, tapes and so on. For this purpose, multi-purpose wall storage units are most useful. Economical of space, they can incorporate drawers, cupboards and shelving for storage and display, as well as housing the radio, record player, tape recorder and television. They are also designed to allow some flexibility of arrangement. If stereophonic sound or hi-fi is to be catered for, it is important to consider the position of loudspeakers in relation to the seating.

Entertaining

You need to ask yourself what kind of entertaining is to take place, on what scale, and how frequently. Does it justify extra seating, a larger dining table, a bar or cocktail cabinet? Or could you improvise for the occasional informal party?

Having listed family, or communal, activities, the next thing is to list individual ones. The possible range is enormous, but some likely ones are:

Studying, letter-writing

These have similar requirements as far as space and furniture are concerned—not just a chair and writing surface, but also adequate storage for books, files and stationery. At a pinch, the dining table will do, with the

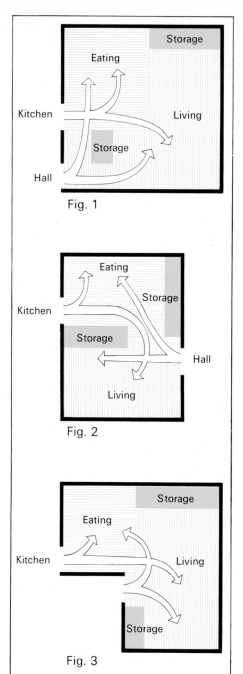

Figs. 1-3. *A simple diagram, with doors and traffic flow marked, will show you immediately how best to zone your space*

storage provided in another room; but a writing desk is much better.

Typing

This has much the same requirements as letter-writing, but anyone who has to type for lengthy periods needs a desk about 75mm (3in) lower than normal writing height. And other members of the family will be happier if the typewriter, and its noise, can be moved away from the general seating area.

Dressmaking, machine knitting

For most women, these are occasional activities, and the dining table will serve. The main problem is storage, particularly of bulky machines; however, these can often be housed, with their accessories, in a movable unit which can double as an occasional table.

Handicrafts, painting

The serious pursuit of any of these interests requires special provision in a separate workroom or studio. Less-demanding hobbyists often use the dining table although, where space permits, it is possible to devise a movable unit, with an adequate work-top and storage space, that can close up like an old-fashioned roll-top desk and leave half-finished work undisturbed.

But before you begin planning consider whether all these activities have to be pursued in the living room. Once the only heated room in the house, the living room attracted all the family's activities. It was too cold to sit elsewhere. In modern homes, however, the rest of the house is not an arctic region to be shunned all winter long. Children's and teenagers' rooms can be made suitable for homework, hobbies, and entertaining friends. An adult's bedroom might double as a sewing room or study. So, before you cram everything into the one main living room, think about using the rest of the space in your home more profitably.

'Zoning' your space

Having listed your family's living room activities, the next step is to work out what you consider the minimum space needed for each, the size of working surfaces, and the amount of storage needed for materials and equipment.

You need also to take into account how often the various activities are carried out, and at what time of day, since if two things are going on at the same time they may clash with each other if, say, one is noisy and the other is quiet.

In working out your plan, try to 'zone' the room or rooms so that noisier activities are in one area, quieter ones in another, messier ones in another. If they are likely to intrude on one another, you may get by with a simple acoustic screen to reduce noise to an acceptable level, or you may have to provide a folding screen or doors to give complete separation.

Working out your plan

You cannot work out your plan in a furniture store showroom; it needs to be

Right: Careful design solves many zoning problems. The split-level living area of this home provides a dining platform, and a study tucks neatly under the stairs.

done in advance, in detail, and on paper. When you are measuring the room or rooms, take down the dimensions accurately and be sure to include; the positions of doors and where they lead to; the positions of windows, whether they face the sun, and the sort of view they overlook; the heights of window sills; the size and position of chimney breasts; and all the smaller, but still important, items such as radiators, power outlets, lights and switches.

Draw your plan to a fairly large scale, say one-tenth of the room size, and cut out cardboard rectangles to represent the surface area of the furniture intended for the room. You can now experiment to see whether, by careful grouping and re-grouping, it is possible to 'zone' the activities logically—and still allow enough space for circulation and cleaning.

Circulation is important. You need a minimum of 500mm (20in) to walk between low units of furniture, more to walk comfortably between taller ones, more still where 'traffic' will be heavy and people must frequently pass each other. However, unnecessary circulation space is wasteful and it is therefore desirable to organise your traffic flow in as simple a pattern as possible (see Figs. 1–3).

If the positions of the doors to the hall and kitchen hamper efficient planning, consider whether it is possible to move or close one or both of them. Try to avoid moving the chimney breast, however; this can be a major, and expensive, structural job.

Once a basic layout has been arrived at, it should be tested for flexibility and whether it will remain suitable for likely future needs.

This experimentation will provide a good guide to the best position of major items which cannot easily be moved, such as wall storage units and dividing screens or doors. It will also indicate to what degree the

furniture must be multi-purpose. The next step will be to decide on appropriate colours, materials and lighting, and the possible use of such devices as mirror walls and floodlit walled gardens, as these can have a profound effect on the character, and apparent size, of spaces.

Left: Open-plan rooms give an impression of spaciousness, and zoning can still be effective. This room has a study built into one end, well away from the main living area.

Below: A floor plan.

Make room for living

'Bed-sitter' is almost a dirty word, conjuring up visions of dingy, badly decorated rooms in converted Victorian mansions, each with old-fashioned furniture and minimal cooking and heating facilities. However, young couples who want a home of their own, but who cannot yet afford a house, are often forced to live in a one-room flat.

Large bed-sitting rooms with shared kitchen and bathroom facilities can convert into workable self-contained flats. Room to work in and storage space, space for sitting and dining in, for entertaining friends, and also a second sleeping area to accommodate unexpected guests, must all be considered.

Whatever furniture and fabrics are bought for a flat like this they must be suitable to adapt or re-arrange at a later time in a larger house. By using white laminated chipboard storage and shelf units which reach up to the

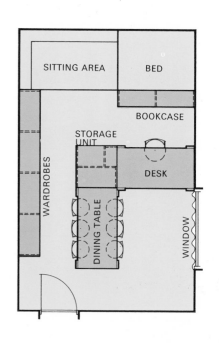

high ceiling, the designers have divided this large room into four specific areas: sitting, sleeping, dining and working. The choice of furnishing materials is economical, consisting almost entirely of large amounts of plain and striped Dralon in bright colours, and yards of plain Dralon carpet.

Sitting area

Instead of conventional armchairs or sofas a raised dais is covered with soft beige carpet and masses of pretty scatter cushions in shades of red, pink and yellow. This forms the sitting area at one end of the long room and a raised shelf round the edge holds lamps, drinks and so on.

Sleeping area

The sleeping area also on the raised dias consists of four mattresses, two of which could be moved along to the sitting area to provide a bed for guests. The walls surrounding this sitting and sleeping area are covered in brightly striped fabric. Since cupboard doors would get in the way roller blinds, in the same colour as the walls have been used to hide the four seperate open wardrobe units which run along one wall.

Dining area

The dining table is made from a door. This is painted white and for special occasions lengths of bright red cotton are used as table mats, giving the table a striped appearance. The table legs are painted red as are the dining chairs. The table is pushed up against a 'tower' shelf unit, which provides ample space for storage without wasting valuable floor area, as well as screening the sitting/ sleeping area from the rest of the room.

Working area

Another white painted door butted against the same storage unit at 90° to the dining table, is used as a desk. Here a work table can be situated out of the way of other people in the room. Books are kept in an open-sided book-case, which camouflages the sleeping area. A roller blind on one side of the book-case screens off the bed from the working area.

Lighting

The window is curtained from floor to ceiling in a sheer Dralon fabric, giving the illusion of a large picture window, while letting in the maximum amount of daylight. At night, lighting is provided by means of small angle and desk lamps.

Centre: The dining table and desk are pushed against the 'tower' storage unit.

Above: The sitting area—a carpeted dias covered with cushions.

Left: *Roller blinds are a substitute for wardrobe doors.*

Below left: *The sleeping area, screened by a book-case which is handy for the nearby desk.*

Below: *Two excellent space-saving ideas – a tiny window bay converted to provide additional seating, and movable units which can be used both for storage and as small occasional tables.*

The spacemakers

Space, you may feel, is either there or not there. And you can do very little to improve something you do not have. With a little imagination and ingenuity, however, you can create not only an impression of more space —which is, after all, half the battle—but also more actual space to use and enjoy.

Space problems in a living-dining area often begin with the furniture. But although a family's activities within this area may be many, complex and even, sometimes, incompatible, the furniture required is basically simple. You need seating, tables, and storage. It is up to you how flexible and appropriate these are. What you cannot afford in a small room is anything useless.

Armchairs

Usually the most bulky furniture in a living room is the seating. Relaxation demands that chairs be soft, low and large. But although massive upholstered easy chairs are undoubtedly the acme of comfort they are also very space-consuming. In a small room these will have to be your first point of compromise.

For day-to-day comfort, two easy chairs are probably sufficient for an average family with two adults. Ideally, the chairs should be light so that they can be easily moved around for different room arrangements as well as for cleaning. Additional seating can be smaller and less dominating—light armchairs, pouffes, and perhaps a couple of large floor cushions. These can be kept in other rooms as well as the living room, and provide extra, informal seating which is especially suitable for children and teenagers. Window seats are attractive and great space-savers, too.

Traditional sofas are not very practical, simply because of their bulk. However, if you have a suitable wall, a long built-in seating unit can take up very little space, and may incorporate useful storage underneath. A convertible couch for sleeping the occasional extra guest will also fit against a wall and double as a sofa. When trying to save space it is often a good idea to 'go to the wall'. Furniture at odd angles, particularly across corners, leaves precious gaps, as does small furniture neatly placed in the middle of a wall, leaving unusable space on either side.

Seating systems designed to be used either as separate chairs or pushed together to form settees of various lengths are particularly suitable for small rooms. Some systems also include low tables and upholstered stools to be used in corners, in the run of seating, or independently. Apart from their obvious flexibility, the main advantage of such uniform systems is that, because the items are related in size, shape and colour, they give an ordered and uncluttered appearance to a room.

This is an important consideration, because it helps to create an impression of space. Think of a traditional late-Victorian parlour, crammed with stuffed birds, ornaments, plants, pictures, mirrors, chairs, lace table mats and chair covers, net, fringes, tassels, and heaven knows what else. However large the room—and many were huge by modern standards—it nearly always looked dark and pokey. The sparse, light furnishings of a Japanese home, on the other hand, immediately make rooms seem elegant and spacious. And while you may not want your home to be quite that austere, a small room will appear larger if its furnishing, colours and

Below: *Main seating arranged along the walls, storage units and light easy chairs save space in this room.*

arrangement are kept simple.

Side tables

'Bitty' furniture like side tables can, in a really tight situation, be kept to a minimum, and should anyway be of a uniform height. One long coffee table will serve a whole block of seating, and occasional tables can be bought in specially designed stacking 'nests' that can be separated out when needed. Shelves or racks for magazines and papers are always useful under small tables. Box tables provide excellent storage for items like sewing, games and toys.

If the family eats informally in the living room, while watching television for example, a table about 60cm (2ft) high may be necessary. But if there is no room for one, a tray for each person will avoid spills and crumbs. These trays can stack out of the way in the kitchen. A trolley, preferably with a drawer, is also useful when eating in the living room and will act as a handy surface by the dining table, too. But make sure when you buy it that it is not too wide to go through the kitchen door!

Extra table tops can be provided in the living room by shelves in alcoves, or by small, hinged flap-up surfaces where needed. These should be between 69cm (2ft 3in) and 76cm (2ft 6in) high—the same as the dining table—for ordinary use. For typing, a height of about 60cm (2ft) is better. As long as it is suitably lit, a surface like this can serve quite efficiently as a desk for homework or letter-writing, and with a drawer fitted underneath or storage unit above, papers, files and so on can be kept neatly out of sight.

Dining area

It is always best to try and organise a dining space that is slightly set apart from the living area—however small it has to be. This will allow some separate storage, and make it easier for two people to carry on different activities at the same time, even if they both have to be quiet ones.

The diagrams show possible areas for dining-living activites, with appropriate storage, in three differently shaped rooms. All of them can be easily opened out into one for entertaining. A simple screen or room divider will help separate them on other occasions. To preserve a sense of space, however, do not choose a divider that is too high or too solid. Boxing up a small space into even smaller compartments will just make everything seem hemmed in. A low cupboard or open shelving is sufficient. It is best to site the dining area near the door to the kitchen, but there is no need to be a slave to convention or planners. If a deep alcove or bay window seems the ideal place to house the table, use it.

The size of table you choose will obviously relate to the size of your family. One that is practical, in space terms, to leave permanently in place will probably not be large enough for some occasions. Tables with hinged, flap ends, or removable leaves, can be placed neatly out of the way, perhaps against a wall, when not in use. If you are really short of space, a flap-up table might be built on to one wall so that it would take up no room at all when closed.

However, there is a 'trap' here: most families need at least six dining chairs, and they must be accessible. If the table stands permanently in place, the chairs should tuck neatly underneath. But a table that folds

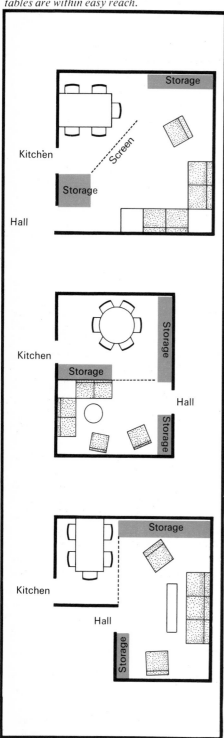

Below: These diagrams show a thoughtful layout for three differently shaped rooms. Ample storage space is provided for, and a simple screen is used to separate the room when required. The majority of the seating is positioned along the walls to avoid leaving unusable space in the corners and occasional tables are within easy reach.

Left: A low storage unit is put to good use in this small living-dining area. It provides useful storage and separates the two parts of the room without intruding on the impression of space. The top can be used as an additional 'table', easily accessible from both areas, when necessary.

rooms. Its storage, if it has any, is usually limited to a couple of drawers, and if you are lucky, a base cupboard. Neither drawers nor cupboard are large enough to hold all a family's table china and cutlery—and anyway, these should probably be kept in the kitchen—and it usually ends up as an expensive, space-consuming platform for ornaments and the fruit bowl. A unit designed not to some purely arbitrary length but to fit the room with shelves and cupboards that are wall mounted, is a far more practical piece of storage for a small dining room. A shelf for stacking dishes can still be incorporated, but this can have a practical heat-proof surface instead of polished wood.

The whole question of storage in any small space has to be considered most carefully. It really will make the difference between a smart and attractive living area and a cramped one. The many different activities of a living-dining room inevitably mean clutter, so, apart from whatever storage you can acquire under tables and seating, you should organise a system which will house tidily books, records, papers, ornaments, toys and all the other essentials of daily life. An odd cupboard here, a cabinet there, and everything else where it falls does *not* make for space-saving.

Wall units usually provide by far the most efficient and versatile answer. Whether floor to ceiling, under windows, across a chimney breast, or into corners and alcoves, the shape of the unit, its design and finish can all be tailored to provide an attractive, original feature to suit exactly the mood and needs of your room.

You can incorporate a drinks cupboard, provide adequate shelving for books, drawers for writing materials and files, dust-free glass display cases for special ornaments, or shelves for plants. You could also build in a fish tank or a television set. (And anything which keeps the television neatly in place without allowing it to dominate the room is welcome!) You can provide special niches for tape recorder, stereo equipment or radio, and ensure proper storage away from sunlight, dust and heat for tapes and records. Sewing, model aeroplanes, children's toys and camera equipment can all be neatly and safely housed. In fact, you can do whatever you like, and if you do it efficiently you will not only have an attractive feature in your room, but also discover that you can do without

away when not in use can leave you with a row of six chairs and nowhere to put them. One or two may stand in alcoves, or go elsewhere in the house, but they can still look clumsy. In this situation, chairs that also fold, or stack, will save a lot of room. So will a built-in bench seat along a wall. These are particularly suitable for narrow refectory tables, and can be made with box storage underneath.

Since dining chairs will also be used as occasional extra seating in the living room, and for all table work, such as studying or machine-sewing, they should be chosen for comfort as well as size. A dinner party or homework can last several hours, and hard chairs with awkward back rests can make sitting on them for that long impossible. Height is important, too. Six inches between seat and table top is about right. These design points are important so that items can double up and do two jobs. You cannot afford the luxury of dining chairs, *and* a desk chair, *and* occasional chairs in a small room.

The larger houses of the past have left an unfortunate legacy to many modern homes. The sideboard—originally a convenient surface for the servants to use to stack plates and food while serving dinner—still remains a space-wasting feature in many small dining

half of the furniture you previously thought was essential.

If you want your storage unit to be free-standing, it might be used to separate your living and dining areas. In this case it will have the added advantage of being accessible from both sides.

Other space-savers

Apart from the furniture plan, other basic factors have to be considered when you are trying to use every inch of space. One of the most relevant is heating. A fireplace, whether for a gas, electric or open fire, will act as a natural focal point in a room and the seating will tend to be grouped around it. This may be comfortable, but not very practical in terms of space. Your seating arrangement will be strictly limited—built-in wall seating might not be at an appropriate angle, for example, and corners of the room may be comparatively draughty and therefore not used. Open fires may also make it impractical to knock two rooms into one because of the heating problems entailed.

To use a small room to its fullest extent, some form of central heating is needed. It allows you a completely free hand over the design of the room and also ensures an even heat, which means that working surfaces or seats in odd corners are just as warm as

everywhere else.

If you are installing central heating, the most effective from the space-saving point of view is underfloor heating, since the heating cables or pipes take up no space at all in the room. They also provide an evenly warmed floor, ideal for small children who use the floor as a play area. If radiators are more practical in your home, choose low, skirting ones which take up least space, and decide very carefully where they will be best situated. One badly sited radiator can take up an entire valuable wall.

Doors and windows are equally important to space planning. And, although most rooms have some inflexible feature that defies real improvement, some can be altered to give more apparent space. An awkward doorway can often be made less conspicuous by fitting a sliding or folding door. And in some cases where the outlook is attractive, a glass door can help create a feeling of spaciousness. The same visual effect can be achieved with windows. Substituting a single, plate glass window for an old-fashioned sash window with small panes can immediately make a room look larger. A carefully placed mirror can work wonders, too.

Continuity of colour, material, and line are vital. This is why plain wall-to-wall carpeting or tiles always seem to make a room expand.

Above: Wall units are usually the best answer to storage problems and take up little floor space. They can be tailored to your needs and can be an attractive feature in a living-dining area.

There is nothing to break the visual line.

Similarly with furniture. A living-dining room in which all the woodwork—dining furniture, sideboard (if you must have one), occasional tables, chair armrests and so on—are all of the same colour, and of as few different heights as possible, looks much bigger than one whose colours and heights are a jumble.

Arranging a room to make the most of available space is a question of careful planning—and compromise. One of the problems often encountered—unless you are lucky enough to be refurnishing completely—is trying to incorporate the often unsuitable furniture you already own. Inevitably, one has items inherited from a parent or grandparent, or that were bought on impulse, or to fit a different house.

But even if you cannot—indeed would not want to—throw everything out and start again, some improvements are always possible. Even a box unit that takes away two cubic feet of clutter will help. And in the long run, the daily comfort and convenience of having a well-organised room, and the family friction avoided by flexible, practical furniture, will be worth any pangs of regret that you feel at parting with the ancient, much loved, but totally impractical object that once filled your room. In a small space, you simply cannot have a huge sofa across a corner with yards of wasted space behind it, nor afford to ignore an alcove which could take shelving and cupboards and work-top but in fact still houses a cumbersome old desk or sideboard.

And if there is something you simply cannot bear to part with, you will have to earn a place for it by perfect planning in the rest of the room.

However intelligently you plan your space to suit your family's various activities, there will still be limitations and problems. But in many ways these provide half the fun as well as the headaches. For they give you the incentive to be imaginative, and, ultimately, the satisfaction of knowing you have solved some problems and disguised others. And in terms of sheer comfort, space-saving can be a very rewarding activity.

benefits will outweigh the initial cost, especially if you have a large growing family with a multitude of interests. It will be far better to concentrate the activities in one spot than having them spread out all over the house and making a mess in several places at once.

Furnishing for fun

Before you put one piece of furniture in the family room, make sure you have a good idea as to what its function will be. For example, do you intend to bar television but encourage contemplative games such as chess? In this case, the seating you choose will not be chosen primarily for its luxury but for its support. If all the activities require a lot of space, then seating should be kept to a minimum and be stackable. If animals are to be kept in the room, priority should be to go deep, strong shelves to take fish tanks, cages and so on.

Whatever the individual hobbies, it is always a good idea to provide as much uninterrupted area of washable work-top as possible. These surfaces should be hinged so that they can be folded against the wall if more space is needed. Most rooms tend to be short on storage; this room will need all the storage space it can get.

Solid wooden chests and wardrobes are less likely to get scuffed and dog-eared than lightly-built modern shelving systems or 'paper' toy chests for example, but they do take up a lot of room. Be sure that they are solid enough to stand up for themselves—even when a young child decides to swing on an open cupboard door or drawer, possibly bringing the whole piece down on top of him. Wherever you have a spare alcove or recess, fill it up with shelves or fitted cupboards, to keep as much floor space clear as possible. Open shelves can be curtained off to keep the room looking neat, or alternatively, a picture or piece of sculpture you are particularly proud of can be spotlit in the alcove to great effect.

Use the largest room you can—this sounds obvious but some families make the mistake of opting for a fairly small area with the idea that it will be 'cosy'. In fact, cosiness can be created in large spaces, too, through *zoning*. You can use screens that slide on tracks to subdivide a largish room so that several entirely different activities can take place at the same time, or slide the screens out of view completely to make use of the entire floor space. Any families keen on theatricals will appreciate this idea immediately—with screens you have an instant auditorium, dressing room, stage and even scenery.

As a general rule, loose furniture should be kept to a minimum (a basic design rule for any room but particularly pertinent here),

Social centre for the family

Modern families tend to have sophisticated hobbies which involve a mass of equipment and materials. If these were allowed to 'stray' all over the house they would cause untold havoc. Small children have their nurseries to clutter up, and specialists have their workshops, but a properly planned 'family room' provides the whole family with a social centre where each member can create his own brand of mayhem. And then, perhaps, you will meet more often than just at mealtimes.

It's no use packing the whole family into the spare room and hoping that everyone will have a marvellous time. Family rooms do have to be *planned*, if only to ensure that they are warm enough, well ventilated, suitably lit, insulated against noise, provided with adequate storage and somewhere to sit, and so on. The 'basics' should be carefully thought out before you try to plan the layout of the room.

Where to put it

You might have a loft that could be converted into a 'den' for the whole family, but noise might be a problem, particularly if you have neighbours with small children who may be trying to sleep while you stay up late playing table tennis or doing something equally noisy. But if you do decide to adapt your loft, make sure that the access provided meets the standard fire regulation requirements.

A cellar would be more soundproof, but then again you might come up against problems with rising damp. A converted loft or a cellar might seem 'trendy', but if you have other spare rooms, then try to convert them instead—it will save you money and temper.

Many American families find the best place for their family room is next to the kitchen, or in an extended and partially divided-off kitchen area. This way, a busy mother can keep her eye on small children without disrupting her work or the children's play. And if the play part of the kitchen is provided with adequate storage space, toys can be whisked away when the toddlers go to bed and the rest of the family take over the room for more adult pastimes. This location would also be the most convenient for partygoers—with the refrigerator handy for chilling drinks and keeping snacks fresh.

In most 'semis' however, this arrangement might not be possible, any room next to the kitchen being used as a dining area or utility room. With space at a premium, you might consider adding on a family room—the

and what there is should be used in conjunction with the screens. The possibilities are endless—subdividing the room in this way you can 'create' areas suitable for study or quiet reading; allow for television viewing while others carry on other reasonably quiet activities; provide completely sealed-off areas to be used as a darkroom, tape-recording area or study; or combine these private 'cells' with public space to allow the room to be used for games. There are a large number of permutations you can work with these sliding screens—just three will be enough for most rooms if they reach from floor to ceiling. To work their arrangement out, draw the room to scale on squared paper (Fig.4) and sketch in the screens in the various possible positions on the tracks. This should give you a guide as to where the furniture and fittings would be best placed—you will realise that there should ideally be a power point in each subdivided area, and that storage, lighting and heating facilities should be evenly spaced and accessible throughout the room with the screens in any position.

Soft lights, sweet music

This is the one room in the house where you can use as many different types of lighting and fixtures as you like. If you use the screen system described above, a variety of lighting effects will add greatly to the comfort and convenience of the room, and won't seem cluttered. One central pendant light is totally inadequate to deal with most activities by themselves, let alone groups of activities going on at the same time. The single central light only casts a hard flat glare on the proceedings, with harsh shadows that can cause

eyestrain. It is best to use local intense lighting, such as spotlights, tracking and angled desklamps to throw light on the work in hand; precise lighting is needed for work such as sewing or marquetry.

Lights can be brought down low over a coffee table by looping their flexes from the central ceiling rose—the subtle glow that this creates enhances the mood of informal conversation or listening to music. Recessed and concealed strip-lighting minimises any glare, and is especially good when positioned just over work surfaces where a spotlight or desklamp might be distracting to the eye. If you intend to use the room almost 'round the clock', then a dimmer switch might be useful to control the intensity of the lights and the mood of the room when it is dark.

And don't forget daylight—this is particularly important if the room is used as a 'den' or study by day. It would be no use at all providing the room with the most sophisticated lighting on the market and omitting to light the room well naturally. The glare from an over-large window can be cut down by blinds, but it is difficult to light a room well if it has pokey little windows, or in the case of internal rooms, perhaps no windows at all. In this case you could perhaps provide a skylight or some dormer windows; it is a false economy in terms of health and comfort to skimp on decent lighting facilities.

If you or members of your family like your music loud, then take precautions to stop it reaching your neighbour. Noise travels in two ways. *Impact* noise—for example, the noise caused by objects being dropped, travels through the actual structure of the building; and *airborne* noise travels through

Above: Simply cushioned comfort for all the family! One-step-up seating makes for easy relaxation in leisure time.

the air in all directions, finding its outlet through any chinks in the fabric of your house such as cracks round old window frames.

Impact noise can be softened through the use of sound-deadening flooring and wall coverings; rubberised finishes; cork tiles; fitted carpets with thick pile and heavy underlay; expanded polystyrene tiles on the ceiling (and perhaps a false, lowered ceiling). If you are feeling extravagant, carry a luxury-floor covering such as shaggy-pile carpet up one or more walls as well.

Think how harsh and hollow average footsteps sound in an empty house with bare boards, and how anything heavy dropped upstairs seems to reverberate down the walls to the rooms below. Noise is more than a nuisance – it can cause headaches and tiredness. If your house is going to be a home then you should admit that noise will be made, and provide for it.

Airborne noise can be 'killed' by checking up on loose window frames, double-glazing your windows, sealing up holes and cracks in the masonry, and providing solid-core, substantial doors. Here again you could 'coat' the door with some soft material such as carpeting or felt; this would help insulate the room against heat loss, as well as noise.

On the level

Any room with all its furnishing at or below eye-level becomes a bore if you spend any length of time in it. Even watching television at the normal height can be irritating if you become conscious of the blank wall and ceiling above. Modern design is emphasising the need to create focal points at different levels in a room, anywhere from floor to ceiling. A television, particularly one of the modern slimline or small portable variety, can easily be suspended from the ceiling. If the ceiling is low enough or lowered you won't have to crane your neck. A movie projector could also be suspended, perhaps in conjunction with one or two spotlights; or you could hang mobiles from the lights to add the interest of gentle movement and colour.

There should be one room where the activities dictate the decoration—pictures painted by the children, sculptures, soft toys and so on just scattered around can provide most of the colour if you wish, or be spotlit as focal points in their own right. Even a blackboard can have pride of place—if you want a more sophisticated look for the room you can always draw curtains over it. Both floor-to-ceiling blackboard and curtaining gives the room the added bonus of versatility.

In very large and high rooms, such as those found in Victorian and Edwardian houses, you could even build a platform, accessible via a ladder, to be used as a mini-library, or general retreat from 'downstairs' activities. Children in particular love the adventure of climbing and hiding, that split-level rooms offer. Or you could set up a room within a room by building (or buying) a sturdy cube—183cm × 183cm (6ft by 6ft) is a convenient and useful size—which could be used as an indoor 'wendy house', or private study, for storing clutter centrally or as a show-piece for

Fig.1. A temporary room divider used to separate the kitchen from the play or a living area. There are three units which slot together to provide work-top, shelves, and cupboard. Together they move on castors.

Fig.2. The 'total look' family room. The three-sided block is the kitchen and eating area, giving immediately onto the larger play area. Note how the floor covering is carried up the opposite wall as well.

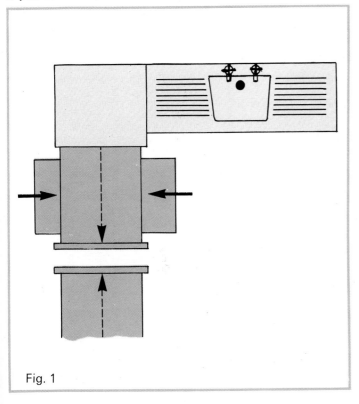

Fig. 1

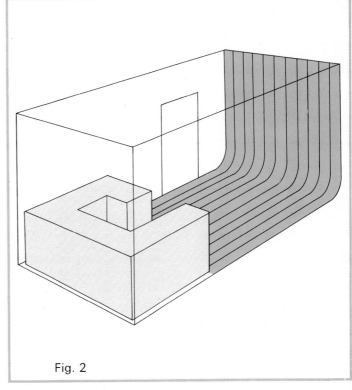

Fig. 2

plants, aquaria and so on. It can be made on castors so it is easily moved for cleaning and if necessary, can be pushed out of the way when the central floor space is needed for a party.

Inflatable furniture is fun and useful; giant blow-up mattresses are now made which cover half the floor and are invaluable for several people to relax on and listen to music. They can be quickly deflated to clear the floor for dancing or games.

The round-the-clock room

Some families, notably those with a wide range of ages, may like to plan a '24 hour room'—one where anyone can feel at home at any time of the day or night. There will always be someone who can't sleep and would prefer to have a drink, listen to music or read without disturbing anyone else in the house. A room like this is best situated next to, or very near the kitchen, and can double as a secondary eating area during the day.

Problems of dual-purpose furniture can be overcome by using one or more 'extension units' (Fig.3) which any handyman can make

easily. Basically it is a tower of combined drawers and work-surfaces which pulls out on castors for easy cleaning. The work-tops are hinged so they can form flaps for writing surfaces, then fold up when not in use. The side facing away from the kitchen can be used for toy storage or household 'business' such as filing bills or typing letters. It could also hold a sewing machine, which is normally too heavy to carry from room to room.

Although separate parts of the room may be used for widely differing functions, you can create a visual unity by accepting that the surfaces must be easily cleaned, and use the same surfaces as for the kitchen in play, leisure and dining areas. Modern laminates

Fig.3. An easily movable extension unit, which combines cupboard, pull-out shelves, and work-surface. This is handy for storing drinks, toys and general clutter—and can be wheeled out of the way when not in use.

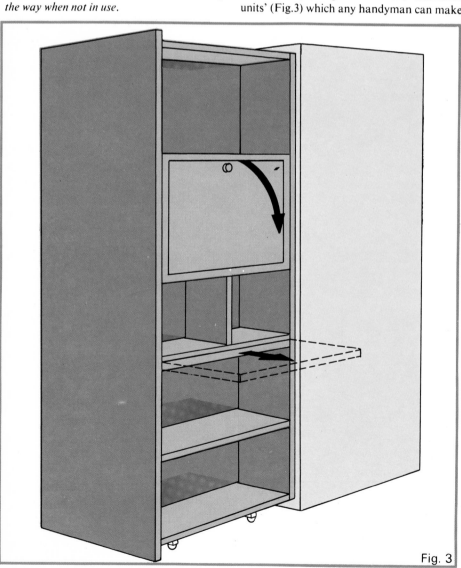

Fig. 3

and plastics provide a comprehensive range of colourful and durable finishes to choose from. Take a single colour over all the walls, floors and work-tops; this helps to create a tidy appearance despite any actual mess. A neutral colour would let personal possessions such as toys, plants, and books provide the splashes of colour needed to make the atmosphere welcoming.

Don't make the mistake of cramming in too many colours or much pattern into this area—it will only make it seem irritatingly 'busy' and too small, despite its real size. A plain, natural material such as cork sheet has the advantage of looking warm and inviting—a pleasing contrast to what otherwise would be a cold, plastic environment. You could use it for flooring and take it up the wall, or similarly, as a ceiling finish carried down the wall.

If any member of your family has the habit of eating in the middle of the night, perhaps it would be a thoughtful move to devise a small, movable 'snack bar', which need only be an adapted trolley housed in an alcove or under a work-surface.

Centre: One end of the room shown on page 34. The colours of the main furnishings are kept to a minimum to allow personal possessions to stand out strongly.

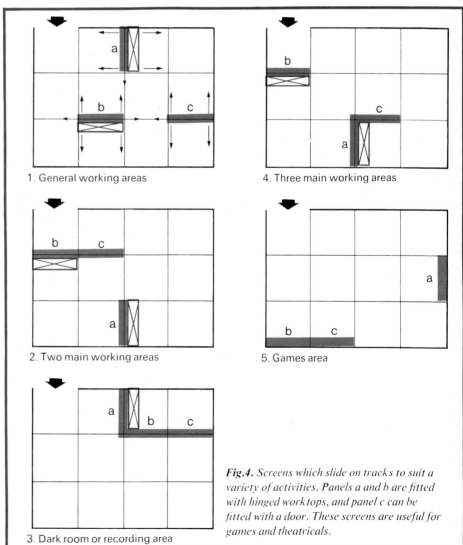

1. General working areas

4. Three main working areas

2. Two main working areas

5. Games area

3. Dark room or recording area

Fig.4. Screens which slide on tracks to suit a variety of activities. Panels a and b are fitted with hinged worktops, and panel c can be fitted with a door. These screens are useful for games and theatricals.

Facelift for an old chimney

Fireplaces and chimney breasts are main room focal points. Without them, room balance may be upset. Adapted for other uses, they can still achieve this balance.

This project is a low-level, room-width storage and seating unit. As shown, it provides a hi-fi console, a drinks cabinet, a magazine or book rack and space for storage under the hinged seats, but it can be adapted to suit the individual family's needs.

Strip lighting over the unit helps make it a visually strong focal point, and the treatment of the carpet—turned up to cover the toe board—combines with the unit's long, low lines to give almost a 'floating' appearance.

The unit is relatively easily built from chipboard or blockboard, with a softwood trim, and can be painted, laminated or veneered.

Closing off the chimney

The first job is to remove the fireplace and hearth, cap the chimney, and block up the fireplace opening except for necessary ventilation holes.

A fireplace is usually attached by metal plates screwed to the wall, beneath the plaster, at its corners and in the middle. Once you have hacked away plaster and removed the locking screws, the fireplace should come away easily. Get some help for this job; fireplaces are often too heavy for one-man handling.

Next, remove the hearth, which may also be fixed by screws through plates. Frequently the area beneath the hearth has to be made good, either by filling with concrete or by putting in local sections of floorboarding. If you have a suspended floor, make sure that in filling any gap with concrete you do not impede the air flow under the floor.

Capping the chimney will prevent rain from entering and obviate any gradual build-up of rain-sodden soot at the base of the chimney, a possible source of damp penetration through masonry walls. You may be able to buy proprietary capping units which can be mortared over the chimney pot, or others which simply slide on. Alternatively, you can mortar on a piece of slate or earthenware.

However, the chimney needs air circulation if it is not to become a dampness 'trap', leading to deterioration of the brickwork and even causing plaster to fall away. So when

you come to bricklaying you should install two air bricks as far apart as possible—for example, one just above the seat of your built-in unit, and the other high up on the chimney breast of the room immediately above. Alternatively, you can use metal or plastic grills, screwed into place over a gap in the brickwork.

Masonry chimney breasts

Ordinary bricks—'commons'—are suitable for bricking in a chimney opening. The bricks should be 'keyed' into the surrounding brickwork, either by removing a brick every three courses or so from the existing brickwork and bonding a brick between new and old brickwork—known as 'toothing'—or by bonding the brickwork by means of metal wall ties. Make sure the new infill brickwork is flush with the original, or at least does not protrude beyond the surrounding plaster, or you will have a problem in getting a flush finish when you come to plaster.

An alternative is to fix plasterboard over the chimney aperture. You nail a timber frame to the brickwork on either side of the opening and fix a sheet of plasterboard, recessed a little to allow for surface plastering, with plasterboard nails. However, such a sheet is vulnerable to heavy knocks.

Timber-framed chimney breasts

In countries where frame houses are the norm, chimney breasts are often built of timber, and regulations insist on a gap between the brickwork and the timber. This automatically provides air circulation around the chimney, and ventilators are unnecessary.

In such cases, rather than trying to patch up the hole where the fireplace has been removed, the 'cleanest' job comes from removing the plasterboard or wood-panel facing from the whole front of the chimney breast. The hole in the framing beneath is then filled with timber jack-studs and nogging, and the whole front re-covered in one piece.

Wiring

Wiring should be done between finishing the brickwork or plasterboarding and beginning plastering.

For the lights, 'loop off' from the nearest ceiling rose and carry the cable through the ceiling into one of the alcoves. Cut a channel

through the wall plaster from the ceiling to a point 3ft above floor level, preferably on one side of the chimney breast, where making good will show up least. Pass the cable through metal or plastic conduit, and 'bury' this in the groove. You can make good the plaster while doing your other plastering.

For the hi-fi unit, loop off a spur from the nearest outlet on your ring-main and carry the cable behind the skirting board to a 30-amp junction box which you will fix below your record deck.

Making good

Once the brickwork mortar has dried out, or plasterboard has been fixed, the opening can be plastered. If you already have some plaster, throw out any which is 'lumpy' (instead of having an even, floury texture); it will not bond to the surface, but craze and break away.

If you are buying new plaster, buy only what you need for the job, since it does not store well and is easily affected by moisture in the atmosphere. For this job, you may need as little as 6.5 Kilos (14lb) or as much as 12 Kilos (28lb) depending on how well you have done the brickwork. Buy by the bag

from the hardware store, rather than in bulk, and if you have any left over make sure it is well sealed.

You will also need a plasterer's metal trowel and wood float, an old paint brush of medium size, and some sort of scratching implement.

If you are plastering over brickwork, first hack back the existing plaster for about 50mm (2in) all round. This will help you feather the new plasterwork neatly into the existing plaster. Now use a vacuum cleaner; the surface to be plastered must be dust-free.

Mix the plaster well, and to a creamy consistency. Now use the paint brush to flick water on to the brickwork until it is damp, but not wet; this will key the plaster.

The first coat is applied to just below the surface of the surrounding plaster. Use the metal trowel with firm upward strokes and covering a short area at a time.

Before the first coat has dried, it must be cross-hatched with a grid of diagonal lines to provide the key for the final, or 'finish', coat. Plasterers do this by knocking small galvanised nails into the back of the float and pushing them through until they are just proud of the face. Unless you are fairly experienced, you might find the trowel or pair of scissors easier.

After the 'scratch' coat has dried, the metal trowel is used to apply the finish coat, again with firm upward strokes. Apply the plaster thinly, and feather it into the surrounding plasterwork so that there are no bumps or ridges. As soon as you have finished, check for irregularities by 'sighting against the light' over the surface and smooth out any that you find—removing them later would be a dusty job!

Next, before the finish coat is dry, flick water on to the surface with the paint brush and polish the work smooth with the trowel.

Decorating over the plaster

'Skim' coats of plaster over plasterboard dry out quickly; thicker plaster needs six months or so. During this time, the plaster can be painted with an emulsion paint, or tiles can be applied; the moisture will gradually disappear. However, an impervious surface (such as a laminate) or one that might stain (such as wallpaper) should be applied only after the plaster is thoroughly dry.

Building the console unit

The seating and storage unit is built as a

Below: The completed unit providing both valuable storage space and an excellent focal point.

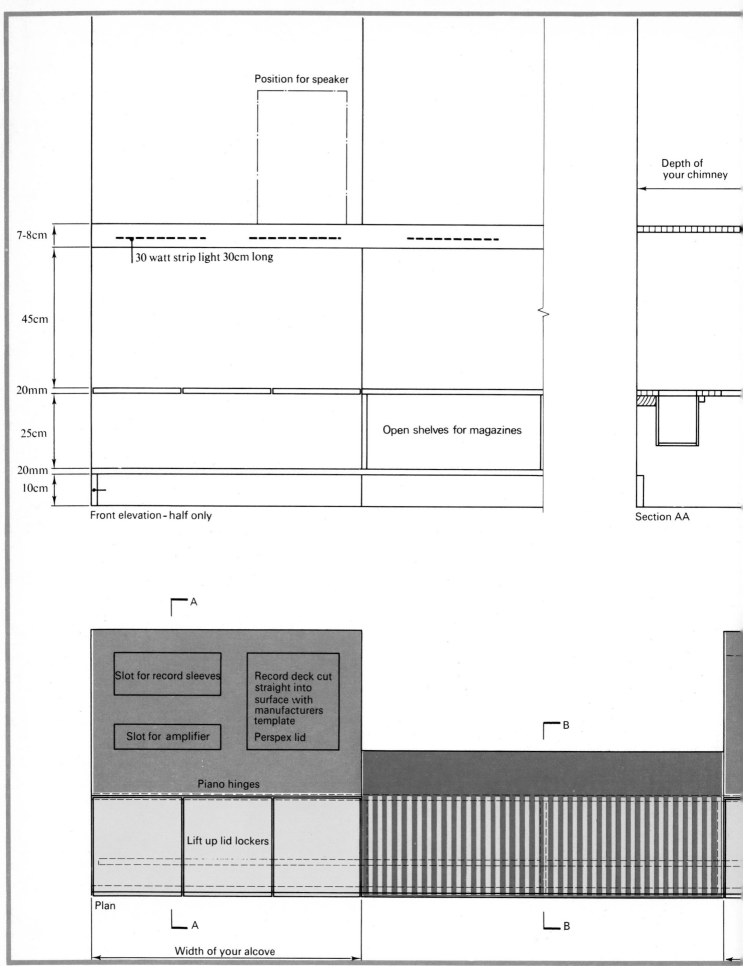

Position for speaker

7-8cm

30 watt strip light 30cm long

45cm

20mm

25cm   Open shelves for magazines

20mm

10cm

Front elevation - half only

Depth of your chimney

Section AA

A

Slot for record sleeves

Record deck cut straight into surface with manufacturers template

Perspex lid

Slot for amplifier

B

Piano hinges

Lift up lid lockers

Plan

A

B

Width of your alcove

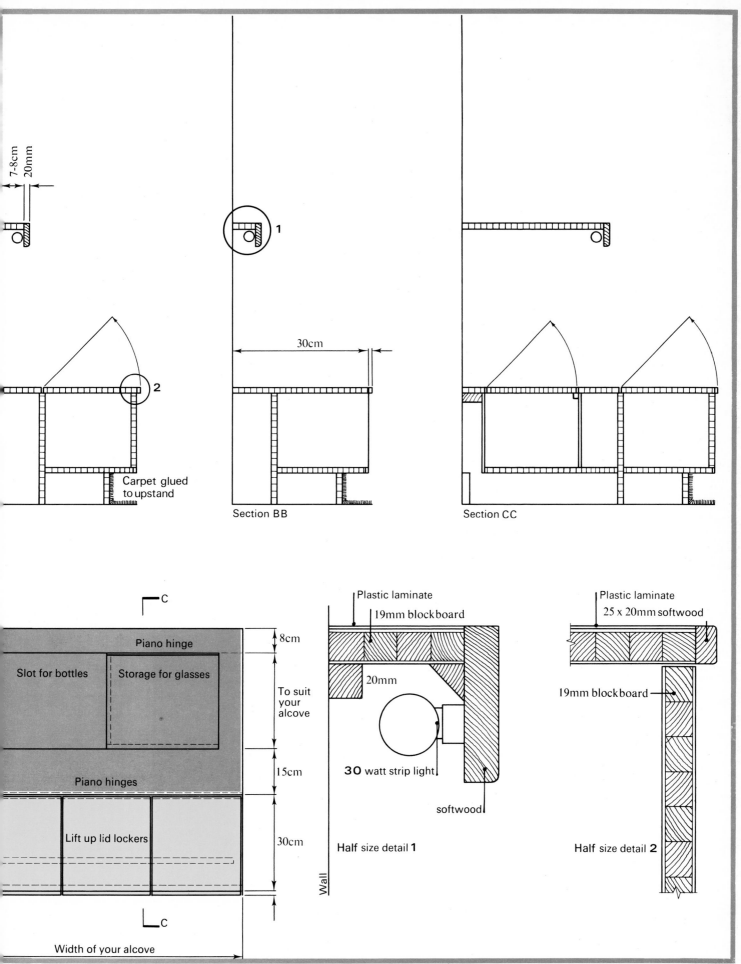

7-8cm
20mm

1

Carpet glued
to upstand

2

30cm

Section BB

Section CC

C

Piano hinge

Slot for bottles

Storage for glasses

Piano hinges

Lift up lid lockers

C

Width of your alcove

8cm

To suit
your
alcove

15cm

30cm

Wall

Plastic laminate

19mm blockboard

20mm

30 watt strip light

softwood

Half size detail **1**

Plastic laminate

25 x 20mm softwood

19mm blockboard

Half size detail **2**

series of four 'boxes', which are then fitted together. Each 'box' is self-supporting, but gains extra strength from being fastened both to its neighbour and to timber battens fastened to the wall.

The unit as illustrated was designed to fit around a standard British chimney 122cm (4ft) wide × 36cm (14in) deep, with 122cm (4ft) alcoves on either side. But as alcoves and chimneys come in all sorts of sizes, the first stage is to modify these dimensions if necessary. The second—or rather, continuing—stage is constantly to check for 'fit' as you go along, and not to fasten any unit until you have tried it against its neighbours.

First, you must establish the accurate sizes of your chimney alcoves, and whether each is 'square' within itself and with the face of the chimney breast. A line stretched taut across the face of the chimney and extended to both sides of the room is the best starting point; then you can use rule and steel square to check dimensions and angles.

If the areas are only slightly out of square, you can make the units a loose fit, later plastering the gaps and turning the wall covering to cover the joint. Or you can chip out small areas of the plaster for an accurate fit. If the areas are markedly out of square, you may have to cut templates to the shape of the alcoves; in this case, the angles where the units meet one another must, at all costs, be made exact right angles to give you essential datum lines.

Making the alcove sections

The alcove sections (coloured red on the plan) are made first, from 20mm (¾in) blockboard or chipboard. Start by cutting the top panels, whose width matches the alcoves and whose depth is the depth of the alcoves plus 152mm (6in).

Both blockboard and chipboard are easily cut with a panel saw, though greater care is needed when cutting chipboard as it breaks up the more easily of the two. Start your cuts on the top faces of the panels, as this will give a clean finish.

Use a try square to make sure that the right angles are true, because otherwise the unit will 'gap' when finally assembled.

The next job is to cut apertures for the integrated hi-fi equipment, the record storage bin and the drinks compartment. Audio equipment for mounting in a built-in unit is usually supplied with a template, so that you can accurately mark out the opening to be cut. Use a padsaw, keyhole saw or power jigsaw to cut the openings. With a hand saw, you will need to drill a pilot hole in order to insert the saw. The power jigsaw will make its own hole.

Save the pieces you cut out to make apertures; they may be big enough to make lids for the storage sections in the front.

The next job is to make, and attach to the tops, the compartments for record storage, bottles and glasses. These are made from 10mm (⅜in) ply, firmly glued and pinned together and reinforced by glued-and-pinned wood bearers (see cross-section A-A). The ply panel that divides the bottles from the glasses is cut 20mm (¾in) shorter than neighbouring 'partitions' to allow for the depth of the lid, which covers the glasses only. On the other side of the glasses compartment, the lid is supported by a narrow wood strip, again recessed by 20mm (¾in).

With the compartments fitted, the next stage is to fasten the hi-fi equipment to the tops, and drill the holes for power and speaker wires. Then the lid for the glasses compartment is cut out, and fixed in place with a piano hinge. (Remember to chamfer one edge slightly so that the top will not jam.)

The alcove units, which have no sides or bottom, are now complete, but before they can be fixed in place two jobs must be done. First the skirting board must be removed from along the outside walls of the alcoves. When the unit is complete, it will be cut to fit snugly against the front, and replaced.

Next, the wall bearers which support the whole unit must be fixed in place. These are of 75mm × 25mm (3in × 1in) timber, plugged and screwed into the wall at a height of 361mm (14¼in). They run right round the chimney breast and alcoves and along each outside wall for the full depth of the alcove units—i.e. the depth of your alcove plus 15cm (6in). Use the spirit level to make sure that the battens are level.

The two side sections can now be dry-fitted in position, but do not fasten them permanently until (a) you have completed the other sections and checked that all four fit together accurately, and (b) you have completed the necessary wiring connections.

Making the front section

The front section (coloured yellow on the plan) is made next. First the bottom is cut; it is 30.4cm (1ft) deep and as long as your room is wide. Underneath the base, a plinth of the same length and 10.2cm (4in) deep is glued and screwed, standing upright and 10.2cm (4in.) in from the front (see section A-A). This upstand is reinforced by glue blocks—short sections of 12mm (½in) angle, glued and pinned at 30.4cm (1ft) intervals in the angle of the joint.

The back of this section is a vertical panel, 36cm (14¼in) high and, once again, as long as the room is wide. This panel is glued and screwed in place and reinforced with glue blocks. Note that it is *not* flush with the edges of the locker lids; half of its width is a bearing edge for sections of the decking.

The front panels of this section are 24cm (9½in) high, and the same width(s) as your alcoves. These, too, are glued and screwed through the base.

Fixing the alcove and front section

Now your front section is complete with its plinth, base, continuous back panel, and front panels; it has no sides. Try it for 'fit' with the alcove sections, checking particularly that the latter sit firmly on their wall bearers when the front unit is pushed home. When you are satisfied, glue and screw the alcove sections on to their wall bearers.

The front section is next pushed into place, and held there by pairs of vertical battens 24cm (9½in) high, screwed and plugged to the wall inside the storage compartments.

Making the centre section

The centre section consists of the final area of decking, and three vertical members—the ends and partition of the magazine rack. The ends and partition are 24cm (9½in) high and 30.4cm (1ft) deep, and are cut from blockboard or chipboard. At the top, they are fastened to the deck piece. At the bottom, the end ones are fastened to 2.5cm × 2.5cm (1in × 1in) battens fixed across the floor of and just inside, the storage compartments. The partition piece is glued along its bottom and skew-nailed into place.

Trimming and finishing

The final stage of building the base unit is to cut the lids for the storage lockers, and fit them on with piano hinges.

If the unit is to be laminated, the entire job can be covered in one 3.657m × 1.219m (12ft × 4ft) sheet. Paper templates will enable the laminate to be marked out accurately for cutting. The openings in the rear section of the unit need special care. It is easiest to bore pilot holes in the laminate and use a keyhole saw to remove these sections.

Full-width sections of nosing, as shown in half size detail 2, are pinned and glued along the top and bottom of the front panels and are slightly rounded for decorative effect.

Building the shelf unit

The shelf unit consists of four members— the front rail or fascia, two alcove panels of blockboard or chipboard, and a 7.6cm (3in) packing strip across the face of the chimney. The fascia is slightly rounded to match the trim elsewhere, and (to avoid screw holes on the face) is clamped and glued in position, and reinforced with glue blocks.

The whole unit is fastened in position by means of 7.6cm (3in) square battens screwed across the chimney breast (see half size detail 1) and around the alcoves.

The great breakthrough

Houses are normally designed for the 'average' family. On the ground floor of British houses, this usually means a separate living room, dining room, hall, and kitchen (in some older houses, a few more rooms are thrown in for good measure). If this type of layout does not suit your needs, or if small rooms are a result, then there is an alternative: knock down one or more of the dividing walls to give you the space you want.

The most popular wall for the 'knocking through treatment' is the wall dividing the living and dining rooms. Often, the dining room is a seldom used part of the house. If this is the case, combining it with the living room will create more space for everyday living, as well as making the house seem larger. If you want to keep some form of division between the two rooms for certain occasions, say if you have children who have to study or want to entertain friends, a simple foldaway screen can be used.

Other walls, depending on the layout of the house, can be removed for an open-plan effect. The wall dividing the kitchen from the

Below: An impressive and spacious living area can be created in many homes by removing the whole or part of the wall dividing the dining and living rooms.

dining area in some homes could be replaced by a breakfast bar, with the seating on the dining side. A pleasant effect can also be achieved, in some situations, by taking away the hall wall and incorporating the stairs in the living area.

Bear in mind that in a cold climate, removing walls can make the house more difficult and expensive to heat. In a hot climate it will help keep the house cool. Either way, unwanted noise will more easily spread throughout the house.

Preparation

Removing an internal masonry wall is not simply a question of hacking the bricks or building blocks away to form the opening. Most internal walls support some other part of the house structure, and this support has to be replaced when the wall is removed. This is done by placing a *lintel* across the top of the new opening to carry the masonry, floor joists and so on above.

In Britain, all structural alterations within the house have to be approved by the local building inspector before work starts. You will have to have plans and calculations passed by him, showing that the structural strength of the wall to be removed will be adequately replaced.

The first job is to determine the function of the wall you are replacing. Few walls are simply room dividers. Even if they are not continued on the next floor, they may still be used to support floors joists, and their removal will require additional strengthening.

The best way to solve this problem is, literally, to get on top of it; in other words, go up to the floor above (or into the loft if you live in a bungalow). By measuring the upstairs room dimensions and comparing them with downstairs, you will be able to tell if your wall supports another. By removing a section or more of floorboards as near as possible above the wall to be removed —obviously this will not be necessary in the loft—you can see how the joists are arranged. In many situations, only a short length of board needs to be removed, say between a pair of joists, and a combination of mirror and torch can be used to carry out a complete examination.

To remove a section of floorboards, you can use either a power saw or a special curved hand saw. Take care not to risk cutting through electric cables or water pipes running across the joists. If you are using a power saw it is best to set the blade slightly *shallower* than the thickness of the floorboard. The thickness can be ascertained by carefully drilling a hole with a hand drill and noting the point on the drill bit when it breaks through the board. Once the cut has been made, the final severing of the board can be done carefully with a chisel.

To enable you to replace the piece of board easily, cut it as near as possible to the joists, so that battens can be nailed to the sides of the joists to carry the replaced board. The location of the joists can usually be determined by the position of the nailheads in the floorboards. Before cutting, however, check that you will not be cutting through the joists as well. Careful probing with a bradawl or drill will normally be a sufficient guide to the exact location of the joists.

Figs. 1 to 7 show examples of most situations you are likely to encounter. In Fig. 1, the wall is not continued above the level of the upstairs floor, but the joists run *across* it and bear on its top. Joists arranged like this are usually lapped above the wall. Such a wall, whether the joists are lapped or not, is usually *load-bearing*, and its removal will necessitate the installation of a lintel.

Fig. 2 shows a situation where the joists run parallel with the wall. At first sight, the wall appears to be non-load-bearing, but check carefully. In some cases the wall may also carry a beam running outwards from some point on it, which may be used to support the joists or other structure. If so,

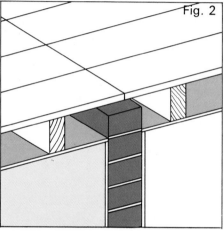

Fig. 1

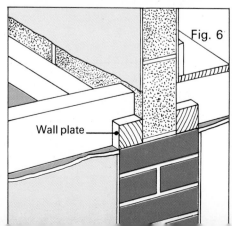

Fig. 2

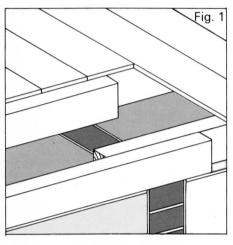

Fig. 3

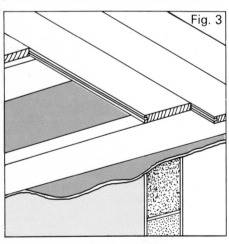

Fig. 4

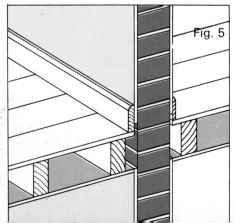

Fig. 5

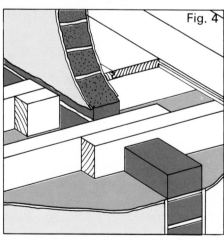

Fig. 6

Wall plate

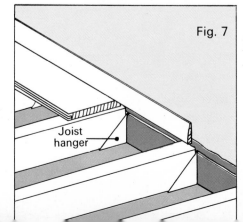

Fig. 7

Joist hanger

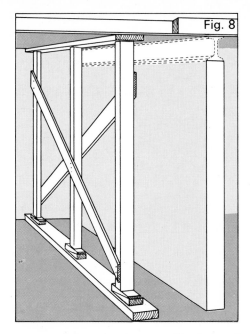

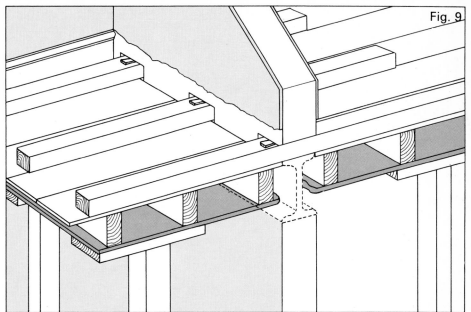

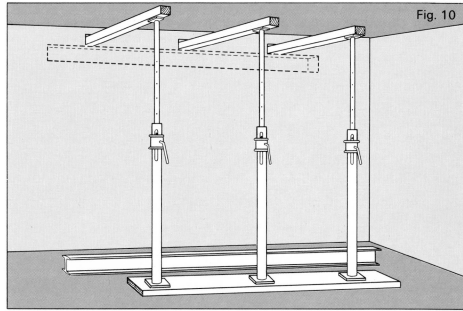

Fig.1. *Joists lapped and supported by the top of the wall.*

Fig.2. *Joists running parallel with the wall. Provided that no structural members are attached, the wall is non-load-bearing.*

Fig.3. *The continuous ceiling lining indicates the wall is a later addition to the house and is non-load-bearing.*

Fig.4. *The wall continues into the room above and supports the ceiling joists.*

Fig.5. *Joists running parallel with a continuous wall.*

Fig.6. *A situation sometimes found in older houses. The joists rest on wall plates positioned on the top of a double-skin wall.*

Fig.7. *Joists supported by joist hangers.*

Fig.8. *Supporting the ceiling using wooden struts (one side shown). A pair of folding wedges is used at the base of each strut to ensure that the struts are not angled out of plumb.*

Fig.9. *When the joists run parallel with the wall, it is sometimes possible to insert the lintel in the ceiling. If so, wooden needles are inserted through the wall immediately above the upstairs floor level as temporary support.*

Fig.10. *In situations where the lintel is to be positioned below the level of the ceiling, needles should be inserted immediately above the intended position of the lintel to support the masonry above.*

the top section of wall carrying this member will have to be retained, and a lintel inserted below it to carry the weight of the floor. This situation may also be found where the wall continues up through the floor. It is not a common one, however. If you have the arrangement shown in Fig. 3, where the downstairs ceiling and upstairs floor surfaces extend *over* the top of the wall, it is likely that the wall has been added later. The wall does not carry any weight, and can simply be knocked away.

Figs. 4 to 7 illustrate examples of walls extended through the room above. A lintel must be used to support the remaining masonry, but it is still necessary to check the position of the joists, so that proper temporary support is given while the wall is removed. This is obviously essential if a major disaster is to be avoided.

Lintels

Once you have determined the function of your wall, you must consider the type and size of the lintel you may have to use, and the way in which it is to be supported.

Various materials can be used for lintels, namely wood, steel and concrete (either prestressed or reinforced). For most knocking through operations within the home, however, the steel lintel, known as an rsj (rolled steel joist), is the one best suited. Although it is heavier than some other types, it is particularly strong and also relatively small in size.

Steel lintels can be obtained in either 'H' section or 'U' (channel) section. They can sometimes be bought second-hand from a demolition yard, but take care to buy one in good condition—a badly rusted one will not be suitable.

The correct size of lintel is crucial. It must be adequate to support the weight, but the dimensions must be such that it can be properly supported at either side of the opening. Two methods can be used for this support. You can either leave some of the wall in place on either side of the opening (often necessary if a folding partition is to be fitted) and rest the lintel on these 'pillars' or, in some cases, fit the ends of the lintel into the adjacent walls. Note however that your local authority may not permit you to fit the lintel into a party wall dividing two houses. If the lintel is supported by an external wall running at right angles to it, the end of the lintel must be supported on the *inner* wall if it is a cavity wall, and halfway into the wall if it is a double brick solid wall.

Where a whole wall has to be supported (in the room upstairs, for example), the width of the lintel must be the same as the width of the wall to provide the necessary support. For example, a 115mm (4½in) thick brick wall will require a 115mm (4½in) wide lintel.

If the outer edges of the wall are left to support the lintel, the length of bearing surface must never be less than the width of the lintel and, preferably, should be slightly more. For example, a 150mm (6in) long surface at each end of a 115mm (4½in) lintel will provide a margin of safety; a 100mm (4in) one will not. It is essential that these supports are strong enough, and your building inspector may insist that they are rebuilt with hard brick.

Once the width of the lintel is established, the depth required to give it sufficient strength must be calculated. The load to be imposed on the lintel, and the depth of the lintel needed to support it, depend on so many things—whether there is a wall above, how your roof is supported, how thick the wall is and so on—so you will need expert advice. Your building inspector may be able to help by quoting from standard tables. However, you will need to give him every possible scrap of information about the dimensions and materials of both your room and its walls, and everything above them, otherwise you will have to consult an engineer.

Supporting the structure

Once your plans have been passed, work can start. The first job is to ensure that the floor and wall, if any, above the opening will be properly supported while you cut away the masonry and insert the lintel.

Two methods can be used, one using a combination of special adjustable steel props and timber planks, and the other using timber alone. Their arrangement will depend upon the type of load-bearing wall you are removing.

Before fixing the supports, however, there is one point to watch. If the opening is to be a wide one, and consequently a long lintel is being used, it may be necessary to lay it at the foot of the wall before you erect your support structure. It will not be possible to start removing struts to enable the lintel to be placed in position once the opening has been made.

In the majority of cases where the ceiling joists run across the wall, whether the wall carries on through into the upper room or not, both sides of the ceiling have to be supported if you intend to position the lintel flush with the ceiling.

To support the ceiling, a line of struts, either timber or steel props, have to be placed every 122cm (4ft) apart and a minimum of 61cm (2ft) away from each side of the wall. If you are using timber, these should be 100mm (4in) square. The load they carry needs to be evenly transferred to the floor, so stout planks should be positioned at the bottom and the top of the supports. These should be about 76mm (3in) thick by 153mm (6in) or 203mm (8in) wide and run the complete width of the room.

Placing supports on suspended ('hollow') floors needs special care. In cases where the joists run at *right angles* to the wall, the base plank can be laid at any convenient position across them. But if the joists run *parallel* to the wall, ensure that the base plank is placed centrally over one of the joists. This, of course, applies only to hollow floors in sound condition. If you doubt that your floor can carry the weight, you will have to remove some of the floorboards and take the struts right down to the sub-floor.

It is essential that these supports replace the strength of the wall, and it will probably be necessary, if timber struts are used, to insert wooden wedges at the bottom of the struts to ensure that they carry the weight properly. It is safer to cut too much off the struts and to use wedges than to have the struts too long and angled out of plumb. These wedges are known as 'folding wedges', and two are used at the base of each strut. Each pair is made from one piece of 100mm × 50mm (4in × 2in) timber about 300mm (1ft) long. This should be cut diagonally through the narrow side, allowing at least 13mm (½in) at the thin end for strength, so that identical wedges 100mm (4in.) wide are produced.

To fit them, the strut should be cut slightly less than 50mm (2in.) shorter than the gap between the bottom and top planks, and the wedges should be driven in from opposite sides of the strut. Make sure that they are the right way round, so that the top and bottom surfaces are parallel (see Fig. 8).

If wood struts are used, cross-bracing

should be nailed to them after they have been placed in position.

Where joists run *parallel* to the wall, and the wall is continued in the upper storey, a different method of support is used. In this case, attempting to support the floor alone would result in the collapse of the upper wall when the downstairs wall was removed. It is the wall itself that needs to be supported. This is done by inserting timber *needles* through the wall and then transferring the load to temporary vertical supports. These needles should be about 153cm (5ft) long and have a minimum size of 100mm × 75mm (4in × 3in). They should be spaced about 3ft to 4ft apart, with one at either end of the wall. This method involves some extra work, but the arrangement of the wall and joists enables you, in many cases, to bury the lintel in the ceiling (see Fig. 9).

Start by removing the skirting on either side of the upstairs wall. Then use a club hammer and cold chisel to remove a brick, or to cut a hole in a building block, to correspond with the proposed position of each of the needles. Insert the needles and pack out any gaps left between the needles and the wall with wooden wedges, pieces of slate or quarry tile. Then arrange your supports downstairs to transfer the load to the ground floor. This time, however, the boards at the top of the props will have to be placed at right angles to the wall, using one board to each strut. Make sure that at least two joists beneath the needles are supported (see Fig. 9).

If you are positioning the lintel lower than ceiling level, and therefore will be keeping some masonry above the opening in the room, support should be provided by needles inserted through the wall immediately above the proposed position of the lintel (see Fig. 10).

Needles must also be used *below* ceiling level if you have the arrangement shown in Figs. 6 or 7, where the joists run to the wall, but rest on wall plates or joist hangers and do not pass through the wall.

Once you have determined the function of the wall you are removing and erected the correct supports to ensure that nothing above the opening will collapse when the wall is removed, you can start on the actual demolition of the wall.

Demolishing an internal wall is a messy business, and a large amount of masonry will have to be disposed of. First decide on which side of the wall it will be easiest to carry out the bulk of the work on. An important consideration here is the place where you are going to dump the debris. Choose the room that gives the easiest access to this point and, if you are going to use a wheelbarrow, try to avoid having to take it through narrow doors or passages, otherwise you may find yourself with more 'making good' than necessary!

It is a good idea to try to contain as much dust and so on as possible in one part of the proposed through room to keep cleaning to a minimum. One of the existing rooms can be effectively 'isolated' by hanging large dust sheets from the temporary supports in that room. Also lay sacking or boards over the floor surface to protect it from falling masonry.

Some form of working platform will be essential for much of the work. It is best to use an adjustable scaffold system at least two planks in width (about 460mm [18in]). This will also be useful, and in many cases essential, when lifting the lintel into position. Never attempt to work off a ladder or pair of steps. As well, you should wear gloves and goggles as protection against splinters.

Knocking through

The first step is to remove any skirting boards, cornices and picture rails on the wall. Do so with care if you are leaving a small section of wall either side of the opening, as you can re-use pieces of them when finishing off.

Any lighting switches or power points on the wall must be removed but first turn off the the power and take out the relevant fuses in the fusebox. If you want to keep the lighting on during the operation, the switch can be carefully removed and held clear of the wall by tying it back to one of the temporary supports. If you are doing this, ensure that it will be perfectly safe and will not get in the way of the demolition work. The cables will be revealed when the plaster is removed, but check that the lighting circuit is *off* when removing the plaster as it is possible that the

Below: Some form of screen, in this case a sliding one, can be used across the opening to re-divide the two rooms when necessary.

cable could be pierced.

Remove the plaster with a club hammer and bolster chisel. If you are leaving part of the wall at either end as supports, it will only be necessary to remove the plaster a couple of inches beyond the intended sides of the opening. At the top of these supports, however, you will have to remove more plaster to allow for the length of the bearing surface for the lintel.

Once the plaster has been removed, and any electrical points or switches taken out, you can start to cut away the masonry. Although the ceiling and wall above will be adequately supported, it is essential to get the lintel in place as soon as possible. This will prevent a possible disaster if one or more of the supports are accidentally dislodged during the removal of the bulk of the wall.

The lintel must bear on a perfectly level and flat surface. It is not sufficient to rest the lintel directly on the masonry, so a concrete *padstone* should be positioned at either end. Its position should be taken into account when cutting away the masonry for the lintel.

Padstones can either be cast in formwork on top of each of the support walls or cut from a 50mm (2in) thick concrete paving slab, which is then placed on a bed of mortar. If you are casting your own, it should be at least 75mm (3in) thick, as it will not be compacted as tightly as a concrete paving slab.

In the situation where the ends of the lintel are to rest on the wall through which you are cutting, the size of the padstone must be equal to the dimensions of the bearing surface. For example, a 153mm × 115m (6in × 4½in) padstone must be used if a 115mm (4½in) lintel is to rest on a 115mm (4½in) thick brick wall. Where, however, one end of the lintel (or both in some cases) is to be taken into an adjacent wall, the padstone must be at least twice the width of the lintel to spread the load properly. For example, your 115mm (4½in) lintel would require a padstone 229mm (9in) wide × 115mm (4½in) deep.

First cut away sufficient masonry to allow for the depth of the lintel plus the padstone (remembering to include about 13mm [½in] for the mortar bed if you are using a piece of paving slab). Use a club hammer and cold chisel about 230mm (9in) long and about 25mm (1in) wide. The first course of masonry is often difficult to remove and may have to be broken into small pieces. Once this course has been removed, however, the remaining strip of masonry needed to be removed at this stage can be cut out by chiselling into the mortar joins and levering each brick or building block loose. In the situation where masonry is supported by needles above the opening, it is wise to wedge temporary pieces of brick or hardwood in the slot as you work along the wall. These will stop the odd brick falling away. Pieces of slate can be used to pack out these supports if necessary.

If you are intending to position one end (or both ends) of the lintel in an adjacent wall, you must work out at this stage how it can be lifted into position. In some situations it may be possible to pass the lintel right through from the other side of the wall. If not, it will have to be swung into position and this may require more masonry to be removed than necessary to position the padstone. You can estimate the amount by using a piece of wood similar in size to the lintel. Attempt to swing it in position as you would the lintel and remove any masonry which may be impeding its progress.

When the slot for the lintel has been cleared, place (or cast) the padstone in position. If you are using pieces of paving slabs on a mortar bed, check each one for level with a spirit level. To ensure that they are both in line, lay a long straight edge across them, and check the straight edge with a spirit level held underneath. If you are casting your own, check the formwork, which should be nailed to the sides of the masonry supports, in a similar way before pouring in the concrete. It is essential that the padstones should be firmly set in place before being subjected to the weight of the lintel, so leave the work for about 24 hours.

Lifting the lintel

The lintel is placed directly on to the padstones and no mortar is used between the two surfaces. Steel lintels can be very heavy, depending on their size, so you will need the help of a few strong friends. Lift the lintel in stages. In many cases, two stages—from the ground to the scaffold platform, set at a convenient height, and then into position—will be sufficient. If the lintel proves too heavy for this, add another stage by placing the lintel initially on suitable supports, say two strong sawhorses, and setting the next stage, the scaffold platform, higher. Make sure that any supports you use will be strong enough to take the weight.

If masonry is being left above the lintel and wedges have consequently been used as additional support, then the lintel must be inserted at a slight angle. Position one end on its padstone and, as you swing the other end across, knock out the supports as the edge of the lintel reaches them.

When in position, any gaps between the lintel and the masonry or ceiling joists above must be packed with suitable slate or quarry tile wedges. These are knocked in as far as they will go, and any protruding ends are broken off. Finally squeeze mortar into any small gaps still remaining. If the lintel has been fitted into an adjacent wall, fill in any gaps between the lintel and the surrounding masonry with suitable pieces of brick and mortar.

Now that the lintel is firmly in place, the rest of the wall can be knocked down. If the edges of the wall are being used to support the lintel, drop a plumb line from the lintel to the floor to correspond with the finished edge of each 'pillar' and mark the wall with chalk along this line. When cutting away the rest of the masonry, avoid cutting right up to this line until last, when it will be easier to obtain a neat edge.

Demolish the wall with the cold chisel and club hammer as described before. When you reach the base of the wall, cut down sufficiently below floor level to allow for a new piece of floorboard or other floor surface to be inserted (see below). The sides of the opening, if supports are left at the edges of the opening, should now be carefully cut and trimmed. Use the bolster chisel this time to help you get a neat edge. If it is a brick wall, some of the bricks may fall out rather than split and the gaps will have to be made good with cut bricks and mortar. An alternative, and much easier, method for obtaining a neat edge is to hire an electric 'chasing' tool. This has a carborundum cutting wheel which will give about a 51mm (2in) cut, so you will have to work from both sides of the opening. Nail a vertical batten each side of the wall as a guide.

Finishing off

Once the opening has been made, all that remains is to make good the sides, top and bottom of the opening, and to fix the skirting boards and so on into position.

The floor surfaces in the two original rooms will need to be joined at the new opening. If your floor surface is floorboards, fix suitable battens at about 400mm (16in) centres across the gap. Bed the battens in mortar on the base of the masonry wall. Check that they are level and in line with a long straight edge and spirit level. When the mortar has set, cut and nail a suitable length (or lengths) of floorboard to the battens.

Where vinyl or linoleum tiles are to be used, first lay a smooth bed of mortar over the masonry, using a sander to take off any high spots, and fix the tiles in position when it has set.

The sides of the opening will require replastering. If the ends of the original wall are left as supports, you can use either angle bead to make neat edges, or the traditional method, using battens as guides.

Unless you consider that a painted lintel will enhance your decor (which is unlikely), the lintel will have to be boxed in. This can

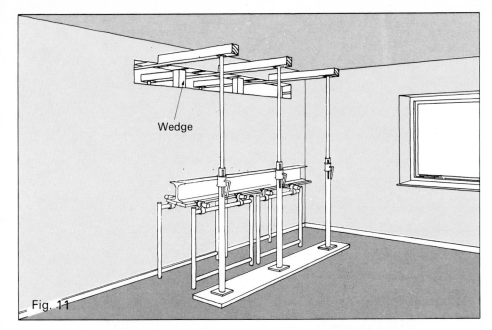

Fig. 11

Wedge

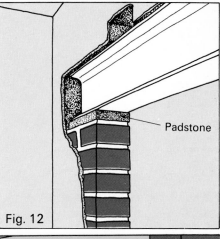

Fig. 12

Padstone

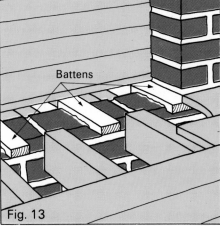

Fig. 13

Battens

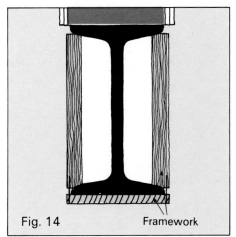

Fig. 14

Framework

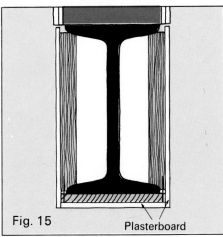

Fig. 15

Plasterboard

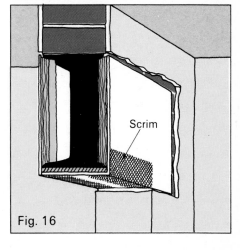

Fig. 16

Scrim

Fig.11. A steel lintel is heavy, so lift it into position in stages. In many cases it will be sufficient to raise it from the floor to the scaffold platform first, and then into position. Note the wedges positioned in the opening for the lintel to support 'hanging' masonry.

Fig.12. Each end of the lintel should rest on a concrete padstone. These can either be pieces of 50mm (2in) thick concrete paving slab, or they can be cast in formwork.

Fig.13. When making good the base of the opening with floorboards, first bed suitable battens in mortar on the masonry base, then nail the boards to them.

Figs. 14-16. Lining the lintel with plasterboard. Wood 'soldiers' are either wedged or bolted into the sides of the lintel and cross pieces nailed to their bases. Plasterboard is then nailed up, the joints are strengthened with scrim, and one coat of finish plaster applied.

be done with plasterboard. To attach the plasterboard, wood 'soldiers', or noggings, will first have to be placed at regular intervals along each side of the lintel. These can be cut very slightly oversize and jammed in place, or attached with bolts passing through the 'web' of the lintel. This latter method is harder work but more satisfactory, as it ensures that the soldiers will remain in place. These soldiers should be slightly wider than the recess into which they fit. This is so that battens can be nailed to them across the underneath of the lintel (see Fig.14).

Once the 'framework' is in position, plasterboard can be cut to size and nailed to it. The joins should then be strengthened with scrim to prevent cracking and the whole surface covered with one coat of finish plaster.

Timber frame houses

Making a large opening in an internal, load-bearing timber stud wall is more straightforward than it is for a masonry wall. As timber frame houses are frequently one storey, it is easier to calculate the load im-

posed on the wall and, consequently, the size of lintel required. (In this case a wood lintel is used.)

The thickness of the lintel is usually equal to the thickness of the wall (normally 100mm [4in]). The depth of the lintel required for most situations is arrived at by measuring the width of the opening, dividing it by twelve, and then adding 51mm (2in). For example, a 244cm (8ft) opening will require a 25.4cm (10in) deep lintel. But this is just a rule of thumb calculation, and you should show sketch plans to the building inspector before drawing final plans.

The lintel is supported by double studs at

49

each end of the opening. The inside stud of each pair is housed 19mm (¾in.) at the top to accept the lintel. In some cases the double studs can be made up by nailing new studs to the existing ones at the sides of the opening. If this arrangement does not suit the size of your intended opening, you will have to fit a pair of new studs either side of the opening and link them to the existing ones with noggings or, if the distance between them is not large enough for noggings, with packers. In any case, you must make sure that the studs are directly above a pair of floor joists, and not just sitting on unsupported floorboards. For extra support, nail in nogging between the joists.

Start by supporting the ceiling with boards and struts. Take care not to jam them in so tightly that the ceiling is moved. Then remove the wall covering and cut out the unwanted vertical studs. Either double up the existing studs at the sides of the opening or fit a new pair of double studs as described above. Skew-nail them to the top and bottom plates.

Once the support studs are in position, the lintel can be fixed in place. Nail it through the studs at either end and also through the top plate, if you can reach this from above.

The structural work is now complete, and the ceiling supports can be removed to give you more room to work. The sides and top of the opening can be covered with plasterboard, and the corners neatly finished with corner moulding. At the base of the opening, you may find that roughly-trimmed ends of floorboards meet where the wall has been. If so, trim them off straight with a flooring saw (or hired 'skilsaw'), and then nail boards across the opening.

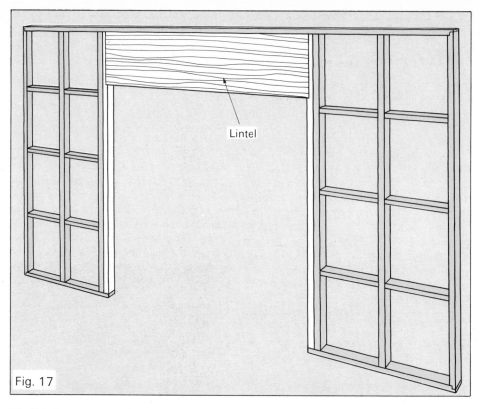

Fig. 17

Fig.17 (above). *An opening through a timber-framed wall. Double studs are fitted at the sides of the opening to support the lintel, which fits into housings cut into the tops of the inner studs.*

Below: *Provided that adequate ventilation is installed to remove cooking smells, knocking away the wall dividing the kitchen and dining rooms can provide a pleasant eating area in many homes.*

Room dividers to make space—and save it

Whitewood cupboards are more than storage units. You can paint them, group them on your walls and link them with vertical boards to make an attractive wall unit. Better still, hang them between vertical boards and decorate them imaginatively to provide a contemporary-style room divider with built-in storage space. You can design your room divider to look exactly as you like and the right size to take all those things you want to store in it.

It is easy to build cupboards into wall units and room dividers; a drill, screwdriver, set-square and saw are about all the tools you need. And this system of hanging cupboards from vertical boards makes the units easy to construct. If the vertical boards project slightly beyond the front edge of the cupboards, it will not be so noticeable if the cupboards are fractionally out of line.

Choosing a type

Room dividers come in all shapes and sizes, but they can be divided into those that split a room completely into two areas, leaving only a gap for access, and those that form only a partial barrier. You must first decide which type you want.

A total barrier, as seen in Fig. 1, consists of a continuous wall of wooden cupboards and provides a reasonably effective sound and light barrier; it would be possible to read a book on one side of it in relative quiet while the television was on around the other side. But this kind of divider inevitably cuts out a lot of light, which may make it unsuitable if there is only one window in a room. If you only want to divide the room into sections to reduce noise, part of the divider can probably be replaced by a glass or plastic

A partial break between two areas is provided by the dividers seen in Figs. 2 and 3. Here the spaces are left in the divider so that you can see through to the area beyond and hear something of what is going on. These spaces can be left completely open, or decorated with house plants or fitted with light shelving. But remember that the cupboards give strength to the unit, and the more spaces are left empty the less robust it becomes. So keep a balance between strength and lightness when you design your divider.

Design

The cupboards can be hung from the uprights at any level. But for the best visual effect they should usually be arranged in horizontal lines. Also for looks, but for strength of construction as well, the top inch of one line of cupboards should, if possible, overlap the bottom inch of the row of cupboards above. (See construction details below.) But note that this is not possible where one cupboard is placed directly on top of another in the same bay of the unit—at least not unless you partly dismantle one cupboard.

A great variety of different room dividers can be obtained by varying the size and number of the cupboards in the unit. But

Below: Room dividers vary from attractive and useful units made from whitewood cupboards to this luxurious purpose-built piece of furniture. Here, the divider is built from the same wood as the ceiling and designed so that it becomes an integral part of the room.

Fig. 1

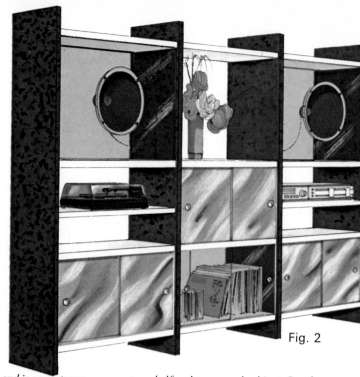

Fig. 2

Fig.1. A gay and practical room divider especially suitable for a nursery. Built from six whitewood cupboards—three on each side —with a space behind each cupboard, this unit looks the same from both sides. It also gives

plenty of storage space and is very strong.

Fig.2. A slimline, single width but less robust divider constructed around three whitewood cupboards faced with foil. Sliding doors fitted

to a shelf make a record cabinet. Speakers fitted here in sheets of plastic could also be fitted in wooden units.

Fig.3. Ten cupboards (five either side) make an

Fig. 3

Fig. 4

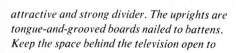

attractive and strong divider. The uprights are tongue-and-grooved boards nailed to battens. Keep the space behind the television open to

prevent overheating.

Fig.4. A slimline divider with a double row of

cupboards placed back to back and hung from very narrow uprights. Stability is sacrificed for looks and so the unit must be securely anchored.

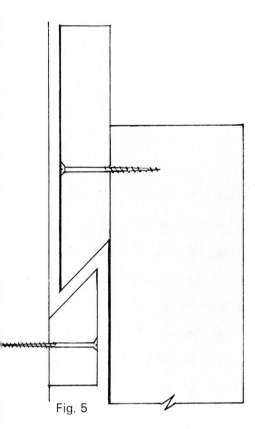

Fig. 5

Fig.5. A side view of a wall fixing. The grooved strip on the back of the cupboard is slipped over a grooved beading fixed to the wall. An equal width of strip along the base of the cupboard holds it vertical.

Fig.6. A varied assortment of units linked together by upright boards can be hung by the method shown in Fig.5.

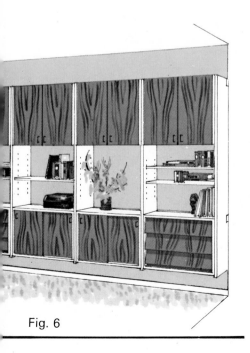

Fig. 6

they should, if possible, all be of the same depth from front to back, so as to give a continuous line to either side of the divider. 300mm (1ft) will be a convenient depth as the cupboards will then hold most average-size loads, such as dinner plates stored flat, but will not make the divider too thick and cumbersome-looking. Note, though, that the sleeve of an LP record is about 311mm (12¼in) wide, and therefore dividers designed to include stereo units need to be at least 330mm (13in) deep.

Buying cupboards

Although attractive units can be built out of the most inexpensive cupboards, you should buy your cupboards with the following points in mind. Get the whole set at the same time and check that all similar units are the same size—especially the length. The cupboards give strength and rigidity to the unit, so buy well-made cupboards that do not rely on the wall for strength. They should always have a back panel, or else you will have to fix one yourself. In any case, most whitewood furniture backs are flimsy, so fix them more firmly by adding some extra panel pins yourself.

The quality of the wood in the cupboards only matters if they are to be painted or varnished, but not if they are being covered with a sheet surface covering such as that described below, or veneered.

Materials for battens and shelves

Most types of board, natural or man-made, can be used to link the units, as long as they are of sufficient length and width and about 20mm (¾in) to 25mm (1in) thick. The final choice will depend on the finish to be applied to the unit. For a divider in a kitchen area, plastic laminated chipboard will often be ideal; and these boards come in a wide range of suitable widths, so that with careful planning no cutting of the vertical edges will be needed, and the boards can be left with a neat manufactured edge on both sides.

If the edges are cut, edging strips will have to be fixed. If the uprights are to be covered with an applied covering when the unit is complete, ordinary 'flooring grade' chipboard will be cheaper and quite adequate. If blockboard is used, remember that the edges have to be faced. For a varnished finish, thick plywood will provide a suitable base. The shelves can be made out of the same type of board as the uprights—or solid timber for strength, or even glass for displaying ornaments.

You can also use solid timber tongued-and-grooved boards for the uprights, but these must be battened together. The battens should be arranged so that they are hidden behind, and also support, the cupboards or shelves (see below).

Fixing units together

The sides of the cupboards must be screwed into each upright in at least four places. With a plywood-covered framed unit, check that the vertical side battens are firmly attached to the rest of the cupboard, for it is these battens which are screwed to the uprights. It will probably be easier to drill through the side battens from the outside of the unit.

Considerable downward pressure will be exerted upon the screws where they enter the uprights. So if these are made of chipboard, drill a hole considerably larger than a screw hole where each screw is to go, and glue in an appropriate-sized piece of hardwood dowel to reinforce the board. If you can put in the dowel across the line of the screw, so much the better, but don't ruin the edge of the board for that reason only. Always insert as large a dowel as you can—but no more than half the thickness of the chipboard.

When two cupboards are joined side by side or back to back, the screws can pass from one cupboard through the vertical board and into the next unit, giving added strength.

If a very strong unit is required—at the sacrifice of a slight loss of looks—then screw battens across the uprights underneath the bottom of the cupboards to provide extra support. If you use T & G boards, you will have to do this anyway.

Permanent shelving installed in any spaces in the unit can be fixed with screws from the opposite side in the same way as the cupboards.

Fixing cupboards to walls

When constructing a wall unit as in Fig.6, you should design it so that the weight of the cupboards is taken by the wall and not by the uprights. The uprights need not then reach right down to the floor; they serve merely to break up the units visually. The system of fixing the cupboards described below and shown in Fig.5 enables the cupboards to be fixed exactly level with each other, and makes it possible to remove the units easily if you want to redecorate behind them. Cut a length of wood say 150mm × 25mm (6in × 1in) lengthways at an angle of 45°. Fasten one length to the wall with the narrowest side against the wall and the slanting edge upwards, so that it forms a long hook. It should be screwed to the wall with plugs and screws every 110mm (4in). Then cut the other batten into pieces the same length as the cupboards. Screw the pieces to the top of each unit at exactly the same level, and with the groove at the bottom and the narrowest side against the unit. Nail a length of narrow batten the same thickness as the top batten to the bottom rear edge of the unit. Then simply lift the cupboard into place and hook the batten at the top over the batten on the wall. The cupboards can be slid along the batten, which allows you to space them as you wish. If you want to have uprights between the cupboards, screw them to one of the cupboards. A notch will have to be cut in the rear edge of each upright to fit over the wall-mounted batten; this will not show when everything is in place.

Height of the units

The easiest way to assemble a room divider is to lay the pieces horizontally on the floor, screw them together and then raise the complete unit to its feet. But the diagonal length from corner to corner of a board is longer than the straight length. So the height of the room from floor to ceiling must be at least the diagonal length of the dividers. If you want a floor-to-ceiling divider, you will have to build it in position, piece by piece, which is harder, or else make it under size and finish it with an extra piece at the top to bring it to the full height, as shown in Fig.4.

A room divider with a solid row of cupboards at the bottom could be raised on a plinth instead. This should contain wide cross-pieces to support the bottom of the vertical boards. But it would be quite difficult to lift a complete divider on to a plinth. You might even have to use car jacks. And the designs shown here, which have gaps at the bottom, would look wrong mounted on a plinth.

Very tall, narrow units such as the one shown in Fig.3 may have stability problems if they are just resting on the floor and not fastened down in any way. The best way to cure the trouble is simply nail them lightly to the ceiling. Three or four nails to every vertical board should be enough, but they must pass through the plaster into a joist.

You can find the joists in a ceiling quite easily by tapping the plaster lightly with a stick—the area over a joist makes a duller sound than the rest—and then drilling a few test holes with your narrowest drill to find the exact spot. When you have found a joist above most of the vertical boards—you may not manage to find one above all of them, but this doesn't matter—skew-nail the top of the board in place as unnoticeably as possible from both sides of the board. Use lost head nails and punch their heads below the surface of the wood. Fill the dents with wood filler if they show. Make good the holes in the ceiling with cellulose filler.

Assembling the unit

Take the pieces if board you are going to use for the uprights and check that one end of each is square. Then cut the other ends to the right length in the following way. If the unit is to reach the ceiling, or if the floor is noticeably irregular, the uprights will not be the same length as each other, because of the slight irregularities in floor and ceiling levels found in all houses. The best way to get these the right length is to mark their positions on the floor, cut them just over length, and (if they are ceiling height) jam them between floor and ceiling as near vertical, and as near their right place, as you can. Then scribe the top to the ceiling as if fitting a shelf into an alcove. Cut ceiling-height uprights to length at this stage, but leave shorter ones alone.

Now prop the uprights temporarily in the place they will occupy and use a long spirit level, or a level and a straight edge, held horizontally between them to make a mark on the edge of each upright at exactly the same level a few inches from the floor.

Number the uprights and mark their left and right sides to make sure you don't get them mixed up. Now lay them down on top of one another in their right relative positions and slide them about until the marked horizontal line is level on the edge of each of them. Then square a line across all the edges at the level of the bottom of the shortest upright, and take this as a base line to measure all distances from, including the total height in the case of uprights that do not reach the ceiling.

Working from the base line upwards, mark across the edge of all the uprights the height of the top and bottom of all the cupboards and shelves at their different levels. Then separate the uprights and square the lines across their faces. You only need to draw lines where cupboards will actually fit, of course, so it is not necessary to square all the lines across all the uprights. Non-ceiling height uprights should be cut to their final length at this stage.

Where cupboards are staggered, as in Fig.1, don't forget to allow for the overlap when marking the uprights.

The next stage is to insert dowels in the chipboard uprights to take the mounting screws of the cupboards and shelves. But you can omit this step if you are using materials into which you can screw directly.

To avoid marking the surface of the uprights, all the cupboards should be screwed to them from the inside of the cupboards themselves, and not from the opposite side of the uprights. Lay each cupboard down on its side on an upright in the position it will occupy, making sure that the overlap at front and back is correct. Drill four or more pilot holes through the strong side battens of the cupboards (not the flimsy ply sides) into the chipboard a short way so as just to mark its surface. At this stage you should number the cupboards so as to be sure of putting them back in the same place during final assembly.

When you have marked all the uprights through the sides of the cupboards in this way, insert dowels under the marks to provide a strong fixing point for the screws. If the board you are using is to be edged later, insert the dowels from the edge wherever possible. If the board is already edged, or the dowel is to be inserted a long way from the edge, put the dowel straight into the face. Make sure you don't drill the dowel hole right through the board. Glue the dowels in with a very strong adhesive, preferably an epoxy resin.

At the same time, insert dowels for the shelf mountings. The easiest way of mounting non-adjustable shelves is on aluminium angle strip. Adjustable shelves should be mounted on proprietary shelf mounting tracks.

If the unit is to be built as one piece and raised into place, lay all the cupboards on their backs on the floor—or, if the divider is to be two cupboards deep, lay the cupboards for one side face down and those for the other side on top of them face up. If the fronts of the cupboards are to be recessed behind the front edges of the uprights, pack the cupboards up on scrap wood blocks to a height equivalent to the overlap you plan to have.

Now insert the uprights between the cupboards and carefully line everything up in its right place. If the uprights are to be recessed behind the cupboards, as in Fig.1, then the uprights will have to be propped up on blocks instead.

Screw everything together and put in the angle brackets and shelf tracks. When everything is assembled, call in at least two helpers, lift up the unit and set it on its feet. Put the shelves on their mountings and it is complete, except for any final decorative work you may wish to do. If the unit seems unstable, you might fasten it to the floor with angle strip and screws.

If the divider is a floor-to-ceiling type, it will have to be assembled upright and in place.

Follow the above instructions up to the point of actual assembly, and then get helpers to hold the cupboards up while you screw them between a pair of verticals. It should be possible, if not particularly easy, to get the whole unit together in this way. It will help if you pre-drill all the screw holes in the dowels before starting work; this should be done through the sides of the cupboards to ensure accuracy. You might also install the shelf mountings at this stage.

Don't attempt to nail the unit to the ceiling joists until it is completely assembled, or you will probably rip the nails out by accidentally pressing too hard on an upright.

Above: An elegant divider can be a partial break between rooms. Thirteen frames are fixed together in columns so that there is sufficient space between them to give a pleasing open effect. On one side, four of these frames —two in each alternate column—are inset behind the others and faced with an attractive grained wood. On the other side these four frames project in front of the rest. The sides of the frames are joined with butt joints and pieces of dowel. The whole assembly is hung from two bars which stretch from floor to ceiling.

Below: An open divider can give both a partial break and plenty of shelf space. This design is particularly flexible and can be easily extended or shortened. Here, three rectangular frames are stood on end and screwed together—but you can easily add another later. Permanent shelves are housed into each frame and provide rigidity (see the shelf at bottom right). In other cases smaller frames fit within the larger frame (see two shelves top right). The divider is stained to contrast with the natural finish floorboards.

An office in the home

An individual home office can solve many problems for you—especially if you run your own business or your job involves working at home. As an ordinary householder, too, you will find it invaluable for the storage of important documents and stationery. A home office clears away those drawers overflowing with papers and you'll be able to lay your hands on such items as stamps, envelopes, insurance and mortgage documents without having to conduct a full scale search—often without success.

The reduced clutter and the resulting increased efficiency of your home makes the installation of a home office well worthwhile. If you run your own business or your job involves a lot of working at home then having an office in your own home is an economic proposition as well as a pleasant convenience. An office at home cuts down travelling time and expense. Also, it is cheaper to use part of your own home than to have to rent and heat a separate office. If you are in the kind of job where the amount of work exceeds what can be done during normal working hours a home office will allow you to get on with it and still be near your family.

You may not run your own business or need to take work home but this does not make a home office any less useful. A well planned home office, tailored to your particular needs, will make a pleasure of writing letters and organising paperwork. And one day you may find yourself handling enough private work, as a salesman or builder for example, to justify adapting it to your commercial requirements.

Types of office

What you expect from your office will have an important influence on its size, design and layout. If you intend to run your own business from home or your job demands that you work at home a lot you'll need a larger office with more generous allowance for filing and storage than if you need it only to help you handle the domestic bills and personal correspondence.

You should avoid placing a business office in a room which your family regularly use, especially if you have small children. Ideally your office should be sited in a separate room—or best of all a converted loft. If your house does not allow enough space for this you can make do by taking over part of your bedroom.

You are less restricted when it comes to siting domestic office facilities as you won't need anything like as much space as that for a business office. Also, a domestic office will only be used from time to time and therefore should cause no inconvenience to the rest of your family.

When it comes to a small domestic office there are a number of ideas for self-contained units. One method is to build compartments into a suitcase. Once you have done this you have a fully portable 'office' which can be taken into any room in your house which is not in use. When you are finished with it you can store it out of the way under the stairs.

The suitcase office may not give you the space you need. In this case why not fit out a trolley as a mobile office unit? This can be pushed out of the way into a corner if you are disturbed in the middle of a job. You don't have to go to the trouble of tidying everything away.

One of the most attractive and versatile of ideas for the small office is the tower unit on castors. If you have a large enough room the tower unit may offer the best solution to your office needs. It can be a square or tubular structure up to about six feet in height and four feet wide. Doors on the side open to provide desk space and reveal office equipment, storage, pin boards and lighting.

The bureau has become a rare sight in the modern home—but it was originally designed to provide facilities for paperwork. Many older bureaux are elegant and soundly made

Below: Unobtrusive service is provided by this small domestic office hidden away behind a room divider in the corner of the living room.

and some are quite valuable. You can refurbish the cheaper ones to fit in with your room. Many bureaux have, behind the hinged and lockable flap or roll-front, an astonishing number of pigeon holes, small drawers and tiny cupboards. They usually have at least three large drawers as well. A suitable bureau will provide you with excellent small office facilities.

If you have an ordinary dressing table with a detachable mirror it can easily satisfy a second function as a desk in your bedroom. What you put in the drawers beneath will depend on your personal needs and on what other storage space you have in the room.

If you are running your own business from home and need a larger office be careful to site it so as not to interfere with the movement of your family around the house. In a bedroom you must be able to undress, hang your clothes up and get into bed without disturbing somebody who is working. In the living room you should be able to come in and out without the need to cross the office area. Build a screen or room divider to separate the office from the rest of the room. You can get many kinds of folding partition made to match your colour scheme. Or, fit sliding partitions which span the width of the room when closed. Sound proofing can be incorporated into this system.

You could use a curtain as a cheap method of screening. Choose a fabric that matches the window curtain. In a bedroom you could have a bed cover in the same material. You can adapt some of the room dividers to incorporate a filing system and desktop.

If you haven't got a spare room or suitable loft for your office the bedroom is usually the best solution, as it offers the most peace and quiet—and may be the only answer if you have children. You can keep a small safe by the bed if you need to have valuable documents at home. The safe can be covered in a fabric that matches the rest of your room and will be useful as a bedside table.

Creating extra space

The room in which you intend to install your home office may not be large enough to allow for it and structural alteration might be necessary. One good way of providing the necessary space is to remove the fireplace and the front of the chimney breast. The side walls of the chimney breast should be retained to provide the frame for the unit. They'll provide excellent supports for your bookshelves and desk. If you wish to keep an open fire the same idea can be used in an alcove to one side of the chimney breast.

Basic requirements

Once you have decided on the type of office you want and on a site for it you can get

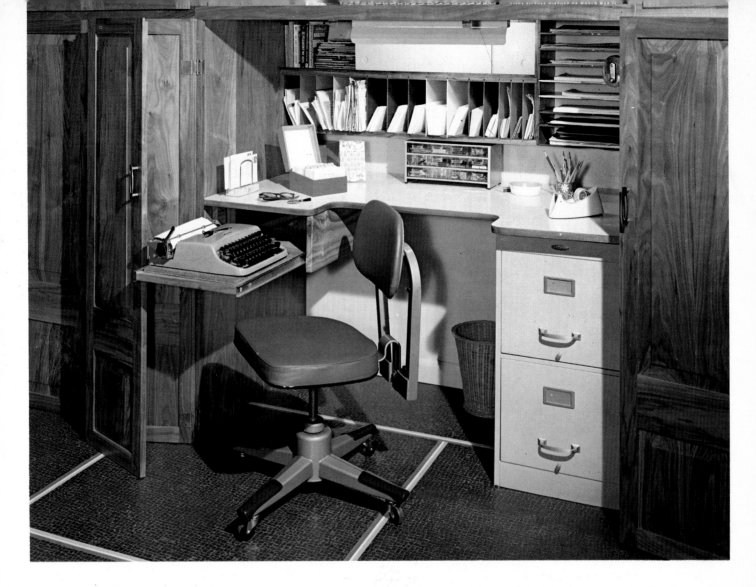

down to planning the details. Make a list of all the items you think you'll need. Some of these are essential in any office—a writing surface, a place to lay reference material, a chair (preferably swivel with adjustable height), versatile and ample storage space, a telephone, a lamp and maybe a typewriter. You will need lighting too; your choice for your home office should be an adjustable lamp which is equally suitable for general domestic use; there is no advantage in choosing the utilitarian types of office furniture when it comes to furnishing your home office. You should position the lamp carefully so you don't work in your own shadow. If you need a typewriter, this should be either a small portable or placed on a trolley so it can be moved out of the way.

Designing the layout

If you set up a permanent office space and use it regularly for business, the telephone will be a central feature. It is important to provide a shelf or table for the phone as a first step in planning your home office. Try to place the telephone, box files, writing paper and diary within easy reach from a sitting position.

The desk you use for typing should be slightly lower than the general office desk—providing the most comfortable typing position. Your main office desk should be about dining table height. The typing desk should have a fairly thin top to provide enough leg room.

Where space is limited you could provide a storable desk by resting a panel of chipboard or plywood, preferably covered with a wood veneer or plastic laminate, on separate drawer units. You can store the separate components of the desk in different parts of the room and eliminate any suspicion of a desk when not in use.

In the case of a built-in office unit there are two possibilities open to you—an exposed or a concealed unit. The exposed unit—which is always on view, and obviously an office, is easier and cheaper to make and you can design it to fit in with the rest of your room. For example, try to make the desk top harmonise, both in terms of finish and approximate height, with other surfaces in the room —such as mantle pieces and window sills. A good idea is to extend any existing bookshelves you may have to provide storage for papers and box files. Wherever possible use

Above: This attractive and well constructed fold-away office provides surprisingly generous facilities in such a small space.

57

matching materials. You could, for example, use the same leather cloth for covering your desk and office chair seat as is used on other chairs in the room.

Concealed units can be designed to fold away or slide into room dividers or wall fitted units. Also you can fit them into cupboards in alcoves or under the stairs. With concealed units you are able to carry out a quick transformation of your room—instantly changing the atmosphere from one of work and business into one of leisure and comfort.

Enclosed units

A completely enclosed and concealed office unit offers the best solution if you cannot devote a whole room to your office. You can for example, build an office into a cupboard. Careful planning of the layout will provide you with enough room for office essentials and a little space left over for non-essential but nonetheless useful items. General lighting is provided by concealed fluorescent tubes—and providing the cupboard is properly ventilated you can easily work undisturbed with the doors closed.

If you don't have such a cupboard you can build an office under the stairs. You only need enough headroom for the stooping position adopted for getting in and out of your chair.

A double-doored wardrobe, either free standing or fixed, can be turned into a serviceable small office. All you need to do is construct a work surface finished in paint or wood veneer matched to the wardrobe. Fix a fluorescent tube inside to provide adequate general light. The inside of the doors can be covered with pin board for notices and a calendar. The work surface can be supported on filing cabinets. When the wardrobe doors are closed all evidence of an office is completely concealed inside the wardrobe.

You should take care over the appearance of your home office. It must fit in with your existing decor. Use plastic laminates rather than paint on all surfaces which are going to receive constant wear. If you do this you'll improve their appearance and save on maintenance costs. Wherever possible go in for bright colours. Lots of office furniture on the market today is gaily painted and imaginatively designed.

A well thought out and soundly constructed home office is of great value to anyone and after you have built yours you'll wonder how you ever managed without it.

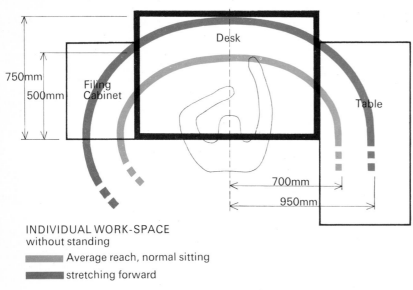

INDIVIDUAL WORK-SPACE
without standing

Average reach, normal sitting

stretching forward

750mm
500mm
700mm
950mm

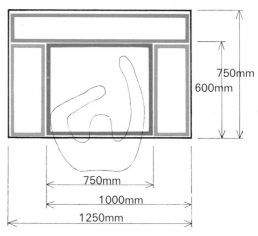

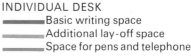

INDIVIDUAL DESK
Basic writing space
Additional lay-off space   Fig. 1
Space for pens and telephone

750mm
600mm
750mm
1000mm
1250mm

Kitchens in tiny spaces

In a tiny kitchen, every inch counts. Room for food preparation, cooking, washing up and storage is at a premium but too often such kitchens are badly designed, lacking storage space and with a thoughtless choice and siting of kitchen equipment. This can be infuriating for the housewife who spends much of her day there. With a little planning, however, a tiny kitchen can be made as pleasant to work in as any other kitchen.

Ideally, to make really efficient use of limited space you should start re-planning the room from scratch. Take a long look at what is already in the kitchen and the type of equipment you have there and you will probably find that much of the space is wasted. A hotchpotch of different-sized storage cupboards, for example, is a great space-waster. An old sink will have very little room below it for storage. A central table in a small kitchen will make traffic jams almost a certainty.

Make a plan

With space at a premium in your kitchen, it is essential that you plan the room thoroughly. The best way to do this is to make a scale drawing of the floor plan of your kitchen on a sheet of graph paper. Mark on it any architectural details—plumbing, electrical points, windows, the door and the way it opens.

Next, cut out coloured pieces of card and mark them to represent the cooker, fridge, sink, cupboards and any other units. Lay these down on the plan and move them about to find the most efficient kitchen arrangement. Once you start doing this it will be easy to visualise how everything can be fitted in, and how to save space.

Basic design

You will gain many ideas from working with your plan, but remember that there are basic design rules for kitchens, however large or small. There are three basic shapes for a kitchen plan—I, U and L shapes. Decide which one is right for your kitchen and fit in the units accordingly.

An I-shaped arrangement is best for really cramped kitchens in passages and very narrow rooms. In this type of kitchen, all the equipment and storage is down one side of the room, making a neat and efficient line.

An L-shaped arrangement is good for a rectangular room, or for part of a multipurpose room where the kitchen can be slotted into one corner. The L-shape can either be fitted neatly around the corner or, if space permits, one 'arm' can be left jutting into the room to act as a serving place or eating bar. But this arrangement is more suitable for a reasonably spacious room.

A U-shape can be used in square kitchens and is often best in a confined space because the equipment can be 'wrapped' around the cook, who stands in the centre and has everything well within reach.

Work areas

Kitchen space must be divided into 4 work areas—preparation, cooking, serving and washing up. Within the framework of the I, U, or L shape, arrange these work areas in a natural progression, so that you don't have to keep doubling back on your tracks when working in the kitchen. For example, you should place the fridge, food storage cupboards and mixer in the food preparation area. Keep pans over or under the sink as they usually need water in them before being put on the stove.

In a tiny kitchen, it is essential that there is a storage place for everything. Items that can't be stored will simply be left cluttering up valuable work surfaces. Serving a meal requires about 0.23-0.37 sq m (2½-4 sq ft) of work surface and you will need 0.28-0.37 sq m (3-4 sq ft) to make a cake in comfort. So plan your kitchen to the smallest detail to allow as much working space as possible to be left permanently free.

When you have planned your kitchen to your satisfaction, you can start fitting in equipment and storage units to suit the work areas.

Above: In a narrow kitchen, folding tables are a real boon. This one slides under the work-top on castors; the chairs fold flat.

Units

You can save a great deal of space by using every inch of wall space from floor to ceiling for storage cupboards. The base units, the tops of which provide a work surface, should all have sliding doors. These take up a lot less room than hinged doors. Base units should stand on a recessed plinth. This will not only make unsightly scuff marks less conspicuous, but will also increase the kitchen floor area slightly, allowing you to work more comfortably as you can get your toes under the working surface.

One problem with base units is that manufacturers' standard sizes will rarely fit snugly into a tiny kitchen. You can build cupboards to your own sizes, or you can use open shelves—cheaper for someone on a small budget—to bridge gaps between units. The top shelf should be level with the other work surfaces.

Corner units are particularly important as there is often wasted storage space here in badly designed kitchens. Corner cupboards with plenty of shelves will gain valuable space.

Over the base unit, shallow midway units, about 100mm × 152mm (4in to 6in) deep will give ample space for jars or tins of food, but leave plenty of working room underneath. Over these units, hanging cupboards can run right up to the ceiling.

Sink

A modern stainless steel sink is shallower, and therefore less space-consuming, than the old-fashioned ceramic sink. If the sink is set into a work-top, you can save a lot of space. Draining racks can be set on either side of the recessed sink, hung on the wall behind it or placed on a tiled window sill over it.

Even in a tiny kitchen, don't stint on the size of the sink, as this is one of the items in most constant demand in a kitchen. If you have a large family a double sink is well worth considering, even in the smallest kitchen. It speeds up washing up, and has many other uses.

Waste disposal

A waste disposal unit will take up far less space than a waste bin, though a cheaper and equally space-saving alternative is a rubbish chute set into the wall near the sink. Rubbish can be 'posted' through a trapdoor on the kitchen side and falls straight down into a dustbin outside. There should be a hinged flap on the outside wall to prevent draughts and the walls of the chute should be tiled to permit easy cleaning.

Cooker

A split-level cooker takes up more space than an ordinary cooker unless it is carefully placed. If you can find room for this arrangement however, the hob and the oven don't need to be next door to each other. This is useful if, for example, you can make use of an old fireplace. The fireplace can be removed and the hob set into the chimney on a fitted unit with cupboards beneath. The oven can be placed near the serving area or on the other side of the food preparation area.

An important point in planning a narrow kitchen is that oven doors are usually hinged on the left and this should be taken into account when placing the oven. Also—don't put the cooker by the door because this can be unsafe, especially with small children around.

Fridge and freezer

A modern, compact fridge with thin wall insulation gives maximum food storage room without taking up too much floor space. Remember that fridge doors are usually hinged on the right, so place the fridge so that the open door cannot obstruct the door connecting the kitchen with the rest of the house.

If you put a deep-freeze cabinet in a tiny kitchen you will have little room for anything else. Freezers can easily be placed in outhouses—the garage or shed—or in the cupboard under the stairs.

Washing machine

If you have to have your washing machine in the kitchen at all, use a front-loading type —this will give you a permanent work surface on top of the machine. A front loader with a built-in automatic spin drier is more compact than a twin tub, though slightly less efficient.

If space is really restricted, consider putting the washing machine in the bathroom. It is just as convenient a place as the kitchen though the machine should be connected to a power point situated outside the bathroom (a power point *inside* would be illegal).

Other equipment

Put as much kitchen equipment as possible away in drawers or on shelves. If you are short of drawer space, you might cover part of a wall with pegboard and use hooks to hang up everything hangable, from strings of onions to pans and egg whisks. This can look attractive and is an excellent way of using a bare wall opposite a line of units in a narrow kitchen.

Lighting and ventilation

Recessed spot lights set in holes cut in the ceiling save space and are especially effective in a low room. Strip lights concealed behind a fascia on the underside of a wall-hanging cupboard over a work surface also look good and work well. A central flourescent strip light is a practical choice for any type of kitchen. Make sure that the lights are placed

Below: In small flats where every square foot counts, a hallway or corridor which would otherwise be wasted can often be pressed into service as a kitchen.

Above: The 'kitchen in a cupboard' is perhaps the most space-saving arrangement possible. It fits into an alcove, and yet holds all you would find in a real kitchen.

so that your work areas are well lit and you are not cooking in your own shadow.

Ventilation is essential in a small kitchen. An open window often is not enough to remove cooking smells. Properly sited extractor fans are a good idea and cooker hoods, which channel cooking smells away, are an excellent buy for a tiny kitchen.

Hiding a 'kitchenette'

A kitchen area in an alcove or corner of a bedsitter or other multi-purpose room is often the most unsightly part of the room, and covering it up or camouflaging it will add greatly to the attractiveness of the whole room.

You can hide a 'kitchenette' of this type behind sliding or folding doors which are closed when the kitchen is not in use. An easier and cheaper alternative is to use roller blinds. The blinds can be fitted from ceiling to worktop level or they can extend right down to the floor. Venetian blinds can also serve this purpose, but they are more costly and harder to raise out of the way.

Kitchens with a difference

With a little ingenuity and planning, you can put your cooking area almost anywhere —in a cupboard, on wheels or on an island.

Kitchen in a cupboard. This type of kitchen is ideal for a bedsitter or other multi-purpose room. It consists of a sink unit with

a cupboard for cleaning materials underneath. On one side of the work surface are boiling rings with a fridge placed underneath. Above the work surface there are shelves, which will hold a plate rack and pots and pans. Hooks can be screwed to the underside of the shelves to hang up cupboards and jugs. The sides of the cupboard are made of pegboard with hooks for holding wooden spoons, colanders, egg whisks and similar items. On the inside of the cupboard doors you can place more hooks for hanging tea towels and pans. Narrow wooden boxes fixed to the inside of the doors will hold cutlery.

The width of this kitchen cupboard need be no more than 1.2m (4ft) and the depth can be as little as 460mm (18in), which makes the unit really compact.

An 'island' kitchen, too, can be very compact and can be an attractive feature. The sink can back onto the washing machine and the cooker and fridge can be arranged on either side, forming an X shape. The gap between the appliances can then be filled with plastic-laminated work-tops so that an octagonal shape is created. Open shelves can be fitted below the work-tops, but if the kitchen island is to be a feature of your room, cupboards with doors are far tidier. Even greater storage space can be provided if you hang an octagonal set of cupboards from the ceiling immediately above the kitchen island.

In a *mobile kitchen* some of the kitchen appliances are fixed into an alcove or roomy cupboard and other appliances are built into a trolley, which can be moved around and brought to the dining area for on-the-spot cooking. When not in use, the mobile unit can be pushed into a seldom used corner.

Fit the sink and the draining board into the alcove or cupboard and place the fridge under the draining board. Above this, fit shelves or storage cupboards and an eye-level oven if there is room, This could be put somewhere else if necessary, of course.

The rest of the kitchen is a mobile unit. It can consist of a square or rectangular work-top with two or more electric boiling rings set into it and storage cupboards underneath. A heavy chopping block can be set into the top of the unit, and vegetable storage provided below. Pans and cooking equipment can be kept under the work-top and small equipment, such as knives, can be put in a drawer just below the work-top, or in racks fixed to the side. Spices and sauce bottles can also be put in racks on the side. The unit must, of course, have a stable base; this should be a frame the same size as the work-top, with castors fitted to it. When you are cooking, the boiling rings can be plugged into a convenient floor or wall socket.

On a smaller scale, you can use a mobile unit instead of a kitchen table. The unit can consist of a large chopping block with vegetable storage and a rubbish bin below.

A *folding kitchen* is a good idea for a bedsitter. In one corner of the room, fit the sink and cooker with shallow shelves above. Then make an L-shaped screen out of chipboard. Fix castors to the bottom and a work-top inside the L (on strong brackets) at such a height that it will fit snugly over the cooker when the screen is 'wrapped' around it.

You will probably have room to fit shallow storage racks around the insides of the two parts of the screen.

The screen is wrapped around the cooker when it is not in use. It will look like a small cupboard and will neaten the appearance of the room by completely hiding all cooking equipment.

One of the most useful space savers in a small kitchen is a pull-out work-top. This can just be a single board that slides out from a main unit like a drawer, or it can have its own flap-down legs. In a very narrow kitchen, completely removable work-tops can be designed to clip on to units right across the kitchen like a bridge.

Wall-hinged tables are also a useful idea if you have an area of wall space at working surface level that you cannot fill. These can be supported with brass chains or—better— by flap-down legs.

Design tricks

A tiny kitchen can be made to appear less cramped by clever use of decoration. You can paint the kitchen in a 'receding' colour such as blue to increase the impression of space. A high narrow room will seem to gain width if you lower the ceiling.

Give storage cupboards a uniform look by painting them the same colour as the walls. Use roller blinds rather than curtains. Horizontal pine boards used on the walls behind the work-top will also give width to a narrow room. One further hint to making the kitchen look and feel as large as possible— don't use too many different types of surface. Use cork or vinyl tiles on both floor and wall, for instance, or ceramic tiles on the work-tops and walls.

Follow the advice offered in this chapter for a specific conversion and your work will be reduced considerably. Also, if you plan with economics in mind, the conversion will be much less costly.

Relating the economic aspects of design to a particular conversion problem requires some thought. What you must do is to plan in a logical step-by-step manner. Say you move into a house which is quite old, and the first thing you want to redesign is the kitchen. Where do you start?

Design economics

The first thing you'll need to know is exactly how much money you can spare to convert your kitchen. Once you have a good idea of your resources—and how much everything will cost—you should look at the kitchen as it is, and decide what initial jobs are essential. For instance, the plumbing may need replacing. Even if the pipes are quite sound, you might want to have the sink somewhere else —and so the plumbing will have to be altered. Remember, the position of the sink should relate to where other fittings are placed, so that the complete kitchen layout will facilitate an efficient flow of work.

Next, have a look at the wiring. In an old house this may need replacing altogether. Even if this proves to be unnecessary, you'll almost certainly need to install new power points. One of the drawbacks of old houses is that the number of power points provided— often only one to each room—is not enough to take the number of electrical gadgets that are commonly used in the modern home. Don't install power points at skirting board level. In a kitchen, power points in this position will cause you to do a lot of tiring bending down. Also, when all the fittings are in place, the points will be difficult to reach at all. Shoulder height is about the right position for power points. If your kitchen suffers from damp, this will have to be seen to before any electrical points are installed.

Once all the necessary alterations have been done to the plumbing and wiring, you can go on to plan the kitchen conversion according to the considerations outlined below.

Planning the conversion

When planning the redesigning of your kitchen, the first thing you'll need to do is to make a scale drawing of the floor area of the kitchen. A scale of 1 : 10 or 1 : 15, depending on the size of the room, should be about right.

With the drawn up floorplan, you'll find it easier to design the layout and positioning of the furniture and fittings. The final kitchen layout should not only result in an efficient work flow being achieved, but should also make the best possible use of the *size and shape* of the room.

The size and shape of the kitchen will go a long way toward determining the type of furniture and fittings that you choose. How much cupboard and drawer space you can afford, as well as the total area of work surfaces, will be governed to a large extent by the room's size and shape. Remember that the height of the room, including such things as angled walls, should be taken into account as well as the floor area. If your kitchen is on the small side, or is an awkward shape, you'll have to compromise a little. Some items, while being desirable in themselves, may have to be dispensed with for the sake of the

Below: *A modern kitchen should have a place for everything and an efficient arrangement of fittings to eliminate unnecessary work.*

overall design.

Once you have a fairly clear idea of what is the best possible layout that will suit your kitchen, you can go on to selecting the furniture and fittings themselves.

Choosing the furniture and fittings

As mentioned before, it is not enough to concentrate purely on the good looks or otherwise, of any particular item. When choosing furniture and equipment for your kitchen, the first question you must ask yourself is 'will it work'? This is where *ergonomics* relates to the problems of design. To recap on this, ergonomics can be defined as the relationship between man and machine. If you bear this in mind, you will see that kitchen furniture must be chosen to satisfy a specific function. Only when you are sure that any item will do the job required of it should you concern yourself with appear-

ance. Not only must the furniture and equipment you select meet their individual requirements, but each item should do so without getting in the way of another item. You should never overcrowd a kitchen. If you do, not only will the efficiency of each item be impaired, but your own ability to work in comfort will be seriously affected. You may think that it doesn't matter too much if your kitchen is a bit crowded. There is nothing worse, however, than spending time, money and effort on any job—only to find that at the end of a day you are no better off than you were at the beginning.

At this point you should consider the *practicability* of your kitchen conversion.

Defining a practical kitchen

A practical kitchen can be defined as a marriage between the furniture and fittings and the structural realities of the room. All

Below: A good example of sensibly arranged kitchen fittings. Cooker and double sink are separated by a laminated work surface, with ample built-in cupboard space. The wall cupboards give extra storage space.

the kitchen furniture and fittings should be chosen with the ergonomics of the situation, as well as size and shape of the room, firmly in mind. Make a list of all the furniture, fittings and pieces of equipment you'd like in your redesigned kitchen. This is where the consideration of *need* enters into the design economic problems of a conversion job. It is almost certain that you will have to eliminate some items from the list of what you'd like in your converted kitchen. Furniture, fittings and pieces of equipment should be chosen according to the priority of need. If you have space left over after the basic essentials of your modern kitchen have been catered for, you can incorporate some less necessary item into the overall design.

Now that you have decided what you have room for in your kitchen, you can begin to choose the particular items.

Cupboard and drawer units

As far as possible, all floor-standing cupboard and drawer units should be built-in. Built-in units are more economical on floor space than free-standing furniture. Also, the construction of built-in units is quite simple, as the kitchen wall forms part of the structure. If a unit is fitted into an alcove, all that will be needed is a top and front.

All cupboard and drawer units should incorporate a work surface. The best covering for a work-top is a plastic laminate material such as Formica. This is washable and scratch resistant. Your cupboard and drawer units should be designed so that all the work surfaces are at just above hip height.

Cupboard and drawer handles should preferably be flush fitting. This will eliminate the risk of you knocking your knees on protruding handles while working. To save space, all the cupboards should be fitted with sliding doors.

As far as wall-fitted cupboards are concerned, they should be fitted at a height that is neither too high for you to reach comfortably, nor so low that you will run the risk of bumping your head. As with floor level fittings, the cupboards should be fitted with sliding doors. For extra storage space, and also to prevent the formation of dust traps, wall cupboards should be fitted to carry on right up to the ceiling. The cupboards nearest the ceiling can be used to store little used, but nonetheless essential, items.

Having catered for the basic storage requirements of the kitchen, you can begin to consider the necessary equipment and where it is all to go.

The kitchen equipment

The most basic piece of kitchen equipment is the sink. Without a well designed sink, your work in the kitchen could prove to be

one long round of arduous and unnecessary toil. If you have room, choose a unit which incorporates two sinks and two draining boards. Also, if you can afford it, it would be a very good idea to have a waste disposal unit built in. On the left hand draining board you should place the dish rack. Choose one that is easy to clean, and gives a generous amount of accommodation for drying crockery.

The type of cooker you select will depend, to a large extent, on the total floor area of your kitchen. One of the most space-saving and attractive designs is the type of cooker with a separate hob, oven and grill. The hob is fitted with a long work-top flanking it, while the oven and grill are set at approximately chest level as part of an oven unit. A domestic refrigerator can be fitted in the same way. If bulky items like the cooker and refrigerator are installed in this manner, a great deal more floor and storage space can be provided. In this way, the total available area of the kitchen will be used more economically. Also, a chest level oven or refrigerator will save you a lot of bending down. This is where ergonomic considerations work in practice. You should be able to use any fittings and equipment with the minimum possible amount of effort and time being expended.

Such things as electric food mixers and coffee grinders need to be stored out of the way—and yet be easily accessible. One of the best solutions is a cupboard which, when opened, pulls out a built-in table—set at an appropriate height for small electrical appliances. The power point for the appliance is fitted into the wall above the cupboard. Such a cupboard unit will eliminate the need to lift and carry your appliances—thus saving you

Above: Here fittings and work surfaces are arranged in a U-shape—probably the best layout for a small kitchen. Always try to make room for a double sink as this helps speed up many jobs in the kitchen.

effort, and reducing the danger of damaging your equipment.

Once you have chosen the furniture, fittings and equipment, and where they are all to go, you can begin to think about the general decor of your redesigned kitchen.

The kitchen decor

As far as possible, all paintwork, paper and floor coverings for the kitchen should be washable.

Probably the best floor covering is foam-backed linoleum, or linoleum tiles. Linoleum is very hard wearing, as well as being a good insulating material against draughts. It is also washable.

As far as the cupboard and drawer units are concerned, all the fascias should be matching, so that the room will not be broken up by conflicting colours and textures. Remember that when you are considering the decor and colour scheme for your kitchen you must bear in mind the *effects of colour, tone and texture*.

The floor covering should be of a dark colour so that dirt and scuff marks won't show so dramatically. If you intend to paint the walls, choose a washable eggshell finish. Where wallpaper is to be used, it should be of the washable vinyl type. If the walls, floor and wood-work are not washable, you will have to redecorate your kitchen after only a few years. The same will apply if the colours you choose are too strong. When strong colours become tarnished, it will be much more noticeable than it would be in the case of more unobtrusive shades. Doors, window frames and sills should be painted with a polyurethane based gloss paint.

For the windows, roller blinds would be more suitable than curtains. Venetian blinds with vertical slats, are also a good choice. The disadvantage of blinds with horizontal slats is that they are a terrible dust trap.

Fluorescent lighting is better in a kitchen than ordinary tungsten bulbs, as more brilliant and even illumination is given.

If you plan your kitchen conversion according to the economic criteria outlined earlier, the job will be done more easily—and with better results. An understanding of design economics will help you plan and furnish your home successfully, while making the best possible use of your resources.

Below: Hardwearing surfaces are a must for any kitchen. Plastic laminate, a tiled table and polyurethane paint are seen here. Notice also the convenient height of the power point.

Adding a kitchen

Kitchens used to be the social centre of the average house, but between the wars their function changed to that of simply being a place to prepare or cook food. More recently, however, the kitchen has reverted to its former role, that of being a secondary eating area as well as a meeting place. Because of this, and because of the increasing use of mechanised equipment, many people are finding that they want to extend the kitchen area of their homes.

There are various ways of doing this. You could, for example, add on a laundry and utility room where everything except food preparation and storage is carried out. Or you could convert the existing kitchen into a utility room and add on a new kitchen—perhaps with space for eating. This last alternative is often a good solution, especially when the existing kitchen is rather small and would not accommodate the full kitchen equipment, space for eating, and people too! It probably would be better suited for converting into a utility room, containing a washing-machine and drier, space for ironing and storage for ironing board, brooms, packets and bottles of cleaning materials and so on.

Utility rooms also normally contain a single-drainer sink which is very useful for hand washing and preparing flowers for arrangement. You might like to house your deep-freeze unit in there if space permits. If the utility room adjoins the kitchen the dish-washer could also be put there though perhaps it could be more conveniently put in the kitchen. Again, this all depends very much on space. With all washing and associated activities (storage of cleaning materials and so on) catered for in this way, the new extension can be given over to preparing, eating and storing food.

Is it realistic?

Before making any final decisions about the feasibility of such an extension, you will have to find out whether it is going to get formal approval from your local authority.

Although any physical difficulties will normally be easily spotted there may be some hidden ones—associated perhaps with underground service pipes. But generally it should be a simple matter to assess whether or not you have room for the extension, and how it will affect the other existing rooms. If, however, the only available site is some

distance from the existing kitchen or utility room, the project may be impractical. It would mean either separating your new kitchen area from the old one by perhaps a considerable distance, or reorganising the functions of your present rooms drastically. Neither of these alternatives is very realistic in terms of convenience or expense.

Assuming, however, that you do have the right amount of space in the right place, you can provisionally earmark it for your extension and investigate other aspects of the work. The possible existence of any underground or other hidden services should be checked out, since they could cause complications later. A small water pipe can usually be re-routed without much difficulty, but if, for example, you discovered a sizeable drain or sewer at a fairly shallow level, then this could lead to major problems.

If the deeds of the property do not throw much light on where underground services are (and often they are sadly inaccurate on these matters), the local authority may be able to help, although in some districts their records may be incomplete or out of date.

Since a kitchen is bound to include at least a sink, you should find out about the location of the drains. Sinks, dishwashers and similar appliances must discharge into a drain connected to a suitable disposal point, that is, a public sewer or some form of

Below: *The twin personality of this kitchen-eating area is emphasised through the use of a dividing storage unit and different flooring.*

private disposal plant such as a cesspool. Any infringement of these rules could land you in trouble.

Regulations and grants

Before you begin building you must get approval from your local authority and from the mortgagee—building society or whatever —of your property.

Depending on the circumstances, financial assistance from public funds may be available to assist individual extension work. In Britain, local authorities can give grants for improving property lacking in amenities or which does not meet with the current housing standard in other respects. If your house is in good condition and has the normal minimum sanitary and kitchen fittings you might not be entitled to a grant, but it is worth making enquiries just in case. Remember that it is a condition of all grants that the work must be approved officially, so follow this up early on.

Layout

Before submitting any plans or drawings for formal approval, you should decide on the layout of the extension. Kitchens can, after all, take various forms—'kitchen' covers a multitude of planning sins—and the choice of shape and size may be dictated simply by the space available.

The work in a kitchen, though of course differing in detail from home to home, is basically the same, following a fairly constant basic pattern. Space must be allotted for *storage* of food (perishables in the refrigerator/deep freeze, vegetables/fruit in a

Fig.1. Floor-plan of a semi-divided kitchen, where a meal can be enjoyed without the sight of dirty dishes but where the second helping is only steps away!

ventilated cupboard or larder, and dry/canned goods in a cupboard), and for *preparation* which usually involves sorting, washing, and cutting. For maximum efficiency a well-lit flat work surface near to the sink is ideal, possibly with a wooden cutting board close to hand. Space and facilities for *cooking* will also have to be provided. The cooker should have a hard working surface next to it—preferably on either side for greater manoeuvrability. You can cook on a conventional combined cooker, or the oven—as is increasingly popular—can be separated from the hob-unit, and mounted conveniently at eye-level.

Once cooked, the food is then *served*, usually on one of the work surfaces adjoining the cooker. Serving hatches are best positioned above or next to this dishing-up worktop. For cold meals and sweets the food is prepared and dished up on a convenient work surface and passed direct to the servery.

After the meal comes the most unpleasant part of what is usually a pleasant occasion—the *washing-up*. So it will be convenient if the sink is near the servery. If you happen to have a dishwasher, this could be well sited near to the sink whether it is a floor or work-top model.

The final stage is the *stacking* of the clean dishes and cutlery. Most people consider the best place is close to the sink—unless of course it is priceless china to be put on display. But often crockery and cutlery are just as handy housed near the dining table, ready for table-laying. If some meals are eaten in the dining room, and some eaten in the kitchen, perhaps at a breakfast bar, then you will have to choose between the two. If you have one 'best' set and one 'only-for-the-family' then you can keep your formal things together, or, if your dining room is some distance away from the kitchen you might find it best to duplicate your sets anyway.

Fitments

There is a wide range of storage cabinets available today, from the inexpensive white-wood types without backs and with un-surfaced tops, to the more highly finished types with hardwood carcasses and laminated working surfaces. Similar cabinets are also available in stove-enamelled steel sheet. (Handymen should have no difficulty in constructing their own kitchen fitments, which can be especially useful if your kitchen is a peculiar shape and difficult to fit with standard sized units.)

Colour will always be perhaps the most personal aspect of design, but it is worth remembering that combinations of white and blue tend to give a chilly effect to the room, whereas yellows, oranges and reds have a decidedly warmer effect. If your kitchen enjoys long hours of sunshine or if you do a substantial amount of cooking it probably will feel over-heated towards the end of a day. This is where choosing the 'cooler' colours is particularly helpful. Conversely, a pokey kitchen that rarely gets the benefit of sunshine will look more welcoming if it has the warmer tones on at least some of its surfaces. But over-strong, or over-emphasised colours can ruin the 'homeliness' of a kitchen, just as much as a chilly look. White fitments usually look very smart against some strong primary colour in the wall or floor covering. Or the main surfaces of the room can be painted white or neutral, and the fitments can carry the stronger colour. It is always difficult to visualise your kitchen from colours in a catalogue, so, if possible, visit a large showroom which will give you a good idea of what your dream kitchen will look like in 'real life'.

Kitchen fitments are produced in standard ranges, which usually incorporate a limited choice of widths and varying arrangements of drawers and cupboards. Most of the better-quality ranges also include special corner cabinets. Shelves often come unfixed so that you can arrange them to suit your height, and most manufacturers produce special cabinets to house refrigerators, oven units and their hobs in the most popular sizes. If you find—possibly because your kitchen is a peculiar shape—that the standard units will not fit neatly together, then this is a good opportunity to add an extra work surface by running one between two fitments or over the tops of several.

Widths of units may vary, but their heights do not. Floor units are around 915mm (3ft) high which is a height that most people find useful—that is, as long as you are of average height. Taller-than-average housewives might find it necessary to raise the standard units on blocks to a more convenient height, while smaller women might like to saw off a

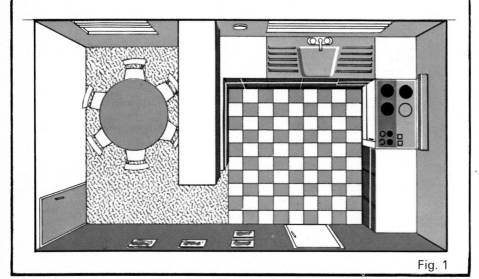

Fig. 1

Right: Greens are good for you . . . Cool green and off-white creates a relaxed atmosphere for both cooking and eating. The shutters help control the heat and light.

couple of inches from the legs or bases of the units.

The standardisation of height helps both the appearance of the kitchen, and its over-all efficiency. Frequently the work-top itself, which continues across the top of several units (such as floor cabinets), is especially made from a single piece of laminate-faced blockboard, thereby avoiding joints in the surface. And the sink-bowl can be let flush into it, instead of having the sink-top inter-rupting the surface and looking ugly. As well as looking neater, this continuous surface is easier to clean, and therefore more hygienic.

Wall units are also made to standard heights, although because they come separate from the floor units you can fix them at various heights to suit yourself. This is particularly useful as the space above a single-height unit is usually wasted and ends up as a mere dust-trap. You could try fixing wall units between the ceiling and the lower units to make optimum use of your wall space. But do remember that there should be a gap of not less than 460mm (18in) between the work surface and the underside of the first wall unit.

In deciding on the layout of your kitchen, you should allow adequate space for circulation, preferably for more than one person to move around in so that a toddler or chatty neighbour is not continually under your feet. Analyses of movements in average-sized kitchens have shown that many miles are travelled in any given day. Often a large percentage of this distance could be avoided by simply re-arranging the fitments—it would obviously be a help if they were not several yards apart or hidden away in nooks and crannies. If you bear in mind the typical work-sequence as given above, then pro-viding an efficient layout should be no problem. It is a good idea to walk through the various stages of preparing a meal to discover the fastest route round your kitchen. Remember, all that is needed is enough space for two people to pass between one unit and another. More space than this will only cause tired feet.

Eating

Many families find it convenient to eat snacks and quick meals in the kitchen itself. On one hand it is practical to reduce the distance involved in carrying food dishes to and from the table. On the other, it does not contribute to the enjoyment of a meal if the debris involved in its preparation is always

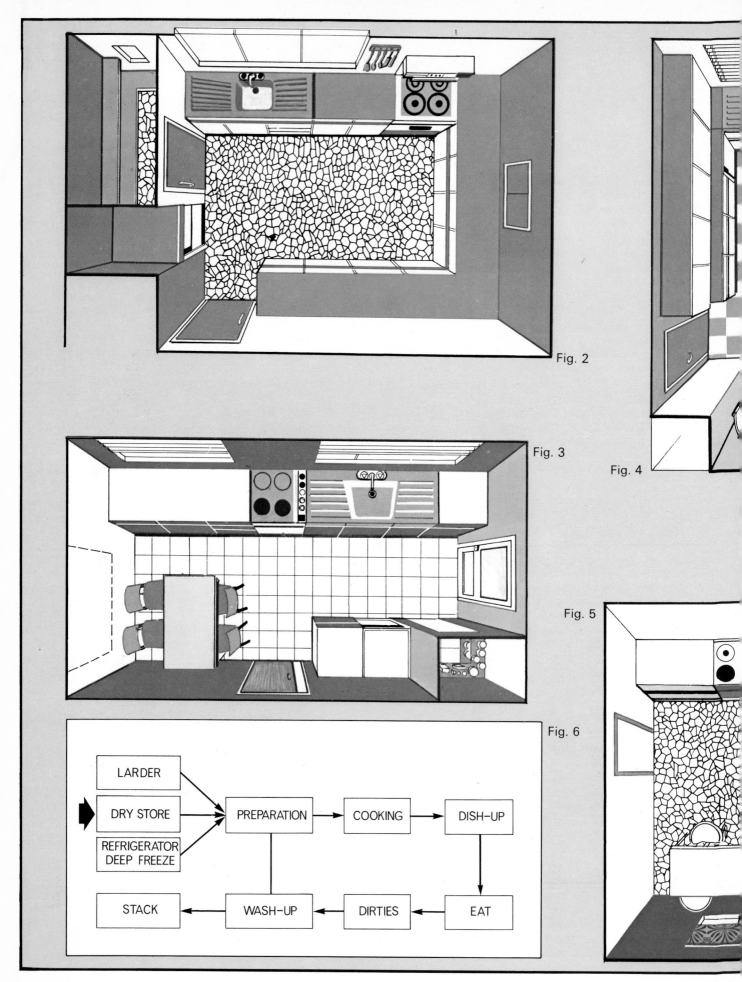

Fig. 2

Fig. 3

Fig. 4

Fig. 5

Fig. 6

LARDER

DRY STORE → PREPARATION → COOKING → DISH-UP

REFRIGERATOR DEEP FREEZE

STACK ← WASH-UP ← DIRTIES ← EAT

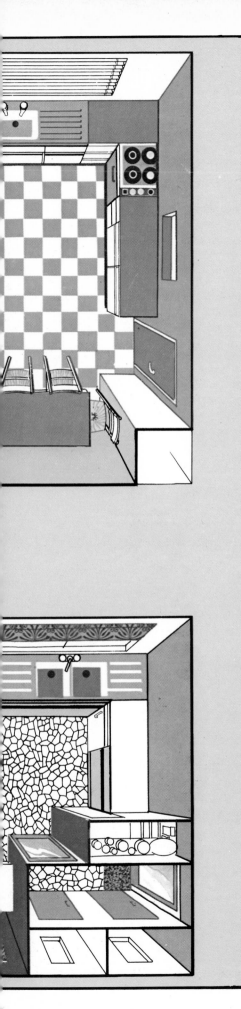

Fig.2. This is a kitchen layout based on the work-flow sequence shown in Fig.6, with all the units arranged for maximum ease and efficiency.

Fig.3. A typical 'galley' kitchen—long and fairly narrow, though everything is within arm's length or a stride away, and plenty of light falls on the eating area.

Fig.4. A square kitchen, with all the fittings hugging the walls—note the wall cupboards overhanging the work surface, for example, leaving the floor area uninterrupted.

Fig.5. An 'L-shaped' kitchen. The bulk of the storage fills one corner, leaving a recess for the eating area. Notice the twin sinks side-by-side for workable washing up!

in evidence. The ideal is probably an arrangement where the distance from the kitchen is kept to a minimum, and the kitchen itself does not obtrude.

There are a number of ways in which this can be achieved. First, you can manage this compromise—if the shape and size of the room lends itself readily to it—with a layout as in Fig.1. With the table as shown the view into the kitchen (with its possible clutter) is minimal. As you are starting from scratch by adding a kitchen it should be easy to plan this sort of shape. The remaining small rectangle can be used as a service lobby or for storage. In other cases, the extension could be the main kitchen, and an existing small room be converted into the eating area.

Second, in a long, rectangular kitchen, especially if there is a door about a third of the way along one wall, the smaller end can conveniently be used for eating, as in Fig.3.

Third, if you want to cut off the kitchen even more from view, you can use a projecting cabinet as a divider. And instead of the upper cabinets being fixed to the wall, they can be held in place by steel corner or angle brackets, leaving an open space above the work-top for serving. If the wall and floor coverings change where this fitment projects, then so much the better, because this in itself will indicate subtly where one area ends and another begins.

A fourth and more drastic way of separating the two areas is to alter the floor level. This is easily done when in the process of adding an extension, but as a general rule, changes in floor level are not a good idea, especially in functional rooms like kitchens where it might be difficult to see the drop of level when carrying a tray. If, however, you do decide to change your floor level, an eating area with its floor about 305mm (1ft)

below that of the main kitchen can look attractive, and separate the two areas most efficiently.

It is better to have the eating-area floor lower rather than higher to reduce the view straight into the kitchen. And there should be at least two steps—as one step can be easily overlooked.

There is a danger that the ceiling may become too high in the eating area, due to lowering the floor levels. In this case you could install a false ceiling which would give an added feeling of individuality to the eating area and improve its proportions. If this solution appeals to you, but you find that the steps present a problem, then you could achieve the same effect by using a short ramp. The gradient should not exceed 1 : 8 so, for example, a 305mm (1ft) change of level would need an 244cm (8ft) long ramp. If space permits this could be very effective, especially if a run of floor cabinets is positioned so that it masks the rough edge of the ramp farthest from the wall.

Blinds can be used to emphasise the difference between kitchen and eating areas. Venetian blinds, for example, could be fitted to a divider or a free-standing panel and form a false 'window' separating the two spaces as effectively but less permanently than a wall. Spring-loaded roller blinds are available in fabric or specially treated paper—both in a range of bright colours and patterns. Alternatively you could use horizontally sliding doors hung on a head track. A lightweight door runs easily and silently on this type of overhead track.

Stale food smells can be especially off-putting if the kitchen doubles as an occasional dining area. You can eliminate them by using a small extractor fan in some convenient position between the cooker—the main offender—and the eating area. These fans are usually fixed to an external wall, collecting the air directly from the room and discharging it into the outside air. Some models can be fitted to a fixed glass pane in a window instead of on to a solid wall. You could also fit the fan in a concealed position, with a duct connecting it to the room or to the outside air. More elaborate but more positive in action, are the fans fitted in or connected to a hood over the cooker. But they may not be quite so effective with cookers having high-level grills. Some types of hood incorporate a renewable filter to collect the greasy fumes.

Laundry room extensions

The advent of automatic washing machines and dryers has meant that domestic laundry activities no longer require constant attention, and can therefore be removed from the rest of the kitchen work. A separate laundry room is safer, quicker, quieter and cleaner than a washing machine operated at the kitchen sink, and makes the whole process more pleasant.

The position of the laundry activities depends, to a great extent, on the existing plumbing in your home. There are also other practical considerations to bear in mind when designing a separate laundry room.

Traditionally, 'washday' has always monopolised the kitchen as well as most of a housewife's time. A wet washday has tended to take over the whole house, with rivers of condensation and a general damp smell everywhere. Modern automatic appliances have gone a long way to alleviate this, and there are now single machines which wash, rinse, dry and air clothes at the press of a button. These are fairly rare, however, and obviously expensive.

Although the average automatic washing machine is installed in the general kitchen area, several inconveniences remain. Dirty clothes come close to food, and clean clothes are liable to acquire cooking odours if not dealt with immediately. The kitchen sink remains in constant use, and a general washday atmosphere prevails. Following the development of automatic laundry appliances, the next logical step is to isolate the whole laundry operation from the food area and place it in a separate room.

The size of a laundry

A home laundry room does not have to be very large in order to be workable, and variations will depend on your individual requirements. An area 2.5m × 2.5m (8ft × 8ft) is sufficient to fit an automatic washer, separate tumble dryer, sink and adequate working surface for sorting, folding and ironing.

For most people, space set aside for a single activity is a luxury, and it may be necessary to incorporate your laundry within a general utility room with washing as the

main function. In such cases the possible sizes will vary considerably.

Since the finishes will be hard-wearing and practical, the room could also be used by children for drawing and painting, or by adults—for wine- and beer-making, for instance. If you are thinking of a secondary function for the laundry room, bear this in mind from the start so that adequate storage space can be included.

Positioning a laundry

You may be limited in your choice of position for a laundry. If none of your rooms is suitable for conversion, consider building on an extension. The position of a conversion or extension should be influenced strongly by the existing plumbing in your house.

Laundries need hot and cold running water and a waste outlet. Position the laundry as close as possible to the existing water supply and drains, as this will enable a simple connection to be made to the water supply. It

Left: The best solution is to have your laundry in a separate room, so that it does not interfere with any other activities. Here an old scullery has been converted by fitting brightly painted storage fitments round the old double china sink unit.

will also reduce, or eliminate, the need for the installation of new drains (underground), which can be very expensive. Ideally the waste pipe (above ground) from your laundry appliances should issue directly into the existing gully (sink at ground level leading to the drain).

You may consider that other factors take priority over the cost of extending a drainage system. Access, for instance, is one which is very important and is influenced by the size of your wash and when you do it.

A housewife with a large family, living in a house, will probably want easy access from the kitchen and to the garden. A young wife with no children, who is out at work all day, and lives in a flat, may find a room off an upper floor bathroom quite adequate for a laundry.

Possible conversions

There are several possible conversions which may not be immediately apparent. A garage which is built into or onto a house would lend itself to being a laundry, providing there is sufficient space elsewhere to build a separate garage. A very large kitchen may become safer, more efficient and better looking if part of it is divided off to make a laundry.

Older buildings often have a network of single-storey outbuildings, including redundant fuel stores and sculleries. These are usually suitable for conversion into a laundry, or alternatively you could demolish them and build a new extension in their place.

When planning an extension, remember to leave adequate external access from the front to the back of the house. This should be at least 915mm (3ft) wide to leave enough room for refuse collection. Avoid placing windows which open outwards onto such narrow accesses, as these can cause serious accidents.

Laundry appliances

Appliances vary considerably in size, and the price range for each type is wide. Your local dealer will be able to supply you with detailed information on the types available, and help you to find the right appliances to suit your needs.

Washing machines. There are four main types of washing machine:

1. *The single washing unit* for rapidly washed small loads. Hand or powered wringers are available and often fit on top of the washing machine. This type doesn't warrant being the centre piece of a laundry, but may well serve as a second machine in a communal room.

2. *The twin tub,* which incorporates a separate washing machine and spin dryer in a single cabinet. The clothes are handled between the washing and the drying operations, and controls have to be adjusted at certain stages. Twin tubs cannot be plumbed in, but are easily stored and moved.

3. *Semi-automatic machines* have an integral washing, rinsing and spin drying tub. The washing does not have to be handled between operations, but controls have to be adjusted at various intervals during the complete programme. Semi-automatic machines can be plumbed in or left mobile.

4. *Fully automatic machines* wash, rinse, and spin dry without the clothes being handled. Some more expensive types automatically tumble dry as well. Once a programme is set, the complete cycle works without any further attention. Automatic machines are usually plumbed in, but this is not essential.

Dryers. There are three main categories of dryer, or drying aid:

1. *Spin dryers* are available as separate machines, independent of automatic and twin tub machines. They do the job of a wringer—extract water from clothes. Spin dryers also rinse clothes, but there is no heat involved.

2. *Tumble dryers* are usually available as a unit separate from automatic washing machines. They take the place of the washing line, and some can be adjusted to air clothes as well. Tumble dryers are usually fitted with a vent which exhausts damp air to the outside.

3. *Drying cabinets* are available in many sizes, and some are small enough to fit under work benches. They consist of a heated and ventilated cabinet with hanging rails fixed inside, and the heat can be controlled to dry or just air clothes.

Ironers. Two main types of ironing machines are available: flat bed or rotary. They are useful for large quantities of simple ironing, but a hand iron is still necessary for complicated garments.

When choosing which appliance to buy, you should consider the available space, the amount of washing you handle, available time, and the amount of money you can spend. Automatic machines require fresh hot water for every load, but with twin tubs careful selection of loads enables the same water to be used several times. Thus a second load can be washing while the first is spin drying, and large quantities of washing are dealt with more quickly and economically than with an automatic machine.

Additional requirements

A well-equipped laundry should have a deep sink for some soaking prior to machine washing, and for hand washing. Provide hanging rails over the sink for drip-dry clothes, and also a draining board if the sink is not large enough to catch all the drips.

A working surface approximately 1.83m × 610mm (6 ft x 2 ft) is necessary for sorting, folding and temporary stacking of clothes. The top should be strong enough to take an ironing machine if required, and should be 864mm (2ft 10in) high for ironing in a standing position. A retractable lower board can be incorporated for seated ironing.

Storage should include a cupboard out of children's reach for bleaches, dyes, detergents, washing powders etc. A tall cupboard is also required if you use a portable ironing board. This should be fitted with an asbestos-lined, ventilated compartment for immediate storage of a hot iron. Provision of storage for dirty clothes, clean linen and an airing cupboard will depend on the layout of the rest of your home. If you are generally short of such space, large cupboards in the laundry could be very useful.

Electrical requirements

When planning electrical outlets, you should consider lighting, appliances, heating and ventilation. Provide a socket outlet for each appliance, not forgetting the iron, and extra outlets for future modifications.

Provide ceiling lighting points so that you are never working in your own shadow. Pull-cord switches are preferable where hands are likely to be wet. Under-floor heating is ideal for a laundry, in which case wiring has to be installed when the floor is being constructed. An electrical extractor fan placed high in an external wall is an asset.

Water

Place the washing machine and the sink as close to the existing water supply as possible. The water can be supplied hot or cold, depending on the appliance and the general water system in your home. If the water arrives hot you save time, especially with an automatic machine which empties after every cycle. On the other hand, extracting water from your household system will rob your central heating or bathroom of hot water. Appliance manufacturers usually state whether hot or cold water should be used.

To obtain water from your main supply, form a junction at a convenient height in the existing pipe. Insert a stop-tap in the extension pipe so that the machine can be moved without having to cut off the water supply to the whole house. Appliances are fitted with a flexible hose for easy connecting and tolerance when finally positioning the machine. You should try to conceal pipes from general view wherever possible.

Machines should be filled at the water pressure recommended by the manufacturers. Consult your water board for local pressures, and they will advise you on the kind of regulating valve you will need, if any, A water softener may also be needed in some areas.

Waste outlets

In Britain the Building Regulations impose certain restrictions on waste and drain pipes. Drains must have a sufficient slope to enable the water to run away quickly. Changes in the direction of a drain have to be fitted with an inspection chamber, and connections to existing drains are best made at such points.

Waste pipes in houses built in Britain since 1966 have to be inside, and this also applies to additional pipes. Additions to houses built before 1966 can be fixed outside along with the original pipes.

Each waste pipe requires an 'S' bend water sealed trap to prevent drain odours from reaching the appliances. However, pipes from different sources (e.g. a sink and washing machine) can meet inside the building so that you only have to penetrate the wall in one place.

Building materials

Building materials used for a laundry extension should be chosen for their thermal qualities as well as structural stability and weather resistance. That means they should be good at keeping the warmth in and the cold out. This will assist the drying and airing process and provide a comfortable, economically run environment. It will also reduce condensation, which occurs when warm, damp air meets a cold surface.

Bricks and building blocks have good thermal qualities. Blocks, larger and cheaper to lay than bricks, may require additional exterior cladding for the sake of appearance. Windows should be large enough for adequate daylight, but too much glass will increase condensation problems, in which case double glazing may be necessary. Have as many openable windows as possible to aid ventilation.

Where flat roofs are used there should be a 152mm (6in) gap between the outer cladding and the ceiling. This will increase the thermal capacity of the roof, especially if the gap is filled with fibreglass insulation.

Beware of the wide range of prefabricated structures which are available. Initially they seem economical, but often they include large areas of glass and corrugated pvc roofing, the thermal qualities of which are

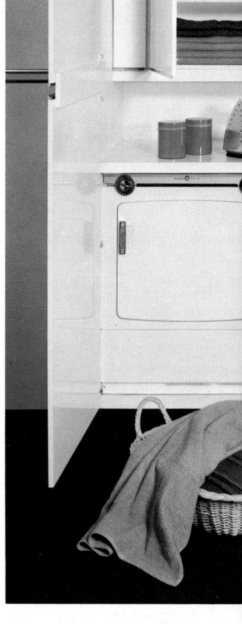

minimal. The walls of prefabricated units often require extra cladding to insulate them sufficiently.

Flooring

Durability and water resistance are the most important considerations when choosing flooring for a laundry room. If the wrong type is chosen, or it is badly laid, it will spoil the whole laundry and be dangerous. A solid concrete construction is preferable, and this must include a damp-proof membrane which will prevent damp from rising to affect adhesives and reduce the thermal qualities of the laundry.

If under-floor heating is installed, use mosaic or quarry tiles on the surface. These will not be affected by the heat which builds up during off-peak periods, whereas plastic

Centre and left: If you cannot spare a whole room for the laundry, a neat fitted alcove can be almost as efficient, providing the floor covering is practical. Make sure there is plenty of storage space for clean linen, washing powders etc. When not in use, the doors close to conceal the area neatly.

more versatile surface for work-tops, but is more expensive than linoleum or plastic sheeting.

Washable vinyl wallpaper is available in a wide range of designs. Do not attempt to use the normal absorbent papers in a laundry. Where painted walls are preferred, these should be gloss or satin finish. Matt finishes are more susceptible to steam and moisture.

Colours must always remain a personal choice, but cool blues and greens help to give the laundry a clean appearance. If in doubt you cannot go far wrong with white everywhere. Ceramic tiles are expensive but help to give a permanent solid appearance which goes well with the designs of most automatic laundry appliances.

If you bear these points in mind when planning a new laundry room, you should be able to produce a practical and attractive addition to your home. As with any major alteration, however, it is important to work out in detail what you want before embarking on the job itself.

floors will soften and dent if they become too warm.

Plastic tiles and sheeting generally provide a good economical floor finish, although some types tend to become slippery when wet. When covering a timber floor in a conversion with plastic, lay a sheet of hardboard over the floorboards. This will eliminate irregularities in the floorboards which show through the surface after some time.

Finishes and colours

A unified and clinical appearance is achieved if the same water-proof material is used on horizontal and vertical surfaces. Linoleum provides an adequate surface for laundries, and this is sometimes available in wall qualities which are thinner than the regular grades. Plastic laminate provides a

Rooms that grow up with the family

Even with space at a premium in modern houses, it is by far the best strategy to give children a room of their own. With any luck this could confine most of the noise and mess to one well-defined area, and encourage children to take a pride in their 'territory'— giving them a sense of independence early in life. And as a child grows older, his need for privacy grows, too. Often he will need somewhere quiet to study, or to enjoy his hobbies, and entertain his friends.

Children's rooms present their own special design problems, often simply because the parents cannot visualise the needs of a child while he is still a tiny baby. Only too quickly they will realise that the tiny cot with transfers of blue bunnies and the pastel-coloured 'nursery' furniture is totally inadequate to stand up to the onslaughts of the average toddler. It is far better to ignore the nursery motifs and furniture altogether— unless you can afford to re-furnish the room completely after a couple of years. Consider instead what the room should be like if it belonged to a six-year-old. That way, time, money and temper can be saved for the first years while the 'den' is taking shape.

The really workable child's room is always

the one which is most adaptable. It takes a lot of thought and visualisation to plan such a room effectively, but not necessarily masses of money. If you do a good job in the preliminary stages then the bonus will be remarkable; once you have made the room secure and attractive to the child then he is less likely to wander into potentially dangerous areas such as the kitchen. Furthermore, it will be easy to maintain and will 'grow up' with him.

Achieving the proper scale

Few things are more frightening or repressive to a young child than a room full of adult-sized furniture looming over him. As a general rule, the less furniture in children's rooms, the better—they need all the floor space they can get. But whatever furniture you do provide, try to ensure that it is in proportion to the child. Again, think of him as a six-year-old, and plan for furniture which will *fit* him.

You will find that manufacturers of 'knock-down' or kit furniture for children will have scaled their pieces accordingly. This usually means that tables will be around 508mm (20in) up from the floor level. Some

Below: *'Kids' corner! The furniture is light but durable, and the decor kept plain so that the child's toys and paintings add the necessary touches of colour. The playhouse acts as a 'garage' for larger toys.*

seats which are as little as 356mm (14in) from the floor actually work as nursing chairs and are firm favourites among young children. If you can arrange for the child to have some of his meals at his own table, sitting on his own chair then you may find he will learn table manners more quickly than if he has to struggle uncomfortably on adult-sized furniture for the duration of a meal.

But it is a fact that the child will outgrow this kind of 'specialised' furniture—unless you plan to have a fairly large family where such pieces will be more or less constantly in use. It is better to buy them in kit form, which can easily be 'knocked down' and stored for the next child, or in cheap materials such as laminated fibreboard (known as 'paper') furniture. Best of all, though, is the new Scandinavian children's furniture which has been designed with versatility in mind. When in a horizontal position a unit can, for example, be a seat and desk combination. When turned up vertically it becomes a storage unit with a work surface. This, and other variations on the theme, is well worth considering for use in a child's room, especially if you have limited space. Although these units are usually constructed in light wood, they are tough and durable.

Pictures

It is no use planning something which is a masterpiece of home design unless the child is happy to stay in it for any length of time. And the quickest way to make him unhappy is to bore him. Providing an interesting environment should be part of the overall planning. Perhaps for a baby of a few months the only visual stimulus needed will be brightly-coloured mobiles dangling over his cot. But as the toddler grows restless and inquisitive, the need for other focal points grows, too. He may show a passing interest in pictures or motifs depicting his favourite nursery rhyme characters but he will almost certainly outgrow them—perhaps before he outgrows the stories themselves. Child experts suggest that children need to be surrounded by pictures full of detail and colour which depict realistic objects and people. Some educationalists go so far as to suggest that even very young children would show more interest in prints of Old Masters than in pictures of teddy bears or whatever.

But whatever you choose, make sure that there is either plenty to look at—a lot of detail in the picture—or enough suggestion to encourage the child's own imagination. Abstracts in vivid colours can hold a child fascinated for hours because he can 'read' into them his own thoughts. For safety's sake, pictures should be mounted on card, rather

than in frames with a glass over them. It is also sensible to hang or fix them at the *child's* eye level, not yours.

Flooring

As soon as children learn to crawl, the centre of their activities will be the floor—and will continue to be so for years. It will be played on, crawled on and subjected to the hardest possible 'consumer' tests! Flooring—the actual floor covering—should be non-slip, warm enough to be walked on with bare feet, as sound-deadening as possible, soft enough to crawl on or sit on for long periods, easily cleaned and, in the long term, economical.

Carpet, even cheap or second-hand carpet, can be destroyed quicker than any other floor covering, by just one small child. *Rugs* on wood present hazards to the child even if the floor has been treated with a non-slip finish. Besides, expanses of floor interrupted by rugs are inferior bases for train sets or other games or hobbies which involve lots of space. (All forms of wooden floors, incidentally, unless immaculately sanded and sealed, are potentially dangerous because of the possibility of splinters working free.)

Rubber, though expensive in the short term, is excellent flooring for the children's rooms because it is relatively soft and heat retaining, and even fragile objects tend to bounce off it.

Cork tiles are also suitable flooring for

Above: A blackboard border inspires tiny artists and keeps at least some of the wall clean. Bunk beds covered in a strong floral design save space and look attractive. Low and high shelves add split-level interest.

children's rooms for similar reasons, although they must be well sealed to prevent spillages seeping between the cork particles and children gouging bits out of them.

Vinyl tiling is probably the most popular type of flooring for 'service' rooms, and few rooms have to be more serviceable than a child's—it is easily wiped clean and fairly durable. Rubber is perhaps the softer of the two but this is a matter of personal taste.

Linoleum is cheap enough to be easily replaced after a major disaster, but it has been superceded in both fashion and quality by the vinyl and rubber types of flooring.

Rush matting would be unbearably knotty to crawl on—such refinements are best left until the child is much older.

Walls

Walls have to be tough. A child expects more of a wall than an adult does and consequently the wall finish must be functional as well as decorative. A child will want to experiment with it. It is yet another surface against which he can try his toys— and his strength. The coward's answer is to provide blackboard as far up as the child can reach at least on some of the walls. This is, however, a temporary solution only and often not a very attractive one.

You may choose to paint the walls but the effectiveness of this depends very much on the type of paint you use. But whatever finish or colour you choose remember it must be lead-free—make absolutely sure of this by checking the label.

High-gloss finishes are perhaps the easiest to wipe clean but many people these days find them the least attractive of all the types on the market. Also, if your child needs a regular nightlight, the reflection can be disturbing, even frightening. Polyurethane paints are renowned for their toughness, and are virtually child-proof. The old stand-by, emulsion paint, is still cheap—temptingly so if you persuade yourself that a child's room will need almost constant redecoration. It will work out more expensive in the end than one treatment in a superior grade of polyurethane, particularly as emulsions are much harder to clean and keep clean than tougher surfaces.

Conventional wallpaper has obvious drawbacks—it can be ripped only too easily— but the newer vinyl wall-coverings have many advantages. They are notably washable, stain-resistant and are available in the brightest colours and an increasing range of attractive patterns. They are also often textured, which provides harmless interest for the child's inquisitive fingers.

Pegboard, which first became popular in schools, has now earned its place in ordinary domestic use. It both protects and enhances walls, and is certainly a useful addition to any playroom. It is more adaptable than blackboard which will undoubtedly be 'outgrown', but pegboard is always acceptable. In the early years you can pin up 'educational' pictures or alphabets—then the child's own schoolwork or paintings. And it will still be useful later, as a display surface for teenagers' posters. Pegboard is also a fairly good insulating material and, mercifully, slightly sound-deadening. If, when the child has become a sophisticated teenager, he will want his walls covered with smarter, more expensive tongued-and-grooved wood panelling, then you will find that the pegboard will be easy to remove and will have contributed to keeping the walls' surfaces in good repair.

Ceilings

It will help to create a cosy atmosphere in a child's room if the ceiling is quite low and, therefore, in scale with him. If you live in a Victorian house with enormously high ceilings you could consider installing a false, lower one and covering it with expanded polystyrene tiles. False ceilings are often used to conceal the complicated wiring of more adventurous lighting systems which may well be called for as the demands made of the room grow more sophisticated. Alternatively you can paint the ceiling in advancing colours to make it *seem* lower.

Safety

Unless you can afford the space and the money to provide your children with separate rooms for playing and sleeping, then it is most likely that their bedroom will fulfil both functions. And in Britain, at least, that usually means upstairs. Windows act like a

magnet to most toddlers, and their danger cannot be over-estimated. They should either be the sort which a child would find impossible to open, or barred. This may sound unreasonably alarmist, but child fatalities due to falls are only too numerous. A large area of glass may be very attractive, but the risks are too great unless certain precautions are taken. Not only may a child open the window and climb out, but a lively youngster may even fall against the glass and smash it. But do make sure that the room has adequate daylight—this becomes increasingly important as the very young child begins to focus his eyes and concentrate on objects. Eyestrain at an early age can result in permanent eye damage.

Top, opposite page: A big, bright and bold room that will grow up with the kids. Simple, uncluttered lines and striking tones will outlast nursery fripperies. The room is divided into separate playing and relaxing areas by the arrangement of main furniture units and grouping colours.

Far right: Bitter-chocolate and orange makes for an unusually sophisticated child's room. Vivid and detailed drawings bring the setting to life, compelling attention.

Right: Well-organised chaos! This child's room has ample space for him to use his imagination without ruining the decor. All the toys have round edges.

Top: A zebra's eye-view of a perfect playroom. The tiny segmented wall unit provides endless opportunities for play, the furniture is in scale with the child, and all the primary colours are well used.

Toys and furnishings should be lead-free, and free from sharp edges and too many loose parts which could get swallowed. Any free-standing furniture (as few pieces as possible should be used) should be light enough to cause little damage if they were to topple on the child, and have rounded corners. Again, 'paper' pieces are ideal here.

But if you do use cupboards which are not fixed to the wall or floor, do make absolutely sure that they are sufficiently heavy to withstand the weight of a child swinging on an open door or drawer. On the other hand, chests should have lids which can be easily lifted by the child himself in case he decides to climb in them and hide—if he is trapped he could easily suffocate.

Electric sockets are best positioned out of the child's reach until he is old enough to respect their potential danger. Wherever they are, they should comply with the standard safety regulations and it would be best if each socket was fitted with a switch.

Although some changes in a child's room

will be inevitable, sensible planning over the basics such as flooring, wall surfaces and work-tops will ensure that these changes are minimal and inexpensive.

Solving storage problems

Just as children are an important part of your household, so their rooms should be an important part of your house. Whether it is brand new and architect designed, or old and in the process of being modernized, one part of the house will probably be changing constantly—the children's room.

Storage will not be much of a problem while your child is still a baby, as a few drawers will usually be enough to accommodate his possessions. But up to the age of eight or thereabouts he will steadily accumulate toys which will inevitably end up under your feet all day. A little preliminary plan-

ning, however, will go a long way in preventing this situation.

Storage units designed originally to be used in the kitchen, for example, may well be of use in children's rooms, especially the kit-type units which can be added to as the need arises. Combinations of drawers, cupboards, shelves and work surfaces, all fixed securely to the wall, will continue to serve their purpose well for many years. Whatever type of unit you use, it must be adaptable because the emphasis on storage will shift from toys to books to clothes to hi-fi-equipment—all differing in shape and size.

In the early years, large, unwieldy toys such as prams or cars can be kept in a 'garage' located perhaps under a work surface, or in a 'drive-in' cupboard. Oddly-shaped toys such as dolls or model aeroplanes can be kept in toy-chests which are

Below: Split-level 'den' for older kids. The play-platform slots into the floor-to-ceiling storage unit and the decor is bright.

now widely available in laminated fibreboard. These are light enough to be moved by a child, but are nevertheless tough and durable. Another excellent alternative is to drop toys into a mobile storage unit which can be wheeled out of the way when not in use.

One commonly unforeseen problem is where to put the tiny objects which inevitably crop up in nursery life. Pebbles, beads, cut-out dolls—these will tend to get lost among the larger objects. Time and temper can be saved by providing very small drawers, even perhaps a toy dressing table, where the child can have fun tidying them away. If there is a place for everything, then everything may—magically—find its place!

After the child has reached the age of five, clothes will begin to be a problem. Up to that time they can nearly always be laid flat in drawers, or in portions of your own wardrobe space. As soon as they have to be hung up the need for adequate cupboard space arises. Outdoor clothes, games-wear and mackin-toshes can be kept in a lobby or hall cupboard —as a matter of policy—to prevent mud and dirt being trodden into the house.

But clothes, and possibly books, are going to be an increasing problem as the years go by. In many old houses there are recesses which can be converted into wardrobes or bookshelf units with a minimum of effort.

Even clothes-rails secured into alcoves and shut off by curtains, are better than nothing. Sliding doors could be used. They are tidier than ordinary hinged doors, but can be difficult for a child to operate and may even be dangerous if they suddenly unstick and trap his fingers.

Books, which are very important to children, should be given ample space and not just piled up in odd corners where they are likely to get torn or damaged. Shelves of differing heights to accommodate varying book sizes can usually be fitted into the versatile kit-units. The shelves should be strong enough to bear heavy loads and, consequently, should be supported underneath at several points and not just by battens at each end.

Whatever type of storage you provide, there will be little point in having it at all unless you make some of it easily accessible to the child himself. This is the first step in ensuring that you will not be his slave with the thankless task of tidying up after him every day until he is tall enough to reach some lofty cupboard!

Sleeping areas

All child experts agree that it is best for the child to sleep in his own room as soon as, and whenever possible. But where there are

Above: Smart space-saver steals the show! Sophisticated pull-out units act as seating, drawers and desk. The simple butterfly mobile and soft lighting add a touch of elegance.

children of different ages the situation becomes complicated. One child's bedtimes may coincide with another's hobby or home-work hours, which is one excellent reason why, wherever possible, the 'den' should *not* be the bedroom.

Assuming, however, that they will be in the same room, it will take considerable ingenuity to ensure peace at the right times. Room dividers are one answer, especially if they fold back almost flush with the walls during the day to allow for optimum floor space and easy cleaning. And often they can 'double' as storage units, or decorative screens.

In the case of extremely high rooms you could even consider erecting a split-level 'deck', accessible via steps or a step ladder (but only for older children—otherwise it may be unsafe). Depending on the age and sense of the children, the lower level could be used as play or work area, and the upper deck as sleeping quarters, or vice versa. A loft, even a small one, could be converted if it leads directly from the main children's room for either of these purposes, providing it has adequate lighting facilities (such as skylights or dormer windows) and good ventilation. But if you are considering any kind of do-it-yourself house conversions, consult your local authority first. There are restrictions on alterations, including (in Britain) fire pre-caution measures, which may frustrate your plans.

Bedding

Future mothers may indulge in fantasies about wicker basket-type cradles, but they

Below: A smallish room very well fitted for growing children. The flooring is tough, and provision is made for studying and play. Colour comes with the child's possessions.

are a total waste of money. Children will outgrow them almost quicker than clothes. Cots, with let-down sides, are old stand-bys for toddlers and there are now many different types on the market which allow for the growth of the child by having removable side 'railings' and extensions which fit on the bottom end. An ingenious handyman could no doubt work out his own version of this.

If you are going to build a cot from scratch then, in Britain at least, there are safety regulations to be complied with. First, 597mm (23in) is the *minimum* height for the inside of the cot with the bars raised. The dropside, when lowered, should not be more than 838mm (33in), and the space between the bars must not exceed 76mm (3in). The dropside fastener should be as difficult as possible for the child to operate, and should

preferably have to be undone at both ends.

Where there is more than one child, bunk beds could be the answer, provided that neither child is likely to fall out nor is frightened of heights, and that the structure is sound and preferably secured to the wall.

A three-child family could find a ready-made answer in the 'slot together' trio of beds which is the latest space-saving idea. They are three separate beds of graded heights so they can be pushed, one under the other, when not in use. The top bed is perhaps a bit too high for absolute comfort, but the advantages seem to outweigh this one drawback.

Remember that hot air rises, so avoid creating a situation where the occupant of the top bunk or raised deck of a split-level arrangement may be trying to sleep in stifling conditions. Ensure that there is adequate

Below: Sunshine all the year round for these lucky children! The bright screen keeps the peace ... Note the drawers under the beds and the sanded 'n' sealed floor.

83

ventilation in the room at all times—preferably some form of air conditioning and not just open windows which, despite health fanatics' claims, do have a habit of causing colds.

Lighting

Good lighting is called for throughout the home, both for added effect and safety's sake. Where children are going to learn to use 'precision' toys and tools (in the early years this may only mean playing with building bricks and paint brushes, but these still demand a great deal of dexterity and concentration from a small child) good lighting is *essential*. This means sufficient daylight for the child to distinguish properly between colours, for example, and artificial light soft enough not to hurt his eyes when he is learning to concentrate on printed pages. In the case of nervous children, nightlights might be needed, which could be no more than strip lighting concealed somewhere out of the child's immediate view while lying in bed. It only needs to be bright enough to remove the fear of dark corners and soften the shadows. Perhaps you could simply leave his room door ajar with the hall or landing light on. (A dimmer switch should be used if the full light is too harsh.) This would be enough to convince most children that they had not been abandoned, and would be useful for other members of the family should they need to go to the bathroom in the night.

As soon as the child begins to sit at a table or desk for any length of time, especially when studying or writing, he will need a source of local light over the work surface such as an adjustable table lamp. A single overhead light is not efficient, nor is it particularly beneficial to anyone's eyes. Moreover it tends to deaden textures and kill colours.

Colour

Colour can do more to make your child like his room than any other single design factor. It can also *appear* to alter the size and shape of a room by highlighting the good points and concealing the bad. A high ceiling can be made to seem lower, for example, by painting it in a warm, 'advancing' colour such as yellow or any of the red tones. Children have an instinctive liking for the primary colours—the brightest and purest colours in the spectrum—and will often tolerate 'wilder' colours than their elders. But if the child's bedroom has to double as play- and study-room, then you may be well advised to use more subdued colours. While bright colours tend to stimulate in the short term, they tend also to tire the eye and distract the occupant of the room. Too much orange and red can positively irritate, in fact.

So perhaps a compromise is called for in multi-purpose rooms. One wall or a few panels could be painted in more vivid colours, while muted colours could be used for the rest. Enough colour may even be provided by paintings and toys.

Supervision and privacy

Ideally the playroom should be close to the kitchen, or wherever the mother spends most of her day, for easy supervision. Best of all would be a playroom actually next to the kitchen where the child can be watched (without feeling he is being spied on), by means of a sliding serving hatch or a dutch door which swings open at a safe height. Meals would be easier to serve, too, and wails of distress would be within earshot. Unfortunately this arrangement is impractical for several reasons. In many homes the room immediately next to the kitchen will be the dining/living room. In some homes the child will be lucky if he has a *bedroom* of his own, let alone a separate playroom, and when he becomes a teenager the last place he will want his room to be will be next to his mother's province!

In the early years the problem will be supervision; later it will be privacy. In a house where the child's room is upstairs a baby alarm could be installed, but the danger here is that the mother will develop an unnecessary concern to listen to the child's every whimper—baby alarms are for strong-minded mothers only! In a bungalow the child may be reached more quickly than in, say, a three storey house, but this is not likely to be much of an asset when the child is in his teens and wants to 'get away from it all'.

No child's room is ever going to be perfect because children change and no two are alike. The best you can do is to provide a few sensible fittings and ideas which will allow for this change.

Bedrooms on two levels

You probably often wish that you had more space in your home—to carry out a hobby, to provide children's playspace, or just to take the strain off a crowded living area. One place where you can find extra space is the bedrooms, which are normally only used for one-third of the day. A two-tier system, using bunk beds or wall- or ceiling-hung beds with study or hobby areas below, will, with a little imagination and planning, provide as much additional space as you need.

Two-tier bedrooms are both functional and attractively different. And compared with the living room or kitchen, a bedroom provides a lot of unused space that makes it an ideal 'overspill area' for family activities.

You do not need much space when sleeping and you are not aware of your surroundings. These considerations should influence you when designing your bedrooms. Ask yourself if the provision of sleeping space is as important as the provision of adult working or children's playing space. The answer will probably be that although it is necessary for sleeping areas to be comfortable, the amount of room allotted to them can take second place in your plans for a dual-purpose bedroom.

Remembering this, one of the best ways of saving floor space is to use the full height of the room, and place beds on the top of a two-tier system. The bottom level is then left free to be used for any purpose you like: a work or study area, or storage space. The height of the top level will depend on the purpose for which the lower portion is being used.

The two-tier bedroom can be used for any number of household activities: an office, a nursery, a hobby room or just for general storage. There is no reason why you should not design your own room units to suit your particular needs. The sleeping arrangements do not have to be confined to children. You could provide spare beds for occasional visitors, or a permanent bedroom-cum-study for student lodgers or other residents.

Change—and children

You can design your two-tier bedroom with either permanent, built-in furniture or free-standing components. The choice is up to you. But if you think you may make major changes later on, free-standing units are preferable. On the other hand, the maximum use of space may be your concern, in which case specially-designed built-in areas are more suitable. If you have a large number of children, you are most likely to want to use both levels of the two-tier bedroom for sleeping, so standard free-standing bunk beds are probably the answer. These lend themselves to the changes in your layout necessitated by additions to the family and the varying requirements of growing children.

The bunks can easily be dismantled when no longer required, or can be taken with you if you move. The most useful kind of ready-made bunk beds can be split and used as normal twin beds which gives you the choice of alternative arrangements as the children grow.

Dual-purpose rooms have to be transformed every day and night and this requires careful planning. In order to prevent regular heavy lifting, some sort of adaptable built-in unit is required. One method is to design two-tier beds where each bed frame has one long side hinged to the wall. These can then be folded upwards to lie flat against the wall during the day. Each bunk is secured in the 'up' position by barrel bolts fixed to the wall which slide into holes in the edge of the bunk. The bedclothes are prevented from slipping by tapes tied across the beds. Two pairs of these should be fixed at each side of the bunk, about 300mm (1ft) from the ends.

Supports for the bunks can be hinged to swing horizontally, so that they are at right angles to the wall when carrying the bunks, and folded flat when not in use. Alternatively, the bunks can be supported from the ceiling with tubular steel rods. Both types of support provide a completely clear floor space underneath, and when the bottom bunk is folded away, the underside provides a useful space for a pinboard or blackboard.

Alternatively, allow enough space under the bunk for a sitting child's knees and leave it down. A board can then be fitted over the bed covers to make a desk, playing surface or climbing platform.

Going to bed can be fun

The two-tier bedroom is particularly suited to children's rooms where there needs to be some room for play. When the children are young there is no reason why bunk units should resemble beds. A child who is reluctant to go to bed may be enticed into a replica of a car or double decker bus. The bed can

Below: This seating area with bunk bed above provides a novel combination of bedroom and comfortable retreat. The arrangement is ideal for a teenager.

itself become a plaything. You need only decorate two ends and one side of the bunks and allow your children's imagination to do the rest.

You can soften any changes from a normal bed to a pair of bunks by decorating the room to look like the cabin of a boat. Here hammocks will make ideal spare beds.

For slightly older children a less adventurous approach is preferable. Making the bunks from the same material will help maintain unity in the room and varying the designs of the bunks slightly will add interest.

A safety chain, which you can cover in fabric to match the curtains, can be used on the top bunk bed. Access to the top berth can be by rope ladder if this novelty is not required.

An alternative access can be made by supporting the top bunk from the floor and not hanging it from the ceiling. If you do suspend it from the ceiling you must use a rigid material, such as tubular steel bars, as supports. Excellent use is made of the space under the bottom bunk by fitting flush drawers which can be used for storing bed linen, clothes or toys.

A solution for a boy's bedroom is to build a platform about 457mm (1ft 6in) high over half the floor area. This has sliding doors fitted to the front and is ideal for storing toys. A second narrower platform can be built on top of the first and against the wall. This should be 610mm (2ft) high and long enough to take a mattress and still leave room for a desk top. There is no space gained in this scheme, but it provides an adventurous journey to the bed and also an excellent play area during the day.

Good looks and comfort

Initially, the thought of placing beds on top of each other may conjure up pictures of impersonal, military type conditions. This need not be so. Consideration of basic design principles—proportions of rooms; lighting; colour; choice of materials—can result in friendly, warm-looking sleeping areas. Careful positioning of furniture will add to general comfort and produce a room which is easily maintained.

Light is sometimes restricted in the bottom berth of a pair of bunks. The occupant can also feel restricted when sitting up. These problems can be solved by abandoning the usual 'one on top of the other' method of arranging bunks.

For example, the bunks can be placed at right angles to each other. The top bunk can be fixed to the wall at one end with a support which can double as an access ladder. The bunks do not have to occupy a corner site, though you will need two supports for the bunk if it stands away from the wall. The

design of the two berths does not have to be the same since, physically, the beds are separate. Matching bed covers will provide the necessary visual link.

Alternatively, the bunks can be placed in line with each other, with the 'foot' of the top bunk directly above the 'foot' of the lower bed. The unfilled space beneath the top berth can be used for storage.

These less conventional arrangements for bunks not only overcome the problems of providing enough light for the lower bunk but they also add interest to plain rooms. They take up a little more space than formally arranged bunks but the added comfort given to the occupant of the lower bunk outweighs this.

It is sometimes difficult to maintain a balance between neatness and cosiness in a busy bedroom. On the one hand lining up objects reduces clutter; on the other hand the room needs a friendly rather than a regimental appearance. Spaciousness and cleanliness can be achieved without the use of alignment if the bunks are cantilevered from the wall. This involves building steel brackets into the brickwork. These support the beds like giant shelf brackets and eliminate the need for any floor supports, and the bunks take on a floating appearance. You can also suspend the top bunk from the ceiling, though you must ensure that *adequate* fixing must be made to the joists above the plaster. You can reduce the bulk look that bunks sometimes have in small rooms by using a heavily patterned paper on the wall and a bedspread in a matching fabric. This will

Above: The simply made platform can be used in other home situations. A high ceiling will provide more than adequate headroom in the sleeping area.

detract the eye from the structure and results in a general flattening effect.

Sleeping soundly

Never underestimate the need for ventilation in a two-tier bedroom. Warm air rises and can cause discomfort to those sleeping in a top berth. Windows are the usual form of ventilation in all houses but they may produce uncomfortable draughts in cold weather and, in large towns where the air is not particularly clean, can do more harm than good. An extract fan in one window and a slightly open room door is the best way of providing an adequate airflow.

Remember, that if you design a free-standing double-decker unit, no matter how thick you make the vertical supports, you will have to install some supports running diagonally to act as braces and prevent swaying and eventual collapse.

Two tiers for adults

A person living in a two-tier bedsitter or small flatlet which doubles as a study room, for example, can spend 24 hours at a time in the same room. An interesting decorative scheme can help reduce any feeling of tedium. One way of creating a visually interesting arrangement is by horizontal zoning—dividing the room around the walls rather than across the floor.

Run a shelf around the wall, level with the top of the bunk. The bedroom area occupies the upper zone of the room and the shelf emphasises this division. Decor in the top part should give a warm appearance with the use of wallpapers and soft colours. The area below should be made more durable looking with the use of painted walls, plastic laminates and cool clean colours. The door will automatically break the division, so provide a unifying factor for the room by painting the whole of the surrounding wall in the same colour, omitting the shelf.

One handy arrangement for a student bedsitter or a home office is to install a desk under a bunk bed—a bed placed far enough below the ceiling to allow you to sit up in bed will still leave plenty of room beneath for this. A fluorescent tube light fixed to the underside of the bunk will provide light for working but it should be fitted with a pelmet to prevent glare.

A room with this arrangement will look much neater if a hinged flap is fitted along the edge of the bunk. It can be raised during the day to hide the sleeping area lowered at night so that you cannot see the work area when in bed.

Another useful idea is to provide storage beneath a bunk bed. This could be drawers or cupboards or a wardrobe fitted with a curtain. The width provided by the bunk will be more than adequate for the storage of jackets which are too often cramped in other wardrobes.

The more you think about it, the more likely you are to decide that a two-tier bedroom has its advantages.

Below: Going to bed is made into a game in this room. Placing the bunks at right angles to each other avoids the regimental aspect of bunk beds.

Left: *Here the platform is a full conversion job, allowing for sleeping area above and living and dining area below. The finished job is an open plan flat from an attic.*

Below: *This cleverly devised arrangement manages to combine the bunks with generous storage space for children's clothes and toys.*

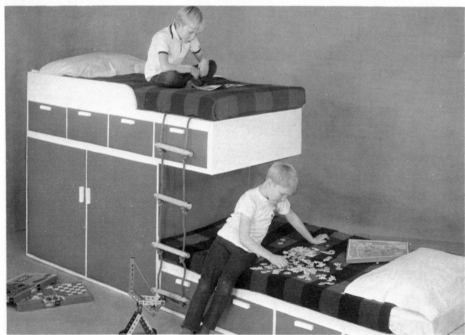

Boxing lesson

The days are gone when baths were tall cast-iron structures with ornate exposed legs. The simple lines of a modern bathroom require the sides of a bath to be boxed in.

Boxing-in a bath is a comparatively simple job and can be done with a wide range of surfaces—ceramic tiles, plastic laminate, tongued-and-grooved timber boarding, or even gloss-painted plywood. None of these presents any serious technical problems.

All these surfacing materials can be mounted on a simple but robust wooden frame fastened to the floor around the edge of the bath. The installation, however, has to meet various requirements.

First, the frame must be strong enough not to warp—this is a serious problem in the steamy atmosphere of bathrooms. The ten-dency of wood to warp in damp air can be reduced by painting all the parts with water-proof paint or varnish on all sides, so that the humidity of the wood remains constant.

Second, it must be properly fastened to the surface it touches, so that it will resist kick-ing, blows from mops when cleaning the floor, and so on. The frame can be nailed to a wooden floor or it can be fastened to a concrete floor with wall plugs and screws, or with masonry pins. Nearly all baths have at least one side or end against a wall, and the ends of the frame can be plugged and screwed to this too.

Third, the outer surface has to be reason-ably watertight, so that water does not seep down behind it and under the bath where it cannot be mopped up. This is simply solved

Below: The bathroom before the bath was boxed in. The old box frame shown here was warped, and had to be discarded.

by setting the panel about 3mm ($\frac{1}{8}$in) back from the outer lip of the bath, so that any drips from it run down the front of the panel instead of seeping through its back and rotting the frame. At the same time, the join between the bath and the wall should be sealed, either with a 'bath trim kit' consisting of narrow tiles with an L-shaped cross-section or (more simply and cheaply) with the white, plasticine-like sealing strip obtainable from any hardware shop.

Fourth, the pipework under the bath must

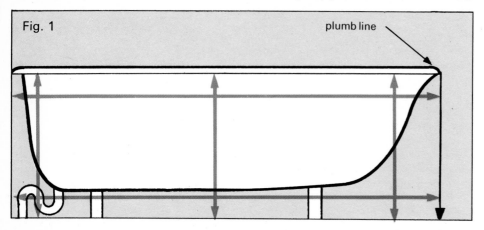

Fig. 1

plumb line

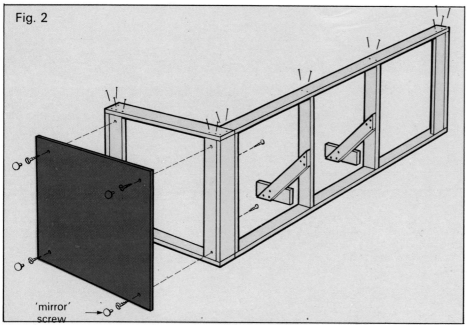

Fig. 2

'mirror' screw

Fig.1. The vertical distance from the bath rim to the floor, and the horizontal distance along the bath, should be measured in several places (marked with red arrows) to ensure complete accuracy.

Fig.2. The basic frame for the bath. All types of panelling fit this frame. It can, of course, be built with as many side and end panels as you need to suit the layout of your own particular bathroom.

Fig.3. A bath with sloping sides and a narrow rim may need a shallower frame than normal to fit into the limited space.

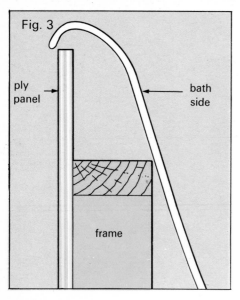

Fig. 3

ply panel

bath side

frame

be accessible for maintenance. This includes not just the taps but also the trap in the waste pipe, which has to be cleaned out occasionally. The best solution here is to screw on the panels with 'mirror' screws, which have decorative covers on the heads so that you don't have to disguise them. Don't use too many screws; six or eight is ample for each panel if it has to be removed from time to time. (It is a good idea to inspect the floorboards under a bath for wet rot every few months.)

Materials

The framing should be made of 50mm × 25mm (2in × 1in) or 38mm × 19mm (1$\frac{1}{2}$in × $\frac{3}{4}$in) softwood throughout. The amount you will need of this, and all the other materials, depends on your particular bath

and bathroom, so you should make a scale drawing of everything you are going to make before you buy anything.

The panelling material depends on what you are going to surface it with. An ideal material for tiling, painting or laminating is 13mm ($\frac{1}{2}$in) WBP (water- and boil-proof) birch plywood, which will last for many years. Chipboard and hardboard are cheaper but less durable. If you do use them, choose exterior grade chipboard or tempered hardboard, both of which are more waterproof than the ordinary kind.

Other materials you can use are a good-quality ready-laminated chipboard (the edges should be given several coats of polyurethane varnish to make them waterproof) or any kind of tongued-and-grooved boarding (this should be thoroughly varnished on both sides—do the back and ends before you put it on).

You will also need some chromed or stainless angle strip to neaten and protect the corners of the box, unless it is tiled or the bath has a wall at each end. Other necessities are surfacing material for the panels, if they are to be surfaced, and plenty of 50mm (2in) oval wire nails, 51mm (2in) No. 10 screws, and 38mm (1½in) 'mirror' screws—the kind with chrome-plated domed covers that screw into a hole in the flat head of the screw.

Measuring

The first thing to do—before you buy anything—is to measure the bath carefully. The space into which each frame must fit should be measured at several points, to allow for the floor not being quite even and the walls being slightly out of true (as they almost certainly will be, even in a well-built house).

Measure the height of the underside of the rim of the bath above the floor in at least three places (see Fig. 1). Then measure the length of the outer edge of the rim of the bath. If the bath is set between two walls, measure this distance from wall to wall; if there is a wall at one end only, measure from that wall to a plumbline (or a small weight on a string) hung over the outside corner. If there is no wall at either end, use two plumblines. Any length beginning or ending at a wall should be measured both at floor level and at bath rim level to see if the wall slopes.

A typical frame for a box around a bath is shown in Fig. 2. To find the length that each side of the frame should have, take the *shortest* measurement of the length of the bath, i.e., the horizontal distance measured at the height where the wall bulges out most. Subtract from 3mm (⅛in) or the thickness of the rim of the bath, whichever is greater; the thickness of the plywood (or T & G boarding) that you are going to cover the frame with; the thickness of the tiles or laminate (if any); and the width of the frame members (at each outside corner of the frame not touching a wall).

This last measurement should be subtracted on *one* side of each corner only, since it allows for the overlap of the frames where they meet at each corner. Note that the frame members are nailed together on edge and not flat (for extra rigidity) so that a frame of 51mm × 25.4mm (2in × 1in) timber is 51mm (2in) wide, seen from the end.

To find the height of the frame, take the shortest measurement from the floor to the lower edge of the bath rim and subtract 10mm (⅜in)—this will make the frame easier to insert. The panel over it must, of course, be the full height and project above the frame a short way.

Measure also the horizontal distance from the inner edge of the bath rim to a point at the same level on the outer wall of the bath. This is to check that the frame will be narrow enough to fit into that space without the bath's outer wall pushing it beyond the outer rim of the bath. On most baths, there should be enough room. If there isn't, you can make the top of the frame lower (see Fig.3) so that it will fit—but don't make it more than 75mm (3in) lower if you are panelling with 13mm (½in) ply or chipboard, or about half that if you are using T & G boarding or hardboard. Otherwise, the panelling may curl at the top. If you cannot fit the frame in and still comply with these limits, you might cut away part of its rear edge to make it fit.

When you have sorted out the size of everything, make scale drawings and from them work out how much wood and other materials you will need. Allow a reasonable amount for waste, particularly with the tiles if you are buying any, because they often break when you are trying to cut them.

Order of work

The frames are so simple to make that no detailed instructions are required. There are no fancy joints, because they would be out of sight anyway, and because the frame is not required to be incredibly strong. A few points to watch: the pieces should be skew-nailed, i.e., the nails should be put in slightly crooked in opposed pairs. This makes them less likely to come apart. All the frame members are set on edge except for the inserts at

Fig.4. The frame should be braced upright with a diagonal strut fastened to a block nailed to the floor. The nails can be driven in diagonally as shown; neatness is not important.

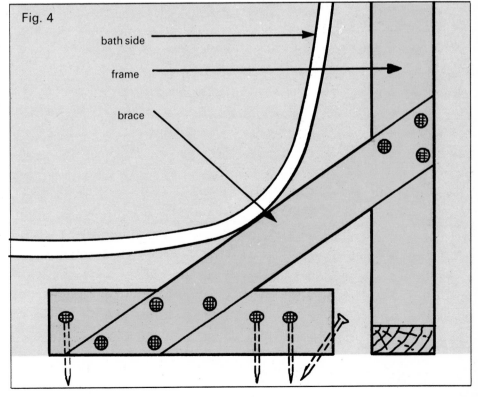

Fig. 4

bath side

frame

brace

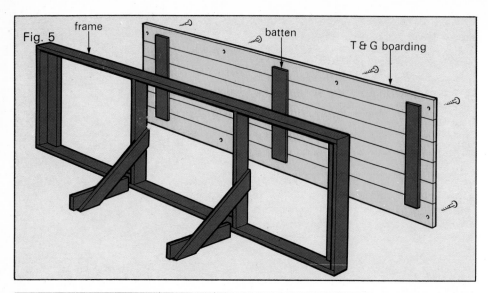

Fig. 5

frame

batten

T & G boarding

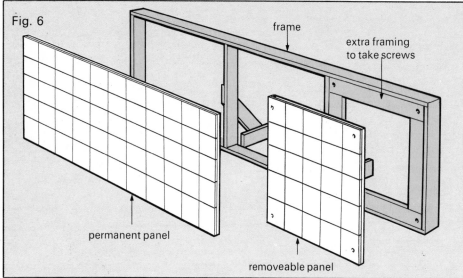

Fig. 6

frame

extra framing to take screws

permanent panel

removeable panel

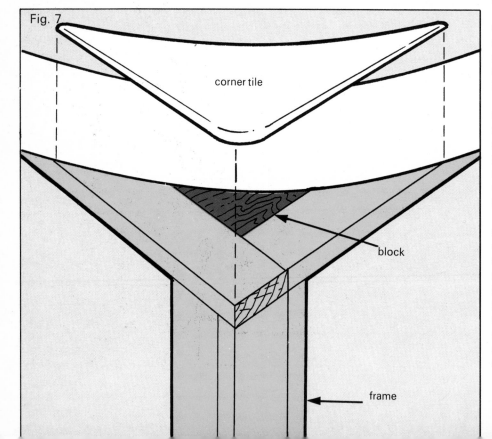

Fig. 7

corner tile

block

frame

Fig.5. Tongued-and-grooved boarding should be made up into a single panel by nailing it to battens. This panel can then be removed in one piece when you want to inspect the pipework of the bath.

Fig.6. Ceramic tiles are heavy, and a tiled panel running along the whole of one side of the bath would be very difficult to remove and replace. The solution is to make a smaller, removeable inspection panel, and attach the rest to the panel permanently to the box framework.

Fig.7. An old-fashioned bath with round corners can be put into a square box by bridging the gap at the corners with a double-round-edged 'corner' tile.

each end, which should be set flat and flush with the front. The purpose of these inserts is to provide something to screw the panels to that is not dangerously near the end of the panels, and so likely to split them.

When the frames are made, mark the floor where they are to go by dropping a plumb line from the rim of the bath at various points. This will ensure that they are vertical but remember that the frames are set back from the place where the plumb line hangs so that there is room for the thickness of the panelling and the slight projection of the rim of the bath.

Fasten the frames to the floor in a suitable manner, and brace them upright with battens running diagonally back from as high up the frame as possible to blocks fastened to the floor under the bath (see Fig.4). The blocks should be made of 50mm × 25mm or 38mm × 19mm (2in × 1in or 1½in × ¾in) timber, and fastened to the floor by very long screws sunk vertically through the top edge, nails driven diagonally through the sides, or small angle brackets or angle strips screwed to both block and floor.

You will probably find it easier to screw the corners of the frame together than to nail them, because it is difficult to hammer a nail sideways into a slightly flexible frame in close proximity to a bath. The ends of the frame must be screwed into plugs in the wall. If the wall is irregular, pack the gaps between it and the frame with scrap plywood.

When the frame is completely installed, cut each piece of 13mm (½in) ply, if that is what you are using, to slightly more than the correct length and height. Then get a helper to hold it steady against the frame with its top edge 50mm (2in) above the bottom of the rim of the bath—mark the back of the panel to help you to locate it correctly. Set a pair of compasses to 50mm (2in) and use them to scribe the bottom of the panel to the floor, or use a 50mm (2in) block and a pencil

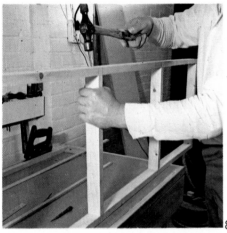

8

9

11

12

Fig.8. *Skew-nailing the frame together. Nails are quite strong enough for this type of construction; there is no point in wasting time on complex joints.*

Fig.9. *Nailing the diagonal struts to the frame. This frame has been set a short way above the floor to provide a toe recess underneath, which gives a little extra standing room to this very small bathroom.*

Fig.10. *Fitting the frames together at the corners of the bath. They can be nailed or screwed together, as you prefer.*

Fig.11. *Check that all the frame parts are straight and level before you go any further. The sloping panel mounted behind the taps drains splashes back into the bath.*

Fig.12. *The finished frame, a sturdy job that will stand up to years of hard use and constant dampness.*

Fig.13. *Fastening a laminated chipboard panel to the frame with 'mirror' screws.*

Fig.14. *The completed job. The bathroom has also been improved by building an airing cupboard round the hot-water cylinder, changing the wallpaper and laying a carpet.*

instead of the compasses.

If the wall is irregular, you will have to scribe the panel to that, too. This should be done after the panel is scribed to the floor, removing as little wood as possible. Trim the other end to length afterwards.

When the panels are the right shape, they can be painted or laminated. Then they can be installed with four, six, or eight 'mirror' screws, depending on the length of the panel. Finish the corners with decorative angle strip and the job is complete.

Special panels

Tongued-and-grooved boards can be nailed direct to the frame if you like. But if you have to remove them to inspect or repair something under the bath, it will be a great bore to prise them off one at a time.

A better idea is to nail them to vertical battens set a short way in from each end, and not quite reaching to the top and bottom of the 'panel' of boards. When the panel is laid against the frame, these battens will fit into the spaces between the frame members, and the boards themselves will lie flat against the frame (see Fig.5). The whole made-up panel can then be fastened on by mirror screws in the usual way. The outside corners can be finished with a metal angle strip or wood moulding to conceal the end grain of the boards, or bevelled at 45° to create a neat mitred corner (this is laborious, but probably worth it).

The tiles should be applied to a normal 13mm (½in) ply panel. The only difficulty here is that the weight of the tiles makes removing the panels difficult, and you might break tiles in attempting it.

If you are content with only one remov-

able panel at the end of the bath, and the tiles are not too thick, then go ahead. Tile the end panel before you put it up, finishing the outside corner with round-edged tiles. Then drill holes (slightly oversize) for mirror screws, using a masonry drill, and put the panel up in the normal way.

If, however, the shape of the bathroom requires you to remove a long side panel to get at the pipes, it is a better idea to have only part of the side panel removable, as shown in Fig.6. Fasten battens all round the inside edge of one bay of the frame, flush with the front, to provide something to fasten the removable panel to. Install the larger, permanent part of the panel with ordinary countersunk screws, and tile and grout it in the usual way. Tile the removable part of the panel before you put it up, making sure that the arrangement of the rows matches that of the permanent part. Then drill oversize holes in the corners and put the panel on with mirror screws. You can wipe grout into the join between the two panels if you like, but it will fall out the first time you remove the panel.

The only other problem you are likely to have is if you are boxing in a very old-fashioned bath with round corners. The best way to deal with this is to treat the bath as if it had square corners. Make the box the same length and width as the bath, so that it projects beyond the bath rim at the corners. Then insert a block behind the corners of the frame, flush with its top edge (see Fig.7) to bridge the triangular gap. Finish the projecting top corner of the box with a white 'corner' tile with two round edges, and its back cut to fit the curve. These baths are nearly always white, so a white tile blends in and makes it look like a modern squared-off bath.

You can sometimes avoid this problem, however; in the case of adding on a bathroom it might be convenient to approach it directly through a bedroom. Here no other landing or extra stretch of corridor would be needed. If you can conveniently add a bathroom next to an existing large bedroom, then you have the instant luxury of a 'master bedroom suite'. Or, if the new bathroom must serve two bedrooms, and the layout of the house does not allow for a corridor, you might consider adding the new bathroom as above but providing two doors—a perfectly satisfactory arrangement, provided that both lock.

Outer space

You may think you have just the right amount of space and in exactly the right place for building on an extra bathroom—but wait. In Britain, town planning standards and building regulation requirements—or in rural areas even estate rules—may all restrict any building close to a boundary. So even if the actual space is not a problem, permission to use it may be. Find out whether you are likely to get 'statutory approval' before starting work or even—ever hopeful—ordering materials.

On the other hand, you may get the 'go ahead' without much trouble, but there may be unseen and unforeseen problems in the shape of underground works—service pipes and cables or other ground conditions. These may make any kind of structural work extremely difficult—or even impossible.

In bungalows it might be especially difficult to find enough circulation space to provide suitable access to your new extension. Here it will almost certainly be necessary to connect it directly to an existing bedroom, or cut a new length of corridor through a room. But in the average two-storey house, a new bathroom would normally be most convenient at first floor level. If you already have some sort of single-storey building such as a kitchen jutting out, or a sun-lounge, or even a garage, then it might be possible to put the bathroom over this.

Most single-storey erections have flat roofs, which means that their joists will almost certainly be too weak to support the extra load on top. You will have to replace them entirely or add larger joists between the existing ones to share the strain. Or if the single-storey part has a pitched roof, you will have to change the roof structure completely —the joists in this case will certainly not be stout enough to hold up a second floor. If the

Adding a bathroom

Adding a second bathroom is no longer the privilege of the very rich—many families today are finding that they need an extra one. Perhaps the family has grown in recent years, and just one bathroom involves queueing at 'rush-hour'.

In many areas the value of land has risen so sharply that it is a good investment to add to your house where space permits, and to improve the standard of amenities in the house to match the greater value of your property. The addition of a second bathroom will usually increase the overall value by at least the cost of the work involved, as well as

adding to your own comfort.

Where to put your second bathroom will be determined by various factors. The most important are: how much access space you have inside your house; available external space; and the position of the drains.

Inner space

Adding a room to a house as it stands normally involves providing access from a hall or corridor—which is, after all, the most sensible thing to do. This is usually done by branching off the main hall or dividing off part of an existing room for this purpose.

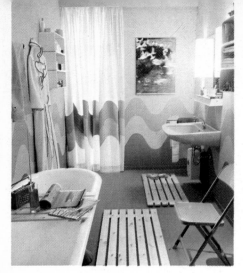

*Above: Going up the wall with a nautical look
... shades of the sea add an original touch to
this simply designed bathroom. Furniture is
kept to a minimum to give a spacious effect.*

pitched roof is high enough, it may be worth
considering forming the new bathroom
within the roof and adding a dormer window.
British building regulations impose *minimum*
sizes for such rooms, however, so it is best to
check with them before attempting any such
'uplift'!

A tall storey

If you have no single-storey to build over,
and still want your bathroom at first-floor
level, then obviously you must construct
some form of support at the lower storey.
Once this is done you could take this opportunity to use the bottom storey area you have
created under the new bathroom—perhaps
as another room or a covered terrace, or even
as a car port. (It would be wasting space
otherwise, and this is virtually criminal these
days!) This would be good policy anyway,
since double the total floor area is added at
much less than twice the cost of a single-
storey addition, because both storeys have
the same roof and groundwork.

The design of this ground floor room will
depend largely on its relation to other rooms
and on other equally important factors such
as aspect, outlook and privacy. It may face
south or west—the sunniest aspects in the
Northern Hemisphere—in which case you
have a fine sun-lounge in the making which
always adds to the value and enjoyment of a
house. Facing other directions (providing it
is quiet), it could provide the older children
with a study, or if it has a pleasant outlook,
the younger ones with a playroom. Or you
could turn it into a utility room or an extended kitchen ... The possibilities are many.

Money down the drain?

Bathrooms have the disadvantage of needing to be connected to drains. It may sound
obvious, but in the first flush of enthusiastic

planning you may overlook this one major
point.

Sanitary fittings must be connected to a
soil stack which is a 100mm (4in) diameter
vertical pipe leading to an underground drain
at an 'inspection chamber'—otherwise known
as a manhole. This runs at a slow gradient
either to a public sewer (the most usual in
towns) or some form of approved disposal
plant. The gradient of the drain should be
neither too steep nor too shallow, otherwise
blockages and difficulties in disposing of the
waste occur. The optimum 'self-cleansing'
gradient is normally taken as 1:40 for a
102mm (4in) diameter pipe and 1:60 for a
152mm (6in) diameter pipe.

In a town you will have to connect it to the
general sewage system or, if this is too far
away or too deep, you will have to connect
the soil stack to another form of approved
disposal. (Working back from the lowest
possible—that is *workable*—connection to
the sewer at the minimum gradient will fix the
lowest level for your new drain.) Alternative
forms of sewage disposal are septic tanks and
cesspools, neither a particularly attractive
system—especially in towns. The local building surveyor will have to approve you using
either of these systems in the first place, and
also all their details such as capacity, construction and location.

A septic tank is really a miniature chemical
treatment plant, and the treated fluid drains
away into the ground. Local authorities will
permit you to use them only when satisfied
that they would be in no way harmful—or
offensive—to other residents in the area.

A cesspool is simply a storage chamber
which must be emptied periodically by a
special pumping tanker—either belonging to
the local authority or operated by a private
contractor. Whoever deals with it, it represents a regular expense, and because of its
obvious limitations should be considered
only as a last resort.

So connecting the waste pipes to a sewer,
or a satisfactory alternative, is crucial when
you are planning to add a bathroom. If you
can connect to an existing drain line, then fine.
But if you can't and must provide new drains,
the cost could prove expensive out of all
relation to the value of the improvement to
your property.

The all-in-one bathroom

Whether or not to put the wc in the main
bathroom or in a separate compartment may
be an issue for the family to fight over, but it
is also a tricky design consideration. To a
large extent it will depend on the size and
shape of the available space and the access.
There may not be room for more than one
door in which case a combined bathroom and
wc is unavoidable. Or you could fit a shower

instead of a bath, which may leave just
enough space to fit a second door and have a
separate wc. The obvious advantage of having
a separate wc is that it *can* be used independently of the bath and other fittings. Remember—while someone is dreaming in the bath
you could have a lengthy wait ...

There is usually, however, no disadvantage
in having the wash-basin and bath in the
same room, though a separate shower is a
good idea, especially for a large family. While
someone soaks in the bath, several others
could take a quick shower at the same time.
This is one good argument in favour of a
shower compartment, instead of shower fittings attached to the bath.

The most workable arrangement, if space
permits, is a bathroom with bath and wash-
basin (and bidet if desired) in one compartment and separate compartments with en-
ntraces for the shower and wc. But if space
really is too tight to allow this, then all-in-one
bathroom does at least have the advantage of
looking a less 'bitty' and sometimes even
more spacious.

Ventilation and light

Building regulations in Britain require you
to make sure that new bathrooms have proper
ventilation—that is, having enough changes
of air per hour. You can do this simply by
opening windows regularly or by mechanical
means such as a small extractor fan. You
could incorporate an electric relay switch,
linking it to the light switch which will start
the fan when the light is switched on and
continue to run for about fifteen minutes
after it is switched off. (This sort of device
makes internal bathrooms, which would normally be cut off from adequate light and
ventilation, a practical project.)

The situation often arises where there is no
external wall available especially in terraced
houses on a limited plot. So part of a large
room could be partitioned off to form an
internal bathroom. Although a naturally

*Opposite, top left: A refreshing look for this
bathroom in simple green and white. The bath
is fitted with a shower attachment, and the
laminate surface is handy for toiletries.*

*Opposite, top right: The Victorians never had
it so good! This stylish period piece enjoys the
added luxury of modern fittings.*

*Opposite, bottom left: This Scandinavian
L-shaped bathroom with the sauna look glows
with warm lighting and the tones of natural
wood.*

*Opposite, bottom right: A separate toilet is
often most convenient and can even be
attractive.*

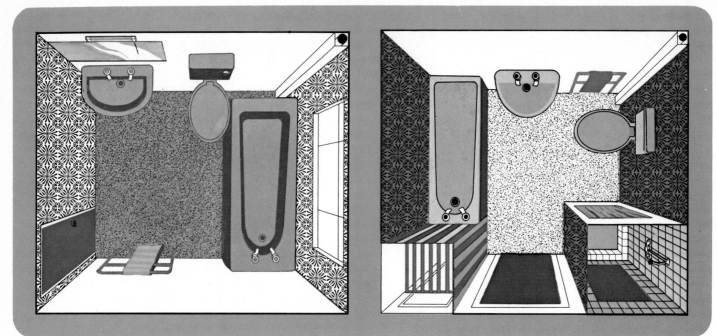

well-lit and ventilated room is always preferable, if the choice is between an internal bathroom or none at all, an artificially ventilated room can be a perfectly acceptable choice. (These are taken for granted in the majority of luxury hotels, where the external walls are given over to bedrooms and the other main rooms such as dining rooms, and the bathrooms are sandwiched between the bedrooms and internal corridors.)

However, if you do have an accommodating external wall it is pleasanter to use it and have a 'real' window. This need not be a large one, because bathrooms are usually small rooms anyway. And the only 'zone' likely to need concentrated lighting is around a mirror —for make-up and shaving—which is best provided by a small fluorescent strip light. If you are overlooked by curious neighbours it might be wise to use some type of opaque glass! There is a wide range of patterned glass

which is often highly decorative as well as ensuring privacy. Some types are more attractive and effective than others: reeded glass, for example, obscures by distorting the view rather than simply blotting most of it out and reducing light transmission like 'frosted' glass, which can also create an unpleasant claustrophobic feeling. But unless you are overlooked by a skyscraper, you may not be over-fussy. Sufficient privacy can simply be achieved by keeping the sill about 122cm (4ft) or 137cm (4ft 6in) from the floor—and using normal clear glazing. This height allows room for bottles and so on to stand on a shelf below the window line, with enough space for a splash-back. High-level windows light the ceiling well, distributing daylight deeper into the room. If you are only concerned about 'instant' privacy—such as when you are actually having a bath—a venetian blind will do, and it would also be useful in controlling the heat in the room if the room faces the hottest way. If you use no artificial ventilation then you should make sure that at least part of the window is openable—for the average bathroom an opening area of about 122 sq cm (4 sq ft) is enough. Most people, unfortunately, do not ventilate their bathrooms nearly enough.

A fitting place

The arrangement of the various fittings is usually decided on the basis of (a) how handy the plumbing connections are (b) convenience in use and (c) general appearance. But in many cases it will be the *plumbing considerations* which will primarily dictate the layout.

It is the disposal of waste matter which usually presents more problems than the supply of water. Supply runs are normally in small-bore tubing which is fairly flexible as to

Above left: Bird's eye view of the average box-like bathroom. The layout is limited by the space available and position of the drains, but flattered by its effective decor.

Above right: The inside story of a windowless bathroom. Here lighting and ventilation must be artificial, but there is no need to skimp on fittings or a bright colour scheme.

Below: A long narrow bathroom given a smart 'split personality' with a step-up to the far end and slatted screens sectioning off toilet and bath/dressing area. The colour is inviting.

Four ways to add on. Whatever type of house you live in, adding on a room often means structural alterations on another floor, too. This gives you the chance to add a new room on two floors at the same time. Adding on any room relies on the same principle.

Fig.1. A 'between-the-wars' semi. The new room—for example a bathroom—is reached through a corridor which used to be an airing cupboard, and the stair window is replaced by a rooflight. On the ground floor the new room can be used as a general utility room.

Fig. 2. An Edwardian semi-detached. On the first floor a window is blocked to provide the new room with a wall, and on the ground floor the new sun-lounge or utility room leads off from the dining room, which has a new window.

Fig.3. A Victorian semi-detached. On the first floor a corridor is cut out of the bathroom to provide access to the extension. This can be lit by a rooflight as well as a front-facing window. On the ground floor the kitchen has a new window in the side wall or a large window in the near wall of the extension.

Fig.4. A terrace house. A new corridor is cut into an existing bedroom. On the ground floor the new sun-lounge is largely glazed.

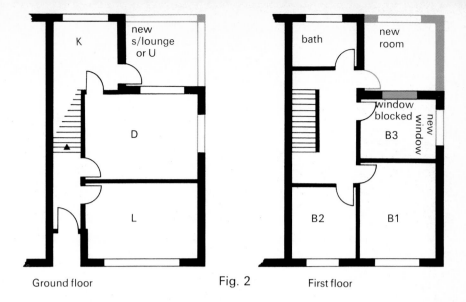

Ground floor   Fig. 2   First floor

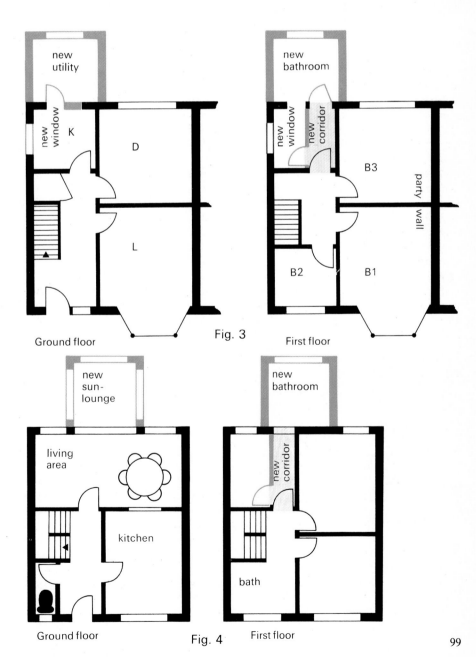

Ground floor   Fig. 3   First floor

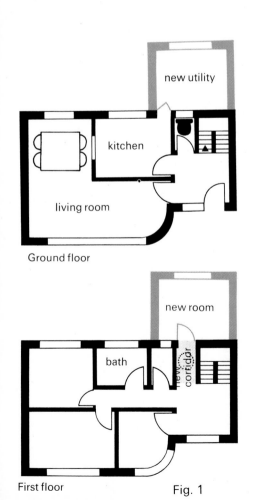

Ground floor

First floor   Fig. 1

Ground floor   Fig. 4   First floor

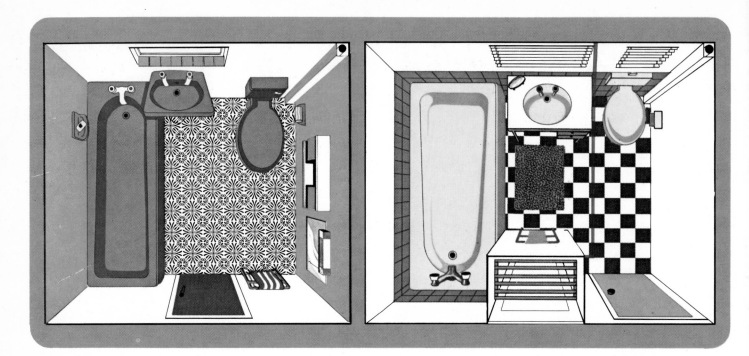

where you could put it. The wc, for example, has a large diameter outlet near the floor and should be positioned as closely as possible to the soil stack it is connected to. This will be in a corner of the room against an outside wall. The soil stack receives the waste from the wc and carries it to an underground drain. A similar pipe which receives discharge from basin, bath, bidet and shower is called a *waste stack*.

Waste stacks have a gulley at ground level which incorporates a 'trap' or water seal to isolate the stack from drain gases—whereas soil stacks connect directly to the drain at a manhole. In Britain, both types of stack must have their tops up above the roof-line to air them.

Above: Sunny sophistication for a luxury bathroom. The area is 'doubled' through the extensive use of mirrors in which you can see the attractive garden-room beyond.

Bidets also have their outlets near the floor, so it is often most convenient to put them next to your wc. Showers and baths, however, are more flexible in this respect, because they have smaller diameter waste pipes and discharge comparatively clean water. Their waste pipes may have to run under the floor surface if the fitting is some distance from the stack. This is quite easily done if you have a suspended timber floor—as long as the pipes run parallel with the floor joists perhaps between the joists. If, however, the pipes must run at right angles to the joists then you will have to cut holes in the joists to hold the pipes . . . and if a long run is called for then this series of holes will in time weaken the joists. In this situation it would be better to raise the fitting, such as the bath, on a shallow platform so that the waste can be run *above* the floor and still have the necessary fall.

The basin is the most accommodating fitting. You can put it almost anywhere in the room, because the waste pipe is the smallest in diameter and it starts at the actual fitting and some distance above the floor. From the plumbing aspect, then, the basin can be farthest from the stack.

As with all extensions and building-on, major home improvements and so on, the building reuglations raise their ugly head. In this case there are restrictions on distances for gradients of waste and supply pipes, and connection points which it would be foolhardy to ignore. These are merely sensible—imagine what would happen if one fitment siphoned off the waste from another for the supply and discharge pipes were too close for comfort! So before you go too far, it is wise to show a sketch plan to the local council to make sure that your layout complies.

Above left: Here the wash-basin over-laps the bath top by a couple of inches to provide easier access to all the fittings. The window gives adequate ventilation and light.

Above right: This galley-style bathroom provides extra privacy for the toilet area by using a screen or room divider. Venetian blinds help control heat by filtering the air and light.

Flooring and insulating your loft

Building on to the side of your house and adding an extension is becoming more and more expensive, what with the cost of having to lay new foundations, walls and roof. Your loft, however, will probably be large enough to create suitable space for living as well as storage at a considerable saving.

There are other advantages in utilising your loft space. At least 30% of the heat loss in the average house goes through the roof. If you use your loft you will have to insulate and plank it, cutting down the major source of heat loss.

Planning considerations

Most of the preparatory work will be done on paper, so you will have to have every loft dimension available. A complete set of measurements must include the length and width of the base; height (from the top of the joists, to the bottom of the ridge timber); the arrangement and number of joists, rafters and any other timbers; the dimensions of the joists, rafters and other timbers; the locations or wiring, pipes, water tanks and other such items.

From these measurements you will be

Below: A typical loft. Because junk tends to accumulate, the idea of converting a loft can present a frightening prospect. But behind the old suitcases and tatty wordrobes, there is really a vast amount of space that could be used for better purposes.

Above: Strengthened floor and roof supporting members, insulation and flooring make up the basis of a useful living area.

able to work out the size of the finished space or room and what it can, or cannot, be used for. In Britain, for instance, half of that part of the ceiling which is above the 1.52m (5ft) mark must be not less than 2.1m (7ft 6in) in height if the room is to be used as a living or bedroom area. Remember that you will lose perhaps 75mm (3in) at the bottom through strengthening the joists and adding flooring. Tack a length of batten across the rafters at a height not less than 2.13m (7ft 9in) from the joists. If you can't do this, then you cannot use the space for living accommodation —in Britain at any rate—but you might be allowed to use it as a children's playroom. There is no height restriction if you only want to use the area for storage.

Modern regulations usually stipulate that some form of vertical interior wall, normally at least 1.35m (4ft 6in) high is required. You are not permitted to use the outside edges of a loft space which has a pitched or sloping roof. (Usually you cannot, anyway, because you must leave in place any struts supporting the purlins, which in turn support the rafters.)

In most cases it will be useful to approach your local authority with sketch plans before you submit any definite plans. They are in a position to know about local building variations and will be quite helpful.

First, sit down and detail your present and future requirements on paper. The more thought you give to the project the more ideas you will get—even more important, you will stumble on aspects that you might want to avoid.

Start at the beginning. How will you get to the loft? It is obviously too inconvenient to get the ladder out of the garage whenever you want to enter the loft. The simplest answer is to have a suitable ladder stored nearby, against a wall and boarded in like a tall cupboard, so that it is quick to get to. On the other hand, there are many proprietary ladders on the market that are specially designed for this job. The basic principle is the same in most cases; the ladder, usually a sliding, concertina or cantilevered type, is installed just inside the loft access door. You are provided with a long pole which has a hooked end. With this pole you push the loft hatch open, hook the end of the ladder and pull it down until it is resting on the floor and rigid. You reverse the procedure when the

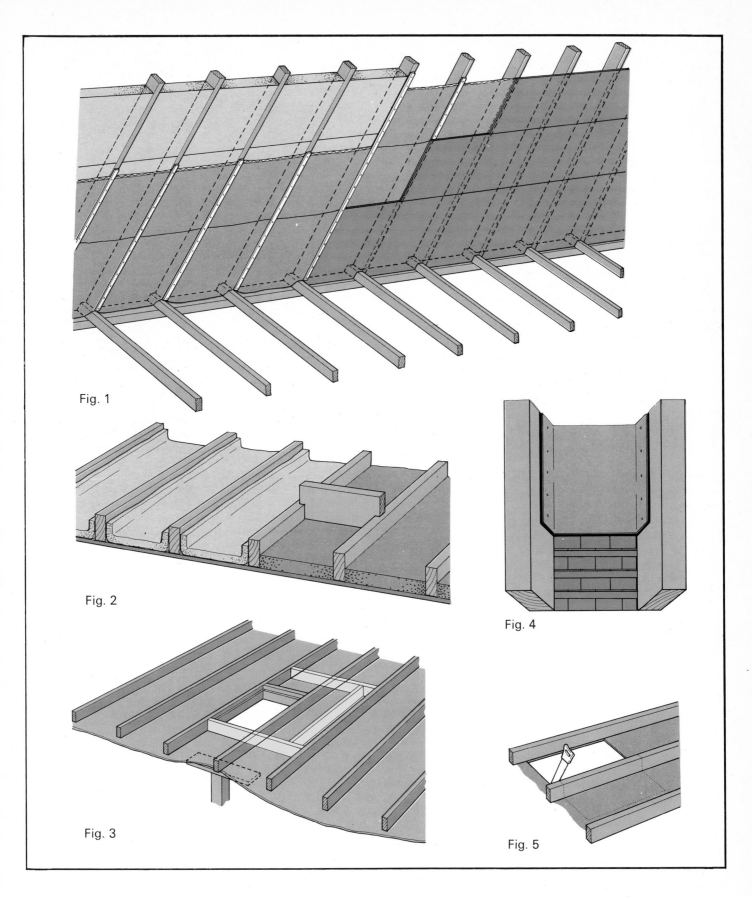

Fig. 1

Fig. 2

Fig. 3

Fig. 4

Fig. 5

Fig.1. *Three insulation methods using foam block, fibreglass blanket and board*

blanketing between the joists.

Fig.4. *Roofing felt can be fixed between the roof joists from the inside.*

Fig.2 *Floor insulation can be done by using either polystyrene granules or fibreglass*

Fig.3. *An outline of the larger loft hatch, showing the joist support.*

Fig.5. *Cutting out the joist and ceiling material to enlarge the hatch.*

ladder is not required. Each brand of ladder is installed by different means, but each comes with its own instruction leaflet.

Although a ladder may be the only way of entering your loft, it does require a certain amount of agility to climb and descend, so that if you convert loft storage space to a proper room later you will have to put a staircase in.

However, the building of a stairway involves problems additional to the intricacies of stairway construction. For instance, in Britain, the building regulations will not permit a simple open-tread stairway (consisting of two heavy planks for stringers with the treads housed in between) above the first floor unless you add a fire escape. In some other countries this restriction does not apply.

The next point is the loft hatch space. In most houses this is only just large enough to allow a person to enter the loft, and will not permit objects much larger than a dining chair to be taken into the loft. So your second consideration is whether to enlarge the access space. If you intend storing only books or similar objects it might be all right as it is, but in most cases it is better when made larger.

Insulation is an important consideration. If you insulate the roof area—the spaces between the rafters—you will satisfy the needs of your storage space, and be well on the way towards the insulation you would

need for a room. It is not essential to insulate the floor area, which will be planked over, although lack of insulation at this point will make your heating system work harder.

Finally, bear in mind that your loft joists were probably not designed to provide a living area and are not strong enough for this purpose, or for heavy storage. In most cases they will have to be strengthened as described later.

Temporary lighting

If you have no lighting point in the loft, you will have to provide a temporary one to allow you to carry out the work. This is most easily done with a roving lead, which is a length of wiring long enough to reach from the loft space down to the nearest plug socket. Fix a plug to one end of the lead, and a wall-fitting bulb mount to the other end. The bulb mount is screwed to a small panel of wood about 150mm × 150mm × 12mm (6in × 6in × $\frac{1}{2}$in). This panel can be temporarily fixed to any rafter, and the plug end and lead can be pulled up into the loft area when you are not working in it. Alternatively, you could fix up something more permanent, with a switch.

Enlarging the loft access

Climb into the loft and examine the existing construction to see how the opening is made—in which direction the joists run, and whether the ceiling finish is of plasterboard or

Above: Although loft space is most often used for a bedroom, it is in fact extremely versatile —as this dining room-library area shows.

lath and plaster. You will find that the opening formed by the builder is framed by two *trimming joists* between the main joists. The easiest way to increase the area is by removing part of one main joist and using longer trimmers, as shown in Fig.3. This almost doubles the length and width of your original opening, and will be sufficient for most purposes.

Commence by marking out the area of the new hatch, by scribing a line across the joist and ceiling where it will be cut.

Temporary support must be provided for the joist that will be cut. This consists of one sturdy upright, with a bracing batten or plank run to the floor, at each end just outside the line of the new opening. Remove the door and lining of the original opening, and prepare the two new trimming joists. These are marked off by direct marking (you lay each length of timber over its intended position while you mark it) and cut on the outside of the marking lines to ensure a tight fit.

Locate the heads of the nails that hold the existing trimmers in place, chisel some of the surrounding wood away so that the heads protrude slightly, then pull the nails out with pincers. Carefully remove the moulding, if any, surrounding the underside of the opening, then prise the trimmers out.

Now cut through the portion of joist that is to be removed. The procedure for this is shown in Fig.5. At one end you can use the existing opening to provide space for the downward thrust of the saw, but at the other end you will have to drill a series of holes, then chisel them into a slot, to provide space for the saw blade. The portion of joist is prised away. Keep it—it can be used as the new trimmer which runs parallel to the existing joists as shown in Fig.3.

Carefully remove the rest of the ceiling material by cutting along the marked lines (the dotted lines in Fig.5) with a panel saw. Do this very carefully so that you don't create any broken edges. With luck you can avoid any re-plastering.

Fit the new trimmers. The two short ones are skew-nailed to the main supporting joists, and the long one is skew-nailed to the two short ones.

Run strips of battening, narrower than the height of the joists, round the bottom inside of the new opening, to provide a lining and a stop for the new door. This battening must be sunk to a depth that will bring it flush with the ceiling below.

Any gaps between the battening and the ceiling can be filled with plaster; or you can run a moulding round the edges to finish it off.

Floor insulation

When converting a loft to a storage or living area, it is not essential to insulate the floor. In fact in some cases it might be a disadvantage. But if you are using the space for storage only, insulating the floor will certainly save on heating bills below, even if the walls or rafters are insulated as well. So before you plank or floor the joists, give some serious thought to the insulation of the floor.

The most popular methods for floor insulation are the laying of polystyrene granules or fibreglass blanket in between the joists. Both methods are shown in Fig.2. You might like to consider a third alternative—installing a false ceiling below. This creates a layer of still air, which is the best insulation of all. A false ceiling, although it entails more work, is particularly attractive if you have high ceilings as it will lower the height of the room. A false ceiling can be constructed quite simply with aluminium angle strip and insulating boards.

In any case, if the roof insulation is to be at all efficient, part of the floor will have to be insulated. This is at the edges where the joists and the rafters meet at the wall plate. Cold air entering up through the cavity wall or blowing in through the eaves can ruin an otherwise perfect job. In this area it is best to lay several layers of glass fibre blankets, covered if possible with sheet polythene or aluminium foil, to stop the draught and seal off the cold zone.

Wall insulation

Whether you intend using the loft for storage or living, you will have to insulate and weatherproof the walls (the spaces between rafters). It must be noted that in all probability you will have to do some re-structuring of roof timbers, and strengthen the joists, and it would be pointless to insulate the walls before this has been done. Wall insulation has been included here for convenience.

The rafters of most modern houses are covered with roofing felt before the roof tiles are laid. The felt not only prevents rain and snow from getting into the loft, but also provides better insulation by preventing draughts. If, however, your rafters are not covered, and the tiles or slates are visible from inside your loft, then this is your first job. It is obviously impractical for a home handyman to remove all his roof tiles in order to cover the rafters with felt; anyway this is not necessary. The felt can be placed in position from the inside as shown in Fig.4. The felt is held in position with tacks or drawing pins, and if a little plastic compound is applied to the side that is secured to the rafter, the seal should be perfect. Always start at the top and work down. Apart from the convenience of pinning the felt at the top

and allowing it to hang down while you continue fixing, any overlap will mean that if rain should enter through a loose tile then it will run down the felt and not be funnelled into the loft space.

There are many methods of completing the insulation of the walls. One is to completely line the rafters with a good lightweight building board such as fibreboard or, even better, a plasterboard with an aluminium foil facing. The foil side should face outwards, to deflect back heat in the summer and the cold in the winter.

Insulating blanket can also be used as shown in Fig.1. This is attached with battening and, if you decide to board the walls later, the boarding can be nailed to the battening, providing a double layer of 'space' sandwiching the blanket and giving excellent insulation.

Between the rafter spaces, insulating material such as fibreglass blanket (as used in Fig.1), solid blocks of mineral wool or cork 50mm (2in) thick, or flame retarded foam polystyrene can be fitted. With this method, some means of holding the insulation material in place must be devised. It is ideal if you are going to board the rafters over, and do both jobs together.

Strengthening the structure

Ceiling joists serve two main purposes. First, by forming the third side of a triangle —the roof rafters being the other two sides— they help make the roof structure stable. In this way the joists act as ties and the main strain, which is at the edges, does not cause any great stress at the centre. Second, the joists provide a means of attaching the ceiling finish of the rooms below. Neither of these functions introduces any great amount of bending stress, apart from the odd occasion when it is necessary for work to be carried out in the loft. Because of this, and for economy, roof joists are seldom deeper than 110mm (4in) and, at normal spacings of 400mm (16in) centres, they are not big enough to provide a stable floor, however well boarded over.

The first job, then, is to provide more rigidity to the joists, if possible by using a method that does not drastically reduce the available headroom—there is seldom much to spare.

Stud and carriage additions, as shown in Fig. 11, are one method of making the joists more rigid. It is particularly useful because studding of some sort will have to be provided in any case to make the vertical walls.

Each stud, which has dimensions of at least 50mm × 50mm (2in × 2in) is connected to a rafter at one end, and a joist at the other end. And the joist/stud joint is further reinforced by nailing to a carriage piece (or hanging beam, as it is sometimes called) as shown in Fig. 11.

This system introduces a new series of triangles, strengthening the roof and reducing the effective span of the joists. For storage purposes, but not usually for a room space, this will usually be sufficient when the joists are boarded over. Note that the bottom joint should be secured with triple-L-grips in addition to nailing. This gives the joint maximum strength.

Where a loft has end walls showing, such as in a gable construction, then a recess should be chiselled out of the wall, and the ends of the carriage piece housed into it. Each end should be liberally coated with creosote or some other wood preservative before housing and mortaring into place. In the case of a cavity wall, the carriage ends can be housed into the inner wall, but make sure that the timber does not bridge the cavity as this might provide a path for damp.

One of the problems in strengthening roof members—and this applies particularly to carriage pieces because of their length—is the difficulty in getting long lengths of timber up into the roof space. Sometimes this can be done through the house and loft hatch, but frequently this is impossible. In such cases it will be necessary to hire a winch from your local supplier and remove several roof tiles to permit the timbers to be winched in.

Although stud-and-carriage reinforcement can be useful and time-saving, it has limited applications inasmuch as it is usually only acceptable for storage space.

If you are building with an eye to creating living space eventually, you will have to use some other method, such as *adding new joists*, as shown in Fig. 10. In this method you actually lay new joists, of suitable dimensions to support the envisaged loading, in between the existing ones. The new joists are set higher than the old ones by laying them on pieces of batten, also shown in Fig. 10. This will prevent them from touching the ceiling finish underneath should they bow downwards slightly. It will also keep them clear of existing wiring and fittings.

There is a simple rule-of-thumb method for calculating the size of the new joists: Take the span measurement in feet, and divide this number by two; call this figure inches, and add a further two inches. This gives the required height of a 51mm (2in) thick joist. For example:

A 12ft (3.7m) span divided by 2 equals 6. Call this inches (6) and add 2in (51mm) making 8in (203mm).
Thus you require 203mm × 51mm (8in × 2in) joists.

To fit new joists, first lay 25mm (1in) strips of timber on top of the existing wall plates as shown in Fig. 10. These are cut into short lengths to fit in between the old joists. The new joists are then laid alongside the old ones and, if possible, nailed to the ends of the rafters. In most cases the tops will have to be bevelled, like the ends of the joists shown in Fig. 11, to fit under the slope of the roof. This is done by making a simple cardboard template to mark the slope on to the joists, and cutting this away with a cross-cut or panel saw.

An economic alternative is to *reinforce the joists* as shown in Fig. 10. You simply secure an extra length of timber directly on top of each existing joist, by screwing at 150mm (6in) intervals. The screws should, in addition to passing through the top joist, screw through approximately $\frac{3}{4}$ the depth of the old joist. If you can also line the sides with plywood to form a composite box beam, you will end up with joists of considerable strength for a modest outlay.

Using this method, the strips added on top of the joists must be at least 75m (3in) high for spans less than 3.7m (12ft), and 100mm (4in) for spans up to 5.5m (18ft).

Construction notes

Always make full use of any load-bearing walls—that is, walls that run continuously down to foundation level. (Some frame walls are no use in this respect, as they run down

Below: '*What you can't conceal, highlight.*' *Matching timber on the drawers and ceiling emphasises the good design of this loft room.*

6

7

Fig.6. *When strengthening ceiling joists in a loft, the most difficult work is around the chimney breast. First, you must secure in place the existing trimmer, which runs across the face of the chimney. Do this by inserting dowels through the existing mortise joints.*

Fig.8. *Next, mortar-in a joist hanger to carry the end of the new, larger joist. Mortise this joist to house the tenons on the 'strap' you will fix on the existing trimmer; fix the joist in place; then fit in the trimmer strap and secure it with wedges through the end.*

Fig.7. *With the ends of the existing trimmer thus secured, you can trim away the tenons which project from the trimmer through the joists on either side of the chimney. Cut with a panel saw, then plane smooth so that the new joists will sit snugly beside the old.*

Fig.9. *With the trimmer strap solidly secured in place by coach screws, the old trimmer has become much stronger. Now you can fit on the joists hangers to carry the joists that butt up to the trimmer—and know they will be solid enough to carry even the weight of a piano!*

8

9

Top: Although too low to be used as permanent living space, a loft room like this is useful for accommodating occasional guests.

Above: Where structural timbers cannot be removed, they can often be 'cleaned up' to add interesting textures to a loft's decor, as in this attractive example.

only to floor level.) This way you can use two short lengths of timber instead of one long one. Timber in short lengths is more economical and easier to use, and nothing is gained by using long lengths of timber and not using the opportunity of lapping over the wall below.

When working around or near any chimney brickwork, bear in mind there are often stringent building regulations to look out for.

First, any exposed brickwork or block-work containing flues has to be rendered externally with a 3:1 mix of sand and cement where it is to be hidden by the new floor. More important, any structural timber such as a joist must *not* rest on any chimney construction and should have an air space of 40mm (1½in) between it and the chimney so that the temperature of the brickwork cannot

be passed to the wood. This presents some problems when you come to insert new larger joists; the way round them is shown in Figs. 6–9. If your building inspector will not permit screws to be used to add extra thickness to the chimney trimmer, you can use coach bolts through both pieces of timber instead. It involves removing a few square inches of plaster from the ceiling below, but this is easily patched.

The next step is to stiffen the joists to stop them twisting. This is done by means of herringbone strutting as shown in Fig. 10, or by nogging, also in Fig. 10. These are placed at 60mm (2ft) intervals.

Flooring

The last task to be considered is the floor finish. This could be tongue-and-grooved boarding at least 25mm (1in) thick and 100-150mm (4-6in) wide. But a more convenient method is to use sheets of flooring-grade chipboard. This is very strong and is obtainable 20mm (¾in.) thick, complete with tongued-and-grooved wedges.

Before laying the flooring, it should be acclimatised to the humidity in the loft. This is best done by laying the boards in position without nailing and leaving them for three or four days.

Laying boards is much easier if you use flooring cramps that enable you to 'squeeze' the boards together before nailing them in place. This is rather specialised equipment, and too expensive to buy for just one job. But it is well worth hiring from your local DIY shop or builder's merchant, since it speeds up the work and makes a better job. Failing this, you will have to use a chisel at each nailing point, to try to cramp the boards together.

As an alternative to boarding, large sheets of chipboard can be used. And although you may experience some difficulty in getting the large sheets into the loft, the saving in time may be well worth the effort. Because they are screwed in place, chipboard sheets are easily lifted should you want to extend, or alter, your wiring. And you are less likely to dislodge plaster from the ceiling below than you would be if you used extensive nailing.

If you do contemplate using large sheets such as chipboard, you will have to find out the spaces recommended by the manufacturers for supporting joists. And ensure that the edges of each sheet are firmly supported and screwed, even if it means adding extra nogging. Whatever material you decide upon, don't use any that is thinner than 20mm (¾in). Even though it may appear strong enough to support weight, it will certainly sag and look unsightly.

Depending on what you intend to use the loft for, the floor can be given two or three coats of polyurethane varnish and left as is.

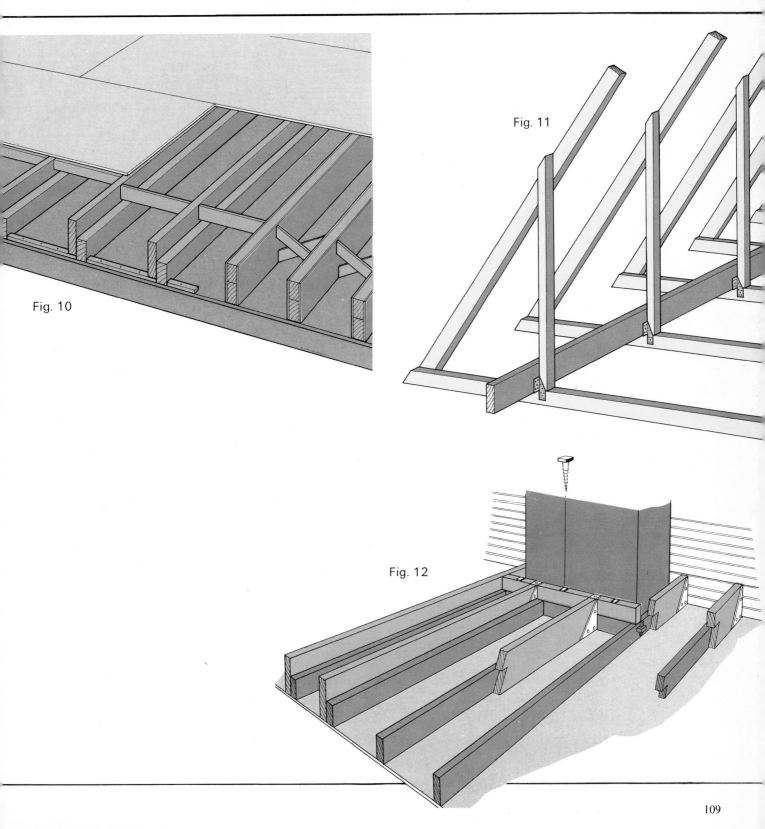

Fig.10. *Various ways of strengthening existing floor joists in a loft, shown in a composite diagram. On the left, new and larger joists are shown fixed alongside the old ones. They rest on strips of 25mm (1in) timber, laid along the tops of bearing walls, so that any sag in the joists will not damage the ceilings below. On the right, the existing joists have been reinforced by screwing on extra strips of timber, and cladding the sides in plywood. Two types of cross-reinforcement are shown— noggings and diagonal struts.*

Fig.11. *A stud-and-carriage-piece construction will help stiffen the floor, but is usually adequate only for storage.*

Fig.12. *How to handle the most tricky job— carrying joist reinforcing round a chimney.*

Fig. 10

Fig. 11

Fig. 12

The power game

One of the dullest and slowest jobs in carpentry is making a large number of identical pieces—sawing the same shape over and over again, hand-drilling row after row of holes, sanding everything to shape, and so on. If you have to do this, you may easily lose interest. So why not speed up the routine work with a power tool?

Power tools greatly speed up some of the most time-consuming work in carpentry, such as drilling, sawing and sanding. Anyone who intends to do a lot of carpentry would be well advised to invest in some kind of power tool, which would soon pay for itself in time saved.

Many types of specialised power tools are made, such as power saws, orbital sanders, lathes and so on. But the average woodworker can save some of the money required to buy this costly equipment by buying a power drill and a range of attachments to fit it.

Power drills

Handy power drills do a lot more than just drill. A huge number of fittings can be attached to the basic drill unit, enabling it to do almost anything that can be done by a specialised power tool—perhaps not quite so fast or accurately, but certainly well enough for general use.

Basically, a power drill is a compact electric motor fitted with a projecting shaft at one end on which is mounted a *chuck*—a revolving clamp that grips and drives drill bits or other attachments. The motor unit is held in the hand by a pistol grip, and the motor is started by pressing a 'trigger' at the top of the grip. For safety reasons, the motor stops if pressure is released on the trigger, but most drills have a locking pin that can be engaged to hold the trigger in the 'on' position.

Electric power is supplied to the drill by a cable that enters the machine through the bottom of the handle. On all modern drills, a complex system of insulation is built in to keep the user from getting an electric shock.

The motor is cooled by a built-in fan that draws air through slots in the side of the drill. These slots must be kept uncovered and free of sawdust, or the motor may overheat and burn out.

Many drills can be adjusted to run at different speeds. The normal type is a two-speed drill geared to run at up to 1,000 rpm and 2,500-3,000 rpm. These two speeds are suitable for most household jobs, and a two-speed machine is probably the best type for the householder to buy.

Variable-speed drills, where the speed can be infinitely varied by an electrical device, are also made, but these are specialist tools. It is false economy to buy a single-speed drill and a separate electrical speed reducer, because although single-speed machines are cheaper, the cost of the two units together will be higher than that of a good two-speed drill.

The most suitable speeds for various woodworking and other operations are shown in the table below.

Drills come in various sizes, which are graded by the capacity of their chuck—i.e. the largest drill bit that can be fitted into it. Common sizes are 6mm ($\frac{1}{4}$in), 8mm ($\frac{3}{16}$in), 10mm ($\frac{3}{8}$in) and 13mm ($\frac{1}{2}$in). The larger machines have more powerful motors. A medium-sized machine—say, 10mm ($\frac{3}{8}$in)—should be adequate for all ordinary jobs, though the smallest may be too light for some.

An indispensable accessory that every drill user will need is an extension cable. This

Speeds for two-speed drills

High speed : 2500-3000 rpm	Low speed : up to 1000 rpm
Drilling :	Drilling
wood up to 8mm ($\frac{3}{8}$") diameter	*wood over 8mm ($\frac{3}{8}$") diameter*
steel up to 6mm ($\frac{1}{4}$") diameter	*steel over 6mm ($\frac{1}{4}$") diameter*
Circular saw	Masonry
Jigsaw	Screwdriving
Sanding	Polishing
Grinding	Paint mixing
Hedge trimming	

Cable sizes for extension cords

For 200-250V drills

Length of extension cable m & ft	Current consumption of drill (amps)						
	0-1	5-9	10-14	15-19	20-24	25-30	
7.5m (25ft)	A	B	B	C	D	E	
15m (50ft)	A	B	B	C	D	E	
30m (100ft)	A	B	C	D	D	E	size of cable required
45m (150ft)	B	C	D	E	E	—	
60m (200ft)	C	D	E	E	—	—	
90m (300ft)	C	E	—	—	—	—	

For 110-160V drills

Length of extension cable m & ft	Current consumption of drill (amps)						
	0-4	5-9	10-14	15-19	20-24	25-30	
7.5m (25ft)	A	B	B	C	D	E	
15m (50ft)	A	B	C	D	D	E	
30m (100ft)	B	D	D	E	—	—	size of cable required
45m (150ft)	C	D	E	—	—	—	
60m (200ft)	D	E	—	—	—	—	
90m (300ft)	D	—	—	—	—	—	

Cable sizes

Letter	Amperage	cross-sectional size (sq mm)	British size
A	6	0.75	24/.20
B	15	1.5	20/.25
C	20	2.5	50/.25
D	25	4	56/.30
E	42	6	84/.30

enables him to use the tool in places remote from a power outlet. Cables are available in standard lengths from 8m (25ft) to 100m (300ft), or you can make up your own. The longer the cable, the thicker it needs to be to prevent power loss. Heavier machines also need thicker cables. Recommended cable sizes are shown in the table. In some countries, though not in Britain, you must also have an isolating transformer if using a power tool out of doors; the shop that supplies the drill can advise you.

Drill bits and fittings

Many types of bit are sold for cutting different sizes and shapes of hole in different materials (see p 114). The 'everyday' sort are *twist bits*, used for drilling all sizes of hole in metal, and holes in wood up to 6mm ($\frac{1}{4}$in) in diameter. The smallest common size

of twist bit is 1.6mm ($\frac{1}{16}$in), and sizes increase in steps of 0.4mm ($\frac{1}{64}$in) up from this.

Larger holes in wood are drilled with *Jennings bits*, which have a wide spiral to remove the surplus wood, and a centre spur or spike to keep the cut accurate when it is being started. *Forstner bits* must be used in a drill press. They cut neat, flat-bottomed holes, but they have to be cleaned out more often than auger bits. *Dowel bits* are like twist bits with a wood-drill-shaped point for extra accuracy.

Very large holes are drilled with *flat bits* [up to 32mm (1$\frac{1}{4}$in)] or *hole saws* [up to 76mm (3in)]. The flat bit has a flat, spade-shaped cutter with a central spur to hold it in place. The hole saw has a revolving toothed ring attached to a central twist bit—the ring removes wood like a revolving

Above: A circular saw being used to rip a length of timber. Always make sure that the blades are sharp; otherwise these machines are liable to stall.

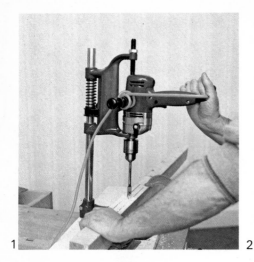
1

2

3

7

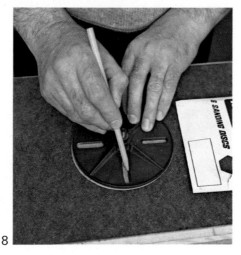
8

Fig.1. A bench stand is one of the most useful accessories for your drill. It allows you to make perfectly accurate vertical holes in wood, metal or plastic.

Fig.2. A jigsaw attachment. Here, a cut is being started in the middle of this wooden door by tipping the saw on its nose and gradually lowering the blade into the wood.

Fig.3. A more powerful integral jigsaw. Here, the saw is being slid along a wooden straight edge to make a straight cut in a sheet of plastic laminate.

Fig.4. When sanding a flat surface, you should hold the rubber disc at an angle to the wood to minimise swirl marks.

Fig.5. The same disc can also be used, with practice, to sand rounded objects. Note how the cable is being held away from the disc.

Fig.6. A drill-powered circular saw being used to cut a bevel, or mitre, along the edge of a piece of timber.

Fig.7 A hole saw cutting large circles out of an aluminium sheet, which is firmly clamped to wooden backing.

Fig.8. An easy way of sharpening chisels without a grinder. First mark and cut slots in a fine-grade sanding disc . . .

Fig.9. . . . then apply special disc cement to the revolving sanding plate and press the sanding disc on to its tacky surface.

Fig.10. Start the motor and hold the chisel tip to the underside of the disc. It will not catch in the slots.

Fig.11. The rapidly passing slots allow you to see, through the disc, whether you are holding the blade at the right angle.

pastry-cutter. Different sizes of ring are available.

Very long holes, such as those up the shaft of standard lamps, are drilled with *shell* or *parrot-nosed augers*. They are generally used on a lathe, and not in a hand-held drill.

Other types of bit include *countersink bits*, for countersinking screw holes, and *drill-countersinkers* or '*screw sinks*', which are specially shaped to drill and countersink (or counterbore) a hole for a particular size of screw.

A *plug cutter* is often used in conjunction with a 'screw sink' to conceal screw heads in wood. The 'screw sink' is used to counter-bore a screw hole—i.e., to recess the screw head some way into the wood—and then a plug like a short length of dowel is cut from a matching piece of timber, glued into the recess over the screw head, and planed flat to give an almost invisible result.

For drilling hard masonry, a *hammer attachment* to a drill is useful. This makes the bit vibrate up and down as it revolves. A *percussion bit* should be used with the attachment. For drilling without hammering, special *masonry bits* are made—they look like twist bits but have cutting tips made of a special hard alloy.

Glass and tiles are drilled with a *spear point drill*, which also has a hardened tip.

Special *right-angle* and *flexible drive shafts* are made to allow drilling in awkward corners that could not normally be reached.

Drilling techniques

Whatever you are drilling, the position of the hole should be clearly marked before you start, and a small indentation made in the workpiece with a centre punch (or, at a pinch, nail punch or big nail), to stop the drill from wandering in the first few seconds of work. Clamp the workpiece down securely, or it may start to revolve.

It is essential that the drill should be at right angles to the surface to be drilled. You can line it up with a try square before you start—though of course the drill always tilts a bit once you start drilling.

Simple drill guides are made (the Wolf 'Drillrite' is an example) that hold the drill at right angles to any flat surface. Or you can buy a drill stand, which holds the drill vertical on a frame. The drill can be moved up and down by a lever. The workpiece is placed underneath on the base of the stand (see Fig.1).

Drill bits should be prevented from over-

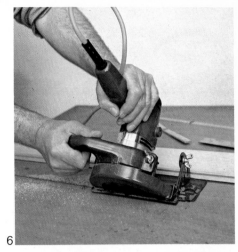

4

5

6

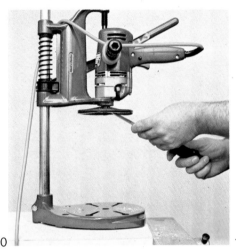

9

10

11

heating through friction. If they become too hot, the metal loses its 'temper' and becomes soft. This is a particular problem with ordinary carbon steel twist bits. Special 'high-speed' steel bits, made for drilling hard metals, are more resistant—but also more expensive. Masonry bits are very prone to overheating.

When drilling wood with a twist bit, remove it occasionally to check that the spirals are not clogged with wood dust, which can lead to overheating. When drilling any metal other than brass or cast iron, lubricate the drill bit frequently to cool. Use oil for steel, turpentine or paraffin (kerosene) for aluminium, turpentine for glass and water for mirrors. When drilling glass, make a small pool of lubricant around the hole in a plasticine ring.

Thin metal should be clamped to a wood backing when being drilled to reduce distortion and keep the drill from jamming as it breaks through to the other side. A piece of thin sheet metal revolving with a drill is extremely dangerous.

Circular saw attachments

These fittings for power drills are very popular, because sawing by hand is a time-consuming business.

Two types are made: *hand-held* ones consist of a 130mm (5in) or 150mm (6in) blade, a frame to hold drill and blade steady and allow it to be slid across the wood to be cut, and a fixed top and retractable bottom blade guard. There is also a *saw table*, or bench-mounted circular saw, where the blade projects upwards through a flat table top.

Unfortunately, neither machine is satisfactory for all types of job. Partly, this is because a circular saw requires a great deal of power to drive it—in fact, rather more power than can be provided by even the largest drill motor. There is a serious danger of overloading the motor to such an extent that it burns out. A drill-driven saw should, therefore, only be used for light work such as battens, mouldings and plywood, and not kept too constantly in use.

Another reason is that, on many jobs—for example, repair work, or where you are fitting architraves or other mouldings—it is necessary to keep removing the drill bit and swapping it for a saw-blade. Often this slows you down to the point where a hand-saw would be quicker.

So that if you intend to do carpentry on a serious scale, a better alternative is to buy a proper *bench saw* with an adequate motor,

which will do everything that a drill-driven saw table can do—and more—faster and more safely. It is used in exactly the same way as the smaller, less powerful saw table, so only the use of the hand-held type of saw is described here.

Using a hand-held circular saw

Saw attachments should only be used on medium- or large-sized drills, and then only for work that is unlikely to overstrain the motor. The 127mm (5in) blade gives a depth of cut of 38mm (1½in), and the 152mm (6in) blade one of 48mm (1⅝in) when set up normally on the machine, and this is about the maximum depth of cut the motor will stand. If the motor shows signs of slowing down or jamming, stop work immediately or you may burn it out on the spot. It is essential that the motor should be kept running at a high speed all the time to keep it from being damaged. Do not press the saw forward too hard, and always start the motor before the blade touches the wood, so that the speed of the motor stays up. You need a straight edge, and some practice, to bring in the blade at exactly the point where you want to cut; sighting straight down the blade will make it easier.

Saw cuts can be kept straight by nailing a batten to the wood you are cutting, and running the saw along it; or by using the adjustable *rip fence* on the saw, which guides it parallel to the edge of the wood.

Four types of blade are available: the *rip blade*, with coarse teeth, for cutting along the grain; the fine-toothed *cross-cut;* the *planer blade*, which gives an extra-neat result, and the most useful type, the *combination blade*, which cuts at any angle to the grain.

These blades will not cut metal, so when using the saw on old wood it is essential to remove all nails and screws. To prevent the blade catching on anything underneath the wood, and to reduce the strain on the motor, set the depth gauge of the blade to only slightly more than the thickness of the wood you are cutting. A circular saw blade cuts on the upstroke, so setting the blade as shallow as possible gives a neater result by flattening the angle at which it cuts.

If the blade of the saw wanders off the cutting line, do not twist the saw to straighten the line. This may jam the blade in the cut, with disastrous results. Take the saw out of the cut, go back a few inches and cut along that section again.

Jigsaws

A power-driven jigsaw is used in the same way as a hand-held coping saw—that is, for cutting curves and complex shapes. Its blade is small and pointed and moves rapidly up and down with a stabbing motion. Various types of blade are available for cutting wood, plastic and sheet metal, but it will not cut very thick boards or sheets. It can manage a 50mm (2in) thick softwood board, or hardwood half as thick.

Jigsaws should not be pressed forward too hard, or the highly tempered blade may snap. But they should be held firmly down on to the material they are cutting to resist the down-stroke of the blade.

The blade is narrow enough to cut 13mm (½in) radius curves, but will not turn a right-angled corner. It can, however, be started in the middle of a piece of wood by tilting the machine forward on its nose and gradually lowering the blade into the wood until it is upright (see Fig.2).

Jigsaws are available both as power tool attachments and as integral tools, hand-held or bench-mounted with the blade pointing upwards.

Sanders

Several types of sander can be fitted to a power drill. The most commonly used is the *disc sander*. A flexible rubber disc is mounted in the chuck of the machine and an abrasive paper disc is fastened to it with a recessed central screw.

The sander is used at an angle, so that only one side of the disc touches the surface being sanded (see Fig.4). If the disc is laid flat against the surface it produces circular marks called *swirl marks*, which may be deep and difficult to remove. Even with the disc used at the correct angle, slight swirl marks are unavoidable.

A special type of disc called the 'Swirlaway'

Below: A selection of drill bits for use with power drills. They all have round shanks to fit in the chuck. Bits for handbraces have square shanks.

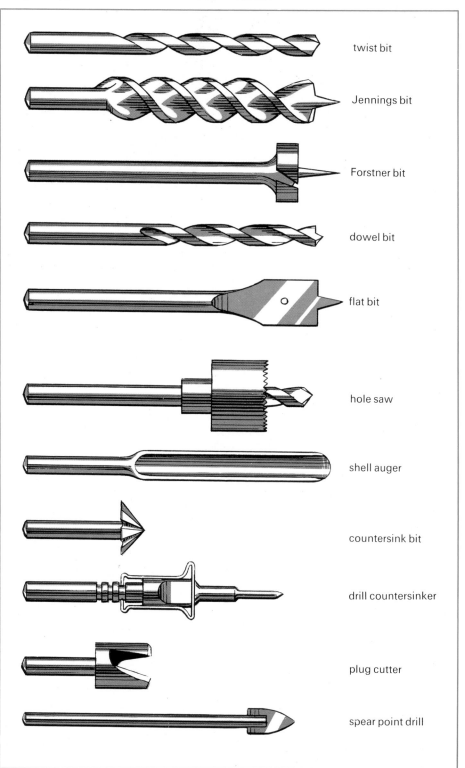

twist bit

Jennings bit

Forstner bit

dowel bit

flat bit

hole saw

shell auger

countersink bit

drill countersinker

plug cutter

spear point drill

reduces these marks to a minimum. The disc is made of metal, and is flat and completely rigid. To give it flexibility in use, the shaft on which it is mounted can be bent at a slight angle while it is turning.

The *drum sander* consists of a wide revolving drum made of stiff foam rubber, with an abrasive belt fastened around its edge. It makes no swirl marks, but can only be used for sanding small objects or narrow strips of wood. On large, flat surfaces it tends to give an uneven result.

The *orbital sander*, on the other hand, can be used to give a perfect finish to any surface. It has a large, flat sanding pad covered by an abrasive sheet. This moves to and fro in a small circle without revolving, so it leaves no swirl marks at all. Orbital sanders are available both as attachments and as integral tools.

The abrasive discs, belts, and sheets for all these tools are available in coarse, medium and fine grades as well as special types such as 'wet-and-dry' and 'preparation' for rubbing down paintwork.

Other attachments

Many highly specialised attachments are available for power drills. These include *rotary files* for finishing the edges of metal sheet, *polishing pads*, made of lambswool, that fit over the rubber sanding disc, *wire brushes* for removing rust from metal, *screwdriver attachments*, useful when a large number of screws have to be driven, and even *paint stirrers* and *hedge trimmers*. Among the most useful are *grinding wheels*, which can save a lot of time in sharpening knives, chisels and plane blades. Special extra-tough wheels are made for sharpening masonry drills.

Anyone who has used both a hand tool and its drill-powered equivalent will appreciate the fantastic saving of time and effort that a power drill brings. Sooner or later, however, he will become dissatisfied with the performance of some of the accessories of his power drill, and graduate to integral tools, as used by professionals.

Integral tools are designed in one piece for one purpose, instead of being a makeshift adaptation. Many have more powerful motors than those of drills, and as a result work faster and more efficiently than their equivalent drill attachments.

In many cases, an ordinary power drill with an attachment is quite good enough for amateur use. For example, the amateur carpenter would not dream of buying a full-size integral drill press instead of his power drill. But with other tools, bolt-on attachments to power drills are inadequate. This is particularly true with circular saws. A drill-driven saw will simply not cope with the strain of cutting large pieces of hardwood. So the

first integral tool that many amateurs buy is a proper bench saw.

The bench saw

Circular saws of this type have powerful motors—at least ½hp—and large blades ranging from 150mm (6in) to 300mm (12in) in diameter. The blade turns much faster than the one on a drill attachment, which not only speeds up the saws' cutting rate, but also gives a cleaner result.

However, both integral bench saw and drill-driven saw table are used in exactly the same way, and if you have a drill-powered saw, you can use these operating instructions provided that you do not overtax the tool's limited power.

A bench saw consists of a flat table top through which the saw blade projects. Wood is slid over the table towards the blade, which is adjustable for depth and angle of cut and protected by a slide-away guard that reduces the risk of you cutting your fingers off—though this is still a tool that must be used with great care.

Wood is fed into the saw at the correct angle by using one of two *guide fences*. One of these, the *rip fence*, is parallel to the saw blade, but can be set any distance away from it by sliding it sideways in a groove up the edge of the table. Wood is slid along it into the blade for straight cutting parallel to the edge, generally along the grain. The other fence, the *crosscut guide*, is for cutting across the width (and grain) of wood at any angle. It does not lock in position, but moves from the front to the back of the table by sliding in a slot parallel to the blade. On the front of the guide there is a protractor. This is set to the desired angle, and the wood is rested against it. Then wood and guide are pushed together towards the blade, which cuts the wood at the angle the protractor is set to.

Both guide fences can be removed entirely if necessary, so that large sheets of hardboard or plywood can be cut without anything getting in the way. It is as well to check the angle of the rip fence from time to time. If it is not exactly parallel to the blade, it may cause the blade to jam when making a cut in a long piece of wood. Some, but not all, bench saws have slip clutches that disengage the motor when this happens, to stop it from burning out.

Of course, the saw is not restricted to making cuts straight along or across wood. It is an extremely versatile tool.

Sawing techniques
Small pieces of wood

It is dangerous to feed small pieces of wood into the blade with your hands, because your fingers get uncomfortably close to the blade and the slightest slip may cause a serious

accident. Wood is very likely to slip on a bench saw, because the tremendous torque of the blade tends to wrench it aside if you are not holding it firmly. This is a particular problem when using the cross-cut guide at an angle.

Small pieces should be pushed towards the blade with a *push stick*—a short lath with a *V* shape cut out of the end so that it can hold the piece of wood firmly (see Fig.12). It doesn't matter if the push stick gets cut, because you can make another in seconds. Fingers are not so easily replaced.

Mitring and firring

Mitring, or cutting wood at a 45° angle to make a mitred joint can be done quickly and accurately. To cut a mitre across the face of a piece of wood—as if making a picture fram—set the protractor on the cross-cut guide accurately to 45°. Then lay the wood against the guide and slide the guide and wood together down the table into the saw blade (see Fig.13).

As a general rule when cross-cutting, wood should be held with both hands on one side of the blade, and the offcut allowed to fall away freely. If you push from both sides, the pressure tends to close up the cut around the blade, causing it to jam and 'buck' dangerously. If you must hold both sides, curve the wood slightly with your hands to hold the cut open.

To cut a bevel, or mitre along the edge of a piece of wood—as if making a box with mitred corners—set the blade at a 45° angle. Many saws have built-in protractors here, too, to ensure accuracy. On some bench saws, the table tilts instead of the blade. Slide the wood and cross-cut guide towards the blade in the normal way, but grip the wood extra firmly (see Fig.14).

Firring is cutting a very shallow taper on a long length of wood so that it is a few inches narrower at one end than the other. It is used, for example, in cutting rafters for flat roofs to create a slight slope for drainage.

Firring is best done by making an adjustable jig out of two moderately long battens. Set them face to face and fasten them together by a hinge at one end and a slotted metal strip fastened with wingnuts at the other. By moving the free ends a distance apart and locking them at this distance with the strip wingnuts, the jig can be set at any shallow angle (see Fig.20).

In use, the jig is slid along the fence together with the wood to be cut. This method is particularly convenient when a large number of identical pieces have to be cut.

Housing joints

Housings and other grooves can be cut very simply (but also very accurately) by setting the saw blade to the required depth of cut and cutting the sides of the groove first, using the fence to keep them straight. Then slide the fence away and remove the wood between the cuts by repeatedly passing the wood over the saw blade. Mark the extent of the groove on top of the wood, or you may cut past the edges. Except with very wide grooves or housings, this method is faster than chiselling by hand, although for a stopped housing you will have to cut the last inch or two by hand, since the curved saw blade cannot reach the inside corner of the housing. It is also more accurate, because the depth of cut is constant all over the groove.

When cutting tenons, wood can be removed in the same way.

Rebates

There are two ways of cutting rebates on a bench saw. One way is to cut along one side of the rebate, using the fence to ensure accuracy, and then turn the wood through 90° and cut the other side (see Fig.15).

This involves two operations for each rebate. A faster way is to mount the blade on 'wobble washers'—a pair of angled washers that make the blade wobble from side to side as it revolves. As a result, the blade cuts a wide groove instead of a neat line. The width of the grooves is restricted by the size of the slot in the saw table, because if the blade 'wobbled' too far it would cut the table. But you can always make several passes to cut a wide rebate.

When you have set the blade on its washers, fasten a piece of old battening to the fence to protect it and move it until the blade just brushes the battening at the apex of its wobble. Now any piece of wood that is slid along the battening will have a rebate cut out of it the same width as the wobble of the blade—or narrower if your adjust the blade to cut farther into the temporary battening fence. The depth of cut can still be adjusted in the normal way.

Great care should be taken when using wobble washers, because the oscillation of the blade makes it even more dangerous than an ordinary circular saw blade. At all costs, keep your fingers well away from it and use a push stick to move the wood you are cutting.

Kerfing

Kerfing is a special technique that enables a piece of solid wood to be bent in a curve. Rows of parallel cuts made across the wood on the inside of the curve through half to three-quarters of the wood's thickness, and all the way along the part that is to be curved. The wood can be bent (see illustration)—though it helps the process if you wet it or steam it as well. Use a cross-cut or planer blade to make the cuts; a combination blade is too coarse and will give a messy result.

Kerfing reduces the strength of wood sharply, and should not be used for load-bearing frames. It is also only suitable for outside curves—that is, with the saw cuts on the narrower radius; the wood *could* be bent the other way but the surface would probably wrinkle unattractively. But when used correctly, kerfing produces a neat curve that is impossible to make by any other method.

Maintenance of blades

Blades should be kept clean and as sharp as possible. After using a blade, rub a little oil or vaseline over it to stop it from going rusty. If any rush does form, take it off with wire wool. The smoother the surface of the blade is kept, the faster it will cut because there will be less friction between blade and wood.

Circular saw blades are very easy to sharpen yourself. You *can* have them sharpened professionally, and some shops run an exchange service, sharp blades for blunt, but you only need a big flat file and a quarter of

12

13

14
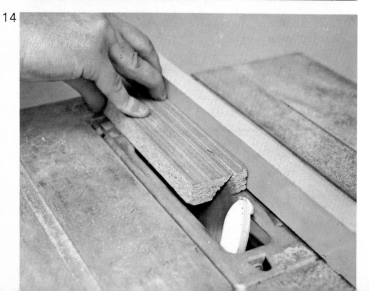

15

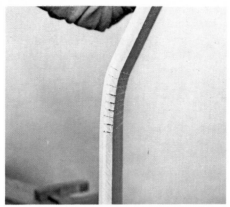

Above: A bench saw is particularly useful for kerfing—bending a piece of wood into a curve by making rows of deep cuts in it.

an hour to do just as good a job as they can.

Rip, cross-cut and combination blades have teeth with squared-off outer ends filed at an angle. Alternate teeth have opposite angles. It is these angles that wear down, and all you need to do is file them back to their original shape. Do not file any of the other surfaces of the teeth or bend them.

Planer blades have straight-cut, pointed teeth which should all be filed straight across, filing the rear edge of each tooth. Otherwise, they should be treated in the same way.

Power saws are sometimes fitted with abrasive cutting wheels for sawing asbestos sheet and other materials. When these become blunt, they cannot be sharpened, but must be replaced.

The bench grinder

One of the most useful tools in any workshop is the bench grinder. It enables all edge tools to be resharpened in an instant—and sharp tools make for easy work. If you have a grinder attachment for a power drill, you will have to set it up every time you want to sharpen something—which is often. In practice, this means that you will not sharpen things often enough. So a bench grinder, which is not particularly expensive, is a good investment.

Another advantage of an integral bench grinder is that it has two revolving shafts—one on each end of the motor. Chisel and plane blades are sharpened in two operations; grinding, to get the blade the right shape, and honing, to put an edge on it. Different grinding wheels are needed for each operation, so having both of them on the same machine speeds up work considerably.

Sharpening is done against the front curved edge of the grinding wheel, and not against the flat circular face. The wheel revolves so that the front edge moves downwards. This keeps sparks and fragments of metal or abrasive from being thrown upwards into

the eyes (but it is still a wise precaution to wear goggles). Adjustable tool rests are provided in front of each wheel to hold blades steady while they are sharpened.

Cutting wheels come in various grades. For most jobs, a medium wheel for grinding and a very fine one for honing should be all you need. Special extra-tough wheels are made for honing the hardened tips of masonry drills.

The wheels are fastened to their shafts by nuts screwing down on to the threaded ends of the shafts. The wheel on the left has a left-hand thread to stop it from coming undone in use. The wheel on the right has a normal right-hand thread.

Sharpening chisel and plane blades

Chisel and plane blades, though completely different in shape and use, are sharpened in exactly the same way. In both types of blade, the preliminary grinding to shape of the edge of the blade should give the ground surface an angle of 25° to the flat face of the blade. Then it should be honed at the slightly greater angle of 30°. The 5° difference saves you from having to hone the whole ground surface. Only the tip is honed (see Fig.21).

To sharpen a blade, first lay it on the tool rest of the grinder with the point touching the stationary wheel, and measure the angle where the point touches. Move the blade until the angle is 25°, and memorise the position of the blade. Now take the blade away, start the wheels and lay the blade lightly against the coarse wheel. High speed and light pressure are the secret of good grinding. Move a wide blade from side to side across the wheel, so that its whole edge is ground evenly.

Grind on one side only until the blade is properly shaped, when the length of the ground surface should be 2½ times the thickness of the blade. Every few seconds of grinding, remove the blade from the wheel and dip it in cold water to stop it from overheating. An overheated blade 'loses its temper' and turns blue. If this happens, grind off the blue part.

The freshly ground surface will be slightly hollow in shape because of the curve of the wheel, but that doesn't matter. The next stage is to hone it.

Find the correct angle of the blade against the stationary wheel as you did before, except that it should be 30° and not 25°. Then start the grinder and lay the sloping side of the blade against the fine wheel—but only for a few seconds. The wheel will turn the edge of the blade over, producing a fine 'burr' on the other side. Cool the blade and lay the flat side *flat* on the wheel (i.e. not at 30°) for a few seconds to turn the burr the other way. Then turn the chisel round again and give the other side a few seconds at 30°.

Some of the many ways of using a bench saw.

Fig.12. *A push stick is used to protect fingers from the revolving blade. The saw is a lightweight drill attachment.*

Fig.13. *Cutting a mitre on a more powerful integral bench saw, using its built-in protractor.*

Fig.14. *Cutting a bevel. A straight-edge is laid along the rip fence to make the cut more accurate.*

Fig.15. *Using the same saw to make the second cut of a large rebate.*

16

17

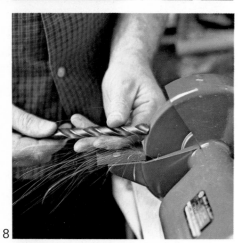

18

19

This will turn the burr again.

Continue doing each side alternately, using very light pressure and reducing the honing period each time. Eventually, the burr will break off, leaving a razor edge.

Blades can be honed several times before they lose their shape and have to be re-ground.

Sharpening twist drills

Twist drills and high speed drills can also be sharpened on a fine grinding wheel. The angles have to be watched carefully, but otherwise the job is not difficult. Do not cool twist drills in water, because the extra-hard steel might crack. Just try not to over-heat them.

There are three important angles that must be maintained on a twist drill. They are marked A, B and C in Fig. 22. Angle A, the angle of the cutting edge to the shaft, should always be 30°. Angle B, the angle of the sloping shoulder of the cutting edge to the horizontal, varies with the size of the drill. For small drills (from 2.4mm to 4.8mm [$\frac{3}{32}$ in to $\frac{3}{16}$ in]) it should be between 20° and 26°. For medium drills (up to 9.5mm [$\frac{3}{8}$ in]) it should be between 10° and 15°. For large drills (up to 15.8mm [$\frac{5}{8}$ in]) it should be between 9° and 13°. As a check on these two angles, if you have got them right, angle C, the angle of the front of the cutting edge to the chisel point of the drill, will always be 130°.

The correct way to sharpen a twist drill is to hold it near the point between the thumb and forefinger of the left hand, gripping it flexibly so that it can be moved about. Rest the left hand comfortably on the tool rest, as shown in Fig.17, and use the right hand to poke it through the improvised pivot you have made with your left hand until the cutting edge touches the wheel.

The front of the cutting edge should touch the wheel first, at such an angle that its whole length is in contact with the wheel. As soon as it touches, push the shank of the drill down with your right hand so that the cutting edge rises, simultaneously twisting the bit a quarter of a turn clockwise (see Fig.18). This movement is necessary to achieve the correct curve and angle on each cutting edge. You can practise on an old twist bit until you get it right. Once learned, it is never forgotten.

Sharpen both cutting edges of the drill equally so that the point is in the middle. When it is, check angle C, which should be 130°. If not, keep on until it is.

Special wood bits should not be sharpened on a grinding wheel, but with a small flat needle file with medium fine teeth. Aim only to preserve the original angle of the cutting edges; these bits are so large that sharpening them is a simple job.

Fig.16. Sharpening a chisel on a bench grinder. The blade is held steady against the tool rest and moved from side to side to keep the edge straight and even.

Figs.17 and 18. The hand movement for sharpening a twist drill has to be learned. The drill is laid against the wheel with the front of its cutting edge touching, then turned clockwise and slid forward and up the curve of the wheel.

Fig.19. Shaping a curved end on a piece of wood with a bench sander—this one is a power drill attachment.

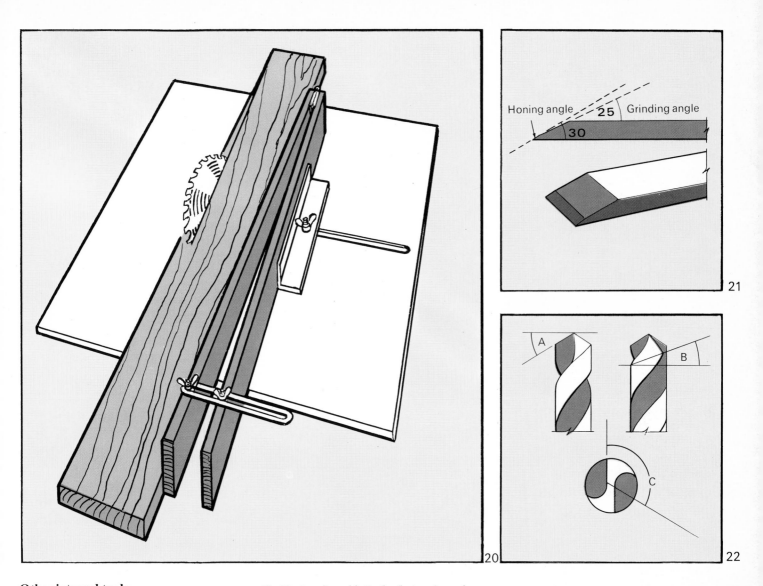

Other integral tools

Most other integral tools are out of the amateur's domain. They are generally larger and more expensive than is suitable for amateur use, and many of them, such as the drill press or orbital sander, can be duplicated satisfactorily by drill-powered accessories.

One that you might come across is a *bench sander*—though even this can be duplicated fairly well with a power drill and a horizontal sanding stand (Fig.19). It consists of a vertical wheel faced with abrasive paper, and in front of it, a horizontal table equipped with guide fences like those of a bench saw.

The purpose of the tool is to sand the ends of pieces of wood at an exact angle— like a shooting board, only more accurate and faster. Only one side of the wheel is used, the side which is moving downwards as the wheel revolves. This holds the wood down flat on the table for maximum accuracy. The wood is fed past the guide fence, which can be set at 90° or 45° (for really accurate mitres) or any angle between.

Fig.20. An adjustable jig for firring. It can be set to a slope of (for example) 1 in 10 by measuring a 2.5cm (1in) gap 254mm (10in) along from the hinge. The hinge must be inset so that there is no gap when it is shut.

Fig.21. Sharpening angles for all types of chisel and plane blade.

Fig.22. Sharpening angles for twist drills—see the text.

Advanced metalworking techniques

Occasionally you will have to tackle a metalworking job which calls for more advanced techniques. Here basic instructions are given for sawing metal bars and hardening and tempering home made tools, together with all you need to know about drill bits, screwthread taps and dies.

The first consideration is how to cut the material. Before this can be done it must be supported firmly. Here a good solid bench vice is vital. Don't be tempted to use a carpenter's woodworking vice—you will spoil the jaws and damage the screw—but use a solid metalworkers' bench vice. As a rule, always buy the largest, biggest and best you can afford since it will make your work so much easier. The weight of a large vice will help to prevent the work juddering during sawing and provides a perfect support. A tight grip on the metal you are to cut is very important; if the metal slips while you are cutting it, at the very least you may break the hacksaw blade and you may also bruise and skin your knuckles at the same time.

Cutting metal

The hacksaw is the best tool for sawing metal, but remember that a hacksaw is not a universal tool. It is only a frame into which you can fit a variety of blades. These blades come in two basic types—ordinary carbon steel and high-speed steel. The latter are more expensive but, used with care, last perhaps three times as long as the more brittle carbon blades.

Blades are also described by the number of teeth they have to the inch. The fewer the number, the coarser the blade, and you must select the right one to suit the job. A good guide is that, whatever you are cutting, there are a minimum of three teeth of the blade in contact with the metal at any moment. This is important when cutting narrow sections because if the blade is coarser than this, the teeth will straddle the metal and chip off. For cutting large sections of steel, the coarser the blade (within reason) the better since the wider gaps between the teeth will allow plenty of clearance for the tiny chips of metal which the teeth remove as they are pushed across the metal. The illustration on the opposite page describes how to select the right blade. When you fit a blade into a hacksaw frame, always make sure that the teeth point forwards, and keep the blade

tight by screwing up the adjuster on the frame—a slack blade is easily broken.

Working with a hacksaw is simple providing you use the correct technique. Hold the saw firmly in both hands with your forearms horizontal. Push the saw forward and pull it back with a smooth, steady movement. Don't saw too quickly—one forward stroke per second is ideal. Do not apply pressure on the back stroke—this does not cut and you will only blunt the tips of the saw teeth.

With practice you will automatically develop the correct sawing technique. When you do you will be able to work with a hacksaw for long periods without fatigue.

If you have to make a long cut through a narrow section, you can turn this blade through 90 degrees in the frame so that the bow of the frame is well clear of the metal.

Drills and drilling

A drill bit is a simple device for making a hole. It is a precision tool made of special hard steel which is hardened, tempered and ground to very precise specifications. The general purpose type of bit has two spiral flutes along its working length ending in a carefully-shaped, ground tip, while the other end comprises a plain steel shank which fits into the chuck jaws of a hand drill or electric drill. Bits are classified under three headings—diameter, type of metal (i.e. carbon steel or high-speed steel), and length.

The diameter is measured in three ways, none of which is directly compatible with the others—that is, it does not have a direct counterpart in another system. The first system of measurement uses fractions of an inch, then comes the metric range measured in millimetres, and finally the letter range, listed from A to Z. Bits are made from either ordinary carbon steel (general purpose bits) or high-speed steel (more expensive, better bits).

The length of a bit is measured in three ways. The ordinary bits which you buy in any tool store are called 'jobbing' bits and these have a set ratio of length to diameter. Stub bits are very short bits for special work. Extended or long bits are just what they say and are made in a variety of long lengths.

There are other variations. Large bits can also be obtained with what is called a Morse Taper Shank. Instead of the usual parallel shank of the normal jobbing or high-speed

bit, these ones have a special tapered end which fits into the tapered chuck of a pedestal drill—used to give great accuracy for toolmakers' work. There are also bits made with various types of flutes. Cabinet makers' bits, for example, have straight flutes rather like a parallel reamer. These are not set on a helix like the spiral sides of an ordinary drill. For drilling soft metals and alloys, the flutes are set on what is called a quick helix—this means that they turn more rapidly around the bit body. For drilling thermo-setting plastics, the flutes are made with a slow helix for gradual twist. Indeed, there are very many different types of specialist bits for particular jobs, but the sort which you are most likely to need are the ordinary engineers' jobbing bits.

Once a bit gets blunt, it can be sharpened on a grindstone, but this takes some practice and a lot of care if you are to do the job properly. Even so, once a bit has been resharpened, it is extremely unlikely that it will bore with the same accuracy as when new. The error may only be small but it can be significant if you are doing work that demands accuracy. Fig.2 shows the parts of a drill and also the form of the ground point.

Drilling metal

The action of drilling metal is to remove material from the hole in the form of two spiral sections and filings. It depends on the type of metal whether these spiral sections are removed as a continuous coil or as fine metallic particles. Soft brass, for example, when drilled leaves two wire strips. Iron and steel, on the other hand, are usually too brittle to assume this form, and so is thrown up as fine lumps. This waste material is known as swarf.

The swarf is formed by the drill point being pressed into the metal while in rotation. The

Opposite page:
Top left: Two types of hacksaw blade, high-speed steel blades and ordinary carbon steel blades. When using a hacksaw there should always be three saw teeth in contact.

Top right: You should lubricate a drill bit when drilling metal to prevent the bit getting too hot. Ordinary lubricating oil is adequate for this purpose.

Bottom left: When drilling metal you should keep the drill as upright as possible and apply some of your body weight to the top of the drill.

Bottom right: The various tools used for cutting threads. At the top of the photograph is a die and diestock, used to cut threads on metal rods. At the bottom are taps and a tap wrench, used for cutting threads in holes.

form of the swarf is also governed by two other factors—the rotational speed of the cutting edge and also the rate at which the drill is pushed into the metal—this is called the rate of feed. There is an optimum cutting speed and a rate of feed for every bit size in every metal—and it differs according to the type of metal.

The swarf flows away from the cutting edge of the bit by passing up the bit flutes. If these passages become blocked, the bit cannot continue to cut the metal because there is no way out for the metal it must remove. If you drill certain types of alloy at too great a speed, the swarf becomes extremely hot—in some cases momentarily molten—and sticks to the flutes, blocking them. Normally this is easily cleared by moving the drill in and out of the hole whilst keeping it turning. If you do this at regular intervals, the flutes should stay clear. In bad cases, the drill must be lifted from the hole, stopped, and the flutes cleaned out with a block of hardwood. Never try to drill a hole deeper than the length of the flutes, otherwise once more this same blockage effect will happen and the drill will stop cutting. If you keep it rotating in the hole, it will generate so much friction that it will become hot. If it gets too hot, the metal will lose its temper and the bit will be ruined.

If you try to drill too large a hole in a thin piece of metal, the drill will jam and, if you are using a power drill, it will probably spin the workpiece round. This could cause you a nasty injury. Make sure, first, that whatever you are drilling is securely clamped in the vice or to the bench. The thickness of the metal should be greater than the point length of the drill, particularly when the bit is 6mm (¼in) in diameter or larger. In other words, do not try to drill a 10mm (⅜in) hole through a piece of 18 gauge metal: if you do the drill bit will jam and could break. It may well tear its way through the metal, leaving either a triangle or a butterfly shaped hole where the side of the drill has broken through in one place, the remaining metal running up the flutes of the bit like a screwthread. This problem arises when the point of the bit breaks through to the other side of the metal before

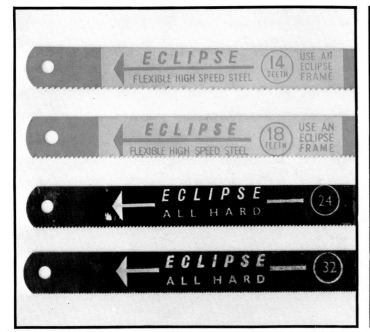

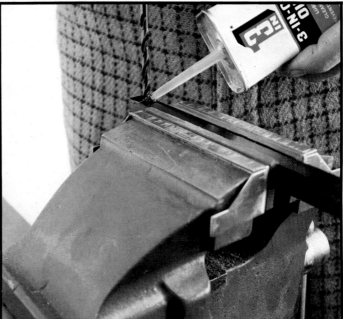

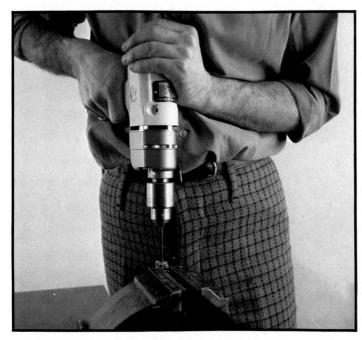

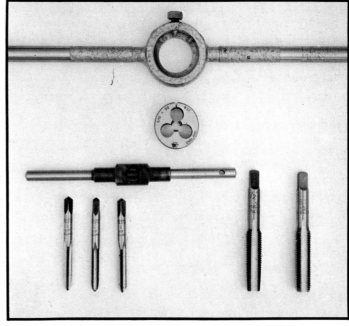

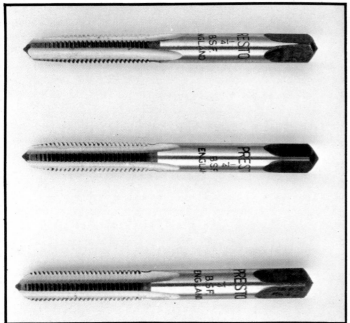

the full diameter of the bit has started cutting.

The best way of drilling large holes in thin metal is to cut them using a tool called a tank —or fly—cutter. If you must drill large holes in thin gauge material, then start by drilling a small pilot hole through the metal and also through two thick pieces of hardwood, say 25mm (1in) thick. Put one of these blocks on either side of the metal, locate the holes by pushing a nail down through the wood so that it passes through the metal and into the other piece of wood. Clamp this sandwich together and remove the nail. Now drill slowly (i.e. at a slow rate of feed) down through the sandwich using the pilot hole to guide the point. You will now be able to bore the thin metal without damage or risk.

Holes smaller than 5mm ($\frac{3}{16}$in) are best drilled in one step without drilling a pilot first. The purpose of a pilot hole is to make it easier to drill thicker metal since the speed of the cutting edge at the centre is virtually nil. By drilling, say a 3mm ($\frac{1}{8}$in) diameter pilot hole first, the point of the larger drill will be guided without itself retarding the progress of the cutting edge. You may think that the way to drill a large hole is to 'go up in steps' starting with a pilot hole and then drilling through with a series of successively larger drills. This may work but as the drills get larger the guidance given from the previous oversize pilot hole gets less and less accurate.

If you have to bore a 13mm ($\frac{1}{2}$in) hole in mild steel, for instance, it is acceptable to drill a 3mm ($\frac{1}{8}$in) pilot, and then open this up to 6.5mm ($\frac{1}{4}$in) before going through with the finished-size drill. But if you were now to go through with a 9.5mm ($\frac{3}{8}$in) drill, the final 'land' available to guide the finished-size drill (the 13mm [$\frac{1}{2}$in]) would be only a matter of 2mm ($\frac{1}{16}$in) each side. This drill is then most

likely to 'wander' and, regardless of the accuracy used in positioning the first pilot hole (the 3mm [$\frac{1}{8}$in]), you could be as much as 2mm ($\frac{1}{16}$in) out of alignment by the time you have finished.

Sometimes you may have to drill a hole in an awkward position where the length of a standard bit is insufficient. Instead of buying a costly long bit (which your stockist may have to order), you can usually get by with the use of an extension drill. These can be made very easily, particularly if you have access to welding or brazing equipment.

To make an extension drill up to, say, 8mm ($\frac{5}{32}$in) in diameter, take a length of 6mm ($\frac{1}{4}$in) diameter silver steel (most good tool stores sell this in 330mm [13in] lengths) and carefully drill a hole down through one end using the drill you are going to extend, that is the 8mm ($\frac{5}{32}$in) drill. Do this by clamping the silver steel vertically in the vice jaws and then get someone to guide your drilling, making sure that the drill is absolutely vertical and in line with the steel. You need only drill down about 13mm ($\frac{1}{2}$in). Now set up the drill bit and the steel rod, preferably packed level using V blocks, so that the shank of the drill is set in the end of the rod. Braze or silver-solder round the join, taking care not to get too much heat on the drill's cutting portion.

For very small extension bits, use silver steel the same diameter as the bits, grind one end to a 45° angle, do the same to the drill shank, support the two pieces in a drilled block and braze together. This is shown in Fig.1. Other ways of extending drills are to braze them into lengths of steel tube of the right inside diameter.

Lubricating the drill

You may have to lubricate the bit while it

is cutting. This lubrication serves two purposes: first it will keep the drill cool—and you should never let a drill get too hot during use —and secondly it helps the swarf to flow freely up the flutes. Engineers use special soluble oil but for the handyman ordinary lubricating oil or even paraffin is adequate.

The metals that have to be lubricated during drilling include hard tool steel (silver steel), alloy steels, low carbon (mild) steel, light alloys, stainless steel and zinc alloys. This is particularly important if the holes are to be deeper than roughly twice the thickness of the drill point. Thin sheet materials need not be lubricated but bar and rod need oil. Let the oil flow down the flutes of the drill at intervals during drilling. DO NOT SWEEP SWARF AWAY USING YOUR HAND. This is a sure way to shred your skin, especially if the swarf is brass which is hard and very sharp.

Cast iron has an almost unique self-lubricating characteristic and can be drilled or tapped without oil of any sort.

Taps and dies

Taps and dies are used for cutting screw-threads in metal. Taps are used to form a thread around the inside of a hole so that a bolt or threaded stud can be screwed in. Generally, they are similar in shape to a drill, but have four straight flutes up the side and

Top left: A taper tap, a second tap and a bottom tap. When cutting a thread in a hole these taps are used in this order.

Top right: Starting to cut a thread on a rod with a die held in a diestock. The stock should be held in as horizontal a position as possible.

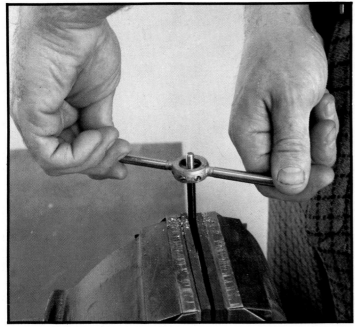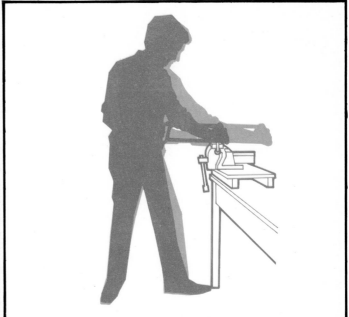

are threaded like the end of a bolt.

Dies are used for cutting a thread round the outside of a round bar so that a nut can be screwed on. They are usually circular in appearance with a cloverleaf-type cut out in the centre.

Threads, whether for taps or for dies, are specified by the form of the thread. In Britain, the three standard forms have been BA (British Association), BSF (British Standard Fine), and BSW (British Standard Whitworth), with the occasional use, particularly in plumbing and gas-fitting, of BSP (British Standard Pipe). In the United States the thread forms are American Fine (AF) and American Coarse (AC). These thread forms are now gradually being replaced by ISO Metric (measured in millimetres) or UNC (Unified Coarse) and UNF (Unified Fine). Whatever the thread form, it can be expressed as pitch diameter and threads per inch (tpi).

Taps are made in three sorts, classified as taper, second and bottom. The taper tap narrows towards the point and, at the point, is only just visibly threaded but as the thread progresses along its length towards the shank end, it becomes more and more pronounced. This sort of tap is used to start a thread in a clear hole in a piece of metal. It is a good general-purpose type of tap to have.

You may wish to tap a 'blind' hole—one which stops part of the way through the metal. Here you must form the thread right down to the bottom of the hole. With a taper tap, this will not be possible. However, this is where the other two forms of tap come into use. You begin by tapping the hole as far as you can using the taper tap. This is then removed and the second tap is used, which extends the thread further down the hole.

Finally this is removed and the bottom tap is used. It follows the firms threads already formed by its predecessors, to cut the final turns of the thread down to the bottom of the hole. The bottom tap has virtually no lead. These three different types of tap are shown on the opposite page.

To cut a thread using a tap, the square end of the tap shank is clamped into a special tool called a tap wrench which has a central jaw to hold the tap. Before you can tap, though, a pilot hole must be drilled first. Since the tap must form a thread in the metal, the pilot hole is smaller than the size of the finished tapped hole. The diameter of the pilot hole is very important: too small and the tap will be difficult to drive, stripping the thread as soon as it cuts it; too large and the thread will be so shallow and weak that it will strip out in use. The proper pilot size for all the sizes of tapped hole are shown in charts readily available from tap and die manufacturers.

Make sure you have the correct tap for the size of the hole by referring to one of these tables. Secure the tap in the wrench and lubricate it with ordinary fine lubricating oil. Insert the point of the tap into the pilot hole, hold the tap upright, and press down evenly on the arms of the tap wrench. Gently but firmly start the thread by turning the wrench clockwise. This is the most critical part of the operation of thread-cutting for if the thread is damaged at this point, the tap may not run straight. Do not lift the tap out and start again if you do not feel it start to bite, but keep a firm pressure on the wrench and keep turning steadily until you feel the teeth start to engage in the metal. Once the tap has cut its way into the metal sufficiently to support the tap and wrench, change your grasp on the wrench so that you are now holding the

Top left: As soon as the thread has been started the grip on the stock is changed. The metal should be lubricated and for every full turn of the stock forward you should give it a half turn back, in an anti-clockwise direction.

Top right: The stance to adopt when sawing metal.

arms between your finger and thumb on each hand. Ease the wrench round with steady turns, and run oil into the hole at intervals. Take care not to jerk the tap and break it.

Do not move the wrench anti-clockwise while cutting. This causes the swarf to jam in the threads and chip them. When the thread has been cut to the required depth, unwind the tap slowly from the hole. Hold the left hand palm uppermost with the first two fingers outstretched into a V and put them under the wrench around the tap so that when the tap comes free of the thread you will be supporting it on your fingers. This will save it from dropping on to the floor and breaking, or damaging the first few threads of the hole as it comes out.

Cutting a thread on a bar with a die is done by holding the die in a special tool called a diestock. This has three screws round one side of a circular recess into which the die fits. The thread in a die is, as with a tap, slightly tapered, so that the threaded hole on one side of the die will be slightly greater in apparent diameter than on the other. Unlike taps, though, there is only one die for one thread. Look carefully to see which side of the die is the 'start' side—if in doubt look closely to see on which side the thread is cut deepest. Drop the die into the stock so that the widest side (the finest thread cut) is on the outside. The other side of the die rests on a rim which prevents the die from falling right through.

Turn the die so that the gap in it lines up with the central of the three screws. If you slacken off the two outer ones and tighten the centre one, you will open the die slightly so that the die will cut a shallow threadform. This will make a tight fit if you subsequently attach a nut. If you slacken off the centre screw and tighten the two outer ones, you will contract the die so that it cuts a deep threadform. This produces a loose fit when a nut is subsequently applied. The best fit is gained by tightening the two outer screws so that they just touch the die but do not force the gap to close. Then if you tighten the centre screw you will have the best thread-forming condition.

To run a thread down a rod, first of all chamfer the end of the rod to about 45° all round using a file. This is so that the diestock can sit on the rod to start the die cutting. Now hold the diestock firmly in both hands and pressing down with firm (but not excessive) pressure on the end of the stock, begin turning it. Do this very carefully until the thread starts. Check that the diestock is at right angles to the rod along the handles, and

also across the width. If you start with a crooked thread, it is almost impossible to straighten and the subsequent nut will sit at an angle to the axis of the rod.

Once the die is firmly engaged, you can concentrate on turning it steadily down the

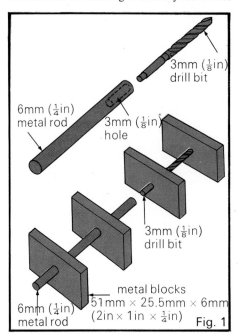

Fig. 1

rod. Lubricate the die with thin machine oil. After every full turn of the stock, give half a turn in an anti-clockwise direction. This breaks off the whiskers of swarf and lets them drop clear through the cloverleaf reserves in the die.

After running a die down a rod, the thread may have very sharp edges, particularly if high-carbon or stainless steels are being cut. These sharp edges are undesirable for some jobs so rub the thread with fine emery cloth.

Broken taps, studs and bolts

Occasionally a tap breaks off in use. If it has snapped off above the surface of the

Fig.1. If you need to extend a drill bit you can braze it into a hole drilled in a thicker piece of metal. The metal blocks hold the two pieces in place while you do this.

Fig.2. The various parts of an ordinary twist drill bit. The two details show the shape of the point from the side and the front. Never drill metal that is thinner than the length of the drill bit point—the point will wander and the hole will not be accurate.

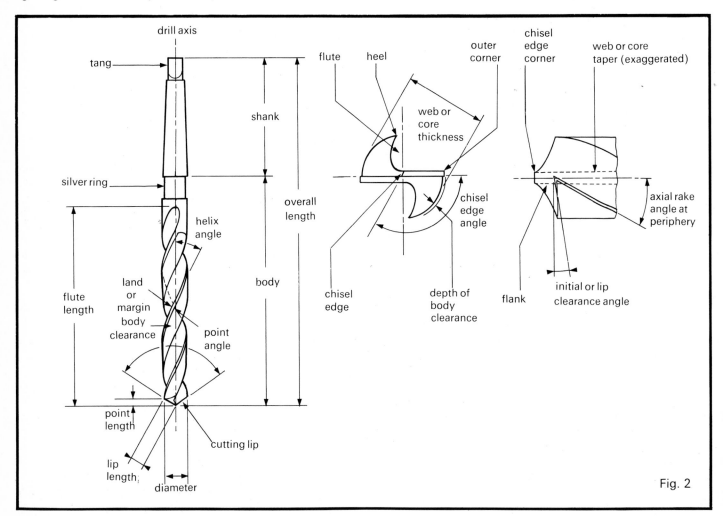

Fig. 2

metal you are working you should be able to remove it with a self-locking pair of pliers or a stout wrench. If it has broken below the surface the job is much harder. If the tap is large you can drive lengths of steel or nails down the flutes and unwind the tap with a wrench. If you can't do this it may be best to leave it and tap another hole nearby.

Alternatively, you may be able to remove the tap, fill the hole and retap it. Carefully drill four holes down beside the broken tap so that the holes break into the area of the flutes. Use a drill about $\frac{2}{3}$ the diameter of the tap to do this. You may now be able to knock the tap round fractionally with a hammer and a punch so that it can be lifted straight out, the cutting edges now being in the spaces created by drilling. You can now drill the hole to a larger size. Tap it for a large diameter stud, (a threaded bar or bolt with the head cut off). Screw in the stud and file it flush. Re-drill and tap' the stud centre to the original size.

Broken bolts and studs, being of a fairly soft material, are easily removed. If they have sheared off below the surface there are two ways of removing them. One is to use a special device called an 'Easiout' extractor. This is a tool with the overall size and shape of a tap, but with a very coarse left-handed screw thread formed on its outside. To use this device, which is made in a variety of sizes to suit the job, drill a hole down through the centre of the broken bolt or stud, wind in the left-handed Easiout until it wedges in—it will do this because it is slightly tapered—and then wind out the broken stud.

The other alternative is to drill out the bolt or stud. Select a marginally smaller drill than the diameter of the piece to be removed, and then either re-drill and tap for the next larger size of thread, or plug the hole and make a fresh one nearby.

Hardening and tempering

If you make your own screwdrivers, chisels or special tools you may want to harden and temper them. They will work better and be far more durable if you do. A hardened steel will cut another metal or, in the case of hand tools, will resist being cut by another metal. Tempering toughens the hardened surface by reducing the excessive brittleness produced by the hardening process. A spring, for example, must be tempered very carefully after forming otherwise it would snap in use because of this brittleness.

High carbon steels, tool steels and, to a certain extent, silver steel, can be hardened by heating in a flame slowly to a temperature just above what is known as the upper critical point. This heat is held for a few moments, and then the metal is quenched

very quickly in brine or water. The actual temperature to be reached is between 750°C (1382°F) and 800°C (1472°F). The metal, at this temperature, has a dull cherry red colour.

Tempering is done by heating the hardened steel to a point below what is called the lower critical point, followed by quick cooling. The higher the temperature used for tempering is the less the hardness and the greater the toughness of the steel. Tempering of tool steel is usually done at temperatures from about 200°C (392°F) to 320°C (610°F).

To temper a chisel or a screwdriver blade after you have shaped and hardened it begin by polishing the metal to remove the black oxidised scale that results from hardening. When the steel is fairly bright, hold the metal in the flame of a gas jet. Heat it to the tempering temperature (see below). Do not heat the tip of the metal, but apply heat to a point an inch or two from the end. Move the flame slowly up and down the metal. Don't allow the metal to get red hot or you will destroy its hardness.

As the metal heats up, temper colours will appear on the surface. These colours will radiate outwards from the heat source along the metal. The tempering range is very small

so you must work slowly and carefully.

The first temper colour will give a yellow appearance to the formerly bright surface of the metal. This corresponds to about 200°C. This will be followed by a change to light brown, then purple and finally blue. At this point the temperature of the metal is between 300°C and 320°C (572°F and 610°F).

If you want a temper for screwdriver blades which will make them hard without chipping, watch for the point where brown/yellow is about to change to dark purple. When this colour reaches the tip, quench the metal quickly in water.

The heat will travel at varying rates according to the thickness of the metal. If it is thick, the temper colour will move slowly: where it is thin it will move fast, so watch for this 'speeding up' as the temper advances down the tapering blade of something like a screwdriver.

As a rough guide, scrapers and scribers should be tempered to pale yellow (220°C or 430°F); cold chisels and screwdrivers to dark purple (290°C or 560°F) and springs to blue (320°C or 610°F).

With the knowledge of these methods at your disposal, the scope of the jobs which you can tackle will be greatly enlarged.

Planning a better workshop

Finding space for pursuing hobbies only too often means 'stealing' it from your living area, and having to break off every time the family wants to eat a meal or watch television. And working in inadequate or cramped surroundings often means being content with poor equipment, which leads to shoddy workmanship and can be dangerous. So wherever possible try to set aside a workshop for yourself, given over entirely to hobbies such as carpentry which need plenty of space and specialist equipment.

A workshop not only alleviates these difficulties, but also provides a place where you can relax for a while away from your daily routine and the rest of the family. If you have a workshop which is properly fitted up, repair and general DIY jobs will take less time and run more smoothly. A workshop is also a good selling point if you decide to move.

Every home should have one

If you are moving into a new house, then the major considerations such as bathroom

fitments, kitchen layout and so on will occupy much of your time and thoughts. But this is precisely the time to recognise the need to plan for areas which will be devoted to leisure activities such as play- or family-rooms, and workshops, particularly if you intend to do most odd jobs yourself.

If you have lived in your home some time and intend to stay there, then a re-allocation of the available space may be called for, especially if your family includes keen handymen.

You may be lucky enough to have a home large enough for you to set up a permanent indoor workshop. But remember that noise may be a problem. The noise you create seems far louder and more irritating to others than it does to you. Cellars are generally the best places to install indoor workshops, as they are often large enough to be split into more than one area for separate activities, and their position underground helps to restrict the spread of noise.

Lofts are less suitable because they tend to become very warm in summer; many hobbies involve some physical effort, which would make working in a hot loft unbearable. You might also have to impose a 'curfew' and curtail night time work there because of sleeping children.

Both cellars and lofts often share the disadvantage of having an over-small entrance —don't be caught making a beautiful wall

Below: A workshop needn't be dull . . . here bright red and the tones of natural wood make the room attractive.

unit which won't go through the door!

Many people use their garage for crafts and hobbies; it is quite suitable for all but the most meticulous and precise work, such as watch mending or scale-model mending. If there is additional car parking space on your premises, it may be worth building a separate carport and converting your garage into a permanent workshop. If you use the garage regularly for heavy carpentry or metalwork, the car tends to spend most of its time outside anyway. However, for most people a garage serves both purposes well

enough.

What you need

The basic general requirements for a combined garage and workshop are: enough space to get in and out of the car when the garage doors are closed; a work bench with a vice; and storage facilities.

The bench top should be 888mm–914mm (2ft 9in–3ft) from the ground, depending on the nature of the work and on your height. A solid old house door with handle and hinges removed, and supported on

trestles or boxes, makes a stable work-top of the right size, and can be covered with a sheet of thick hardboard or plywood. If the door has recessed panelling, cut a hole in the covering sheet to coincide with the sunken area of the door panels, filling any gaps with strips of timber. This will make a recess in the bench top deep enough to take any tools in current use.

A badly made bench is more trouble than it is worth. It must be rigid during normal use, either because of its own weight or because it is fixed to the wall or floor. Ideally it should be free-standing with ample walking space all round, but where this is not possible aim at having at least one long side and one short side free from obstruction. Position the vice on the bench so that it is in a good light for detailed work, and in such a way that it can grip long pieces of material without obstruction. It should be offset to one side of the bench to leave as much clear work-top as possible.

Careful consideration of the space which remains after you have parked the car will give you far more accessible storage space than you first thought possible. If you fit shelves along the wall next to the driver's side of the car and 1.5m (4ft 10in) from the floor, they will be above the height of the open car door and the average person's shoulder. This enables shelves to be fixed along one whole wall but remain accessible when the car is parked. A car parked as close as possible to the wall on the passenger's side will leave enough space to fit shelves on that side of the garage 914mm (3ft) from the floor beside the car bonnet and still leave space to open the car doors. A bench along the short wall opposite the garage doors will enable you to use the wall space above the working surface for keeping regularly-used tools.

Workshops that stand alone

Old buildings can be modernised and re-designed for specific types of work, or equipped with the basic essentials of good lighting, working surfaces, water and electricity supplies so that they are easily adaptable for many hobbies. Don't be afraid of the initial expense incurred in having water and electricity laid on, because in the long run it is cheaper than late extensions. You are also more likely to give regular use to somewhere that is well-equipped and comfortable.

The ideal solution

Where there are no existing buildings suitable for conversion, a new building designed specially as a workshop is a dream well worth pursuing (convincing your family of this will probably be easier if your

plans include a children's area). Once you have made the decision to build, do not skimp on the size or complexity of the building. Your garden will probably already have separate sheds, fuel store and garage.

Rather than adding to this list by building a workshop, consider the possibility of having a single multi-purpose building incorporating all your outhouses. This will look tidier, and also reduce maintenance costs. If the building stretches across the bottom of your garden, you could perhaps reach it via the garage, as in Fig.2. In this example, the clean 'studio' area is kept well away from the garage. The workshop in the centre is equipped simply so that it can serve as an over-spill area for either the garage or the studio with a minimum of alteration. Such a building will have a fundamental influence on your property, and will give an opportunity to landscape your garden during the building stages.

Once you have chosen where to set up your workshop, you can begin to plan what is going to go in it in detail, but as with all the designing that you carry out for your home, resist the early temptation to let your enthusiasm run away with you. Spend your time and thought not only in drawing up your plans, but also in writing down a list of all the things you would ideally like to have in your workshop. When making your final decisions consider the following: function (this should take precedence over appearance); lighting; heating and ventilation; storage; and floor treatments.

Don't worry if your furniture and equipment do not all 'line up' visually, but let considerations of safety and function dictate the layout. For instance, if a particular operation suggests that you need a bench at sitting level and one at standing height, or that you need a working surface beside you as well as one in front for ease of assembly, then design the layout in this way.

There will always be some equipment which imposes strict limitations on your arrangements, for example, equipment that must be permanently fixed, like a vice, or requires running water, as in photography. Some machines require a minimum amount of space around them, like a circular saw used for cutting large sheets of material. Multi-purpose workshops will impose so many limitations that you will have to decide on the most important factors—the first of which must *always* be safety.

Lighting

Good lighting is vitally important. Have windows as large as possible, though bearing in mind that they will increase your heating bills in winter if they are *too* large. Position precision equipment and your main work-

bench close to the natural light, taking care that your body will not cast a shadow over your work. To provide light from the same direction throughout the day, place electric lights between you and the windows.

Put power points as close as possible to working areas—preferably above the bench top, rather than close to the floor. This avoids stooping which can be dangerous in confined spaces.

Heating and ventilation

Heating and ventilating a home workshop can be a problem. But do not neglect them; their importance is usually underestimated. Irritability when you are too warm, and lack of control when your hands are cold, will lead to shoddy work and can be dangerous when working with machinery.

Whatever type of heating you use, it will be cheaper in the long run if you insulate old buildings.

A common mistake is to fit a free-standing electric fan, which just moves stale air around the room, instead of a proper extractor set in an outside wall. Ventilation ducts such as airbricks should also be fitted to let in fresh air to replace the extracted stale air.

Storage

You can never have too much storage space. In fact, it is worth providing a specific space for every tool. You can paint a silhouette of each tool directly behind its resting place, and thus see at a glance exactly what is missing. You stand a far better chance of holding on to your collection of tools this way. Storage of raw materials such as timber needs early consideration, especially large sheets or planks, which take up valuable space. A gap between work bench and wall will cater for them, provided there is adequate ceiling height to manoeuvre them in and out. Large offcuts can be stored in wall racks, and small ones in trolleys 'parked' under a workbench. Very long pieces of timber can be kept well out of the way on ceiling racks.

Flooring

Floor treatments are an important factor in workshop safety. Avoid shiny surfaces near machines; beware of smooth concrete, which becomes especially slippery when covered in saw-dust. Liquid treatments are available which harden the surface of concrete, thus reducing wear which creates a great deal of dust.

Different floor-coverings can help distinguish between separate areas in a workshop, especially if some are 'danger zones' near sharp or powerful equipment, or power points. Some flooring has a sound-deadening quality which is particularly useful in a

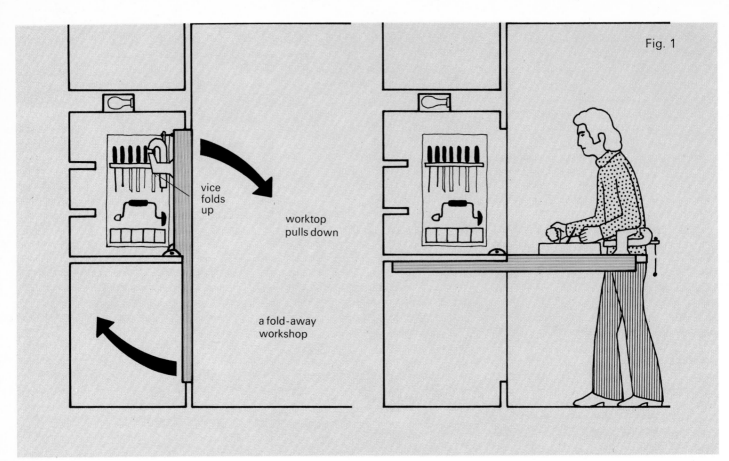

Fig. 1

vice folds up

worktop pulls down

a fold-away workshop

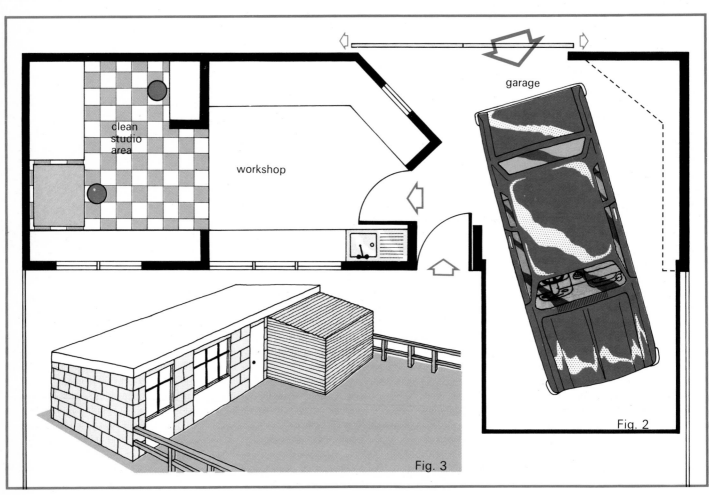

clean studio area

workshop

garage

Fig. 2

Fig. 3

Fig.1. A fold-away 'mini' workshop specially good in confined spaces.

Fig.2. This workshop is in the garden and is reached via the garage.

Fig.3. All the outhouses are collected together in this 'complex'.

Right: A spacious workshop, supplied with running water, adjustable lighting, and plenty of storage space. The floor covering is distinctive and easily cleaned.

confined space where hammering and sawing will be the order of the day. The problem is, however, that most flooring which absorbs noise tends to absorb oil, too, so buy cheap vinyl sheeting and lay it over felt. The cheaper varieties are perfectly acceptable in workshop conditions and when they get too dirty, you can afford to throw them away.

Any areas you want to keep specially clean you can raise about 152mm (6in) above the general level, as long as the step is well away from the machines.

Although function is of primary importance when designing a workshop, a smart and attractive room will be more comfortable and inviting. Line up open storage and cupboards as uniformly as possible, and choose wall coverings which are appropriate to specific activities. For example, carpentry tools look attractive against timber slats or naturally finished plywood panels. Brick walls and quarry-tile floors harmonise with clay modelling and similar hobbies. This may seem a superficial point of view, but remember that pride in your working environment is reflected in the work you do.

At the same time, do not over-furnish your workshop to a point that makes it hard to clean.

Outside finishes

When choosing materials for the outside of your building, remember that many exterior quality materials also make an attractive interior decor. Besides, using the same material inside and out is economical. It is no accident that this approach is now fashionable in many types of architecture, and for several reasons other than economy. For example, combining bricks and timber with plastic laminates in an interior help to soften the harsh appearance of many plastics. Asbestos is another 'exterior' material that comes indoors successfully. Its fire resistance makes it an obvious choice if you are going to use your workshop for welding or iron-work. It also provides an attractive neutral colour and rough texture.

Pick materials which are going to be seen from the outside to harmonise or contrast dramatically with your garden. Rough timber treated with dark creosote, and used with pale concrete building blocks and brightly-coloured fibreglass infills under windows or above doors, is an example of a combination of natural and artificial materials that is very easy to maintain. Go for contrasts in texture as well as in colour.

Paving the way

'Concrete' usually conjures up impressions of towering skyscrapers and similar giant constructions, but the very qualities that make concrete so valuable in large scale projects are just as useful to the handyman for home improvements.

The durability of concrete is only one of its qualities. In terms of weather resistance it is virtually indestructible, and it is impervious to most kinds of chemical attack. But concrete's greatest asset is its versatility. Its range of uses includes drives, garages, paths, fencing, patios, walls and even complete buildings. And all can be produced in a wide range of coloured, textured and profiled finishes for infinite variety.

Composition of concrete

Concrete is made from cement, aggregate (sand, gravel, pebbles, crushed stone) and water in varying proportions.

Sand is described as 'fine aggregate' and should be the 'sharp' variety, as distinct from the 'soft' bricklayer's sand used in bricklaying mortar. Gravel, pebbles and crushed stone are described as 'coarse aggregate', and consist of particles varying in size between 5mm and 19mm ($\frac{3}{16}$ in and $\frac{3}{4}$in).

The cement most often used is Portland, which is light grey in colour. Also popular is white cement, which can be used on its own or with a colourant to provide a wide range of colours. There are also many cements of a more specialised nature, such as quick-setting cement, and masonry cement, which sets slowly and is used for certain types of brickwork.

Laying a concrete slab

A concrete floor slab—cast on site, without digging foundations—is a straightforward job even for the inexperienced. The technique is the same whether you are laying a drive, a path, or a foundation for a small building. You begin with a mould formed by laying planks or other sheets of timber (the formwork) round the edges of the area to be concreted. The formwork is held in place by stakes driven into the ground, and protruding up to the top of the formwork (page 133). The interior of the mould or formwork is then filled with a concrete mix that is allowed to set before the timber is removed.

The choice of materials for formwork is dictated by the shape of the concrete slab required. If the edges are to be straight, or angular, as is usually the case with drives and foundations for buildings, the formwork can be laid in simple timber planking. But if curved edges are required—and for paths this usually gives a more pleasing outline—then the formwork will consist of strips of flexible plywood, or even hardboard that can be pegged into a curved shape.

Concrete should not be laid in frosty weather, for reasons given later.

129

Tools and equipment

The basic tools needed for laying the average path or drive are:—

Shovel. A medium-sized one. For concreting, if you are in any doubt select the larger size; the work is too heavy for small tools.

Bucket. The sturdy metal or rubber variety. A thin plastic bucket tends to buckle when filled with water.

Claw hammer and nails. For securing the stakes to the formwork timber or sheeting.

Straight edge. A sturdy piece of timber about 2m (6ft) long, and 75mm × 50mm (3in × 2in). Check by holding it up to your eye that it is absolutely straight. Reject it if it curves, but high spots can be planed down.

Spirit level. A 1m (3ft) builder's level.

Tamper. For tamping or compacting (Fig.E) the concrete after it has been laid. The tamper must be wider than the width of the work. It could be just a plank, but if the width is such that two people would have to work it, then the tamper must have a handle or some other form of grip at each end.

Saw. For cutting the formwork.

String. Used with stakes for outlining the formwork.

Formwork and stakes. Sufficient timber or sheeting to provide the side supports of the mould. The stakes must be sturdy; at least 40mm × 40mm (1½in × 1½in) and long enough to cover the depth of the concrete plus about 300mm (12in) for driving into the soil.

Not essential, but still of value for finishing the surface are:—

Brooms. One hard and one soft, for providing a smoother finish.

Wood float. For working the surface after tamping and providing a smoother finish than the brooms can provide.

Steel float. For the smoothest finish of all.

Calculating quantities

Estimating is a relatively simple procedure, but it does pay to take care and double-check.

If you are using metric measurements, multiply the area in square metres by the thickness in millimetres, and divide by 1000. This will give the amount required in cubic metres. If you are using imperial measurements work out the area the drive or path will occupy in square feet, multiply by the thickness in inches, and divide by twelve. This will give the amount required in cubic feet. For example: a path 30m (90ft) long and 1m (3ft) has a depth of 75mm (3in). So the quantity required would be:

$$\frac{30 \times 1 \times 75}{1000} = 2.2 \text{ cu m} \quad \text{OR}$$

$$\frac{90 \times 3 \times 3}{12} = 67\tfrac{1}{2} \text{ cu ft}$$

To convert cubic feet into cubic yards, divide by 27.

To convert cubic metres into cubic feet, multiply by 35.3.

When you order the cement and aggregate, it will be supplied either in cubic centimetres or cubic feet or in 25kg (½ cwt) or 50kg (1 cwt) bags. If ordering bags, assess on the basis that a 1 cwt bag of cement or aggregate contains approximately 1¼ cu ft.

The volume of concrete, after water has been added to the dry mix, reduces by about 25%, and this must be taken into account. For example:

50kg (1 cwt) bag of cement ⎫ Yields about
76 cu cm (2½ cu ft) of sand ⎬ 171 cu cm
114 cu cm (3¾ cu ft) of coarse ⎪ (5⅝) cu ft of
aggregate ⎭ of concrete

Preparing the site

Strip off all topsoil and vegetable matter, level the area and ensure that the surface is even. It is most important to obtain an even surface over the whole area. Dig out any soft spots and fill with aggregate well rammed down. If the sub-soil is of soft clay, it is best to provide a sub-base of firmer material such as aggregate or well burnt clinker, compacted by rolling and ramming down hard.

If the slab is to be laid over an existing concrete, asphalt or gravel area, level the old surface and fill any depressions. Should the old surface show signs of cracking, it should be broken up, otherwise the new floor might crack over the same places as the old.

The prepared area should extend at least 152mm (6in) beyond the edge of the finished slab, so that space is left for preparing the formwork.

Pegging out

Paths are often far more attractive if the outline is curved. The pegging procedure for a curving path is explained by Fig. B. Pegs are driven in at the four 'corners' of the path, and line is stretched between, giving you a very long, thin rectangle. The line is then marked at equal distances along the long edges, and pegs inserted at each point. Then you move the corner pegs, with the line still attached, an equal distance farther out from the sides of the path; the stretched line is already marked, and pegs are inserted in between each pair of marks.

You will now have two staggered rows of pegs, one on either side, in which the sheeting can be 'weaved' to produce the formwork outlined in Fig. B.

If you want a single, curving outline, or a circle, this can be drawn in the earth in the same manner as drawing with a compass. A peg is inserted at the point of centre, or, as shown in Fig. A, at the middle of the straight side. Tie a length of line to the peg, stretch the

line to one end of the straight side, then tie the end of the line to another peg, which is held in your hand. Your hand-held peg can now be used to scratch a circular groove in the earth, providing you keep the line taut as you swing round. Support pegs are then driven in round the outline.

A popular layout is a square path, with an inset into which flowers or trees, are planted. The pegging out is done in exactly the same way as that for outlining a square, except that an additional square form is laid in the middle, as shown in Fig.D.

Setting the formwork

The path or drive is cast between timber planks, or sheeting, staked to the sub-base. In the case of an angular outline, use 1in or 25mm thick timber if possible. Stand it on edge so that its width matches a curved outline, you will need something more flexible than planks. For a very wide curve, as in Fig. A, thin plywood strips would do the job, but short curves, as in Fig. B, require something even more flexible, such as hardboard. The fact that the hardboard is not 25mm (1in) thick does not matter, because curves make material much more rigid.

If 25mm (1in) planks are being used, the stakes are driven in at 1 m (3ft) intervals, but if the planks are thinner, place the stakes at 300mm (12in) intervals. When plywood or hardboard is being used, place the stakes on the inside and outside of each curve (Fig. B) or, if the curve is long (Fig. A), at 230mm (9in) intervals.

The thickness of the slab—and of course the depth of the formwork—will depend on its intended use, and the nature of the soil. For light use such as garden shed foundations, and paths that will not see mechanised traffic, a thickness of 75mm (3in) is

Right: A composite illustration showing a variety of uses for concrete paving. The path in the top left corner has been laid in solid, staggered sections, with the crazy paving effect pointed in with a trowel. The patio is a solid concrete slab, with the 'tile' effect created in the same way. From the patio, an attractive line of circular slabs inset into the earth leads past the tree, which is surrounded by an octagonal slab and a slatted bench. A stepway of rectangular slabs leads the way to a straight concrete path. (The greenhouse is light enough to be moved along the path when the soil is exhausted.) A square slab, with ornamental chippings pressed in, has a square inset studded with pebbles to support the clothes line pole. At the top right, a concrete drain well outside the garage is shown. This is bordered by bricks laid on end and is surrounded by a concrete path.

suitable on normal firm soil. For garages, drives and workshops, 100mm (4in) is a good average. On soft clay subsoil, the thickness should be increased by 25mm (1in).

Once the planks, or sheeting, have been laid on edge round the outline of the base, and fixed to stakes driven into the soil, the spirit level should be used. It is at this stage that a slight fall in the surface of the path, if required, can be incorporated if drainage is required in a specific direction—away from the house, for instance. The amount of fall can be determined by placing the level along the top edge of the formwork at frequent intervals.

Make sure the formwork is firmly staked, otherwise it might be displaced during compacting. This applies particularly when plywood or hardboard is being used.

Concrete mixes

Although an average concrete mix could be used for most purposes, certain types are more suitable for particular projects, and the proportions of sand and cement must be adjusted accordingly. The mixes shown here are suitable for different kinds of concrete work outdoors.

Where strength or resistance to wear is important, it is best to use mix 'A'. Where a lower grade will do, mix 'B' could be used. Mix 'C' is a fine concrete suitable for very thin sections or for bedding mortars. Mix 'D' is for bedding paving stones. All proportions are by volume.

A, 1 part cement, 2 of sand, 4 of coarse aggregate.
Suitable for paths, pools, steps, fencing and edging.
B, 1 part of cement, 2½ of sand, 4 of coarse aggregate.
Suitable for foundations, garage floors, drives, filling for garden rollers, and thick walls.
C, 1 part of cement, 3 of sand.
For formal or crazy paving less than 2in or 50mm thick. This is also the mix for brick laying mortrar if soft sand is used.
D, 1 part of cement, 5 of sand.
A stiff mortar mix for bedding paving.

Pre-mixed concretes

Many handymen make up their own concrete mix, although for small jobs it is more usual to buy a bag of dry mixed ingredients that requires only the addition of water. Dry mix can be bought from a builders' merchant or DIY shop and is usually sold in 50kg (1 cwt) bags, although some places sell bags as small as 3kg (7lb). As the cement in the mix deteriorates with storage, buy only enough for the job in hand.

The dry mix is sold in a variety of proportions to suit different work, so when you order make sure you specify exactly what you are using the mix for.

For large jobs, such as for the foundation of a garage or for a long driveway, ready-mixed concrete is the answer. This has the correct amounts of cement aggregate and water mixed in a central plant, and is delivered, ready to lay, in special agitator lorries.

Ready-mix can be ordered in most places through a builders' merchant and, in theory, can be obtained in any quantity. But in practice, quantities of less than 4 cubic metres (4 cubic yards) is uneconomical for the supplier.

A quantity of ready-mixed concrete can be delivered when it is most convenient, so that a large concreting job can be done in stages. And if there is access to the site, the agitator lorry can place the concrete directly into the formwork or trench, thereby saving a lot of back-breaking labour.

If you do order ready-mixed, have your site ready before the concrete is due to arrive. And make sure that you have sufficient labour to handle the job quickly— 1 cu m (1 cu yd) of concrete weighs about 2 metric tonnes (2 tons) and in warm weather it may become unworkable in as little as an hour.

Mixing concrete

All preparatory work on the sub-base should be completed before the concrete is mixed.

If you are mixing by hand, rather than using a concrete mixer, mix on a clean, smooth surface. An old sheet of plywood or hardboard is excellent. Alternatively, you can work on a section of path or patio, protected if need be with a heavy layer of polythene sheet.

Blend the cement/aggregate until the pile is a uniform colour with no patches of sand or cement. Make a well in the middle of the pile and pour in a little water. With a shovel, work the inside walls of the well into the water until the water has been absorbed; then add more water and continue until the mix is just wet enough to place and compact. An easy way of checking this is to pat the surface a few times with the bottom flat of the shovel; after this compacting, the surface should be smooth and close-knit.

Avoid using too much water, as this will weaken the concrete and cause shrinkage as it hardens. But the mix must be workable enough to be put in the moulds and compacted without leaving air-holes, which will result in honeycombing and loss of strength.

Laying and compacting

Fill the formwork mould with mixed concrete, spreading evenly and making sure that the corners and edges are well filled by tamping the mix with the sole of your boot, or a heavy piece of timber. After filling, the concrete should stand proud of the formwork by about one-fifth of the depth of the slab. This allows for compacting.

Tamping, or compacting, (Fig.E) should start as soon as possible. With an area as wide as a drive, the tamping beam should be at least 230mm by 50mm (9in by 2in), and at least 300mm (1ft) longer than the width of the formwork. It will have to be fitted with handles at either end so that it can be worked by two people. A heavy duty tamper, with handles, is required for someone who is laying paths every day. But if you are only doing a one-off job, then one of the simple designs in Fig. E could be built in a few minutes, and dismantled just as quickly.

A smaller piece of timber is used by one person for narrow sections such as paths.

The tamper should be held level, then raised and dropped on the concrete, moving it forward by half the width of the tamper each time. Cover the area twice in this way and you should produce a surface that is well smoothed and level with the top of the formwork.

After compacting any excess concrete can be removed by working the tamping beam along the formwork with a side-to-side sawing motion. This will also show up any holes that need to be filled in and re-compacted.

The concrete surface, after tamping, is perfectly suitable for most drives or paths. But if a smoother surface is required, this should be started as soon as tamping has finished.

The most common method of finishing is to brush the surface with a soft, or hard, broom (experiment on a small portion to see which effect you prefer). Alternatively, work the surface with a wood float. Start at one end—using a thick plank across the formwork as a gang-plank if necessary—and slide

Right: Most of the techniques and formwork shapes for raised concrete slabs are outlined here. (A) Formwork and marking technique for a semi-circular slab. (B) A 'wavy' path. The outline is slightly exaggerated here. Note the pegging and outlining procedure along the long sides of the formwork. (C) Method for a raised circular slab. (D) The usual formwork for laying a drive, path or patio. The formwork in the middle shows how to set out boxing for a planting area. Levels are indicated by laying a straight edge (the white plank) across the formwork, and gauging with a spirit level. (E) Two useful temporary tampers that can be built easily and quickly, and then dismantled to save space. (F) A float easily made from two pieces of wood.

the float, using a circular motion, across the surface. A smoother finish can be obtained by following the wood float with a steel trowel, then giving it a second trowelling after 2-6 hours, when the surface is firm.

Setting and curing

Fresh concrete should not be allowed to dry out too quickly. If this happens, its strength will be reduced and cracking and 'dusting' will occur. Keep concrete damp after laying by covering it with a polythene sheet for 24 hours as soon as setting has completed sufficiently to prevent marking.

Concrete goes through two stages before reaching its maximum strength. The first stage is 'setting', which is the initial reaction caused by the activation of the cement by water. In normal weather, setting takes about seven days, but hot weather could shorten the time to four days, and cold could extend the period to ten days.

It is easy to see when setting has completed because the concrete turns 'green', and literally takes on a greenish tinge. When this happens the concrete is starting to 'cure'.

When curing is complete, the concrete loses its green tinge and is said to have reached maximum strength, although it will actually go on getting stronger for up to 20 years. The complete cycle for setting and curing takes about 28 days.

The formwork could be removed once the concrete has set, but if possible leave it in place until curing has completed.

If it is unavoidable, you *could* start building on, or using, the concrete before it has cured. But it might crack badly if the maximum weight it is intended to carry is used during this time.

Avoid laying concrete during frosty weather. Water in the mix will expand on freezing, and this is likely to make the concrete break up.

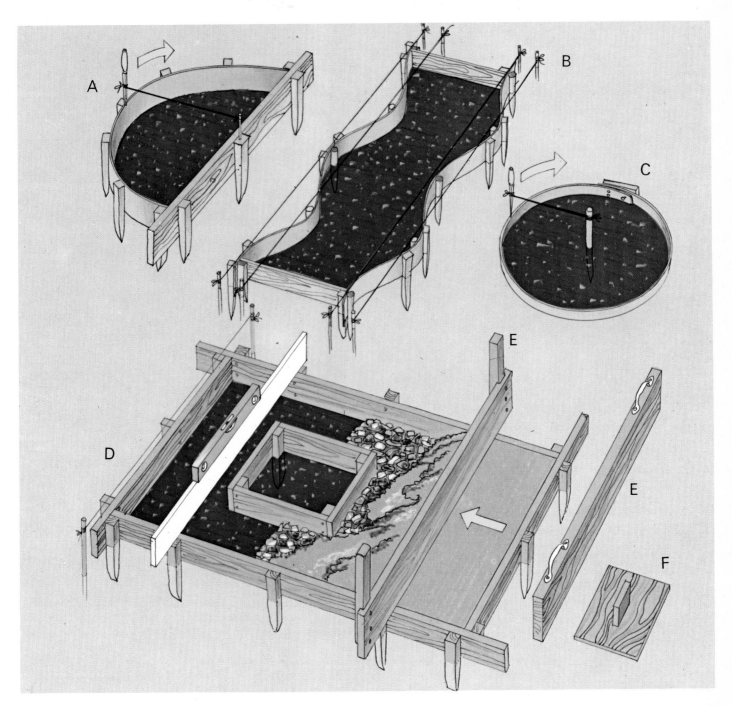

Pergolas and rustic fencing

A pergola draped with flowering plants will enhance any garden and not only is it attractive, it can be placed to give seclusion to a favourite spot or cut off an unwanted view. When pergolas and fences are carefully planned they make a garden a more beautiful and intimate place.

There is no strict definition of what a pergola is and the variety of designs, some of which are shown in Figs. 1-4 is endless. At its most basic, the pergola consists simply of a single line of upright posts which are linked at their tops by thinner horizontal sections. Various patterns can be created by adding more poles between the uprights, or by combining conventional trellis work, so that even this simple structure is capable of great variation. By bridging two parallel lines of uprights a simple arch is created which can be built over a path to provide an attractive covered walk.

Really, the only limitations on pergola design are provided by your imagination. As the designs become more complex, the finished structures should perhaps be more properly called arbors, but the construction techniques and materials remain the same.

The well designed pergola is an attractive feature in itself, but it is seen at its best when clothed in climbing or trailing plants. Because it will be a prominent feature of the garden a lot of thought should go into its location. A simple design can be set in the middle of a lawn to provide a feature of interest; or it can

Top left: *A fence with a difference. Paling stakes, drilled and 'threaded' to the main posts with dowelling.*

Bottom left: *Double-sided ranch style fencing, with the boards stepped alternately, forming a patio corner.*

Top right: *Rustic fencing simply trellised to form an attractive boundary. The hedge forms an integral part and acts as both screen and background.*

Bottom right: *Plain fencing painted in four harmonising colours.*

act as a divider between, say, a flower and vegetable garden. A pergola may also be used to hide an unsightly view. The arch type structure is best situated over a path or gate, and will give added emphasis to these features as well as providing an attractive covered walk.

Materials

Traditionally, a pergola is made of rustic posts which have the bark left on. This rather limits the type of wood which can be used, as few woods combine the ideal qualities of durability, tight bark, and workability with an attractive appearance. Larch and birch poles are probably the most suitable timbers for the rustic pergola and easily obtained. However, if you do not insist on undressed timber, the range of materials is much wider. Dressed pine poles which have been suitably treated are ideal.

All the timber mentioned so far is left in the round, but a more contemporary design can be created using squared and planed timber. Cedar is a good choice, not only because of its attractive colour, but because its high resin content makes it naturally rot resistant. Squared deal is suitable, but oak, while very durable, is difficult to work.

Your choice of materials should be dictated by the style of your garden and for this reason brick and stonework can be used for the uprights in a garden which is both formal and modern. The rustic pergola is obviously suited to a traditional flower garden.

Whatever materials you choose they must be thoroughly weather proofed with a horticultural grade preservative and should be strong enough to support fairly heavy weights. The length of the horizontal sections is not vitally important, but the uprights should be cut long enough to insert 610mm (2ft) into the ground and provide 1.8 m (6ft) clearance overhead.

Treating the timber

Where bark covers the posts it provides its own protection against damp and most fungal attacks. The only parts which require treatment are all the cut ends. These may be coated in hot pitch, burnt with a blowlamp, or dressed with a proprietary horticultural grade preservative such as a copper naphthenate solution. Special attention should be given to the base and this must be treated to a height of 152mm (6in) above its proposed ground level.

Dressed and squared timber is not only sealed at the cut ends but must be painted all over with a resistant varnish.

If creosote is used, the wood must be left to dry for several days, otherwise the creosote will damage plants.

Joining timber

One of the attractions of rustic posts is their natural appearance, so that there is no need to fix the sections together with elaborate joints. The simplest method is nailing or tying the timber with strong coated wire. However, a more attractive method for joining rustic posts which also gives greater strength, is to use simple joints as shown in Figs. 5-6. These can be cut roughly with a billhook or axe as well as with a saw. The bridging sections of a covered walk do not bear any weight and can be nailed to the horizontal sections as shown in Fig. 7.

Squared timber presents a more formal appearance, and is best jointed together with simple joints. Non load-bearing sections can be slotted together as shown in Fig. 2.

Erecting a pergola

The main uprights should be inserted 610mm (2ft) into the ground; more if the soil is very loose and sandy. In heavy soils the excavation hole must be kept as small as possible and when the post is inserted the surrounding soil should be well compacted. To allow water to drain away from the base of the uprights place a layer of stone at the bottom of each hole. A stronger foundation, which reduces timber rot, is made by setting the upright in cement. If brick or stone

Below: This otherwise ordinary driveway has been transformed by the addition of a pergola that is very easy to make.

Fig. 1

Above left: A most attractive pergola, with piers of natural stone, and trellis work along the sides for the plants to climb.

Fig.1. This is just one example of the many different designs you could use or adapt for your garden.

uprights are used they must be set on proper concrete foundations. The size of these will depend on the type of surrounding soil; in a compact soil they should be twice as wide as the piers they support, in a light, sandy soil a larger foundation is necessary. Where timber sections join the piers they are fixed to the brickwork by bolts cemented into the top of each upright.

Pergolas are assembled in situ and the construction is easy if all joints have been cut correctly. Care should be taken when spacing all sections to ensure a uniform pattern.

Circular pergolas

It is possible to build a pergola which is completely round, but a lot of difficulty will be encountered in cutting the rim sections to the correct size and shape. However, an attractive alternative is the polygonal pergola shown in Fig.3. This structure has six sides, but the number can be varied. The uprights and rim sections would need to be 100mm (4in) thick and though rounded timber could be used, squared dressed timber would be easier to assemble neatly.

The top of this structure can be bridged with thinner sections, or a spoke pattern can be created with timber sections radiating from a centre post as in Fig.3. The rim sections are mitred and the angle of this mitre is calculated by dividing the number of sides into 360°. The roof sections are housed in slots cut into the centre post and are notched where they meet the rim sections.

An ingenious handyman gardener will be able to devise variations of the polygonal design but should bear in mind that the spaces between sections should be large enough to allow climbing plants to grow unobstructed and in good light. Too much elaboration is unnecessary, because when the finished pergola is clothed with climbing plants the details of the patterns are obscured.

Rustic fences

The overall appearance of your garden owes a lot to the type of fencing which surrounds it. Not only are fences decorative, there are styles which lend seclusion to a garden, or provide protection from wind and rain. Before choosing a fence, look at your own garden and decide whether it is too exposed or too enclosed and cramped looking. Then choose a design of fence which not only looks good but which is suited to your particular garden. This section concentrates on helping you choose rustic fencing that best complements the traditional garden; which not only gives detailed information on all types of fencing, but also describes the techniques necessary for erecting a fence.

Perhaps the simplest type of rustic fencing is that shown in Fig. 1, which is made of hazel branches woven between and nailed to 1.8 m (6ft) horizontal sections. The drawback of this type is that it is not very strong and is best situated against a well-planted hedge. Wattle fences, which have a basket weave construction, are sturdy and rustic in appearance. They can be purchased in sections which are fixed to oak stakes driven into the ground.

Another simple rustic fence, shown in Fig. 11, is easily made using many of the techniques used in the construction of rustic pergolas—it can also be bought through some garden suppliers. It is generally constructed from undressed larch or pine fixed in a repeated diamond pattern. The uprights should be 76-102mm (3-4in) thick while the design work between them is of thinner section—about 38-51mm ($1\frac{1}{2}$-2in).

Of course this type is almost wholly decorative, giving no protection against the weather or stray animals. A rustic fence which retains the natural look yet provides seclusion and weather protection is the interwoven type. Fig.10. illustrates a larch weave fence which is sturdy, attractive, and virtually wind-proof. A more sophisticated design which meets the same needs is double-ranch. This is constructed from chestnut boards

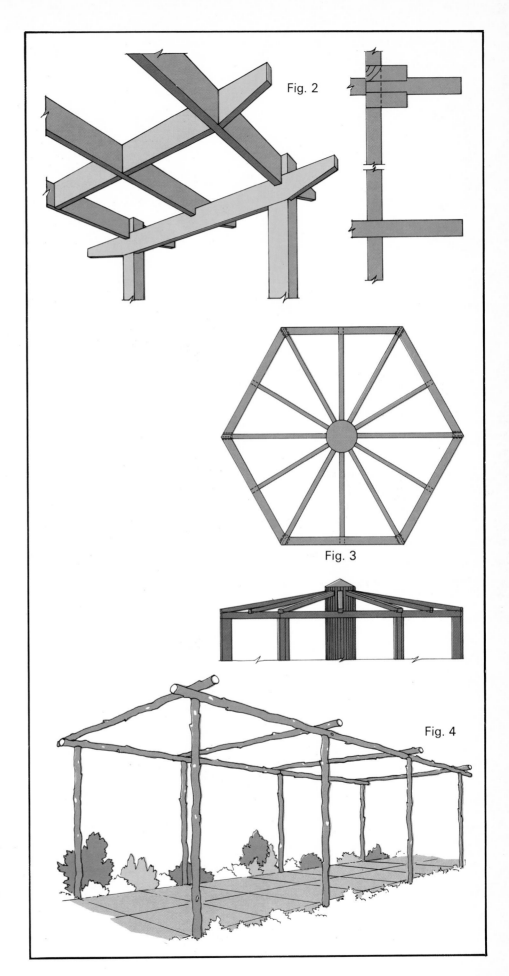

Fig. 2. *Squared timber can be jointed at the tops in the same way as bottle partitions in wooden crates.*

Fig. 3. *Construction outlines of a polygonal pergola. There is no need for a centre pole if you run the top members straight across.*

Fig. 4. *A simple, popular, and very effective pergola design—similar to the one in Fig. 1.*

137

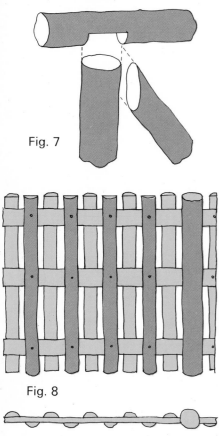

Fig. 5

Fig. 6

Fig. 7

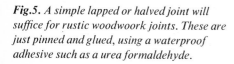

Fig. 8

Fig. 9

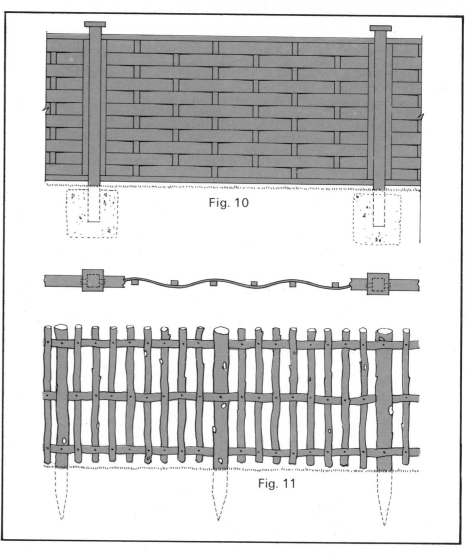

Fig. 10

Fig. 11

Fig.5. *A simple lapped or halved joint will suffice for rustic woodwork joints. These are just pinned and glued, using a waterproof adhesive such as a urea formaldehyde.*

Fig.6. *Verticals are housed into the horizontal members, then pinned and glued.*

Fig.7. *Bracing members are just pinned and glued—no joints need to be cut.*

Fig.8. *A simple rustic fence.*

Fig.9. *A modern design of pergola, showing many interesting features, and incorporating a screen wall and a barbecue.*

Fig.10. *Interwoven wood strips provide a peep- and wind-proof screen.*

Fig.11. *A fence with 'woven' timbers.*

which overlap to prevent casual passers-by looking into the garden. It is sold commercially, but, you can build your own.

Where privacy and shelter are not the most important considerations a more open fence can be erected. The palisade type is popular and lends itself to both traditional and contemporary styles. This can be a very sturdy construction which has a neat and formal pattern but which retains its natural look by the use of split larch poles, the bark left on.

There is no reason why more than one type of fencing should not be used in gardens. For weather protection and seclusion a high solid fence can be erected round the garden, while different areas inside the garden can be fenced off with more open designs. In this way a garden takes on a well planned aspect, and if fences and pergolas are planned carefully with your own garden in mind, even a smallish garden becomes a more interesting and intimate place.

Making more of a mini-garden

In towns, the word 'garden' is often misleading. Often the American term 'yard' would be more descriptive. Plenty of town back gardens are merely small square or rectangular patches between two rows of back-to-back terrace houses—each one, probably, with a frontage of no more than 15ft. Sometimes, too, such a garden is found in the central well formed by an extension or as an integral part of an architect-designed complex of new housing.

These mini-gardens need treating in quite a different way from larger ones. For a start, paving almost always looks better than grass in a confined space. (A combination of children and wet grass can result, anyway, in a sea of mud in no time at all.) A scaled-down version of the conventional herbaceous border planted down one side looks not only boring but cramped. And left completely alone, such a backyard is nothing but an eyesore—especially when seen through living room or dining room windows.

Garden walls

Almost always, a tiny garden is enclosed; and one or two of its walls may be formed by the back or sides of another house.

This enclosure is often an advantage. High walls shut off noise, besides giving privacy—plus a lot more gardening space. But as the brickwork will be seen when the last leaf has fallen from the last creeper, it is important that walls are treated as an integral part of the garden itself.

If you wish to extend your walling, woven wooden palings (which need creosoting to protect then from the weather) are comparatively cheap, but not particularly versatile. A good brick wall is much more satisfactory. In many places, too, the heights of side walls, and the materials in which they may be built, are limited by local authority regulations; fireproof materials are often preferred, or compulsory, when a wall is on a boundary.

Brick walls, provided they are in good repair, can be colourwashed in any of the pale, pretty, sugar-almond colours that are almost as light-reflecting as white. Although white itself is fresh and gay, it goes dirty extremely quickly; and on a grey winter's day looks cold and depressing. The hint-of-a-tint given by the admixture of pink, ochre, or turquoise—even a cupful or two to the gallon makes a difference—to the basic white paint gives a warmer, slightly 'Mediterranean' look. In warmer, crisper climates, white walls or palings look brilliant in sunlight.

This Mediterranean look can be backed up by using pretty bits of ceramics or glass—for instance, lining an alcove in the wall with tiny, brilliant blue Italian glass mosaic tiles. Then there are small, fairly cheap, weather-proof ceramic ones that could cover a projecting ledge to make a plant table. Even an unpromising basement area wall can be prettied up by painting it a light, gay colour and hanging a few random Portuguese or Spanish patterned tiles.

A piece of mirror in the garden is another simple but effective idea. Try a tall one to reflect a narrow little cypress tree, or a square one angled behind an urn full of spilling geraniums. A generous slab of mirror on a wall behind a wide-spaced trellis supporting a tangle of blue morning glories, for example, can appear to add yards of beauty to a tiny garden. Be careful, though, to use mirror just far enough from a cultivated area that the rain cannot splash it with mud streaks.

Levels

In a tiny garden, you should 'think vertically' as well as 'thinking horizontally'. In other words, it is important to create a series of points of interest at different heights.

If you want to pack the garden with plants and flowers, this means aiming for the effect of standing in the middle of a flower basket, with a lot of blooms at eye or shoulder level, rather than looking down on flat, ground-level beds, such as you might use in a larger garden.

Achieving different flowerbed levels usually means a lot of hard work at first. Topsoil must be carefully removed. A foundation of rubble, gravel, or builders' debris must be built up and shaped into a miniature landscape of hills and valleys, then the topsoil replaced over this foundation. As there will now be a greater surface area to cover, more topsoil must either be bought, or brought up sack by sack from the country. (Most town topsoil is stale; so take advantage of this preparing stage to add whatever is needed, from moisture-retaining peat to fertilizer.)

Once the beds are made, they can be broken up into small separate areas by brickwork, or paths made from flagstone pieces. These paths are not just decorative: they provide firm squatting-stones when you want to plant or weed. Lilliputian terraces, like small fields or vineyards descending a hill, can be equally effective, especially with hanging or trailing plants. Brick edging can be used here, or dry stone walling made from pieces of flat stone, or paving chips too small for any other use.

A corner for leisure

If you prefer to devote the whole of a tiny garden to a flat space for children's play, sitting about, or sunbathing, it becomes even more important to concentrate a lot of the interest higher than the basic ground level to avoid a 'walled-up' feeling. Should you be lucky enough to have a tree growing in one corner of the garden, you have a ready-made solution; if not, you could plant your own tree; concentrate on climbing plants—perhaps growing a vine or wisteria right up the side of the house; fix pots to the walls; or site plant boxes on the top of walls to trail foliage downwards.

Materials

A plain sweep of lawn looks magnificent in the open spaces of a large garden; in a tiny one, a certain amount of cunning and intricacy works best. Even the Japanese, masters of the simple, single-spray-in-a-vase school of flower arranging, avoid this approach in their tiny gardens; each one is a balanced, but complicated, little masterpiece.

In a paved garden, try a few contrasting materials. A sunburst of bricks around a tree, a miniature patio area near the house, covered in heather-brown quarry tiles, or old-fashioned cobblestones to outline or emphasise the paving itself, add a richness to an

Above: A tiny back garden made a blaze of
colour by a terrace banked high with bright
shrubs and greenery at different levels.

otherwise boring area.

In Britain, beautiful old paving stones with
varying grey-gold colours and slightly
irregular surfaces can be bought cheaply
(especially if broken or damaged) from local
councils who are replacing pavement surfaces. Almost anywhere, you can find
mellow old bricks from a house that is being
demolished or converted. Although this
material can be chipped or broken, and
sometimes needs hours of work to strike off
old mortar, its textured surface or matured
colouring are much more attractive than the
flat regularity of cement or concrete paving.

In a paved garden, allowance should
always be made for drainage. You can
arrange this by making a very slight slope
towards a central drainage hole or small grid,
or towards several cracks between paving
stones which are not cemented together, but
loose-filled with gravel or sand.

Providing a focus

All tiny gardens need some kind of focus—
if only to remove the impression of standing
in a small square box. Trees, water, plants,

statuary, all (though not all together!) make
good focal points.

A focal-point tree should be the sort that
is a good shape even when the branches are
bare, or should be an evergreen.

Views vary on the use of water in gardens.
Streams and small lakes are one thing; small
stagnant-looking pools covered with a
floating debris of leaves and insects are
another. Part of the charm of any garden is
movement (think of swaying branches, bird
flight) so that running water is always a
delight—the sunlit fountains in the stone
courtyards of Spanish houses are perfect
examples. Fountains may be beyond our
reach, but a birdbath is within reach of all—
perhaps an old stone one, perhaps a new but
weathered-looking fibreglass one, placed on
the edge of a banked-up terrace bed. Plant a
small shrub, some ferns, or a few small,
bright flowers nearby, and you almost have
the effect of a miniature pool.

Statuary, which can mean anything from
an exquisite small bronze to a stone urn,
heightens interest in any garden. Few people
can afford really superb pieces—but anyone

who can afford to consider a piece of sculpture might reflect that it is often seen at its best out of doors.

There are, too, all sorts of smaller items that enhance a small space, from a sundial bought when an old house is demolished to a modern fibreglass urn whose shape and pattern are taken from an eighteenth century mould. Large terracotta flowerpots, in different shapes and sizes, are particularly flattering—and are cheap. Even a clutch of chimneypots or drainpipes, of different widths and heights, grouped together and planted with ivy or geraniums, can make a decorative and interesting focal point.

Plants

Focal-point plants should have a very definite shape. The stiffness of a large yucca, the dark formality of a little cypress, are good examples. Remember that pencil-shaped trees, such as flowering cherries, block out less light from the rest of the garden. The sort with angular bare branches, like figs or magnolias, let light through in a dappled pattern, as well as providing interesting shapes.

Although what can be planted in a garden depends to a large extent on the type of soil, climate, rainfall, and so forth, successful planting of a small garden depends on certain other factors as well.

As most very small gardens are in towns, with high walls surrounding them, they usually get very little light indeed. This means using plants that thrive in dark conditions. This, in turn, means depending on greenery rather than blooms.

Space is usually so limited that bare earth looks much more desolate than in a larger garden. Coat flowerbeds between plants and shrubs with tiny, quick-spreading ground-level green plants; this will also stop weeds growing.

In a mini-garden, each plant is an individual. A permanent one must pay its way in terms of shape or foliage for most of the year, if it is not to leave a gap like an extracted tooth when flowering time is over. Others may be best planted singly, or sparingly, otherwise their effect may be to pull the rest of the garden out of scale, when they are not

Top left: A small yard livened up by introducing both paved and grassed areas surrounded by bright white walls.

Below left: A sophisticated angle for a corner garden! The goldfish pool adds a cool note to the paved outside lounge.

Above: Using the subtle shades of green against moss and mellow stone. The light shines attractively through the foliage.

in bloom. In a tiny area, three yellow crocuses give just as much of an effect of spring as an orchardful in a country garden. For brilliant colour, or scent, a few bedding-out plants or seedlings can be installed in chosen sites, in tubs or urns.

Lighting

One of the advantages of a tiny garden is that it can so easily be floodlit. Just one lamp, tucked beneath the house window, and beaming on to the plants opposite, may be all that is needed. Or it could be set at ground level behind a statue, to throw this and the surrounding shrubs into relief; or spiked into a flowerbed to illuminate some particularly decorative bloom.

The dramatic effect of the interplay of light and shadows in a small, lit-up garden creates a living picture-wall for anyone indoors in the dining or sitting room. It is especially effective if you are entertaining—and is, incidentally, a burglar-deterrent.

For outdoor lighting, always use the correct, specially-designed, outdoor plugs and sockets – a safety precaution which really must be taken.

An extra room?

If you are short of living space, you may wish to treat a small back garden primarily as an extra living room, or as an extension of a kitchen-dining room, especially in warm weather. In this case a glazed (or better still, double-glazed) door into the garden gives a sense of extra space and continuity where a conventional wooden door would act as a view-stopper.

Sometimes it is possible to use flooring to add to this sense of continuity. Quarry tiles on the kitchen floor can be continued outside to form a small patio, and possibly link up with cobbles and brickwork to make a patterned garden 'floor'.

The mini-garden that is used as a 'room' has to provide several of the functions of a real room. Warmth, privacy and shelter can be given by high walls or palings. For a verandah effect, cover a third or half the garden with a pergola or some other roof structure. This can be glazed, fitted with pull-down slatted wooden or canvas sunblinds, or twined with climbing plants.

If there is sufficient shelter, outdoor cooking may be possible. This could be on a brick barbecue built along one wall, or on a simple brick or tiled counter top fitted with outlet sockets for various plug-in appliances. (Remember to use special outdoor plugs and sockets.)

In an extra 'room' of this kind, seating is important. Mini-gardens often belong to smallish houses so that, while there is plenty of attractive garden furniture available, finding somewhere to store it is a problem. An alternative to the white-painted iron seat, or teak bench, that can be left out all year round, is built-in seating. A brick or concrete block bench down the length of one wall can be softened with a scatter of gingham cushions for impromptu outdoor meals, and double as a parking place for glasses if you have a small drinks party—or even, since your outdoor room is still a garden, as a table for plant pots!

Opposite page
Top left: A town plot seen as a quiet 'retreat'. The fine old urn acts as focal point, centred in paving, and the whole area framed in greenery.

Top right: Hanging baskets and ground-level flowers hide an ugly spot. The colour is relieved by restful foliage.

Bottom left: A terrace given a distinct character through the skilful use of stone, evergreen and flowering shrubs.

Bottom right: Spiky and smooth shrubs provide variety in a small garden.

The mix and match suite

This living room suite has modern styling, is extremely versatile and is easy to make. And it also gives you a choice of two styles; either a formal suite with integral settee such as the one illustrated below, or with 'staggered' legs so that the chairs can dovetail to form a settee, form a corner unit, or even run along a wall and into a corner if required.

This suite, made up of a settee, chair, stool and coffee table, is modern in design and possesses a number of useful construction features.

It is also a simple carpentry job for the experienced handyman.

The construction of the stool is identical to that of the coffee table except that the stool is finished with a plywood sheet to take a cushion, while the coffee table is fitted with a decorative top.

Construction details

These units are constructed mainly of utile. This is a medium priced wood, similar to mahogany, and is suitable for most joinery projects.

You may, however, prefer a lighter or darker wood, or one with a richer grain, in which case most hardwoods will do. If you have no experience in the selection of various woods, talk the matter over with your timber merchant because the correct wood for a specific job depends not only on appearance but also price, type, and how it will eventually be finished.

Basically the main frame consists of 100mm × 25mm (4in × 1in) PAR (planed all round) hardwood that has been radiused (all corners rounded off).

Where frame members cross by lapping, they are joined with four bolts as in the illustration cover. The positioning of the drill holes is extremely critical and it is essential that a drill hole template be made as in the illustration. This will ensure that drill holes match perfectly.

Where main frame members butt against one another, they are joined with three dowel rods drilled and fitted in dovetail fashion. Here again, the positioning of the drill holes—in this case to take the dowel rods—is extremely critical and it is essential to use a dowel jig if the members are to be joined level and at right angles.

Start the construction of the furniture by first deciding whether you want to build the 'formal' suite or the 'dovetail' suite — the construction outline of which is in Fig.5.

Place the lengths of timber for assembling one unit of furniture to one side, and examine these for 'matching'. This is done to ensure that all timber surfaces that can easily be seen—such as the outside faces of legs or rails—harmonize with one another, For instance, the leg timbers might come with a prominent grain on one side, and little or no grain on the other, which could present a jumbled visual appearance if fitted at random. Mark the 'inside' of such timbers lightly with a pencil to identify them.

Cutting the timber

Cut all lengths and right angles accurately to their final dimensions. This is easily achieved by nailing three lengths of batten round the edges of a leg so that it forms a three-sided stop. Next construct a 'bridge' that will exactly span the leg from side to side; this will require two short pieces of batten, and one piece sufficiently long to span the width of the leg and be nailed securely on to the two shorter battens. The whole assembly, shown right, can be made in a few minutes. The bridge is held in place by a cramp at the correct distance along the leg, rail or arm, and will enable you to cut several lengths of timber to the same length while guiding the tenon blade at right angles.

Using a try square and marking knife, carefully mark one of each leg, rail (and arm, if required), to the correct length. Do this carefully to ensure that you do not make a mistake—you can measure as many times as you like, but you can cut only once!

The cutting should be done with a fine toothed tenon saw with at least 14 points to 25.4mm.

Radiusing

Radiusing consists of rounding the corners of timber to eliminate sharp edges. It is done here to soften the lines of the furniture which, by design, tends to be angular in appearance. The radius, in this case, is carried out to the extent that only the corners are rounded off, not the complete edge.

While it is a simple technique, radiusing requires a certain amount of skill and care if you are to avoid bumpy, undulating edges, If you have not done this before you should either get your timber merchant to supply the

timber ready radiused—this will cost more and not all merchants will do it—or practise on some spare pieces of wood until you get the hang of it.

To radius by hand you will need a marking gauge, 12.5mm ($\frac{1}{2}$in) bevel edged chisel, hammer, smoothing plane, block plane, fine toothed flat tile, and grade 0 glasspaper.

Set the marking gauge at 6.2mm ($\frac{1}{4}$in) and run a *light* line at this depth along the edge of each piece of timber, including the ends. Repeat this by drawing another line, in between the first line and the edge, setting the marking gauge at 4mm ($\frac{5}{32}$in). You will now have two parallel lines marked all round the edges of the timber.

Place one of the pieces of timber in a wood vice so that one long edge is upwards. If you do not have a wood vice, the piece can be cramped to a table top, but in this case the edge will be placed horizontally, which is slightly more inconvenient as you will have to turn the timber over to radius the edge opposite the one being worked.

With the smoothing plane, chamfer the corners of one long edge down to the 4mm ($\frac{5}{32}$in) line. Do not forget to plane with the grain, not against it, and make sure that your strokes are long and even to prevent the radius from being irregularly shaped and bumpy. Repeat this along the corner of the opposite edge. You should now have a piece with flat bevels on both edges.

Now, still using the smoothing plane, round the same corners down to the 6.2mm

Opposite page above: *Individual units can be placed together to form larger units, provided the legs, arms and rails are constructed in accordance with the plan in Fig. 6.*

Opposite, left: *A simple jig can be made to ensure that the dowel holes are bored accurately.*

Opposite, right: *A completed corner joint showing the positions of the dowels and the bolts.*

Top right: *This simple jig ensures that timbers are cut square and to the correct length. It is easily made in a few minutes and makes a valuable work aid.*

Right: *Radiusing the end of a timber. This has to be done very carefully because you are working on end grain and this splinters or splits easily.*

Fig. 1: *If you have no wood vice, radiusing can still be done by cramping a timber to a table top. Some carpenters prefer to radius in this position.*

($\frac{1}{4}$in) line. Use a very light, smooth stroke for this because if you plane deeper than the line you will have to end up rounding the edges completely.

When you have radiused the long edges of all the timbers, finish off the work with the fine glasspaper.

Next, you will have to radius the ends, which is slightly more difficult because you are working with end grain, and this is liable to splinter or split much more easily.

Lay a rail, leg or arm down on the bench or table top and, with the hammer and chisel, take a traingle of wood off the tip of each end corner down to the first marked line.

With the block plane, chamfer all round the end, down to the first line. As you are working on end grain, do not plane along the line as you did with the side edges because the wood will only splinter. Use the plane starting from the first marked line and work away, over the end of the timber (illustrated) Check that the curvature is uniform. If it is, continue with the block plane, chamfering down to the second line all round. After a final check, glasspaper down to a fine finish.

Applying a protective coat

At this stage it is best to apply a protective coating so that any stains or marks that occur as the result of working can easily be wiped off. For economy, dilute the coating. A varnish consisting of clear polyurethane and turpentine or turpentine substitute in the proportions of 1:1, is perfectly adequate. Rub off all pencil marks and finger marks first, and wait for the coating to dry thoroughly before starting work again.

Drilling bolt holes

Mark out the positions of all the bolt holes with something that is easily erased, such as chalk. Now run through a 'trial assembly' to ensure that the bolt holes are in the correct positions. When you are sure that all the

pieces have been marked in the correct places, put each piece in turn in a drilling template and mark each drill hole position positively, with an awl or a drill bit, through the template holes.

Drill the holes for the bolts through each marked position. It is essential that the holes are dilled through at exactly right angles and for this you will need a vertical drill stand. It is possible to drill the holes by hand, but this is a hit-and-miss technique that will almost certainly prove to be ineffective.

Next counterbore the tee nut and screw

Fig. 1

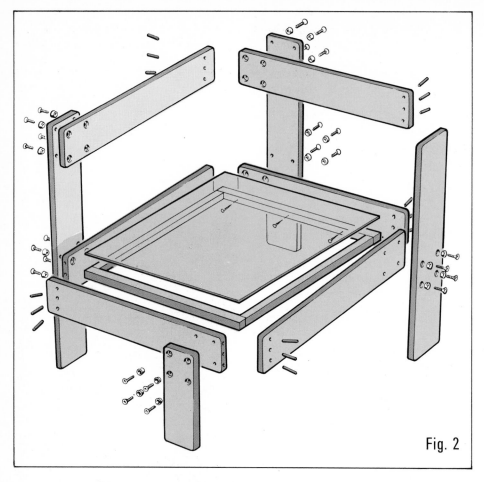

Fig. 2

cup recesses. The depths to which the recesses are taken will depend on the type of bolt and nut used. And of course the counterbore bit, in each case, should be of a diameter equal to either the nut or cup, whichever is being used.

Dowelling preparation

The dowels are drilled and inserted in dovetail fashion. Once again, mark the intended dowel hole positions with chalk and 'trial assemble' the unit. It will be even easier this time because you can insert the bolts—tightening them gently by hand—to hold part of the unit together.

Insert each piece of timber in turn in the dowelling jig and drill holes through the *outside* timbers only. Note that the internal holes—which in all cases are drilled in the edge or end grain—are drilled when the unit is being assembled. If you drill both external and internal dowel holes together, it is almost certain that they will not match the bolt drill holes exactly when assembling, and necessitate some ugly alterations.

The dowelling rods must now be slightly chamfered. This consists of planing a 'flat' along the length of the rods. The chamfer allows air and excess glue to be forced out of the dowel holes when the dowel is being inserted. If this is not done, it will be impossible to insert the dowel to the full depth because of the excess glue.

Cut the dowelling into lengths of 70mm (2¾in). Then, to facilitate the insertion of each dowel, radius or 'round' one end. The method is the same as sharpening a pencil and can be carried out with a trimming knife or block plane.

Fig.2. An exploded view of a corner chair. This one has 'staggered' legs, enabling it to dovetail with other units.

Fig.3. A more orthodox armchair. The legs are symmetrical and cannot dovetail with other chairs, but a stool or table can be fitted in on either side.

Fig.4. Cramping a corner for dowelling. The outside dovetail dowel holes are drilled first, then the clamp is removed for the middle dowel.

Fig.5. One of the corner legs, 'A', is only dowelled. 'B' shows a bolted and dowelled corner, 'C' a 'T' nut in place, 'D' plan view of a stool or table.

Fig.6. Two corner chairs and a backed chair, with staggered legs. They can dovetail together as shown. Note that if the leg positions of any of the units are altered, they will not fit together.

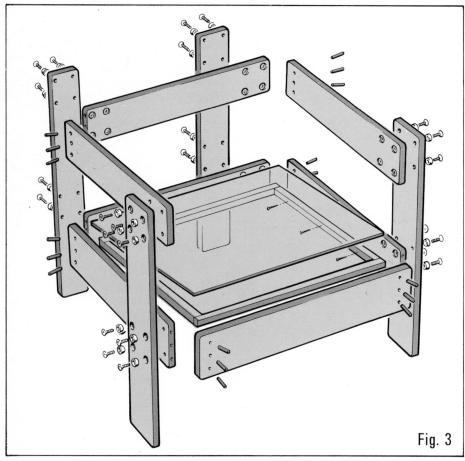

Fig. 3

Assembly

Place a dab of adhesive in all the screw cup holes and insert the screw cups. Insert the four bolts through the two timbers for one of the joints, and tighten down with your fingers the pronged tee nuts on the ends of the bolts. Then screw them in fully. Repeat this for all the lapped joints. You will now have several parts of the unit ready, and these have to be butt-joined with the dowelling.

Position two of these parts so that they are ready for drilling the dowel holes. This is quite simple because they will be at right angles to one another. Now cramp the corner together as shown in Fig.4; the near end of the clamp, pressing on the surface containing the dowel holes, will be fixed directly over the middle dowel hole. When the assembly has been cramped firmly, place the drill bit in one of the exposed dowel holes and drill through into the second timber. Repeat this on the other hole. You have now drilled the holes for the dowels that actually 'dovetail' towards the middle dowel. Smear some adhesive round the dowels, and put some of it into dowel holes. Tap the two dowels in position. There will be a small portion of dowel protruding, but ignore it at this stage—it will be planed down later.

Having completed the dowelling for the outside holes, the clamp can be removed. Now drill and fit the dowel for the centre hole. This procedure is repeated for all the dowelled joints.

While the glue is setting, measure and cut the battening for the seat or table top supports, and also measure and cut the seat or table top to size. When the glue has set, align and fit the battening. These are simply drilled and the holes countersunk. Apply glue to the side that contacts the unit frame, then screw securely. Following this by pinning and gluing the table top.

The battening, in the case of seat supports, does not have to be located critically. A fraction of an inch of deviation will be obscured by the cushions. But a table top is a different matter. If the battening is not placed exactly you will have a sloping table top!

For the table, first cut or plane the top to size, then place it down on a flat surface. Turn the unit frame upside down and place this over the table top; the whole unit will now be upside down, and the top of the table will be level with the top rim of the table frame. You can now measure and fit the battening from the underneath.

Finishing

Plane the protruding dowelling down carefully to prevent marking the timber, and finish off with glasspaper.

Smooth all the remaining surfaces with grade 0 glasspaper and wipe all over with a cloth damped with turpentine to remove any dust. Then go over the timber with fine steel wool and wipe again with the cloth.

For the final finish use wax and polish, a polyurethane varnish, or paint. Allow varnish or paint to dry thoroughly before fitting domes of silence or similar coverings for the bolt heads.

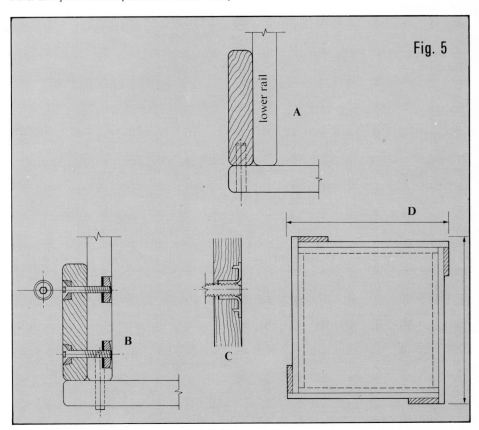

Fig. 5

lower rail

A

B

C

D

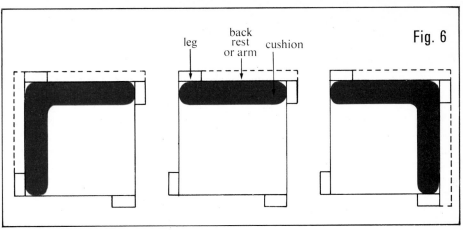

Fig. 6

leg

back rest or arm

cushion

Fig. 4

Getting more 'mileage' from storage space

Space is a very expensive commodity these days. The trend is for today's householder to have less and less of it, and more and more belongings with which to fill it. But well-planned storage will enhance the appearance of your home, prevent deterioration of your possessions and save time and money. And ill-considered storage is not only wasteful but can even be dangerous.

Unfortunately, good storage is initially expensive, but even so it should be a central part of your long-term planning for the whole house.

New brooms, new rooms

Enthusiasm often runs high when you are about to decorate your new home. For economical and practical reasons you may have possibly decided to complete one room at a time. You may have chosen a colour scheme, ordered the wall storage unit you have longed for, and chosen the chairs that you would like. But beware: you are already in danger of preparing a room of which you may be justly proud, but which will be inadequate for your needs within a year.

During the early stages of creating a home, storage will not usually present many problems. The builder or previous occupant will have left enough shelves and cupboards to cater for your initial needs. Items such as step-ladders and brooms are in constant use; while books, records, glasses, spare linen and maintenance equipment can be put in a 'spare room' for the time being. But as time goes by, your stock of such items increases. You may realize for example, that a seat-cum-storage unit would have kept your sewing materials neatly, and wish you had made the wall storage unit deep enough to take your record player. By the time you have lived in one house for many years, you will be ready for a massive 're-think' about your storage problem, which could well be getting out of hand by now!

The planning stages

Even the most careful planning leads to 'overspill' storage. If you wish to have an efficient, attractive home you must keep this to a minimum, making sure that it consists only of items which are not in regular use, such as camping or other holiday equipment. The only way to ensure this is to face the fact that storage is a problem. Consider your requirements throughout the whole house before you start work on the first room. By doing this you will be able to harmonise your storage with the other decor and to position equipment close to where it is used.

Let your experience of other people's homes influence you—how do they deal with this problem? But avoid letting it dictate your own decisions. Think carefully about how you work and where you relax at home, and plan accordingly. Think also about any special features your home may have—for example, the distance you live from the shops may determine whether you need a deep freeze to store food. Such a planning exercise may delay your decorating by a whole week, but it may save you years of domestic chaos.

Two basic approaches

You can approach your storage requirements in two main ways. First, if your home is a new building with few of the alcoves and recesses found in older houses, you can make a feature of your fitments. A battery of cupboards gives a clean and efficient appearance to a kitchen. Open stacks of books contrasted against glass, or pot ornaments and plants, give a warm and friendly appearance to a living area.

Secondly, if your home is of the older type, with chimney breasts and plenty of nooks and crannies, you can use these spaces for cupboards and hide away storage. Doors fitted flush with existing walls and coloured to match the general decor will blend into at room. Initially this approach may provide you with more cupboards than you need, but very soon you will find the extra space invaluable. There is a large variety of free-standing dual-purpose furniture which harmoniously painted can add to the no-storage illusion.

Main storage categories

The first step in over-all planning is to divide your possessions into four main categories.

1. Items which are constantly in use (especially kitchen equipment). These must be easily visible, accessible from a normal standing position and close to the area in which they are to be used. They should also be situated so that they cannot be obstructed by other objects—for example, on shelves just deep enough to take the required article.
2. Items which are used regularly: general cleaning and maintenance equipment; refer-

ence books, hobby tools and games. These should be accessible from a standing position and can be kept in a central store.
3. Seasonal items like sportswear, deckchairs and Christmas decorations. These are normally stored for well-defined and limited periods and are best kept away from the daily living area. Lofts and high cupboards are better than cellars which are often damp. You should consider temperature extremes for items like plastic emulsion paints, wines and beers, and wooden objects (which may spoil and warp).
4. Hoarded items: What you 'hoard' will depend on personal taste—one man's treasure is another man's junk. But the general rule is that if you cannot find a use for it—throw it away. However, because everybody has their own idea of what is valuable, you plan your storage carefully and you can afford the luxury of keeping your personal treasures.

Waste disposal

Short-term storage of waste presents its own problems, especially where central heating has made open fires redundant. Each room should have a portable waste container of some kind. The most hygienic type for the kitchen, if you do not have an automatic waste disposal unit, is the specially made bag suspended from a metal ring. It can be fixed to a wall or the inside of a door. When full, the bag is discarded with the contents and replaced by a new one.

Positioning your storage

The next step in planning is to decide where you are going to keep the bulk of your storage. The best thing is to measure each room and draw the floor areas on a piece of graph paper or to a scale of 13·302mm ($\frac{1}{2}$in-1ft). Draw the rooms on the paper in the same relative positions as they are in your home, including entrances and any hatchways. Indicate other features such as sinks, chimney breasts and windows which will influence the position of your storage. Write on each floor area on the drawing the proposed function of each room, then consult your list of possessions in their categories, and allocate adequate storage space to each room. Check these spaces against areas which will be needed for walking, sitting and any specialist activities. Remember that the most direct routes are usually the best. Once this is done you can modify your storage allocation if necessary.

You may find that an existing cupboard does not suit your plans, so if it presents major limitations then seriously consider altering it to fit your scheme. When you have finally decided on an arrangement, shade in, or stick coloured papers over, the storage areas and

Above: Slimline storage, sunshine colour! Tall, pull-out drawers hold larger objects, while slot-together segments top the lot. They are open-fronted for show-off storage.

make a note of which items are to be stored in each area.

Nooks and crannies

Builders usually leave a new home with a minimum of flexible shelving, which is expected to cater for all needs, and the lazy planner may not think to improve on this situation. Even in an ultra-modern home where the architect or builder may have provided what he considers the optimum storage space, you may be able to take a closer look around the house and even find nooks and crannies which can be used. Check existing cupboards to see whether the space

can be used more economically, for example.

Then look for extra room. The space under the staircase of many houses is ripe for development, for example. Your house may have a door in the kitchen, leading to a larder under the highest part of the stairs. In Britain, there may also be a door in the hall leading to a meter cupboard under the lower portion. Larder arrangements, which often have three or four deep shelves can be classic examples of wasted space—it is better to 'slim' down all but the bottom one so they are only wide enough to take single items, this can more than double the amount of easily accessible storage space.

It is a good idea to leave enough space between the floor and the bottom shelf for a vegetable rack.

If you do this you may have enough space to take as much as 10in off the width of your

larder, which can be reached from the hall-way. It is usually adequate for storing daily outdoor clothing on hangers for a family of four. There is sufficient space above the hanging area for a shelf to take gloves and scarves. If you remove the panelling from the remainder of the stair side and fit a series of narrow flush doors you can use all the space under the stairs for everyday use. The central portion is good for most cleaning and maintenance equipment, including brooms and an ironing board. The lowest end portion is ideal for storing shoe cleaning material in a removeable box.

When you have made sure that you are using all the available space in your home, choose the room which you intend to furnish and decorate first. Consider in more detail those areas set aside for storage. Think carefully about the nature of the items that

Above: Look, no cupboards! But cunning decorating 'disappears' the fitted units, which form one whole wall, while the room-divider provides a showcase for oddments.

Below: A tower of strength for focal point storage . . . this unit is walk-around, elegant, and provides a 'home' for television, hi-fi, and other cumbersome equipment.

you are storing: how they are best handled, their weight and to what they are most vulnerable—undue pressure, for example, or temperature changes.

Think also about what is involved when you use a piece of equipment. For instance, when you are positioning a record player, consider where to put the lid while you are placing the record on the turntable. Where will you keep the record sleeve when the record is playing? You will probably wish to store your records close to the player; and you will need to keep the whole unit away from inquisitive children and boisterous party-goers.

Grouping units

Always try to use the wall for storage, rather than the floor, because large empty floor areas create an illusion of space. On the other hand, avoid having all your storage units hugging the walls. If you have the space, put a unit at right angles to the wall; this can act as a room divider accessible from both sides.

If you have a variety of items stored openly, the room will look tidier if you place the shelves in groups rather than scattering them evenly over the wall surface. Although there are cases where specially built units are necessary, try to make at least some storage flexible and easily adaptable.

Types of storage

Cupboards, shelves and drawers each have their good and bad points.

Cupboards are clean and generally look neat. However, doors can be a nuisance. Sliding doors—which are, admittedly, wonderful space-savers, tend to limit the view into a cupboard but they are easily obstructed by tightly packed clothing and by small objects stuck in the tracks, and they can do damage to delicate equipment. Doors with horizontal slats or louvres are expensive and attract, rather than repel dirt. Two kinds of doors which may solve difficult problems are concertina-action and 'up-and-overs'. If you have eye-level wall cupboards it is always worthwhile taking them up to the ceiling. This prevents a dirt trap and provides valuable long-term storage space.

Shelves are usually cheaper than cupboards and offer easy access to their contents, but the amount of work and skill involved in making good shelves is often underestimated. They tend not to show their weaknesses until long after they have been put up. The 'box' method is a good way of making shelves and it makes a variety of objects look neat and compact. The vertical pieces act as dividers or book ends and form supports to prevent the shelves from sagging. If the whole unit is made soundly it will require far fewer fixing points than conventional shelves would.

An economical way of making shelves is to incorporate them with a storage board. The plywood back can hold an assortment of items which are clipped on with spring fasteners or hung between pairs of nails. The triangular plywood supports are strong and economical and also help to contain the contents. Do not forget the undersides of your shelves, which will be useful for hooks and for fixing screw top jars. Simply fix the lid of the jar underneath the shelf then tighten the jar into the lid in the normal way. Start saving matching jars and they will make for tidy and attractive storage in the kitchen or workroom.

Drawers tend to be expensive and can be a nuisance unless they are a good fit. The best place to position them is below working surfaces where they can use awkward space economically and their contents can be seen easily. Sometimes it is possible to buy good sets of drawers cheaply from second-hand shops, but check first for dry-rot and wood-worm. By painting them and changing the handles they can be successfully incorporated into your fitted storage units.

Cupboards, shelves and drawers can be free-standing, fitted or built-in. Consider the following points before making any decisions.

Free-standing units have the distinct advantage of allowing you to alter the layout of your rooms frequently. You can also take them with you if you move. Although they probably require more knowledge and skill to make than other types, there is a wide variety available on the market. Dual purpose seats, and tables which are either portable or fitted with castors, can be quickly transferred between rooms. The principle of using 'dead' space under furniture, especially beds, is ideal, if space is very limited. Often capacious drawers can fill up the space under beds which would otherwise just be a dust trap.

Fitted furniture, by definition, is usually screwed to the wall or floor, but it can be removed if you wish. There is an excellent range of units on the market suitable for all kinds of storage requirements.

Built-in furniture is an integral part of the structure of a building, and is strictly permanent. If you intend to carry out any structural work yourself and you are in any doubts then consult a specialist.

Choosing suitable storage

If you never allow personal preferences to influence your decisions all the fun would go out of home planning. However, there are certain practical aspects to consider before making your final decisions. Considerable research has led to a guide on dimensions for storage in the home (see chart). Storage of

Above: Antique anti-clutter unit for this difficult attic wall. The structure is very simple, but the wood is carefully chosen to blend in with the old books and gold glow.

Below: Cutting corners for efficiency . . . Double-hinged doors fold back for maximum accessibility. The enlarged space houses the more unwieldy kitchen utensils easily.

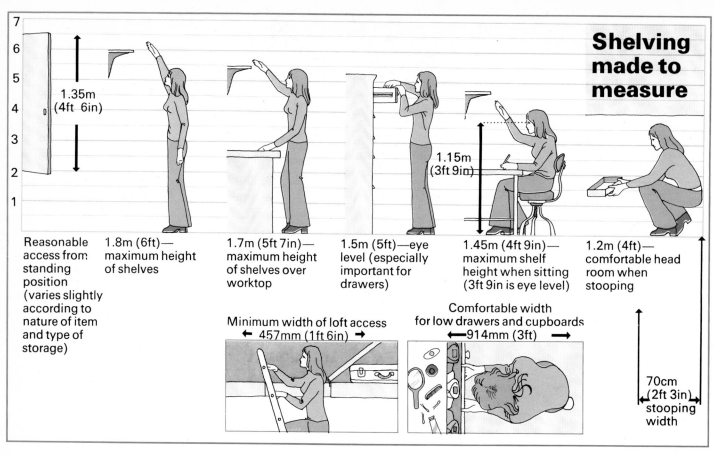

Shelving made to measure

Reasonable access from standing position (varies slightly according to nature of item and type of storage)

1.35m (4ft 6in)

1.8m (6ft)—maximum height of shelves

1.7m (5ft 7in)—maximum height of shelves over worktop

1.5m (5ft)—eye level (especially important for drawers)

1.15m (3ft 9in)

1.45m (4ft 9in)—maximum shelf height when sitting (3ft 9in is eye level)

1.2m (4ft)—comfortable head room when stooping

70cm (2ft 3in) stooping width

Minimum width of loft access
← **457mm (1ft 6in)** →

Comfortable width for low drawers and cupboards
← **914mm (3ft)** →

any constantly or regularly used items needs to take the dimensions into account. Take care to compare your height with that of the average person before using the guide—you may have to modify it. Consider furniture in relation to surrounding objects in order to avoid awkward postures when retrieving articles.

Remember, good storage means easy accessibility—not accessibility with great effort. Here the human element is often neglected, even by professional designers. It is no good working out exactly how many packets you can fit into a cupboard, or how many carefully folded items of clothing you can pack into a drawer if sooner or later when you are in a hurry, you bring down the whole shelf full of packets—or leave the clothes out chair.

When you are planning your storage, be honest and imagine yourself in your daily work around the house. Take time to consider practical aspects, and allow both these things to influence your decisions. If you do you will be rewarded with a considerable saving in time and money. You will also allow the rest of your furniture and decorations to be seen at their true value.

Left: A room with a view—inside! A few choice utensils are set off by the white tiles, orange kitchenware and gingham blinds. Sometimes things are better left unstored.

Unusual storage space

The days of the utility cupboard are gone. Modern storage is fun, yet functional—everything still has a place. With the help of imaginative ideas, a well-planned storage unit can become a major feature of a room, rather than something which has to be hidden.

You can treat storage in one of two ways. Either it can be so unobtrusive that it doesn't look like a storage unit, or it can make a big splash with everything on show. A neat cupboard fitted into an alcove can house ample hidden storage space, or open shelves can display small objects like glasses or books to become part of one large piece of furniture.

When you move into a new house, don't tailor yourself to suit what storage exists; it should be designed for you and for your needs. For instance, open shelves are best for tidy people, while the untidy ones are probably happier if they can shove all their junk away behind closed doors. So tidy people can remove doors from fitted cupboards and liven up the shelves inside, while the untidy ones can hide any open shelving units with the help of bright ideas for using blinds and doors.

You can find a variety of storage units in shops, ranging from reasonably priced whitewood shelves and matching cupboards, through units in acrylic, glass, wood or fibreglass, to expensive modular units, superbly made and created by some of the world's top designers. The trick is to take a good look at what there is, particularly in the more exclusive furnishing shops, then to adapt the ideas that interest you according to your budget.

Cheap mass-produced whitewood shelves can easily be made to look quite different with cunning treatment. Cover them with wallpaper to match the walls behind—fiddly work but worth it; or paint them in a colour such as shocking pink to make a feature of them.

Storage towers

The Continental idea of a living tower is a good example of a capacious unit which does not take up a lot of space. This is a floor-to-ceiling storage unit which stands in the middle of a room, good to look at from all angles, decorative and functional. The supports can be anything from wooden planks to slim chromed pipes and the shelves can be glass, acrylic or wood.

Storage towers are usually square, but they can be round, and often have one or two small cupboards let into them to house drinks, records or correspondence. They can be given a stark modern treatment and used as a display point for models or special ornaments, or can be crammed with everything from a record player, TV set and books, to drinks, glasses and china.

Right: Deep plastic drawers fixed on the underside of a table top are handy for small tools and utensils.

Above: New angle on storage and seating. The clean white shelves form backing for a cushioned corner in complementary blue.

Make your own storage

You can emphasise the width or the height of a room and give it a totally different feel by clever use of the horizontals or verticals on a floor-to-ceiling shelving unit for books and ornaments. Make a low room seem higher by fixing the vertical supports as little as 1ft apart, making extra lines from floor to ceiling, then give them more emphasis by picking them out in a contrasting colour or even covering them in a bold-striped wallpaper.

If you want to make a room feel wider, emphasise the horizontal lines instead. Don't have a group of short shelves all different sizes; instead, keep the horizontal lines as long as possible, so that the room looks wider. Instead of breaking up these lines with vertical supports, mount the shelves on touth brackets or battens. If you are trying to achieve this effect with an existing unit, paint the vertical supports in a colour that matches or merges with the walls behind, then pick out the shelves in a bright colour, or cover them with a gay felt or hessian.

A small trolley, designed for carting meals from kitchen to living or dining room, could easily be turned into a storage place for the television set or record player and records. Fix slatted racks to the lower tray, making an ideal place for storing records, and the trolley takes on quite a different personality. The advantage of keeping a television set or a record player on a trolley is that it can be wheeled away into an unobtrusive corner when it is not in use.

You can make your own modular units by adapting cheap household items; try some of these simple suggestions.

Orange boxes and tea chests. Choose only sturdy boxes, and pile them together like children's bricks to form a unit. Use a group of six or nine, piled on top of each other, glued and screwed together. Cover each box with lining paper and paint it, or use patterned wallpaper or sticky-backed plastic to hide the rough wood finish. You can use these boxes for any kind of storage from books and toys to kitchen things or even jumpers and heavier clothes.

Oil drums or beer barrels. The circular shapes of these containers will make an unusual storage unit. Cut in half, they can be put on their sides, piled one on top of the other and held firmly inside a frame made from planks. Try four bolted together then set into a frame, or make them into a tall pillar with six, one on top of the other. A tringular unit with three on the bottom, two next and one on top inside a frame, painted in a bright colour, is an original idea.

Brick and plank units. You can make attractive but cheap bookshelves using smart planks supported at each end by three or four bricks. Use cheaper wood for a unit in the kitchen, and cover the shelves with sticky-backed plastic.

Plastic and acrylic. Ideas for making storage units out of plastic bowls and buckets are given on page 295. Another unusual idea is to make storage cubes out of sheets of acrylic. Remember that it scratches easily, so these cubes are best if used in a purely decorative way or for storing something soft like sheets and towels.

Storage pyramid. Another eye-catching idea is to make a storage pyramid, using two ladders as supports. The ladders should be fixed firmly into a pyramid shape, joined at the top by slotting them together after cutting out grooves, and bound for a firm join. Fix them securely against the wall with a strut or bar so that they remain steady, then add shelves using the rungs as supports. The length of the shelves must keep to the shape of the pyramid, and be screwed to the rungs for safety. The final touch is a coat of polyurethane seal or paint in fresh-looking white or a bright colour like yellow or blue. In the kitchen the pyramid can be used for casseroles, pots and pans, or elsewhere as a gay display unit for toys, books or ornaments.

A new look for existing storage

It is easy to give a different look to old storage shelves and units, without going to the expense of replacing them with something new.

Louvred doors always look smart, so hide a deep storage alcove by fixing louvred doors across the front. The inside of the cupboard should look as good as the outside, so fix a light inside to show up a bright wallpaper, or paint it in a warm red or a cheerful green. Red is a particularly good colour in a hall, so if you are building a cupboard unit for coats and outdoor things, give this a different look by painting it red.

Deep storage cupboards are invaluable, as they can be turned into anything from a bar to a mini-sewing room with a flap-down work-top and fold-up chair. Hang the iron and ironing board on the wall, add shelves and a spotlight, and there you have a compact sewing corner that is easy to tidy away when necessary by flapping everything flat and closing the doors.

You can make a study corner in the same way, fitting a shelf deep enough to hold a typewriter, a strong light for working by, and more shelves or drawers for filing and paper. You can brighten up the inside of the cupboard by covering the door panels with sticky-backed plastic, on which you can stick important reminders which would otherwise spoil the paint.

Another good way of dealing with a very deep cupboard is to make a shelving unit on the back of the door. Make sure that the door is strong enough to support the extra weight of full shelves, and that you fit heavy duty hinges. This method can double the storage space of a deep wardrobe or a kitchen cupboard.

In the wardrobe, hanging clothes can be at the back, with shelves above and below; then a shallow shelving unit can be built on to the back of the door for the rest of the clothes or sheets and towels. In the kitchen, the back of a deep cupboard could be used for bulk-bought items and heavy tins, and the door storage could house lighter groceries like spaghetti and packet soups and sauces. Alternatively, racks could be fitted inside the door to hold backing equipment or small storage jars.

Industrial easy-to-assemble shelving units, though often associated only with offices, can look splendid in the home. They can be used in any room and painted to match the colour scheme, so that they blend with the wall behind. They can be unobtrusive if treated properly, and they are not expensive.

Decorative treatments

Here are some quick ideas for brightening shelves and cupboard doors. They will quickly add a fresh look to any piece of storage furniture.

Pop art shapes. You can transform the plain doors of a large fitted unit by painting bold pop art designs on them such as a huge circle in a gay colour. Decide how large you want the circle to be and where it is to go, then measure a piece of string half the required diameter. Attach one end of the string to a pencil and tack the other end lightly to the cupboard door. Simply draw the pencil round in a circle, then paint away. Use any colour you like—an orange circle on a white background, or a bright white circle on a deep purple cupboard door and so on.

Friezes and borders. Either buy a paper frieze or a wallpaper border print, or paint your own border with wide stripes of paint. These can be used on door panels in a large fitted cupboard, or to give a framed effect outside the door frame.

Felt, hessian and tweed. A successful idea for an old kitchen dresser is to line all the shelves with felt or other material. It adds a touch of colour, makes the dresser look different, and prevents china from chipping.

Pelmets and scallops. For an old fashioned, cottagey look, make scallops from oilcloth or gathered pelmets out of fresh-looking gingham, then tack these onto the front of plain shelves in the kitchen. Any plastic-coated material is a practical choice, because it can be wiped down easily, and the pelmets do not have to be removed for cleaning.

Below: *Super-efficient storage for this organised corner. Note the drawers under the bed and the shelves on the back of the door. Every inch is used wisely.*

Bottom: *Pull-out toy boxes fit under the bed.*

Space under the stairs

More often than not the space under the stairs tends to be a glory hole, where awkward things are thrown because they have no other home. With a little thought, this space can be put to good use, and become an organised storage area, particularly if it is closed in.

The inside of the door is an ideal place for storing tools, where they are out of sight, but within easy reach. Cover the back of the door entirely with pegboard; work out where each tool is to be hung, then paint its shape on to the pegboard before fixing up hooks to hold each tool in place. This ensures that each tool gets put back in the right place, and you can see at a glance if one is missing.

Another way of using open space under the stairs is to make a narrow storage cupboard. This is a neat idea if you want to add a feeling of width to a passage. Make the highest part of the space under the stairs into a cupboard or telephone corner. Cut out a sheet of blockboard the same shape as the sloping part and, using a power saw cut in it two doors with rounded corners. These doors should follow the sloping angle of the stairs. Fix the cupboard front in place against a frame, then cover it with a patterned wallpaper matching that used on the stairs and in the hall. Add brass knobs on the cupboard doors, and there you have a storage unit that saves as well as gives space.

Living rooms

You can create an impressive effect with books by constructing a shelving unit which covers one complete wall. If you can't spare a whole wall, fill the alcoves on each side of the chimney breast with fitted shelves cut to exactly the same length and depth as the recesses. If you paint the shelves to match the walls behind, the books or ornaments will provide all the necessary colour and pattern.

Fitted seating units are ideal places for concealed storage space. Build a low seating unit 305-457mm (1ft-1ft 6in) above the ground, cover it with foam cushions, and either fit drawers underneath, or make flap-up lids to the base so as to make full use of the space. A seating unit which runs along one whole wall, or is built in an alcove, can be livened up by creating a 'curvy' shelf effect above it. Either fit a sheet of hardboard, or paint a wide stripe on the wall above the unit in the shape of an arc. This should start low on one side, curving up to leave enough headroom for people sitting down, then run down again on the other side. The interesting shapes left above the arc on each side can be filled in with shallow horizontal shelves, giving a contoured effect.

Shelves don't all have to be joined together. You can make separate cubes or boxes from planks of wood, then hang them individually on the wall in strategic places for a stunning arrangement.

Kitchens

Even everyday items like vegetables can be made to look exciting if they are stored in an unusual way. A bright treatment for a vegetable rack soon turns it into something

special that is a pleasure to look at. The treatment can be a simple coat of spray-on paint, or it could be sticky-backed plastic in a gay pattern stuck on to strips of hardboard which are then fixed to the sides of the rack. Remember not to cover the whole rack up, as air circulation is important.

Kitchen storage is rapidly being accepted as something which doesn't have to be hidden away, and hanging arrangements of pots and pans, and even fruit and vegetables, combine to give a kitchen a cheerful appearance. For something different, try hanging baskets of fruit and vegetables above an eating corner, or suspend a shelf on chains from the ceiling and use it for storing pots and pans. If you don't want to display storage jars on open shelves, keep them all in one or two deep drawers, then write their contents on the lids, so you know what's inside.

Children's things

Children should have plenty of low open shelves on which to store all their possessions. Under the bed you can keep a row of wooden boxes, all on wheels, which can easily be pulled out when it's time to put things away. These can also double as play things, because, so long as they are stable, they can be used as toy cars and trains. If you are making boxes for this purpose, make sure they are tough enough to withstand rough handling.

If you make it fun for a child to put his things away, he will automatically be tidy, and enjoy it. For instance, make a teddy bear storage cupboard. First draw a gently rounded bear about 914mm (3ft) high on a sheet of blockboard. Cut out the bear shape with a circular saw and jigsaw, and make his tummy into a door. Fit the blockboard on to an open cupboard, and finally paint it in a bright colour.

A simple toy box can be transformed into a climbing frame by cutting round holes in all four sides. Fix castors on the bottom and weight the base for stability. Then, when the child has finished playing and climbing, his toys are placed in the box, which can be easily wheeled into a corner for neatness.

You can gain storage space in a childrens' room by giving it a 'cabin' treatment. Build a bunk above low cupboards which hold clothes and toys, and fix a stable ladder for access at bedtime.

Mobile storage

Storage doesn't have to be static. One of the most versatile ideas is to have mobile units. These could be as simple as a small kitchen cupboard on wheels with a chopping block fixed on top and vegetable racks inside, making vegetable preparation easy.

Open shelf units on wheels or castors can be used to hold radios, television sets or record players in the living room. A trolley with an electric ring incorporated in the top can be used to transport food from the kitchen to the dining room for dinner parties.

Different shapes

You can choose other shapes than verticals and horizontals when planning storage units. Shelving units look more exciting in triangular shapes, and books stored on diagonal shelves add a completely new angle to a room.

You can make a real splash with this kind of storage so that it takes up an entire wall, a treatment which is particularly effective in a dark kitchen. If you are making a right-angled group of shelves, then fixing them up at an odd angle, it is best to draw a sketch to scale of what you want before you begin. Then you can get the shelves just right. When they are firmly fixed together, the unit can be fixed on the wall at its odd angle.

Before you begin designing any shelf unit which relies on odd angles for its effectiveness, remember angled shelves are successful visually only if all the angles are regular. So measure them extra carefully with the help of a T square.

More different ideas

Ugly shelving units which seem to have no redeeming features other than the storage space provided can easily and effectively be hidden behind blinds or folding doors. The cheapest method is probably to fit a roller blind over the front of an open unit. Blend it with the rest of the decorations by making it up in a fabric that matches the curtains or covers in the rest of the room.

If you have no linen cupboard, but need somewhere to store your clean linen, construct an open shelving unit in the bathroom or on a landing. Place a wicker basket on each shelf, line the baskets with cotton to protect the contents from dust, then fill them with linen. Put towels in one basket, pillowcases in another and so on, choosing colours which look good next to each other. Integrate the whole unit by spray painting the baskets for a stunning effect.

The space by a passage window can be put to good use by fitting a bench for flower arranging just under the window sill. Cover the shelf with sticky-backed plastic and fit plastic pull-out tray drawers under the worktop. Keep a plastic rubbish bin underneath for debris, and flower arranging need no longer mess up the kitchen.

Colourful plastic canisters can be strung together to form an attractive storage unit for magazines and newspapers. Make your own

canisters cheaply out of cardboard tubes, covered with felt or sticky-backed plastic, then knot them together like a rope ladder.

A neat idea for tools is to gouge out holes in blocks of polystyrene, and store hammers and screwdrivers handle end down inside them.

Why not go through your house with some of these ideas in mind? Take a fresh look at existing storage and try to work out what can be done to improve it.

Above: *Storage can be hidden away behind discreet doors or put proudly on display. Here a whole wall of segmented shelves holds books, ornaments and oddments to great effect as a strong focal point.*

A new look for old chairs

When all the old upholstery has been removed and the chair frame cleaned and repaired, the interesting stage of upholstery can begin. Although using rubber webbing and foam is easier and quicker than the traditional webbing and springs, it still pays to take time over attaching them. Keep on adjusting the tacks at the various stages until the shape of the foam is just right.

Webbing the seat

Because the rubber webbing takes the place of the original webbing and springs, it is attached to the top of the seat frame, rather than the bottom as before. Mark the position for each strand on the back, front and side rails, and sand down the inner edges of the frame so it will not cut the webbing.

Using the webbing straight from the roll to avoid waste, place it in the position of the first strand, with the cut edge just inside the outside edge of the back rail. Tack it down, using five tacks placed in a straight line 6mm (¼in) from the cut edge. Be careful to position the tacks at right angles to the frame, and to tack them down so that their heads are completely flat on the webbing, so they cannot cut into it.

Each strand of webbing should be $\frac{9}{10}$ the length of the distance it spans and stretched to fit; so, after fixing the strand at the back, mark this measurement on it and stretch it until the mark is in the middle of the front rail. Tack in position, placing the tacks on the mark. Cut off the webbing 6mm (¼in) outside the tacks.

Attach the other strands in the same direction, then interlace the cross strip with the other strands. Because weaving the cross strand in and out will use extra webbing, it is best to interlace it through the main webbing first, then tack one side. Mark the place where it reaches the opposite rail unstretched and measure $\frac{1}{10}$ of the total measurement back from this. Stretch and tack down on the second mark.

Padding the seat

If the front legs are higher than the seat frame, cut a piece of 1in foam to the size of the chair, and stick it to the frame.

Cut out the foam biscuit to the shape of the seat, plus 20mm (¾in) all round. Mark the position of the back uprights, but do not cut the foam away. Mark the centre of each side of the foam and of the chair.

Make enough 152mm (6in) wide calico strips to fit round the perimeter of the foam, making those for the sides and front long enough to overlap at the front corners by 76-102mm (3-4in). The strip for the back edge should just fit between the uprights.

Fold the strips in half lengthwise and apply adhesive along them from one long edge up to the crease. Mark a 76mm (3in) wide border round the edge of the top of the foam, omitting the area of the uprights, and apply adhesive to it. When the adhesive is tacky, stick the calico to the foam, with the crease level with the edges.

Put the foam on to the seat, matching the centre points. Roll the excess foam under so

Fig.1. To support the upholstery, webbing is placed across the seat. The gaps between strands should equal the width of the webbing.

Fig.2. So that the webbing is stretched the right amount, $\frac{1}{10}$ of its total distance unstretched is marked in from the end.

Fig.3. The webbing can then be pulled so that the mark comes to the point where it should be tacked down. Five tacks are used for strength.

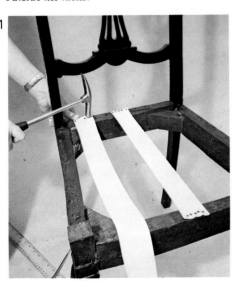

1

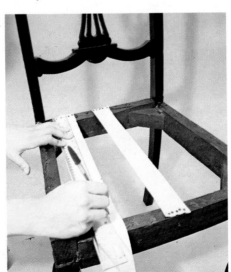

2

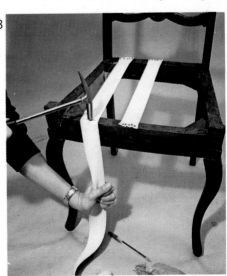

3

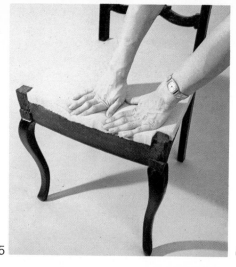

4

5

6

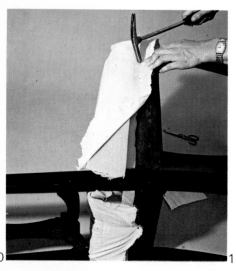

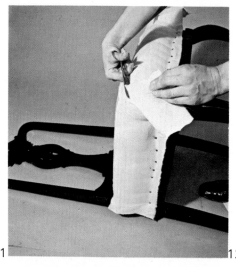

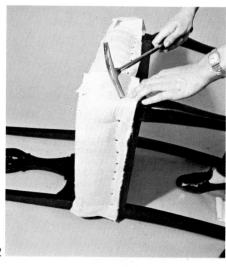

10

11

12

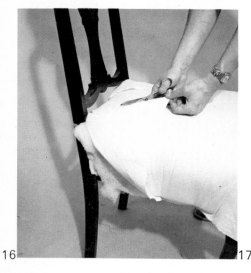

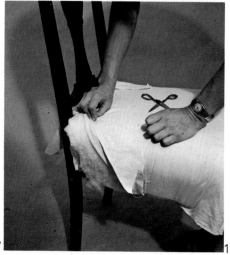

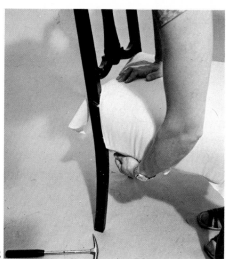

16

17

18

Fig.4. *Rubber webbing is so strong that cross strands are not necessary, although one can be put at the back for extra support.*

Fig.5. *To build up the frame to the level of the extended front legs, a piece of foam the exact size of the seat is stuck in position.*

Fig.6. *The main foam padding is attached to the chair by wide calico strips which are stuck to the foam and tacked to the chair.*

Fig.7. *To fit the foam at the back uprights, it should be slashed diagonally in from the corners and wedged in between them.*

Fig.8. *To get a good shape, the foam is cut larger than the seat and its sides squashed down and held in place by calico strips.*

Fig.9. *So that they can be adjusted if necessary, the tacks holding the strips are widely spaced and not driven right home yet.*

Fig.10. *After the main tacks are in on each side, more can be put in between. The sides of the foam must still be kept level with the seat.*

Fig.11. *To finish the front corners, the strips are cut so they can be wrapped round the other way and tacked or stuck down.*

Fig.12. *The wavy line of tacks may look untidy, but it will prevent the strips from ripping along the grain of fabric through strain.*

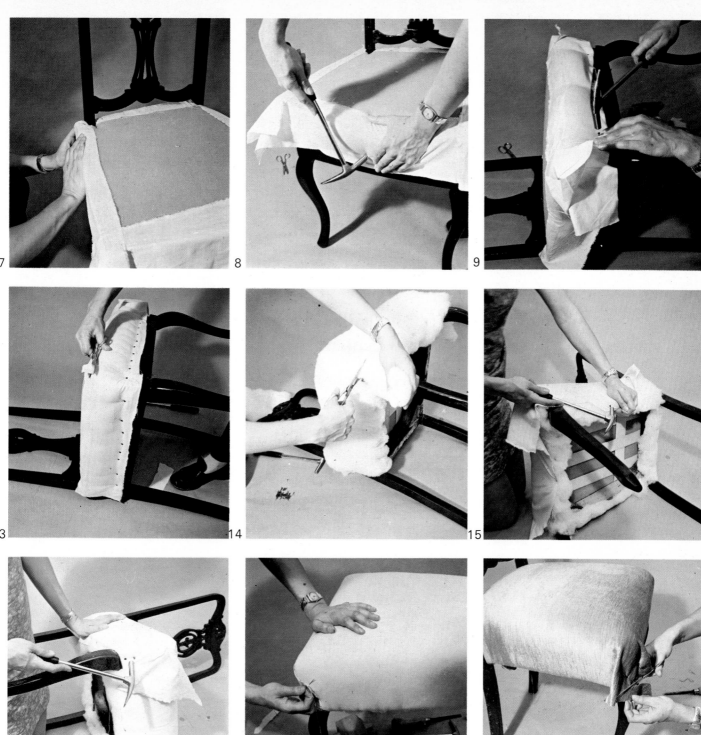

Fig.13. *The excess fabric can then be trimmed off. Do not trim it too close to the tacks, however, or it may pull away.*

Fig.14. *On the chair where the cover finishes below the seat, wadding should be tacked on to pad the edges of the wood.*

Fig.15. *The next step is to put on the inner calico cover. This is held in place at first by one temporary tack on each side.*

Fig.16. *To fit the inner cover at the back uprights, fold back the corner diagonally so that the fold just touches the wood.*

Fig.17. *Slash the fabric diagonally from the point to within ½in of the fold. Fold it level with the uprights and trim off the excess.*

Fig.18. *Tack the fabric down, pulling it as tightly as possible at the back corners. You may then have to adjust the other tacks.*

Fig.19. *When the inner cover is completely taut and smooth, the fabric at the front corners can be finished off as for the strips.*

Fig.20. *After the excess fabric has been trimmed off, the piece wrapped round can be stuck down or held in place with stitching.*

Fig.21. *To finish the front corners of the top cover in a double pleat, pull down the point of the fabric and tack it in place.*

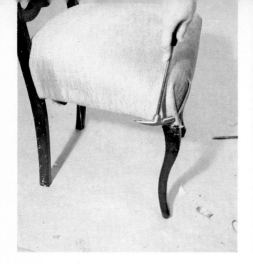

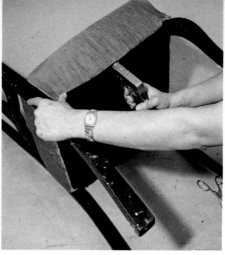

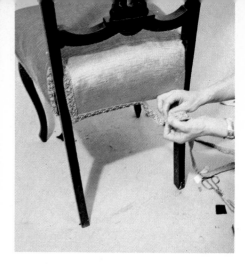

Fig.22. *Fold under the excess fabric neatly in two inverted pleats. Some fabric inside them can be trimmed away so they will lie flat.*

Fig.23. *To hide the 'works' under the seat, a piece of black fabric should be tacked or stapled on. Cut it away to fit round the legs.*

Fig.24. *The final touch is to attach braid round the edge of the seat. Stitch down the mitres at the corners for a neat effect.*

that it does not hang over the edge of the seat frame and tack down the calico strips. To fit the foam at the uprights, simply slash it diagonally at the corners and wedge it between them (Fig.7).

Cut a piece of wadding to fit over and down the sides of the foam with 12mm (½in) turning, or long enough to reach below the chair to pad the edges if the upholstery finishes underneath. Tack in a few places, slashing and overlapping it at the corners.

Fitting the cover

Place the calico inner cover over the wadding and attach it with tacks. At the back uprights, fold back the fabric diagonally so that the fold just touches them (Fig.16). Slash diagonally from the point to within 12mm (½in) of the fold. Fold under the slashed fabric, trimming off the excess, so that the folds are level with the uprights and tack the fabric down. Finish the front corners of the calico by slashing them diagonally from the corner to the edge of the foam. Fold each piece round the corner, press as flat as possible and tack down (Figs.19 and 20).

Fit the top cover in the same way, but making pleats at the front corners. If the cover finishes part way down the frame, trim the raw edge to within 6mm (¼in) of the tacks and cover with braid or gimp. If the cover finishes under the seat, tack it 12mm (½in) from the edge and trim off the excess fabric to within 6mm (¼in) of the tacks. Otherwise attach the braid around the bottom of the seat.

Finish the underneath of the seat with a piece of black hessian. Cut it to the exact size of the seat frame, turn under 6mm (¼in) on each side and place it centrally under the seat. Tack in position, mitring the corners for a really neat finish.

Learn to paint

It isn't for nothing that carpenters scathingly refer to paint as 'long putty'. Many a botched woodwork job has been rescued by first-class painting. Equally, a bad paint job will ruin the finest woodwork. And come the time that you want a project fit for exhibition in the 'I Did It Myself' show—it is infuriating to see it spoiled by a stray bristle, an ugly run, or worse. Yet careful preparation, and the observance of a few rules, can make your next painting project the most successful yet.

Choosing a brush

A good brush is a good investment—not just in better mileage, but in helping to preserve your good temper. A cheap brush is often stiff, making it difficult to avoid ugly brush marks on the finished job. If the bristles are too thin to pick up a decent load of paint, you may be tempted to dip too deeply into the paint—the result will be a clogged-up brush which you cannot get clean and which will drop flecks of old paint on to the next painting job. And a cheap brush will also shed an infuriating number of bristles—at least a couple of which you will not notice until your otherwise immaculate gloss paint coat has dried out.

To be good, a brush does not have to be the most expensive one in the shop. But its bristles will at least be plump (to pick up a sufficient paint load), soft to the touch (to avoid brush marks), and long (to apply the paint smoothly). The best brushes are those

with natural bristle—hair of hog or boar. This bristle has naturally split ends, which provide a grip to hold the paint and help it go on smoothly. Synthetic fibres are smooth and hold paint less efficiently. The bristles on a good brush taper slightly at the end.

General-purpose paint brushes range in width from 13mm (½in) up to 102mm (4in). For most indoor gloss paint or varnish work a 50.8mm (2in) brush is easiest to handle, while a 25.4mm (1in) brush is used for detail work, such as drawer handles and narrow edges.

New brushes shed hairs, and often contain odd bits of bristle and factory dirt. To keep this rubbish out of your painting the brush should be 'flirted', that is, flicked against the hand, and then washed in warm, soapy water and rinsed in clean water. Lay it flat to dry out.

Most professional painters break in a new brush by using it for priming or undercoating. This allows them to deal with the odd stray bristle where it matters least. They also keep one set of brushes reserved permanently for white or pastel paints, since darker pigments left in the 'stock' (handle) may 'bleed' into lighter paintwork.

Materials required

For painting a whitewood Welsh dresser, the paint tools required are:
1. Paint kettle. **2.** Brushes—50.8mm (2in) and 25.4mm (1in). **3.** Glasspaper—grades

Fig.1. 'Flirting' a new brush by flicking the bristles against the hand. This removes loose hairs, odd bits of factory dirt and any debris from storage before you begin to paint. Starting with a clean brush helps to avoid getting rough patches on the finished paintwork.

Fig.2. Raising the nap by applying a slurry of filler and adhesive as thinly as possible. It is applied to best effect if you work a small area at a time both with and against the grain.

Fig.3. Applying a stiff filler mixture with a flexible scraper to close up deeper cracks, pressing it firmly into the cracks to prevent it from falling out later, and feathering it out over the edges to form a continuous and smooth surface for the paint.

Fig.4 Smoothing the wood surface by sanding down lightly with glasspaper after the filling dries out.

Fig. 5. Cleaning the unit with a suction head attachment on an ordinary household vacuum cleaner. The surface must be totally free from fluff and dust.

Fig.6. Raising the unit clear of the floor by tacking wooden blocks to the base of the unit. This will prevent your brush from picking up dust from dust sheets, or ink from newspapers, and thus spoiling the painted surface.

Fig.7. Masking tape is used to prevent paint from seeping into the dovetail joints, which could make the drawers hard to open or, possibly, jam.

Fig.8. Straining off bits of paint flakes and pieces of paint skin by pouring from the tin into a paint kettle through muslin or an old nylon stocking. Old paint often needs this treatment.

0 and 1. **4.** A cellulose-based filler, such as Polyfilla. **5.** Small sponge or duster for surface cleaning. **6.** Patent shellac-based knotting for treating knots. **7.** Thinners—for which to buy, see instructions on the paint tin. **8.** Pva adhesive, which you will mix in a thin solution with the cellulose filler to 'raise the nap'. **9.** A flexible scraper to apply this mixture. Also, you need newspaper or dustsheets to protect the floor.

Wood preparation

Whitewood furniture is made from deal or pine. It sometimes shows knots, it often has the exposed end-grain of plywood showing, especially on door edges, and the timber itself is somewhat coarser than more expen-

1

2

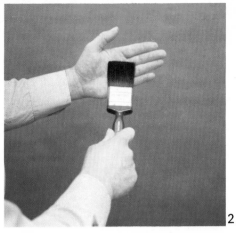

3

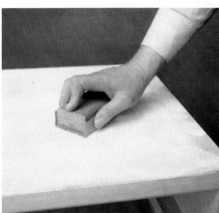

4

5

6

7

8

sive woods. But careful preparation will give it a uniformly smooth, durable finish.

If the woodwork has any knots, these have to be treated to prevent resin from 'bleeding' through the paintwork. Paint them with a thin coat of the shellac-based knotting, and leave it to dry.

Next raise the nap. Make a paste from 28g (1oz) of the cellulose filler and the same volume of the pva adhesive, mixing with water to the consistency of cream. Apply it to the wood as thinly as possible with a scraper, working both with and across the grain. Work a small area at a time, as the filler hardens rapidly. When this has dried, rub down the surface with grade 0 glasspaper.

This treatment ensures that the surface of the wood is completely smooth. Whitewood tends to swell when moistened and so it is wise to raise any uneven fibres deliberately and sand them down before priming. The filler will also cover any small dents in the wood and close any tiny hair cracks that otherwise would not be obvious until they had been painted over. If any deep cracks are still visible, fill these with a stiff mixture of the cellulose filler and water, following the instructions on the packet. Give it at least an hour to dry—from a pale grey colour, it will turn white—before sanding down very lightly with grade 0 glasspaper.

Before you paint

The traditional three-coat indoor paint method consists of a lead-free primer, with undercoat and topcoat. Buy, if you can, from a store with a fast turnover of paint; pigment settles during storage, so the fresher the paint the easier it is to mix. If in doubt, stand the tin upside down for a day or so before using it, to help loosen settled pigment.

Prise off the lid by levering at several points around the rim, being careful to avoid distorting the tin. If the lid is not airtight, any remaining paint stored in the tin will form a skin. (Any skin in an old tin should be lifted out in one piece by running a stick around the edge; otherwise the skin will break up and leave bits on the paintwork. If necessary, strain the paint through a piece of muslin or old nylon stocking to remove lumps and other debris.)

When you have finished pouring paint from any tin, hammer the lid back on to provide an airtight seal. A block of wood big enough to cover the whole lid makes the best hammer; a carpenter's hammer will sometimes distort the lid and prevent it from closing properly.

Always mix paint thoroughly, with a circle-and-up movement, so that all constituents are evenly distributed. If using a thinner, do so sparingly; too much can spoil both the depth of colour and the gloss. A newly opened tin of paint normally needs no thinners at all.

Before you begin work, check the light. Daylight is by far the best, but if you must work at night try to pick the brightest place—the kitchen, probably—in the house. Under poor artificial light it is easy, particularly when using a white gloss finish to leave unnoticed 'thin' patches and spoil the job.

Next, protect the floor with newspaper or dustsheets. Never wear woollen clothes, as loose fibres will settle on the paint. Remove fittings, such as knobs or handles, from the unit. Remove the drawers and stand these on end; it is easier to paint a horizontal than a vertical surface, since there is less risk of 'runs' or 'curtaining'.

Now fix wooden blocks under the base of the unit to lift it clear of the floor. This will prevent your brush from picking up dirt from your newspaper, or fluff from your dustsheets. Vacuum clean the unit to get rid of any dust.

Priming

Always work in a set order. If you live in a house where wood-boring insects are particularly troublesome, start by painting the underside of the unit. It is nearest the floor, and therefore most vulnerable. If not, forget the underside and start on the back—where, while you get into your stride, any faults will

Fig.9. Holding a paint brush in the correct way. Grip firmly and, to prevent unsightly 'curtaining', do not dip the bristles in too deeply.

Fig.10. Applying topcoat with smooth strokes, along the grain of the wood. Breaking the strokes, or dabbing too lightly, will cause curtaining—ugly 'sags' in the surface coat.

Fig.11. Each successive band of paint slightly overlaps the one before. It should be laid on firmly, cross brushed, then finished with the lightest possible strokes. This will ensure that the final finish is smooth and even.

Fig.12. Tackling the tricky edges with a 25.4mm (1in) brush.

Left: The simple lines of this Welsh dresser are enhanced by a smooth and professional paint finish. Using one colour over all, the effect is both homely and sophisticated. The unit can be 'dressed up' to suit your individual tastes and need not be restricted to the kitchen—it is a handsome addition to any living area. When correctly applied the gloss paint gives the unit a high-quality sheen which is delicate enough to take subtle lighting to good effect. The unit merges well with period or modern decor.

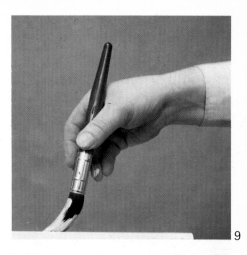

9

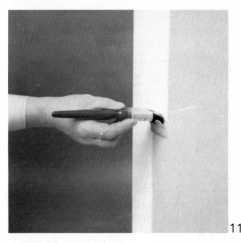

10

11

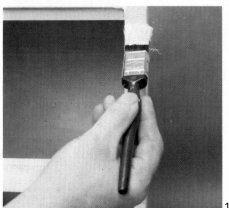

12

show up least—and then do the sides. Next, paint the larger top and front areas and, finally, the narrow dividing strips. Never paint the slides on which drawers run—or they won't.

The primer comes first. Its function is to bind loose particles and form a tough, non-porous surface for the undercoat. Pour into the paint kettle just enough primer to cover HALF the depth of bristle in your brush. There should never be more paint than this in the kettle. By using a paint kettle you avoid the inevitable consequence of painting from the original tin—a build-up of thick, sticky paint around the rim which prevents you from getting an air-tight seal when you close the lid. And, by filling the kettle to the right depth, you avoid overloaded, clogged-up brushes which are hard to clean.

Dip the brush into the primer. Wipe off any surplus paint on the inside of the kettle—not the rim—and lay on the primer with firm strokes along the grain of the wood. Do not be too timid; a firm, wristy action will spread the primer into a thin, but even, coat.

Allow 24 hours for the primer to dry. Then rub it down with grade 0 glasspaper, working along the grain of the wood, until you have a smooth finish. Wipe off the dust with a rag dampened with thinners. Clean the paint kettle and brush with thinners—the back of the paint tin will tell you which kind.

Undercoating

A good undercoat is, more than anything else, the basis of a good paint job. Any 'pimples', rough patches or unevenness of colour in the undercoat will show through the gloss paint, particularly if this is in one of the lighter shades. So the objective in undercoating is a velvet-smooth surface and an absolute evenness of colour.

White and the reds, particularly, are likely to show up all imperfections. For white, two coats of undercoat are best. For red, the evenness of colour will be improved if a tube of tint colour the same shade as that of the topcoat is mixed in well with the undercoat.

With the paint in your paint kettle at the right depth, dip in the brush and wipe off any surplus on the inside of the kettle. Beginners often make the mistake of dabbing on too much paint too lightly; this causes the ugly, sagging effect known as 'curtaining'. The correct way is to make the paint spread as far as you possibly can while still looking even in colour.

Paint first *with* the grain of the wood, holding the brush quite firmly and without lifting it except where it naturally rises from the surface at the end of a stroke. Without reloading the brush, and pressing much more lightly, work backwards and forwards *across* the grain. This avoids a striped effect

by eliminating the first brush marks. Finally, 'lay back'. Holding the brush almost flat with the work, brush so lightly that you can hardly feel the bristles touching the painted area, and in one direction only—with the grain, and working from the newest edge of the paint (the 'wet edge') back towards the previously painted area.

When you load your brush for the second time, start applying the paint, not on top of the existing wet edge, but one brushload away from it, and work back towards the already-painted bit. This avoids a build-up of paint in one place—the prime cause of curtaining. The strokes, on a wide flat surface, should be about 305-457mm (12-18in).

Edges are tricky; they catch the tip of the brush and release a globule of paint around the corner. Avoid this by stroking *towards* edges, where possible, rather than away from them. If you do cause a run in this way, wipe the paint off your brush and 'spear' off the run by pushing (instead of drawing) the brush. The same trick is used to pick up any stray bristles that appear.

Allow 24 hours for the undercoat to dry. Sand off any pimples, brushmarks or other irregularities with grade 1 glasspaper, and remove the dust with a thinners-dampened rag. If the undercoat is uneven in colour—remember, the gloss coat will probably not correct this—repeat the whole procedure. It is well worth the trouble to get a first-class job. Once the undercoating has been completed, clean brushes and kettle thoroughly once more.

Topcoating

Gloss paint is stiffer than undercoat, so needs to be applied more firmly—although the final laying-off strokes should be, if anything, even more delicate than before. It is important, too, that each new brushload should reach the previous one while the wet edge *is* still wet, and not sticky—with gloss paint, runs and curtaining can happen very

easily. Otherwise, the technique is the same as for the undercoat.

One point is worth watching, however; because of its shiny surface, gloss paint can play tricks in poor light, and for this stage of the job only daylight is really good enough.

Gloss paint is touch dry from three to six hours after application, but takes 16 to 24 hours to dry thoroughly. Edges subject to wear or knocks are best left alone for two or three days while the paint really hardens.

Care of brushes

Poor maintenance, tests have proved, wears out paint brushes much faster than painting does—and there is nothing like a dirty brush for ensuring that the next paint job will be a shoddy one.

If you have to leave a particularly long job unfinished in the middle of a coat, brushes full of paint can be left for a day or two suspended in water. Never let a brush stand on its bristles, since this may 'cripple'—distort—the ends. Suspend the brush by slotting a piece of wire or wood dowel through a hole drilled through the handle. For longer periods, of three or four days, thinning agents should be used instead of water. When resuming painting, rough-dry the brush on a piece of clean board to remove excess water or thinning agent. It is important to remove thinners, since they dilute the paint and produce a patchy surface. However, it is always best to finish a coat of paint completely, as resuming the work half-way through will produce an uneven result.

Brushes should be cleaned thoroughly after each change of paint. Working from the stock towards the tip, scrape off excess paint with the back of a knife and sluice the brush in thinners or a proprietary brush cleaner, finishing off with warm water and soap or detergent, and then clean water. Once dry, the bristles should be wrapped in clean newspaper, fixed with a rubber band, and the brush stored flat. Exposed bristles are subject to attack by moths.

Paperhanging

For your first attempt at paperhanging, choose walls which are free of awkward obstructions like doors and windows. Move as much furniture as possible from the room, put the rest in the middle and cover it. Give yourself plenty of time—paperhanging can't

be rushed—and try to work in daylight.

Materials required

For preparing the walls you will need: *1.* Bucket. **2.** Sponge. **3.** Glasspaper wrapped around a cork block. **4.** Plaster filler. (Use a

Fig.1. *Folding lining paper concertina fashion makes a long length easy to handle.*

Fig.2. *Holding the folded lining paper with the left hand leaves the right hand free to smooth it to the wall (reverse this if you are left-handed).*

Fig.3. *Matching the left-hand side of the paper to the right-hand side of the cut piece ensures that a drop repeat matches when the pieces are on the wall.*

Fig.4 *Using a plumb bob to establish a true vertical line.*

Fig.5. *Pasting from the centre to the far edge of the paper. The edge overlaps the board to prevent paste getting on the face side.*

Fig.6. *The paper is pulled back so it overlaps the near edge of the board. The paste is then brushed out to this edge.*

Fig.7. *When the paper on the board is pasted, the right-hand edges are brought over to make a large fold.*

Fig.8. *When the whole length is pasted, the left-hand edges are brought over to meet the first fold.*

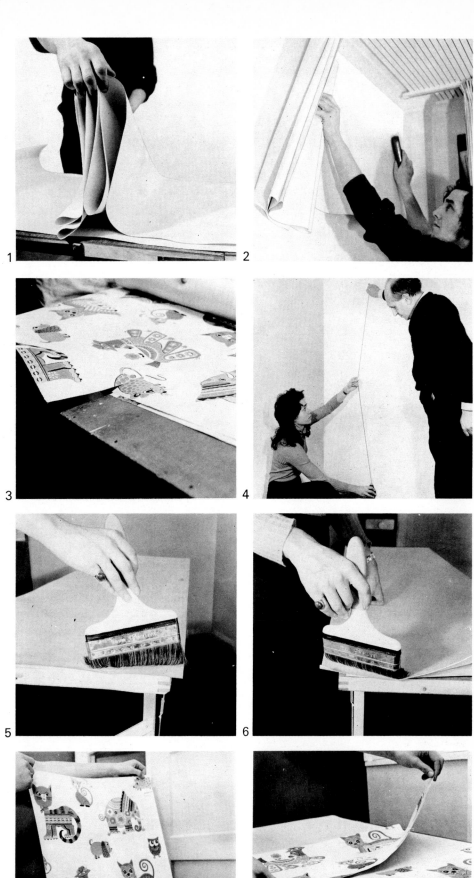

cellulose-based proprietary brand.) **5.** Lining paper. If your walls were previously papered you will also need: **6.** An old distemper brush. **7.** A broad stripping knife. **8.** Chemical stripper (optional).

For putting up the paper you will need: **1.** Plumb bob, chalked line and chalk. **2.** Scissors with 280–305mm (11–12in) blades. **3.** 1m (3ft) rule. **4.** Soft pencil. **5.** A table or board supported on trestles. (The board should be at least 600mm (22in.) wide and 1.8m (6ft) long to provide an adequate surface for pasting. An old flush door suspended across two chairs could also be used.) **6.** Adhesive. (Most manufacturers give advice about which adhesive to use for the type of paper.) **7.** Buckets in which to mix adhesives. (Plastic ones are better than metal.) **8.** Pasting brush. **9.** Paperhanger's brush. (Have two brushes, if possible, to save delay if one has to be washed, after picking up paste). **10.** A hop-up or stepladder, plank and strongly built box (to make a platform from which to reach the top of the walls safely). **11.** Seam roller.

Quantities of paper

A roll, or piece, of standard British wallpaper is about 10m (11yd) long and 52cm (21in) wide. This covers an area of approxi-

9

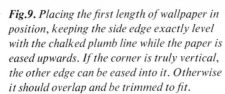

Fig.9. Placing the first length of wallpaper in position, keeping the side edge exactly level with the chalked plumb line while the paper is eased upwards. If the corner is truly vertical, the other edge can be eased into it. Otherwise it should overlap and be trimmed to fit.

Fig.10. When the excess paper overlaps for the right amount at the top, the paperhanger's brush is used to hold it in position by smoothing it into the angle of the wall and picture rail.

Figs. 11 and 12. Smoothing down the centre of the paper and then out to the sides in a series of arrowhead movements.

Fig.13. Using the back edge of the scissors to run along the paper in the angle made by the wall and the picture rail.

Fig.14. The top of the paper is eased away from the wall and the excess trimmed off along the crease line. The paper is then smoothed back into position.

Fig.15. Matching the pattern before smoothing the second length into position. The pieces should be placed edge to edge and not overlapped.

Fig.16. Using a seam roller to give a firm butt edge when the paste is nearly dry.

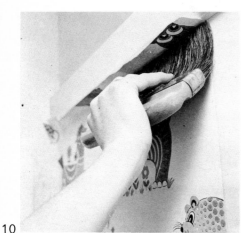

10

11

ROLL CHART

Height in metres from skirting	Measurement round the walls in metres, including doors, windows, etc.												
	10	11	12	13	14	15	16	17	18	19	20	22	24
	Number of rolls required												
2	6	7	8	8	9	9	10	10	11	12	12	14	15
2.50	8	8	9	10	10	11	12	13	13	14	15	15	16
3	9	10	11	12	13	13	14	15	16	17	18	22	25
3.25	10	11	12	13	14	14	15	16	17	18	19	22	25

12

13

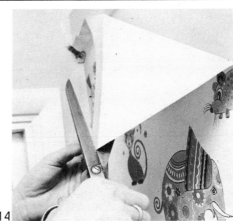

14

Left: A brightly coloured wallpaper, patterned with animal motifs, is ideal for a child's room.

mately 5 sq m (6 sq yd or 57 sq ft), but some is usually wasted through cutting and matching patterns. Most papers are ready trimmed but if they are not, this can be done by the retailer. To estimate how many rolls of paper you need, measure the total length right round all the walls you want to paper, and the height of the room from skirting board to ceiling (or to cornice or picture rail). Match these measurements against the chart given below.

Rolls of paper are produced in batches, so check that they come from the same one (each has a serial number), as rolls from different batches may vary slightly in colour-

ing. If you buy a 'job lot' of paper in a sale, always buy more than you need to cover wastage by matching patterns or through damage.

Preparing the walls

Walls must be carefully and throughly prepared in order to make paperhanging a complete success. New wallpaper slapped on top of old is by no means certain to stay up, and is likely to bubble and blister. The walls should be as even as possible, and completely clean and free of grease.

Newly plastered walls containing lime can be papered if they are perfectly dry. Coat the

area with an alkali-resisting primer which will neutralise any active lime in the plaster. Alternatively, use one of the papers which have been specially treated for use on new plaster; a lining paper would be useful here.

Distempered walls should be washed down with soapy water to remove all grime.

Painted walls should also be washed down with soapy water to remove all grime. When dry, gloss-painted walls should be keyed by thorough scouring with coarse glasspaper (this slight roughening of the surface will help the paper adhere securely).

Previously papered walls should first be stripped by soaking the paper well with warm water and an old distemper brush. A chemical stripper may be added to the water—but if the chemical splashes the paintwork, wipe it off straight away. While the paper is still wet, use the stripping knife to ease it off a little at a time. Properly soaked paper will come away from the wall easily and cleanly. Once all the paper is off, wash the walls with soapy water, rinse with clean water and, when dry, sand them lightly to remove surface blemishes, small pieces of paper, old paint drips, and so on.

Making good

Fill any holes and cracks with a proprietary

5

16

167

cellulose filler and when it is completely dry smooth it with glasspaper.

The next step is to 'size' the walls. This prevents them from absorbing the paste too quickly, allowing time to position the paper on the walls correctly. To make size, dilute the adhesive you intend to use according to the manufacturers' instructions (the packets usually give instructions for making it up for both size and adhesive). Coat the walls with it, using a pasting brush.

Adhesive

Make up the adhesive according to the directions given on the packet at least 20 minutes before you want it. This gives it time to absorb the water properly and become completely smooth. Always make up a complete packet at a time to ensure a correct consistency—any paste left over can be kept in a completely airtight jar and be used for touching up, if necessary. Don't mix batches of paste.

When the wallpaper is cut, it is a good idea to test for colour-fastness on a waste piece. If the colours do run, take extra care not to get paste on the surface of your cut pieces.

Lining the walls

For a really first-class wallpapering job, always use a lining paper under the wallpaper. It provides an ideal surface of even porosity, to which the wallpaper and its adhesive will marry, particularly if the wallpaper is heavy (the principle being that paper sticks to paper more firmly than to plaster). Heavy papers, especially embossed ones, have a tendency to stretch as their fibres first absorb the paste but shrink on drying. This can mean that the joints (joins between pieces) open because the paper loses its grip on the plaster surface. Lining paper prevents this happening. Another advantage of lining papers is that they can disguise a 'bad' surface, as well as having some insulating value.

The method of pasting and hanging lining paper is similar to that for wallpaper (see below—make sure you paste the rougher side, so the smooth side is outermost). It is best hung horizontally as the finished effect is smoother. This makes the paper rather difficult to handle on a long wall, so you should fold the paper, without creasing, concertina fashion (always with pasted side to pasted side). Start in the right hand corner of the wall and, holding the paper with your left hand, brush it out with your right hand (reverse this if you are left handed). If you prefer to hang the paper vertically, stagger the joints with those of the wallpaper to avoid the possibility of ridges. Like wallpaper, lining paper should be butt-jointed (i.e., the pieces are positioned edge-to-edge,

with no overlap).

Using the plumb bob

As few corners, cornices, ceilings or picture rails are really straight either vertically or horizontally, it is wise to use a plumb bob to check them and, if necessary, to establish a true vertical line for the position of the first piece of wallpaper.

The easiest way to do this is to chalk the string to which the plumb bob is attached and then suspend it from the top of the wall, about 20in from the corner of the wall nearest the light. (As you hang wallpaper, always work progressively away from the light, so that any imperfections or slight overlaps will cast a shadow.)

When the weighted end of the plumb bob is still, hold it against the wall and pluck the string from the wall and let it snap back to mark the line (this is much easier to do if someone helps you).

To find a true horizontal line for hanging lining paper, use the 914mm (3ft) ruler to draw chalk lines at right angles to the vertical. Check the line with a spirit level if you have one.

Cutting the paper

Unroll the wallpaper face ('right' side) upwards. Measure the length required and cut off 51-102mm (2-4in) below this (the additional amount is for easing the paper at the top and bottom). If the paper is patterned, find the first complete motif and cut off 25-51mm (1-2in) above. Measure the length, and cut off 25-51mm (1-2in) below. These extra amounts allow you to position the paper accurately, and to ease it in at the top and bottom.

Cut the next length, checking that the pattern matches exactly at the top and sides, again allowing the additional inches at top and bottom. Lay the cut lengths on top of each other. Cut 2-3 lengths before pasting. Turn the pile over, so that the 'wrong' side now faces upwards, with the first cut length on top.

Pasting the paper

Arrange the pile of paper centrally on the width of the pasting board, so that a little board shows on either side of the paper and the top edge of the paper is on your right. If the paper is longer than the board, have the overhang on your left. Push the top length only so that its far edge slightly overlaps the edge of the board (Fig.5). This is to avoid getting paste on to the board, and then on to the face of one of the other sheets.

Apply a liberal brushful of paste along the centre of the length of the paper, and brush out to the far edge. Always brush outwards, as there is a danger of paste getting on to the

face of the paper if you brush inwards. Slide the paper towards you, so that the unpasted side now slightly overlaps the near side of the board. Brush the paste from the centre to this edge.

When the length on the table has been pasted, lift both the corners on the right edge and bring them over to make a large fold (Fig.7), without creasing (the pasted sides will be facing). Gently draw the paper along the table until the unpasted portion is flush with the left-hand edge of the board. Paste this length as before and then bring this section over and down to meet the first fold (Fig.8).

As each length is pasted, place it on another table to 'rest'. This lets the paste soak in—the time depends on manufacturers' instructions—and the paper becomes supple.

Hanging the paper

Lift the first length of paper over your arm and carry it to the wall. Unfold the top half and, holding the length carefully, place the top edge in position, easing it upwards until the 25-51mm (1-2in) excess overlaps at the top. Keep the side edge exactly level with the plumb line. If the corner is vertical, ease the paper into it exactly. Otherwise let it overlap into the corner.

Smooth along the top of the piece with the paperhanger's brush to hold it in place. Now smooth down the centre and out to the sides in a series of arrowhead motions (Fig.11). This movement eliminates air bubbles, and spreads the paste evenly on the wall. Don't brush from side to side, as this could move the paper out of position. Try not to over-handle or stretch the paper. If any paste seeps out from the sides of the paper, wipe it off with a rag. Keep the paperhanger's brush completely clean, and don't let any paste get on to the 'right' side of the paper.

Check again for correct placing, then unfold the bottom section and smooth it out, brushing it as before, until the whole length is completely flat without creases or blisters. The bottom edge will overlap the skirting board.

Run the back edge of the scissors along the paper into the angle between the wall and the cornice or picture rail. Ease the top of the paper from the wall gently, and trim off the excess paper along the crease. Now repeat the procedure at the bottom, where the wall meets the skirting board. If you overlapped the paper into the corner, trim off the excess in a similar way. Smooth the paper back into position.

Hang the next pieces of paper in the same way, butting the edges together (do not overlap them) and carefully matching the pattern. Run the seam roller down the joint when the paste is nearly dry.

All you should know about glazing

Glazing repairs seem to fall into the category of 'tasks that are put off until tomorrow'—many people simply do not know where to begin. Both timber and metal framed windows are easy to repair, however, with a few techniques.

Warm weather is the time to tackle those external glazing repairs needed around the house, such as replacing cracked panes of glass, renewing crumbling old putty, and repairing leaking skylights or lean-to roofs.

Improvements can also be made, such as installing wholly or partially glazed doors in a hallway or on a landing to give better illumination to these areas. Or, you might want to insert plastic circular, cord operated, ventilators in kitchen or bathroom windows to improve ventilation and reduce condensation. Whatever your plans, warm weather is the best time to handle glass, since it may be brittle to handle in cold weather, and more apt to crack or leave jagged cutting edges.

Special considerations

Removing broken glass requires care at all times, but especially when working above ground level. If doing so, place obstructions around the area below and warn others to keep children and pets away from the area. Whenever possible remove sashes and frames and work on ground level.

Putty glazing to wooden frames

In a wooden door or window frame, the glass is held in the rebate with putty and special nails called sprigs, or occasionally with panel pins. To remove the broken glass, first loosen all putty and fixings around the outside edge, in front of the glass. A glazier's hacking knife is useful to use here or an old screwdriver and chisel. Remove panel pins or glazing sprigs, or drive them well below the wood surface with a hammer.

Now, wearing thick gloves of some sort, such as gardening gloves, remove the old pane of glass; be careful that the glass does not fall out of the rebate. Broken or loose pieces can be pried out and detached with pliers, working always from the top so that loose bits do not fall on to your hands (see Fig.6). Once this is done, clear out about 3.17mm ($\frac{1}{8}$in) of putty around and behind the glass; you should now be down to bare wood.

With the glass removed, smooth the rebate

with glasspaper, and give it a good coat of primer. Allow this to dry before proceeding —about four hours usually.

Reglazing

Begin by measuring the rebate—each side, top and bottom separately—and the two diagonals. Use a steel tape and take the measurement from the inside edge of each rebate. Deduct 1.6mm ($\frac{1}{16}$in) off each side or 3.17mm ($\frac{1}{8}$in) all round if the pane is more than .37sq m (4sq ft) to allow for glass expansion within the rebate.

Now, cut the glass. Avoid using old or

Right: Putty glazing to metal frames is basically the same as to timber frames, but there are a few small differences.

Fig.1. It is essential that all rust be removed from the rebate and the inside painted with a rust-inhibiting paint.

Fig.2. A special non-hardening mastic putty is used in metal frames. Apply it in the same way as for timber frames.

Fig.3. Metal frames require small expansion pieces fitted in the bottom of the frame rebate. Remember to allow for these when cutting the glass.

Fig.4. Special glazing clips must be fitted into holes in the sides of the frame.

Fig.5. These clips have a shape resembling a bent 'S'. They spring into place and press on to the face of the glass to hold it in place.

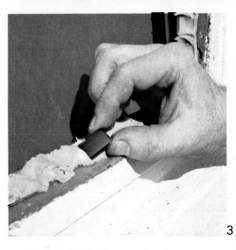

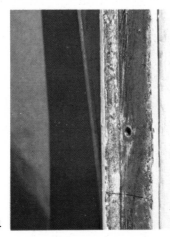

weathered glass for reglazing, as it may be brittle and difficult to cut accurately. After cutting, any sharp edges can be smoothed down with an oil-stone which has been wet with turpentine, water or oil. Once the piece is ready, mark the glass top on the outside face so that it is ready to offer up correctly into the rebate.

Roll a lump of putty in your hands until it is soft and easy to work. If the putty is too oily, wrap it first in newspaper to absorb some of the oiliness. With your thumb, lay a continuous strip of *bedding putty* about 3mm ($\frac{1}{8}$in) thick all round the back of the rebate against which the glass will be placed (see Fig.10). With sprigs or panel pins to hand, place the glass in the rebate, bottom first, leaving an equal space all round the edges and press it gently against the back putty. *Never* press from the centre. Squeeze out the surplus putty until a thickness of about 1.6mm ($\frac{1}{16}$in) remains between the back of the glass and the rebate.

To fix the glass in place, tack the sprigs or panel pins into the side of the rebate, against the face of the glass. Fix one close to each corner and space the others equally—about 150mm (6in) apart—around the pane. Use a small hammer to knock the sprigs in and keep it touching the glass as you work, so that you do not knock the glass and break it (see Fig.13). Cut off the excess back putty around the rebate with the putty knife.

A strip of weathering putty must now be placed around the outside of the pane. Knead the putty in the hands as before and lay a thick continuous strip into the angle of the rebate against the face of the glass. Lubricate the knife with water to keep the putty from sticking to it.

Hold the putty knife in one corner of the window with the blade against the rebate and the tip resting on the glass at an angle of 45°. Cut the excess putty off all round the pane in one clean stroke, so that a slope is formed to allow the rainwater to run off, and tidy the corners with a square-ended filling knife to form a mitre (see Fig.17). Finally, all the putty surfaces may be brushed over with a damp, soft brush.

After two to three weeks, the putty may be painted over, using an oil undercoat and finishing coat to match the existing paint-work. Allow the brush to run over the putty onto the face of the glass about 3mm ($\frac{1}{8}$in) to seal the join.

Putty glazing to metal frames

The procedure is the same as described for wooden sashes with three important differences:

1. A special putty for glazing to metal frames is necessary.

2. Small bits of plastic strips are needed to

Fig.6. Always protect both hands and wrists when removing old glass from a frame, and begin at the top to prevent pieces from falling on top of you.

Fig.7. Using a hammer and chisel, hack old putty down to bare wood.

Fig.8. Any odd pins or awkward pieces can be removed by using an old pair of pliers.

Fig.9. Once you have removed the putty and smoothed the rebate with glasspaper, brush out bits and pieces with an old brush.

Fig.10. Using the thumb and a ball of putty held in the palm of the hand, lay a continuous strip of bedding putty about $\frac{1}{8}$in thick round the rebate.

Fig.11. Place the glass into the rebate by pivoting it in from the bottom.

Fig.12. Press the glass pane in evenly from the sides—never from the centre.

Fig.13. When inserting glazing pins into wooden frames be sure to keep the hammer flat to the surface of the glass.

Fig.14. Once the glass is in place, trim off the excess putty on the inside of the window.

Fig.15. A thick, continuous strip of weathering putty is now needed around the outside of the pane, against the glass.

Fig.16. Lubricate the putty knife with water. Holding the blade against the rebate with the tip resting on the pane, trim away the excess putty.

Fig.17. Tidy the corners to make mitred edges for the water to run off.

set in the bottom of the rebate to allow for expansion.

3. Sprigs are not used; the glass is held in position by spring clips which look like a bent 'S'. These are hooked into the rebate and press onto the face of the glass. It is important to retain these for re-use.

Special notes

When all the glass and old putty has been removed from a metal frame, there may be rust present in the rebate. No matter how little, this must be removed and bare metal exposed with wire wool or emery paper. Treat the bare metal areas with a rust inhibitor as soon as they have been exposed and, when dry, prime the whole rebate with a metal primer. If this is not done, the ex-

6

10

14

pansion of the rust in the rebate will eventually crack the glass.

Steel windows may tend to distort and twist in shape from the effects of heat and cold. In such instances they will not shut properly and the glass will crack. Do not attempt to reglaze if this appears to be the situation, since you will first need to consult a blacksmith to straighten and square the sashes.

Some steel and aluminium windows have metal glazing beads fixed to the exterior with grub screws. Before attempting removal of a glass pane, lubricate these with a drop of penetrating oil; it will make the job much easier.

In some cases the glass in windows is still

sound, but the putty on the face has rotted away. To repair this simply chisel out all the remaining putty, rub the rebate smooth up to the glass, prime it and when dry, proceed as described in the section on applying weathering putty under **Reglazing**.

Glazing with wooden beads

Wood glazing beads may be used as a substitute for the sloping putty around the outside of a window. You will still need to use bedding putty (see above) between the glass and the rebate, but in this case it need not be quite as thick—about 2mm ($\frac{1}{16}$in) thick—as for ordinary glazing with putty.

Materials needed: Prepared softwood beading—square, splayed, quarter round, or other shape as required—panel pins 19mm-25mm ($\frac{3}{4}$in-1in), and glazing felt.

Glazing lightweight glass in small areas

Measure the top, bottom and sides of the rebate separately and then the diagonals to check that the frame is in square. Cut four lengths of beading slightly over-size for the sides, top, and bottom, and mark these accordingly. (Cutting slightly over-size will help the lengths to fit snugly when mitred.) Smooth off any roughness with glasspaper and carefully mitre the ends using a mitring block and dovetail saw. Paint the backs and mitred corners with priming paint.

Lay the beads flat. Take one and gently tap two panel pins part way into the centre of the bead width, about 25mm (1in) from the face of each mitre. When you have worked out the direction the panel pins should run in, remove them and drill the nail holes; this will prevent the wood from splitting. Continue doing this, positioning the pins at equal distances, about 150mm (6in) apart, along the length. Do the same for the remaining beads and check to see that the beads fit into the rebate. Spread bedding putty as described above, place the glass in the rebate leaving an equal expansion gap around each edge. Holding the glass firmly with the palm of the hand and pushing a side bead squarely into place with the thumb, gently tap the pins down to the face of the bead with a hammer. Do not fix the beads permanently until all four are in position. Similarly, fit the opposite side bead, then the top and finally the bottom, checking that the glass has not slipped down. With a centre punch and the hammer gently punch the heads of the pins about 16mm ($\frac{1}{16}$in) below the bead surface.

Use a square-ended filling knife to fill in these indents with putty or filler and smooth off. A final rubbing over with glasspaper and the beads are ready for priming. Finish with an undercoat and an oil-based top coat.

Glazing heavier glass in larger areas

Panel pins will usually do an adequate job of fixing the glazing beads around heavier glass over a fairly large area (especially on curved beads, such as quarter round), but a more secure job can be achieved by using either screws, or cups and screws. The cups and screws are usually made of brass or white metal, and they look especially good fixed on natural or varnished hardwood. Another interesting visual effect can be achieved by using glazing beads which are slightly raised or proud of the edge of the glazing rebate.

Any rattling of the glass in the frames from wind or vibration can be avoided by using adhesive glazing felt which has been cut to length and set into the rebate before the glass is positioned.

To fasten the glass with screws, or cups and screws, measure all the rebate sides as before, cut the beads to length, mitre and smooth them off as necessary. In the same positions as previously described for panel pins, drill clean holes through each bead. Once this has been done use the countersinking bit in the drill to countersink the holes to the size of the screw head. If the cups are used, omit the countersinking as the head of the screw is driven into and recessed inside the cup.

Spread bedding putty as before. Now, with sufficient screws, or cups and screws, to hand, place the glass in position together with a side bead held firmly in the angle of the rebate. Drill slightly, using a bradawl, into the rebate through each of the holes you have made in the bead. This will help to give the screws a good grip.

Fasten the screws, or cups and screws into these holes and proceed to drill and fix the screws into the beads along each of the remaining sides, checking the position of glass as you work. If screws without cups are used, the head should be driven well down into the countersinking and filled as described for panel pins. Smooth and paint as before.

Repairs to lean-to roof glazing

Lean-to roofs glazed into a timber frame-

work are apt to cause some trouble. The timber frequently warps, and the putty dries out and shrinks, permitting water to enter tiny crevices. Eventually, this water leaves unsightly stains all along the wooden frame. Cracking of the glass is also quite common, and leaks may occur between the roof and the main wall of the house, even though a strip of lead, zinc or felt called a 'flashing' is positioned there to form a weather-tight joint.

If the timber frame has warped, it may be the cause of any cracked glass. In this case you will need entirely new frames before you can do any reglazing. The techniques for reglazing are described in **glazing to wooden frames.**

To repair water leaks, first wash off the roof surface and allow it to dry thoroughly. Apply some self-adhesive proprietary glazing tape, such as Sylglas, as directed onto the glazing bars. Press it firmly in place to exclude all air bubbles and extend the tape over the putty onto the glass; allow the ends to lap the frame by at least 25mm (1in). Continue taping around the frame in the same way. There is no need to use new putty if you are using the glazing tape.

Cover the flashing well with at least two coats of cold bitumastic to stop any leaks between the roof and the main wall of the house.

Let the sunshine in

Glass is one of the most versatile building materials. Modern glass production offers a wide range of glass for glazing purposes, both plain and decorative, which are relatively inexpensive, and easy to obtain.

Simple glazing techniques requiring the use of few tools are quite simple to learn, and when coupled with a basic knowledge of the different types of glass and their uses, will enable you to use glass to its best advantage in decorating.

Special considerations

All building materials are to some extent controlled by building regulations and local by-laws. In new building works and where any alteration is carried out, the size and the type of glass and its position in the building may have to be considered with regard to fire resistance, heat and sound transmission. If in doubt, consult the local building authority.

Choosing the glass

The thickness of the type of glass required is always related to the size of the sheet, and to the degree of exposure to wind and consequent suction loads on the surface. Manufacturers produce readily available tables which give the correct weight and thickness of glass to be used for particular purposes. Most glass used for domestic glazing in Britain is 4mm ($\frac{1}{8}$in) thick.

The glazing quality of the glass you are using is also an important consideration to make. Sheet glass has three grades: OQ-Ordinary Quality; SQ-Selected Quality; SSQ-Special Selected Quality. For general

glazing purposes, the OQ grade is suitable.

Types of glass

Sheet glass

Use for normal glazing work, this is a clear, drawn glass. Since the opposite sides of a pane are never perfectly flat, and parallel, some degree of distortion is inevitable.

Sheet glass is commonly used for domestic glazing and is available in thicknesses from 3mm (just under $\frac{1}{8}$in) to 6mm ($\frac{1}{4}$in).

Float glass

This type of glass is made by floating molten glass on a bed of molten tin. Such a process produces a glass similar to plate glass, but its higher quality dispenses with the need for additional polishing and so it has generally superseded plate glass.

Float glass comes in thicknesses from 5mm ($\frac{3}{16}$in) to 25mm (1in). As this glass is quite free from distortion and is strong, it is often used for domestic purposes, especially for large picture windows and table tops.

Float glass is also produced in plain or tinted decorative forms, by using various processes including acid etching, electro-float and sandblasting. Additional decorative effects are obtained by the introduction of certain materials into the molten glass mix to alter its light and heat transmission qualities.

Mirrors are also made from float glass of the SQ grade, which has been moisture-proofed, silvered and edged in a variety of ways by machine and hand grinding.

Patterned glass

This range includes glasses with several different decorative finishes which are frequently used for 'modesty' purposes in

Fig.1. Stack glass at a shallow angle against a wall with protection at the sides and bottom.

Fig.2. The proper method for one person to carry a sheet of glass—note the protective gloves.

Fig.3. To cut a straight piece, check to see that the glass edge is true with a T-square.

Fig.4. Mark out cutting measurements with a crayon, felt-tipped pen or chinagraph.

Fig.5. Cut glass with even-pressured strokes and always protect the wrists.

Fig.6. Use the cutter as a fulcrum or place a batten beneath the cut and press down to break.

Fig.7. Find the centre point of a circle by marking out diagonals on the area to be used.

Fig.8. Use a radius cutter with a central suction cup to mark out the circumference.

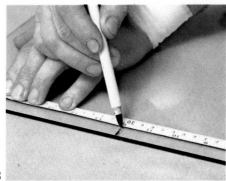

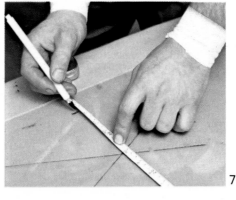

bathrooms and toilets. They are specially designed to allow light through while obscuring vision. One typical example is rough-cast glass, which is smooth on one side and obscured on the other.

These glasses, which are usually produced by passing liquid molten glass through rollers, are available in a variety of styles such as *arctic, cotswold, reeded, autumn, flemish* and *patchwork*, in either plain or tinted versions. The degree of transparency and light diffusion desired will largely determine the type to be used. Thicknesses generally are between 3mm ($\frac{1}{8}$in) and 5mm ($\frac{3}{16}$in).

Wired glass

This glass has a metal mesh embedded into it to reduce the risk of injury from falling bits of glass. It is also accepted as a fire retarding material. The mesh may be of a square (Georgian) or diamond pattern.

This type of glass is often used in porches and garage roofs where breakages may occur, because the wire mesh helps to hold the glass together if it is broken.

If you intend to re-use this glass, you may find it difficult to cut, and for this reason it is advisable to buy it already cut to size from a merchant. Wired glass is available in 6mm ($\frac{1}{4}$in) thickness only.

Toughened glass

Float, sheet and even some patterned glasses can be toughened by a special process which can increase the strength of the glass by four or five times. Is particularly suitable to use for doors and similar areas where there is a danger of impact, since it shatters into granules instead of sharp splinters if it is broken.

Profilit glass is a strong, translucent glass used mainly outdoors for carports and the like, although it can be used indoors.

Solar control glass reduces the transmission of heat, light and glare from sunlight. It comes in a range of colours in float, laminated, rough-cast and patterned form.

Diffuse reflection glass, commonly known as non-reflective glass, is coated on one side to reduce the amount of light reflection and thus improve viewing. It is frequently used for picture framing.

Handling glass

As long as correct methods are followed and care is exercised, glass can be handled quite safely. Experts recommend that gloves should be worn when handling glass, but they should not be too stiff, since it is necessary to be able to feel the glass to handle it with complete safety. You may also use folded newspaper or 'rubbers', such as pieces of old inner tube, as improvised 'laps' when carrying glass. Wrist bands are a further recommendation.

Always handle the glass gently but firmly; never grip it tightly. To reduce the danger of breakage, carry glass vertically and never carry it balanced on your head. When negotiating sharp corners or winding staircases, be sure to allow plenty of room for the glass trailing behind you.

When stacking glass, place it on lengths of timber which have been laid over a flat surface, and rest it at a shallow angle against a wall—25° is about right. Cushion it with newspapers or rugs and be sure that it is not kept in a place where it might be knocked over by wind.

Carrying glass sheets

One person: Small sheets may simply be tucked under the arm so that the lower edge is supported in the protected hand. Larger sheets may be carried as follows: position the centre of the bottom edge of the sheet of glass in one hand. Rest the upper portion of the sheet against the forearm and shoulder and hold the top edge of the leading sheet with the other hand.

Two people: Large sheets can be carried as follows: The person in front should adopt the same position as described above for one person carrying a large sheet. The person at the rear should then support the glass with one hand cupped around the lower corner holding the bottom edge, and rest the back edge into his shoulder. The top edge is held with the other hand. The two people must be careful to walk in step at a slow pace, taking special care at changes of level and when turning corners.

While glass can be carried up ladders—supported by a second person for large sheets— this should be avoided as it can be extremely hazardous in the event of a strong gust of wind. If repairing a broken window pane, it is much easier and safer to reglaze it by removing the sash and doing all the reglazing at ground level. If this is not possible to do, always work on ladders with a helpmate, never alone.

Transporting glass

Glass sheets can normally be transported quite safely in a car. Small panes should be laid flat on a rear seat over a blanket. Turn the edges of the blanket just over the glass sheet, but do not cover the glass entirely—keeping it fully visible will help to prevent accidental damage. Glass carried in the boot of a car should also be wrapped in a blanket for protection. If you are carrying two or more sheets of glass, interleave them with paper or cloth.

Larger panes can be carried on a roof rack. They should be supported on a piece of blockboard at least 19mm (¾in) thick and then covered over with a blanket. Lash the glass and the blockboard firmly to the roof rack.

Measuring and marking glass

Always double-check your measurements before cutting glass. If fitting glass for a door or window rebate, do not assume that the frames are square. Measure each side of the rebate and the top and bottom separately, noting any discrepancies between opposite sides. Deduct 2mm (³₃₂in) from each of four

9

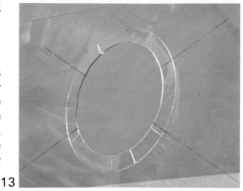

13

Fig.9. Tap the glass gently around the circumference to loosen and spread the cut.

Fig.10. Cut a safety circle about ¾in (19mm) in from the outside circle.

Fig.11. Cross-hatch the centre of the innermost circle for ease in breaking out.

Fig.12. The centre can now be broken out into a receptacle by tapping with the glass cutter.

Fig.13. The inner circle has been removed and the safety ring is cross-marked for removal.

Fig.14. Remove this safety ring by gently pulling out pieces with a pair of pliers.

Fig.15. Rough edges on the finished piece can be smoothed with a wet Carborundum stone.

Fig.16. To find the precise point for drilling, cross-measure from the outer edges of the glass.

Fig.17. Use a spear-point bit to make a small indentation for the drill at the cross mark.

Fig.18. Build a small ring of putty around the indentation to contain the lubricant.

Fig.19. Fill the ring with lubricant and drill the hole at slow speed—here with a handbrace.

Fig.20. Just before the hole breaks through the glass, stop for a moment and clean away loose bits.

Fig.21. Finish by arrising the edges with a medium and then a fine Carborundum stone.

Fig.22. To cut a circle out of glass, use a radius cutter set at the appropriate distance.

17

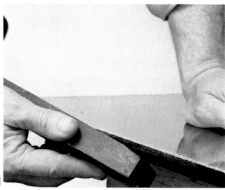

21

Fig.23. Spread the cut by pulling gently with a pair of pliers around the circumference.

Fig.24. After using the pliers, tap along the underside of the cut with the straight cutter.

Fig.25. Work around the circle making safety cuts at each corner. Do not cross the circle.

Fig.26. Tap again to loosen and spread. The piece should come cleanly away.

Fig.27. Continue working around the entire circle until you have removed all the outer pieces.

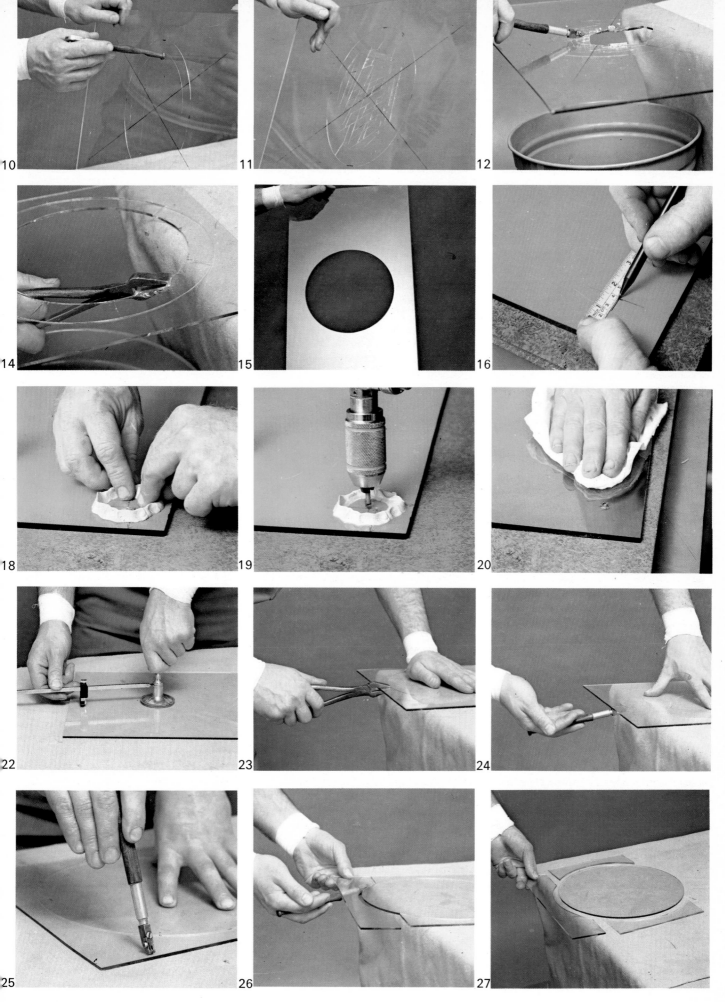

dimensions—i.e., 4mm ($\frac{5}{32}$in) these from the total length and the total width—to find the correct cutting size. This will allow for any possible expansion of the glass in the window frame.

Preparations for cutting

Great care is needed when cutting glass. Professional glass cutters wear protective wrist bands, since a splinter of glass could cause serious injury. It is advisable, then, either to wear wristbands or to wrap your wrists with household bandages or something of the sort before cutting glass.

You will also need a large, flat surface to lay the glass on, such as a kitchen or dining table. Place the blanket on the table to protect it and the surface of the glass from being scratched.

Where odd shapes must be cut, always make a template first from a stiff card, carefully checking its accuracy. Be sure to make this 3.2mm ($\frac{1}{8}$in) smaller all round than your measurements to allow for the distance between the edge of the cutter and the cutting wheel.

A steel wheel glass cutter is adequate for nearly all types of glass cutting and is also much cheaper to buy than the traditional glass cutter's diamond. Try to choose a cutter on which the wheel is clearly visible while the tool is in use, as this will promote greater accuracy.

If you anticipate doing a large amount of cutting, you may find it useful to buy a good T-square to guide the cutter through the stroke. You will also need a ruler or steel tape for measuring. To mark the glass, a felt-tipped pen, chinagraph pencil or crayon can be used.

Straight cutting

Before doing any cutting, clean the surface of the glass by wiping it with a proprietary glass cleaner, such as Windolene, or with some methylated spirits. Mark the cutting lines on the surface and *re-check the dimensions before cutting*.

Lubricate the glass cutter beforehand by wiping it over a piece of felt which has been soaked in light machine oil. Hold the cutter so that the handle rests between the first and second fingers and the bottom of the hand remains clear of the glass. With a straight edge held 3.2mm ($\frac{1}{8}$in) from the marking line (to allow for the thickness of the wheel), score the surface of the glass along the line with the cutter. Cut with a firm, smooth stroke, drawing your arm back while keeping the rest of your body still. Do not backtrack, as the glass may break at a point other than where you want on your cutting line.

The scoring should be completed in one operation—the object being to score the

surface of the glass evenly so that the piece can be easily snapped apart. Once the score mark is made, lift the glass and tap it gently from underneath along the length of the mark. Then position the edge of a small batten, about 50mm (2in) wide, directly under the cutting line. Place your hands on the glass surface, one on either side of the line and as close to it as possible, and press down slowly and firmly with your fingertips until you get a clean break along the cutting line.

Where you need to remove small strips or pieces of glass, score the line as before and then, using the jaws of a pair of pliers, break off the waste pieces in small bits. Do not use the notches along the outside of the cutting wheel for breaking off small segments of glass—they are intended only to be used as gauges.

Curves and angles can also be cut by scoring the glass to the shapes required from cardboard templates. Once the glass has been scored to the shape, tap it carefully from the underside and then, gripping the piece firmly on each side of the score marks, snap evenly downwards to break the glass.

Cutting circles

A special instrument called a *radius cutter* is needed to cut accurate circles in glass. This cutter is best used with the glass resting on a flat surface, although it can be used on a window which is already in position. It consists of a cutting wheel mounted on an adjustable arm which revolves on a central pivot fastened to a suction cup.

The first step in cutting out a circle is to find the centre point by marking diagonals on the piece from corner to corner. If the circle is not to be in the centre of the sheet, mark out a rectangular area where it will be and work accordingly within this area. Do this with a felt-tipped pen or crayon and then measure off the exact radius of the circle to be cut along one diagonal, beginning from the point where the diagonals cross.

Fix the suction pad of the cutter on this central point where the diagonals meet and set the arm so that the cutting edge just reaches the length of the radius. Now scribe the circle, holding the cutter firmly and applying even pressure all around. Once this is completed, move the cutting edge in about 19mm ($\frac{3}{4}$in) and scribe a second circle—this is known as a safety circle because it helps keep the edges of the glass from splintering and cutting your fingers.

Using the metal tip of an ordinary glass cutter, tap the underside of the glass upwards towards the cuts. Work slowly and carefully around both circles—the object of doing this is to open up the cuts so that the eventual removal of the waste glass is both clean and neat, without any splintered edges.

With the ordinary glass cutter, divide the safety circle into wedge sections. Cross-hatch these wedges and use the head of the cutter to tap out a small piece of glass from underneath. Carefully break out the glass in the safety circle with a pair of pliers.

Finally, tackle the outer circle. This should first be marked with a series of scores at about 25mm (1in) intervals, but take care not to mark the glass beyond the outer circle. Break out these pieces with pliers.

Drilling glass

Normally, the only type of glass you will need to drill will be mirror glass in order to provide holes for the fixings. Special bits, made expressly for the purpose of drilling glass, should be used with a hand drill or brace. Power drills are generally not suitable (unless fitted with a speed reducer) because the speed should not exceed 350 revolutions per minute.

First, lay the glass on an absolutely flat surface. Mark the drilling position by pressing the tip of the bit on to the glass. This is to fracture the surface which will, to some extent, prevent the bit from wandering while drilling. Remember to start on the *non-reflective* side to prevent damaging the silvering. Lubricate the end of the bit with turpentine and begin drilling, keeping the drill at right angles to the surface. Do not use too much downward pressure as this will break the glass. The powdered glass thrown up by the bit will turn the turpentine white and, when this happens, more turpentine should be added. A useful tip is to make a small 'well' around the drill hole with a ring of putty to contain the lubricant.

Proceed carefully as the bit nears the other side, but do not stop turning or you will run the risk of splintering the glass around the edge and ruining the piece.

Removing rough edges

After the drilling has been completed, any rough edges can be smoothed away using two Carborundum stones—a No. 121 fine and a No. 122 medium. You will also need a natural pumice stone, some pumice powder and a wood block. Both the Carborundum and the pumice should be kept wet at all times when being used.

The first stage, called 'arrising', removes the sharp edge. Use the medium stone for this, holding it at an angle of 45°, and rubbing it downward in one direction. Once the edges have been arrised, the flat part of the edge can be ground with the face of the medium stone. Rub it up and down, keeping it in contact with the glass at all times. Follow this with the fine stone to produce a sheen. Basic polishing can now be done with the pumice stone.

Ideas with mirrors

Without a looking glass a room is only half alive. From great sheets of glass that cover a whole wall to the tiny little Victorian nonsenses, framed in shells, that you sometimes come across in junk shops, they all have a part to play in adding a touch of glamour to a room. Mirrors are space-makers that are able to give the illusion of added dimension; decorators and reflectors of light; objects of light and beauty when properly used—but capable of appearing as ugly holes in the wall when their function is misunderstood or abused.

Mirrors as space-makers

Mirrors create space through illusion, by deluding you into believing that where you know there is a wall there is space. Properly used, these slabs of mirror make you feel that you could walk straight through them into an unexplored dimension.

To do this successfully the mirror has to be placed where, structurally, if there were no wall, you *could* walk on. It is no good putting one beside a window which looks out over the garden. The mirror will reflect the room and, since the eye is no fool, it will do a double-take when it sees garden and room in the same dimension. For a moment you will be surprised, then you will realise the deception. But, placed on an inner wall where you could expect more rooms beyond, a mirror

Above: A wall of sliding doors covered with mirror glass creates an illusion of extra light and space in this bedroom.

177

will have a quite different effect.

These deceivers should be used so that there is a reason for their end and their beginning. For maximum impact, they should begin at the floor (not at the skirting, because the floor should appear to run right into them), reach up to the ceiling and to the end of the wall on both sides. If you do not want a mirror that wide, or if it does not reach from wall to wall, you must provide a reason for its not doing so.

One way is to set the mirror into panels that cover the rest of the wall. These panels can either be made of wood or be papered to match the rest of the room. Another way is to curtain the rest of the wall, hanging the curtains on rings suspended on brass poles fixed at ceiling height. Both of these effects make the mirror appear to be an integral part of the wall, not an afterthought added at random. A large framed mirror will also

be infinitely more satisfactory than fixing a plain sheet of glass to the wall. The framed image is very much more telling than that which, for no apparent reason, suddenly stops with the edge of the glass. You are dealing with illusions, remember.

Line the alcoves on both sides of a fireplace with mirrors, from floor to ceiling and wall to wall, then—providing that you arrange your possessions so as to give a satisfying reflection—you will feel that you can walk straight past the chimney breast into the space beyond. Or, if your living room seems to come to an abrupt end in a hard-looking wall, try putting a slab of glass in the middle of the offending wall. Set it in panels, or curtain up to its edges, possibly adding a swag or two of the material over the top, rearrange the furniture until the reflection pleases you, and your blank wall will disappear. This is a good treatment for

Below: The use of mirror glass along one wall of this dark, narrow hall makes it look brighter and wider.

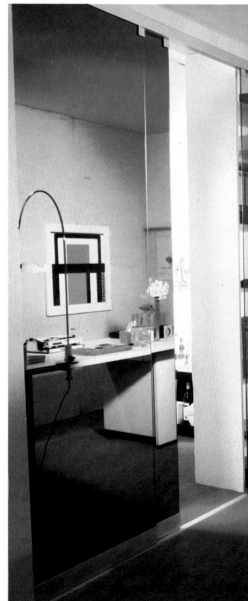

a dead-end wall at the end of a hall.

But if you do feel like covering one whole wall of your living room with mirror glass—and this can be most effective—it is really better that it should be the wall *behind* the sitting area rather than the one *facing* it. It can be very distracting to have to watch your own reflected antics for an entire evening.

Experiments

The bathroom, or a tiny cloakroom without a window, are perfect arenas for more adventurous experiments with mirrors. Try lining all the walls of the bathroom with them (forget what was said earlier about window walls—the eye will be far too busy staggering about in infinity to worry about that) and mirror the ceiling as well. As long as there is something worth reflecting, you can transform a dull room into a fascinating kaleidoscope of images.

Do not be put off by the bathroom fitments. There is nothing intrinsically ugly about a lavatory or bidet. The shapes, as shapes, are quite pleasing aesthetically, but familiarity has bred contempt. An attractive floor covering of either carpet or tiles, decorative jars or plants and pretty towels will add to the reflection.

Or, if you feel that this is overdoing it, a sheet of mirror over the vanitory unit will create light and space as well as look good. Fix it hard up against the walls and to the top of the unit, and then try another on the wall behind you.

Mirrors as reflectors of light

Mirrors can be invaluable in helping to lighten and brighten dark corners or even whole rooms. Two mirrors placed opposite

Centre: Smoked mirror glass on sliding doors gives a subdued reflection in this study, and the smoked glass partition enclosing bookshelves adds to the illusion of space.

Below: A circular skylight above a landing lightens the whole stairwall.

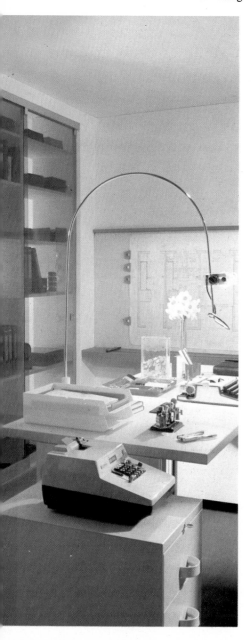

Right (*top to bottom*): *Coloured, frosted, or etched glass can be used effectively in bathrooms—either to hide an ugly view or just for decoration.*

each other, butting up to the window wall, for example, will give a room the illusion of greater width and will also make it lighter, by 'bouncing' the light further back into it. This is a very good way of brightening up a long, narrow bedroom, or any dark, confined areas such as a hall.

If you panel the sides of a dormer window, in an attic, for instance, with mirror glass, the natural light will be greatly increased by reflection. Lining the whole deep reveal of a window with mirror glass will have a similar effect.

A little cubby-hole of a room, say a cloak-room, or any dark place with a hopelessly inadequate window, will be transformed if you cover the ceiling with mirror glass and let it reflect light from strip or spot lights.

Why use glass mirrors?

Glass, lovely as it is, is dangerous stuff to work with, as well as being very heavy. But you need not use glass at all. Silvered acrylic sheeting comes in sheets of up to 2.4m × 1.2m (8ft × 4ft), the mirrored reflection is undistorted, it is half the weight of glass, and it is practically unbreakable. It can be cut with an ordinary saw and fixed with screws or with a special sticky tape. It comes in fifteen colours, including colourless and some stunning brownish colours. It is also almost immune to condensation. This seems the ideal material for a mirrored door that saves so much space in a tiny bedroom. There is even a specially toughened grade that is bullet-proof; hardly necessary in most homes, but it should be able to withstand the rough treatment reserved for nursery walls.

There is a semi-rigid pvc sheeting which can be stuck on flat surfaces to produce a fairly good image. This might be used on ceilings, as it is light and easy to handle. It can also be stuck to curved surfaces, when it produces those fascinating distortions usually only to be found in fairgrounds. A mirrored material made of very strong tery-lene treated with a special reflecting product is also available. It is stretched on an alu-minium frame over a resilient backing board. The result is a gleaming, perfect mirror surface that is unbreakable in the way that glass is breakable. It is, however, easily punctured or cut, therefore its use should be limited to situations where this is not likely to occur. This material is ideal for ceilings; its virtues for that purpose being its extreme lightness and the fact that it is immune to condensation. It is easily fixed by means of impact fabric pads (such as Velcro). It comes in 15 standard sizes, or specials up to 1.2m (4ft) wide can be made to order. It is impervious to heat from lights, and apertures to take ceiling lights can be cut into specials.

Plastering

Repairing cracked plaster sometimes turns into a much bigger job than expected: you find a whole wall that needs replacing.

Plastering a complete wall or ceiling is a fairly ambitious job and some skill is required to produce a true, flat surface. If you doubt your ability, it would be a good idea to experiment first on a suitable 'hidden' surface like a garage wall or ceiling.

Plastering a wall

It is unlikely that your wall will be perfectly flat and upright, so the first job is to find the high spots and determine whether or not the wall is out of true. To do this, hold a spirit level on the back of a long straight-edged rule and move it systematically over the wall.

Once you have prepared your surface, taking particular care to ensure that it has a good key, mix your mortar floating coat and start to lay 'screeds' on the wall. These are strips of plaster about 200mm (8in) wide which act as depth guides. They also break up the wall surface into easily manageable sections (see Fig. 7).

With the steel laying trowel, lay the first screed a little over 13mm ($\frac{1}{2}$in) deep, from the floor to the ceiling on one side of the wall. Take it right up to the end of the wall. If this is a reveal corner, and you are using a length of angle bead to make a neat edge, place the bead in position *before* you lay the screed. If you are using the more traditional method, leave the reveal until you have floated the whole wall.

When you have laid the first strip, use a straight-edged rule about 1.8m (6ft) long to rule it off. Hold the rule vertically and move it gently up and down from the outer edge of the screed inwards. Test for plumb with the straight edge and spirit level, and adjust, if necessary, with a little more careful ruling. Add more mortar if required. The ruling should reduce the thickness to about 13mm ($\frac{1}{2}$in) if the surface is good. A screed similar to the first one should then be laid on the other end of the wall. You should lay a minimum of two vertical screeds although, for ruling off later, it will help you to lay additional screeds at about 1.5m (5ft) intervals.

Now lay a horizontal screed about 50mm (2in) from the floor to join the vertical ones. Use the latter as guides when ruling off this screed. Another horizontal band should now be laid about 1.5m (5ft) from the floor and ruled in the same way. The final screed should be laid across the top of the wall, flush with the ceiling, and ruled. The screeds should now be smoothed with the wood float.

The sections between the screeds are then to be filled in flush. Deal with one section at a time and apply the floating mortar with the laying trowel. Rule off each section using the screeds as guides. Fill and re-rule if necessary. (The 50mm (2in) strip at the bottom of the wall can be left if skirting board is to be used).

When the whole wall is covered, clean the internal angles with the laying trowel, and wash down any adjacent surfaces smeared with mortar. Finally, go over the entire surface with the devil float to flatten any small bumps and to key the surface.

If you are using a sanded floating mix, allow it to dry for 24 hours; a lightweight plaster will take about four hours.

If you are using the traditional method, any reveals in the wall should now be plastered with both the floating and the setting coat.

Before applying the finish plaster, it is wise to test the surface for suction. Brush water on to a small section of the wall and watch what happens. If it is 'sucked' straight through, there is excessive suction. As this can have a disastrous effect by weakening the final coat, it will have to be remedied. Throughly dampening the wall will be sufficient in many cases, but if the suction persists, brush on a weak mixture of water and pva bonder—one part bonder to six parts water is about right—and follow up immediately with the setting coat.

When you are ready to apply the setting coat, mix up some finish plaster in a bucket and pour it on the spot board. Then clean out the bucket and fill it with clean water so that it is ready for another mix. Start to skim on the plaster with the laying trowel. First skim a band, about a trowel width, along the top. Then skim over the whole wall in vertical strips, up to the band already laid. When the wall is covered, use the wood float to put on another thin application, again with vertical strokes. Work systematically from the left to the right (if you are right handed) and keep the seams well pressed down.

Now, still using the wood float, put on another thin application, but this time use horizontal strokes. At this point use the feather-edged rule to rule out the internal angles. Any seams still visible should be smoothed over with the wood float. If you are using an anhydrous plaster such as Sirapite, a little water will help for this, but do *not* use any at this stage if it is a hemi-hydrate.

The final application of finish plaster should now be put on the wall. Use the steel trowel and lay a 'tight', or firm, coat with long vertical strokes. Then wash the trowel and sprinkle a *little* water over the plaster. Quickly follow up with the trowel and smooth over the whole area. Use the angle trowel to finish the internal angles and, finally, scrape any unwanted plaster off the floors, adjoining walls and the ceiling before it sets.

Plastering ceilings

Solid ceilings are plastered in basically the same manner as walls. Solid ceilings are rare, however, and either plasterboard or some form of lath is usually fixed to the ceiling joists before plastering.

Plasterboarding ceilings

Plasterboard consists of a gypsum core sandwiched between paper liners. Various types are designed to take plaster, and it is advisable to read the manufacturer's instructions regarding fixing and plastering before you start work as there can be small variations to the instructions given below. Most plasterboards, however, have square edges and these need 'scrimming', or reinforcing, after the boards are placed in position. Most can also be plastered with one 'thick' (about 5mm [$\frac{1}{16}$in]) coat of finish plaster. The plaster *must* be a hemi-hydrate.

Various sizes of boards are available and it is sometimes useful to obtain a variety to minimize wastage. But as it is easy to cut, one of the standard sizes, say 1.2m x 2.4m (4ft x 8ft) is a convenient size to work with. Plasterboards also come in two thicknesses 9.5mm and 12.7mm ($\frac{3}{8}$in and $\frac{1}{2}$in). The first is suitable for most situations, but where the distance between the centres of the ceiling joists exceeds about 350mm (18in), the latter should be used.

Some ceilings are very uneven and it may be necessary to counter batten them to provide a new level surface on which to nail the plasterboards. The first battens are nailed at any convenient spacing and are used to form fixing points for a second set of battens which are then fixed ar right-angles to the first ones.

This second set of battens are fixed at centres to suit the width of the plasterboard and they are levelled by driving thin wooden

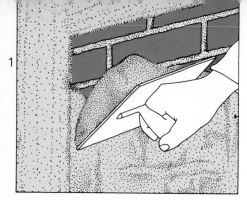

1

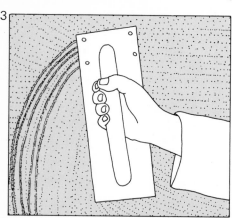

2

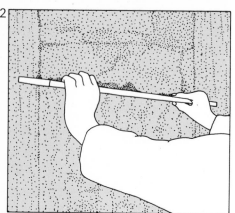

3

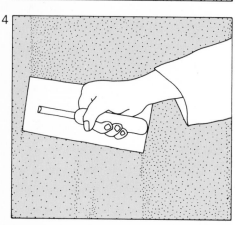

4

5

6

packing pieces between the battens where necessary.

The ends of the boards can be butted up to the walls or the plaster can be chipped away so that the boards can go right up to the brickwork. In the former method jute scrim is applied to the angle to reinforce the plaster.

When fixing the plasterboards to the joists do not use ordinary galvanized clout-head nails as these large, flat heads cut the paper covering of the boards. Use only the proper plasterboard nails which have a slight bevel underneath the head rather like a counter-sunk screw head. These small-headed galvanized nails should be 30mm (1¼in) long for 9mm (⅜in) thick boards and 40mm (1½in) long for the 12.5mm (½in) boards. Place the nails 12.5mm (½in) from the edge and at 150mm (6in) centres.

Fixing to the ceiling

Plasterboards over which you intend to plaster can normally be nailed either across or along the joists. For large areas it is often desirable to position them in both directions so that long joins, which may cause cracking, are avoided wherever possible. It is particularly important to ensure that the joints are adequately nailed to the joists. You should leave an 3mm (⅛in) gap between the boards for scrimming.

Before starting work, it is a good idea to draw a plan of the ceiling and work out roughly how your boards will be placed. This will help you to arrange them to minimize cutting, and also to ensure that they are sufficiently staggered.

If you are working alone you will need the help of a 'dead man's hand' in addition to the normal tools and working platform. This is simply a long piece of straight-edged wood, about 50mm x 25mm (2in x 1in) to which is fastened a cross piece about 600mm (2ft) wide. The bottom of the batten rests on the floor and the cross piece is wedged against the plasterboard to hold it in position. Your hands are then free to nail the board to the joists.

The easiest way to cut plasterboard is to score the face side deeply with a knife along a straight edge and then lay the board, with the cut side uppermost, over the edge of a

Fig. 1: Filling in between the screeds using a steel trowel to apply the mortar.

Fig. 2: As each section is filled in it is levelled off with the straightedge using the screeds as a guide.

Fig. 3: The surface is then smoothed and scratched with a devil float which has nails protruding to scratch the plaster and form a key for the next coat.

Fig. 4: Finish plaster is applied to the wall in vertical strokes.

Fig. 5: Final smoothing is done with the steel trowel and a little water applied by a brush.

Fig. 6: A special angle-trowel can be used to finish off the corners of the wall.

Fig. 7: Horizontal and vertical, plumbed screeds, act as depth guides and divide the wall into manageable sections.

Fig. 8: The doorframe is wider than a partition wall and the plaster finishes flush with the woodwork. the joint may then be covered with an architrave moulding.

Fig. 9: Plaster is finished at an external angle by fixing a temporary batten up the reveal allowing it to project to the thickness of the plaster required. When one wall has been plastered, the batten is taken off and fixed to the plastered side so that it projects over the reveal. It is then used as a guide for plastering around the reveal.

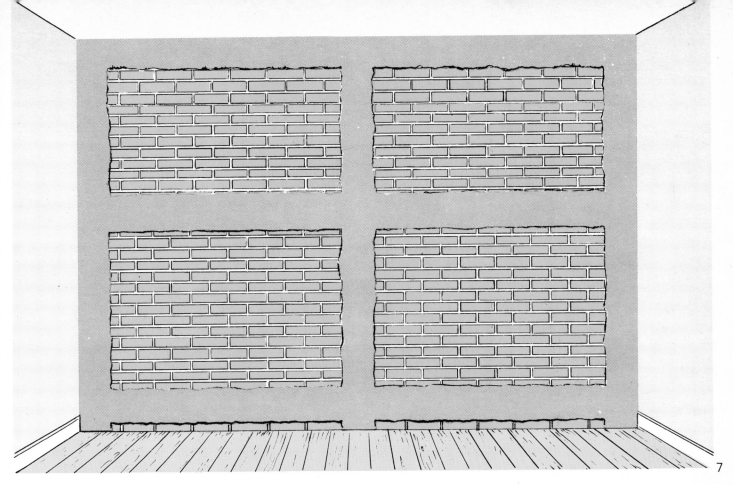

7

table or bench so that the cut is in line with the edge. Snap the core by pressing down sharply, turn the board over and cut the paper on the other side along the crease. Alternatively, you can use an old saw, but this is slower and more tedious.

Scrimming

Before plastering, the joints are reinforced with 90mm (3½in) wide jute scrim which is fixed in position with finish plaster. (A cotton scrim is available, but it is designed for use only with boards that do not carry a coat of plaster). First cut the scrim to the required lengths and then mix up a small quantity of finish plaster—about half a bucketful for an average ceiling—and place it on the spot board. Transfer some to the hawk and spread a little along one of the

joints with the laying-on trowel, making sure the plaster is pressed into the gap. Place one end of the scrim at the beginning of the joint. Guide the scrim with one hand and press it firmly into the plaster with the trowel, keeping the centre of the scrim over the gap. Do the same with all the joints, leaving the edges of the ceiling until last.

When the scrimming is completed, start to lay the finish coat. Treat each section separately, and use the steel trowel to skim on a thin application up to, but not over, the

scrimmed joints. Follow up with further applications with the wood float, now covering the entire ceiling surface until the plaster is at least 5mm ($\frac{3}{16}$in) thick. Firmly lay on a little more fresh plaster with the steel trowel, filling in where necessary. Use the gauging trowel to fill in the strip between wall and ceiling if required, and smooth with the steel trowel.

Finally, smooth over the entire ceiling with a clean trowel, using water sparingly. Once the surface is finished, smooth the corners

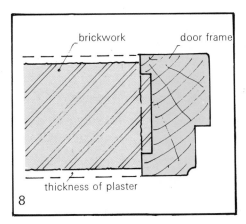

8

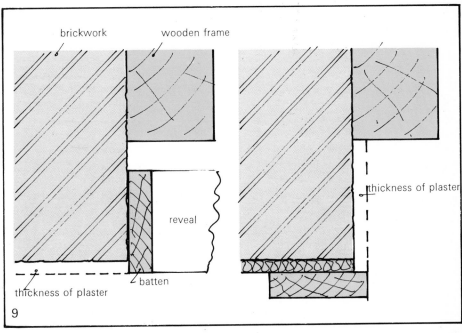

9

Fig. 10: Cutting plasterboard.
A score a line with a knife
B break the board along the line by bending it over a batten or the edge of a table, like breaking glass.
C The board can also be cut using an old saw.
D A bottle or other round object can be used for drawing round holes which can be cut out with a padsaw.
E Rough edges can be smoothed with a piece of sandpaper and a wooden block.

Fig. 11: Dry lining: fixing plasterboards to brickwork using dabs of plaster as adhesive.

Fig. 12: Dry lining method 2: Fixing plasterboards to wooden battens using adhesive.

Fig. 13: When dry lining using method 2: the spaces between the battens can be filled with insulation material.

Fig. 10

between wall and ceiling with the angle trowel.

While you are plastering bear in mind that a hemi-hydrate plaster sets rather rapidly, so you will have to work quickly.

Lathing ceilings

Lath can be used as an alternative to plasterboard as a base for ceiling plaster. Various types are available, but the most common are 'expanded metal lath' and 'K-lath'. Wood lath has largely been replaced by these.

Expanded metal lath is a metal diamond-shaped mesh which is fixed in position with galvanised clout nails or staples. It comes in 2.7m × 600mm (9ft × 2ft) sheets and can be cut with tin snips. When fixing to the joists, stagger the sheets to avoid long joins, and overlap each about 13mm (½in). Wire any unsupported joins with galvanized wire at frequent intervals.

K-lath consists of a mixture of metal wire and paper. It is also cut with snips and fixed with galvanized nails or staples.

Wood lath is made up of strips of timber about 1.2m × 25mm × 6mm (4ft × 1in × ¼in). The strips should be nailed about 6mm (¼in) apart *across* the joists, and the joints should be staggered wherever possible.

Plastering on lath

Before the normal floating and setting coat, a 'rendering' coat has to be applied directly to the lath. If you are using a light-weight finish coat, a plaster such as Carlite Metal Lath should be used. If using this plaster, however, you *must* use the same material for the floating coat.

Using a sanded mix is more complicated, but it does enable you to use a slower-setting finish plaster, such as Sirapite.

To mix a sanded rendering coat, first prepare a lime mortar by mixing three parts of sand and one part of lime with water (use a bucket as a measure). Hair, or a special nylon fibre made for the purpose, should be added to this mix to strengthen the finish mortar. As a guide, if you have used three bucketsful of sand and one of lime, mix in about one handful of hair or fibre. Allow this mix to stand for about 24 hours, then mix six parts of it to one part Portland cement (you can use plaster of paris instead of cement if mixing a small amount). Add water, but only enough to make the mix fairly stiff.

When applying the rendering coat, press it on firmly with the laying trowel so that the plaster firmly 'keys' with the lath. If you are plastering over wood lath always apply the plaster in the direction of the joists, so that you plaster *across* the 'run' of the lath.

Once the lath has been covered to a depth of about 6mm (¼in), key the surface well and leave it to set.

Now mix your floating coat and lay screeds around the edges of the ceiling with the laying trowel. Rule them in with the feather-edged rule. Divide the ceiling into manageable sections with further screeds if required. Then proceed to fill in the sections and rule them flush with the screeds. Smooth over and key the surface with the devil float, and clean out the corners with the laying trowel.

When dry, skim on a thin layer of finish plaster with the steel trowel. Go around the edges first and then apply strips from one side to the other. Follow up with the wood float, using strokes in the same direction. Then put on another layer, this time crossing the previous strips at right angles. With the steel trowel, lay on a final coat and then smooth all over. Clean out the corners where the ceiling meets the walls with the angle trowel and, finally, wash down adjacent plasterwork if required.

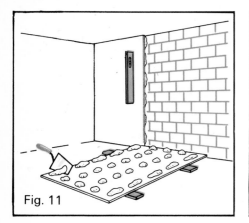

Fig. 11

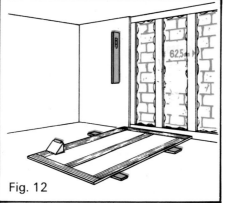

Fig. 12

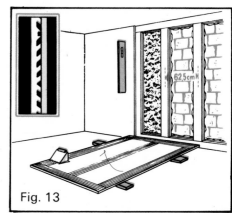

Fig. 13

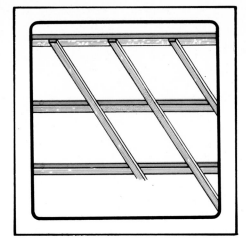

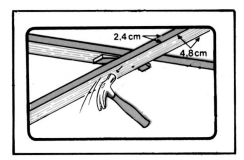

Figs. 14-15. *Some ceilings are very uneven and it may be necessary to counter batten them to provide a new level surface on which to nail the plasterboards. The second set of battens are levelled by driving thin wooden packing pieces between the battens where necessary.*

Make a timbered feature wall

Natural timber boarding can be used to decorate any room in a house—from a living room to a bathroom. The colours and patterns which can be achieved with different wood grains and board profiles are almost limitless, and since timber is long-wearing, redecorating problems will be minimised.

Most woods used for building purposes can be used for decorating interiors. The choice of timber, therefore, should depend on cost, availability and appearance. Many softwoods are very pale in colour, while hardwoods range from the creamy yellow of ash, beech or sycamore to the richer browns of mahogany, cherry and walnut.

When choosing a wood for timber lining, it is important to consider the moisture content of the wood; timber which has a high water content will shrink and warp in a heated room.

Solid timber planks, or boarding, are cut to one of several standard profiles. Square-edged planks may be used, but tongued and grooved—or 'T and G'—planks are more commonly used for internal timber linings, as they allow for easy formation of interlocking joints. Different groove designs, such as rebated, V-jointed, squared and extended shiplaps, are available in lengths which will fit the height of an average room. On a long wall, however, horizontal boarding may need to be joined end-to-end.

Planks may be between 13mm-25mm ($\frac{1}{2}$in - 1in) thick. Normally, they are between 76mm-152mm (3in -6in) wide. The thickness determines both the rigidity of the boarding and the spacing of the fixings. Allowance for movement of the planks is made when the tongues and grooves are originally machined. The tongue is made not to extend the full depth of the groove.

Design considerations

So much depends on the use of the room, its size, shape and lighting, and on personal choice, that it is difficult to lay down rules for choosing internal linings. The basic factors which should be considered are: whether to line the walls and ceilings in wood (a later chapter explains how to line ceilings with timber boards) or only one or the other; whether to cover all the walls with timber or to leave some in a contrasting finish; what kind of wood to use; the angle at which to fix the boards—vertical, horizontal, or diagonal; and the extent of coverage that is desired—the full or partial height of the walls.

Another point to consider is that if furniture in a room is a jumble of pieces of different heights, horizontal boarding will tend, unfortunately, to accentuate this aspect by providing guidelines for the eye. On the other hand, rooms such as kitchens and laundry rooms, which usually have worktops and appliances all about 914mm (3ft) high, will usually look better with horizontal boarding. It helps make their (usually small) walls look longer.

A final consideration is your own skill. A beginner will find it quite easy to board one plain wall to make a 'feature wall'. But covering a whole room involves a range of problems—replacing door and window architraves, for example—and requires a bit more skill, or experience, or patience at any rate.

Preparatory work

Before fixing any planks to new walls, be sure that the walls are dry; newly plastered walls will take at least two months to dry and concrete walls will take at least four months to dry before planks can safely be fixed to them.

The method of fixing internal timber linings will depend primarily upon the type of wall to which they are to be fastened.

Masonry walls, such as unfaced or plastered bricks or lightweight building blocks, will need to have a timber framework of battening attached directly to their surfaces. The linings will then be fixed to these.

Timber frame walls will also need battening, unless the studs (vertical members) and noggins (horizontal members) are close enough to make battens unnecessary. You can find the studs and noggins by driving nails at intervals across, and up and down, the walls. Mark a pencil 'x' every time you strike solid timber; soon you will be able to rule a grid pattern on the wall to show where solid 'nailing' is available.

Re-wiring and re-plumbing

You may want to put in some new light fittings or move existing ones or, if you intend to line a kitchen or bathroom, you may need to rearrange the pipework. Any work of this sort should be carried out at the 'bare wall' stage rather than later, to avoid damaging the wall planking. Also, it is advisable to mark the wall surface where any new

Above: A small, rather confining bedroom can be made to look rich and cosy with timber lining on all walls.

wiring has been buried under plaster. This will help you to avoid accidentally severing or damaging cables when drilling or nailing the battens.

Wall preparation

Protection against damp. If the walls to be panelled have a tendency to dampness or will be subject to condensation—as they would in a kitchen or bathroom—you may prevent this from affecting the panelling by treating the boards with a special damp-proofing compound. There are many proprietary, damp-proofing compounds available, both liquid and solid, including bitumen-based emulsions, siliconised resin-based liquids, and pvc-based sealants. Select one which is easy to apply and follow the makers' instructions. You can also use 500-gauge polythene

sheeting as a vertical damp-proof membrane, or aluminium foil, or heavy-duty bitumen-impregnated paper, glued to the wall with neat pva adhesive.

Alternatively, treat the panels and the battens, before fixing, with a wood preservative. (Be sure to buy a clear, not a coloured variety.) This will protect the timber from damp, and fungal and insect attack—particularly important in warmer climates where insects are more prolific and damaging.

Insulation. If necessary, you can insulate against heat and sound by inserting a quilt or blanket of thick, flare-free expanded polythene sheeting, fibreglass, mineralised rock-wool quilting, or cork panels between the wall surface and the new panelling.

Conditioning the timber

Ideally, keep all timber in a dry, damp-free store, preferably in the room in which it is to be used. Store it for at least a week before using it, to allow the wood to acclimatise to the room's general temperature and to permit

excess moisture to evaporate from it.

Calculating quantities of battening

Estimating the amount of wood needed for the battens is a fairly simple procedure. Battens are continuous lengths of sawn softwood, sometimes available insect-proofed. about 50.8mm (2in) wide × 25.4mm (1in) thick. If using boarding about 12.7mm (½in) thick, battens should be fixed at 610mm (2ft) centres when horizontal (ie, for vertically-fixed boards) and 457mm (16in) centres when vertical (i.e., for horizontally-fixed boards). If using boarding about 25.4mm (1in) thick, horizontal battens can be at 762mm (2ft 6in) centres, and vertical ones at 610mm (2ft) centres.

Either way, remember that there is always one more batten than there are spaces between battens. Allow also for two pieces running in the opposite direction to the battens—these are to form a 'frame' round the outside of the wall (Fig.2). Allow 10% extra for waste.

Fixing the battens

The positioning of the battens will depend on the style of boarding you want to use. For *horizontal* tongued-and-grooved boarding, the main battens should be fixed to run vertically. For *vertical* boarding, you will require horizontal battens. For *diagonal* boarding, either vertical or horizontal battens may be used.

It is desirable that battens present a plane (dead flat) surface for the planks to fit evenly over, but it is not necessary, and normally

Below right: Timber boarding used as in this kitchen, for walls, storage units and a dining shelf, will help disguise awkward features and unify the room's appearance.

Fig.1. When an adjoining wall is 'out of true' (shown here in exaggerated form) the first board must be scribed to fit the curve or slope. See that the board is vertical—it too may have a curve which you must straighten—as you nail it temporarily. Then trace the outline of the wall by running a wood block and pencil down the wall. Cut the board down the pencil line, and move it over into its correct position.

Fig.2. Fixing diagonal boards to vertical battening. Note that you must also have top and bottom battens: these are to give you nailing for the ceiling moulding and the skirting board, as well as for the ends of the T & G boards. Whichever way your boarding is to run, you always need to 'frame' the wall with the outside battens.

not practical, to go to great lengths to achieve such a level surface. Neither walls nor timber are ever perfectly true. Any major irregularities in a wall can be corrected by packing the battens with scraps of wood to the correct level, or by shaping a batten to fit over a 'high spot'.

There are several methods of fixing battens to walls, depending upon the type of wall you have.

On *masonry walls*, battens may be fixed with 50mm (2in) No. 10 masonry screws and fibre or plastic proprietary wall plugs such as Rawlplugs. Space the screws about 381mm (15in) apart. If the walls are made of concrete or very hard brick, you may wish to

hire a percussion drill, especially if you are covering a large area. Otherwise, an ordinary electric drill set to run at a slow speed and fitted with a high-speed masonry bit, or a Rawlplug tool for tapping holes, may be used.

Houses which have a *timber framework* may need additional noggins (cross members) between the studs (vertical framing members), or vice versa. If after examining your wall, you find that noggins are too far apart to take vertical planking, you have two choices: 1, to batten the whole wall as for a masonry house, nailing the battens with 63mm (2½in) flathead nails; or 2, to remove the existing wall lining and provide extra

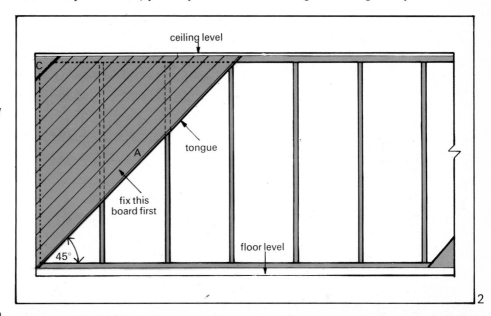

noggins between the studs.

If, on the other hand, the studs are too far apart to take your proposed horizontal boarding, battening across the face of the whole wall is the best course.

When putting up battening, it is necessary to treat each wall separately. Begin by removing the skirting boards and protruding ceiling mouldings from the wall.

The first thing you need is a 'frame' of battening right round the wall (Fig.2). Start by loosely fixing a horizontal batten across the top of the wall, 25mm to 50mm (an inch or two) down from the ceiling. Use a spirit level to check that it is reasonably level, and fix it permanently in place. Now fix a second batten about 76mm (3in) up from the floor, checking that it, too, is reasonably level.

Next, cut two vertical battens to fit between the horizontal ones. Theoretically, these go right at the ends of the wall. But before fixing them permanently, check with a spirit level held vertically to see that they are plumb (straight up and down). If not, your wall is slightly out of plumb; bring each batten back into plumb by fixing it (or one end of it) slightly out from the corner.

Once the 'frame' round the outside of the wall is completed, you need only to fill in the intermediate spaces with battens at the correct intervals, as given above. Try to keep them reasonably level (or plumb, as appropriate), because straight battening will make nailing easier when you come to the top boards.

When you come to doors and windows, battens will be needed around the edges or frames to secure the ends or edges of the planking. Batten offcuts should also be used where new light switches or power points are to be fixed. If surface wiring is to be bridged by battens, notch them to fit over the wires. Remember to fix additional battening where wall-hung furniture or units are to be positioned.

Selecting and matching panelling

All natural timbers vary in colour, grain and figuring, so there may be some slight variation from plank to plank. To get the most pleasing effect, stand the boards against

Above left: *A plain room can be given a distinctive appearance by the use of T & G boards, in this case fixed diagonally.*

Fig.3. *Cramping vertical boarding. Drive the chisel point into the batten and pull it upright to squeeze the board against its neighbour. This helps to eliminate ugly gaps as the timber dries.*

Fig.4. *Since the last two or three boards cannot be cramped, fit them together into a bow shape and 'spring' them into place with your fist.*

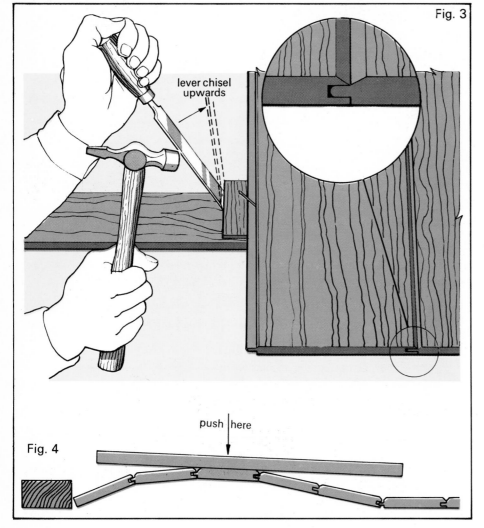

Fig. 3

lever chisel upwards

push here

Fig. 4

the wall and arrange them to suit your own taste before cutting and fixing them.

Scribing

If the wall is out of plumb or is slightly curved, it may be necessary to trim your first board to fit exactly into a corner. To do this hold the board against the corner, flush to the butting wall and the ceiling; use the spirit level to make sure it is truly vertical. The exact contour of the wall is then traced off on to the board with a pencil (Fig.1) and the board trimmed or cut accordingly. This process of tracing an angle or contour directly on to a board is called *scribing*. The advantage of scribing over measuring is that any unevenness in a surface will automatically be transferred in outline to the piece being traced.

For trimming the edge of a board, use a sharp plane with a fine set. Then sand over

with fine glasspaper to smooth the edge.

Fixing T & G boards

Vertical positioning

Begin at an internal corner of a room and scribe to fit the groove side of the first board into the corner, as described above. Remember to leave about a 6.35mm (¼in) gap at the ceiling and floor levels for air to circulate. Keeping this first plank vertically true, begin pinning about 6.35mm (¼in) away from the corner edge. Skew pin the board at about a 45° angle into the support framework behind, using 32mm (1¼in) lost-head nails, a small hammer, and a nail punch to push the nailhead well below the surface of the board. Work down the plank from ceiling to floor, pinning at intervals to correspond with the battening behind. Any holes can be filled with a suitable wood filler.

On the other side of the plank, place pins

Above: Natural grained furniture combined with timbered walls for a striking effect.

along the tongue of the board and skew pin with a hammer and nail punch (Fig.3). Fit the groove of the next board over the tongue, thereby hiding the nail heads. Next, part drive the nails in this board, and *cramp* the board up close to the preceding one using a chisel (Fig.3). Cramping should always be done on the tongue of a T and G board, as any marks will be covered by the groove of the next board. It is necessary to cramp tightly; otherwise gradual shrinkage of the timber will make your wall open up at the joints. When you come to the third board, cramp and nail from the bottom up instead of from the top down—cramping always in the same order will gradually 'skew' your boards out of line.

When you reach the last two or three

boards to be fixed along a wall and into a corner, do not cramp them. Instead, cut them a little oversize and fit them together in a slightly bowed shape (Fig.4). Then bang or 'spring' them into place with your fist. These last boards will need to be pinned through their surfaces, and the holes filled with wood filler.

Horizontal positioning

Horizontal T and G boards are fixed in the same general manner as vertical ones. It is best to position the first board 25mm to 50mm (1in to 2in) above floor level, with

Above: A narrow hall and archway gains warmth and richness from all-over timber.

Below: One timbered wall, plus matching shelf unit, makes a pleasant kitchen.

the tongue upwards. This board should be skew pinned into the underlying battens through the surface of the timber about 12.7mm (½in) up from the bottom edge. It should then be skew pinned through the battens along the edge of the tongue so that the groove of the next board will cover the pins. Use a spirit level over this first board to see that it is level.

Continue fixing the boards up to ceiling level, cramping each board and checking your boards every once in a while to see that they are level. If they are slightly out of line, you can make adjustments by cramping very closely where necessary. Just below the ceiling, leave a 6.35mm (¼in) gap for air to circulate.

If you cannot buy boards which will fit the entire breadth of your wall, you will have to join two or more lengths. Use a *splay joint*, so that no gap shows at the joint. Stagger the joints so that they fall randomly across the wall.

Diagonal positioning

An unusual and often effective means of fixing boarding is diagonally. Visually, the best angle to fix diagonal boarding is at 45°.

Instead of beginning with short lengths of board in a corner, begin at a position along a wall where your first board will be a full length one (you can save short offcuts to fill in the corners later).

To establish the length of the full-length boards required, cut 45° angles in two boards with a mitre block. Be sure to cut these angles in the direction in which you want the boards to slope. Position these boards one beside the other and hold them against the wall, adjusting them until they are straight and you get the correct length. Fix them together by nailing two short battens across them. These boards will give you a gauge from which you can measure the first full-length board. The others can be marked from this —but check as you go that the lengths do not need to vary slightly because the floor and ceiling are 'out'. If your walls are very high, it is not advisable to attempt to cover them in diagonal boarding, since you may not be able to buy long enough timber to avoid a jumble of joints.

For boards which are to slope from left to right, work from left to right across a wall, with the tongue on each board facing towards the right. Hold your first board in place with nails partly driven through the surface of the timber on the right-hand side only. This first board (A in Fig.12) is fixed loosely so that later boards can be 'sprung' into position, as previously explained. 'Secret fix' the remaining full-length boards into position by skew-nailing them through the tongues and punching the nail heads below the surface of the

timber. Cramp each board as you go along and check, occasionally, to see that all the boards are at the correct angle of 45°.

To fill the top left-hand corner (above board A in Fig.12) start by temporarily stacking a row of offcuts against the wall along the left-hand edge (you will need to hammer in a few nails to keep these boards up) until you can accurately judge the size of the board that will fit into the extreme corner (C in Fig.12). Cut this board, which will be a right triangle, about 6.35mm (¼in) oversize along the two sides forming the right angle, and fix it in position. (Cutting the board oversize will ensure a tight fit later.)

Once you have fixed board C into the corner, you can remove the offcuts from the wall and with boards which have been cut to the correct size, work progressively back towards board A, cramping each board along the tongue-side as you go. However, the last three or four boards should not be nailed into place at first. but 'sprung' into position. If the last board does not quite fit, the tongue-edge may be smoothed with a plane slightly so that it can be eased in. After these boards are in place, nail them through the surface and punch in the nailheads. Fill the holes with a wood filler.

To fill the bottom right-hand corner, follow roughly the same process. When you have six or seven boards to go, stack offcuts as you did before until you can ascertain the size of the corner piece (see Fig.12). However, do not fix the corner piece first. Rather, work from left to right, springing the last three or four boards into place and surface nailing them.

Doors and windows

When fixing timber boarding around doors or windows, one of the most important considerations is to see that the unsightly rough edges of the planks do not protrude

Opposite page: Internal timber lining comes in a variety of styles, using either T & G boards or cheaper square-edged planks.

Fig.5. Conventional, v-jointed T & G.

Fig.6. Flat surfaced, extended tongue T & G.

Fig.7. Concave surfaced, extended tongue T & G.

Fig.8. 'Board-and-batten'—hardwood batten over square-edged planks.

Fig.9. Square-edged planks with moulding fixed to one board at joints.

Fig.10. Square-edged planks fixed over hardboard which has been pre-painted in a contrasting colour.

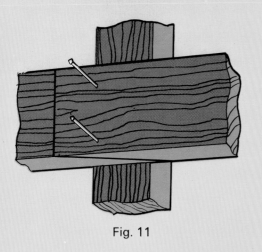

Fig. 11

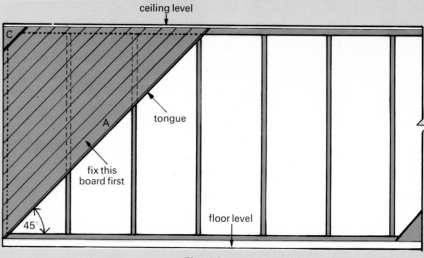

ceiling level

C

A

tongue

fix this
board first

45°

floor level

Fig. 12

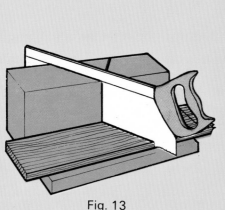

Fig. 13

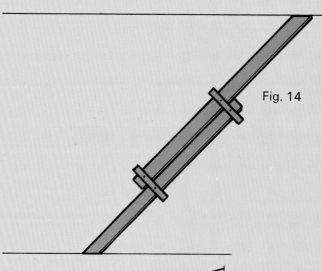

Fig. 14

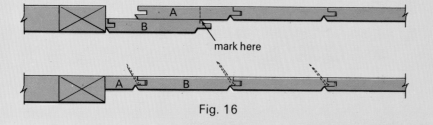

old architrave in next room

door frame

packing pieces

masonry wall

door stop

batten

T & G boarding

door

corner moulding
(old architrave
removed)

Fig. 15

Fig.11. *A splay joint leaves no gap between boards joined lengthwise. It is made by clamping two boards together and sawing through both before trimming them to the final length.*

Fig.12. *For diagonally positioned boarding, fix full-length boards first and use offcuts to find the size of corner pieces.*

Fig.13. *Use a mitre board to hold timber that is to be cut at a 45° angle.*

Fig.14. *To find the size of a full-length, diagonally fixed board, cut 45° angles in two boards, hold them against the wall and when the correct length is found, fasten them together with short battens.*

Fig.15. *A cross-section through a wall and door frame, showing how the old architrave has been replaced by a square-section corner moulding.*

Fig.16. *Boards must be scribed to fit around architraves. Fix 'A' loosely where the last full-width board will fall, and using 'B', scribe the portion of 'A' to be cut away. Then spring the boards into place and surface nail.*

A

B

mark here

A

B

Fig. 16

beyond architraves or flush edges. Usually, the thickness of the battens plus the thickness of the planks will be greater than the thickness of your architraves. If you have doors or windows which are set into walls without any architraves, you will encounter the same problem. And anyway, most elaborate moulded architraves will look awkward set against this sort of boarding.

Such problems can be solved by first removing all existing architraves. Try to pry them off from their external edges so as not to damage adjoining woodwork. Windows may present many more problems than doors, since you will have to remove not only the architraves but also the window sills (or trim them flush with the wall surface).

On *masonry* walls, replace the old moulding (or, in the case of doors and windows without any architraves, make a new moulding) with square-section timber 25mm × 25mm (1in × 1in) (or whatever size necessary) which will be slightly thicker than the *combined* thickness of your battens and your planks (see Fig. 15). The same procedure will work on *timber* walls, but only if 'nailing' is available around the door or window— either to existing studs or to battens which you provide.

When putting up vertical planks around a door, work progressively across one side of the wall from a corner to the door, then across the wall space above the architrave, and then across the wall on the opposite side of the door to the end of the wall. If you are

planking around a window, follow the same plan—side, top, side—and then fill in the area across the bottom of the window. To fit boards around the corners of architraves, scribe and cut boards as in Fig.16.

When putting up horizontal boarding around doors, begin on one side of the door and work up the wall to the top of the architrave, butting the boards against the architrave as you go.

Then, work up the wall on the other side of the door in the same way. Finally, fix boards across the wall area above the architrave, staggering any splay joints which you may need to make. For boarding around windows, follow essentially the same procedure, beginning with full-length boards at the bottom of the wall and working up and around the walls on either side of the window and then across the top of the window. It is important that you stagger any splay joints across the wall so that they do not make an unsightly line.

Fixing the boards diagonally around doors and windows often is not visually pleasing, and problems can arise in matching the slope of the boards and the angles. Consider carefully before you attempt to fix diagonal boarding on a wall area broken by doors and windows.

If you do fix diagonal boarding, be absolutely sure that you measure and cut your boards so that they can be butted smoothly against any architraves and are all positioned at a 45° angle.

way to obtain the colour you want. With wallpaper, hours of searching through pattern books may fail to produce the colour required in a suitable pattern. But with paint the availability of a wide range of standard colours and the facility for precise mixing of special colours make it possible to obtain an exact choice.

Mistakes can be corrected more easily with paint as well. If you find, for example, after hanging one or two pieces of wallpaper that the scale of the pattern or the general effect is not as anticipated, it will be necessary either to live with your mistake, or to reject the whole supply outright and buy fresh stock. If, however, a sample panel of paint indicates the colour is strong or the hue needs adjusting, it is a simple matter to mix in the appropriate corrective colour.

Always prepare a test panel and check this before proceeding with an entire room, since a small pattern on a colour card can give a false impression of the effect over large areas.

Varieties of paint

All paints are basically similar in composition—consisting of a pigment mixed in a suitable medium, with various additives to improve certain qualities.

Hard gloss oil paint uses linseed oil as its medium, mixed with pigment, a thinner to improve workability, and a drier to speed up drying. A traditional finish for woodwork, it is usually applied to walls only when a durable, washable surface is required. Before beginning to paint it is essential that the wall is dry, since the paint forms an impervious film which will not allow moisture to evaporate; if dampness is present, it will normally cause blistering and flaking of the paint layer.

Because it is non-absorbent, a gloss paint surface on walls or ceiling in a room subject to high humidity will cause condensation—in severe cases water will collect and drip from the ceiling and run down the walls. It is not, therefore, a very suitable material for kitchens and bathrooms, although in the past it was often used in these areas because of its washability. Today, however, there is a wider choice of more suitable finishes, made from various synthetic resins and marketed under different trade names. Condensation in kitchens and especially in bathrooms will occur to some extent, no matter what type of wall covering you choose to use.

Enamels formerly meant paints designed solely for applying to metal or clay surfaces which are fired at high temperatures to produce a stoved finish (vitreous enamel), but the term is often used loosely today to describe a superior hard gloss paint for normal use. It is especially good to use on flush surfaces such as cupboards or on areas where

---

Choosing wall coverings

Walls account for the largest surface area of a room, making the choice of a decorative finish very significant. Whether it be mosaic tiles, flock wallpaper or vinyl paint, the finish will influence the entire room's character.

The choice of wall decoration is dependent upon suitability of appearance, amount of maintenance needed, and cost. Living areas and bedrooms, for example, have relatively minor maintenance problems and the choice for these rooms is likely to be made mainly on the basis of the colour, pattern and texture required for the particular room. A painted or wallpapered surface might be the most likely choice, although other appropriate finishes could be wood panelling or boarding.

Rooms which are liable to high humidity,

such as kitchens and bathrooms, need a more durable surface capable of withstanding water splashes, detergents or grease marks and regular cleaning. Tiles, plastic laminates or, in the less vulnerable areas, vinyl wall coverings, would be suitable choices for these areas.

Paint or wallpaper?

In rooms that do not require a particularly durable surface, and have suitable wall surfaces (such as smooth plaster with no cracks), the least expensive wall decoration will usually be a painted finish. This may also be the best choice on other grounds. The advantages of paint are that it is readily obtainable from stock without special ordering, inexpensive, can be applied by a competent handyman, and it is the least frustrating a fine finish is wanted. Most gloss paints can be thinned with mineral turpentine substitutes, but it is important to follow the manufacturers' directions as some have complex compositions.

Emulsion paint is, in some cases, an adequate alternative to gloss paint. Apart from its tendency to induce condensation, a gloss paint finish is often unsuitable for walls because of its shiny appearance, which emphasises any slight irregularities in a wall surface. Most interior walls look better with a matt or slightly glossy eggshell finish.

The development of emulsion paints, in which particles of the medium are dispersed in water, represented a great advance for the home decorator, since they combine the advantages of a flat finish oil paint with the convenience of a water paint for thinning and cleaning of brushes. Most modern emulsion paints are composed of a synthetic resin emulsified in water. The finished surface of these paints is very durable and will withstand frequent cleaning.

Even more resistant to dirt and moisture are co-polymer or plastic emulsion paints such as those which provide a vinyl finish. These form a continuous surface of plastic 'skin' and must be applied to walls that are smooth and free from grease, flaking paint and paper. *Oil bound water paint*, or distemper, is similar to conventional emulsion paints, but is cheaper and not nearly as durable.

Acrylics represent the latest development in emulsion paints and can be used almost anywhere—even on damp external walls.

Thixotropic paints are 'jelly' paints with a dense medium which thickens the consistency of the paint, largely eliminating the problem of paint drips. A further advantage to the handyman is that the increased thickness of the paint film results in a greater opacity, so that one coat is often sufficient to produce a uniform tint. The most professional looking results, however, will be obtained by building up several thin layers of paint. Thixotropic paints come in a wide range of colours in gloss, emulsion and vinyl finishes.

Cellulose paints must be applied with a spray gun for best results and are not very suitable for domestic use. They are best used on metal and other surfaces which will need a high gloss finish.

Stone paints have small particles of stone mixed in an emulsified resin base. Their normal use is for external brick or rendered surfaces, but they can be used internally to improve the appearance of a brick or a cement rendered wall.

Many other paints have been developed for special situations. These provide rust, damp, fungus, fire, or acid and alkali resisting finishes.

Varnishes and sealers are used where exposed natural surfaces, such as wood, stone or slate, need protection. They are transparent and usually based on linseed oil or polyurethane resins. When the natural surface is to be retained, but the colour needs improving, a varnish incorporating a stain can be used.

Primers. To obtain a smooth finish, the top coat of paint must adhere thoroughly to the wall surface. Some surfaces, such as old plaster, may vary in their porosity, and if a top coat paint is applied directly onto this surface, it will produce a patchy finish. Primers, therefore, are used as base coats to provide uniformly absorbent surfaces for later coats of paint, and to seal in alkalis or other chemicals which might affect the decorative finish. Primers are usually white or pink.

Undercoats. One or more coats of undercoat are usually necessary on new walls to build up the colour to a dense uniform level. Normally they are fairly thin, but have a high pigment content to give good opacity, and they dry to a matt finish. Existing paint, if it is in good condition, will need only one undercoat and one top coat in most cases. It is important, however, to ensure that existing coats are adhering properly and are being uniformly absorbed. Be certain that new paint is compatible with the old paint you are working over, as some paints react with chemicals in other paints.

Wallpapers

If a texture or a pattern is preferred to a flat colour, some form of sheet wall covering is indicated. The cheapest material of this type is wallpaper. There are several different kinds of paper available in an incredible range of patterns.

The largest selection is still to be found in the standard range of wallpaper with flat printed patterns. These include stripes, abstract forms, geometric shapes, floral and pictorial patterns and regular small-scale designs which give the appearance of texture. Patterns are often available in a choice of colourways.

An increasing number of wallpapers are now treated to make them spongeable. Some are even claimed to be washable, but the extent to which a printed paper surface can be cleaned is inevitably limited; if severe dirtying is likely, a more durable surface should be selected.

The range of patterns available in ready-pasted wallpapers is also steadily increasing. These are generally more costly than standard wallpaper, but may offer savings in time, effort and equipment.

Wallpapers with an embossed texture to simulate a woven fabric, or with other raised patterns, are useful for covering walls or ceilings with uneven surfaces or with minor plaster cracks.

Some extra-stout embossed papers have patterns which stand out in high relief. These can be used very effectively with oblique lighting, which will emphasise the pattern by casting strong shadows. They are best used in small areas to accentuate a panel of wall, rather than as a general surface over an entire room.

There are several other variants on the basic printed paper finish. Some manufacturers produce a range of papers with a metallic surface. These often have patterns of stripes or geometric shapes embossed on the surface, which produce varying degrees of reflection from different angles. They should be used with caution as they can be overpowering and too showy. For many rooms the wall surfaces, while looking attractive in themselves, should act as a background for the furnishings. Too strong a colour or pattern on the walls can produce a harsh and disjointed effect. Metallic papers are often best restricted to small areas, like corridors, where a dramatic effect is wanted.

Flock papers are made by printing the pattern in a glue and dusting the surface with fine shreds of coloured felt which adhere to the surface, and produce a raised velvet effect. They are a modern imitation of handmade papers of the eighteenth and nineteenth centuries and, as such, they are used in rooms which seek to reproduce this period. The designs tend to be traditional and rather large in scale and are not really suited to modern, bright and clean interiors. They are also expensive and need careful hanging to ensure that the pattern in adjacent lengths matches.

Vinyl wallcoverings

In kitchens, laundry rooms and bathrooms, where water may splash on walls, or where walls will need frequent cleaning as in playrooms, a surface which can withstand regular wiping down is needed. The new vinyl-faced wall-coverings are excellent here. The vinyl surface is available on either a paper or a fabric backing—of these, the paper-backed types are cheaper and quicker to hang, as they need only a heavy-duty paste. The fabric-backed types normally require a special adhesive, but they are more stable and less likely to stretch unevenly in the hanging process. Some vinyl wall coverings are available read-pasted.

The extensive choice available includes plain colours and patterns with a flat surface, or embossed surfaces that simulate canvas and other fabric finishes. Some patterned vinyl wall-coverings tend to be rather large in scale, and these can be used successfully only on a large wall.

Other materials

One of the high quality, and consequently more expensive, wall finishes is *hessian*. This is a natural woven material which comes dyed in solid colours with or without paper backing. Hanging requires care and patience, especially with the backless type, as the special adhesive used tends to penetrate the material and appear on the surface in uneven patches.

A hessian covered wall has a warmth and character quite distinct from that of vinyl and paper decorations, but being a natural fabric, it is more difficult to clean.

Another rather costly, but high quality, wall finish which offers an unusual and pleasing appearance, is composed of very thin slices of *decorative hardwood* mounted on a flexible backing. The thinness and small size of the wood pieces enables the paper to be hung in the same way as woven materials, again using a special adhesive. It can also be used loose as a screen or blind.

Natural grass papers enjoyed popularity some years ago when they were first introduced from the Far East. They are composed of strips of natural decorative dried grasses stitched to or mounted on a backing and are hung in the same way as the woven fabric described above. Being a natural product, the pieces vary slightly in width, thickness and colouring, but it is precisely these qualities which give grass papers their distinctive character.

The surface of grass paper is surprisingly hardwearing, but it is not easily cleaned due to its coarse texture, and it is expensive. If, after some time, you wanted to change the decoration and paint your walls, you would have to strip off this paper, as it cannot be over-painted. The same also applies to woven fabrics and the hardwood material.

The best surface for areas which must stand up to regular cleaning with detergents is *ceramic tiles*. These are made of fired pressed clay which is then glazed and fired again to give a high-gloss or matt finish. They come in an enormous range of plain or mottled colours.

There is also a choice of tiles decorated with screen-printed patterns. Some of these are self-contained designs and can be mixed into a wall of plain tiling to add a decorative effect. Others are designed to form a continuous pattern, while still others, based on Spanish or Portuguese handpainted tile designs, can be used either individually or as part of a regular repeat pattern.

These tiles are usually about 6mm ($\frac{1}{4}$in) thick and 110mm ($4\frac{3}{4}$in), or 152mm (6in)

Decorating uneven wall surfaces, such as brick ones, can present problems. Most wallpapers and tiles will not adhere properly, and many paints are unsuitable if the walls are susceptible to damp.

Top: *A brick-walled vanity area painted with several coats of white emulsion.*

Bottom: *A feature brick wall covered with a special copper foil paper.*

square, with various other sizes available to order. Tiles with one or more rounded edges to fit around wall perimeters are also manufactured.

Relief tiles, which have a pattern moulded into the surface and are usually glazed with a plain colour, are also available in sizes similar to those above, but these are about 13mm ($\frac{1}{2}$in) thick. As with heavily embossed papers, they will be seen to best advantage if lit from one side or from above to produce a strong 'modelled' effect.

Tiles are traditionally fixed by bedding in a cement and sand mortar mix on a hard, flush surface, but one of the proprietary mastic adhesives may be quicker and easier to use. The joints are pointed in plaster or portland cement, unless there is any danger of movement in the surface to which they are fixed. If this is the case, a mastic compound should be used.

Polyvinyl chloride tiles are made in sizes similar to ceramic tiles, and are also available in panels moulded to simulate a group of individual tiles. They are fixed with an impact adhesive and are good to use in bathrooms, since their warm surface reduces the likelihood of condensation. The surface is, however, more liable to damage by scratching and knocking than a clay tile, and will not withstand abrasive cleaners, such as detergents or scouring powders.

Another attractive and suitable wall finish for bathrooms is *mosaic*. The true vitreous mosaic composed of a small square of glass or vitrified clay is very expensive, but *ceramic mosaic* with an eggshell finish and various other cheaper types are available. These are usually sold in panels about 300mm (1ft) square, covered with a temporary paper facing which is washed off after the mosaic is fixed.

Like ceramic tiles, they can only be fitted to a hard flush surface, and are fitted with adhesive in the same way. The joints between the pieces are filled with white cement or other recommended grouting medium after the paper has been removed. Generally, the pattern of small pieces provides sufficient visual interest, and panels of uniformly coloured pieces are preferable to those with a mixture of colours. Some manufacturers produce panels composed of cushion-shaped square pieces, rectangles or hexagons.

Bathrooms usually need at least one *mirror* and the opportunity can be taken to form part or the whole of a wall surface as a mirror. Apart from its practical use, a large wall mirror can be effective in increasing the apparent size of a small bathroom, especially if it extends the full width of the wall at eye level.

A conventional, silvered plate glass mirror can be used, but this should not be fitted above a bath or other source of steam, or it will quickly mist over with condensation. This can be overcome by using a sheet of silvered plastic which is marketed at approximately the same price as the glass type. Glass mirror can also be obtained in the form

of tiles which will fit in with the pattern of ceramic tiling.

Stainless steel, an increasingly popular surface for sink-tops, utensils, dishes and tableware, is also available in tiles and can often help to relate the walls to the other surfaces in a kitchen.

The other popular material for vulnerable areas of kitchen walls is *plastic laminate sheet*. Laminates come in a wide choice of plain, or mottled and marbled colours, woven and geometric patterns, and wood-grains. They are made from compressed layers of resin-bonded paper, topped with a layer carrying the printed decoration and a clear melamine coating.

It is a very versatile and durable material and can be cut to most shapes. Impact adhesive can be used to fix it to any rigid smooth backing, such as blockboard or chipboard. The edges of the backing material are usually lipped with matching laminate, which is available in strips about 25mm (1 in.) wide in a variety of popular colours. The surface is very hard and tough and will withstand regular cleaning and normal domestic liquids. A cigarette resistant grade is also obtainable.

Since laminates can be used for tabletops and worktops as well as for wall facings, it is possible to feature a consistent colour and pattern scheme which will help to give the room a unified appearance.

The very thin, *flexible vinyl sheeting* which usually comes with a self-adhesive back protected by a cover piece, is not suitable for permanent wall facings or splashbacks: its use should be restricted to covering shelves and other areas where splashing and high humidity do not occur.

A similar material which is available mounted on hardboard, however, could be used as a wall facing. It is fixed by nailing to wood grounds plugged to the wall, or by glueing with an impact adhesive to a hard, flush surface. The wearing characteristics of this surface would not, however, approach those of plastic laminate sheet or ceramic tiles.

In some rooms, such as a child's playroom or a study-bedroom, pinboard wall panels can serve a useful as well as decorative purpose. Inexpensive insulating fibreboard sheets, nailed to wood grounds or fixed with plaster dabs to the wall, can be used and can be painted or faced with a vinyl wallcovering.

A more durable and more expensive wall of this kind can be made from a suitable floor finish, such as cork tiles, or linoleum. Cork tiles can be fixed with adhesive to a smooth wall surface. Linoleum, (which should be heavy quality, at least 3mm ($\frac{1}{8}$ in.) thick) is obtainable in tile form which can be similarly fixed, or in wide sheet form which should be stuck and pinned to a rigid backing of blockboard or chipboard. The composite panel is then fixed to the wall by screwing into wood grounds or plugs. The panel should be trimmed with a narrow hardwood moulding.

Above: Bathrooms, *usually being quite small and fitted with awkwardly shaped fixtures, are a challenge to decorate. This confining bathroom is painted all over in a warm red paint and decorated along one wall with mirrored cabinets to give an illusion of space.*

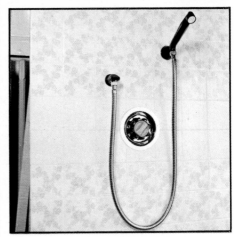

Design considerations

Every room is a separate problem, and every family will have its own views on the most suitable treatment. Generally it is wise to spend plenty of time deciding on the colour and material. When choosing a material for wall decoration, any shortcomings of the room should be borne in mind.

Avoid cheap material or tools; they often take up more time than better ones and can lead to poor results.

Do not skimp on preparations. Tiling on an uneven wall will never look satisfactory, and a painted surface will ruthlessly reveal inadequate preparation and undercoating. Take into account the use and wear the surface will receive and select the material accordingly. It is very disappointing when a whole room is spoiled by one or two vulnerable areas which will not stand up to cleaning.

Left: This shower has been added in a 'spare' corner, and tastefully decorated with ceramic tiles, red and black paintwork and a matching shower curtain.

Above top: A shower fitted into what was previously a cupboard and tiled throughout in patterned ceramic tiles.

Above centre: Contrasting plain white and patterned tiles as the backing to a detachable head shower.

Above: The simple jointing in fitting a shower need not spoil the wall covering.

The glamour wall

An alcove or room panelled in wood can give your house a special charm. You don't have to go to the difficulty or expense of fitting individual boards, though. It is easier and cheaper—but just as effective—to face your walls with plywood or hardboard that has a veneered or simulated wood finish.

A wide range of large sheets of this type of panelling is readily available, or can easily be ordered, from most DIY shops. The price varies with the type, but the cheaper kinds are so reasonably priced that you could probably afford to do an entire room with them.

Types of panelling

The cheapest panelling of all is hardboard sheet with a simulated wood-grain finish printed on it; there are bevel-edged grooves in the sheet to imitate the join that is found with interlocked tongue-and-grooved boards. The sides of the board finish with the bevel edge of a fake board so that all you have to do is place two sheets side by side to hide the join. These sheets are best fixed to an entire wall and edged with a skirting board at the bottom of the wall, and stained and varnished hardwood moulding round the sides and top of the wall. Alternatively, polystyrene or plasterboard coving can be fitted against the ceiling.

At the dearer end of the range is plywood sheet with a genuine wood veneer. These are usually plain sheets without any bevel-edged grooves and do not give the impression of boards joined together. Practically all veneered plywood is supplied with a finished surface and does not require any further treatment apart from final varnishing. However, some veneers are supplied unfinished and these must be sanded, stained, sealed and then varnished. These veneers look especially attractive if they are divided into small rectangular sections by a framework of matching hardwood moulding.

Fitting sheet boarding

First calculate how many sheets you need. Most rooms in modern houses are 2.45m (8ft) high (or less), so the standard-sized 2.45 × 1.22m (8 × 4ft) sheet will reach from floor to ceiling. You will therefore need one sheet for every 1.22m (4ft) of wall if you set them with grain running vertically. If a single feature wall less than 2.45m (8ft) long in an alcove or in a small kitchen is panelled, two sheets can be fitted sideways, one above the other.

If the wall is longer than 2.45m (8ft) it would be difficult to match the ends of the sheets together because there are no bevelled edges at the ends of the sheets only at the sides. You will have to link them with a moulding covering the join, which may look strange. Otherwise, horizontal boarding appears to widen a room and can look most effective, especially where kitchen units or other furniture on the same wall are of a uniform height.

If the units are of varied height, horizontal boards are best avoided as they only emphasise the different levels. Instead, hang the boards so that they run vertically and so harmonise better with the units.

On a sound, flat wall the sheets can be fixed with adhesive. Use a general-purpose impact adhesive because, though you must position the sheets correctly 'first time', there is no need for elaborate propping to hold the sheets while the adhesive dries. Strip the wall of any wallpaper or paint to avoid the possibility of the weight of the sheeting from pulling the paper or paint from the wall. With a straight edge, check to see that there are no bumps or sharp curves in the wall. If there are, battens will have to be fitted to the wall as a base for the sheeting, as described below. Turn off the electricity supply at the fuse box and remove any light fittings or power points that will get in the way of the panelling.

Then get someone to help you. Hold the first sheet in place against the wall in one corner. Use a spirit level—or better, plumb bob—to make sure that the board is hanging vertically. Then check that the corner of the wall is square enough to take the sheet; you can neaten the join in the corner later by fixing a strip of hardwood moulding so it does not matter if one of the sides is fractionally out.

If the corner is too far out of square, you will have to scribe the edge of the board to it. Cut the board by scoring with a sharp marking knife and then cutting with a fine toothed saw. This will give a clean edge to the cut.

If you have removed an electric fitting from the wall, mark and drill a hole in the sheet to allow the electric wire to pass through if it is a surface-mounted fitting, or cut a square hole with a pad saw for a flush-fitting switch. Now hold the sheet against the wall again to check that it will fit into the corner of the room. Then draw around the edges with a pencil, being careful especially about your vertical line, and take the sheet down.

Now spread impact adhesive on the wall in a band about 50–75mm (2in or 3in) wide on the inside of the outline you have just drawn. Then run strips of adhesive either vertically or horizontally at approximately 600mm (2ft) intervals inside the outline. If a light switch is to be set in the sheet, spread some adhesive on the wall around the hole you have cut. Now spread impact adhesive on the sheet of plywood (or whatever) in bands corresponding with those on the wall and wait until both lots are touch dry.

Get someone to help you again and position the sheet as accurately as possible while holding it so that it is just clear of the wall. Then press it in place starting at one corner and side, checking that as you press it in place it fits right up against your pencilled marks. Repeat this with the next and following sheets, trying each in place 'dry' before you apply the adhesive.

When fixing a sheet to a second wall at right angles to a wall that has already been covered with the sheeting, check carefully to see that both edges of the second sheet are exactly vertical or horizontal. If the corner is out of true you will have to scribe the sheet to it as before.

Finishing off

For a neat finish, fit mouldings round the sides and top of walls. You may prefer to replace your existing skirting board with a hardwood one matching the panelling.

On an internal corner, where the angle between the two walls is 90 degrees, fit a quarter-round moulding. First cut the moulding to length and sand it if necessary. If you are going to stain it, do it now. Then seal it with a coat of varnish mixed with an equal amount of white spirit. Give it as many coats of varnish as you think necessary. Then fit it in place either with adhesive (if the boards beside it are pre-finished, you will have to scrape off some of the varnish) or moulding or panel pins. Knock the moulding pins in with a light hammer and then use a punch so that the heads are recessed into the beading.

It is difficult to make a neat finish on an external corner, so fix a piece of L-shaped beading in place to cover the join (see Fig.1).

Battening uneven walls

On a crumbly or uneven wall it is best to fix rows of battens at 406mm (16in) centres, or a spacing that is an even fraction of the width of the boards. Attach the panelling to it using either adhesive or panel pins. For the battens use softwood strips about 50mm × 25mm

(2in × 1in). Cut them to size and fix them to the walls with No.8 screws that are long enough to extend into wall plugs set in the masonry behind the plaster. A batten is needed round the top, bottom and sides of the walls. Between these, battens can run either vertically or horizontally, whichever is more convenient. If panel pins are to be used to fix the sheet to the battens they will be placed in the grooves so that they are hidden as much as possible. In this case ensure that the battens run across the simulated boards and not with them, as it will then be easier to arrange for the pins to pass through the battens. There must always be a batten where the sides of two adjoining sheets are to meet. If the battens run across the width of the sheets, cut pieces of batten the length of the distance between the battens and fit them in place where the two sheets join (see Fig.2).

When facing a single wall, take the battens right up into the corner of the wall, but when facing two walls at 90 degrees to each other there is no need to overlap the battens in the corner. It is sufficient for the surfaces that face into the room to meet each other, as in Fig.4—but they must meet because there is no way of filling any cracks. At an external corner, such as around a chimney breast, the battens should overlap as in Fig.4.

If there are light switches or other electrical fittings on the wall, back the hole cut in the sheet with a piece of wood the same thickness as the battens, and larger than the size of the fitment to be replaced, to bring the fitting out to its proper level. This piece of wood may need to be cut out to take the switch box, or drilled to take the flex in the case of a surface-mounted fittings.

Position, mark and cut the sheets as

Above: Simulated wood-panelled sheets give a warm richness to any room, and provide a 'natural' background against which to set a favourite picture or piece of furniture.

before. If fixing the sheets with panel pins, knock the pins in with a light hammer and punch, or better still a 'push-pin' tool, being careful not to mark the surface of the sheet. If the sheet is under tension because the wall is uneven, there is a danger of the panel pins pulling through the sheet. In this case, use adhesive on the battens as described previously in the section on fixing the sheets directly to the wall. The other advantage of using adhesive is that you are less likely to damage the surface of the sheet and there will be no pins to spoil its appearance.

Framed panelling

Wood-veneered panels set in a hardwood framework are more expensive than sheet boarding, and more time consuming to cut and attach to the wall, but they look extremely smart. If you find the look of full-height panelling too heavy, the panelling can be taken up to a level 1m (3ft 3in) from the floor. The size of the framework in which the panels are set, and the size of the panels, can be varied to suit your taste. Panels 500 × 400mm (20in × 16in) and a framework between them 50mm (2in) wide make a suitable combination for many rooms.

There is no need actually to cut the sheet of veneered ply to the size of the panels. It can be left the full height of the panelled area and the framework glued to its surface to give the impression of panelling. Provided the grain of the veneer is not too strongly marked, so that a distinctive streak goes under a strip of framing and 'surfaces' on the other side, the illusion of separate panels set in a frame will be very realistic. Joins between pieces of ply can be anywhere, as convenient, provided they fall under a framing strip. Nail heads can be concealed in the same way.

If the wall is flat, and sound, you can use 50mm × 12.5mm (2in × ½in) framework, and fasten the ply behind this directly onto the wall. If glue is used, the wall must be stripped of wallpaper and paint. If the wall is crumbly and uneven, the ply must be glued to a framework of battens. If these are arranged to fall behind the front framing, this can be pinned to the battens with small 'lost head' nails punched below the surface. This is a stronger method of construction than glue by itself. The small dents left by the pins can be filled over with wood stopping tinted to match the framing.

To find the amount of hardwood needed for the framework, calculate the length of one of the horizontal and vertical pieces on each wall. Decide how many panels high and wide the wall cladding is to be. One more horizontal piece of framing is needed than the number of panels in the height of the cladding, and one more vertical piece than the number of panels in the width.

The vertical pieces of hardwood are not continuous lengths but a number of short pieces set between the horizontal strips. Consequently, slightly less wood is needed for the vertical strips than your calculations will give, but this saving will probably be offset by general wastage in cutting.

If the battening lies directly under the front framing, you will need exactly the same amount of wood for it as for the framing.

Installing framed panelling

To install the panelling, use a spirit level and straight edge to draw a horizontal line on the wall to mark its top edge. You must start from this horizontal line and work downwards even if the ceiling or floor is not itself horizontal. Cut the hardwood for this horizontal length and pin it lightly to the wall

Fit the bottom horizontal length of hardwood in position. Then cut and fit two vertical pieces up either side of the wall and between the two horizontal lengths. If the wall is out of true, scribe these to fit into the corners with the inside edges vertical. Next, cut and fit the rest of the horizontal pieces. Then cut and fit the vertical pieces between these horizontal lengths. Draw round the inside of the framework with a pencil. Then take it down piece by piece, numbering the back of each strip of hardwood, and write the same number beside its position on the wall, so that you know the correct position to replace it in. Sand, stain, seal and, if wanted, varnish all the lengths.

Fit the battening (if any) to the wall over the pencil marks in the same way. Apply adhesive to the battens, or to the wall if no battens are used. Place the veneered panels firmly in position and refix the stained framing firmly over it to complete the panelling. Use 'lost head' nails to mark the framing as little as possible. Punch the heads below the surface.

General construction details

The alcoves on either side of a chimney breast are usually just wasted space. In this project, the recesses and breast are panelled to make a feature of the area, and fitted with shelving and storage units to make good use of the space.

In this instance the chimney flue has been blocked up, and the fireplace opening used for other purposes, but you could just as easily panel round a fireplace that is in use.

Briefly, in this project the walls are battened, panelled, and fitted with shelving brackets to which storage cabinets are fixed. The shelving brackets are used to hold two cabinets—there could be more—and in this case one is used as a casing for a record turntable, and the other for storing the records. But they could be used for other purposes or for general storage.

The panelling used here is of the pre-finished plastic-coated variety that is sold in large sheets. This material has certain advantages over normal tongued-and-grooved boarding in that large areas of wall can be covered quickly; and the chores of sanding

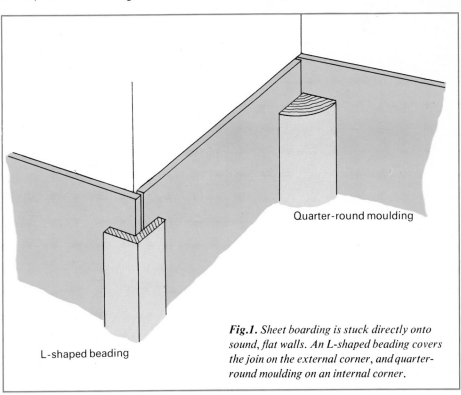

Quarter-round moulding

L-shaped beading

Fig.1. Sheet boarding is stuck directly onto sound, flat walls. An L-shaped beading covers the join on the external corner, and quarter-round moulding on an internal corner.

and varnishing or painting are eliminated.

Battening strips are nailed to the wall at 400mm (16in) centres, and the panelling is attached to this with panel pins. The battening is of 19mm × 50mm (¾in × 2in) timber and must be purchased PAR (planed all round). This is because unplaned timber often varies in dimensions.

The shelving consists of proprietary adjustable shelving strip. An example is shown in Fig. 8, but there are many similar types on the market.

The shelf brackets that hold the cabinets obviously support a considerable weight, so their fixing strips are screwed through the panelling into extra strips of hardwood batten which are in turn screwed securely to the wall.

Laminated chipboard is the material used for the cabinets. Like the panelling, it is pre-finished and requires no final treatment and very little maintenance. The cabinets shown here are half the length of the alcove, and this would of course vary with the dimensions of your own alcove. These units are 1.08m (42½in) in length, 343mm (13½in) deep from front to back, and 381mm (15in) high.

The alcove shown here has had a platform built into the corner, as shown in Fig. 7. This was built to allow a skirting radiator to run across the alcove without having to be fitted into the corners. You could build such a platform if you wish and use it to support the lower cabinet. But this is not necessary; it is cheaper and far less work to fit the cabinet on

shelf brackets.

Materials

The panel and shelf support battening is of 19mm × 50mm (¾in × 2in) timber. Use hardwood for the shelf supports, which will take a heavy load. The other battens can be made of the cheapest softwood.

The panelling can be of any variety. The type chosen here is a popular one with a plastic coating that imitates wood grain. Ask your dealer to show you all the varieties and surfaces he can obtain, so that you can select something to harmonize with the rest of the room.

The cabinets are of 19mm (¾in) thick plastic-laminated chipboard, but you may prefer the type that is surfaced with a real

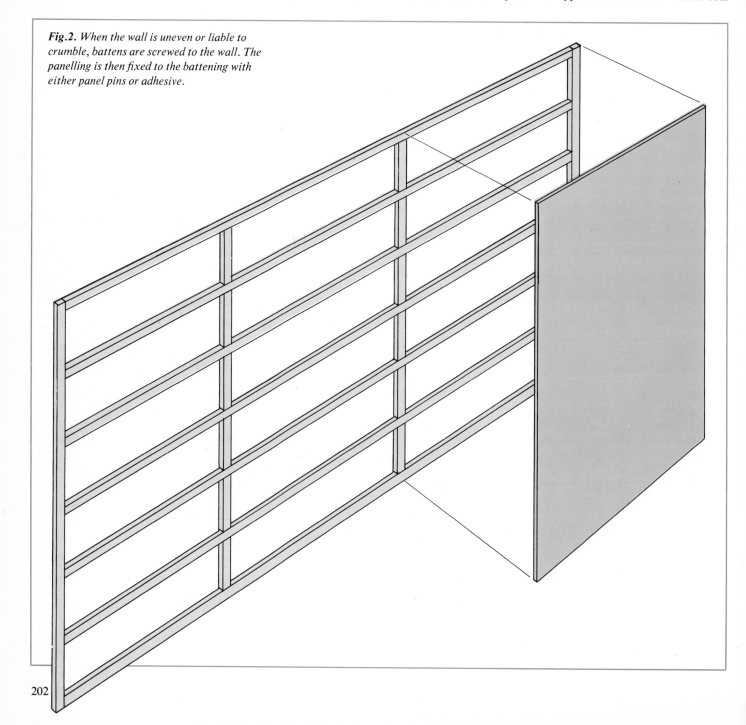

Fig.2. *When the wall is uneven or liable to crumble, battens are screwed to the wall. The panelling is then fixed to the battening with either panel pins or adhesive.*

wood veneer. This is cheaper, but must be heavily varnished if it is to wear well.

Adjustable shelving strips and brackets of the type shown in Fig. 8 are available in a wide variety of proprietary makes, but the principle in all cases is the same. Securing strips are screwed to the wall, and shelf brackets clip or slot into the strip. The brackets used here have flat tops with screw holes at intervals to allow the brackets to be screwed to the bottoms of the cabinets.

Preparing the walls

The battening that holds the panelling, and the pieces that anchor the shelving strip, must be plumb vertical; otherwise the shelf brackets will not be horizontal and the cabinets or shelves will slope up or down. For this reason you will have to use a plumb line to check the angles of the alcoves, and the battens may have to be packed or wedged underneath before they are nailed in position.

Even when a wall is otherwise vertical, it often has hollows in the plasterwork. If these are ignored, the battening and the panelling will be nailed into these depressions and the result will be areas of undulating surface that look unsightly when lit from an angle.

Mark out any hollows in the wall so that when you nail the battening in place you can place packing pieces (pieces of thin plywood, hardboard, or even cardboard) underneath the battens at these points. This marking out should be done with either a 1.2m (4ft) builder's level or a straight edge at least as long. Place the straight edge along the wall at intervals and with a piece of chalk mark the edges of the hollows. When you have finished you can outline the outside line of the hollows. By placing the straight edge over these marked hollows you should be able to estimate how much packing you need for the whole job.

Now mark out the lines the battening will follow. These are spaced at 409mm (16in) intervals as shown in Fig.13. At the same time, decide on the heights of the shelving brackets that will hold the cabinets, and any others you intend to fit. The height of the brackets to take the lower cabinet is a matter of perference, but bear in mind that the distance between the top of the lower cabinet and the bottom of the upper cabinet must be at least 380mm (15in) to allow the lower cabinet to be used freely, and the lid to open fully. Having decided on the heights of the shelving brackets, mark the locations of the support or shelf battens as shown in Fig.13.

Fitting battens and shelf supports

The quantity of battening required for the panelling and shelf supports can be estimated by measuring the lines you have marked on the wall. Add about 10% for wastage when ordering.

The panel battening is secured to the walls by masonry nails driven in dovetail fashion as shown in Fig.5. The nails must be long enough to go through the batten and plaster, and penetrate the brickwork underneath to at least a depth of 25mm (1in). The nails are driven in at approximately 380mm (15in)

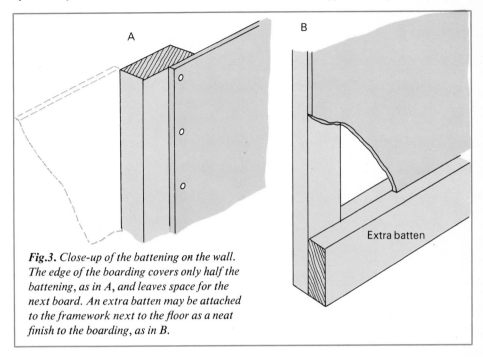

Fig.3. Close-up of the battening on the wall. The edge of the boarding covers only half the battening, as in A, and leaves space for the next board. An extra batten may be attached to the framework next to the floor as a neat finish to the boarding, as in B.

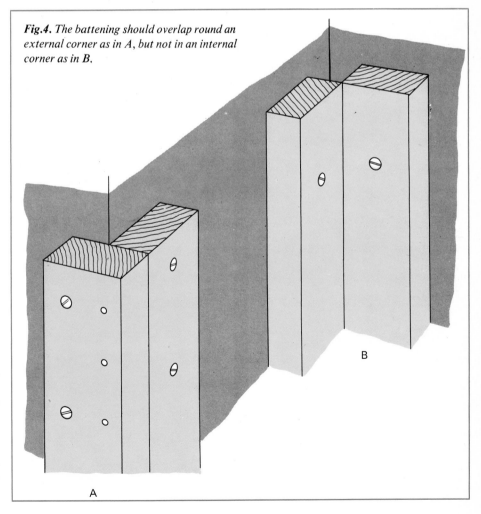

Fig.4. The battening should overlap round an external corner as in A, but not in an internal corner as in B.

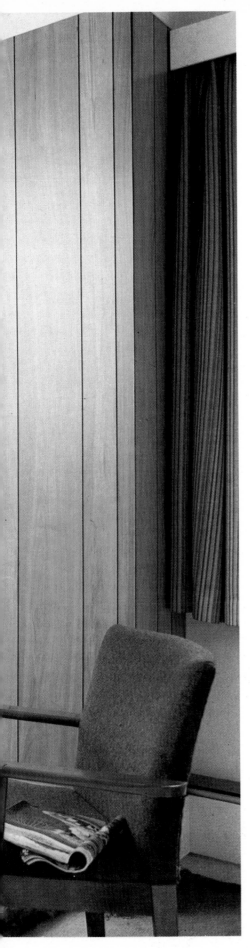

intervals.

Battening for the shelving strips will have to be fixed more securely because of the loads it will carry, so these should be screwed into the wall with No.10 screws set in fibre wall plugs such as Rawlplugs. As with the nails, the screws have to penetrate at least 25mm (1in) into the brickwork, but they must be placed closer, at 75mm or (3in) intervals.

Electricity

It is almost certain that at least one of your alcoves will have a power point or switch in it, which will have to be brought out flush with the panelling. The method of doing this is shown in Figs.9 and 10. When you are ready to fit the panelling, turn off the supply to that particular point and unscrew the holding screws. Lift the point out and nail a square of battening round its position to support the panelling, as shown in Fig.9. Cut a sheet of panelling to fit that section of wall and cut a hole in it where the point will be located, as shown in Fig.10. When the panelling is nailed in position, pass the point through the hole and screw it into the surrounding batten through the panel.

The panelling

The sheets of panelling will have to be accurately cut to size. Do the cutting with a fine-toothed panel saw or general-purpose saw. When cutting, the face side of the panel should be uppermost—if you try it the other way round the surface will chip or splinter. Make sure that each panel is firmly supported underneath when sawing.

Place each sheet carefully in position and nail it to the battening with 19mm ($\frac{3}{4}$in) panel pins dovetailed at 75mm (3in) intervals. Use a nail punch of the appropriate size to drive the heads below the surface. This will avoid dents in the panel caused by the hammer head.

At the edges of the panelling, spread a little wood-working adhesive along the underside of the edge, and along the top of the battening. This will prevent the edges of the panel from lifting slightly between nailing points, which they might otherwise do after a while.

Fitting panelling to a flat wall is comparatively simple, but the finishing of external corners is always a problem. The easy way out is to fit a covering angle piece over the corner, as shown in Fig.14. But the neatest way is to join the edges so that they follow through as in Fig.6. In this method a 45-degree angle is planed along the reverse edge of board A, and along the face of board B, making the join look like the other imitation joins in the panelling. The V-shaped groove formed by this method will have to be

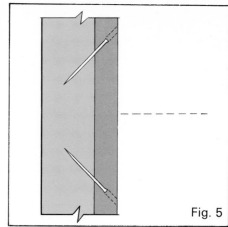

Fig. 5

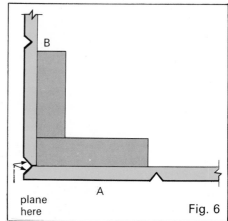

B

A

plane
here

Fig. 6

painted black to match the others.

Above: Detail of the storage arrangement. Because of the flexibility of the adjustable strips, the layout can be changed in minutes.

The shelving strips

These are the vertical strips into which the shelf brackets fit. They are screwed to the support battening using 25mm (1in) screws.

After you have fitted one strip, make sure that every adjacent strip is lined up so that the shelf bracket holes are in line. To do this, fit a shelf bracket to the strip you have just fixed to the wall, and one at the same height on another strip. Hold the loose strip in place while a straightedge is placed along the two shelf brackets. You can now adjust the correct level of the loose strip with a spirit level, as shown in Fig.8.

The cabinets

The construction of the cabinets is comparatively simple, but there are a few points to bear in mind if you decide to alter the dimensions shown. First, the cabinets must be large enough to accommodate their intended contents easily. This might be obvious, for example, in the case of fitting a record or tape deck. But did you know that if you want to store 12in LP records with their covers, you must allow 323mm (12¾in) each way?

Throughout the cabinets, mirror screws

with decorative heads are used to save the trouble of recessing and hiding the heads of ordinary screws. As chipboard has no great holding power, the method of glueing fibre plugs into the screw holes has to be used. All the joints are simple butt joints. The exposed edges of the boards should be covered with iron-on veneer edging strip, or pieces of plastic laminate cut to the correct width and stuck on with contact adhesive.

Full construction details are shown in the exploded views in Figs.16 and 17. The top or record cabinet is divided into three compartments by the insertion of two partitions. Access to the records is through a drop front, not a lid, and two stays are fitted so that the front, when open, also serves as a temporary shelf.

The bottom cabinet holds the hi-fi unit. This has two compartments, each with its own lid. The lid covering the record-player deck is hinged in the middle as shown in Fig.17 so that it can be folded right back

7

8

Fig.5. If the panels are nailed to the batten in dovetail pattern, and the heads 'lost' as shown, the marks will be nearly invisible.

Fig.6. When fitting panels to external corners plane two edges to match the other panels.

Fig.7. This shows the pattern of the battening, with some of the alcove panelling glued and nailed in position.

Fig.8. When fitting the adjustable shelving strip, fit one piece, then adjust with a spirit level laid across to ensure that the shelf brackets, when fitted, will be placed level.

Figs.9 and 10. If an electric point is already on the wall, unscrew it and lift it out, then fit battening all round as shown. Cut a hole in the panelling, pass the point through the hole and secure the point to the surrounding batten through the panel.

Fig.11. To cut right-angled slots in panels, drill a hole through every corner, pass a coping blade through one of the holes, fit the blade to the saw and proceed as shown.

Fig.12. A turntable fitted into one of the cabinets. Note how a drop-flap has been fitted to the front to allow better access.

Fig.13. The orange framework shows a typical pattern for the panel battening. The brown vertical strips represent battens placed as anchors for shelving strip screws.

9

10

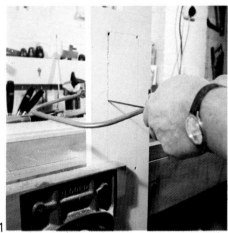

11

12

without interfering with any shelving above. But if the clearance above it is enough, this feature can be dispensed with. This same compartment has a 63mm (2½in) drop-flap section, as shown in Fig.12, to allow easy complete access to the front of the deck, where the controls are in most designs.

Obviously, if other equipment such as a tape-recorder is installed in this space, the requirements will be different and the boxes will have to be altered to match. But the basic design is so simple that you should have no trouble altering them, or for that matter, any other part of the unit.

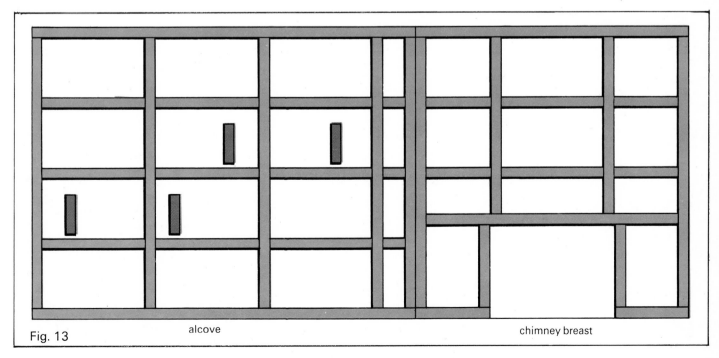

Fig. 13   alcove   chimney breast

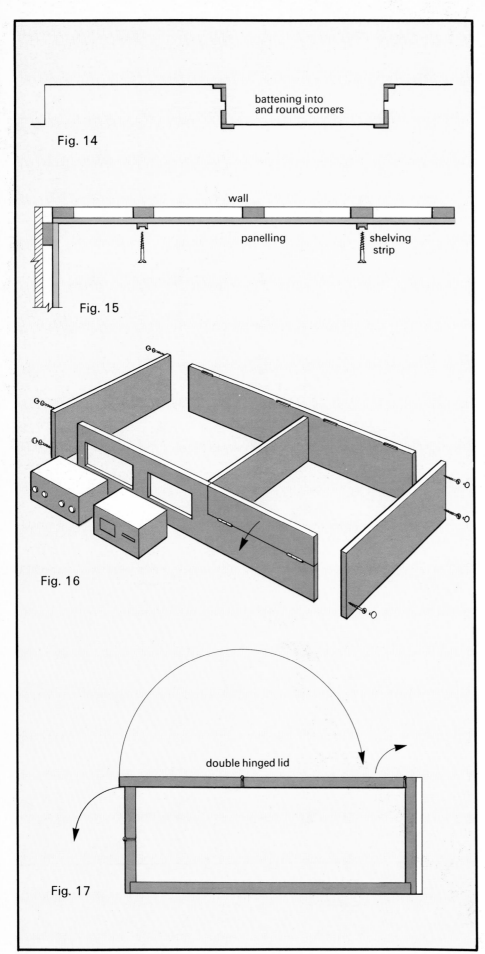

Fig. 14

battening into
and round corners

wall

panelling

shelving
strip

Fig. 15

Fig. 16

double hinged lid

Fig. 17

Fig.14. Battens must be nailed to the wall on each surface of a corner to provide a nailing surface for the battening.

Fig.15. Cutaway view from the top of the panelling. The main battens hold the panels, with separate battens for the shelving strip.

Fig.16. An exploded view of the cabinet carcase that holds the record player turntable, amplifier and tuner.

Fig.17. Side cutaway view of the complete cabinet. Note how the lid is hinged in two places to clear the shelf above.

Stick on glamour for your kitchen walls

One of the traditional places in which glazed tiles are used is the kitchen because they are durable and easy to clean. They also help, because they reflect light, to make the kitchen a bright place in which to work.

Types of tiles

The choice of ceramic tiles is wide. The standard sizes are 108mm (4¼in) square × 4mm ($\frac{5}{32}$in) thick, and 152mm (6in) square and 6mm (¼in) thick. Mosaic tiles, in a panel of 50 on a scrim backing, are the third of the widely used types, and usually measure about 55mm × 25mm × 4mm (2⅛in × 1in × ⅛in).

Tiles are available in many plain colours, many of which match equipment in a British standard colour (they have a BS identification number). Floor tiles, 13mm (½in) thick, can be obtained to match or complement them. 'Effects' tiles—patterned, textured and sculptured—are also obtainable in a wide colour range, but may not always be available 'off-the-shelf' and have to be ordered. Tiles used near cookers should be treated by the manufacturer against heat, or be ⅜in thick.

Calculating the number of tiles

There are three basic types of tile. The first is the 'bulk', or 'field', tile. These usually have spacer lugs on the outer edges so that they are separated by 4mm ($\frac{1}{16}$in) from each other. These gaps are filled, after tiling, with a white compressible material called *grout*, which gives a neat patterned effect.

RE tiles have one rounded edge and are used to give a neat finish at the edges of part tiling and on external corners of window reveals. *REX* tiles (for round edged external angles) have two adjacent rounded edges and are used to finish the top corners of part tiling and splash backs.

To calculate the number of tiles needed, allow three 108mm (4¼in) tiles per row for every 330mm (13in) of wall to be tiled, or 72 tiles for every 840 sq mm (square yard. With 152mm (6in) tiles, allow 6 tiles to 914mm (1yd), or 36 to 914mm sq (1 sq yd). Allow at least five extra tiles for breakages and cutting in. For the number of RE tiles,

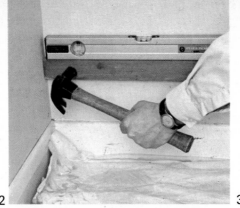

measure the length of the area for which you need them and allow three 108mm (4¼in) or two 152mm (6in) per 304mm (1ft). Deduct the number of RE tiles needed from the total number of tiles for the whole job.

Other equipment

Adhesive. This is available in a powder form to which you add water, or ready-prepared in cans. 4.55 litres (1 gallon) contains enough to cover 4.6-6.4mm (5-7 sq. yds.) on a good surface.

Notched spreader. Small metal or plastic spreaders are usually supplied by the adhesive manufacture, but if you plan a lot of tiling, a notched trowel will make the work easier.

Tile cutter. This can be a simple wheel cutter; or a scriber with a tungsten-carbinet tip; or a tile-cutting kit, consisting of a cutting platform, a small try-square and wheel cutter and a cutting tool rather like a pair of pincers. The more elaborate tile-cutting machines used by professionals, are also obtainable.

Pincers. These are used to adjust the shape of the tiles and to nip out small sections.

Plumb bob or *builder's spirit level.* These are used to establish accurate working lines.

A *lath or batten,* the same length as the longest dimension of the area to be tiled.

Grout. A 454g (1lb) quantity, mixed to a fairly stiff paste, will cover an area of about 1.8 sq m (2 sq yd) of 108mm (4¼in) tiles and 4.1 sq m (4.5 sq yd) of 152mm (6in) tiles.

Sponge or *tiler's squeegee,* for applying the grout.

Other useful items are a *radius cutter* for making large holes, or a *tungsten-tipped* drill for small ones, and a *carborundum block* or *tile* for shaping and smoothing cut edges.

Preparing the surfaces

First, remove any cupboards that you intend to tile behind (see 'Tiling around obstacles', below). Remove any unwanted screws, hooks, brackets, old pipes or other 'rubbish' and, if you have unsightly wiring on the wall surface, cut it back into the wall. If the skirting boards are battered, you may also decide to restore or replace them. Against a bright new surface, any unsightly old items will 'scream'.

The area should be dry, clean, flat and firm. Fill out any cracks and irregularities with cellulose filler or plaster, and rub down to a flat surface when dry. Newly plastered surfaces should be completely dry and, if dusty, brushed down with a wire brush to remove any loose material, If the surface is porous, a sealant primer should be used to prevent absorption of the adhesive into the plaster.

If the surface has been previously painted and the paint is sound, you can tile straight on to it (score gloss paint to help adhesion). Otherwise, strip the paint with a sanding block and medium glasspaper.

It is possible to tile over old tiles if they are sound and the surface is firm and flat. But

Fig.1. Measuring the tile height from the floor for the starting line.

Fig.2. Fixing the lath along the line.

Fig.3. Marking the vertical at the end of the wall to line with the last full tile.

Fig.4. Driving the adhesive over the surface to form ridges.

Fig.5. Starting at the intersection of the lath and vertical line.

Fig.6. Checking the tiles' alignment.

Fig.7. Fitting in a part tile.

Fig.8. The other section of the tile is placed on the adjacent wall to continue the pattern.

Fig.9. Fitting in a 'buttered' tile.

Fig.10. Using a sponge to rub the grout into teh joints.

Fig.11. Removing the excess grout.

Fig.12. Drawing a round-pointed stick along the joints for a good finish.

because old tiles are usually 13mm (½in) thick and bedded on to mortar, tiling over them will produce a bulky effect and you may be restricted to half tiling. In this case, it is

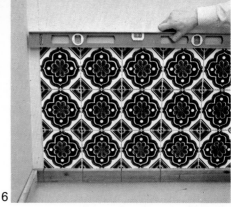

4

5

6

10

11

12

well worth considering chipping off the old tiles and their backing mortar, making good the surface and starting afresh. A club hammer and a bolster will make short work of the old tiles, or an electric rotary hammer can be hired to remove a large area.

Building boards, such as plywood, chipboard and plasterboard, provide good tiling surfaces, but must be removed, stiffened and replaced to prevent them from sagging and warping. Appropriate battening of 75mm × 50mm (3in × 2in) timber at about 304mm (12in) centres, horizontally and vertically, will give the necessary rigidity. If the board has a rough side, use this as the surface for the tiles. Use a heavy duty adhesive, and seal the untiled side—an ordinary paint undercoat can be used—to prevent moisture from the adhesive from seeping through.

For floor tiles, the surface must be dry and well brushed, and sealed with an anti-dusting agent. Newly laid concrete surfaces must be completely dry—allow a month for each inch of depth. If the floor is solid and uneven, clean it and relevel it. If necessary, remove the surface and re-screed the floor, or use a proprietary self-levelling compound. Timber floors also need to be levelled.

Setting out the work

If you are *tiling the walls*, remember that most floors are slightly out of level. So use a lath or batten as a base line because if you start from the floor or skirting board, you may find the tiles go out of true. First measure the height of a tile, including its spacer lugs, from the floor or skirting board. Fix the *top* of the lath or batten securely along this line to the length of the area being tiled. Check its accuracy with a spirit level. Take one tile, stand it on end, and run it along the floor beside the batten to make sure the batten is not too high—you do not want to fit tiny silvers of tile at the bottom if the floor is uneven. If the batten is too high, lower it, and then re-level it with the spirit level.

Next, mark out tile widths on either side of the centre point of the wall. This will give an equal tile cut at the ends, and should avoid having to make very short awkward cuts. Mark a true vertical line at the end of the wall, corresponding with the outer edge of the last full tile space.

Now repeat the procedure on any walls which meet the first one. But this time, if the wall length does not match an even number of tiles, try to space them to avoid finishing with two very narrow pieces in the same corner. And see if you can have complete tiles on either side of window reveals as it will save cutting.

You start work at the intersection of the batten and left-hand vertical line, beginning with the bottom row and working upwards. 'Obstructions', such as sink units, window reveals, and half cuts for the corners and top of the wall, are left until last.

If you are *tiling the floor*, the tile positions are set out with chalk lines, and you start tiling in the middle.

Fixing the tiles

Apply the adhesive to the wall or floor, rather than to the tiles, as this is easier and cleaner, and will give a more even surface. Use the spreader or trowel to spread it on the surface to a depth of ⅛in, covering only about 1 square yard at a time. If you apply more than this, it will dry out before you have tiled it. With the serrated edge of the spreader, drive the adhesive over the surface to form ridges which will give good suction and adhesion to the tile backs.

For awkward areas, and part tiles, the backs of the tiles may be 'buttered' by spreading the adhesive on to them to a depth 2mm (1/16in).

Press the tiles firmly into place, without sliding them—this would merely remove the adhesive from the wall or floor. Any adhesive which squeezes on to the surface of the tiles can be removed later with a damp cloth. Between each application of adhesive, check the horizontal and vertical alignment of the tiles because they are liable to creep. When wall tiles have set, remove the battens and fit tiles into the remaining space, cutting them to fit if necessary (see below).

Tiling around obstacles

Where possible, remove fixtures such as cupboards; if this is not possible, tile to the sides of the unit, leaving the tiling immediately above them until later. Then fix a batten along the top of the unit so that the top of the batten aligns exactly with the bottom of the tiles on either side. Continue to tile along

13

14

15

16

17

18

19

either side, and above the batten, and when these tiles have set, remove the batten and cut tiles to fit below.

A similar method is used for window reveals and doorways. Use round-edge tiles on the reveals of the openings, rather than on the face of the side wall. as this will help keep the vertical lines in true. As neither RE nor REX tiles have spacer lugs, cut small pieces of card and insert them between the tiles. Remove them when the tiles have set. Any part tiles should be nearest the window, with the spacer lugs facing those tiles already in position.

Cutting and shaping tiles

Use a felt-tipped pen to mark the tile where it is to be cut. For a straight cut, score the glazed surface with the tile cutter, using a straight-edge as a guide. With the glazed side uppermost, place a matchstick or small piece of wood under and along the scored line, put your thumbs on both corners and apply even pressure downwards. The tile will snap cleanly along the scored line. For a shaped cut, cross scratch the area to be removed and use pincers to nibble away the part, taking small 'bites' at a time. Smooth off any unevenness with the carborundum block or file.

Near the edge of the tile, a round hole can be made by marking the line round a coin, and scoring it, and the area inside it, with the tile cutter. Nibble away the waste area with pincers. Small holes can be made with a tungsten-tipped drill. Larger holes or patterns can be cut by drilling a series of holes in line to the shape required and removing the section.

To make a hole in the centre of a tile, mark its position and then cut the tile in half. Use pincers to nibble away the semi-circle in each half. When the halves are placed together, the join will be barely discernible.

Grouting

When all the tiles are in position, wait at least 12 hours (several days if tiling over old tiles) and then grout the joints. Use a sponge to rub it into the joints with a semi-circular movement. Remove any grout from the surface of the tiles with a damp sponge. When the grout has almost set, draw a round-pointed stick across the joints. Finish by polishing the tiles with a soft dry cloth.

Fig.13. Using a try square and scriber to score a straight line.

Fig.14. If you are doing a lot of tiling it is worth using a special cutter which scores the surface and breaks the tile in one action.

Fig.15. Nibbling away small sections of the tile with pincers.

Fig.16. Smoothing the cut edges with a carborundum file.

Fig.17. Another special tile cutter cuts circles for pipes.

Fig.18. Small holes can be cut in tiles by using a drill with a tungsten tipped bit.

Fig.19. For awkward areas and part tiles, the backs of the tiles should be 'buttered' with the adhesive.

Step-by-step to underfoot glamour

Vinyl tiles have been popular for several years, especially for kitchens, where they provide a tough, practical flooring. Now self-adhesive tiles do the same job, with the added bonus of being even easier to lay. They are one of the simplest means of giving your kitchen a 'lift'.

Vinyl tiling is both durable and easily maintained. Normal household spillages can be wiped up with a damp cloth, and keeping the floor sparkling is a simple job with warm water and a mild detergent.

Types of floor

The two most common types of floor are the solid floor and the suspended floor.

The solid floor consists of a concrete screed laid over a block of site concrete. Between the two layers of concrete there should be—and in new houses, there is—a damp-proof course, usually of polythene sheeting. Its function is to prevent damp from entering the house.

The suspended floor is the type built of wooden planking—sometimes plain boards, sometimes boards that fit together with tongue-and-groove joints. This planking is laid on floor *joists*, which rest in turn on the sub-floor structure. In Britain and some other countries, this consists of masonry *sleeper walls* on which the joists rest; in yet other countries, a system of timber sleepers and *stumps* or *jackstuds* is used.

Preparing timber floors

A suspended timber floor usually provides a rather unstable surface on which to lay floor coverings.

In newly-laid floors the timber will almost certainly shrink, unless the timber is well seasoned and the builder has taken the trouble to cramp up (squeeze together with flooring cramps during the nailing process) only three or four boards at a time. Too often, the opposite is the case: the timber is on the 'green' side, or damp from exposure at the building site, and boards are cramped up ten or a dozen at a time—a system giving far too little pressure to get them really tight.

Older floors often show where the individual boards have 'cupped' through years of natural timber shrinkage, producing ridges across the surface and cracks between the boards. Even if they are not sharp enough actually to crack vinyl or lino, the ridges will cause uneven wear on the surface, which soon shows up as streaky marks. And air will seep through the cracks between the boards, in extreme cases making the house draughty.

In any case, timber is always subject to some seasonal movement. It expands during humid weather and contracts again when the weather is dry, loosening the floor covering.

To help counteract these problems, American homes are sometimes built with double floors. One skin of flooring is laid diagonally and nailed to the floor joists, and the other skin laid lengthwise and nailed to the first.

A less costly way of providing a double floor is to lay hardboard over the existing one. First, any loose floorboards are dovetail-nailed to the floor joists, and any 'proud' (protruding) nailheads are punched well below the surface. Then the floor is sanded to remove any bumps and ridges. For the odd high spot, you can use the rotary sanding head of a power drill, but the ridges on cupped boards require either an orbital hand sander or a larger commercial sander (either of which you can hire).

When buying hardboard, you need only the standard 5-6mm ($\frac{3}{16}$-$\frac{1}{4}$in) thickness, but it must have been correctly treated to prevent moisture coming through the floor and making it warp when laid. In Britain, you can ask for 'flooring' grade, or buy standard hardboard and temper it yourself by brushing or sponging water on to the mesh side and leaving it for 24 hours to dry out. In more humid climates, however, you may need oil-tempered hardboard; ask your dealer's advice.

Buy the hardboard in whichever size (or combination of sizes) will be most economical, but you will probably find it easier to lay in 600mm (2ft) or 1200mm (4ft) strips than in large sheets. Stagger the joints so that they do not run right across the room. For securing the hardboard, use countersunk screwnails (threaded nails) in the standard 16mm ($\frac{5}{8}$in) size, at 106mm (4in) intervals.

Preparing solid floors

Hardboard is not usually necessary on a solid floor—although in some countries it is widely used to provide a slightly more resilient surface, less jarring to walk on, than the concrete would be.

However, solid floors, although obviously more stable and draught-resistant than wooden ones, must have a smooth surface if they are to act as the base for vinyl or lino. Minor cracks and indentations can be filled with a mixture of pva adhesive and cellulose filler, diluted if necessary with a little water to make it workable, and pressed firmly into place. Larger cracks should be chipped out to 12.5mm ($\frac{1}{2}$in) wide and filled with mortar. Odd high spots will need to be chipped off with a heavy hammer and cold chisel.

Really uneven solid floors are a more difficult problem. In Britain and some other countries, you can buy a self-levelling compound which neatly solves the problem: you apply a coating at least 12.5mm ($\frac{1}{2}$in) thick; and as it dries it levels out.

Where this is not available, you will need to surface coat the whole area to bring it into level. First, coat the floor completely with a proprietary bonding agent, following the manufacturer's instructions. Then use a mix of sharp sand and cement in a ratio of 4:1 by volume, mixing with just enough water to turn it to the consistency of brown sugar, and apply a coating at least 12.5mm ($\frac{1}{2}$in) thick; any less might crack and break away.

To keep the depth consistent, use shallow formwork to divide the floor area into bays. After tamping and levelling off, wait for the concrete to dry before removing the formwork and making good.

New tiles on old

It is generally bad practice to lay new vinyl tiles on old, because an adhesive layer between vinyls produces a chemical reaction which causes movement between the two layers. Old lino, vinyl sheeting or tiles should always be stripped off before new flooring is laid.

Calculating quantities

Self-adhesive vinyl tiles are usually 253mm × 253mm (9in × 9in) or 305mm × 305mm (12in × 12in). To work out the number you will need, first measure the length and breadth of your room and 'round up' the measurements to the nearest foot.

Next find out, by dividing the length of the wall by the wall width of one tile, how many tiles you need for a row along the longer wall. Example:

Longest wall: 3.8 m (12ft 6in)
Rounded up to nearest foot: 4 m (13ft)
Width of the tile: 229mm (9in)

Therefore the number of tiles per row is 4 m (13ft) divided by 229 (9)—answer, $17\frac{1}{3}$ tiles. Or, rounded up to the nearest whole number, 18 tiles.

Now do the same for the shorter wall. If

for example it is 2.5m (8ft 3in) long, one row will need 11 229mm (9in) tiles.

Finally, multiply the number needed for the longer row by that for the shorter row to give you your total—in this case, 18 longer wall × 11 (shorter wall) to give a total of 198 tiles.

If your room consists of two or more rectangles, calculate separately the quantity for each rectangle; then add the totals together.

This method also works for hexagonal tiles, provided that you measure them from centre to centre (Fig.7) and not from side to side.

When buying, you need to allow about 5 per cent extra for wastage. If you have had to 'round up' several of your measurements already, you will probably have an adequate margin for saftey. If not, add the 5 per cent at the end of your calculations.

Setting out the pattern

When laying a patterned floor with tiles in contrasting colours, it is a good idea to prepare a design sheet in advance. Draw your room to scale on graph paper, using one

Below: Vinyl tiles used in a dignified setting. They create a smooth look for the entrance hall, enhancing the overall decor.

Fig.1. Starting the tiling job at the datum point—where the chalked lines cross at the centre of the room.

Fig.2. With the blue tile pushed against the wall, the white one is being used as a template. It is laid on top, and one row further in, so that . . .

Fig.3. . . . the blue tile can be cut accurately to fit against the wall.

Fig.4. How to get around awkward corners and projections: cut a whole tile to the pattern of a cardboard template.

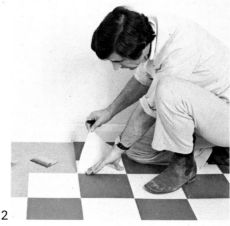

square on the sheet to represent each tile: for example, each square on the graph paper could represent a 229mm × 229mm (9in × 9in) tile. Then use coloured pencils to set out your pattern.

This method helps you to see that your pattern will 'sit' centrally on the floor, and to avoid errors such as bold diamonds whose corners are cut off by a wall, or edging strips which fall an uneven distance from the skirting boards.

Later, when you come to lay the tiles, you can check the design on the floor by loose-laying enough tiles to cover one quarter of the room. This will allow you to make any adjustments necessary, either because you have measured wrongly or because the room itself is slightly out of square.

While working out your plan, remember that tiling (or any other floor covering) should finish at a line halfway under the door of the room when the door is closed. It is at this line that it meets the door covering in the adjoining room or hall.

(You will need a covering strip to prevent the tile edges being damaged.)

Setting out the tiles

Before you begin tiling, keep the tiles inside the house for about 48 hours. Especially in winter, this will make them easier to lay

because the warmth assists adhesion.

However, if you have under-floor heating this should be turned off 48 hours before you begin work, and not turned on again for 48 hours after you have finished.

Check through each box of tiles before you begin, to make sure there are no variations in colour.

For the tiling operation itself, you will need: 1, A chalk line to mark out the room. 2, A pencil. 3, A sharp handyman's knife and scissors. 4, A straight-dege. 5, A square of hardboard to make a scribing board; for the dimensions, see 'Fitting Awkward Tiles' below. 6, A carpenter's rule or a steel tape. 7, A rolling pin.

The first step is to mark the guide lines to which the first tiles will be laid. Rub chalk along two lengths of string long enough to measure the length and width, respectively, of the room. Using the carpenter's rule or steel tape, measure accurately the halfway points on opposite walls, excluding any bays or recesses. Next, tap a nail into the floor or skirting board at each of these points.

Now stretch a chalked line tauntly between one of these pairs of nails. Hold the string in the middle and let it twang against the floor so that it leaves a straight line chalked accurately across. Now chalk a similar line in the crosswise direction.

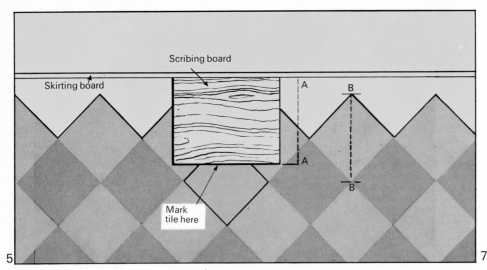

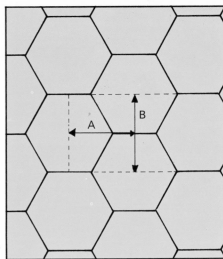

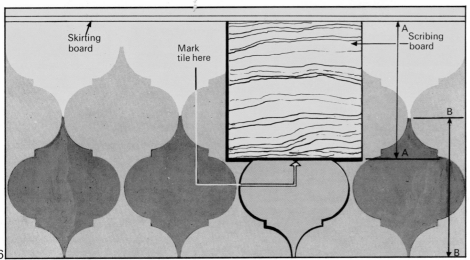

Figs. 5 and 6. *Where the skirting board is not parallel to your lines of tiles, the last row of tiles must be 'scribed' to fit. Make a scribing board from a piece of hardboard. Its length (A-A in the diagrams) must match the effective width of one row of tiles (B-B), and is not necessarily the same as the width of one tile. Place the tile you want to cut one row further from the wall than where it is to be laid. Place the scribing board on top of the tile, with one end pushed against the skirting. Now you can cut the tile to exactly the size you require.*

Fig.7. *To calculate the number of hexagonal tiles needed, measure them from centre to centre, not corner to corner.*

Next, dry-lay (without adhesive) enough tiles to cover one quarter of the room, and re-position the chalk lines if necessary. If the room is out of square—and most rooms are, however slightly—try to place the inaccuracies where they will show up least. (As a general, but not invariable rule, remember that the longer the wall the more any tiny, but progressive, variation will tend to show up. So keep your rows parallel to the longer walls unless this throws up a serious discrepancy elsewhere.)

Once you are satisfied that you have positioned the pattern to best advantage, rub out the original chalk marks. Twang in a new set, and then go over them with a pencil and straight-edge so that they will not disappear as you work.

Laying the tiles

The point where your two chalked (and now pencilled) lines meet in the middle of the room is the *datum* point. This is where your tile-laying starts.

Peel the paper backing off the first tile. If necessary, trim the edge carefully with the handyman's knife or scissors. Fit the tile

exactly into one of the right angles formed by the crossed lines. Press down the first edge firmly, then place the rest of the tile. When it is in place, use the rolling pin to get it down hard and flat.

Each tile after the first one is butted up against the preceding ones, pressed down along the joins, and then stuck down over the rest of its width.

As you go, make frequent use of the straight-edge to see that the tiles are staying in line—there is nothing so ugly as tiles that have 'stepped' slightly out of line—and, every two or three rows, measure the distance to the wall at several points to make sure that your rows are not gradually twisting out of straight.

Fitting awkward tiles

When you come to the final rows, beside the skirting boards, first tile those areas requiring the largest pieces of cut tile. A wrongly-cut tile can always be re-cut to a smaller size, but—obviously—not to a larger!

Cutting the last row is not difficult if your line has been running exactly parallel to the wall. You simply flip the tile over, upside down and end-to-end, and rule the line showing where to cut.

If the line is not running exactly parallel to the wall, the simplest method is to use a scribing board. This is a simple rectangle of hardboard whose width is made to suit the tiles you are using. You place the tile opposite to where it is to go, but one row further out. The scribing board lies on top of the tile, with its back pushed against the skirting board (Figs. 5 and 6). Since the board is the same width as one tile, all you need do is to mark along the front edge of the board to show where the tile must be cut.

Where a tile must be cut two ways to fit into an internal corner, you can use the same procedure: you simply scribe twice, once in each direction.

For more intricate fitting, such as around

216

Above: Three examples from hundreds of patterns you can copy—or invent yourself.

pipes, the best method is to cut a profile from a sheet of cardboard. When it is a snug fit, trace around it on to a tile to give you your cutting lines.

After tiling, divert 'heavy traffic' from the room for 48 hours. Avoid washing the floor during this time, to allow the flooring to settle.

Later maintenance presents no particular problems. Vinyl tiles have a slight sheen and do not need polishing. But if you require a higher gloss, use a water-based emulsion.

Avoid using harsh abrasives or bleach, as these ruin the surface of the tiles.

Cork, vinyl or wood blocks

The decorative effects of flooring are often overlooked, but a floor can make or break a room's appearance. Tiling floors is quite easy, and you can choose from cork, wood-block, or vinyl tiles.

Natural finishes

Cork and wood are natural products with intrinsic properties of durability and resilience which are not always present in man-made materials.

Cork is the tough, elastic outer tissue of a variety of oak tree. Cork tiles used for flooring are made from carefully selected cork chippings, strips or granules which are compressed under heat and bonded together with resins. The natural cellular composition of these cork tiles makes them 'bouncy', elastic and hard wearing.

Another characteristic of cork tiles is that they feel warm and comfortable to the touch —even bare feet will not recoil. They also help to deaden sound, provide good grip, and are resistant to most stains and weak acids. The tiles can be used anywhere in the house, but are particularly suitable for bathrooms, kitchens, nurseries and hallways where their non-slip qualities are most likely to be appreciated. One place they must not be used is on floors which are electrically heated to above 80° Fahrenheit or 27° Centigrade, since the adhesive which is used to fix the tiles in place is likely to melt and cause them to buckle.

Cork tiles come in various sizes and thicknesses, the most popular one being 305mm × 305mm (12in × 12in) and 3.17mm ($\frac{1}{8}$in) thick. They may be purchased completely unfinished, wax-coated, or vinyl-sealed to a matt or a sheen finish. Unfinished tiles should be wax polished after they have been laid, or given at least two coats of polyurethane varnish to seal their otherwise porous surfaces. Wax-coated and vinyl-sealed tiles need no further special treatment for sealing.

Unsealed or wax-coated tiles, which come in a range of shades, tend to look bleached out when exposed to strong sunlight for long periods of time. To restore them to their original appearance, sand the surfaces and reseal them. Vinyl-coated tiles, in addition to the usual, natural shades, come in a range of bright colours which have been sealed in by the vinyl coating and will not fade in sunlight.

Cork tiles can be simply maintained, once they have been properly sealed, either by going over them with a damp mop or, in the case of waxed tiles, by occasional re-waxing.

Decorative parquet *woodblock* floors can give a very luxurious appearance to a home at moderate expense, and do away with the need for carpeting. As a natural product, timber is particularly hard-wearing and, like cork, has good insulating properties.

Woodblock flooring is usually supplied ready-dried to a specific moisture content in order to prevent major distortion of the wood after the floor has been laid. It is available in different sizes and thicknesses, in solid blocks, or in thinner plywood blocks with veneered surfaces. As with cork tiles, they can be purchased ready-sealed, or they may just be machine-sanded, ready for finishing with a proprietary polyurethane seal after laying. Some blocks are tongued-and-grooved and are simply loose laid, needing no further fixings. Others are square-edged and ready to fix on a mastic bed.

Both hardwoods and softwoods are used for this type of flooring, ranging from the exotic mahogany and teak to the 'local' oak and walnut. Different patterns can be introduced by using the colour and graining in the chosen blocks to their best advantage. Usually the simple designs, such as basket-weave, are the most effective.

Solid hardwood block flooring can be used in living areas where hard wear is expected, such as hallways and playrooms; but softwoods and plywood parquet tiles are not really suitable here.

After several years of hard service, all that is needed to renew the appearance of the wood blocks is a light sanding and a new surface seal.

Manufactured flooring

Unlike wood and cork, vinyl flooring is a man-made material. It is produced in sheet form, or in tiles which are either ready for fixing onto a mastic base or self-adhesive.

As a floor covering, vinyl is very hard-wearing, flexible, resistant to water, grease and oil, and easy to clean. The disadvantages of using vinyl tiling are that it is not resilient, does not have good thermal or acoustic insulating properties, and is often cold to the touch. In rooms which tend to be cold, vinyl tiles may be damp because of condensation on their surfaces.

Vinyl tiles are produced in a variety of colours, textures and designs which will not fade or blur. Because they are inexpensive, you can afford to lay the same type of floor tiles throughout the house and achieve an overall decorative effect.

Cleaning the tiles is best done with a mild detergent solution. Avoid using solvents, paraffin (kerosene) or harsh abrasives, as these will damage the surface of the tiles. If you want a sheen, use a water-based wax emulsion.

Sub-floors

It is extremely important that all sub-floors should be level, dry and clean, no matter what the final surface finish is going to be. Meticulous care taken at this stage will ensure a perfect and lasting finish. There are no short cuts—each problem must be overcome, including damp-proofing, levelling, sanding, nailing down or removing old surfaces.

Calculating quantities

Cork or vinyl tiles are usually 253mm × 253mm (9in × 9in) or 305mm × 305mm (12in × 12in). To find out the number of tiles you will need, you must first measure the length and breadth of the room. Always round your measurements up to the nearest *whole* figure. Next, divide the length of the room by the width of one tile to find out how many tiles will fit along this wall. A wall 2.743m (9ft) long, for example, will require twelve 229mm (9in) tiles. Do the same for the width of the room and multiply the two final totals together to give the number of tiles necessary to fill the area of the room.

If your floor is unusually shaped, divide the areas into separate rectangles, calculate each rectangular section separately and add your totals together. And remember that tiles should finish at a line half-way under the door of the room, when the door is closed.

This method also works for hexagonal tiles if you measure them from centre to centre and not from side to side. Always add an extra five per cent to your calculations for possible wastage.

Patterns

If you want to work out a pattern sequence for tiles, you can do so quite easily by drawing your room measurements to scale on a squared paper planner or graph paper. Use one square on the grid to represent one tile and then use coloured pencils to shade in your pattern or design. You can always adjust the pattern or amend any errors in calculations by dry-laying the tiles on a portion of your floor before finally fixing them.

Preparing cork and vinyl tiles

Pre-finished *cork* tiles or factory-waxed ones do not need special conditioning, but unsealed cork tiles do. They expand and contract depending on the humidity in the air. Condition them by spreading them over the floor in the room where they are going to be laid, and leave them for at least 24 hours.

Vinyl tiles should be kept in a warm place for at least a week before they are laid, If you have under-floor heating, it should be turned off 48 hours before you begin work and kept off for a further 48 hours after you have finished. This applies to both vinyl and cork tiles.

Laying materials required

1, Special flooring adhesive suitable for using with sealed cork tiles or with vinyl tiles, and a notched spreader, or 2, Neoprene-based special cork-tile adhesive—if you are using unsealed cork tiles.

Laying cork or vinyl tiles

Once you have found the *datum* point in the middle of the room you may begin laying your tiles. Start by spreading the flooring adhesive over the floor, about a square yard at a time, from the datum point. Use a notched spreader to give the adhesive a ribbed surface which will grip the tiles well. In order not to obliterate the guidelines, spread the adhesive up to, but not over them.

Position the first tile so that one corner and edge register exactly with one of the right angles made by the two guidelines on your floor and gently press it home so that the tile bonds evenly to the floor. Continue tiling in this way, butting the tiles closely to one

Above: A basketweave-design woodblock floor combined with a carpet strip makes this narrow room look inviting.

another and checking continually to see that the tiles are not running out of line. Be careful not to let the adhesive 'go off'; it will stay sticky for about 15 minutes, but may set more quickly in a warm room.

When you have completed tiling a square yard area, smooth over the tiles with a decorators' rubber roller or a felt-covered block.

Remove any adhesive from the tile face immediately—a damp cloth will remove adhesive from vinyl tiles or sealed cork tiles.

Unsealed cork tiles are highly porous, however, and the adhesive is extremely difficult to remove from them, so be especially careful when you are laying these.

You will find that you will have to cut the tiles to fit around projections, at skirting board edges and into door thresholds. To get around pipes and other obstacles first cut a profile from a piece of cardboard. When this fits accurately, trace its outline onto a tile to give you the correct cutting lines. Fitting tiles at skirting board edges or at thresholds

is best done by a process known as *scribing*. For this method of direct measuring you will need to use a scribing board made from a piece of cardboard cut to suit the size of the tiles you are using.

After tiling your floor, try to avoid walking over it for 24 to 48 hours to allow the tiles to set firmly.

Conditioning parquet flooring

Acclimatize the wood blocks by spreading them over the floor in the room where they will be laid. Leave them for at least one week before permanently fixing.

Some proprietary woodblock floors, suitable for loose-laying, can be ordered with a sheet of heavy-duty polythene. This will protect them from damp ,especially if laid on concrete floors. Others may come with a cork cushion underlay which forms a resilient bed for the wood blocks. Still others, such as square-edged ones, need a cork expansion strip along the walls.

Loose-laid woodblock tiles

Always follow the manufacturer's instructions carefully. If it is necessary, lay your polythene sheet or cork underlay, cork side down. Leave a 12.7mm (½in) gap between lengths of the underlay to allow for expansion and around skirting board edges.

The starting point for loose-laying interlocking blocks is the corner of your room with the largest unbroken stretch of wall. Begin by making up a nine-or-twelve-block section to form a large square. Saw off the tongues of all panels which will butt against the skirting board and position the square up to the chosen corner. The angle is likely to be out of true, so line the panels up with the longer wall. Any small gap along the shorter wall can be corrected later by fitting moulding around the skirting board. At this point check to see that your skirting board is firmly secured so that you have something

Opposite page: The unusually styled woodblock floor in this room gives it a richly textured appearance. The insets show some basic techniques for loose-laying conventional oak parquet tiles.

Fig.1. Begin with a test square.

Fig.2. Knock in blocks with a hammer and a small board.

Fig.3. For close areas use an edging tool.

Figs.4 and 5. Marking the bottom of an architrave cut out with a chisel to avoid the skirting.

solid to support the blocks against.

Once your large test-square has been laid, the rest of the blocks are fitted against it (Fig.1). Position each panel, remembering that the grain of a block should be at right angles to the one next to it. The block is knocked into place with a hardwood board (to protect panel edges) and a hammer (see Fig.2). Gentle tapping is all that is necessary to fix the flooring in place; if a board seems to be stuck, it is probably due to a piece of dirt or small obstruction. Gently remove the impeded block, clean out any obstruction, and then knock the block into place. Always be sure to fit blocks so that you are hammering towards one or the other of your original two walls.

When you have to fit boards around projections, do so with a paper template in the manner described above for laying tiles. This can then be traced over the block to give the correct cutting lines, and the unwanted portion removed with a fine-toothed panel saw. Odd-shaped windows or corners may be cut to fit quite easily in this way. Blocks which are to be fitted up to the last two walls will need to be scribed to fit properly into place, using a scribing block which is the width of one panel. Corners can be cut to fit by scribing along the two sides where the block will meet the corner angle. Any panel pieces which must be specially cut to fit properly should be fitted *before* preceding complete panels are finally knocked into

Above: A subtly patterned, vinyl tiled floor can effectively set off a room's decor.

Inset: When laying tiles, spread the adhesive over a square yard at a time. Butt the first tiles close to the guidelines.

Left: Many delightful patterns can be created using hexagonal cork tiles in two contrasting colours, as shown in these four examples.

Below: Natural, honey-coloured cork tiles make a room look sunny.

place. End pieces should be cut and fitted *before* you begin a new row of blocks.

After the odd shaped pieces are cut, the rough edges should be sanded down and coated with some pva adhesive before they are put into place. The adhesive will help keep the joints from opening.

When fitting blocks close to the walls, special edge-fitting tools, usually supplied by the manufacturer, may be used. These are helpful wherever it is too narrow to allow a full hammer blow to knock the blocks into place (Fig.3).

Architraves and doorways

If you are laying woodblock flooring in two adjoining rooms, you should treat each room separately and finish them so that the blocks finish halfway under the door when it is closed. When you reach door architraves it is often easier to saw an appropriate amount off the bottom of the moulding to allow the block to fit underneath it, rather than to try to shape the block to fit around the architrave. Use the depth of the panel as a guide for cutting the moulding and scribe the panel to fit into the area underneath the architrave (see Figs. 4 and 5).

If the flooring on the other side of the doorway is lower or higher than the finished level of the woodblock floor you will need to use a *diminishing strip* across the threshold to even out the two levels. These can be ordered with the flooring and are merely tapered lengths of wood grooved on one side to meet the panel tongues.

Panels at thresholds usually have to be cut to fit, and they will need to be fixed to the sub-floor—either with a pva adhesive, or with 25mm (1in) losthead panel pins, or with masonry nails punched below the wood surface, depending on what the sub-floor is. If using masonry nails, the panels must be drilled for these beforehand.

The diminishing strip should be butted up against the threshold panels, and then may be pre-drilled and fixed with wood screws which can be driven straight into floorboards, or into Rawlplugs if you have a masonry floor. Brass wood screws are most practical to use as they will not rust. If wood screws are not used, the strip may be fixed with a rubber-based adhesive.

Skirting boards

If you find that you have slight gaps

between your flooring and your skirting boards, cover them with moulding. Fit any moulding that you do use so that it also covers any extra polythene underlay you may have put down. Polythene protruding over the moulding should then be trimmed off.

Square-edged woodblock flooring

There is one type of woodblock flooring which is square-edged and is fixed onto a mastic bed. Full directions are normally supplied from the manufacturers, but basically, the techniques you will need to use —squaring off the floor, applying the adhesive, scribing blocks to fit odd places—are the same as those for laying cork and vinyl tiles.

Finishing

If you have scuffed your floor a bit while laying it, marks can be removed by rubbing them gently with dry steel wool. If you want to, you can then touch them up with a polyurethane seal. Wax-polishing may be carried out at intervals to give the floor a smooth protective surface finish.

Carpet laying made easy

The estimating and laying of wall-to-wall carpeting can be a tricky job in a large or awkardly shaped room, and here it is probably best left to the professional. But in many average-sized, simply shaped rooms, it is practical—and more economical—to tackle it yourself.

Carpets with a foam backing, whether of the tufted, bonded or needle felt type, can all be successfully fitted by an amateur. Those with a heavy foam back—medium or high density—are particularly easy because they can be loose laid: simply cut to shape and placed in position without any securing at the edges.

Carpets without foam backing are much more difficult to lay, because often the edges need binding to prevent fraying and, if the carpet is of the woven type (Wilton or Axminster), the carpet must be stretched during the fitting. This stretching is done in order to make the backing really taut, thus keeping the pile upright—essential if the carpet is to look good and wear well. Stretching is an art and requires skill (and developed muscles) if it is to be done well. For this reason many carpet manufacturers will not recognize complaints about the performance of their carpets unless they have been fitted by a professional. However, since expert fitting is costly, there are occasions when you may want to tackle it yourself.

To stretch the carpet fully and evenly over a large area it is worth hiring a professional carpet stretcher, known as a knee kicker. For smaller areas, it is possible to make a form of kicker (see below), or even to use the prongs of a garden rake or fork.

The edges of unbacked carpets have to be secured in position. This can be done by turning them under and tacking them down, in which case the carpet should be 76mm (3in) wider and longer than the area being covered. This method, however, cannot be used on concrete floors. Alternatively (and this way is more efficient, but also more expensive), tackless gripper may be used. This is a wood or metal batten—in 4ft lengths—which is fixed round the perimeter of the room, and has two or three rows of prongs on the upper side to grip the backing of the carpet. The carpet should be 10mm (⅜in) wider and longer than the area being covered.

With either method of fixing, the underlay should be approximately 76mm (3in) shorter and narrower than the dimensions of the area to allow for the width of the batten or turn.

Home-made knee kicker

To make a carpet stretcher, you will need: a 300mm (12in) length of timber 100m × 75mm (4in × 3in); a piece of plywood 150mm × 75mm × 19mm (6in × 3in × ¾in); 55 25.4mm (1in) nails; 4 38mm (1½in) No. 8 screws; padding (foam or rubber) to cover the end of the timber; tacks to secure the padding.

On one side of the plywood mark a frame 25.4mm (1in) in from the edge. Inside the frame mark a grid of 13mm (½in) squares. Make holes for the screws (Fig.2). Then at the corners and intersections of the grid, hammer the nails through the plywood so that the points of the nails project 6.5mm (¼in) on the other side.

Lay the timber flat with the 102mm (4in) side as the base. Place the plywood on the timber as in Fig.2, with the points of the nails facing uppermost. Position the edge of one of the 152mm (6in) sides of the plywood level with the short end of the timber, and centre it on the timber's width so that 25 .4mm (1in) of plywood extends on either side (Fig.2). Screw the plywood to the timber. Tack the padding over the other end of the timber.

Measuring and estimating

Even if you are having the carpet fitted for you, or are fitting it yourself but getting the store to estimate the quantity, it is worth making a plan and making your own estimate as a double check. Often the store may be able to save on the amount needed, but if their estimate exceeds yours by a great amount it is advisable to recheck your own and then query it with the store.

To make a really accurate plan, use paper drawn up in 25.4mm (1in) squares, each square representing 305mm (1ft). Measure the room carefully with a steel tape and then draw the shape to scale on the paper. Mark all recesses and projections, and then measure the diagonals of the room to check on the squareness of the corners (they will be equal if the corners are true right angles). Then decide on the width of carpet you are going to use, and where pieces cut out—for a fireplace or bay, for example—could be used to fill in elsewhere.

Broadloom carpet is made in seven standard widths. It is the easiest type to lay in simply shaped square or rectangular rooms because joining is not necessary. You simply buy the length required in the nearest width beyond that of the room.

Body carpet is made in two standard widths. In an oddly shaped room with alcoves and projections it can be more economical than broadloom because there is less wastage, but as seaming the joins can be tricky it is often better in the long run to use broadloom for the main area of the room and buy matching body carpet to fill in alcoves.

In all cases, the width of the carpet should go across the width of the room, and the length—and therefore the pile and pattern—should run down the length of the room towards the door, if this is in one of the short walls. Any join in a doorway should be along the line of the door when it is closed, and never at right angles to it.

Laying the carpet

Remove all the furniture and any doors which open into the room. Prepare the floor and make good the surface as for vinyl tiles. If the floor is concrete, cover it with tarred paper before the underlay to prevent dust from coming through. If the floor is boarded, cover it with felt paper.

Rubber-backed carpet

Unroll a little of the carpet to check on the direction of the pile and pattern, turn it and

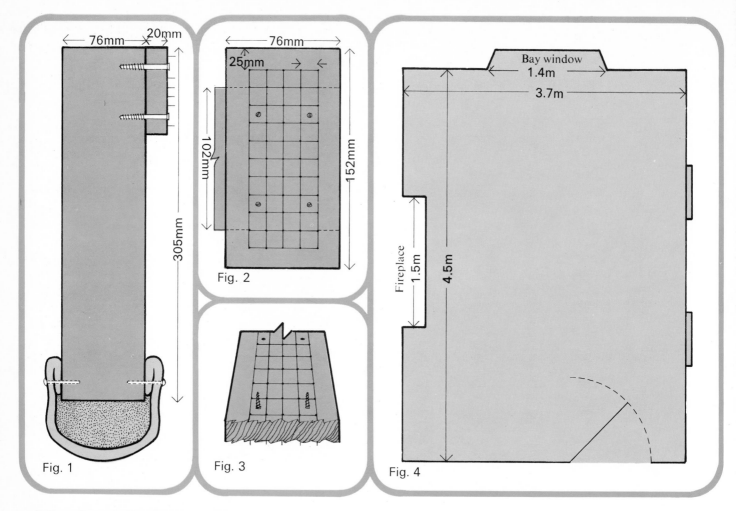

Fig. 1

Fig. 2

Fig. 3

Fig. 4

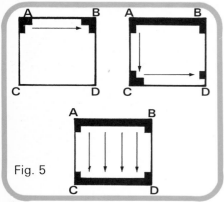

Fig. 5

Fig.1. *A home-made knee kicker may be used to stretch small areas of carpet.*

Figs.2 *and* **3.** *The grid marked on the plywood gives the positions of the nails, which are knocked right through the wood. Their tips grip the carpet when it is being stretched.*

Fig.4. *In this room, it would be best to buy a 3.7 m × 4.6 m (12ft × 15ft) carpet 'square',*

and use the offcut from the fireplace for the bay recess.

Fig.5. *To stretch a carpet, secure it at corner A, stretch to B. and secure along the wall between. Stretch to C and then to D. Stretch from wall A-B and secure wall C-D. Then secure wall A-C, stretch to wall B-D and secure that.*

start at the opposite wall if necessary to get them running in the right direction without rerolling the carpet.

With the edge of the carpet butting up to the wall, unroll the carpet evenly. Tread it out flat as you progress, but without pulling the edge away from the wall. If it starts to go out of line, reroll the carpet and begin again. If you discover that the corners are out of true, let the edge of the carpet run up the wall slightly and trim it to fit afterwards. Do not attempt to adjust a large area of carpet when it is rolled out because its weight makes it almost impossible to do so evenly.

When the carpet is almost in position, trim

off any excess with a metal straight edge and sharp knife. To make a clean cut, press the straight edge into the carpet between the tufts of pile and run the knife along its edge in one continuous motion. When large areas have to be cut out, mark the line with chalk, allowing an excess margin of 2 5 mm (1in). Cut out the main part, fit the carpet back into position and trim off the margin to fit it exactly.

To make a join, fit both pieces of carpet in position and check that the pattern fits, that the pile is running the same way, and that the edges butt exactly. If they do not, overlap pieces and cut through both, using the

straight edge as a guide. Then roll back the edge of one piece and stay tack it to hold it back. Measure the width of the carpet tape, and mark a line with chalk on the floor at a distance of half the tape's width from the edge of the carpet piece still in position (Fig.9).

Roll back this second carpet section and stay tack it back. Cut off the right length of adhesive tape and position one edge on the line so that the tape is on the side of the *second* piece that you rolled back. Stick the tape down or anchor it at each end with tacks. Replace one of the carpet pieces and press it down firmly on half of the tape.

Unroll the other piece and press it down carefully so that the edges butt firmly and the pattern, if any, matches exactly.

Next, slide the joined edges towards each other, making a slight peak and thereby exposing the cut edges. Apply a thin bead of joining cement along one side and then flatten out the carpet again. Remove any excess joining cement with cement solvent and leave the seam to set for about an hour.

Unbacked carpets

If using the gripper method of fixing the carpet, nail, screw or glue the battens to the floor at a distance from the wall of slightly less than the carpet's pile height; the points of the gripper should be slanting inwards to the wall. Fix battens right round the perimeter of the room, and not just where the ends of the roll will be.

Fit the underlay in position (rubber-backed hessian should have the hessian side uppermost). If you are turning and tacking the edges of the carpet, the edges of the underlay should be 38mm (1½in) away from the wall on all sides. If you are using gripper, the underlay should butt up against the inside edge of the batten. Staple or stick (with latex based adhesive) the underlay in position and join it on the underside with adhesive tape where necessary.

Turn and tack method

6

7

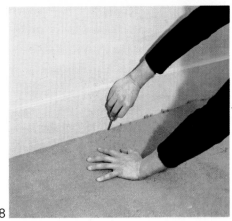
8

9

10

11

Fig.6. The underlay should butt up to the edge of the gripper batten.

Fig.7. The knee kicker is used to push the carpet over the prongs of the batten which grip the carpet backing firmly.

Fig.8. The edge of the carpet is poked down into the gulley between the gripper and the wall.

Fig.9. To join carpet, fold back one piece and mark a line at a distance of half the tape's width from the edge of the other piece.

Fig.10. Fold back this piece and stay tack it. Position the tape with one edge butting the marked line and tack it down at each end.

Fig.11. Press both the carpet pieces firmly down on to the tape.

Unroll the carpet as above, but position it so that a 38mm (1½in) margin overlaps on to the wall on each side. Secure it temporarily in one corner with a tack and stretch the carpet taut (see Fig.5). Retrim the margin to 38mm (1½in) if necessary, and coat the edges on the backing with latex adhesive to seal them and prevent fraying.

Turn under the margin, press the folded edge against the skirting board and then tack it down, using 13mm (½in) tacks at approximately 127mm (5in) intervals. Use 25mm (1in) tacks at corners, where there is extra thickness.

Gripper method

Unroll the carpet as above, but position it so that 10mm (⅜in) margin overlaps on to the wall at each side. Secure the carpet temporarily in one corner with a tack and stretch the carpet taut (see Fig.5). Retrim the margin to 10mm (⅜in) if necessary and coat the edges on the backing with latex adhesive to seal them and prevent fraying. Use the knee kicker to push the edges of the carpet over the prongs of the gripper and down into the gully between the batten and the skirting board (a screwdriver will make this job easier).

Finishing off

All carpets should be well secured at doorways to prevent both accidents and wear. This is most easily and neatly done with a binder bar, which should come immediately under the door when closed. One kind of binder bar is a 'cove' of metal which is screwed to the floor. The edge of the carpet is fitted into the recess and secured on to the prongs on the bottom lip. The top of the binder bar is then hammered down (with a wooden mallet) to close it over the edge of the carpet.

A simpler form of binder bar is a metal strip which is placed over the edge of the carpet and screwed into the floor. With both kinds, it is possible to secure the edges of an adjoining carpet at the same time.

When the bar is in position, check that the door will open and close smoothly over the carpet. If necessary, plane off just enough of the bottom of the door to make it clear the carpet without rubbing it. Rule the line to which you intend to plane, rather than guessing, and always plane 'from sides to middle' so that the plane does not rip off the edge of the door. Be careful not to plane off too much or you will create a draught problem.

Timeless tiles—for a fresh new look

If you are bored with linoleum and vinyl for utility-room floors, try glazed tiles or quarry tiles for a distinctive and practical floor. Quarry tiles are plain, matt-surfaced tiles, but they come in a range of colours and can be arranged in attractive patterns. They will give a permanent and ageless look to any style of room, but are a particularly suitable way of providing a hardwearing, water- and fireproof floor for a kitchen or bathroom.

Glazed ceramic tiles are available in a much larger range of colours, and often have patterns embossed on them. They will make an attractive floor to an entrance hall, or any room where more visual impact is required than can be given by quarry tiles.

Glazed and quarry-tiled floors should last a very long time; quarry tiles in particular are virtually indestructible as there is no glazing or pattern to be worn away. The extra work involved in laying ceramic tiles, rather than other types of floor coverings, is well worth the effort. Both types of tiles have to be fixed firmly on a sound base, or they may come loose or crack; the ideal method is to lay the tiles on a screed of concrete as thick as the tiles themselves and to *grout*, or fill in between them, with white cement. The weight of the screed and the tiles can create serious weight problems on a timber floor, but it *is* possible to lay tiles on timber provided the floor is strong.

Before deciding to lay ceramic tiles, consider the following points carefully. Tiles laid on a solid floor will usually raise the floor level by at least 25mm (1in). With suspended wood floors, a concrete base should first be laid. The effect of this is to raise the floor level, usually by at least 63mm (2½in). This means that there will be a small step between the rooms, which can be hazardous; it is advisable to slope the other floor up to the level of the tiles. If the doors open inwards to the room being tiled, the bottom of the door will have to be cut off to allow the door to swing over the tiles. And if you tile a kitchen which has a number of fitted units at working surface level, the addition of tiles on a suspended wood floor will effectively reduce the working surface level by at least 51mm (2in). You can avoid this by removing the units, laying the tiles all over the floor, and then replacing the units on top of the tiles. You could use chipboard instead of tiles under the units to save money and weight, but then you can't move the units later.

The combined weight of the tiles and the cement screed on which they are set is considerable. You must therefore ensure that the floor is sound, that the span of the joists does not exceed approximately 3.6 m (12ft). If it does, it is inadvisable to lay tiles unless the floor is first strengthened.

Types of tiles

There are numerous tiles to choose from and the price range is wide. Quarry tiles are at the cheaper end of the range. They are made from clay which has been fired but not glazed; the finish is flat but hardwearing. Although other colours are obtainable, the most readily available is red, or reddish brown. The surface is normally smooth, but tiles can be obtained which have a non-slip, ribbed or studded surface .The normal shape for quarry tiles is square, but tiles in hexagonal and octagonal shapes are also on sale. The commonest type of all is the 152mm (6in) square tile, which is mass-produced and therefore constant in size. Some other sizes and shapes are hand-made and may therefore vary slightly in size. Quarry tiles usually have plain square edges, so that they can be fitted edge to edge, or round edges for use where the tiles end, for example in a doorway. *Coving* is also available (see Fig.2). These L-shaped tiles enable you to make internal corners, and so take the tiles a short way up the wall to create a skirting board. The corner is rounded to make it easy to clean the sides of the room.

Glazed tiles are more expensive. They can be obtained in a wide range of colours and the surface may be plain or have a pattern embossed on it. They are usually obtainable in 150 or 200mm (nearest inches equivalent: 6in or 8in) squares, and the thickness varies from 6mm (¼in) and 9.5mm (⅜in) for wall tiles to 13mm (½in) and even 16mm (½in) for floor tiles. Always ensure that you purchase floor tiles and not wall tiles by mistake. Coving and corner pieces are available to match the commoner types of glazed tile. Some manufacturers, however, produce coving and edging strips in a plain colour that matches the background of their patterned tiles.

Tools

To lay your tiled floor you will need a trowel to mix the cement with, a metal float to smooth it, a hammer, a tile cutter, a pair of pincers, and a block of wood or a mallet.

Cut three battens 13mm (½in) thicker than the tiles being laid, an inch and a half or more wide and about 1.5m (5ft) long. Mark on each of them a line the width of a tile plus 1.6mm ($\frac{1}{16}$in)—half the normal gap between

Above: *Attractive and practical quarry tiles in this entrance hall contrast well with the colour and texture of the carpet.*

tiles, away from one end. Then mark the rest of the batten at regular intervals corresponding to one tile width plus one *whole* gap, i.e. 3.2mm (⅛in). These battens will help keep the tiles in line and correctly spaced when they are laid.

Now make a levelling board. Take a piece of timber 100mm or 150mm × 25mm (4in or 6in × 1in) and cut it to the combined length of six tiles, the gaps to be left between them and double the width of the battening you have already. Cut a rebate in the corners at opposite ends of one long edge (see Fig.3); the depth of the rebate should be the thickness of the tiles less 3mm (⅛in), and the width a little more than the width of the battening you are using.

Quantities of tiles

To find the number of tiles you need,

divide the room into squares, and measure the length and width of each square. Divide the width of each tile plus the width of the gap between them into the length and width of the square. This gives you the number of tiles needed to bridge the length and the width of the room. If the answer is a fraction, round it *up* to the next whole number. Multiply the two numbers together to give you the number of tiles needed to cover each square. Do this for all the squares in the room and add them together. Add another 5% for breakages. If you are using different tiles to make a patterned floor, draw a plan of your room, divide it into squares the size of your room and plan how many of each type you need on the drawing.

Floor preparation

If you already have a solid floor in the

room to be tiled, simply take up any existing floor covering and clean the floor. A solid concrete ground floor is the best base for tiling. If the floor is slightly uneven this can be put right when laying the cement screed, as described below.

Suspended wooden floor

It is possible to lay tiles on a wooden floor, but it is not worthwhile taking short cuts. Floorboards, even if they are sound and the span of the joists is less than 3.5 m (12ft), give as you walk on them. In comparison, tiles hardly give at all. So if you fit your tiles directly on the boards you run a high risk of them cracking or coming loose.

You should therefore lay a solid, rigid layer of concrete on top of the floorboards. First check that the boards and joists are sound, then temporarily remove any doors opening inwards. Remove the skirting boards.

Cover the floor with sheets of 19mm ($\frac{3}{4}$in) thick chipboard and nail it down firmly so that there is no gap between the joints. The chipboard will dampen some of the movement of the floorboards. Then cover the chipboard with a layer of polythene sheeting —there is no need to nail it down. This will allow the chipboard and the concrete to move against each other a little without undue stresses being set up. The next stage is to take some expanded metal or chicken-wire and staple this to the chipboard to make a reinforcement for the screed. Do not put in too many staples or you will restrict the movement of the floor under the layer of screed. Use just enough to hold the reinforcement in place.

Take two lengths of 13mm ($\frac{1}{2}$in) thick battening as long as the width of the room and nail one of them temporarily in place along the wall opposite the door. Nail another one parallel to it and 600-750mm (2ft or 2ft 6in) away. Find a straight edge, preferably a fairly robust piece of wood, that will reach between them.

Make up a fairly dry cement mix with three parts of sand to one of cement and trowel it into the space between the battens. Then level it off by scraping the straight edge along the tops of the battens.

Wait until the screed you have laid is half-dry (this will take about two hours in normal weather), then remove the batten farthest from the wall and refasten it another 600mm (2ft) from the edge of the screed. Mix and lay another strip of screed in the same way, running the straight edge along the batten you have moved and the edge of the first strip of screed. Leave the other batten against the wall for the time being.

Continue in this way until you have laid a 12.7mm ($\frac{1}{2}$in) thick coat of screed all over

the floor. Remove the batten against the wall as soon as the screed is dry enough to walk on, then fill the gap where it was with more screed. You should now have a completely uniform layer of screed all over the floor.

This technique ensures that your tiling job will last for a very long time. If you are not particularly concerned about durability, or if you are doubtful about the ability of the floor to bear the weight of tiles *and* screed, you can dispense with the screed altogether and stick the tiles direct to the chipboard with an epoxy resin adhesive. This may come loose after a few years, but this short cut will save you a lot of trouble.

Positioning the tiles

First divide the room (excluding any bays etc.) into quarters. This is done by taking two pieces of string longer than the width and length of the room and rubbing them with chalk. Then, if the corners of the room are square, measure the halfway point along each wall and hammer a nail into the floor at that point. Tie the string to the nails on opposite sides of the room. Take hold of the middle of each string and raise it from the floor, then let it 'twang' back into position so that it leaves a chalked mark on the floor. Mark this line in pencil.

If your room is out of square, it is usually best to position the tiles so that they are parallel with either the longest wall or the wall with the door. This will be the base wall. Measure the length of *one* of the walls adjacent to the base wall, using the largest available set square and a long straight edge. Divide the length by two to find the mid-point, and drive a nail into the floor at that point (see Fig. 4). Do not measure the length of the other wall adjacent to the base wall. Instead, draw another line out from the base wall at right angles, measure the same distance along it, and knock in another nail. It does not matter whether these nails are against the side wall or a short way from it. As before, tie a chalked string to these two nails and mark the floor. This line will be parallel with the base wall. From the mid-point on the base wall draw a line at right angles to the wall opposite. The point where these two lines meet can be treated as the centre of the room, and the two lines as dividing the room into roughly equal quarters.

Now lay the tiles on the floor in the position in which they will later be cemented. Lay a quarter of the room beginning with the section farthest from the door. Start from the 'centre' point and work towards the walls. Leave space between the tiles for grouting with white cement later. You can regulate the gaps by laying the tiles along one of your previously marked battens. 3mm ($\frac{1}{8}$in) is

usually a sufficient gap, but if you are using large, hand-made tiles it is better to leave 6mm ($\frac{1}{4}$in) gap to allow for variations in the size of the tiles. Don't cut the tiles to fit round the edges yet, but check that the rest of the tiles look right, especially if the individual tiles form a pattern. If they look wrong, re-arrange them as you see fit.

Repeat this with the other three quarters of the room, then take all the tiles up again.

Laying tiles

Clear the section of the room you are going to tile first, and paint the screed with a concrete bonding agent such as Unibond. Take two of the battens you have already prepared and place them at right angles to each other with one end of each at the 'centre' point so that the inside edges of the battens follow the

lines already drawn on the floor. Place the third batten parallel with one of the first two battens but just over the width of six tiles nearer the wall. (See Fig.5). Fix the battens in place with heavy weights, or better with an impact adhesive. But use only just enough adhesive to hold them in place as they will be removed later.

Take some more cement mix (three parts sand to one cement) and fill the space between the battens with cement to a thickness of slightly more 13mm ($\frac{1}{2}$in). Then take the levelling board already prepared and place it across two battens so that they fit into the rebates cut into two corners of the board. Then press downwards and drag the board towards you. The cement screed left behind will be approximately 16mm ($\frac{5}{8}$in) thick. Lay the tiles on the screed alongside

one of the battens, but leave a gap between the tiles and batten half as big as the gap there will be between the tiles (use a piece of cardboard the right thickness as a guide). Repeat this round the other three sides. Then fill in the centre, leaving the full gap between the tiles (use a thicker piece of board). The tiles will stand above the battens by approximately 3mm ($\frac{1}{8}$in). So now take the wooden block and knock the tiles down into the cement until they are level with the top of the battens. If the cement is too stiff to let you do this, pour a *little* water between the tiles. Ensure that they are still in line by running your piece of board between them, and that they are lying flat by running a straight edge along the bettens. Then remove the battens and repeat the procedure, starting from one side of the square already laid.

Above: Dark coloured tiles on the floor look good with white fitted kitchen units and reflect the warmth of the accessories. Use ribbed tiles for a non-slip surface.

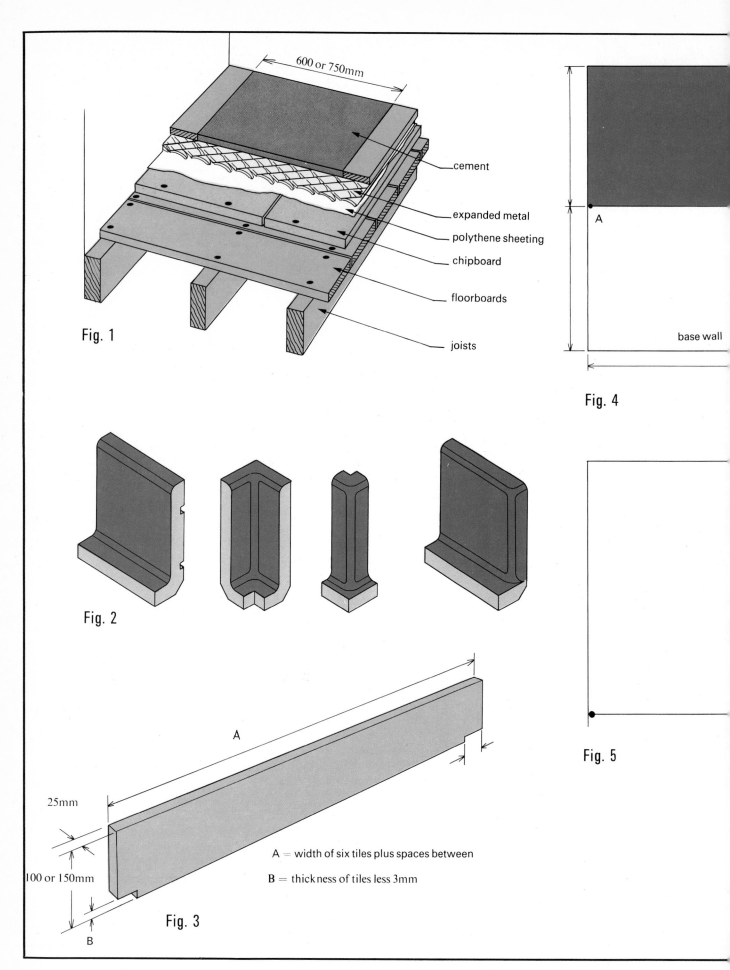

600 or 750mm

cement

expanded metal

polythene sheeting

chipboard

floorboards

joists

Fig. 1

Fig. 2

A

25mm

100 or 150mm

B

Fig. 3

A = width of six tiles plus spaces between

B = thickness of tiles less 3mm

A

base wall

Fig. 4

Fig. 5

230

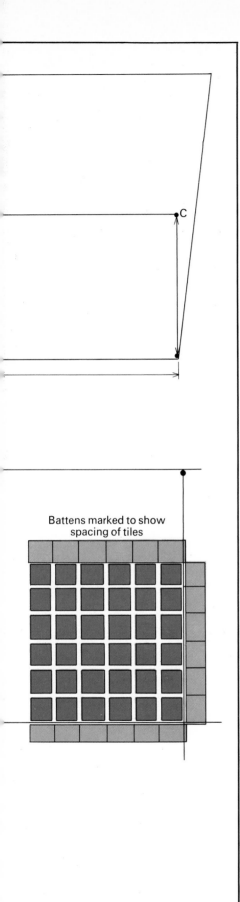

Battens marked to show spacing of tiles

When placing the battens for the second section line them up with the section already laid. Sprinkle neat cement against the edge of the wet cement mix under the tiles already laid, so that the next lot of mix bonds properly to it.

Cutting floor tiles

As you work towards the walls of the room, the last row of tiles will normally have to be scribed and cut to fit. Take the tile to be cut and place it directly on top of one of the tiles in the last row nearest the wall. Take another tile and place it on the first tile,

Fig.1. Cross section of a rigid layer of concrete laid on top of a suspended wooden floor before laying the tiles. The cement screed will sink through the expanded metal and form a single rigid concrete layer.

Fig.2. Various pieces of coving to make a neat finish between the floor and wall.

Fig.3. A wooden levelling board.

Fig.4. Chalked string is used to divide an irregular shaped room into quarter for tiling. Nails A and B mark the mid-points of the base and left walls. Nail C is half the length of the left wall from the base wall.

Fig.5. The section of the room furthest from the door and the 'base' wall is tiled first. The tiles are lined up with the battens.

parallel with the wall and twice the width of the normal gap between tiles away from the wall. If you are fitting coving, allow also for the width of this and a backing of cement. Draw a pencil line on the first tile along the edge of the second tile. This will show you where to cut the first tile.

To cut the tile, take a metal straight edge and place it on the line just drawn. Take the tile cutter and score deeply along the line. Then, with a hammer, tap the reverse side of the tile along the scored line until the tile breaks along the line. If you are cutting a curved line, cut to the nearest straight line, and then use pincers to bite away at the tile till it is the shape you want. For awkward-shaped corners, first cut the shape on a piece of paper and then mark it on the tile.

Finishing

Leave the floor to harden thoroughly. Then take some white cement, which is sold specially for the purpose, and mix it according to the manufacturer's instructions. Use a plastic sponge to spread the cement all over the cracks and a flexible plastic or wooden ruler to smooth the surface. Allow the grout to dry slightly, but not too much, then clean the surface of the tiles with a damp sponge, or by sprinkling sawdust or sand on it, rubbing it around with a soft-bristled household brush, and then sweeping it off with the same brush. Do all this before the grout hardens completely, or you will have to remove it with dilute hydrochloric acid.

Sufficient means of support

When you want to fix anything to a wall, whether it be a simple tooth-brush holder or a large cabinet, it is vital that a secure attachment is made. This is easy when you know the correct method of fixing to use.

Invisible fixings

There are two types of 'invisible' fixing for shelves: those that are unseen from above, used for shelves below eye level, and those which are genuinely invisible from any angle. The first kind is easier to build.

Shelves that run the full length of a wall or alcove, and which can be supported at each end by other walls, are much easier to fix unobtrusively than free-standing shelves with open ends. Small glass shelves in alcoves can be held up by virtually invisible clear Perspex supports that plug into holes in the

wood or plaster at each end (see Fig.5).

A wooden shelf mounted below eye level can rest on horizontal wood strips plugged and screwed to the wall (see Fig.9). Provided these strips do not come right to the front of the shelf, and their ends are trimmed at an angle, they will not be noticeable. A long shelf can also be given extra support by running a strip along the back. If it is more than 2m (6ft) long and carries heavy loads, one or more brackets may be needed in the middle of the shelf to stop it from twisting and sagging. These brackets can also be hidden—see below.

A shelf running between solid walls and mounted above eye level can be fixed in such a way that nothing shows at all. The supporting strips at each end of the shelf are made either of very narrow wood strips

(narrower than the thickness of the shelf) or of aluminium angle strips. Instead of resting on the strips, the shelf is grooved at the ends and slides on to the strips, effectively concealing them (see Fig.10). If the grooves are 'stopped' (do not reach all the way to the front) nothing will be visible.

Grooves in the ends of shelves should be cut with a plough plane, if you have one. The end of a piece of blockboard is hard to plough neatly because the joints between the blocks impede the plane blade. The best way to do it is to make deep cuts with a marking knife to mark the edges of the groove, then to set the plane blade very fine and alter its

setting very slowly.

If you don't have a plough plane, the grooves can be made just as well with a narrow mortise chisel the same width as the groove.

This method is very suitable for blockboard shelves, because they are quite thick and will conceal a wide, strong supporting strip. It is important that blockboard shelves are made with their internal blocks running *along* the shelf, or they will have little strength. These shelves are normally edged to hide the blocks and make the front look neater. In this case, the groove can be cut right across the shelf and its front masked

Above: A simple white-painted shelving unit can set off your crockery or ornaments to their best advantage.

232

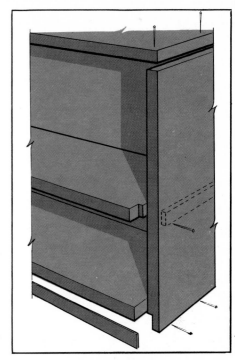

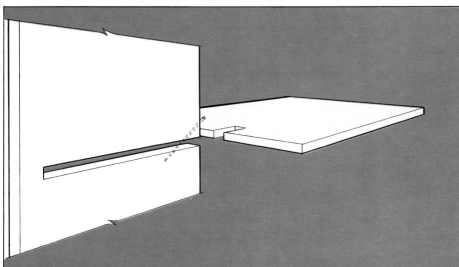

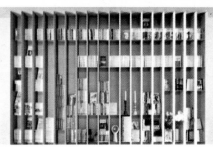

Above Left: Boxed-in shelves.
Fig.1. *Housing joints are often used to make this kind of shelving.*
Fig.2. *Cheap, light ''egg-box'' shelving made of plywood can give a dramatic effect, as shown above.*
Below Left: Vertical spacers strengthen shelving and give it variety.
Fig.3. *The shelves are supported by housing joints, the spacers pinned.*

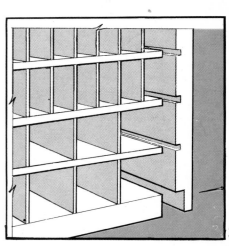

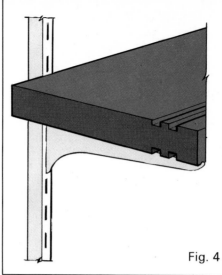

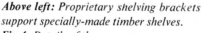

with edging strip.

All these techniques can also be applied to shelves mounted around inside and outside corners (see Fig.11). The shelf on one side of the corner acts as a brace for the shelf on the other side. However, both ends must be firmly attached to their mounting and not just resting on it, for the force exerted by pressing down on one end of a corner shelf may lift the other end. A shelf resting on wood strips can simply be screwed to them. One slotted into invisible mountings is harder to fix, unless the mounting strips are very wide and can have a screw passed through them from above. It may be easier to plug and screw the shelf to the wall instead. A small 'pocket' cut out of the less visible side of the shelf, with a screw passing through it into the wall at an angle is one solution (see Fig.12).

Free-standing shelves

Shelves which do not have their ends supported by a wall are harder to fix unobtrusively. Most people putting up this kind of shelf settle for small, nest brackets, but if you feel you must have invisible fixings, there are solutions to the problem.

The simplest method is suitable only for timber-framed stud walls—common in the United States, Australia and New Zealand. Few houses in Britain have this type of wall, except in the 'box room' over the stairs, but a few recently-built houses have stud partition walls. Large coach screws—at least 230mm (9in) long and 9mm ($\frac{3}{8}$in) thick—are screwed into the studs, which are generally 400mm (16in.) apart. Once they are firmly screwed in, their heads are sawn off. Holes the diameter of the screws are then drilled into the shelf from the back edge and the shelf is then slid on to the screws (see Fig.13). This fixing method is very strong, provided the timber for the shelves is twice as thick as the screws, and provided the screws project about two-thirds of the width of the boards.

Another similar method for brick or breeze-block walls uses steel angle brackets—the flat solid steel kind, not the U-section type made of sheet metal. The horizontal parts of the brackets are slotted into the shelf as the coach screws were. The only difference is that the slots in the shelf are rectangular, rather than round. These slots are made by drilling several holes and cutting out the wood between them with a long, narrow chisel. It is easier to make the slots too wide and insert narrow pieces of wood as a wedge to hold the shelf firm to the brackets.

The other half of the bracket is harder to hide. One solution is to plug and screw it to the wall and hide it with a backboard. If

Above left: Proprietary shelving brackets support specially-made timber shelves.
Fig.4. Details of the support.
Left: Glass shelves are ideal for ornaments.
Fig.5. They can be invisibly fixed on clear plastic 'buttons'.
Below left: Hanging shelves supported by roof beams are strong enough to take heavy loads—and there are no awkward brackets.
Fig.6. How it works.

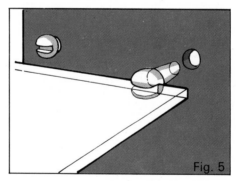

there are three or more rows of shelves and the backboard runs behind them all, it can be quite a decorative feature.

A more satisfactory way of hiding the brackets is to recess them into the wall 6-13mm (¼-½in) and cover up the recess with cellulose filler. A neat, shallow channel can be cut in a plaster wall with an ordinary carpenter's chisel, though you will have to sharpen it afterwards. The blade should be held at an angle so that its cutting edge always points towards the centre of the channel. Then, if the blade slips, it will damage the plaster *inside* the channel instead of making a long gash in the wall. Once the channel is cut, use proprietary plugs and screws to fix the bracket to the wall.

As brick is much harder to cut than plaster, the above method is probably not worthwhile for a brick wall.

Brackets should not be placed too near the ends of shelves or they will make it liable to sag in the middle. A proper position for a pair of brackets under a free-standing shelf is roughly one-quarter and three-quarters of the way along it. With this arrangement, neither the middle nor the ends is very far from a solid support. A shelf should always be fixed rigidly to its brackets to stop it from tipping up if the end is pressed down.

Featured fixings

If you cannot hide the fixings of your shelves, the best thing to do is to bring them out into the open and make a feature of them. One way of doing this is to buy a ready-made shelving system, which has the great merit of being adjustable. If this doesn't appeal to you, there are many good-looking fixings you can make yourself.

If you have period furnishings, plain timber brackets are probably the most suitable. A typical design, intended to be made out of 15mm (⅝in) thick hardwood, is illustrated. The shape can, of course, be varied to taste, provided that the vertical depth of the bracket is at least half the width of the shelf. The bracket is best fastened to the back plate with a mortise-and-tenon joint as shown, but can be screwed on from the rear if you prefer.

One of the simplest ways of holding up shelves, and one that looks particularly good with modern furniture, is to run verticle boards up the ends of the shelves to turn them into a wall-mounted box (see Page 233). All the shelves except the top one should be attached to the vertical boards by stopped housing joints, and the top shelf rebated at each end. This construction, which makes the shelves look like a bookcase, is very strong. (In good carpentry, shelves are never supported by just the strength of nails driven into the ends.) A backboard, even of hard-

Right: A highly original shelving idea: three wooden shelves drilled at the corners and hung from thick, knotted ropes. But you need plenty of confidence to put a tall, fragile oil lamp on them.

Fig.7. If you can't hide brackets, why not make a feature of them; the curved plywood brackets are held to the shelves by dowels.

Fig.8. Shelves look good in alcoves, and are easy to install there. One of the simplest alcove mountings; screw-eyes and wall plugs.

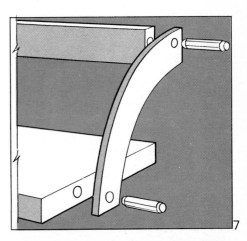

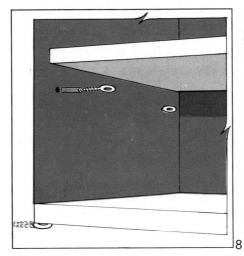

235

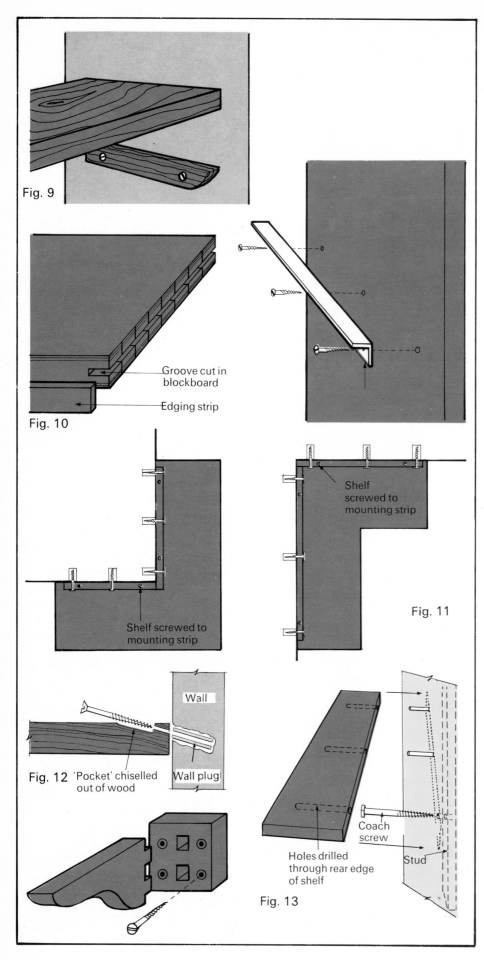

Fig. 9

Groove cut in
blockboard

Edging strip

Fig. 10

Shelf screwed to
mounting strip

Shelf
screwed to
mounting strip

Fig. 11

Wall

Fig. 12 'Pocket' chiselled
out of wood

Wall plug

Coach
screw

Holes drilled
through rear edge
of shelf

Stud

Fig. 13

Figs. 9-13. *Various methods for mounting shelves, all of which are described in the text.*

Fig.14. *When using fibre plugs in plastered walls, always ensure that they are firmly positioned in the masonry, not merely in the plaster surface.*

Fig.15. *Nylon plugs have 'teeth' which when the screw is tightened, expand to grip the masonry. They are particularly suitable for fixing to aggregate blocks.*

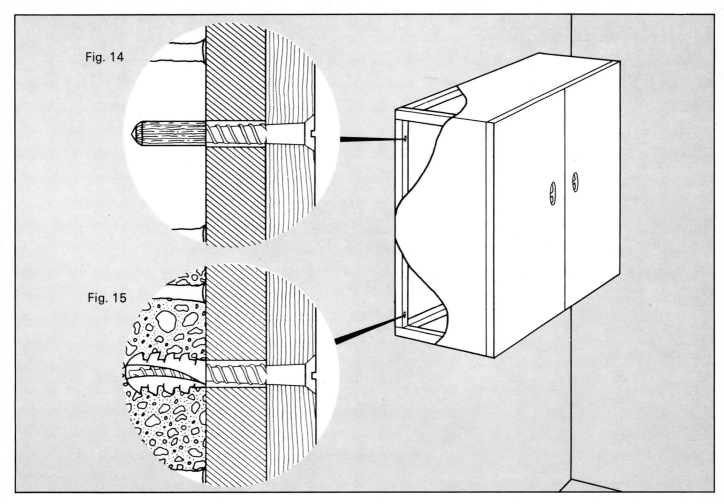

Fig. 14

Fig. 15

board, fitted behind the unit makes it even more stable, by acting as a brace. In a long unit, short vertical 'spacer' boards can be put between the shelves to hold them apart. An attractive random effect can be created by placing these boards at irregular intervals.

There are many other methods of giving your shelving an interesting appearance. For example, the method illustrated on Page 235 uses heavy rope to hang the shelves from rings at the top of the wall. The rope is knotted under each shelf; the height of the shelves can be adjusted by reknotting the rope. This method is too flexible for fragile ornaments to be put on the shelves, but it is ideal for books or magazines.

One of the most convenient types of shelving consists of large open-sided boxes that can be stacked on each other. As long as the boxes are not stacked too high, they provide a strong, stable storage space that can be rearranged to any shape. If all the boxes are made the same height, but some are twice or three times as wide as the others, an enormous variety of arrangements can be made to suit any use.

A wide variety of fixings are available for interior and exterior use. The choice of fixing will depend largely on the weight of the object to be fixed, and the type of wall or

ceiling it is to be attached to. There are three basic methods of fixing: for solid walls, masonry nails and plugs and screws (or bolts in the case of very heavy objects) are used, and for hollow surfaces such as panelled walls or ceilings, cavity devices can be used.

Fixing for solid walls

Solid walls are generally made of either brick, concrete, or lightweight cellular or aggregate building blocks. Attaching objects to brick and concrete is usually straightforward, and a secure fixing can be made with masonry nails or any of the standard types of plug and screw fixings. In the case of cellular blocks, an adequate fixing can be made by simply drilling and driving in a screw. Care is needed, however, when fixing to aggregate blocks as these do not provide as secure a bedding as the other materials.

Masonry nails

These can be used to fix such things as shelving battens, picture rails, skirting boards and studs for wall panelling to most types of solid surface in the home. They are tempered to prevent bending and can be nailed straight

into the wall with a hammer. Special cartridge tools which fire the nail into the wall can be obtained. These are particularly useful where large quantities of nails need to be driven.

Two types of nail are available. One has a straight shank and the other a twisted one, which improves penetration into hard materials and helps keep the nail firmly in place.

When nailing, always drive the nail in at right angles to the wall and ensure that the nails are long enough to penetrate at least 13mm or $\frac{1}{2}$in and not more than 19mm or $\frac{3}{4}$in into the masonry. If the wall is plastered add the thickness of the plaster to the length of the nail required. To prevent them from snapping, nails with straight shanks should be *gently* driven into the wall with light hammer blows aimed to hit the head of the nail straight on. With twisted shanked nails, start the nail off with light hammer blows, and then use heavier blows to drive the nail home—they are stronger than straight-shanked nails and will not break so easily. If possible, wear goggles as protection from flying chips of masonry or broken nails.

Wall plugs

Most household objects can be firmly

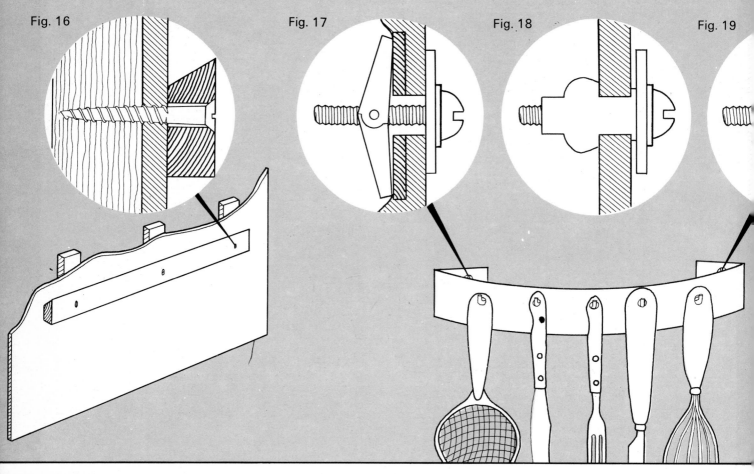

Fig. 16   Fig. 17   Fig. 18   Fig. 19

Fig.16. Fix large, heavy objects to hollow walls by bridging the studs with a batten. The object can then be screwed to it. Alternatively, the top edge of the batten can be bevelled, as shown here, to accept a similar, but inverted, batten on the object. The object's weight will keep it in place without further screwing.

Fig.17. Spring toggles have arms which open behind the wall and spread the load when the bolt is tightened. They make an ideal fixing in lath and plaster walls.

Fig.18. Rubber Rawlnuts can be used in both hollow and solid walls. The rubber sleeve expands when the bolt is tightened.

attached to solid walls with one of the many types of plug and screw fixings available. They all require a pre-drilled hole, which can be made with either a hand boring tool or a tungsten carbide-tipped masonry drill.

To make a hole with a hand tool, first tap the tool with a hammer through any plaster and then use firmer blows when the masonry is reached. Twist the tool slightly after each blow to ensure a neat hole and to stop it jamming. Once the required depth for the plug has been reached, remove the tool and blow out any dust.

If you are using a masonry drill, you must use either a hand brace or an electric drill with a speed reducer. With some drills this is built in, but an attachment is available to reduce the revolutions of a fixed speed drill. As you drill, press firmly so that the bit bites into the masonry. Remove it from the hole a few times and clear away any debris. Take care to keep the drill steady or the hole will become larger than required. If this does happen, you will have to pack it with a suitable filler (see below).

A percussion drill is desirable for use with concrete as it saves time and wear on the drill bit. This can be hired but, again, an attachment for converting an ordinary drill is available.

Plugging the hole

The most common types of plug are those made of fibre. These are suitable for most applications in the home, but should not be used where extreme moisture or heat is likely to be encountered. In these circumstances, aluminium or metal plugs specially treated against corrosion should be used.

Fibre plug sizes are numbered to correspond with the size of screw and boring tool to be used. If there is a fixing hole in the object to be secured, its size can be a guide to the size of screw required. As a rule, the longer the screw the greater the strength of the fixing, so if you are in doubt about the security of the object, use the largest suitable screw and plug.

The correct size of fibre plug for any screw is the same length or slightly longer than the length of the thread. When boring the hole, drill about 3mm or ⅛in deeper than the length of the plug so that the screw can be tightened fully home without the point touching the end. Two other things must be remembered when making the hole. First, if the plug is to be inserted into a plastered wall, ensure that it is firmly bedded in the masonry, not merely positioned in the plaster—ideally it should be sunk right into the masonry to avoid fracturing the plaster surface (see Fig. 14).

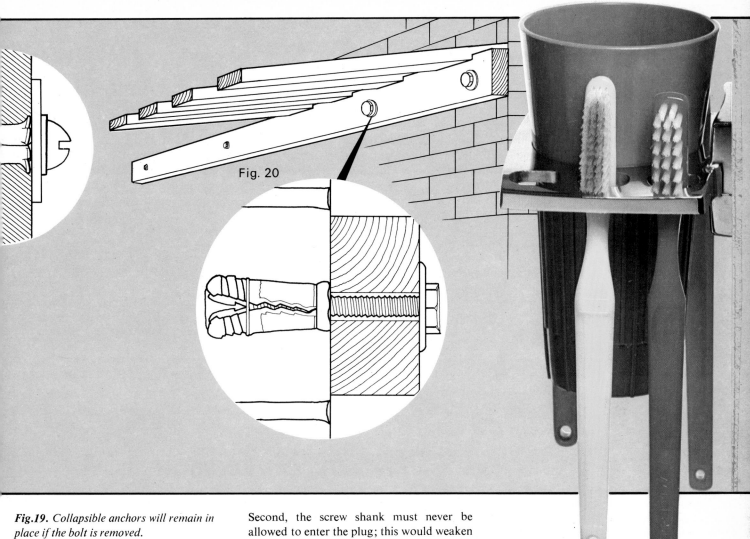

Fig.19. Collapsible anchors will remain in place if the bolt is removed.

Fig.20. Heavy construction timbers, such as the wall plate for supporting rafters shown here, should be attached to walls with masonry bolts. When the bolt is tightened, a plug is drawn into the metal outer body, which then expands to grip the masonry.

Second, the screw shank must never be allowed to enter the plug; this would weaken the fixing and the masonry. If the thickness of the article to be secured is less than the length of the screw shank, sink the plug further into the wall.

When the hole has been made, first insert the screw a couple of turns into the plug and then push the plug into the wall. Then tighten the screw until the shank is about to enter the plug. Withdraw the screw, attach the fixture and then screw it up tight.

Plastic wall plugs are also available and come either as strips which you cut yourself, or in pre-cut lengths. They have the advantage of being rotproof and waterproof, and are colour coded for size.

Aggregate blocks

The main problem encountered when attaching objects to walls made of aggregate building blocks is obtaining a firm anchorage for the fixing. Although light objects can often be adequately fixed with standard plugs and screws, it is safer to use one of the many nylon plugs designed for the purpose. These have 'teeth', or ridges, which grip the surrounding material, and 'fins' which prevent the plug rotating while screwing. They will also take screw shanks with little distortion, and can be used in normal masonry.

Another device that is useful for fixing to aggregate blocks is the 'Rawlnut'. This has a rubber sleeve which, when the bolt is tightened, expands and compresses against the surrounding material. It can also be used for fixing to other types of masonry and is suitable for hollow surfaces.

Wooden plugs

Home-made wooden plugs can be used in place of proprietary ones but apart from the difficulty and tedium of carving each one by hand, they are more likely to work loose than other types of plug. They can be, however, a useful temporary substitute. If you are making one, ensure that it fits tightly in the hole and then drill it before insertion. A slight taper at the end will help it to fit right to the back of the hole.

Overlarge holes

Sometimes holes are distorted either through bad drilling, or through wear if they are being re-used, and will not take a wall plug. If this is the case, you will have to plug the wall with a special filler made for the purpose. To increase the strength of the fixing, scrape out the inside of the hole with a nail so that it is larger than the mouth. Then moisten the filler to a plastic consistency, mould it into a suitable shape, and force it into the hole, making sure that all parts of the cavity are filled. When the filler has been inserted, pierce the hole for the screw. A tool for packing and piercing is normally provided. If light objects are to be fixed, the screw can be driven home before the filler has set, but objects likely to pull the screw from the wall should be left until the filler has hardened. This filler can also be used as a substitute for wall plugs in all types of masonry.

Supporting heavy weights

Where very heavy furniture and timber used for construction purposes are to be attached to solid walls, expanded masonry bolts should be used for secure fixing. These are inserted into a suitable hole and, when the bolt is tightened, it draws a plug up into the outer body of the bolt, which then expands and grips the masonry.

When positioning the holes, avoid drilling in the mortar between bricks and in the corners of the bricks themselves. Bolts up to 10mm or $\frac{3}{8}$in diameter are suitable for 230mm or 9in thick brickwork; 6mm or $\frac{1}{4}$in is the largest recommended size for a 115mm or 4$\frac{1}{2}$in brick wall.

Hollow ceilings and walls

Many interior wall and ceiling surfaces are created by fixing some form of lining, such as plasterboard, to timber supports. The fixings described above, except for the Rawlnut and some nylon plugs, are not suitable for use on these surfaces as they would simply fall out.

In some cases, objects can be attached by screws passing through the lining into the timber supports. To locate the position of the studs or joists, tap along the wall or ceiling with a hammer—a 'dull' sound will indicate a stud. Before drilling the screw hole, probe with a fine drill or bradawl to confirm you are in the right position.

Often, however, the proposed fixing point will not correspond with a timber support (or you may not be able to find them!) and you will have to use a special fixing.

Fixings for hollow surfaces

A large number of fixings are available and all are designed so that some form of support

is provided *behind* the panel when the bolt or screw is tightened.

A metal type of fixing is the metal 'toggle'. These either rely on gravity to open the toggle when the fixing is pushed through the wall, or are spring loaded. Gravity toggles should be used for hollow wall fixings only as they would not spread the load evenly on a ceiling. Spring toggles, however, are suitable for both walls and ceilings.

To attach an article with both these fixings, first undo the toggle and then insert the bolt through the object to be fixed. Attach the toggle to the end of the bolt, fold it flat, and push it through the hole. Once on the other side of the panel, the toggle opens and is drawn against the back of the panel when the bolt is tightened. Unfortunately, these can only be used once, as withdrawing the bolt will cause the toggle to fall into the cavity. This feature also applies to nylon or plastic anchors, which are used with screws instead of bolts.

For a more 'permanent' type of fixing, a nylon toggle is available that remains in place when the screw is removed. This is

made up of a toggle bar, a slotted collar which remains on the outer surface of the panel, and a ridged nylon strip which joins the two. The toggle is first pushed through the wall panel and the collar is slid along the strip into the hole. The strip is then cut off flush with the collar and the screw is inserted.

Alternatively, you can use one of the anchor devices with a flange which remains on the outside of the wall to prevent the body of the fixing being lost in the cavity if the bolt is removed (see Figs. 18 and 19).

Heavy fixings

Lined walls are obviously weaker than solid ones, and great care must be taken when fixing up heavy objects. If there is too much stress on an unsupported wall board, it could rip away from the studs. To make a secure fixing, locate the timber studs (see above) and attach a batten to the surface of the wall with No. 12 screws. The studs may be 300, 400, or 600mm (12, 16, or 24in) apart. The object can then be screwed to the batten.

Electricity in the home

Electricity comes into the house from the mains electricity system via a 2-wire service cable usually laid underground, but in rural areas it often comes via an overhead service cable.

The cable terminates in a sealed unit containing the Electricity Board's service fuse, and mounted on the same board is the electricity meter which registers the electricity consumption in units (KWHs). Fixed close to the meter is the householder's consumer unit containing a double pole main switch and the circuit fuses, though in some installations miniature circuit breakers (MCBs) are fitted instead of fuses.

The consumer unit is linked to the meter by a pair of large size PVC insulated and sheathed cables, one red, the other black in colour. There is also a green, or green yellow PVC insulated earth conductor running from an earth terminal block in the consumer unit to an earth terminal which is usually an earthing clamp secured to the metallic sheath of the Electricity Board's underground service cable. In some older installations the earthing clamp is on the mains water pipe (which may no longer be used as the sole means of earthing).

Where the Board is unable to provide earthing facilities an earth leakage circuit breaker (ELCB) is fitted in conjunction with an earthing rod driven into the ground outside the house. This circuit breaker is a double pole main switch which automatically trips and cuts off the electricity to all circuits when a line/earth fault (a live conductor coming into contact with earthed metalwork) occurs in the installation. This ELCB is normally wired into the mains between the consumer unit and the meter but some consumer units incorporate this as the main switch. The electricity supply throughout the UK is standardised at 240 volts AC 50 Hz and is a 2-pole service. One pole is termed the live (or line) the other is termed the neutral.

As the neutral is solidly connected to earth in the mains distribution system the live pole has a voltage of 240 volts above earth and the neutral is at potential which means zero volts between neutral and earth. It is because the neutral is earthed that anyone who is standing on a concrete floor or on the earth itself or in contact with earthed metalwork and touches a live wire or contact will receive an electric shock of up to 240 volts which can be fatal. Or if metalwork such as

the casing of an electric kettle or heater is not properly earthed and through a fault becomes live with mains electricity, a person touching it will receive a serious electric shock.

Normally, should a live conductor come into contact with earthed metalwork a heavy surge of current results and this blows the fuse or trips a circuit breaker, so cutting off the electricity feeding the fault.

Electrical terms

Although there are numerous terms used in electrical engineering those which really concern the householder are volts, amps and watts. A **volt** is the unit of electrical pressure which as already explained is standard at 240V in the UK from the mains supply. Apart from being lethal this comparatively high voltage makes it essential that all flexible cords, cables, switches, socket outlets and other accessories used in home installations are of the correct type designed for 240V, working without any likelihood of leakage of dangerous currents which would result in fire and shock. In addition it is imperative that electrical work is done properly and is correctly maintained to prevent leakage of dangerous currents.

The **amp** is the unit of current, and this determines the sizes of flexible cords and cables and the current capacity of electrical wiring accessories, that is, switches and socket outlets.

The **watt** is the unit of power and represents the electrical loading of a lamp or appliance and therefore the current consumption. The watt is the product of the voltage and current; multiply the volts by the current and the result is the wattage. 1000 watts equal 1 kilowatt. A 1KW appliance switched on for one hour consumes 1KWH (1 unit) of electricity.

Electrical appliances are usually rated in watts (or KWs). To calculate the current in amps when the wattage is known, so that the correct size of flexible cord or cable is chosen, divide the watts by the voltage. For example, a 2-bar electrical fire having a loading of 2000 watts consumes 2000W ÷ 240V = 8.4A.

Home wiring

The home electrical installation is divided into a number of circuits each having a specific current rating. The current ratings are determined by the current ratings of the circuit fuses or MCBs in the consumer unit and protecting the circuits. There are five standard ratings: 5, 15, 20, 30 and 45 amps but rarely does a consumer unit include all five ratings. Some homes only have 5A circuits, for lighting only, but most have 5A and 30A fuses: the 30A being for ring circuits supply-

ing 13A socket outlets, and a separate 30A fuseway for the cooker and another 30A fuseway for the instantaneous shower unit. Immersion heaters are usually supplied from either a 15A or 20A fuseway and night storage heaters from 20A fuseways usually from a separate consumer unit under time-switch control set for the overnight cheap rate. Where the cooker is of extra large size it is supplied from a 45A fuseway.

Circuit fuses

Circuit fuses are in two types: rewirable, using fuse wires, and cartridge type where the fusing element is enclosed in a cartridge similar to but physically larger than the fuse in a 13A plug.

The cartridges are of different dimensions according to their current rating. This, unlike a rewirable fuse makes it impossible to uprate a fuse by inserting one of higher rating which could lead to overloading the circuit wiring, which in turn could result in a fire. The fuse units of both types are colour coded according to their current rating. The colours are: white (5A); blue (15A); yellow (20A); red (30A); and green (45A).

Mending fuses

Always have a card of fuse-wire available, these cover the most popular current ratings: 5, 15 and 30 amps. Make sure you rewire a fuse with the correct size fuse wire using the colour code as a guide to the size required. For cartridge fuses, always have at least two spares of each current rating in the consumer unit. Locate the 'blown' fuse and remove the fuse holder. Take out the bits of old fuse wire or the old cartirdge and insert the new one, taking care not to stretch the fuse wire on tightening the terminal screw, as this would decrease the current rating, lead to heating of the wire and premature failure. Before replacing the fuse holder in the consumer unit try and find out why the fuse 'blew'. If the new fuse blows immediately there is a fault in the circuit which requires attention.

Miniature circuit breakers (MCBs)

An MCB is simply a single pole switch which automatically trips (switches-off) when there is a fault in the circuit or serious overloading. To restore the current you simply switch on the MCB but if there is a fault in the circuit it is impossible to close the circuit breaker until the fault is rectified. MCBs can also be used to switch off individual circuits when required, or leave a circuit supplying a freezer or refrigerator switched on when leaving the house for an extended period.

House wiring cables

The fixed wiring in a house supplying the

various circuits is usually flat, twin-core and earth PVC sheathed with some sections of a lighting circuit such as 2-way switching being wired in flat 3-core and earth PVC sheathed cable. The sheath is either grey or white.

Within the sheath of twin-core and earth cable are two PVC insulated, current-carrying, copper conductors: one red, one black and an uninsulated copper conductor positioned between them. The red conductor is normally used as the live and the black as the neutral, but the return wire from a switch to the light of a lighting circuit although live when the switch is 'ON' is a black wire which needs a red sleeve slipped over each end.

The uninsulated wire is the earth conductor and its bare end within a switch or any other accessory must be enclosed in a green yellow PVC sleeve, so that it does not make contact with a current carrying terminal. Core colours of a 3-core and earth cable are red, yellow and blue, and when used in a switch circuit the ends of the blue and yellow conductors must be enclosed in red sleeving. Sizes of cables used in home wiring are 1.0mm², 1.5mm², 2.5mm², 4mm², and 6mm².

Home circuits

The various circuits in a dwelling are detailed below.

Lighting circuits

A lighting circuit is wired in either 1.0mm² or 1.5mm² cable using either of two methods. One is the **loop-in system** where the cable from the 5A fuseway runs to each ceiling rose or other lighting fitting and terminates at the last on the circuit. From each light a cable is run to its switch which if a 2-way switch, a 3-core and earth cable is run from this switch to the second 2-way switch.

The other method is the **joint-box system** where each light and its switch requires a separate 4-terminal joint-box. The cable from the 5A fuseway runs to each joint-box in turn and terminates at the last joint-box in the circuit. From each joint-box a cable is run to the light and another cable to the switch.

A lighting circuit may supply up to a maximum of 12 lampholders which is the equivalent of about eight lighting points.

Ring circuits

A ring circuit is wired in 2.5mm² cable. The cable starts from the terminals of a 30A fuseway, runs to each socket outlet it is to supply and returns to the consumer unit where it is connected to the same terminals as the first end of the cable. Cables termed spurs may branch off the ring cable at socket outlets or joint-boxes to supply remotely positioned outlets. A ring circuit may supply an unlimited number of 13A socket outlets but any one ring circuit is limited to supplying a floor area not exceeding 100m² (120yd²). The socket outlets may be either singles or doubles and for a fixed appliance such as a wall heater a fused connection unit is fitted instead of a socket outlet.

Circuits for electric cookers, immersion heaters, instantaneous water heaters and other appliances having loadings in excess of 3000 watts, run direct from fuseways in the consumer unit, having current ratings suitable for the loadings of the appliances and wired using cables of appropriate sizes.

Portable appliances

A portable electrical appliance is connected by its flexible cord to a 13A fused plug. Of the two ratings of plug fuses 3A (red) and 13A (brown), the 3A fuse is fitted for appliances having loadings not in excess of 720 watts. For appliances having loadings between 720 watts and 3000 watts, 13A fuses are fitted into the plugs.

Flexible cords are made in a wide range of sizes and types. When you renew a flex on an appliance make certain that the new flex is of the same size and the same type as the original. Most flexible cords are 3-core for fitting to 13A 3-pin fused plugs, but some all-insulated appliances such as mowers, hedge-trimmers and power tools are also fitted with 2-core flex as no earth connection is required. When fitting a plug the brown core is connected to the live terminal and the blue to the neutral terminal. The earth terminal of the plug is left blank.

DIY wiring

Most householders with a mechanical turn of mind are able to do small wiring jobs such as adding a light or a socket outlet.

Adding a light

To add a light to an existing lighting circuit you require: a length of 1.0mm² 2-core and earth PVC sheathed cable; fixing clips; about 15cm (6in) of green yellow PVC sleeving to slip over the ends of the bare earth wires; a loop-in ceiling rose; flex and moulded lampholder; one 1-way rocker switch together with a mounting-box; either a plastic-box for surface mounting or a plaster-depth metal-box for sinking into the plaster for flush mounting.

Pierce a hole in the ceiling where the new light is to be fixed and also a hole immediately above the new switch position. If you are installing a ground floor light, lift the appropriate floorboards for running the cable, and where necessary drill holes in joists 5cm (2in) below the tops of the joists.

Decide from which loop in the ceiling rose you are going to feed the new light and switch. From this light run the cable under the floorboards or in the roof space as relevant, to the new light position and pass about 15cm (2in) down through the hole pierced in the ceiling. Remove the existing ceiling rose but leave the wires connected. Pass the end of the cable through the hole in the ceiling and cut the cable, leaving about 15cm (6in) for connections.

From the new light position run a length of cable to the switch position, down the wall leaving about 15cm (6in) for connection at the switch. At the new light, connect the flex and lampholder to the ceiling rose, thread in the ends of the two cables and fix the rose to the ceiling using batten wood fixing between the joists if necessary. Strip off the cable sheath within the rose and slip green yellow sleeving over the bared end of the earth wires and connect these to the earth terminal.   Connect the red and black wires and replace the cover of the rose.

Prepare the end of the new cable at the existing ceiling rose. Connect the red to the live terminal, the black to the neutral terminal and the sleeved earth wire to the earth terminal. Refix the ceiling rose. At the switch position run the cable down the wall using clips for fixing it to the surface or it may be sunk in the plaster direct. Remove a cable knockout in the box. Thread in the cable and fix the box. Prepare the end of the cable as for the ceiling rose, and slip sleeving over the bare earth and connect it to the terminal in the base of the box. Connect the red wire to one of the terminals. Slip red sleeving over the end of the black wire and connect this to the other terminal. Fix the switch to the box using the screws supplied. Turn on the power.

Adding a 13A socket outlet

For an additional 13A socket outlet you require a length of 2.5mm² 2-core and earth PVC sheathed cable, a single or a double 13A socket outlet and a 1-gang or 2-gang mounting-box which can be either a plastic-box for surface mounting or a metal-box for sinking into the wall.

Select an existing socket outlet on the ring circuit. With the power switched off release the socket from its box and raise a floorboard near the socket and another near the new socket position.

From the existing socket run the new cable by passing it up behind the skirting board and then under the floor to the new socket where it is run up behind the skirting. Remove a cable knockout from the new box. Thread-in the end of the cable and fix the box, which, if flush will be in a chase cut into the wall.

Prepare the end of the cable by removing the sheath within the box and connect the green yellow sleeved earth wire to the earth terminal, the red wire to the live terminal and the black wire to the neutral terminal of the socket. Fix the socket to the box using the screws supplied. At the existing socket prepare the other end of the cable likewise and connect the wires to the respective terminals alongside the existing wires of the same colours. Refix the socket to its box and turn on the power.

Planned lighting to enhance your home

Your eyes are sensitive and delicate instruments. They scan your surroundings more efficiently than radar to provide an enormous amount of information. But they are totally dependent on one thing. Light. The reflection of light enables the eye to interpret distance, size, colour, shape, texture and movement—and the quality of this light is all-important. Not only can bad lighting spoil the appearance of your home (under a flat light velvet can look as dull as the cheapest denim) but it can also make it inefficient—and dangerous.

To plan your lighting you must consider exactly what you need it for. Are you an amateur painter, a cook, or a carpenter? You will need suitable lighting for each hobby or activity. Is your living room open plan where the family wants to knit, do homework, and doze all at the same time? Decide what has to be lit—a work surface, a draining board, a tabletop—then how it should best be lit.

The lighting in your home deserves very careful consideration. And yet, examples of bad lighting are all too common. Often, the only source of artificial light in a living room, for example, is the single, centre light fitting. Numerous, different activities are carried out daily under this one, pitifully inadequate light. Even reading may be difficult, if you find you are sitting in your own shadow, with the light throwing distracting reflections off mirrors or other shiny surfaces.

Glare, high contrast, under-lighting, working in your own shadow—all are examples of bad lighting which can cause headaches, eyestrain, and inconvenience, and may even cause accidents.

Lighting for safety

Safety should be of first importance when planning the lighting in your home. Potential accident spots must be clearly lit at all times, especially if there are very young, elderly or short-sighted members in the family. Stairs usually present the main hazard. All stairs whether a full flight up to another floor or a couple of steps between levels, should be lit so that the beginning of the flight, and the nosings of the treads are quite obvious. Although you may know about those two unexpected steps down to the kitchen, a visitor could trip on them and fall.

Staircases are best lit from the tops of the flights so that the rises are in shadow and the nosings are accentuated. To avoid too deep a shadow on the risers, however, an infill light below the flight is also recommended. And it may be necessary to keep stairs and halls lit artificially during the day, as they often have inadequate natural light sources.

Few people consider the necessity for special night-time lighting, but it can be important. A child may have a nightmare and need reassuring; you may have to go to the bathroom; the telephone or front door bell may ring. Many emergencies can occur in the middle of the night.

Switching on lights at their normal level of intensity in a blackened room can cause temporary blindness—enough for someone to misjudge the top of the stairs. So, at night, a much lower lighting level is required for safe movement. The staircase, corridors, bathroom and telephone area can be lit effectively with 15 watt night lights and at this wattage, the cost of running the lights all night would be negligible. Regular night risers—people on shift work, or mothers with young babies to feed, for example—might also find an additional low wattage switched light useful, that they can turn on by the bed.

The hall

A hall can often benefit greatly from careful lighting as it is so often a dull, long and narrow corridor with no attractive feature. The first impression of your home needs to be bright and welcoming, and so have plenty of light here. A bright ceiling fitted downlighter is effective and downcast shadows will not matter so much in this part of the house. Otherwise try a cluster of beautiful glittering glass lamps, or a glowing ceiling lit with concealed indirect uplighters combined with attractive wall bracket lights. As halls are for 'passing through', you could try a more daring and experimental approach than would be appropriate in the living room. Just be careful not to have a brilliant lamp glaring at eye level.

The kitchen and bathroom

The kitchen is one room in the house where emphasis must be on *efficient* lighting. The work surfaces must be lit to avoid shadow and glare—but this does not mean it should be twice as bright as anywhere else in the house. The point is proficiency, not brute force. A single, central pendant is not the answer. If possible, light fittings should be directly above the work surfaces but shielded from direct view.

Strip fluorescent lighting, positioned out of sight underneath wall mounted cupboards, will shine directly onto work surfaces giving a good clear light. And fluorescent ceiling fittings are ideal for general lighting in the kitchen area. You might also consider fitting small lights inside deep storage cupboards.

Carefully placed spotlights, or tracking lights fixed to an overhead rail are also very efficient and provide lighting without glare in the kitchen. These tracks enable special light fittings to be clipped into any position on the track and can be angled at stove, sink, table, and work surfaces. (Lighting tracks, in fact, can be very useful throughout the house—as supplementary lighting in a study or workroom for example.)

Generally, there is little call for flexibility of lighting in the kitchen. But if chores such as the ironing are done there, then the tracking or spot lights could be swung into the appropriate positions. Open plan kitchen/living rooms may need a lower, more subtle, level of illumination at times, for a cosy supper or to flatter a sophisticated dinner party.

If you entertain only occasionally, then a portable light fitting that gives a soft, coloured light in the dining area can be effective. Or a pendant light, which is height-adjustable, will light the dining table effectively for both formal and informal occasions. But again, without supplementary lighting—picture lights, wall lights, or even candles—there will be a considerable, glaring contrast between the background and light fitting which can be tiring. To eliminate this, and help create a cosier atmosphere you could use a dimmer to lower the wattage of your single light.

The bathroom mainly needs a good, general purpose, overhead light, combined with mirror lights. A fixed bowl shade will not be affected too much by steam. And for very small bathrooms there are combined light/heat fittings which are useful.

Lighting the bedroom

A centre light is generally not adequate on its own in a bedroom and most people have bedside light fitments. The traditional, shaded light, however, can cast shadow and spread a diffuse light over the whole room. Although the effect may be attractive, many people enjoy reading in bed and it can be infuriating if your partner is reading when you want to sleep and the light disturbs you. This can be prevented by fitting low voltage

spot lights at each side of the bed. The light will be bright enough for reading, can be angled in a suitable direction, and will leave the rest of the room in deep shadow. A soft, hidden light behind a bed alcove will add a glamorous touch.

Mirrors, particularly make-up mirrors, always need to be lit clearly. Lights positioned at either side of the glass will fall directly on the user and avoid too much glare. Or a strip light along the top is an adequate alternative; there are some effective ones available on the market which incorporate electric shaver sockets.

Living areas

The living room and dining room are likely to call for flexibility of approach. The lighting requirements of a family breakfast will be very different from those of a sophisticated dinner party in the same dining room. And you may want the option of lighting only certain areas of an open plan room, so that you can 'lose' the kitchen while dining, or simply highlight the areas you need.

The variety of effects you will need can best be produced by using several different lighting methods, each of which has a wide range of practical and decorative uses.

With *direct lighting*, such as spotlights, 90% of the light falls downwards and, although it can be very harsh, it gives a strong clear light where needed. This is ideal for reading or paper work. If the fittings are imaginatively positioned, this strong light will also bring out the form and texture of

Above: Imaginative lighting in a modern kitchen where efficiency is at a premium, and lighting without glare necessary for comfortable working. The concealed tubes throw adequate light on the work surface, making for fast, safe food preparation.

objects illuminated, and can be effective when directed onto a special ornament or other room feature. *Semi-direct lighting* also falls mainly downwards but gives a softer effect as some of the light diffuses around it.

General-diffused lighting is equally distributed upwards and downwards. This is the effect you get from most glass fitments, and round paper lampshades for example. The light is usually quite bright and generally useful, but it usually needs to be supplemented for activities that need strong light and dimmed for intimate atmosphere.

Semi-indirect lighting has to be used with care. It throws a small amount of light downwards and tends to give a rather dull, flat effect. (And yet, with a pendant fitting, this is the most commonly used lighting in the average living room.) In attractive wall or movable fitments, however, semi-indirect lighting can give a gently relaxing background light.

Ceilings would seem to benefit most from *indirect lighting* as it gives more than 90% upward light, but it does produce a shadowless, completely dull appearance. Depending on colour and intensity, it could vary from being bright and practical in the kitchen, to being soft and warm in another room. Otherwise indirect uplighters can add a touch of glamour to a wall of long curtains as long as they are positioned safely away from the fabric.

Choosing the fitments

When considering any particular room, bear in mind that several types of distribution and fittings may be better than just one. There are some important general points to bear in mind; glare should be avoided and lamps in the fittings should be shielded from view. Too great a contrast between the light fitting or lighted object and its surroundings is likely to cause discomfort, and sometimes eyestrain and headaches. Even the flame of a candle on a dinner table can cause considerable glare if there is no background lighting, because of the extreme contrast between the candle flame and the surrounding darkness. Television should not be watched in a totally dark room for the same reason.

When choosing your lighting fitment, do be careful to consider the effect of the lighting and not just the look of the lamp. A beautiful standard lamp that will grace the corner of your living room may have a totally impractical effect, casting huge shadows, or giving a glaring light. So often additional lighting fitments are just added to a room, apparently haphazardly, around the furniture. You end up with an uninteresting effect and yards of trailing leads.

Daylight is constantly changing in colour and intensity. Similarly, artificial lighting

should provide contrast. Pools of light, reflected light, lower levels of lighting—all can add interest to a room and break up different living areas.

Lamp shades are also important. Large ones allow greater diffusion of light. Their colour will greatly affect the light, too. 'Warm' colours—reds and yellow tones—are generally considered attractive. Blues and greens can be used to great effect for special positions provided they are backed with warmer shades in the rest of the room.

Table lamps should always have shades large enough to cast a pool of light over sewing, book or table.

Fluorescent fittings are particularly suitable for providing a good economic source of light. But be careful about choosing the colour of fluorescent tubes as they can easily give the wrong effect. 'De luxe warm white' tubes are the most suitable for domestic purposes because they are the closest tube colour to tungsten lighting, and also reflect colour well. Nearly all fluorescent tube manufacturers produce tubes specially designed for giving good colour, but some can appear much colder than 'de luxe warm white'. If you want strip lighting in the living room or bedroom, a particularly warm tone of light— the red tones—may be needed. Tinted fluorescent tubes, such as pink or peach give a soft, attractive light. The 'colder' tones, however, can be useful to bring up blue or green shades of decor or foliage.

Tungsten tubes have none of the disadvantages associated with fluorescent lighting, such as buzzing, flickering and delayed starting, but they are more expensive both to buy and run.

Although principally intended for the shop fitting and display market, spotlights can provide interest and atmosphere in a room. (But be careful about positioning them, or someone may get the impression he is being put through the third degree!) The development of tungsten halogen lamps (probably more familiar to most people in projectors), has enabled tiny spotlights to produce a very high output.

Tracking light systems, which can hold several spotlights at different angles, also have adaptors for taking lowload appliances such as food mixers, sewing machines or portable electric drills. Because of the possibility of overloading too many fittings into the track, it is preferable to have it installed by a qualified electrician. Should you decide to install one yourself, check that the current carrying capacity or the cable is adequate for the purpose, and that an appropriate fuse is provided in the circuit.

Another by-product of the shopfitting market is the general availability of colour spotlights. You have only to think how

Opposite, top left. Clever use of glass and light. The spotlights throw light on to the mirror and the face, without glare.

Top right. Good bedhead lighting enables the late-night reader to enjoy his book without disturbing his partner.

Bottom. Planned daylight in a distinctive manner, with large corner picture windows framing the natural greenery of the garden.

colour television can portray the whole colour spectrum simply by the projection of red, green and blue onto the screen to realise the enormous potential of colour lighting. With imagination—and discretion—you can change the whole atmosphere of a room by the use of colour filtered light.

Wall brackets and wall mounted fittings are particularly useful for such rooms as the living room, where you need semi-indirect light from above and behind.

Using daylight

Do not forget daylight. It is as much a part of planned lighting as the most sophisticated artificial light. Where the opportunity arises of influencing or dictating the positioning of windows, these should be carefully planned to achieve a good balance of light in the building. Very large windows are not necessarily the answer. Large rooms are for the most part better lit with more than one window, preferably in different walls. But the positioning of windows involves far more than simply its effect on the daylighting of the interior; orientation, view and the external design appearance of the house are also major considerations.

As well as the actual positioning of windows, think of the window space as potential decoration through the curtaining and colour of the window frame. A deep room with a single window, be it large or small, should not be decorated in dark finishes if the room is habitually used in daylight. Remember, too, that glare from an over-large window can be softened by hanging fine net curtains in front of it.

Do not neglect the exterior of your house. A pretty garden can look dramatic and glamorous when carefully lit and give a visual extension to your living room. Lights

Left: Softly diffused light enhances a mellow setting by emphasizing the yellow tones. It is reflected off the white walls to fall equally upwards and downwards.

plug per room, and perhaps a couple of wall light outlets on either side of a fireplace or in an alcove. It is all too easy to allow your choice of lighting to be moulded by what is there—and obvious—rather than plan out exactly what each individual room needs. After all, planning takes time and energy. But if you can find enough of these to bother, the rewards will be considerable.

When choosing your lighting fitments, try to decide what you want before you go shopping. Department stores tend to be discouraging to new ideas. Their lighting departments are usually a blaze of fittings, all switched on at once, with little attempt to demonstrate individual effects. It is hard to visualize what a specific fitment will look like away from all the others in the shop and hanging in your home. Confused and unsure, one can so often end up with buying the same style fitment or lampshare as before, with the feeling that it is better to be safe than sorry.

Spotlights

Although a new lighting scheme has ultimately to be planned for the whole house, it can be tackled gradually. One of the easiest, cheapest and most effective experiments you can try is to purchase and place a spotlight. Theatrical designers and shop window dressers have realized—and exploited—the dramatic potential of spots for many years. A figure on the stage, or a garment in a shop window, can be made arresting and dominating by the simple expedient of focusing spotlight on to it.

Spotlights are now supplied specifically for the home and, used with a little imagination, they can do much to enliven a room. Because they are fully adjustable, both vertically and horizontally, even one lamp, carefully placed, can be used to illuminate a favourite painting, for example, and then turned to throw intense local light on a work surface such as a desk. Apart from wall fittings, they can be placed on the floor as elegant uplighters, fitted to standing frames or ceiling tracks, or clamped to a bedside fitment for a reading lamp.

Domestic spotlights are mostly small, neat and unobtrusive. The light and not the lamp catches the eye—or should if it is properly placed. As well as ensuring that they do not give a blinding light, spots must also be positioned away from fabrics or any inflammable materials as they produce a considerable heat.

by the side of the drive reveal it quite clearly at night.

Lighting can be fun, formal, and flattering. Experimenting with it is fun, too, but the secret often lies in simplicity. A single spotlight focused on a favourite picture is a simple idea, but can be more effective than a dozen badly placed standard lamps. Planning lighting carefully can give your home a new dimension.

Because of the technicalities involved, many people tend to fight shy of making drastic changes to the lighting in their homes, preferring to leave it to the experts. But

traditional lighting in the home is usually conservative, and often inadequate. By exploiting the potential of the many different fitments that are readily available, you will be able to achieve both effect and efficiency in your lighting system—and without completely rewiring your home.

Unless you are lucky enough to be in on the planning stage of building a new house, you will probably find that your home has been wired unimaginatively. Builders tend to be conventional and provide only the standard lighting points in the traditional positions—a centre ceiling light, one wall

Normally, spotlights are fitted with special, internally silvered reflector lamps, but you can also buy general service lamps adapted with clip-on auxiliary reflectors. Versatility is the great merit of spotlights. Installation is simple: they screw into place, and are wired like any other wall or pendant light. Some have pushbutton switches, so they can be wired into an unswitched circuit, without the need to run new cables back into the switch for other lights in the room. If you want to fit them to the ceiling, spotlights should be sited one to two feet from the wall. Placing them depends on what you want to illuminate. Spotlights should 'spot' something—be planned to pick out one area or object. Installed at random, much of their effect is lost.

Flourescent lights

Fluorescent tubes are often considered boring, dazzling and useful only for kitchens. This need not necessarily be the case. They can have many effective and efficient uses in the home and are always worth considering because of their cheapness to run.

The slightly chilling effect they sometimes have can be eliminated by using one of the warmer shades such as 'De luxe warm white'. 'Warm white' provides a high light output (measured in lumens per 305 sq mm (1 sq ft)) and is very efficient in large kitchens. It is 'sharp' enough for work surfaces where efficiency is important, and yet warm enough to be comfortable to work in. 'Natural' is closest to day-light but is probably the least acceptable for domestic use since it gives a cool, blue-white appearance.

Daylight itself reflects 'true' colours because it contains all the colours in the spectrum: red, orange, yellow, green, blue, indigo and violet. Artificial light, in general, contains a much narrower range of colour, which is why fabric shades, for example, look so different under department store lights. Artificial light gives either a cold or a warm effect and you must know what is best for your needs. Candlelight or firelight contains more natural red/orange and gives people a healthy, flattering glow. Fluorescent blues tend to have bluey tones which give a colder effect. This is why they are often recommended for use in purely service rooms where you need a good light rather than an intimate atmosphere.

Despite its occasional chilliness, fluorescent light has much to recommend it. Because the length of tube eliminates light shadows, a 40 watt tube gives approximately the same amount of light as a 150 watt metallic filament bulb and spreads the light over a wider area. And with an estimated life of 7,500 hours, a tube lasts at least seven times longer than a bulb.

Another advantage is that the tube never gets overheated; you can even fix one behind a pelmet with no danger of your curtains catching fire. Fluorescent tubes are available in a range of lengths from 30cm to 244cm (1ft to 8ft) and your choice of length depends on the output needed. For example, a 15 watt 15in. tube would be ideal for lighting a bathroom mirror, and a 40 watt, 1.2m (4ft) tube would be fine for a small kitchen.

The installation of fluorescent fittings presents no particular difficulties. The body of the unit is screwed to the wall or ceiling through distance pieces, designed to provide a space of about 6mm ($\frac{1}{4}$in) between the back

Above. *Dramatic use of whole-house and surrounds lighting, with spotlights under the roof and special porch fitments to give a welcoming blaze of light.*

Right. *Living area enhanced by the use of several types of lighting. Recessed and pendant lights are supplemented by a global lampshade, showing through the open door.*

of the unit and the surface to which it is fitted. This is to allow some circulation of air round the tube. The wiring is equally straightforward, being clearly marked on the terminal block fitted inside the unit. Some fittings have push-button switches so that they need not have a switched electrical supply and these are particularly useful for fitting over a bedhead.

While unshielded tubes are not ugly, they have a stark, utilitarian air, and you may prefer to use them only in less sophisticated areas, such as a workshop or kitchen. The tubes can be made more attractive, however, by fitting them with diffusers, although some output efficiency may be lost as a result. There is a wide range to choose from: extruded reeded plastic, natural raffia, and various fabric finished diffusers. They are designed to give a soft upward light, with a stronger downward light to illuminate areas of special interest. Diffusers usually clip to

the tube itself, or to the fitting, and are easily removed for cleaning.

Ceiling lights

Fittings that are mounted on the surface of the ceiling, or even recessed into it are a comparatively modern development. They can be spotlights, or more conventional fittings with diffusing glass or louvres which are excellent for general lighting. Spots are ideal for reading because they provide beamed, concentrated light; the light shines directly onto the book and the reader is not sitting in his own shadow. These lights can be grouped to provide high light intensity where it is

needed, giving reflected light throughout the rest of the room.

Not many people will want to start cutting holes in their ceilings to accommodate recessed light fittings. A less messy and inconvenient alternative would be the installation of a false ceiling beneath the existing one. This may be worth considering if your present ceiling is either badly cracked or very high (more than 2.5m [8ft 6in]). Tackling a whole ceiling can be an ambitious project, but you may be able to fit a false ceiling across part of a room. This is particularly easy in a house that has a reinforcing beam in some of its ground floor ceilings, support-ing a bay or ground floor extension. This would enable you to fit a false ceiling to the depth of the beam. With two or three concealed lights built into your new ceiling, there would be no ugly cables showing and there would be the effect of softly diffused light.

Try to forget about the traditional habit of placing a light in the centre of the ceiling. Several lights dotted all over the room are more interesting than a single fitting, although an off centre ceiling light can only be really efficient if other lights are available to illuminate the rest of the room. Greater flexibility can also be achieved with ceiling lights if they are fitted with a dimmer switch. These simply replace your present switch and enable you to raise or lower the level of lighting by simply turning a dial. In this way, you can, for example, tone down powerful reading lights for relaxing.

New ideas

Even in the more conventional lighting fields—such as ceiling mounted or suspended fittings—there is a wide range of choice and something to suit every taste.

The bayonet-type fitting, suspended on a flex, remains the most popular. Designs are available to suit the mood of every room and they have the advantage of being extremely

easy to fit. The flex need no longer be the ugly, twisted, silk-finished type. A single tubular plastic insulation looks more attractive and can be wiped clean.

Rise and fall units—ceiling suspended lights which are height adjustable—are also useful and versatile. When used in the 'up' position they provide general lighting. In the 'down' position they throw a pool of light into a limited area, creating an intimate atmosphere. They are most commonly used for dining table fittings and are particularly suitable for this, although they could also be used over a desk top or sewing machine, for example.

Many people choose a standard lamp for a reading light or to cut down glare when watching television. These will be more efficient if fitted with a large shade, which gives a wide pool of light. Small shades also tend to make bulbs overheat, thus shortening their lives, because they prevent the free circulation of air around the bulb.

How much light do you need?

The various activities carried out in the average home require not only different types of lighting, but also different amounts of light. In technical terms the requirements are expressed in *lumens* per square metre. (To convert them to lumens per square foot, divide by 10.)

For general use a living room should have a light intensity of 100 lumens per square metre (10 per square foot). Light reading requires 200, prolonged reading (or studying) 400. Sewing or close work calls for 600

Above: This unusual pendant light is made of plastic and is designed to hang low over the table, thus covering the whole surface with a soft light.

lumens per square metre. You could achieve this necessary versatility by having a ceiling light fitting which provides sufficient light for general purposes, supplemented by spots or table lamps. Additional light will be needed near or above chairs or work surfaces.

The average requirements for other rooms are kitchens—200 lumens per square metre (particularly over work surfaces); bedrooms —50 lumens per square metre with provision for a 200 lumens headboard light for the late night reader. Most other rooms, including landings and halls need about 100 lumens. Stairs, at their treads, ought to have 50-100 lumens to be absolutely safe—with control switches at both the top and bottom of the staircase.

It is simple to calculate the wattage required to provide these standards of lighting as long as you know the efficiency with which the lamp converts electrical energy into light—in other words, the number of lumens per watt. A fluorescent tube provides about 50 lumens per watt. So, for example, if the light intensity needed in a kitchen is 20 lumens per square foot the wattage required using a fluorescent tube will be $20 \div 50 = 0.4$ watts per square foot. Thus, one 40 watt fluorescent lamp will provide the equivalent of 20 lumens per square foot over an area of 100 square feet (0.4×100). Metallic filament bulbs are far less efficient than fluorescent

Top: Concealed strip lighting is most useful over worktops, where proper light is essential for safety and efficiency. With a concealed light there is no glare. This fitting has its own extra socket for irons, mixers or other kitchen equipment.

Centre: A wall-mounted desk lamp which can be adjusted to several angles, throwing intense local light on the work area.

Below: (main picture). Unshielded tubes need not necessarily be ugly. This tube gives a soft enough light in which to work, with no uncomfortable glare and a neat line.

Inset: Tube lighting fitted with a diffuser, used to soften any glare and improve the appearance of the light.

Left: Planned lighting for bedroom and bathroom, incorporating different types of fitment. The bathroom mirror is flanked by strip lighting, and the general lighting is provided by fluorescent tubes fitted with diffusers. Bracket lights equip the bedhead.

point has very severe lighting limitations. But a few simple changes can work wonders. Rid yourself of the centre light and replace it with three ceiling mounted spots in the darker end of the room, away from the window. These could be served by a dimmer switch, and supplemented by a table lamp, and/or a fluorescent tube concealed behind a pelmet or in a shelf recess. Or try splitting one lighting outlet, such as the wiring for a wall light, to provide wiring for two mounted spotlights. These could be served by the same switch. If you decide to mount the cables on the surface, look for unobtrusive routes. (Burying them behind skirting boards and plaster tends to upset your decor.) You could run them behind curtains, along the top of a skirting board, or down the corners of the room. Securing clips with hardened steel pins—such as Dylon clips—are small, easy to use and make a neat job of fixing cables to walls.

When you plan the lighting of any room, aim for variety of effect. Daylight is always interesting because it is constantly changing in intensity. Artificial light should try to be just as interesting, just as adaptable. With a little care, your lighting will add greatly to the efficiency, mood and atmosphere of your home.

lamps, producing approximately 12 lumens per watt.

Daylight has hundreds of lumens per square foot but it is generally easy on the eye because it is so evenly distributed.

Rewiring

Unless you are building a new house or having your home completely rewired—when you can merely give the electrician your instructions—you may find that efficient, effective lighting involves some rewiring. However, do not be too ambitious. It takes an expert to rewire a house, especially the complicated rewiring you may need to achieve your best planned lighting. Use your own ideas but, unless you have every right to consider yourself an expert, leave the actual rewiring to a professional. Many useful improvements can be made very simply by adapting your existing circuits—preferably with the minimum of damage to your decor.

For example, a lounge which is fitted with one central pendant light and a single power

Lighting for dark rooms

Dark, dreary rooms need not be a problem if you decorate them with imagination. Use colour as your main ally, together with well planned lighting and mirrors, to conjure up a feeling of more light. Extra windows, naturally, are the best way of letting in more light to dark rooms, and you may be able to afford to alter or enlarge the windows in your house. This is more of an upheaval than ingenious decorative treatments, however, and entails structural alterations.

Plan what you are going to do. If one of the rooms in your house is dark, and you want to brighten it up, don't simply increase the wattage in all the light bulbs and paint the walls and ceiling white. There are more

subtle—and more effective—treatments for dreary areas, and each room must be dealt with according to its function, shape and size.

Using colour

You can obtain colour charts specially planned to help you create light colour schemes for dark rooms. Different rooms need different treatments, so consider what

Right: Make a dark room seem much more bright and cheerful through the use of mirrors, mirrortiles and other shiny surfaces such as in this unusual bathroom.

effect you want to achieve before you go ahead. For instance, an all-white scheme in a living room can make it seem light and airy, but an all-white bathroom would be cold and clinical without the addition of bright pictures, towels and other accessories.

Choose cheerful colours like daffodil yellow for tall, dark rooms, or brighten them up with a gay wallpaper, paint the ceiling in one of the paler colours of the wallpaper and use masses of white on the woodwork and furniture. Low, dark rooms often look best with a white ceiling, but if you want to paint it the same colour as the walls, you can avoid a lowering effect by picking out the cornice in brilliant white, and add bright-looking furniture in white, sky blue or yellow.

Using bold colours in a dark room needs special care. Bright red in a small hall looks warm and welcoming, but it can also look dark unless it is mixed with a lot of white plus a big mirror and strong lighting. Remember that pale colours like white, grey and pastel blue are space givers, whereas more dense colours like emerald green and scarlet or orange advance, making a room seem smaller.

In the northern hemisphere, north- and east-facing rooms need warm colours to help them feel sunny, so yellows and oranges are good dominant colours. South- and west-facing rooms will be sunny anyway, even if they are dark, so you can safely use cooler colours like white, pale blue or very pale green.

Heavy colours like black and deep brown should be used sparingly in a dark room, although one wall covered in chocolate brown hessian will give a warm feel to a room. A black-covered kitchen bench could be too sombre in a dark kitchen, but if you choose orange, blue, or even white, the work-top will act as a reflective surface, making

the dull room lighter.

Window treatments

Enlarging windows is the most positive way of creating more light in dark rooms. If you don't want to widen your windows, a less major operation is to lengthen them to floor level and put in French windows in the basement and ground floor rooms. Long windows can also be put in bedrooms, but this is not a good idea in a child's room. A small fake balcony outside, attached to a strong pair of brackets, will make the window look more natural; this could take the form of a wrought iron railing, or a big painted brass fender with room for a trough of flowers inside.

To catch more light in a ground floor room, change a plain window for a bow-shaped one, or a larger bay window. Installing a bay window would mean extending the walls outwards to take in the shape of the bay.

You can add more light fairly simply by changing the type of window inside the original frame. Small-paned or leaded windows can be replaced by ones with larger panes, but remember that the glass will be more expensive to replace if it gets broken. Many Edwardian houses still have coloured or stained glass panes, particularly in hall or living room windows. If you swap these for plain glass, more light is easily let in.

Remember that altering a window will change the whole appearance of a house from the outside. Well thought-out enlarged windows will add a feeling of light both inside and outside the house. But windows that do not blend with the design of the house, especially if it is a decidedly period one, can ruin an otherwise attractive front, although they may improve matters inside.

Curtains and blinds

The main rule to remember in a dark room is never to use dark curtains or blinds. Light window coverings will help reflect what daylight there is in the room. Don't half-draw curtains; instead, make the rail long enough so that the curtains can be pulled back to clear the edge of the window frame, thus letting in as much light as possible.

Blinds are particularly good in dark rooms because they can be neatly rolled up in the daytime so that they don't obscure the light at all. Shutters are another good choice, because they fold neatly out of the way. In a dark bathroom, you can make your own shutters out of figured hardboard, painted white, or use white-painted louvred shutters. They can be left closed during the day for privacy and will still let in a certain amount of light which can be supplemented by a

concealed tungsten strip light behind them if necessary.

It is best to keep the feeling of light coming through a window in a dark room by painting the frame white, both inside and out. If you need net curtains, choose a crisp white rather than a pastel shade; the heavy fish net type let in more light than the more dense plain ones. A pretty effect can be achieved by using a thick Nottingham lace with a fairly open pattern to let in the light.

Lighting

Well-planned lighting can transform a dark room, and there are several tricks to remember if you want to make the most of it. One is to put table or standard lights near the window, even on either side of it. Placed in this way, they will increase the feeling of light coming through the window.

Hidden lighting behind a curtain pelmet is another useful trick. This gives a good background light, helps to frame the window, reflects a light-coloured ceiling, and again will help to increase the feeling of daylight in a room. Strip lights used in this way, or fitted behind a false cornice, should be tungsten tubes, which give a more natural light than fluorescent tubes. Main lighting over the rest of the room can come from table lamps.

One or two spotlights reflected on to the ceiling will help brighten up a dark room. Highlight a dark corner with an eyeball spot let into the ceiling (expensive to instal, but worth it) and add to the effect with a huge jug of pale grasses or gay flowers.

In a dark hall, living room or kitchen, use lighting hidden above a suspended ceiling. Hidden strip lights above a work surface help in a dark kitchen, but more light will be needed at ceiling level for general illumination.

Rooflights

Rooflights or skylights are invaluable for giving extra light, particularly at the top of a stair well, or let into a flat or sloping roof over a dark room. If you do fit one into a flat roof, you will need to alter the positions of the joists to make room for it—a square one is the easiest. One of the problems which arise with rooflights is that they let in water if they have not been fitted properly. In order to make your rooflight watertight, fit a cowling with a lip around to keep out the rain.

Mirrors

A well-placed mirror is another great help in a dark or gloomy room. The best method is to hang a large mirror on the wall opposite the windows so that it reflects the light coming into the room, doubling its effect. Just as a light near a window will increase light, so will a table light placed near a mirror. The mirror reflects the light again and again, creating an impression of much more light.

Full length mirrors transform a dark hall, passage or landing, particularly if they are placed so that they reflect bright, sunny furnishings. In a minute, dark bathroom, you can go further and have a complete wall of mirrors. Add a strip light concealed behind a fake pelmet above the mirror, casting light down where it is needed.

Look for huge old mirrors in junk shops and use them as bedheads in dark bedrooms. If you cover all the doors of a fitted row of cupboards with mirrors, it will help to create a feeling of more light and space.

Dark areas

Basement rooms or flats can be brightened up considerably by decorating the area outside in light colours. The simplest and cheapest way is to paint everything, brick walls, steps, doors and dustbin cupboard in a light colour such as white or yellow. Dark-leaved climbing plants will darken an area, so choose the type with variegated leaves if you want greenery outside the window. Plant white-painted tubs with bright flowers like marigolds and nasturtiums and arrange them on the outside window sill or at the base of the wall if you have full-length windows.

Mirrors can be used here, too. Fix a mirror on the area wall opposite the window; the bigger the mirror the better. Any old cracked or damaged mirror will do, and you can arrange a 'frame' of plants around it to make the area seem larger. If you don't want to have to look after plants all the time, try painting a bright flowery mural on the area wall opposite the window. Even a simple yellow sun on a blue background looks effective, and makes a light-hearted treatment for a dull area.

Ideas room by room

Hall and stairs. You can increase the light cast over a dark hall and staircase by letting in a fan light or small window above the front door. You can create a feeling of light and depth by papering the ceiling in the hall with a bright, geometric paper. Add plenty of white, particularly on the woodwork, plus a mirror to reflect all the light things. Borrow light from the rooms leading off the hall and landing by fixing glass panels in doors, or by installing 'windows' in the walls. These can be disguised as shelving alcoves inside the rooms, and help to let more light on to the stairs.

White-painted banisters will look less heavy and dark than natural wood, and an open staircase with a light carpet will give a brighter, more spacious feeling. Don't obscure the window on the landing, but help it by fixing hidden lights behind plants or ornaments strategically placed to highlight corners.

Living rooms. Large windows, combined with fresh-looking curtains or blinds, warm lighting and a pleasant colour scheme all help to emphasize brightness in otherwise dark rooms. Be careful in your choice of furniture, however, as big heavy pieces like a mahogany desk or dark leather-covered sofa can be too over-powering if you want light. Don't mix too many different colours together, as this looks messy; a plain colour will usually create a lighter feeling than a pattern, particularly where carpets are concerned.

You can create a much brighter appearance simply by painting the floorboards white to reflect the ceiling, then adding shaggy mats, Spanish rugs or rush matting to make it more practical. Use plenty of table lamps with white shades to create the maximum amount of light, with spotlights in dark corners, and concealed lights in alcoves or behind curtains as back-ground lighting.

Dining rooms. The dining room is often the darkest room in the house, and if you tend to use it only in the evening, this does not matter too much, as then you can rely entirely on artificial lighting. If you have a young family, a dining room needs to be a light and airy place, and often a one-colour treatment is the most effective, with the walls, ceiling, floor and furniture painted in the same gay colour. At night the appearance of the room can be changed dramatically by the addition of a patterned tablecloth with matching blinds at the windows, and softer lighting. A low hanging light over the dining table will focus attention on it. If you think blinds are too harsh, hang fake curtains at each side of the window; these will frame the blind, but will not obscure the light by day.

Kitchens. As well as a gay colour scheme and wisely chosen lighting, you should look for accessories like tiles—for worktops or floor, storage jars and pretty pots and pans which will add brightness to your kitchen. However, you must remember that while a plain flooring in a pale colour like white or yellow may reflect extra light, it will need a lot of cleaning if it is not to look tatty. Instead of a dark flooring, however, go for an attractively patterned sheet vinyl, which will look bright but not show every speck of dirt.

One of the best ways of lighting a low kitchen is to fit downlighters into the ceiling. They don't encroach on the headroom, but are particularly efficient if they are placed strategically above worktops, cooker and

sink. Another way of letting in more light is to fit a larger than average serving hatch, thus borrowing light from the adjoining room. In a kitchen, gloss-painted walls combine extra reflected brightness with ease of cleaning.

Bedrooms. Bedrooms should feel warm, so a pale colour is usually best avoided, even for a dark room. A lot of white in a north-facing bedroom is a particularly bad idea, and it is better to choose a sunnier colour. If you want the impression created by white, choose beige or oatmeal, which give a light feeling without looking cold. You can create an attractive effect by using a patterned wallpaper, preferably on a white background. Make up the curtains and bedspread in the same fabric, if possible to match the wallpaper, and pick out all the woodwork in white paint. The ceiling can be painted in one of the paler colours of the wallpaper, with a matching carpet. Carpets are expensive, though, and a cheaper way of brightening the floor is to paint the boards in a light colour to match fabric or wallpaper used elsewhere, whether it is yellow, sky blue or pink.

Bathrooms and lavatories. Oddly enough, one of the best ways of dealing with a dark bathroom or lavatory is to decorate it in deep vibrant colours. These will help to make the room seem warmer, and when combined with plenty of strong lighting it will become much brighter. Since you are often scantily clad when you are in the bathroom, it is important that it is a cosy room, so try to avoid the traditional pastel shades of pink, blue and green if your bathroom tends to be cold. Here a deep chocolate brown with bright towels and blind will create a more inviting feeling.

Lavatory windows usually have frosted glass in them, so the view out is not important. A permanently-closed blind which matches the wallpaper will give a warmer feel, and a bright, low light hanging from a dark painted ceiling will minimize the lofty feeling of a very tall room. You can achieve an unusual effect very cheaply by papering the walls of a lavatory or bathroom with newspaper. Paint one or two coats of clear wallpaper lacquer on top to give a washable surface, and you have a bright black and white room.

Obscured glass sometimes keeps out more daylight than net curtains, so check whether you really need frosted glass in your bathroom and lavatory windows. If you are overlooked, you may find that only the lower part of the window needs to be obscured, and that the top can be fitted with clear glass.

Don't resign yourself to having dark, dreary rooms. Use the ideas given here to transform the dull parts of your house into bright, welcoming rooms.

Heat insulation

There is a tendency among builders to skimp on the insulation that they should be installing in every new house, but you can remedy this in your own home at a cost of a few pounds. Proper heat insulation is a 'must' in any climate from the Arctic to the tropics—in cold weather it keeps the interior of the house warm, and in hot weather it keeps it cool.

If you live in an average British semi-detached house with central heating you may be wasting as much as three-quarters of your fuel in heating the air outside your house. It has been estimated that in a house of this type, only 25% of the heat produced goes to heat the rooms. Of the rest of the heat, 25% goes through the outside walls, 20% through the roof, 20% through windows, doors and chimneys, and 10% through the ground floor.

In a terrace house, slightly less heat is wasted than this, and in a detached one, slightly more. In a modern house with large windows, even more heat may be lost. In any case, the annual waste of money is enormous.

In a hot climate, of course, the problem is quite the reverse—to stop the sun that beats down on the roof from making the house interior too hot. In some countries, there has been a trend since the Second World War to make roof pitches (slopes) lower and lower—sometimes as little as 16°. This reduces the volume of air available as 'insulation' between roof and ceiling, and helps make the running of an air conditioning system more expensive than it would otherwise be.

The answer to both problems is efficient insulation. Insulating a house properly can reduce heating bills by 35% while keeping the rooms at the same temperature, or can make the house much warmer without using more fuel. Similarly, insulation can reduce substantially the power consumption of an air-conditioning system—or, in a moderately warm climate, even make one unnecessary.

The greatest fuel savings made by insulation are in houses with central heating. Provided the insulation is done economically, it should pay for itself in two years' saving on fuel bills. In houses with local heating, such as coal or gas fires, people tend to heat only the rooms they use most, and the saving is not so great. But insulation will still make the house more comfortable.

Many postwar British houses have a certain amount of insulating material already installed. But standards are not very high as a rule, and adding more insulation is generally worthwhile.

Value for money

An important factor in deciding whether insulation is worthwhile or not is, of course, the cost of installing it. For example, sales-men of double-glazing systems often claim that their glazing halves the heat loss through windows. This sounds impressive until you realise what a small proportion of the total area of a house the windows occupy. Halving the heat loss through them might reduce heating bills by comparatively little. If this is the case, then obviously it would be better to spend the money elsewhere.

Before installing one type of insulation rather than another, it is a good idea to find out the relative costs of various methods of insulation, and how efficient they are. The efficiency of an insulating material is expressed as a 'U value', and the brochures put out by insulating-material manufacturers gen-

Right: Pouring loose fill insulation between the joists in a loft. This type of insulation does not irritate the hands as some types do, so the man who is laying it is not wearing gloves.

Below: Levelling off the insulation with a cardboard 'rake'. You will have to make this yourself to fit the space between the joists in your house, and to reach to the right depth below their tops.

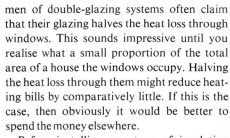

erally state the improvement in U value obtained by using their material. U value measures the amount of heat that passes through a material in a given time, so a high U value is undesirable and a low U value is desirable. For example, a properly-insulated loft floor may have a U value as low as 0.08. If it is not insulated at all, the U value averages 0.43 in post-war houses.

The U values quoted by manufacturers for their products are average figures for houses in normal positions. If your house is in a very exposed position, such as on a hill or overlooking the sea, the U value of even the best insulation will be raised, and therefore worsened, by the winds whistling around your roof and walls. You will need more and better insulation. Similarly, if your house is in a sheltered valley and surrounded by trees, you will not need so much insulation to keep it warm—though in fact the more insulation you have, the more heat you save.

Draughtproofing

Heat insulation will be largely wasted if your house is draughty. It is no good warming the air in a house if the wind just blows in and replaces it with cold air. Curing draughts is cheap, quick, and easy.

It is not only old houses that are draughty. Modern ones, too, have cracks and gaps through which air can pass. Even if you cannot feel a draught, heat may be pouring out wastefully and being replaced by cold air—a process that loses you money as well as comfort.

Even a well-fitting door lets in an amazing amount of cold air unless it is properly sealed around the edges. Wooden window-frames, especially in old houses, are no better. In particularly draughty houses, more heat may be lost in this way than any other.

Many types of door seal are sold. The cheap kinds work just as well as the expensive ones, but do not look so good. One of the cheapest is a simple felt strip that is hung from the bottom of the door by a strip of adhesive-backed plastic. This type is particularly good for irregular floors, because it does not get caught as the door moves.

More expensive draught excluders are often attached to the threshold itself and not to the door. They are generally made of metal, and are screwed or pinned to the threshold so that they line up with the bottom of the door. The great advantage of this type of excluder is that it keeps rainwater from seeping under outside doors.

The sides and top of a door may be nearly as leaky as the bottom, but need a different type of sealing. One highly effective type that can be used around doors and windows consists of thin metal strips that are nailed to the frame where the door or window touches it.

After nailing down, they are bent outwards so that they press hard against the door or window to provide a tight seal. Some types of strip come with instructions and a special bending tool. They are quite easy to install. Others must be put in professionally.

A cheaper alternative for doors and windows is self-adhesive foam plastic strip. This is bought in rolls and simply stuck to the door or window frame. Be sure to clean dirt and grease from the place where it is to be stuck.

A chimney takes a lot of heat from a room if there is no fire in the fireplace. Closing off the chimney opening is an advantage, but it should never be blocked completely, or it may cause condensation and damp patches on the walls. The fireplace can be closed off with hardboard or some similar material, leaving a tiny gap at the bottom to ventilate the room without too much heat loss. Or, better still, it can be bricked in for a neater appearance, so long as ventilation bricks are provided.

In draught-proofing, ventilators such as air-bricks should never be blocked up. Even the best-insulated buildings need a small flow of air; without it, condensation or dry rot may result.

Insulating ceilings

In most houses, the cheapest and most efficient insulation is that installed in the roof cavity or loft.

One way is to fill the gaps between the ceiling joists with lightweight loosefill insulation, which is simply poured in from a bag. It may be made of vermiculite, cork or polystyrene foam granules.

Loosefill insulation is not suitable under draughty roofs with open eaves. The wind blows it away. But in calm air it insulates as well as anything else. A 50mm (2in) layer gives a U value of 0.15; a 75mm (3in) layer gives a U value of 0.10.

A 76mm (3in) layer is an ideal amount, except in very cold or very hot climates. 50mm (2in) is reasonable, but less than that is simply not worthwhile. In Britain, the material comes in standard-sized 13kg (28lb) bags. One bag covers 2.3sq m (25 sq ft) to a depth of 51mm (2in) or 1.6sq m (17 sq ft) to a depth of 76mm (3in). These measurements take the ceiling joists into account, so when you are measuring the floor area of your loft or roof cavity, measure the total area and do

Right: Only a quarter of the heat produced by a central heating system stays inside an uninsulated house. The rest pours through the walls, roof and floor to the outside air. The proportions of escaping heat shown are typical for a British house, but vary with particular buildings.

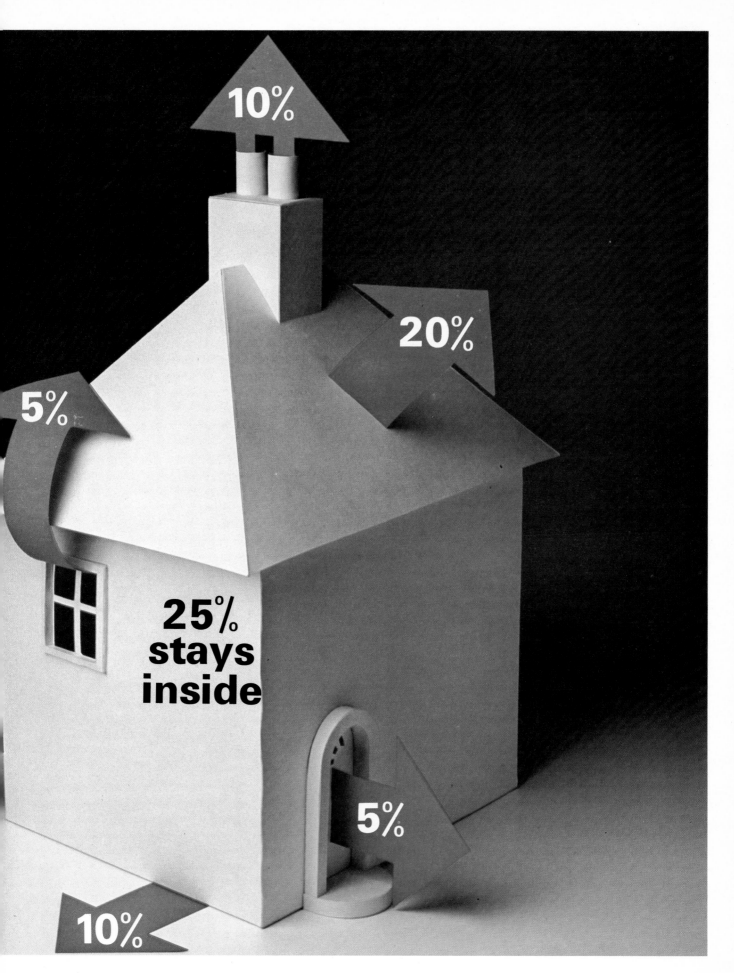

Above: Fibreglass matting used for loft floor and cistern insulation. To avoid skin irritation, you should wear old gloves.

not subtract anything for the area taken up by the joists.

When you have filled one space between a pair of joists, level the granules off to the correct depth with a piece of cardboard cut to fit between the joists and slid along them to act as a rake. This will show you whether you have poured in the right amount, and provide a guide for all the other spaces.

Make sure that you cover every part of the area with an even layer of granules. Even quite a small gap will lose a surprising amount of heat. The only gap should be the trapdoor leading into the loft from the room below. In most houses, the joists form a box shape around the trapdoor, so you will not have any trouble with granules falling through. If not, you can box off an area between the neighbouring joists.

If your loft or roof cavity is too draughty for loosefill insulation, the right type to use is fibreglass matting, which comes in rolls in several standard widths. Choose a width slightly wider than the space between the joists, so that it fits tightly without gaps. If

you cannot get the width you need, it is easy to cut pieces to shape with a handyman's knife. Cut the strips too long as well as too wide, and tuck the ends up under the edge of the roof for a better seal. You can glue a small piece of matting to the top of the trapdoor to seal that off as well.

Fibreglass matting comes in several thicknesses from 25mm; U value 0.16 (1in) to 100mm; U value 0.08 (4in). There is also a wider version that goes over the top of the joists. It is easier to lay, but you cannot see the joists after it is laid, so next time you go up there, there is a danger of putting your foot through the ceiling.

Lagging

Insulating the loft floor is effective, but in cold climates it makes the loft itself very cold indeed; little of the heat that used to penetrate can now do so. If the cold-water cistern is up there, as it is in most British houses, you will have to lag it—wrap it up—to stop it freezing in winter. Leave a space in the floor insulation under the cistern so that a little heat reaches

it from below.

The cistern itself can be lagged with various materials. A special type of fibreglass blanket is sold for the purpose. There are tank-lagging kits available that use cut-to-size polystyrene foam boards to fit all standard sizes of cistern. The boards fasten together with clips that are supplied with the kit. Holes can be cut for the cistern's pipes with a handyman's knife. Measure the exact position of the hole from the two nearest edges with a ruler. Cut as small and neat a hole as possible, and cut out a strip of board from the hole to the edge of the board so that you can slide the board into place over the pipe. When the board is in position, put the strip back and clip it down.

Join the edges of the floor insulation to the sides of the tank insulation so that no heat seeps through the gap. Remember to lag the top of the tank as well as the sides.

All water pipes in the loft must be lagged too. Two types of lagging are sold. Bandage lagging is a flexible strip of fibreglass or mineral wool sandwiched between layers of paper or plastic. It is wrapped around the pipe in an overlapping spiral. It is important to overlap each turn, leaving no gaps, and to continue the lagging all the way from floor to cistern. Gaps may allow the pipe to freeze.

The other type of lagging is a straight, hollow tube of foam plastic or rubber. It is slit down one side so that it can be slipped over the pipe. The slit is held shut with adhesive tape. Foam plastic lagging cannot be used for hot pipes, because it melts.

Attic roofs

If you have a loft with an impossible number of water pipes in it, so that it would cost too much to lag them all, you may prefer to insulate the roof instead of the floor. This keeps the loft warm. If your loft is used as an attic room, and has floorboards, you will have to do this anyway.

The easiest and cheapest way to insulate an attic roof is to use fibreglass matting similar to that used for a loft floor. It has to be held in place by hardboard nailed to the rafters. The same rule as before applies about width: the matting should be slightly wider than the space between the rafters. It should not stick out at the ends, however, or it will get in the way of the hardboard.

A simpler, but less efficient way to insulate the roof is to omit the matting and nail up insulation board instead of hardboard. Many types of insulation board are available. The types backed with aluminium foil conserve the most heat, but cost more than the others.

as felt or rubber, either between the support clips and the wall to which they are fastening the pipe, or by using them as a sleeve between the pipe and the fixing clips. Also check that there is room for the pipes to expand where they pass through ceiling joists or partition walls, and that pipes to central heating radiators do not rub against the floorboards; when you turn on the heat, they will squeak as they expand.

Resilient pads can also be used to help stop noise from large musical sources, such as pianos or large stereo speakers, being carried into other rooms. Though most of such noise is airborne, and needs different treatment, some of it can be carried by the building structure—sound travels surprisingly well along, or through, some surfaces. This element of the sound can be reduced by standing the piano on resilient pads, or fitting a similar baffle between a speaker and the floor or wall.

Noise caused by footsteps and banging doors can also be a source of irritation and can often be limited quite easily. Impact noises from footsteps can be reduced by laying a resilient floor finish such as cork, rubber, foam-backed vinyl sheet or thick-pile carpet on an underlay. The noise of doors closing can be muted by fitting a self-adhesive strip to the rebate of the door frame, so that the door is cushioned when it is closed.

The methods described above can successfully cut down much structure-borne sound, but excessive noise, whether it is internal or external, carried through the structure of the house or airborne, requires more extensive treatment.

Sound insulation

Unfortunately modern houses tend to be built with lighter materials than older ones, and the result is less, not more, insulation against unwanted noise. Older houses have a greater amount of protection because of their thick brick walls, but badly fitting doors and windows and uninsulated roofs all enable noise to enter. But the cure for the noise problem is not simply a question of shutting out the outside world. Interior noises, such as vibrating pipes, banging doors and footsteps reverberating throughout the house all contribute towards discomfort.

Installing sound insulation in your home can be cheap and simple, or involved and expensive. It depends on the source of the noise (or noises if you are particularly unfortunate) and the extent to which you wish to remove it. Bear in mind, however, that it is practically impossible to stop excessive noise completely, though you can make it acceptable.

Controlling noise

The most effective way of overcoming noise is to eliminate or reduce it at its source. This will obviously be impossible if your problem is traffic or aircraft noise, but many irritating internal noises that are transmitted through the structure of the house can be stopped with little effort.

One of the most common forms of unwanted internal sound is that made by parts of the plumbing system, particularly WC and water-

storage cisterns refilling. In many cases a satisfactory reduction in noise can be achieved by simply attaching a length of plastic pipe (if one is not already fitted) from the ball valve outlet to near the bottom of the cistern. This will enable incoming water to discharge below the waterline and not splash on to it. Another method to cut down the noise is to fit a 'silent' ball valve.

Another common source of noise in the plumbing system is vibrating pipes. This can usually be cured by fixing resilient pads, such

Fig.1. For really effective sound insulation, the inside of the roof should be lined, and the floor covered with glass fibre, or mineral wool.

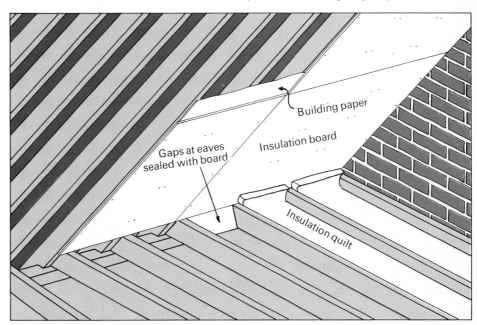

Building paper

Insulation board

Gaps at eaves sealed with board

Insulation quilt

External noise

External noise is in the form of airborne sound, and in most situations attention to the windows and external doors will have the most effect in preventing it entering the house.

Most noise enters buildings through the windows. If the noise is not excessive, merely sealing any gaps, however small, between the frame and the wall opening with a mastic filler or suitable cover strip, and fitting draught excluders, may reduce the noise to a satisfactory level. Fitting heavier glass will also have an effect on the insulation, but if the noise problem is severe, then it will often be necessary to fit double windows.

The type of double glazing usually fitted for heat insulation is not very effective as a sound barrier, as it normally has only a narrow gap between the two panes of glass. To be really effective, the window should consist of two separate frames of 6mm ($\frac{1}{4}$in) float glass with a wide air space between. This should preferably be about 203mm-228mm (8in-9in)—a gap of less than 100mm (4in) will not be effective. The sides of the air space should be lined with sound-absorbent material, such as 13mm ($\frac{1}{2}$in) fibre board, which should preferably be mounted on battens with a small air space behind. To prevent condensation occurring on the inside of the outer pane, some silica gel crystals can be placed on the bottom to absorb moisture. It is no use leaving the usual anti-condensation hole in the inside frame, because this will let sound through—and insulation is only as good as its weakest point.

For the most efficient sound insulation, a double window should be permanently sealed and ventilation provided by mechanical means or by a window facing a quieter direction. This will not be convenient in many situations, but inner window units can be obtained which slide open. With any system that is not permanently sealed, fit draught excluders to the outer window, and ensure that the joint between the frame and the walls is properly sealed.

The other major route through which sound will enter the house is through the external doors. Whatever you do, some sound will inevitably enter this way as it is not possible, of course, to permanently seal the doors. Noise can be minimized, however, by fixing a flexible draught strip to the bottom edge of the

Fig.2. This diagram shows how noise spreads throughout the house. Some noise is airborne, but some of it is transmitted through the house structure itself.

Fig.3. A lining of quilt and then some form of wallboard, mounted on battens or studs, will reduce the amount of noise passing through a masonry wall.

door, which will 'take up' irregularities in the floor surface, and by fitting resilient foam strips into the rebate. The joint around the door frame should be sealed as for windows.

If additional soundproofing is required, a porch which totally encloses the door will

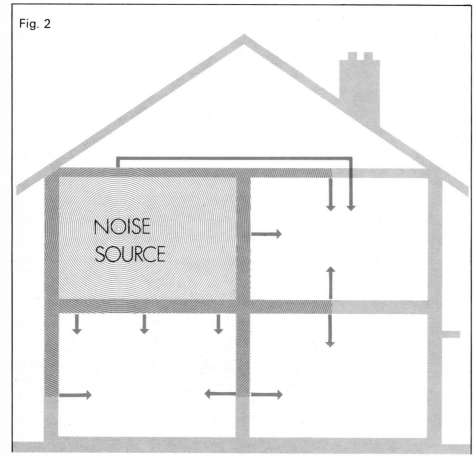

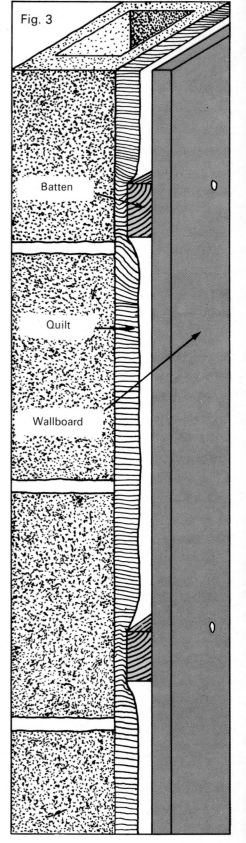

Fig. 3

Batten

Quilt

Wallboard

provide an effective sound barrier—a large volume of 'dead' air—as well as having many other uses.

In some houses, particularly older ones, sound can penetrate through the roof. A covering of glassfibre or mineral wool laid between the joists will provide both sound and heat insulation and so would be a worthwhile investment. Also cover any gaps in the eaves with insulation board or wood battens. As an alternative to lining the ceiling with insulation materials, or in addition to it if the noise problem is excessive, you can fix plasterboard or insulation board to the underside of the rafters if the roof is unlined. (To stop any leaks or dirt from disfiguring the lining, a layer of building paper, well lapped at joints, is a good idea.)

Internal noise

Although most unwanted sound will probably come from outside the house, it is often desirable to install some form of sound insulation to reduce noise within the house itself—as anyone with a houseful of young children will know!

Before embarking on major, and perhaps expensive, changes, first consider whether the careful use of sound *absorbent* materials will be adequate for your needs.

When a sound is made in a room, the ear first hears the direct sound, and then that reflected from the walls, floor and ceiling. This reflected sound reinforces the direct sound (it all takes place within a fraction of a second) and is called *reverberation*. The larger the room and the harder and more reflective its surfaces, the more reverberation will occur. Adding sound-absorbent material reduces the effect and helps to reduce the intensity of the sound passing through to adjoining rooms.

In most cases, the best place to add absorbent material is the ceiling, as carpets, curtains and upholstered furniture all contribute towards sound absorption. The most common type of absorbent material suitable for ceilings is acoustic tiles. Various types are available. They are usually 300mm (12in) or 600mm (24in) square and are made of ordinary wood fibre, mineral fibre, or special lightweight plasters. They are light in weight and most can be attached to the ceiling with a suitable adhesive, although some require pinning as well. Acoustic tiles come in a variety of patterns, such as regularly spaced holes, random holes, continuous slots and broken slots. The purpose of all forms is to expose the maximum area of absorbent surface to the sound. It is important not to destroy the texture of the surface by filling it in with paint. Most of these tiles are already decorated, but if further decoration is required, two *thin* coats of emulsion paint

Fig.4. An insulated 'double stud' partition wall. Two sets of studs are used, and an insulating quilt keeps one side of the wall separated from the other.

Fig.5. A floating floor is separated from the joists by quilt.

Fig.6. Increasing the weight of a floor with a layer of dry sand will improve insulation against airborne sound.

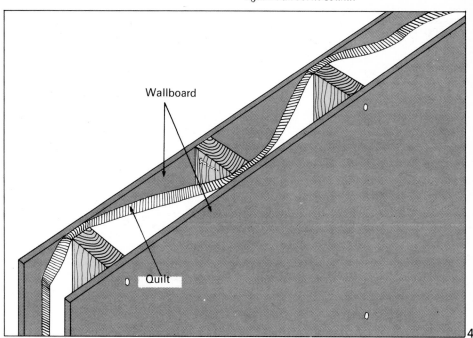

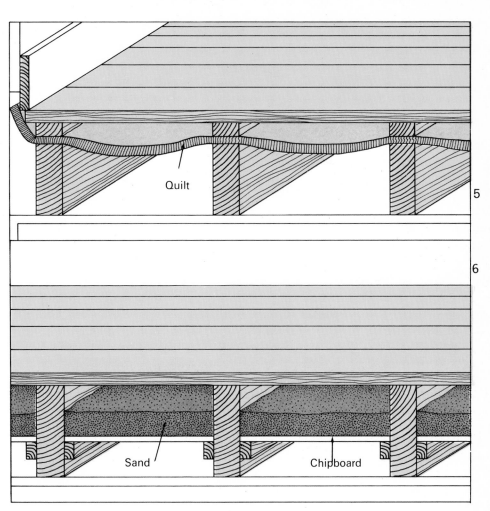

should be used.

Similar materials are also available in the form of boards. These come in standard sizes, like plasterboard, and have to be pinned or screwed through the existing ceiling into the joists. It will help to locate the position of the joists and mark them with pencil lines on the existing ceiling first before offering up the boards. An alternative method is to attach 50mm × 25mm (2in × 1in) battens to the ceiling first, and then fix the boards to them. The gap between the acoustic boards and the original ceiling will slightly increase the sound absorption properties.

Sound absorbents are, however, limited in their effectiveness, and it may be necessary to take other steps to cut down the level of internal noise.

Insulating walls and ceilings

Generally, walls transmit mostly airborne sound, and floors both airborne and structure-borne sound. The denser a material is, the less readily it will vibrate, so the denser and thicker the wall, the more effective it is as an insulator. In existing houses it is not usually possible to increase the density of a dividing wall significantly, and improvement in sound insulation must be achieved in other ways.

The sound insulating properties of a solid partition wall can be considerably increased by lining it with plasterboard or other building board on timber battens or studs. A 25mm (1in) thick layer of resilient quilt—fibreglass or mineral wool—should be sandwiched between the masonry and the battens. When fixing the battens or studs, use as few masonry nails as possible to keep direct contact with the masonry wall to a minimum. It is essential that all gaps in the board surface, and between it and adjoining walls, ceilings and so on, are filled as noise can penetrate through the smallest hole.

Timber stud partition walls are poor sound insulators—the board panels act like large speaker diaphragms. The sound transmission can, however, be greatly reduced by forming a double stud partition (see Fig.4). In this, two sets of alternating studs, each faced with plasterboard or similar building board, are separated by a resilient quilt which winds in and out of the studs.

The nature of sound transmission through floors is more complex, as both structure-borne impact noise and airborne noise occur. Sound is passed through the floor itself, and the structural floor members transmit noise to the walls on which they bear.

If impact noise through a suspended floor is severe, and cannot be satisfactorily reduced by the use of a resilient floor covering, then you may have to install a floating floor (see Fig.5). The floor surface is attached to 50mm (2in) square battens which *rest* on the floor

joists, a 25mm (1in) thick continuous layer of quilt, such as glassfibre or mineral wool, being first laid over the joists. The quilt should be turned up at the edges of the floor to isolate the floor surface from the walls. Once the quilt has been laid, the battens can be placed in position and lightly nailed to the joists. This nailing is purely to hold the battens in position as you lay the floor surface. It is essential that these nails are removed progressively from the battens as you nail the floor covering down, otherwise the effectiveness of the insulation will be reduced. Make sure that the nails you use to fix the floor covering to the battens will not penetrate the quilt or joists.

If you have installed a floating floor, it will be necessary to remove a certain amount of wood from the bottom of any doors because of the raised level. A ramp will also be required to avoid a 'step' down to any adjacent floor surface.

A suspended floor can be made more resistant to airborne noise by increasing its weight. A common way of doing this is to lay a heavy 'pugging', such as a 50mm (2in) thick layer of dry sand, between the joists (see Fig.6). First check with your local building inspector, however, that your joists will be adequate to support the additional weight. Sand is very heavy.

In many cases, the ceiling lining will not be strong enough to carry the weight of the sand layer, so it will be necessary to attach a suitable platform between the joists first. This can be 13mm ($\frac{1}{2}$in) chipboard positioned on supports nailed to the sides of the joists.

This method of insulating suspended floors can, of course, be combined with a floating floor to give insulation against both structure-borne and airborne noise.

It is also a good idea, as the floorboards will be up, to check that there are no gaps where the joists pass through a partition wall—another way for noise to be transmitted. Fill in any gaps with mortar.

Plumbing: how to measure/cut/fit new pipes

How many times have you wanted to fit items like a new washbasin, sink or storage cistern, but have been put off by the thought of having to move or extend water pipes? With modern materials and jointing methods, basic plumbing work is well within the capabilities of the average handyman.

Metal pipes used in modern domestic plumbing installations are usually made of copper or stainless steel. Older houses, however, may have lead or iron pipes. When replacing or extending part of the system it is advisable, for ease of fitting, to change to copper or stainless steel if you have the older pipes.

Tools required

Few tools are needed for general plumbing work, but one or two special items are needed for some jobs. The main tools are:

Hacksaw. The junior hacksaw is quite suitable and is useful for cutting pipes in awkward places. A *pipe cutter* is a more sophisticated alternative, and more expensive.

Files. Two, a flat one and a round one, are required. These are used for removing the burrs from the inside and outside of pipe ends after cutting.

Adjustable spanners. Two are needed for making joints with 'compression' fittings, one to hold the fitting while the other tightens.

These should be about 250mm (10in) long—anything larger will increase the risk of thread stripping.

Stillson wrenches. Two are needed if you are undoing iron pipe fittings, which can sometimes be rusted solid.

Bending springs. These are available for $\frac{1}{2}$in and $\frac{3}{4}$in pipe and for 15mm and 22mm pipe. If larger sizes need bending, a bending machine will be required. This can usually be avoided by arranging suitable fittings at any bends. If not, you can hire a bending machine from some D-I-Y shops and hire firms.

Blow torch. Used for soldering 'capillary' fittings and for joining lead pipes to modern ones. The gas canister type is satisfactory and fairly cheap to buy.

Measuring pipes

If the pipe you are extending or replacing is to be straight, use a steel tape or rule to measure the amount of new pipe to be fitted. Should any bends be required in the 'run' of the pipe, a suitable length of string can be used to estimate the length of pipe needed for the bend. Always allow two inches or more extra for each bend to be made.

Cutting pipes

Copper pipe used for domestic purposes is the light gauge, hard-temper type, and can be cut easily with a hacksaw. Take care, however, that adequate support is given to the pipe on either side of the proposed cut so that no distortion occurs during the final stage of cutting.

If you are using a vice to hold the pipe steady, wrap a thick piece of cloth around the pipe to protect it from damage. Another method is to hold the pipe on top of your left foot (if you are right handed) to steady it while cutting. This method enables you to cut the pipe where you are working and so avoids frequent journeys to the workbench. But you need a straight eye!

When using the hacksaw, use only gentle and even pressure and take care to make a straight cut—a crooked one will impede good joint making later. Stainless-steel pipes are much tougher than copper and more pressure is needed to cut them with a hacksaw.

A pipe cutter has the advantage of producing a straight, clean cut more easily than a hacksaw. A typical one has three toughened metal wheels mounted on a frame to form a triangle. The circumference of each is tapered to form a cutting edge and a threaded spindle is attached to one of the wheels for adjustment. To cut the pipe, insert it between the wheels and position them over the cutting point. Adjust the cutters so that they grip and turn the tool a couple of times round the pipe. Then tighten the spindle to deepen the cut and continue turning, re-tightening as you go, until the pipe is severed.

Once the cut has been made, the burrs, or jagged edges, left inside and outside the pipe end must be removed. If they are left, they can restrict the water flow and create unwanted turbulence within the pipe. They can also make the actual jointing of the pipes much more difficult, if not impossible, particularly where capillary fittings are used. To remove them, use the flat file to clean off the external edge, and the round file for the inside. Many pipe cutters have an accessory for this. Also bevel the outside edges of the pipe slightly with the flat file as this will enable the pipe to fit tightly inside the fitting.

Making a bend

Using bending springs is a simple job which requires little practice to achieve successful results. The spring should be inserted into the pipe so that the middle of the spring roughly corresponds with the proposed bend point. If this means that the spring will disappear into the pipe, attach a length of nylon cord or thick string to help you remove it after the bend has been made.

In many cases the easiest way to make the bend is to place the pipe, with the spring inserted, just below your kneecap and, holding it either side, *gently* pull it towards you.

Fig. 1. Pipe cutters make a straight, clean cut with little effort.

Fig. 2. Cutting pipes on your foot with a hacksaw avoids frequent trips to the workbench.

Fig.3. Use the flat file to clean off burrs from the external edge of the pipe, and also to bevel it slightly.

Fig.4. Internal burrs are removed with the round file.

As it is difficult to correct a greatly overbent pipe by this method, first underbend and then check the angle before proceeding.

If the pipe proves too tough to bend this way, obtain a thick piece of wood, about 100mm × 50mm (4in × 2in) and about 610 mm (2ft) long, and drill a hole near one end slightly larger than the diameter of the pipe. Chamfer the lower edges of this hole with a suitable tool (the round file will do). Then place the bottom of the wood on the floor or workbench, insert the pipe in the hole, and then press down on either side.

When the bend has been completed, the spring is sometimes difficult to withdraw. This can be overcome in two ways. The first is to insert a screwdriver through the eye at the top of the spring and unscrew it anti-clockwise. The other method is to overbend the pipe slightly, then correct. This loosens the 'grip' and the spring can then be pulled out.

Connectors and fittings

An extensive range of fittings is available for joining pipes together and for connecting them to taps, cisterns and so on. Straight connectors, bends and tee junctions are most commonly used for joining pipes. In addition to these there are 'tap' connectors designed for fitting to male iron threads (taps and ball valves), 'tank' connectors which have two flanged surfaces for attaching to the side of a water storage cistern, and various adaptors for changing from iron or lead pipe to copper or stainless steel. Fittings are also available which are designed to permit a reduction in pipe bore. Other, not so common ones, include drain-off cocks, stop ends, blanking-off discs, swept tees, and obtuse bends.

This is not a complete list of available fittings. Manufacturers issue catalogues of their fitting range and it is well worth acquiring a copy for reference purposes.

For joining copper or stainless-steel pipe, two types of fitting can be used—compression and capillary.

Compression fittings

Compression fittings are the most common

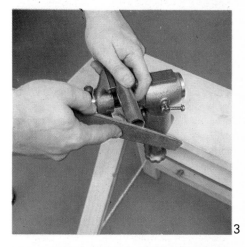

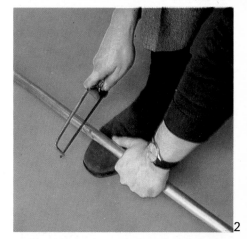

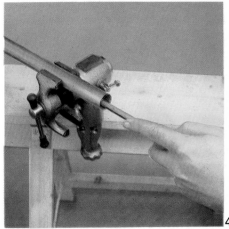

type and the easiest to use. Two types are available: 'manipulative' and 'non-manipulative'. The first is seldom used nowadays for domestic purposes. A special tool is required to 'bell out', or force open, the ends of the pipes, which are then compressed against the fitting body, when the nuts are tightened, to make the joint.

Non-manipulative fittings rely on the compression of a soft metal ring, known as a cone, olive or ferrule, against the external wall of the pipe to create the joint between pipe and fitting. No 'working' or distortion of the pipe itself is required, and so the work involved is much easier.

5

6

To make a joint with this fitting, the pipe ends must first be cleaned up, as previously described, with the files. Place the nuts on to the pipes, and then the cones. The cones have two chamfered faces, and if one of these is longer than the other, the long face must be placed towards the pipe end. Each pipe is then inserted into the fitting as far as it will go. A 'stop' moulded into the fitting will determine the depth of entry.

You must ensure that the pipes do not 'creep' out of the fitting while the joint is being made. Once they have been pushed in, scratch them next to the fitting with a nail or other sharp object. This will show up any movement.

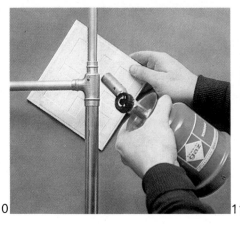

10

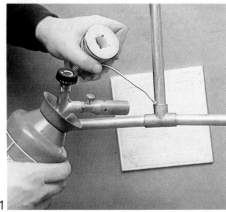

11

Before sliding home the cones, it is wise to smear a little non-toxic jointing compound on the cone. Manufacturers do not stipulate this, but it helps to ensure a watertight join.

Once the cones are inserted into the fitting, the nuts should be engaged on the threads and tightened as far as possible by hand. Two or three turns with an adjustable spanner on each nut are generally sufficient to complete the union. Use the second spanner to hold the body of the fitting while you tighten each nut. Do not overtighten or either the threads may strip or the olive may be forced into the pipe, making a bad joint.

Although the procedure described above is basically the same for all makes of non-manipulative fittings, it is wise to read any instructions supplied by the manufacturer before starting work.

Capillary fittings

More work is involved when making joints with this type of fitting, but they have the advantage of being cheaper and less bulky than compression fittings.

There are two types: one has a ring or reservoir of solder incorporated during the manufacturing process and simply needs the application of heat to seal the joint; the other type, known as 'end feed', has to have molten solder introduced at the fitting mouth.

Before you start to make the joint, make

sure that the surrounding area will not catch fire when you use the blow torch. Use asbestos mats (if you do not have them, spare pieces of ceramic tile will do) to cover any adjacent material liable to catch fire.

To make a capillary joint, after cutting and preparing the pipe, thoroughly clean the inside of the fitting and the surfaces of the pipes, otherwise the solder will not adhere. Use a rag to remove any grease or dirt and then burnish them to a bright finish with either fine wire wool or fine glasspaper.

A suitable flux recommended by the fitting manufacturer should then be smeared over the outside of the pipes and the inside of the fitting. Take care that no areas are left bare. Now insert the ends of the pipes into the fitting, ensuring that they reach the integral stop, and make a scratch mark on the pipes next to the fitting to indicate any unwanted movement. Either the fitting or the pipes should then be twisted to help 'bed in' and distribute the flux evenly. Wipe off any excess left outside the joint.

Heat should now be evenly applied to the whole fitting area with the blow torch. With pre-soldering fittings it is only necessary to continue heating until a ring of solder appears around the circumference of the fitting mouth. While not strictly necessary, an added precaution against leaking is to run a piece of cored solder around the mouth of the still-hot joint.

End-feed fittings should be heated until they are sufficiently hot to melt the solder wire, which is introduced around the mouth of the fitting. Once the solder starts to melt, slowly take it round the fitting mouth until the fitting overflows and will accept no more. Leave a ring of solder around the edge of the fitting as before. Once the joint has been completed, using either fitting, leave it for at least two minutes to cool and harden. Finally wipe off any flux left on the exterior of the joint.

If you are using stainless-steel pipe, special precautions must be taken to make a satisfactory joint. Ordinary flux used for copper is not satisfactory; an 'aggressive' flux is necessary to remove the oxide film which forms more quickly on stainless steel than on other metals. Several types of flux, in liquid and paste form, are suitable, most of which contain an acid base. As these are highly corrosive, they should be handled with care, and any excess left on the external surface of the pipes and fittings *must* be removed. The pipes should also be flushed out as soon as possible to remove any traces of flux from the inside of the pipe bore.

The other difference concerns the application of heat. This should be directed on the fitting only, and not on the pipes. This is because the thermal conductivity of stainless steel is lower than copper and any heat applied to the pipe will not be effective.

7

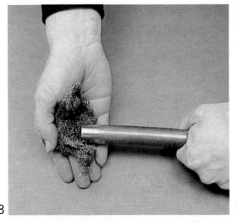

8

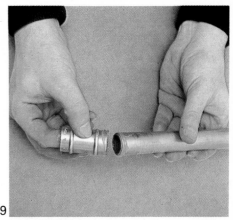

9

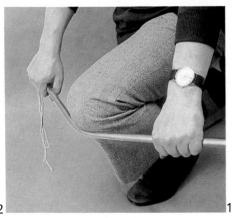

12

13

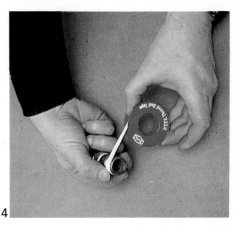

14

Fig.5. The component parts of a compression tee joint.

Fig.6. Fit the nut and then the cone on the end of each pipe to be joined.

Fig.7. Before inserting the pipe into the fitting, smear a little non-toxic jointing compound on the cone to assist a good join.

Fig.8. When making a capillary joint, the pipe must be burnished to a bright finish.

Fig.9. Before inserting the pipes into the fitting, smear flux evenly on the outside of the pipes and the inside of the fitting.

Fig.10. Pre-soldered capillary joints only require to be heated with a blow torch to seal the union. A ceramic tile gives protection against accidental fires.

Fig.11. Solder has to be introduced at the fitting mouth if end-feed capillary fittings are being used.

Fig.12. In many cases, pipes can be bent, using a bending spring, below your kneecap.

Fig.13 and 14. When joining iron pipe to new materials, either plumber's hemp and jointing compound or ptfe tape must be wound round the pipe threads.

Iron pipe

Where alterations or repairs are made to iron pipe, it is wise to adapt the immediate area of the existing system to either copper or stainless steel. This avoids the difficult job of threading new pipework, which requires the use of stocks and dies. These are not easily obtained and need considerable skill to achieve a satisfactory result. When connecting copper pipes to galvanized iron, use a special fitting designed to prevent 'electrolytic' corrosion.

Iron pipes and fittings have to be loosened with a pair of Stillson wrenches. A great deal of pressure is often required, especially when joints are rusty. If necessary, you can use heat or penetrating oil to free stubborn joints, using the hacksaw as a last resort. When undoing the fitting, use one wrench to hold the adjacent pipe as you apply pressure with the other.

Several fittings are available to adapt iron pipe. These have compression or capillary fittings at one end, and usually female threads at the other. When connecting to iron pipe, either plumber's hemp and jointing compound or the more modern ptfe tape must be wrapped around the threaded end of the pipe, to ensure a watertight join, before the nut is fitted and tightened.

If you are using hemp, first smear the thread with jointing compound, and then 'tease' out a suitable length of hemp. Wind this tightly around the pipe in the direction of the thread usually clockwise, starting about one thread back from the end of the pipe (see Fig. 13). Do not use too much hemp or it will be forced off the thread when the nut is tightened. Ptfe tape should be bound around the thread at least a couple of times, again in the direction of the thread and leaving the first thread or so clear. The nut should now be engaged on the thread and tightened with an adjustable spanner to complete the joint.

All about plastic plumbing

Key to fittings shown in the photograph:
1. *13mm (½in) copper pipe from pressure main*
2. *Stopcock*
3. *13mm (½in) metal socket to 9mm (⅜in) cold water pipe*
4. *9mm (⅜in) adaptor pipe to 13mm (½in) drain cock*
5. *9mm (⅜in) × 9mm (⅜in) × 9mm (⅜in) tee joint or junction*
6. *9mm (⅜in) cold water pipe*
7. *Adaptors to bib cock*
8. *Pipe support clips*
9. *13mm (½in) copper hot water system*
10. *PVC mixer taps*
11. *38mm (1½in) polypropylene waste outlet and tubular 'S' trap*
12. *38mm (1½in) high temperature pvc waste pipe*
13. *Swept tee junction*
14. *Access plug for cleaning rods*
15. *Self locking boss for joining waste pipe to soil pipe*
16. *104mm (4in) plastic soil pipe*
17. *Wall fixed retaining clip*
18. *Expansion joint*
19. *Soil pipe branch to WC*
20. *WC connector with rubber seal*
21. *Connector to pitch fibre pipe*
22. *Washing machine waste pipe into*
23. *. . . gully raising piece. This connection is not permitted in new houses*
24. *PVC gully trap*
25. *Connector to pitch fibre pipe*
26. *Rainwater pipe and shoe (27)*

With a certain amount of skill, and the use of plastic plumbing, you can make a successful job of most new plumbing and drainage installations and repair work around the home. The development of plastic plumbing materials has now made the job much simpler, and the materials themselves have some important advantages over the more traditional metal alternatives.

Plastics are now used for many aspects of plumbing, including cold water systems both above and below ground, waste and soil pipes, drainage systems and complete rainwater systems. Items such as lavatory cisterns, baths, sinks and basins, cold water storage tanks and even one-piece drainage inspection chambers are also available in plastic. Most manufacturers can supply comprehensive literature on their products and it is well worth acquiring a selection for reference.

Lightness and durability are, generally speaking, the main advantages that plastics have over metals. Even large diameter drain pipes can be handled easily by one person. The pipes are, too, usually made in longer lengths than other types, so fewer joints are required and this helps to simplify installation.

Plastic pipes have the added advantage that

the properties of the plastics used for cold water supply pipes safeguard against the risk of the pipes bursting if the water inside freezes. The water is actually less likely to freeze in the first place because plastic is a much better insulator than metal but if it does, the elasticity of the plastic permits the pipe to expand a little without breaking. Plastics do not corrode, and the inside of the pipe is very smooth, so there is little chance of deposits building up inside and obstructing the flow of water. If a plastic water system does fail, it is more likely to be because of a faulty joint rather than a fault in the pipe itself. Another bonus is that plastic pipes are less susceptible to 'water hammer'—so you won't have to worry about strange noises in the night!

The comparative lightness of plastic not only makes installing pipework much easier but it also pays dividends when you are installing a large piece of equipment like a water storage tank. Anyone who has attempted to install a heavy, bulky galvanized-metal storage tank in a loft will know the problems involved in getting it into position. Now you can obtain a special polythene tank that can easily be installed in the loft by one person—and it can also be squeezed through a loft hatch smaller than its own dimensions.

Plastics are not, however, the ideal plumbing material for all requirements, despite their many advantages. Most plastics cannot be subjected to much constant heat, so their use is normally confined to pipework and fittings for cold water services, drainage pipes and for such things as waste and soil pipes where the pipe will not be full of hot water for any length of time. Research is, however, being carried out to find a plastic suitable for hot-water supply systems and central heating systems, and there is every indication that this will be successful. Until specifically hot water pipes become available, however, you must be careful how you use plastic pipes and follow the manufacturer's instructions as to when you can fit them.

Plastic also has a fairly high coefficient of expansion, which means that special care is needed to ensure that the pipes have room enough to expand and contract during temperature fluctuations. Also, plastic pipes, unlike metal ones, are not suitable as earthing points for electrical installations.

Plastic pipework

Various types of plastics are used for pipework and it is important to know the correct type for the particular job in question—a plastic suitable for one application may not be suitable for another. Before starting any work it is very important to check with your local authority that the material you intend to use is acceptable.

Plastic pipes can be made of polythene, polypropylene, polyvinyl chloride (pvc) and acrylonitrile butadiene styrene (abs) and there are different types within some of the groups.

Polythene (or polyethylene) pipes are available in two forms—low density polythene and high density polythene. The latter is more rigid and can be subjected to marginally higher temperatures, but neither is suitable for carrying hot water. Low density polythen pipes larger than 50mm (2in) in diameter must not be used below ground as their softness would result in the pipe being crushed by the surrounding earth. Small diameter

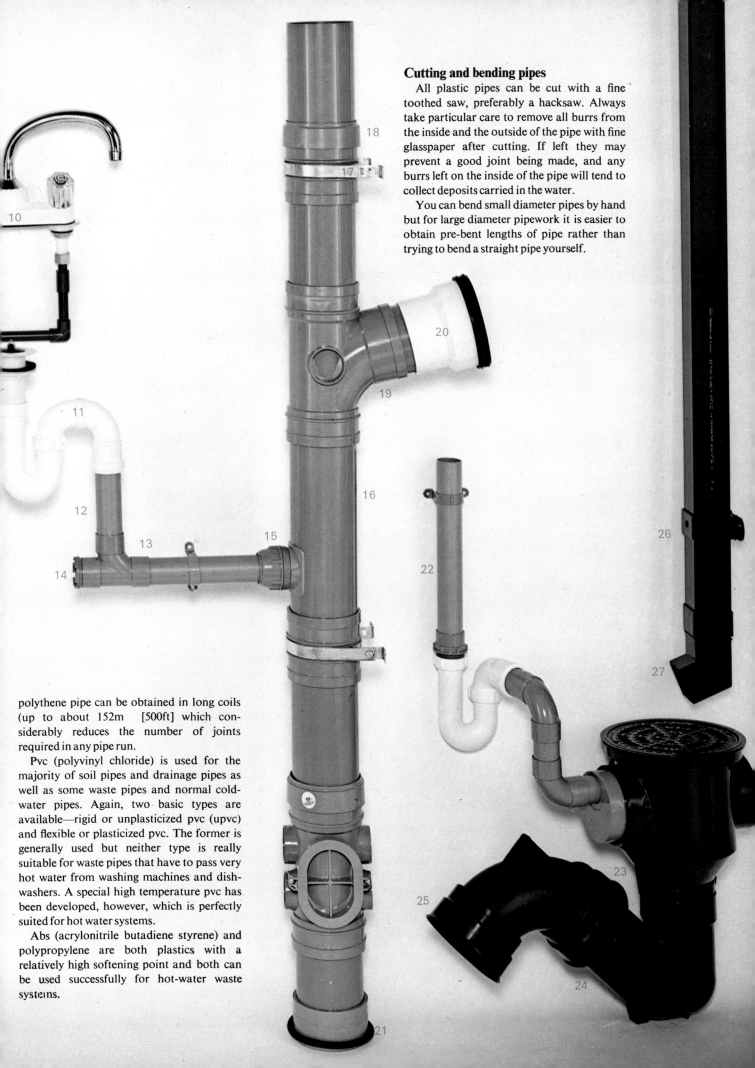

Cutting and bending pipes

All plastic pipes can be cut with a fine toothed saw, preferably a hacksaw. Always take particular care to remove all burrs from the inside and the outside of the pipe with fine glasspaper after cutting. If left they may prevent a good joint being made, and any burrs left on the inside of the pipe will tend to collect deposits carried in the water.

You can bend small diameter pipes by hand but for large diameter pipework it is easier to obtain pre-bent lengths of pipe rather than trying to bend a straight pipe yourself.

polythene pipe can be obtained in long coils (up to about 152m [500ft] which considerably reduces the number of joints required in any pipe run.

Pvc (polyvinyl chloride) is used for the majority of soil pipes and drainage pipes as well as some waste pipes and normal cold-water pipes. Again, two basic types are available—rigid or unplasticized pvc (upvc) and flexible or plasticized pvc. The former is generally used but neither type is really suitable for waste pipes that have to pass very hot water from washing machines and dish-washers. A special high temperature pvc has been developed, however, which is perfectly suited for hot water systems.

Abs (acrylonitrile butadiene styrene) and polypropylene are both plastics with a relatively high softening point and both can be used successfully for hot-water waste systems.

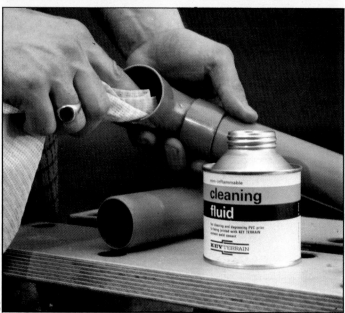

The method of bending depends on the type of plastic used. Polythene pipes can be bent either cold or hot. If you are bending low density polythene pipe cold, the radius of the bend must not be smaller than eight times the external diameter of the pipe. Note, however, that clips should be positioned close to the bend to stop the pipe straightening out. If you apply heat to the pipe the bend will be permanent, and you can form a bend with a radius as little as three times the external diameter of the pipe. Use either boiling water or a blowlamp to heat the pipe. If you use a blowlamp, take care that you move the flame continuously over the whole length of the bend—if you don't the pipe will melt.

An internal bending spring must be used to maintain the shape of the pipe while it cools.

High-density polythene pipe can be bent using either of the methods described above, but note that as it is more rigid, the radius of the bend needs to exceed ten times the external diameter of the pipe if it is bent in a cold state, and six times the external diameter if heat is used. As this type of polythene has a higher softening point, use a blow-lamp rather than

boiling water, again keeping the flame moving.

Pvc and abs pipes have to be bent using a blow-lamp, but in this case a bending spring is not required. It is important to note that heat must never be applied near the mouth of a pipe, as small distortions may occur and prevent a good watertight joint being made. If you require a bend right at the end of a length of pipe, start with a longer piece of pipe, form the bend away from the end and then cut off the excess.

Joining plastic pipes

There are three types of joint commonly used for jointing plastic pipes—compression joints, solvent welded joints and joints made by a rubber sealing 'O' ring contained in a socket or special fitting. Always use the joint provided by the manufacturer for the system you are using and read the accompanying instructions very carefully before starting work as there may be slight variations on those given below.

Compression fittings are generally used for

Figs.1 to 5. How to solvent weld a plastic pipe fitting.

Fig.1. First cut the pipe to the required length with a hacksaw. A piece of paper wrapped around the pipe will guide the blade, giving a neat, square cut.

Fig.2. Chamfer the end of the pipe to a 30° angle. Remove any burrs from the inside of the pipe with a sharp knife.

Fig.3. Clean both surfaces with cleaning fluid. Then abrade the surfaces with a fine abrasive. Steel wool or glasspaper is ideal but do not use a carborundum based abrasive.

Fig.4. Apply solvent cement. The brush strokes should run along the length of the pipe, at right angles to the ends.

jointing polythene pipes. These fittings are of the non-manipulative type which means that you do not have to widen, or bell out, the end of the pipe when using them. The fitting may

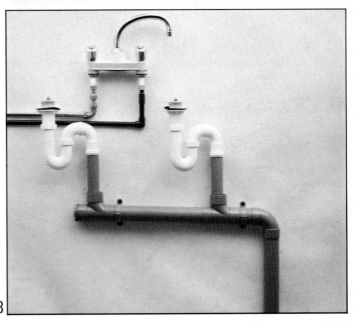

Fig.5. Put the pipe straight into the fitting without twisting either component. Then leave the joint to set.

Figs.6 and 7. Making a hole in a soil pipe to connect a self locking boss. This allows you to connect a domestic drainage pipe to the soil pipe. The hole in the soil pipe is made with a tank cutter. The boss is self locking so you do not have to fix it from the inside of the soil pipe. Solvent cement is also used with this joint.

Fig.8. The plastic pipework for connecting a double sink unit. The lower grey pipe runs to soil.

be made of plastic or metal, but note that the type of compression fitting used for jointing metal pipes is not suitable for jointing plastic pipes together as the plastic, being flexible, cannot be clamped firmly in the body of the fitting.

With compression fittings for plastic pipework a special sleeve is inserted inside the pipe end to prevent it becoming distorted when the nut on the fitting is tightened. If you have difficulty inserting the sleeve, carefully apply heat to the end of the pipe. This will soften it sufficiently to allow the sleeve to be slipped in.

To assemble the joint, start by placing the nut and then the compression ring on each pipe end. Insert the sleeve and then push one pipe end into the body of the fitting and tighten the nut by hand. Finally use a spanner on the nut but be careful to avoid overtightening (a couple of turns should be sufficient). Then repeat the procedure for the other pipe end to complete the joint.

Solvent welded joints are easy to make and exceptionally strong. A chemical is coated over both surfaces of the joint which welds the plastic surfaces together and, provided the instructions are followed carefully, there is little that can go wrong. Socketed pipes, or a special separate fitting, are used with this method.

First ensure that the surfaces to be welded are completely clean and grease free. Manufacturers usually supply a special cleaner for this. Then coat the two surfaces thoroughly with the special solvent cement. Note that you should always use the solvent recommended by the manufacturers as some solvents are not suitable for particular plastics. When both surfaces have been coated all that remains is to insert the spigot end of the pipe into the socket of the other or into the special fitting as far as it will go (a 'stop' is provided to prevent you pushing it too far). Then give the pipes or pipe and fitting a twist to distribute the solvent evenly. Wipe off any excess solvent squeezed out of the joint and leave the joint for between 12 and 24 hours (according to the manufacturer's recommendations) before testing.

The advantage that rubber ring-sealed joints have over other methods is that allowance is made within each joint for thermal expansion (see below). With this joint an 'O' or 'D' shaped rubber ring is first inserted into a groove in the socket end of one pipe (or into a separate fitting). A special lubricant—soap can be used if the manufacturer does not supply one—is smeared over the spigot end of the pipe and the pipe is then pushed firmly into the socket or fitting as far as it will go. It is particularly important to ensure that the rubber ring does not become displaced during fitting, so the two pipes must be perfectly in line during this operation. Note that the end of the spigot should be chamfered to about 15° for easy insertion. This chamfer is normally included in the spigot end during manufacture, but if you have to cut the pipe use a file to chamfer the cut end.

When you have pushed the pipe right up to the stop, withdraw the pipe a certain distance to allow for an expansion gap. This gap varies according to the material used. Some manufacturers put a mark on the pipe near the end and others give instructions as to how far to withdraw the pipe.

Installation details

The manufacturer's instructions regarding the installation of their pipework should be closely studied and followed exactly. The main factor to take into account is thermal

movement. If your pipes are jointed with the ring seal method you have no problems as allowance is made, as described above, for expansion in every joint. You must still, however, be careful that no tight restrictions are placed on the pipes themselves. Pipe clips (spaced at manufacturer's recommended intervals) must not be so tight as to restrict the expansion of the pipe. You must also leave suitable gaps wherever pipes pass through walls.

The solvent welding method of jointing, however, prevents any movement in the joints and allowance has to be made elsewhere in the system. This is done by incorporating special expansion couplings at specified distances apart.

Providing you take particular care to read all instructions thoroughly the actual physical work involved in installing a plastic pipework system is quite straightforward and easy, and you will have a system that should be maintenance free and exceptionally long lasting.

Super ceilings in timber or tiles

Timber cladding a ceiling gives a really expensive look to any room if it is executed and finished well. The resilience and lasting beauty of this type of ceiling treatment makes the job well worth tackling. This article tells you how to do it—and how to tile a ceiling perfectly as well.

Tiles and timber cladding are popular forms of ceiling treatment. The ceiling is an awkward surface to work with, but the right technique and materials simplify the job a great deal.

Timber cladding

Three main types of board are used for timber cladding. These are:

1. *Tongued-and-grooved* (T & G) boarding is timber specially cut and rebated so that one section slots into and interlocks with another. It can be bought in standard lengths or cut to specification by the supplier. A variety of widths and thicknesses is available, the most popular for indoor use being 100mm (4in) wide by 19mm ($\frac{3}{4}$in) thick. They are usually supplied already sanded, but unfinished.

The advantage of T & G boards over ordinary square edged planks is that they can be fixed through the tongue—this is known as 'secret' fixing, as the nails do not

pierce the surface of the board.

2. *Finished timber* is supplied in a variety of lengths, widths and thicknesses and does not come sanded.

3. *Laminated boards* are plywood or hardboard panels faced with a laminated wood grain design. They are most commonly supplied in 2.44m × 1.22m (8ft × 4ft) panels, usually 3mm ($\frac{1}{8}$in) or 6mm ($\frac{1}{4}$in) thick, and have grooves cut down the face to give the effect of solid wood. They have to be fixed through the surface.

Design considerations

You will have to decide which way you want the boards to run. Ceiling cladding usually seems to look better running the length of the ceiling—the effect is far less bitty than if you ran it sideways. However, you may wish to alter the existing proportions of the room, by running the boards across the room. This can make a narrow room appear wider.

The sawn ends of the boards will have to be disguised in some way and other decorative features of the room may facilitate this. If, for example, you have a wall that is 'all window', consider running the sawn ends to it and disguising them with a pelmet above the window.

If you decide to run the boards the long way across the ceiling (and if the joists run across the room) you can fix them directly to the joists either with brass screws or nails. If you use screws, ensure they are of sufficient length so that the whole of the screw thread will be firmly bedded in the joists.

Should you wish to lower the ceiling slightly, fix battens at right angles to the direction you want the boards to run, by screwing them either along or across the joists.

Before you do anything, however, find out what alterations you will have to make to the light fitting. You will need to fix a new ceiling rose to the boards—if there is any loose flex above the original rose this will be a simple task, but if there is not, some rewiring will be necessary.

Fixing battens

The first task is to locate the ceiling joists. These are normally uniformly spaced across the ceiling and the distance between the centres is usually 410mm (16in).

You can bore through the ceiling at different points with a bradawl to find them. Or, if you have access to the area above the joists, as for example, through a loft, you can drill small holes down the sides of two adjacent joists through the ceiling. Find the centre of each of the two joists. By measuring the distance between them, you can ascertain the spacing of the rest of the joists. Mark off their positions by snapping a line.

The ideal material for battens (if you decide to use them) is 50mm × 25mm (2in × 1in) prepared timber. Fix the first battens around the perimeter of the ceiling. If you are laying the battens parallel to the joists, simply align them with the marked centres of the joists and screw them into place. Countersink the drill holes in the battens.

An ideal distance between centres of battens if they are to run at right angles to the joists is 406mm (16in), because it exactly matches a 1.2m (48in) panelling width. Snap a line between the centres of each of the end joists of the ceiling and make marks at 406mm (16in) intervals along these two lines.

Providing support

One problem with timber cladding a ceiling is that of supporting one end of the board while you are fixing the other end. A way of overcoming this is by building a 'dead man's hand' which can be used to wedge the boards temporarily in position.

Fixing the boards

For a flush finish

If you want a flush, modern finish without a cornice or scotia, the boards must be cut to

fit snugly against the side walls. It is virtually
impossible to achieve a perfect fit at the ends
of the boards. So these are butted against a
length of square-section timber whose thickness matches that of the boards. For example,
if the boards are 19mm (¾in) thick, you use
19mm × 19mm (¾in × ¾in) end pieces.
This allows you to scribe the ceiling boards
to fit exactly against the end pieces at both
ends of the room. When all the boards are
scribed and cut, the end pieces are fixed,
and left in place. Since they are the same

thickness as the boards, they are quite
unobtrusive.

Begin by fixing the end piece at one end of
the room only. Nail it to either the ceiling
joists or the battens, whichever you are
using. Now temporarily nail to the wall, at
the other end of the room, a temporary support board which will hold one end of the
planks in position while you mark, and later
fix, them. For reasons given below, the thickness of this board (Fig.1) *must* be the same
as that of the end pieces. But it can be wider;
for example, where you are using 19mm ×
19mm (¾in × ¾in) end pieces, the support
board can be 19mm × 50mm, 76mm or
102mm (¾in × 2in, 3in or 4in).

The next stage is to make the first ceiling
board a snug fit. First, cut a length of board

to just under the length of the ceiling. Scribe
it along its *length* to fit against the side wall.
If you are using T & G boards, remember
that the grooved side must go against the
wall. Remove the waste wood with a finely
set smoothing plane and, if necessary, a
spokeshave.

Now scribe one *end* to fit against the end
piece you have already fixed to the ceiling,
and trim it with a tenon saw. Slide the other
end of the plank in, on top of the support
board; push the scribed end against the end
piece; scribe the other end (using the support
board as a guide); remove the plank from the
ceiling; and trim it to length.

Now fix the plank permanently in place.
If you are using ordinary planks, push the
first one into place, and fix it with 50mm

Above: A welcoming sight on a dark night. A perfectly clad ceiling gives further effect to the smooth outlines and rich opulence of this room.

Centre: The polished surface of the ceiling boards forms a pleasing contrast to the sanded floorboards. The timber cladding also increases the apparent length of this room.

Below: White painted ceiling cladding in this room makes the most of the light from the small window and blends well with the older decorative features of the room.

(2in) nails driven through its surface. Drive the outside row of nails at an angle which will help push the boards against the wall. Drive the inside row at the opposite angle. (Dovetail nailing of this sort is much stronger than straight nailing.) If you are using T & G boards, skew nail them through the tongue, cramping each board.

Subsequent boards are fixed in the same manner as the first. After the last few boards are fixed in place ('*The last board*', below), the temporary support board is removed. Then the second end piece is cut and fitted into place.

For a trimmed finish

Instead of a flush finish as described above, you may prefer to use a wooden scotia, or moulding, around the perimeter of the room—if only because this method is considerably easier.

In this case an exact fit around the edges is not necessary; the scotia will cover any gaps. But you must still make sure that your boards are cramped tightly.

Most beginners make the mistake of trying to mitre the corners of scotia for a neat fit. It seldom works—as the scotia is nailed home it is forced apart, and you get an ugly gap in the corners.

The last board

The method of fixing the last three boards on a ceiling is the same as that for walls. Lightly fix the boards to the battens and scribe the last board. Remove the boards, shape the last one and fit the three of them together in a slightly bowed shape. (You will probably need assistance to do this.) 'Spring' or knock the boards into place with your fist and surface fix them.

Laminated boards present no difficulty in fixing—simply treat them as wide planks. You must, however, ensure that the edges of

the boards are square or the joins in the ceiling will look unsightly. If you do not wish to work with 2.44m × 1.22m (8ft × 4ft) panels, use a fine toothed panel saw to cut the boards, working from the finished side. The lighter panels can be fixed in place with panel pins.

Ceiling tiles

Ceiling tiles come in a variety of sizes, patterns and materials.

1. *Wood fibre* tiles are produced in a variety of different surface finishes and often have

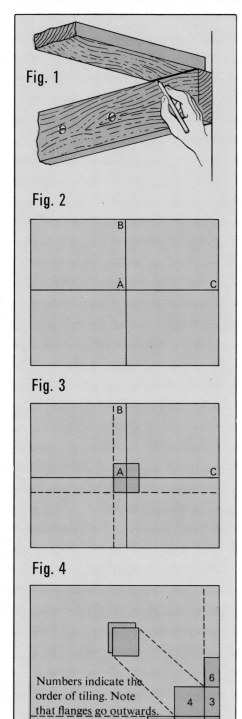

Fig. 1

Fig. 2

Fig. 3

Fig. 4

Numbers indicate the order of tiling. Note that flanges go outwards.

tongued and grooved edges which enable them to be interlocked after they have been 'secret' nailed. Often the surface is pitted or irregular to increase their sound absorption properties—indeed they are generally marketed as acoustic tiles. They can be fixed with adhesive direct to the ceiling or stapled or pinned to wooden battens.

2. *Cork* tiles, more usually used on floors and walls, can also be used effectively on ceilings. They should be used in a dry atmosphere and must be glued to the ceiling. At least half of the surface area of the tile should be covered with adhesive.

3. *Carpet* tiles are produced specifically to cope with floors that incur a great deal of traffic. They can, however, be applied direct

Fig.1. Scribing the shape of the wall on one end of a ceiling board. The temporary support board, along which you scribe, is fixed firmly to the wall and is as thick as the end pieces which later replace it.

Fig.2. If you use ceiling tiles without flanged edges start tiling at or near the centre of the ceiling. Divide the ceiling and snap a chalk line to mark the lines.

Fig.3. If starting at the exact centre will leave a very narrow border, snap new lines half a tile's width inside the dividing lines and start tiling from this point.

Fig.4. To tile a ceiling with flanged tiles, start in one corner, first estimating the size of the border lines.

Above: A ship's cabin effect in this room is reinforced by the knotty timber on the wall. The ceiling tiles add an extra touch of warmth to the compact room even if their arrangement is 'all at sea'.

to ceilings, but remember that you are paying for their hardwearing properties for use on a surface where this is unnecessary.

4. *Polystyrene* tiles are cheap to buy and easy to apply, but they do present a fire hazard. They should never be used where there is a risk of fire—as there might conceivably be in a kitchen or workshop area.

Preparation

Ceilings that are to have tiles glued directly to them must be dry and free from grease and dust. If in doubt about the suitability of the ceiling surface apply a few tiles, leave them for 48 hours and then remove them. If any of the ceiling paint or paper comes away the ceiling must be stripped.

Where to start

If your ceiling tiles do not have flanged edges, the first one should be applied as near to the centre of the ceiling as possible. To find the centre, snap lines to mark off the ceiling into quarters (see Fig.2). Count the number of tiles that will fit along lines AB and AC. It is unlikely that your ceiling will measure an even number of tile widths along either line, so there will need to be a border of tiles cut to fit the smaller space at the edges of the ceiling.

If the space left over is *more* than half the

width of the tile, fix the tiles from the centre of the ceiling. If it is *less* than half the width you would finish up with two narrow border strips which would look unsightly and disproportionate. In this case, mark new lines half a tile width from the centre line and work from that (see Fig.3) so that you finish with only one row which is at least half a tile wide.

If you are using flanged tiles you must lay the first one at a corner. The border around the outside edges should, for appearances sake, be at least 152mm (6in) wide. Measure the distance across the ceiling at several points. If the distance includes an odd number of inches, the width of the border should be 152mm (6in) plus the half odd number. Calculate the width of the border along the long and short wall. Snap a line to mark these distances from, and parallel to, the long and short wall.

Cut the corner tile slightly bigger than the corner space, and then scribe it to fit exactly between the snap lines and the walls. Then cut the tile to the scribed shape using a tenon saw, with the grooved side of the tile on the waste side of your cuts. Staple or fix this tile into place if you are using battens, or glue it.

Fix subsequent tiles in the order shown in Fig.4.

Applying the adhesive

Always use the adhesive recommended by the tile manufacturer. Apply a dab of adhesive to the four corners of the tile about two inches away from the edges. Smooth the adhesive over the tile with a stripping knife. Then apply a cone-shaped blob of adhesive to the centre of the tile and to the centres of the smoothed over adhesive at the edges. Hold the tile to the ceiling about 25mm (1in) from its final position and press and slide it into place.

Many types of ceiling tile are pre-finished, so ensure that your hands are clean enough not to mark the surface. If there is any difference in colour between one box of tiles and another, the variation will be diminished somewhat if you use tiles from different boxes in rotation.

Finishing the ceiling

When you have tiled up to the borders, scribe the tiles to the shape of the ceiling and wall angle. Flanged tiles can be eased into place without difficulty.

give extra strength—provided they run *upwards* from the hinge side.

A matching rebate is cut into the two middle rails, and across the stiles that meet them, to provide a weather-tight joint where the two halves of the door meet.

Setting out

If the two halves of a Dutch door were made separately, they would almost certainly not be parallel when they were hung. So you make the whole door in one piece, using stiles which are over-length, and cut it in two when construction is nearly complete. This means that you must set out the height of each half by measuring over the *rails*, not by measuring down the stiles. Remember to allow an extra 12.7mm ($\frac{1}{2}$in) for the overlap in the middle; your doors will 'shrink' by this amount when you rebate them together.

The stiles should be cut about 50.8mm (2in) too long. This will allow for 12.7mm ($\frac{1}{2}$in) waste at each end and 25mm (1in) in the middle. The inch in the middle allows adequate room for waste. The gap in the middle of the door will resemble a narrow 'letter box' when the door is assembled. The rails must also be cut slightly over-size; the waste is removed after the mortise and tenon joints are completed.

At this stage the areas of the joints in the stiles and rails can be marked. Lay the two stiles together with their long edges butting. Measure and mark a point in the middle of the stiles' length. On each side of this point measure and mark 12.7mm ($\frac{1}{2}$in) towards the ends of the stiles. Square lines through these points.

All measurements for the areas of the joints must be made from these squared lines. For the area of the joints in the upper part of the door mark from the top squared line. To mark the area of the joints in the lower part of the door measure from the other squared line.

From the respective squared lines measure and mark half the length of the finished door towards the end of the stiles. From this point marked in the top part of the door measure and mark 102mm (4in)—the width of the top rail—back towards the centre of the stiles. From the points marked near the ends in the bottom part of the door measure and mark 203mm (8in) back towards the centre of the stiles. This indicates the width of the bottom rail. Returning to the central squared lines, mark off towards the ends of the stiles the width of the two middle rails—114mm (4$\frac{1}{2}$in) for the rail in the top part of the door and 102mm (4in) for the rail in the lower part of the door.

Working from the middle, mark out each rail using the same method as for the stiles. The first pair of squared lines should mark

---

Going Dutch

Dutch doors, traditionally seen in farmhouses and rustic country cottages, can be both an attractive and functional addition to various rooms in the more conventional home.

Dutch doors are doors that are separated into two pieces across their width. This enables one half to be opened independently of the other. Traditionally Dutch doors were ledged and braced but any design, providing it incorporates a middle horizontal rail, can be copied as a Dutch door.

Standard British doors are 1.98m × 0.76m. (6ft 6in × 2ft 6in). The size of the door you build will obviously depend on the size of the door you intend to replace. The construction involves quite advanced jointing techniques and very accurate rebating.

Construction

A Dutch door consists of a frame composed of four horizontal members, or rails, and two vertical pieces, or stiles, which run the whole length of the outsides of the door. The top rail of each part of the door is made from timber of the same size. For standard

doors and all but very large doors pieces of 102mm × 38.1mm (4in × 1$\frac{1}{2}$in) timber are ideal. The bottom rail of the top part of the door is slightly wider than the rail it meets to allow for a 12.7mm ($\frac{1}{2}$in) matching rebate to be cut. 144mm × 38.1mm (4$\frac{1}{2}$in × 1$\frac{1}{2}$in) is ideal for this rail. The bottom rail of the finished doors should equal the finished width of the two middle rails—203mm × 38.1mm (8in × 1$\frac{1}{2}$in) being about the right size. The bottom rail is double haunched mortised and tenoned into the stiles, and the other three rails are single haunched mortised and tenoned (Figs.3 to 4).

The space between the rails and the stiles is filled with tongued and grooved boards, or 'matching'. These are pinned to rebates cut into the inside edges of the stiles and rails. Dutch doors are usually made with braces—diagonal pieces of timber the same width as the stiles, placed on each half of the door along the matching. The braces run parallel to each other, are fixed to what will be the back of the door, and their top faces, when fixed, are flush with the top faces of the stiles and rails. Braces are not essential but they do

the length of each rail between the stiles; what is left over 102mm (4in and a bit) is for the tenons, which run right through the stiles and protrude slightly on the other side.

Now lay the rails and the stiles together in the positions they will occupy in the finished door. Mark the top surfaces and the edges that are to be rebated. This will avoid the danger of cutting joints or rebates the wrong way round.

Cutting the mortises

The next step is to cut the mortises in the stiles. Fig.4 shows the shape of the haunched mortise and tenon which will later be cut on the ends of every rail (except the bottom rail) in the finished door. The mortises should be cut to accommodate this shape. The tenon is one third the thickness of the rail—in this case 12.7mm ($\frac{1}{2}$in). The tenon also has a stepped shoulder which is equal to the depth of the rebate which will later be cut on the inside edge of the stiles and rails. The depth of the rebate, given the measurements stated earlier, is 12.7mm ($\frac{1}{2}$in). The haunch in the tenon is about one third the length of the tenon—which equals the width of the stile. So the mortise has three depths, the main part of the tenon going right through the stile, the stepped shoulder entering to a depth of 12.7mm ($\frac{1}{2}$in), and the haunch entering to a depth of about $1\frac{1}{3}$in.

In the case of this complicated joint, do not cut the whole mortise yet. Cut the part that accommodates the main piece of the tenon but simply mark out the area of the haunch and the stepped shoulder. These can be cut to depth after the full shape of the tenon has been cut.

The single haunched tenons can now be cut. The shape and dimensions of these are shown in Fig.4. Then finish cutting the mortises, trying the tenon in the joint from time to time until the stepped shoulder and haunch are cut to the right depth.

The next step is to cut the mortise and tenon joints in the bottom rail and bottom of the stiles. Fig.3 shows the shape and dimensions of these double haunched mortise joints. The tenon has two tongues, a stepped shoulder and a haunch.

First mark out the position of the mortises. Cut only that part of the mortise that will

receive the two tongues of the tenon that go right through the stile.

Then cut the tenon. Score a line with a handyman's knife and straight edge along the squared lines you have previously marked on the ends of the bottom rails to indicate the width of the stiles. Set a marking gauge to one third the thickness of the rail. On the narrow edge of the rail score a line from the squared line to the edge of the rail, with the marking gauge. Continue this line on to the end grain and along the bottom edge to the squared line. Repeat this process with the block of the gauge flat against the opposite face of the rail.

The tenon can now be cut to the shape and size shown in Fig.4. On the side that is not to have the rebate, saw down the scored line through the end grain. Stop the cut when you

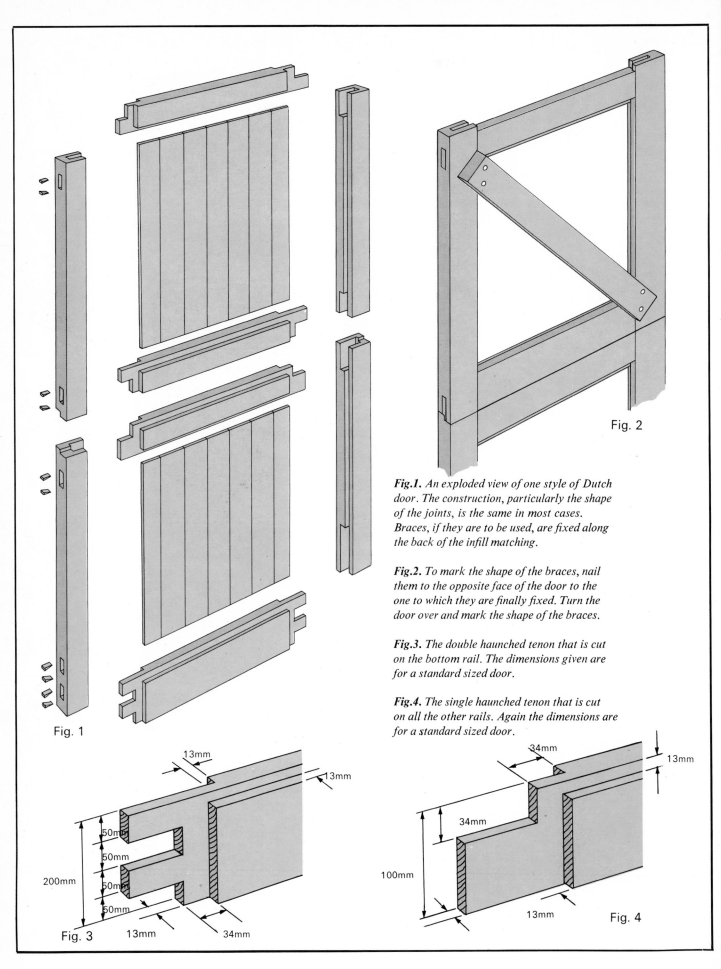

Fig.1. An exploded view of one style of Dutch door. The construction, particularly the shape of the joints, is the same in most cases. Braces, if they are to be used, are fixed along the back of the infill matching.

Fig.2. To mark the shape of the braces, nail them to the opposite face of the door to the one to which they are finally fixed. Turn the door over and mark the shape of the braces.

Fig.3. The double haunched tenon that is cut on the bottom rail. The dimensions given are for a standard sized door.

Fig.4. The single haunched tenon that is cut on all the other rails. Again the dimensions are for a standard sized door.

Fig. 1

Fig. 2

Fig. 3

Fig. 4

13mm

13mm

50mm

50mm

50mm

50mm

200mm

13mm

34mm

34mm

13mm

34mm

100mm

13mm

Right above: This Dutch door's finish attractively contrasts with that of the table to add an extra touch of old fashioned charm to this room.

Right below: Here the Dutch doors, together with the table, chairs and tiled floor, give this otherwise modern kitchen a farmhouse look.

reach the squared line. Then saw down the squared line through the face of the rail until you reach the original cut at right angles. Remove the waste. On the opposite face—the one at right angles to the edge to be rebated—mark inwards a distance that equals the depth of the rebate. This will indicate the size of the stepped shoulder. Square a line through this point and on the two edges. Saw away the waste as before.

Next mark out the positions of the two tongues on the existing single tenon. From the top of the tenon mark it into quarters along the end grain. Square lines through these points onto the face of the tenon. Mark the distance of the haunch, which is one third the length of the tenon, from the original squared line towards the end of the tenon. Cut out the waste down to this line to the shape shown in Fig.4.

Now complete the mortise that will receive the double haunched tenon.

Cutting the rebates

The inside edges of the rails and stiles are rebated to receive the tongued and grooved matching. The rebates are cut to a depth that equals one third the thickness of the timber—12.7mm ($\frac{1}{2}$in) if 38.1mm ($1\frac{1}{2}$in) timber is used. Their width along the wide surface of the pieces should be about 12.7mm ($\frac{1}{2}$in)—giving you plenty of room to pin the matching in place.

The rebates can be cut the whole length of the inside edges of the rails with an ordinary rebate or plough plane. But along the edges of the stiles the rebates run to 12.7mm ($\frac{1}{2}$in) inside the squared lines that were marked to show the area of the joints. This will form a corner between the rebated stiles and rails. On the ends of the stiles mark a distance of 12.7mm ($\frac{1}{2}$in) from the original squared lines towards the ends. From the squared lines that denote the position of the middle rails mark inwards 12.7mm ($\frac{1}{2}$in) towards the central waste area. Square lines through these points part of the way across the top surface and on the edge to be rebated.

The rebates can now be cut in the stiles between these points. Stopped rebates are difficult to make with either an ordinary rebate plane or a plough plane. This is because the body of the plane projects about 75mm or (3in) in front of the blade and

about 130mm or (5in) behind it. This means that you cannot stop the rebate accurately at the point required. A special type of rebate plane, called a bullnose rebate plane, is specially made for stopped rebates. Or you can do most of the job with an ordinary rebate, plane and finish off with a chisel.

Assembling the door

The skeleton framework of the door can now be fitted together. Assemble the door on a perfectly flat surface, and check that the two parts of the door are the correct size. (Remember the 12.7mm ($\frac{1}{2}$in) rebate still to come in the middle!). When satisfied glue the parts together with a waterproof glue such as Cascamite. Do not use pva adhesive as this is soluble in water and is, therefore, not weatherproof. Check that the door is square with either a large square or by measuring the diagonals. These will be exactly equal if the door is square.

The next step is to drive thin wedges from the outsides of the stiles into the mortise and tenon joints with a mallet. Do this before the adhesive dries. The wedges will make a tight fit between the mortise and the tenon. If the door is not square the fault can be rectified by driving the wedges home with extra force at suitable corners.

Cramp the assembly using sash cramps with waste wood blocks between the shoes of the cramp and the edges of the stiles. Wipe excess glue from the surfaces of the doors.

Cutting the braces

The length of the braces will depend on the size of the door. Their width should equal that of the stiles, and their thickness should fill the space between the matching and the back of the frame, so that stiles, rails and braces are all flush. Cut the braces several inches over-size. Lay the braces across the rails so that they 'cover the corners', and lightly nail them in position. Turn the door over, and direct-mark the braces by running a marking knife around the corner. With a saw and smoothing plane cut down to these lines. Fig.2 shows the braces nailed across the rails. Now remove the braces until matching has been fixed.

Now sand the back surfaces of the matching with either an orbital (not rotary) sanding device fitted to an electric drill or glasspaper wrapped around a wood block.

Now fix the braces. They can be glued into place first. Then nail them to the matching,

nailing through its surface. Pin the braces to the stiles and rails by angling the nails.

Separating the two parts

The assembly can now be cut in two. Separate the two components of the door by sawing through the stiles into the middle waste area. Saw away any waste that protrudes from the ends of the stiles and remove any parts of the wedges and tenons that stick out at the joints.

The rebates in the meeting rails

Cutting the rebates in the meeting rails is the final step in the construction of a Dutch door. Set the rebate plane to half the thickness of the meeting rails. Take the top half of the door. Cramp a waste block to the end to which you will be planing. This will avoid damaging the end grain of the stile. Lay the body of the plane along the face of the middle rail that will be the back of the door. Cut a rebate along the rail and two stiles to a depth of 12.7mm ($\frac{1}{2}$in).

Then cut the rebate in the lower part of the door. The process is the same, but the body of the plane must lie on the surface of the rail that will be in the front of the finished door. Cut this rebate to a depth of 12.7mm ($\frac{1}{2}$in) also.

Ledged and braced doors

Ledged and braced doors are usually seen outside the home where their strength provides necessary security on garages, sheds and other outhouses. If constructed carefully and well designed, though, a ledged and braced door can add an interesting and attractive touch inside the home.

The basic construction of ledged and braced doors is simple. The face of the door consists of vertical lengths of timber, called battens, which are butted together along their long edges. They are held together by ledges, horizontal pieces which are as long as the door is wide. Most of these doors also have braces, pieces of timber that run diagonally between two ledges. These always run *upward* from the hinged side; they give added strength to the door.

There are many designs for ledged and braced doors, some of which are shown in Figs.2-6. If the door does not have to be particularly strong—for a cupboard, say—you can do away with the braces. You can use

only two ledges, one near the top and one near the bottom of the door.

Another variation is a framed, ledged and braced door. This has stiles and rails jointed together, with the battens glued and pinned into a rebate cut on the inside edges of the stiles and rails. The construction of this type of door is basically the same for making Dutch doors though, of course, the door is not cut in two.

Most British doors are 31mm (1$\frac{1}{4}$in) thick, and if your door frame will only take this size you can build the door to this thickness. Doors on outhouses, however, need to be fairly solid for security, and for one of these you may wish to increase the thickness to 38mm (1$\frac{1}{2}$in); you can then use 19mm ($\frac{3}{4}$in) timber for all the pieces, which will be more convenient and less wasteful than using two different thicknesses of wood. The width of the timber depends largely on the design you choose but 100mm (4in) is a common size for ledged and braced doors. Doors made from

wider boards tend to look heavy and unattractive.

Tongued-and-grooved boards are often used for battens. These help to provide a weathertight seal. Square-edged boards can be used but these are not as weatherproof, especially when they shrink and gaps appear between them.

For example, if the door width is 762mm (2ft 6in) and you intend to use 100mm (4in) battens, this width will be approximately bridged by seven 100mm (4in) and one 63mm (2½in) battens. The door would look odd if you simply put the 63mm (2½in) batten at one edge of the door. In this case you should use eight 100mm (4in) battens, cut two of them down to just over 75mm (3in) and put one at each side of the door.

Cut the boards a little too long and the outside boards just over width. If you are using T & G boards, paint the tongues and grooves before you begin the assembly of the door. (*But see* 'Designs with a difference' below.) Paint the edges of square-sectioned timber also. This makes the door more weatherproof.

The battens should be fitted together tightly and the ledges nailed to them. To do this, you will have to cramp the boards together. Two or three sash cramps would do the job, but you may not have any. An alternative is to nail a long, reasonably straight piece of timber to the floor parallel to the skirting. Do not drive the nails right home. The distance of this piece from the skirting should be the planned width of the door plus, say, 50mm (2in).

Cut four wedges, each of which should be a little narrower than 50mm (2in) (or whatever distance you have chosen). Lay the battens on the floor between the nailed-down strip of timber and the skirting, then force them together with the wedges, used as 'folding wedges' in two pairs (see Fig.7).

Fixing the ledges

Now mark out on the battens the finished length of the door and the position of the ledges. To do this, mark a line across the battens in the middle of their length. Take all measurements from this line. On each side of the line, measure half the planned height of the door. Square lines through these points across the battens.

Now mark the lines that will indicate the position of the ledges. If you intend to use three ledges the middle one should run across the centre of the door. On each side of the central squared line mark a distance equal to half the width of the middle ledge. Square lines through these points. The top and bottom ledges can be between 25mm-75mm (1in and 3in) away from the top and bottom of the finished door. They should not be farther away, or the ends of the battens may become damaged when the door is in use. Mark out the positions of the top and bottom

ledges from the central squared lines.

Before assembling the door further you will have to decide how the braces, if they are to be used, will be jointed to the ledges. If you intend to use simple butt joints you can go ahead and fix the ledges, as described below. If you want to notch the braces into the ledges, as shown in Fig.3, you will have to cut the ledges to shape before you fix them. The distance of the point where the braces meet the ledges from the ends of the ledges is a matter of design. Fig.3 shows one design and indicates the positioning and size of the notches.

Once the ledges have been cut to shape, you can fix them to the cramped-up battens. *Lightly* pin the ledges to the battens in the marked positions. Use oval nails to do this, nailing through the edges of the ledges into the battens. Release the cramps, or knock out the wedges if you are using them, and turn the assembly over. Place rough pieces of wood underneath the ledges to hold them away from the ground.

Now nail through the battens into the ledges. Use nails about 6mm (¼in) longer than the combined thickness of the ledges and battens. Nail through the door into the rough pieces with oval nails. Then turn the door over, knock off the rough pieces and *clench*, or bend over, the nail points with a nail punch. This pulls the ledges and the battens together tightly. Remove the oval nails that were used to fix the ledges temporarily to the battens.

Ledged and braced doors sometimes sag a little when hung. You can reduce this distortion by screwing the central and the two outside battens to the ledges as well as nailing them.

The door can now be cut to size. Saw along the marked lines that indicate the top and bottom of the door. Plane off the excess wood on the long sides of the outside battens.

Fitting the braces

If you have designed your door with braces, these can now be cut to size and shape and nailed in place. Remember that braces add to the strength of a door only if they run *upwards* from the hinged side.

If the braces are to butt against the ledges, mark on them the points where the brace ends meet the ledges. Cut the braces slightly over length and nail them temporarily *over* the ledges, so that they cover and protrude beyond the points marked on the ledges. Near the end of the brace lay a straight edge and line it up with the edge of the ledge—the edge to which the brace will run. Draw a line along the straight edge. Repeat the process at the other end of the brace. Remove the brace from the assembly. With a tenon saw, cut down the lines marked at the brace ends.

Once you have cut the brace to shape and

Basic construction

The first step in the construction of most designs of ledged and braced door is to butt the edges of the battens together. You will first have to decide how many battens you need to make up the door. You may have to cut some of the battens narrower than the rest. In doing this you must ensure that the arrangement of the battens is symmetrical.

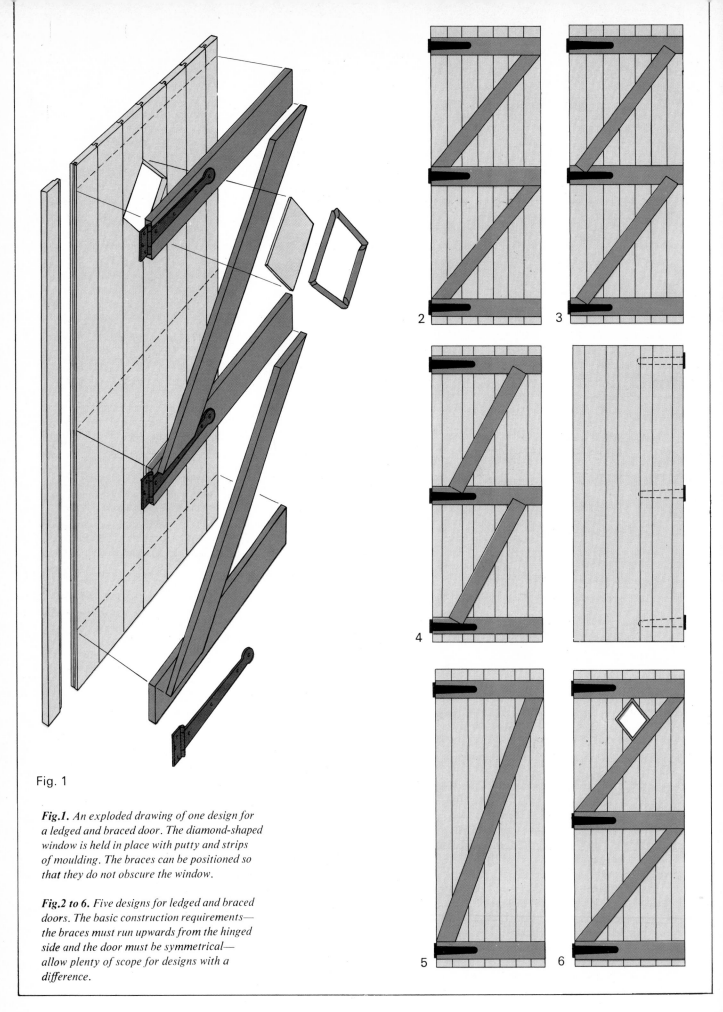

Fig. 1

Fig.1. *An exploded drawing of one design for a ledged and braced door. The diamond-shaped window is held in place with putty and strips of moulding. The braces can be positioned so that they do not obscure the window.*

Fig.2 to 6. *Five designs for ledged and braced doors. The basic construction requirements— the braces must run upwards from the hinged side and the door must be symmetrical— allow plenty of scope for designs with a difference.*

284

tried it for fit, cut the other brace to length in the same manner. Lightly pin the braces to the battens and follow the procedure outlined above to enable you to nail through the batten into the ledges.

Insert braces

If the ledges have a V-shaped notch cut into them, cutting the braces to shape will be a little more difficult. It involves reproducing the V shape on to the end of the braces, but at a different angle (see Fig.8). To do this, mark a line along each ledge to indicate the maximum depth of the V, and across each ledge through the point of the V. Nail the braces lightly in place over the ledges and draw a line to indicate the edge of the ledge. Now mark on the brace the maximum depth of the V and the position of its point. The place where these two lines cross will be above the point of the V. Draw two lines from this point to the line indicating the edge of the ledge. Repeat this at the other end of the brace. Remove the brace and cut it to shape.

If you have cut the V shape in the ledges accurately, you can use the first brace to mark out the second. If in doubt, though, repeat the process outlined above. Nail the braces in place.

Designs with a difference

A simple variation is to use two different widths of batten for the door face, placed alternately across the door. The assembly is exactly the same as for a conventional door. Make sure that the arrangement of the battens does not spoil the symmetry of the door.

Fig.1 shows a door with a diamond-shaped window in the centre of the top half. The hole for the window is cut after the ledges are fixed, but before the braces. The braces must be positioned so that they do not obscure the window.

To make this type of door lay the battens together in the manner described above and cramp them together. Mark out the position of the ledges. Then mark out the diamond shape. Its size is largely a matter of taste, but it should not be too large or the door will lose some of its rigidity. An attractive size for a door 762mm (2ft 6in) wide is 305mm (12in) along the vertical and 203mm (8in) along the horizontal.

Assemble the door in the manner described above. Mark out the diamond with a pencil. At the four corners, drill a 6mm ($\frac{1}{4}$in) hole. The diamond shape can then be cut out with a power jig saw or, if you do not have one, a pad saw.

An alternative is to cramp the battens and mark out the position of the ledges. Do not fix them yet. Mark out the diamond shape and number each of the battens. Release the cramps. The battens in the centre of the door

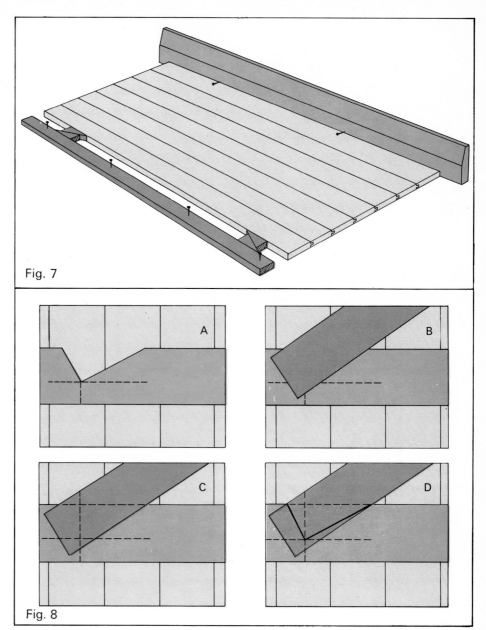
Fig. 7

Fig. 8

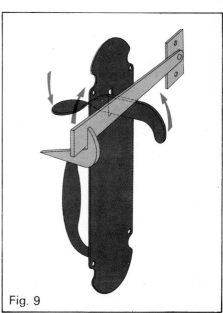
Fig. 9

Fig.7. One method of cramping the door battens while you fix the ledges. A piece of timber is nailed to the floor. Pairs of wedges are knocked in place between the timber piece and the door edge. This pushes the door firmly against the skirting board.

Fig.8. If the braces are to be inset in the ledges, cut the ledge to shape and fix it to the door. Mark it as shown in A. Lay the brace over the ledge (B). Sighting the marks on the ledge, draw intersecting lines on the brace (C). Draw lines joining up this intersection with the points where the brace meets the edge of the ledge (D). Then remove the brace and cut along these lines.

Fig.9. Where security is not really important a thumb latch will hold the door closed.

will have part of the diamond marked on them. Cut along the lines with a tenon saw. Re-assemble the battens in their correct position, lining up the pencil marks that indicate the position of the ledges. Re-cramp the battens and assemble the door in the usual way.

If you intend to cut the diamond by this second method, and you are using T & G boards, you should not paint the tongues and grooves before the initial assembly. If you do, it will be difficult to get them apart again. They can be painted when you reassemble them after the diamond has been cut.

Once you have cut out the diamond, you can reassemble the rest of the door, including any braces. These do not have to run right to the ends of a pair of ledges, so you can avoid obscuring the cutout for the window. When the door is assembled and cut to size, fit a glass pane into the window.

Your glass stockist may be prepared to cut the glass to shape for the window. Fit strips of wood moulding around the sides of the diamond from one side of the door to give a firm fixing for the window, then fix the glass in with putty. If the sides of the diamond have been irregularly cut, rebated moulding will disguise this. The method of fixing the moulding is basically the same as that for fitting new panels into panelled doors.

Hanging the door

Ledged and braced doors are hung with tee hinges. The long part of the hinge is screwed to the ledges. If the door is fairly heavy and has been built from thicker timber than that suggested above a heavier type of hinge, known as a Scotch tee hinge, may be necessary.

You will also need to fit some kind of lock, bolt or latch to the door so that it closes securely. A barrel bolt is the most commonly used on ledged and braced doors. These are made from iron, brass or bronze, but for purely functional purposes an iron bolt is sufficient. The length of barrel bolts varies between 75mm and 380mm (3in-14in) but a 150mm (6in) bolt is sufficient for most types of ledged and braced door. The plate of the bolt is screwed to the door and the metal socket or staple is fixed to the door frame. The bolt is pushed into this socket to secure the door. If the door frame is thick, the bolt can slide directly into a hole drilled in the frame.

A thumb latch will hold the door closed, but does not lock it. The components of a thumb latch are shown in Fig.9. A rim lock is the most secure way of locking the door. These are easy to install, the main part of the lock being screwed to the door and the keep, or smaller part, to the door frame.

Panelled doors made of solid timber move more than modern ones made from man-made boards. Softwood ones move more than hardwood ones. And of course, wide doors move more than narrow ones (in actual distance, not in proportion to their width).

The way to estimate the right clearance is to leave a minimum of 1.6mm ($\frac{1}{16}$in) round the top three sides of the door, and at least 3mm ($\frac{1}{8}$in) at the bottom (but more about clearance *under* doors later). Then you can add to this figure 0.8mm ($\frac{1}{32}$) for each factor that might make the door expand an extra amount—for example it if is an outside door, in a centrally heated house, or if it is made of solid timber panels. The average clearance for an inside door is about 3mm ($\frac{1}{8}$in) on the top three sides, and 6mm ($\frac{1}{4}$in) at the bottom.

There used to be a British joiner's rule of thumb that you should be able to get an old penny (just over 1.6mm [$\frac{1}{16}$in] thick) between a door and its frame all round. This was before central heating, however, and the gap is a bit small by today's standards. But it is a good way of measuring if you can find a coin of the right thickness for the clearance you need.

The method for fitting a standard-sized door into a standard-sized frame is as follows: first, buy a door of the correct size and leave it in the room where it is to be fitted for a couple of days to let it adjust to the prevailing humidity. New doors with solid timber rails and stiles (this includes many flush doors) often have the top and bottom ends of the stiles (vertical side pieces) left uncut, and these projecting *horns*, as they are called, should be sawn off and planed smooth.

When the door has acclimatized itself, offer it up to the hinge side of the door-frame and examine the edge of door and frame to see if they are parallel. Many frames are leaning or curved, even in new houses. If the frame is really irregular you may have to scribe the door to it, but otherwise an ordinary plane and your own judgement should be enough to make it fit. Make sure that you don't remove so much more wood from one end than the other that the door is no longer vertical; an occasional check with a spirit level should guard against this.

If the door is not too tall to fit into the door frame at this stage, hold it up with a couple of wedges underneath it while you check it against the frame. If it is too tall, rest it on the floor and put wedges under it only when it begins to take on the right size and shape (see Fig. 1).

After the hanging edge of the door is cut to shape, do the same with the top, then the bottom (remembering to remove more wood than for the sizes). Then raise it to its correct

---

Getting the hang of it

Doors and windows have two purposes: they open to provide access or let in air, and they shut to keep out rain, draughts and sound. So they must open easily and shut firmly, which means that they must be fitted very accurately into their frames.

Hanging doors and windows is not particularly difficult, and there are only a few facts and procedures you need to know about to get it right every time.

The most important part of the job is getting the door or window to fit properly into its frame. They do not fit exactly; there has to be a clearance all round to allow for expansion in wet weather, and to keep the door from scraping against its frame when it is opened and shut.

Doors do not open straight as if they were being lifted out of their frame. They swing slightly outwards as they pivot on their hinges, and the lock side of the door, opposite the hinge, has to be cut away to allow for this movement. Different kinds of hinges cause the door to move in different

ways, and you have to know how a particular type of hinge will make the door behave.

The hinges themselves have to be installed strongly but accurately, so that the door does not sag or hang at an angle. It is not hard to put them in correctly when you know how.

Fitting doors and windows

These instructions apply to doors and windows alike, except where stated.

Doors (and wood-framed windows) invariably expand slightly when the humidity rises. If they are painted, or sealed in some other way, it slows down the rate at which the humidity affects them, but they still change size.

Outside doors are obviously more affected than inside ones, but even so, inside doors in a house that is centrally heated during the winter or air-conditioned during the summer, may change their size quite noticeably from season to season, perhaps by as much as 1.6mm ($\frac{1}{16}$in).

height on wedges, and shape the last side, which is the side with the lock.

Finally, run a coin around the top three edges of the door to check that there are no tight spots.

Non-standard sizes

Most door frames in houses less than about a century old are in standard sizes, and you

The best solution is to dismantle a door and re-cut the joints to alter the size—if you can be bothered to do it. It is a laborious job, however, for door manufacturers use good glue and strong joints deliberately to stop their doors from coming apart.

Altering the size of window frames in this way is nearly impossible for the amateur. They will almost certainly have to be made to measure by a professional joiner.

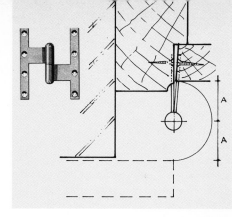

5

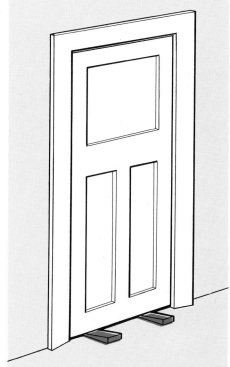

1

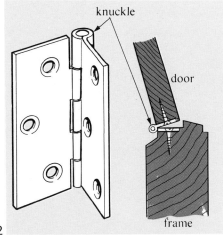

2

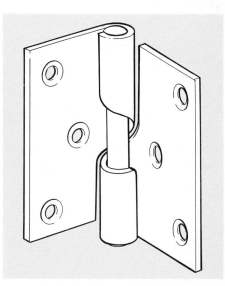

6

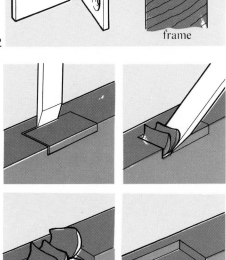

3

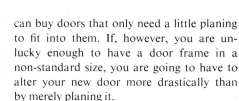

4

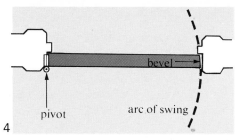

7

can buy doors that only need a little planing to fit into them. If, however, you are unlucky enough to have a door frame in a non-standard size, you are going to have to alter your new door more drastically than by merely planing it.

Nearly all doors, including flush (flat-surfaced) modern doors, have some kind of supporting framework of stiles and rails to strengthen them and keep them from sagging or warping. This is held together by mortise-and-tenon or dowelled joints. If you remove more than, say, 13mm ($\frac{1}{2}$in) from any side of the door, there is a danger of cutting into one of these joints, and this could seriously weaken it.

One way round this problem is to order a specially-made door, but this might turn out to be expensive. Ask a builders' merchant and see if you think the job is worth the money. If not, you could just buy a large piece of 19mm (¾in) blockboard, apply an edging strip all round and use that as a door. It might, however, warp a bit because of not having a proper frame.

Fig. 3. Cutting in a butt hinge. First the outline is cut round, then the wood is chiselled out to leave a flat bottom.

Fig. 4. The edge of a door must be bevelled, because the position of the hinge pivot, or knuckle, makes it swing outwards.

Fig. 5. A stormproof hinge, which fits into the L-shaped space between some types of casement windows and their frames.

Fig. 6. A rising butt hinge, which raises a door a short way as it is opened.

Fig. 7. The top of a door on rising butts must be bevelled to allow it to clear the frame as it rises during opening.

Fig. 1. A door propped up on wedges to bring it up to the right height while it is being fitted into its frame.

Fig. 2. A typical butt hinge. The screw holes are offset to keep the screws from splitting the wood of the door and frame.

287

Above. These two doors must be hung at exactly the same height to avoid giving the installation an untidy appearance.

Fitting the hinges

Nearly all doors and casement windows are hung on butt hinges (see Fig.2). These come in a good range of sizes from 25mm (1in) long, used for cupboard doors, to 150mm (6in) long, used for heavy front doors. Most ordinary-sized doors use 100mm (4in) hinges. For really large doors —the front doors of some Victorian houses are a case in point—you can use three hinges instead of two, with the third hinge halfway between the other two. This also helps to prevent warping.

To fit a pair of hinges, first position the door in its frame in the exact position it will occupy, propping it on wedges to hold it

steady. Then make a mark on both door and frame (and at the same level on each) 150mm (6in) from the top of the door and 230mm (9in) from the bottom. For small casement windows, halve these measurements.

Then take down the door and draw round one flap of the butt hinge with a marking knife to mark its position on both door and frame. Top and bottom hinges should be positioned *inside* the lines you have already marked. The hinges should be set so that the 'knuckle' (pivot) is just clear of door and frame.

When you are satisfied that the position of the hinges is correctly shown, set a marking gauge to the thickness of the hinge flap and mark the front surface of door and frame to show how deep the cutout for the hinge is to be. Be very careful not to mark it too deep.

Some marking gauges will not adjust far

enough to make such a shallow mark. One solution to this is to put in a new metal spike at the other end of the arm of the gauge in such a position that the sliding part of the gauge can move right up to it. You could make a good spike from a small panel pin sharpened with a file.

Now chisel along all the marked lines to ensure that the wood will be removed cleanly (see Fig.3). Then turn the chisel bevel-edge down and make some diagonal cuts to the correct depth to make it easier to remove the wood (see Fig.3 again). Finish the cutout neatly by slicing out the raised wood chips from the spindle with the chisel held right way up. Using a broad chisel improves accuracy.

Place a hinge leaf in each of the cutouts to ensure that it fits with its upper surface flush with the edge of the door or frame. If the cutout is too shallow, and the hinge stands proud, remove more wood. If it is too deep, you will have to pack it out with a piece of veneer or ply—but this is *not* recommended and it is much better to cut too shallow and work down.

When all the hinges leaves are set in properly, drill *one* hole through each side of each hinge into the door and frame. Drill through the centre hole of each hinge leaf, using a bradawl on small hinges, a drill of the correct size for the mounting screws on large hinges. Don't drill the other two holes in each side yet.

Prop the door up on its wedges and mount it temporarily on its hinges with one screw per hinge leaf. Then open and shut it —gently, so as not to tear the screws out— to make sure that it is not catching on anything. You will almost certainly find it does catch on the lock side, because the projecting hinge knuckle makes it swing slightly wide. The remedy is to bevel the edge of the door slightly with a plane (see Fig.4). Nearly all doors and wood-framed windows are bevelled in this way.

Open the door as far as it will go to make sure that it does not catch on the floor. If it does, you will have to plane a bit more off the bottom edge.

The door should fit flat into its frame and stay there without having to be held. If it sticks and has to be forced, or swings open of its own accord, the screw holes are wrongly sited. Take the door off and plug the misplaced holes with glued-in dowels. Let the glue dry and try again.

When you are satisfied with the fit, take the door down, drill the remaining holes and refit it with all its screws. Make absolutely sure that all the countersunk screw heads are in the whole way, or the hinge will not fold flat. If they stick out, file the heads flat—this is cheating, but it works.

The installation is now completed except for any locks or bolts. These come in a multitude of shapes, sizes and types, but any good-quality lock comes with instructions.

Other types of hinges

Special problems in fitting doors and windows may call for special types of hinge. For example, a door or window that has to fold flat against a wall needs a 'parliament' hinge. This has an offset pivot that moves the door well away from the face as it opens, allowing it to be opened much further than normal. It makes the door swing very wide in the first few inches of opening, so that the lock side needs a heavily angled bevel cut on it.

Casement windows often have a rebated edge and frame to keep the rain out. These must have a special L-shaped hinge called a 'stormproof' hinge (see Fig.5). Unlike butt hinges, these come in left- and right-handed versions, depending on which way the window opens (though of course, they are generally bought two pairs at a time for paired windows). They are installed in the same way as butt hinges, but the window frame can be a looser fit than usual, since the rebated front seals it.

In houses with irregular floors or thick carpets, there is often a problem with the door catching on the floor as it opens. If enough wood is taken off the door to clear it, the wind whistles through the huge gap underneath. The solution is to use 'rising butt' hinges, which raise the door as it opens (see Fig.6). To stop the top of the door from catching on the frame as it rises, a special tapered bevel has to be cut along one-third of the length of the top edge of the door at the hinge end (see Fig.7).

The only way to get the shape of the bevel right is by trial and error, removing a very little wood at a time. The length, angle and depth of the bevel vary with particular installations. The hinge is installed like a normal butt hinge, so if you hang the door temporarily on single screws and keep taking it off, planing a bit more wood off and replacing it, you should soon get the shape of the top edge right.

Certain types of hinge are installed in plain view on the front (or back) of the door. These include the long sheet-metal hinges found on cottage and outhouse doors, and special self-closing spring hinges, which have such huge pivots that it would be impossible to hide them. Both types are very easy indeed to install, because the screws are exposed and you don't have to keep taking the door off to get them positioned correctly.

Fitting a mortise lock

The security of your home is almost completely dependent on the locks with which it is fitted. Despite the increased number of break-ins, many householders still depend on inadequate and antiquated locks to safeguard the home. Mortise locks—types of which are approved by insurance companies—provide good domestic security and are easy to fit and maintain. This chapter describes the various types available and how to fit and maintain them.

Judging by official police statements, it is surprising how many householders still depend on inadequate locks to safeguard their homes. They tend to think that the sight of a lock—any lock—will deter the would-be burglar, even though their homes may be filled with valuables. Of course, this isn't true; some types of lock, such as rim locks, can be opened in a matter of seconds by the professional burglar equipped only with a few bits of plastic and wire. This is not to say rim locks and other types have no uses; fitted in conjunction with a proper security lock, they give added home protection.

What types of lock then, give the sort of protection which insurance companies insist on? The variety is so large as to be bewildering, but the most secure locks all incorporate certain features which will baffle anyone but a Houdini.

Firstly, a secure lock, apart from having a sturdy construction, has a mechanism complicated enough to defy attempts to 'pick it'. Generally it incorporates several levers or tumblers arranged in such a way that only a particular and unique pattern of key will open it. Secondly, the lock is recessed into the door in such a way that only the keyhole is visible on both surfaces of the door. This prevents anyone from unscrewing the lock or forcing it with a lever. Several types of locks incorporate these features, but the one most commonly used is the mortise lock.

What is a mortise lock?

Though their locking mechanisms vary,

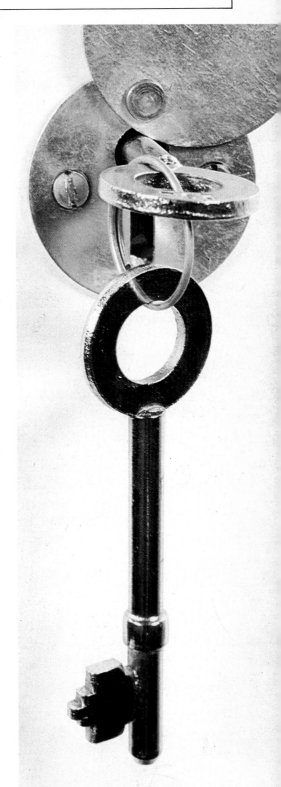

Right. Before they will accept a household insurance policy, most insurance companies insist on all your external doors being fitted with an approved mortise lock.

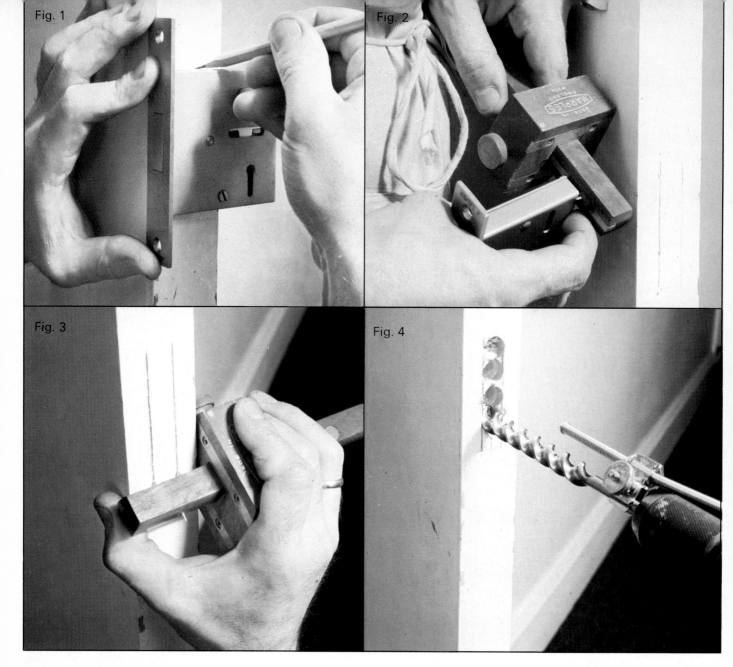

Fig.1. *The mortise lock is best located at the midpoint of the door. Mark out the position and depth of the lock.*

Fig.2. *With a mortise gauge, calculate the width of the lock, then adjust the stock so that the two spurs are centred for marking.*

Fig.3. *Scribe out the width of the lock, with the stock face parallel to the door edge.*

Fig.4. *After marking in the bore centres with the aid of a combination square, bore out the mortise with a brace and auger bit fitted with a depth stop.*

they are all intended to be recessed into the door. Not only does this give greater security, it allows a neater finish to the door. Some mortise locks are fitted with handles and latches, others, usually called deadlocks, are

without these features and consist only of a bolt and its locking mechanism. Mortise locks for sliding doors are available and these are fitted with hooked bolts which lock in position over a catch on the striker palte.

Doors and locks

No matter how thief-proof your locks are, they give only an illusion of security if they are fitted to flimsy doors. Sometimes, locks which would deter a master criminal are fitted to doors which can be broken down by one hefty push. Mortise locks have the advantage that even if a housebreaker removes a door panel he cannot open a mortise bolt from inside, except with the proper key. However, before fitting the lock, the householder should examine the door not only to see if it is sturdy, but also to see whether it will take a mortise lock.

Mortise locks are recessed into a solid base and for this reason cannot be fitted to some

types of hollow door. All solid doors are suitable for modification and most hollow doors are fitted with a solid wood panel in the lock area, which is capable of taking a recessed lock. If your home is equipped with hollow doors, you must check on the presence of this plate by tapping the door round the proposed location of the lock. If it sounds hollow then it is unsuitable, unless you add a solid wood core to the lock area. If it sounds solid it is probably suitable, but to make sure, bore one or two holes from the edge of the door to a depth of 100mm (4in).

Choosing a mortise lock

Always buy a type of lock which is approved by insurance companies. They are more likely to accept an insurance risk on a house fitted with these locks and, in the event of a break-in, view a claim more favourably. Don't assume that burglars only break into houses that are filled with valuables; virtually every house possesses something of value—such as a television or record player.

Although your choice of mortise lock will be determined by how much security you want, a general guide is—fit deadlocks on external doors and latched mortise locks on internal doors. Even a mortise lock can be picked or sprung by an expert, but the chances of this happening are remote if you choose a lock with a complex mechanism. This is largely determined by how many levers and/or tumblers the lock is fitted with, and this number is usually stamped on the faceplate.

Fig.5. Clear waste wood from the mortise with a chisel. Hold the chisel parallel to the long sides and make small cuts till you have cleared down to the marked lines.

Fig.6. When the long sides have been made plane, take a chisel of the same width as the lock and clear the short sides. Work carefully and keep testing the lock for fit. It should just fit with no play. When you are satisfied that the mortise has been cut out to the correct size, insert the lock in preparation for marking out the face plate rebate.

Fitting a mortise lock

This is a simple operation well within the capabilities of any handyman. As in all aspects of carpentry though, special care should be taken in marking out, and only the correct tools for the job used. First work out where the lock is to go. In most cases it should be fitted midway up the door, which allows space further up for the addition of a rimlock or safety chain. If another lock is already fitted at this point, it can easily be unscrewed and located higher up.

Mark out the position of the lock and its area, by holding it against the door at the correct location, as shown in Fig.1. Remember to allow for the thickness of the face plate and mark in the correct position of the keyhole. Now, using a mortise gauge, calculate the width and height of the mortise and mark out these measurements on the edge of the door. Particular care should be taken to centre the mortise in the door so that it is the same distance from both surfaces.

Most of the mortise can be cut out by boring with a brace fitted with a bit exactly the same width as the lock. To assist in boring accurately, a centre line is drawn down the area to be cut away and the centres of the holes marked in. This is best done by carefully marking out with the aid of a 45°

combination square or adjustable bevel gauge as follows. Lay the bevel edge against the side of the door, and adjust its position so that one edge of the rule meets one corner of the area to be cut away. Draw a line from this point to meet the opposite side, then reverse the square and, using the same technique, draw in another line from the point where the first line crossed the edge of the mortise housing. Repeat this procedure along the whole length of the area to be cut away, then mark in the points where the diagonal lines cross the centre line to give the bore centres.

Fit the bit with a depth stop so that the depth of each bored hole can be gauged correctly. If you do not possess this fixture, an alternative is to tie a piece of tape to the bit at the correct point. Bore out each hole to the required depth, ensuring that the bit is held at right angles to the door edge. A simple way of checking that the bit is held horizontally is to place a large washer over the bit. If the washer moves towards you as you drill, the bit is held too low; if the washer moves towards the door, the bit is held too high. The bit is horizontal when the washer does not move.

When you have bored the mortise out, clear the hole with a chisel. Keep to the

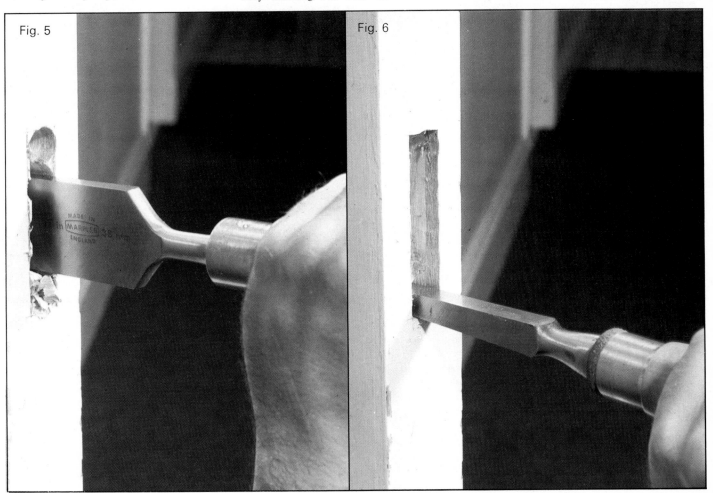

Fig. 5 Fig. 6

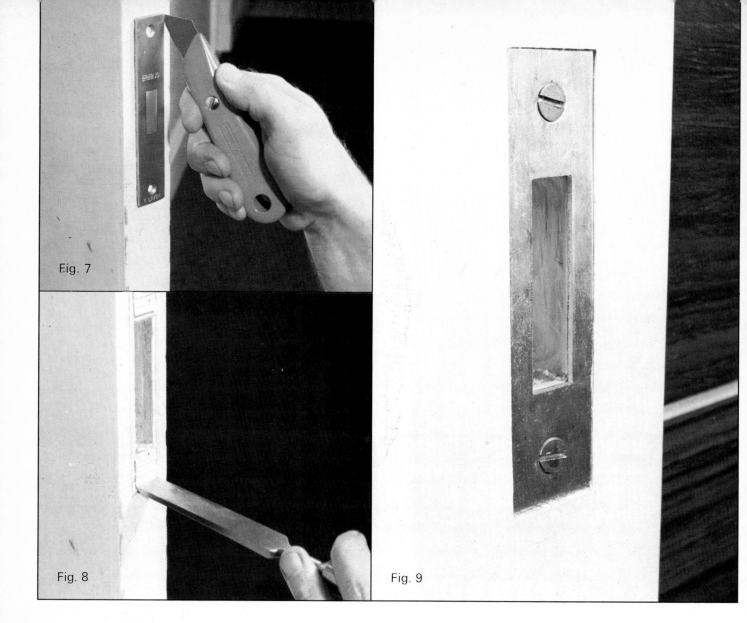

Fig. 7

Fig. 8

Fig. 9

marked lines and don't try to remove too much waste wood at once. Instead, chisel out a little at a time and keep testing for size by fitting the lock into the mortise. The lock should just fit with no play.

After checking that the previously marked locations of the keyholes are correct, remove the lock and bore them out with a bit slightly larger than the diameter of the keyhole on the escutcheon. Do not bore right through the door from one side; reverse the direction of boring before the bit emerges through the wood. Clean up the keyholes and, if necessary, cut them to shape with a coping saw.

Now insert the mortise lock in position and test the action of the key in the lock. If it turns smoothly, fit the escutcheons in position over the keyholes. Secure the lock in the mortise by fixing screws through the holes on the face plate.

Cutting the face plate rebate

Insert the lock into the mortise so that the face plate is flush against the edge of the door. Mark out the extent of the rebate by

Fig.7. With the face plate flush against the edge of the door, mark out the extent of the rebate by marking round the face plate with a handman's knife to the required depth.

Fig.8. Remove the lock and, using a chisel with a blade of the same width as the face plate, make a series of cuts down the length of the rebate, then, holding the chisel at a shallow angle, remove each section.

Fig.9. Insert the lock again and, when you have bored out the keyhole on both sides of the door, screw it into position. Now make the mortise for the bolt.

marking round the face plate with a handyman's knife to the required depth.

Take a chisel with a blade exactly the same width as the rebate and make a series of cuts down the length of the rebate, as shown in Fig.8. This allows the rebate to be cut out in small sections. Hold the chisel at a flat angle against the door and remove each section with very light blows from a mallet.

When the rebate has been cut to the required depth, clean up the edges and insert the lock but do not secure it with screws.

Fitting the striker plates

The striker plate is recessed in the door frame in exactly the same way as the lock. To mark the correct position, first turn the key to extend or 'shoot' the bolt, pull the door to and mark out round the bolt (and the latch if the lock is fitted with this feature).

Following the same procedures that were used to mark and cut the mortise for the lock, cut out the recesses for the bolt and the striker plate and screw this piece into place. The fitting is now complete and the lock ready for use.

Maintenance

Like any other fixture with moving parts, the lock should be lubricated at least twice a year. A light oil or powdered graphite inserted into the mechanism through the keyhole should ensure the smooth operation of the lock.

292

Security

In the metropolitan area of London alone there were 46,087 household break-ins in one year. Of these, a little less than half were 'walk-ins' representing an increase of 10.2% on the previous year. The remainder were forced entries which, surprisingly, showed a slight drop from the previous year.

According to New Scotland Yard this does not mean that burglars are getting less bold, only that householders are increasingly careless and making the burglar's job literally as simple as walking through a door.

This is a worldwide phenomenon that the man in the street shakes his head over and thinks he can do little to avert. In the case of domestic buglaries this is simply not true. No matter where you live there are several precautions you can take to safeguard your property. These are often inexpensive and largely a matter of sheer common sense and forethought. Just remember that it *can* happen to you, and if you neglect to take every possible precaution then it is unfair to complain about the inefficiency of your local police. Burglary prevention is mainly in your hands.

Burglary is big business

A professional thief can burgle a flat in sixty seconds. He knows where you are likely to hide money, keys, chequebooks and so on. An 'amateur' will take longer and will probably make more mess. Organized gangs of burglars can strip a fair-sized house of all its furniture, including large items such as television sets and hi-fi equipment in a matter of an hour or less, and make away with the goods in a truck which is ready and waiting. Your property then passes on to crooked dealers and—only too often—completely out of your life.

It is no use imagining that you can catch a burglar by creeping bravely around in the dark clutching a poker. The personal risks are too great, and, besides, most domestic burglaries take place in broad daylight—mainly in the afternoons, in fact. Too often an open window, or a kitchen door left ajar while you 'pop out' for a few minutes is an open invitation to crime. But a few minutes are all that's needed to cause a great deal of personal distress. However rich you are you can never afford to lose what the thief will take. And no matter how poor you think you are, there will always be something he will consider worth taking.

Safe as houses

Before going to bed, the average householder goes through the ritual of locking his doors. This is usually the only precaution taken and, up to a limit, it is all well and good. But there are other things to consider. 28% of thieves enter property from the front of the house, 7% from the side, 62% from the rear of the premises and 3% from the roof. Can the thief approach your house from the rooftops of adjoining property? Are your skylights and dormer windows fitted with adequate locks? Are *all* your windows fitted with locks (not just flimsy catches)? Do you ever leave a window open—no matter how small—for your cat's convenience? Remember, it may be convenient for a 'cat'-burglar, too. Very little is 'impossible' for a thief to get through if the opening is there.

In ninety-nine cases out of a hundred only a small section of glass is broken, the thief inserts his hand and releases the catch, thus simply opening the window for entry. Dramatic window smashing is rare. *Key-operated* window locks are the answer, because the thief would have to smash the glass, causing some danger to himself and making a tell-tale noise. Remember the greatest risks for a burglar are noise and delay. These locks are effective deterrents—always supposing, of course, that you don't leave the key in the lock!

Fighting forced entry

Modern doors tend to be very flimsy, and it is no use whatsoever fitting an expensive, good quality lock to a feather-light door. The chances are that you will find yourself coming home to a smashed door and your lock lying intact on the floor! Hollow core doors which are packed with material no more sturdy than bits of egg-box will always give way under brute force, if the burglar is really determined.

Panel doors should be between 4 5mm and 51mm (1¾in and 2in) thick. Even if you fit a good lock (such as a British Standard lock) to a door thinner than this then you may have *weakened* it and the lock could be torn off whole more easily.

There are basically two types of lock—a mortise lock which, in the U.K., should at least comply with British Standard require-ments, and a rim fitting lock which is fitted to the surface or rim of the door.

A mortise deadlock is the most likely to be burglar-proof. Manufactured to the strictest specifications under British Standard rules, this type of lock *has* to be good. It must withstand attacks from skillfully wielded jemmies, be resistant to side pressures of 3,000 pounds and end pressures of 2,000 pounds and be able to thwart at least five minute's attack from a steel saw. Each lock carrying the 'kite' mark will have undergone rigorous tests—and passed them. All you need to do is fit them correctly and even here you are helped because all these mortise deadlocks come with detailed instructions on how to fit them. Every outside door should be fitted with one.

Remember though, that the strength of the lock depends on the strength of the door. While there is no need to armour plate your door, you could strengthen it by fitting strips of sheet steel or iron round its edges especially where the lock is going to go.

It makes sense to lock internal doors in houses which have been split up into flats, but police often advise householders of the average 'semi' *not* to lock internal doors, only the main outer ones. The reasoning behind this is simply—if a thief goes to the trouble of breaking into your house in the first place he is not going to be frustrated by flimsier internal doors. He will simply smash them in, causing further unnecessary havoc. Unfortunately some insurance firms disagree with this viewpoint, so find out what your own insurance company feels about this.

All external doors should also be provided

Fig. 1: An exploded view of a mortise lock.
1 The latch which is operated by the handles.
2 Holes for the latch spindle and the key.
3 Lever handles fit onto the square spindle to operate the spring loaded latch.
4 The face-plate of the lock is let flush into the door stile.

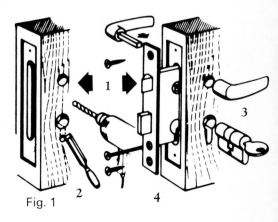

Fig. 1

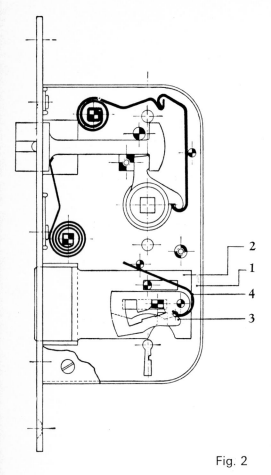

Fig. 2

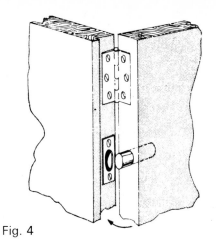

Fig. 4

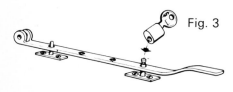

Fig. 3

Fig. 2: A section through a mortise lock, every make is different.
1 The outer casing.
2 The bolt which is operated by the key.
3 Levers which hold the bolt in the locked or un-locked position. The more levers there are the better the lock.
4 Springs holding the levers down against a peg on the bolt until they are lifted by the right shape key.

Fig. 3: A casement lock which fits on to the peg of the stay.

Fig. 4: Metal pegs can be fitted into the rebate of a door frame so that they will protrude into holes in the edge of the door when it is closed and prevent its being prised off its hinges.

with *bolts*, preferably both at the top and bottom—the old-fashioned padlocks are no longer considered effective against such skilful odds. A door-chain not only keeps a thief from the door but a potential attacker, too. Casual 'callers'—especially on old people or people living alone—can turn out to be vicious thugs capable of inflicting grevious bodily harm, sometimes in order to make off with just loose change or a radio. Most dwellings in New York—a city notorious for its soaring crime rate and violence—have peepholes or 'doorviewers' fitted in their front doors. They are an excellent idea anywhere—you can lift a flap and see the caller, satisfying yourself that he is a bona fide repair man or whatever before attempting to let him in. And do not be afraid to ask anyone—even someone claiming to be a policeman—to prove his identity before allowing him in your home. You may have everything to lose through undue timidity on your part. These precautions may sound alarmist and frightening, but face facts, crime *is* both alarming and frightening.

Man's best friend?

It is surprising how many householders still rely on dogs to guard their homes. But the chances are that if your dog wags his tail at a visitor you let in through your front door, will also wag his tail at the unwelcome visitor who climbs through the window. Pets are *not* guard dogs and even 'trained' house dogs cannot be expected to act like police dogs. And, like people, they are liable to be silenced—sometimes only too effectively. Dogs are also unpredictable, so it would be foolish to rely on them alone.

Alarming burglars

A burglar alarm on full show, say, on the outside of a building, will nearly always deter the 'amateur or casual thief. But if yours is the only alarm in the area it may well advertise the fact that you have something

worth stealing. It could act as the go ahead or challenge to the professional buglar. Whether or not to put your alarm on display or hide it away will depend on how many other similar devices are in evidence in your neighbourhood, and as always, on your common sense.

There are many types of burglar alarm system on the market, varying widely in price and efficiency. It is a business which, unfortunately, is easy game for the confidence tricksters. Some people are so keen on security that they are incredibly gullible. So check that the firm where you buy your alarm is reputable. In Britain your local Crime Prevention Officer will know of the best firms.

Burglar alarms can work in three stages: they detect through various devices such as pressure mats: they control or 'decide' whether to give a signal or not and then they finally give a signal. They range from the simple bell type most people are familiar with, to highly sophisticated ultra-sonic devices which can be expensive and may not be really practical for general domestic use. Most types miss out the middle or 'decision' stage because of the mechanical complexity involved.

The main types of alarm are bell systems, which rely on neighbours or public spirited passers-by to report the alarm, the telephone system which will ring the emergency 999 automatically, one which will ring through to the security department of the firm which installed or sold it (this is most common in the U.S.A.) and, in Britain, alarms which ring through directly to the local police station (this does not apply to the Metropolitan area).

An alarm system may be purchased outright but with a maintenance agreement (this is essential or your alarm may go 'on holiday' without telling you), or you can buy part and rent part, or you can rent all of the equipment and, in Britain, claim a tax rebate on it.

Technology v thieves

One of the newest burglar detecting devices is based on a principle whereby a passive infra-red mechanism is triggered off by body temperature. This could be placed in a door or window frame. The problem is—when is an intruder not an intruder and merely the master of the house? The most up-to-date devices include a shunt key and lock which will by-pass the system when bona fide occupants insert their own shunt key.

Another alarm which is both effective and unobtrusive is called the 'inertia switch'. It is basically very simple, being a ball-bearing balanced on three special spikes and wired up to the signal. You can set this in a window frame and paint over it. Any massive vibration or unduly heavy knock on the window will dislodge the ball from the spikes and set off the alarm. It is nicely controlled so that heavy winds will not affect it, and they come with shunt-out locks, too.

One of the oldest methods of protecting property—the man-trap—is now illegal. Bluffing, however, is not, and a sign reading 'Danger High Voltage', which could act as a deterrent, is perfectly permissible—as long as it isn't *true*!

An ounce of prevention . . .

It is a good idea to make a comprehensive list of the serial numbers (and any distinguishing marks) of your valued possessions, such as television sets, cameras, bicycles and so on.

People are continually taking the most absurd risks and then wonder why their property disappears. Everyone knows that they *should* stop their newspapers and milk being delivered when they go away—doorsteps cluttered with congealing milk and newspapers are as good as a 'Vacant' notice. Everyone can see how stupid it is to leave notes on the front door telling expected friends what time they will be back. Everyone knows what risks they are taking popping out for a few minutes leaving the door ajar, and how insane it is to leave even small amounts of cash on a table by a window.

seal them. A sanding machine is reasonably cheap to hire, but before beginning make sure that gaps between the boards are plugged—or dust and draughts will whistle up—and check that there are no protruding nails. These must be hammered down or pulled out. After sanding, the boards must be sealed with one of the proprietary brands of floor sealer. A clear polyurethane alters the colour least.

Another way of treating a wood floor, if the original boards are too poor to use, is to cover them over with hardboard panels. Hardboard, like other wood flooring, has the advantage of standing up to considerable wear and tear—vital in a living room or hall. Although it is usually used only as a sub-floor for tiles, linoleum, and so on, it is perfectly successful on its own, *provided* that it is laid absolutely flat and level, stuck down firmly with adhesive and nails, and given coats of sealer when completely clean and dry. A hardboard floor in panel form will

---

Furnishing on a next-to-nothing budget

If there is one thing more difficult than furnishing on very little money, it is furnishing on practically no money at all. Jokey things like orange boxes (if you can still find them) are all very well in their way, but most home-makers, from newly-weds to flat dwellers, want the place to *look* like home—not like a camp site.

Unfortunately, there are certain things that only money can buy. Where plumbing, central heating, and structural alterations are concerned, the best things in life are far from free. There is *no* cheap way of installing a bidet, a boiler, or a back addition to the main living room. But apart from these major items, there is usually a way round.

Flooring

The cheapest thing of all, if your floorboards are in good condition, is to sand and

Below left: Turning the tables on plastic! This ultra-modern table is simply four up-turned washing-up bowls topped with a glass sheet. Matching buckets provide 'occasional tables'.

Below right: A library to bowl anyone over . . . The 'bookshelves' are ingeniously stacked and brightly-coloured bowls, fitted into deliberately conspicuous piping.

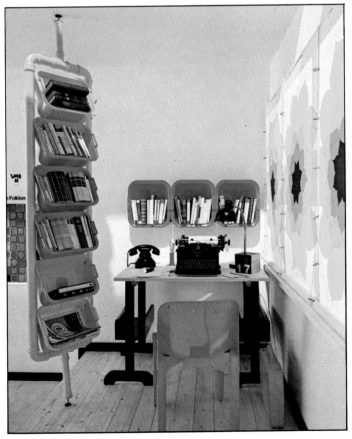

cost a matter of only a few pounds.

For stairs, wood (unless custom-made as a complete staircase) is on the whole undesirable. It is noisy, and more slippery than carpet. One of the cheapest ways to cover stairs is to use second-hand carpet; and the least expensive way of getting this is to go to a shop or store that specialises in selling off carpets that have been used in exhibitions. Some of the carpet will be useless, through wear and dirt, but when this is cut away the rest is generally in good condition. However cheaply you have bought the carpet, it is false economy not to use an underlay—as otherwise dirt that comes up through the floorboards will mark it with indelible lines.

In a bedroom, polished boards teamed with rugs are always successful. But, because bedroom flooring does not have to be so tough, something softer can be used if the boards are in poor condition. Felt can add a dash of brilliant colour, and is, of course, far cheaper than carpet (though generally its life is shorter). The cheapest felt of all is the industrial-waste sort; this is tough and strong and comes in varying shades of brown.

Other floor covering could be rush matting (best in the country, where you can take it out and shake or brush it clean—remember also to sprinkle it with water occasionally); cheap, plain-coloured lino with diamonds, lozenges, circles or whatever, with a darker colour 'dropped in', to give a Roman-marble-

floor look (try chocolate and beige, orange and cream, black and tobacco); or good old floor paint. This comes in several colours—and white especially gives a light look to a room—but it does chip or scratch a bit. (It is best bought from a marine shop, where it is known as 'yacht' paint.)

Walls

There is, really, not much to choose between the prices of the different makes of paint—apart from the fact that beautiful, original decorator colours often cost more than the ordinary standard ones, and that chain-store paints can be the best buy of all.

Even having a gallon of emulsion (which covers a lot of wall) mixed to the exact colour of your choice usually costs very little extra.

Wallpaper is something else entirely; costs vary enormously from roll to roll. One of the cheapest ways of covering walls is to use ordinary brown wrapping paper; this can be bought in huge rolls from paper mnaufacturers.

Heating

Central heating is expensive, but insulating—the first real step towards cheaper warmth—can be comparatively cheap. Most of the heat escapes through the roof, so (if it has not already been tackled) this is the place to start. Short of foam injection of cavity walls (usually possible in newish

Above: Even old cardboard boxes can be pressed into service to provide valuable storage space.

Below left: At first glance merely a bright and 'trendy' room—but look again at those colander hi-fi 'speakers'; plastic-tub storage and the other fruits of plastic budgeting.

Below right: A battery of sunshine-coloured colanders cleverly used as light fittings. The laminated fibreboard chest of drawers achieves distinction through its colours.

Louses, and very expensive at that) cork, plasterboard, and wall fabrics give more warmth than paint or paper. An alternative to double-glazing (which, costwise, is the highest in terms of value-for-money) is either to put old shutters back into working order or to have thick curtains lined and interlined, or two rows of curtaining. Whichever you choose, remember that a sound principle of insulation, whether from heat, cold, or or noise, is to trap a layer of air between two layers of material. 'Material' may mean anything from tweed to glass depending on the limits of your budget and your personal preferences.

Lighting

The cheapest way of lighting a room is to have several lengths of flex from a central

Right: *Curtaining off a corner can give you both a wardrobe and a bright focal point. The white wall makes even ordinary objects stand out and seem interesting.*

Below left: *Surely the strangest linen cupboard around! Simply fix those versatile buckets onto the back of a door and pop in your towels or whatever. It saves space, too.*

Below right: *Empty oil-drums sprayed to look like expensive chrome, bright boxes supporting painted slats for seating, and paper decoration make up this budget room.*

ceiling point looped to wherever you want them, with the lights dangling as low as you like from them. (Note, though, that this does mean *looped;* as soon as you fix flex along a ceiling or wall you are creating 'permanent' wiring out of the flex, which is illegal.) The shades could be cheap paper lanterns, or wire frames which you can cover with raffia. Make sure they are hanging over a piece of furniture, like a coffee table, or someone will bang into them. Both shades and flex usually look best in white. Cheap bulbs, and shades in attractive designs are always available at chain stores.

Furniture

Buying second-hand furniture is one of the most obvious, and still one of the most successful, ways of saving money. Chairs, in particular, can be found at phenomenally cheap prices. In large second-hand stores, dining chairs can be picked up for small sums. They may not be particularly pretty, but stripped and lacquered a bright colour, with the seats recovered (try navy blue and emerald, black and tobacco brown) they look extremely presentable. Most pre-War furniture has the merit of sound, solid construction. For an extra-comfortable sack chair, make a 'sack' of canvas or shiny pvc, and buy polystyrene granules by the cubic foot.

Of new furniture, the cheapest in Britain is white wood, although kit furniture is sometimes more durable and it pays to compare the two before you buy. Again, this can be painted, stained, or lacquered. Foam rubber blocks, covered in tough, cheap and washable canvas, can make anything from push-together seating or sofas, to divan mattresses to stack on the floor.

Some office furniture is cheap as well as durable. So are chipboard tables on trestles that can be bought from builders' merchants. Cover one of these with a tablecloth, and you have a good-sized dining table.

Coffee tables or storage systems can be made from chipboard, and supported on anything from aerated concrete blocks (cheap and paintable), or brick to cheap brackets.

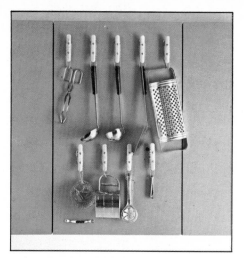

An ancient filing cabinet—again from a secondhand furniture store—painted in bright gloss coach paint (as used for car bodies) makes an excellent storage place for toys. Or an old, second-hand trunk can be painted, and stuck with transfers or cut-outs.

Keep an eye open, too, for shopfitters rebuilding premises in your neighbourhood. Often, old counters and shelves which will provide useable timber are available for little cost.

In a bedroom, a thick felt curtain across one wall, hung from a track in the ceiling or from a rod and rings, comes much cheaper than any wardrobe. Clothes can hang from moveable dress rails, which you can buy through mail order; other clutter can go in anything from cheap Moroccan rush baskets to shoe boxes or plastic cutlery trays. Jewellery looks fine hung from hooks on a felt or hessian pinboard on the wall.

Materials

The rule here is 'never skimp'—or it will *look* cheap. Be as lavish as possible with quantities, but use cheap materials.

Curtain lining materials, when lined and interlined so that it hangs in thick, 'extravagant' folds, has the dull sheen of expensive-looking satin. Hessian is extremely cheap, does not need lining, and comes in attractive, earthy-looking colours. Calico bought by the bundle can be used in its original creamy state, or dyed. Deckchair canvas has the

Top: Rows of door handles and chain loops hold up shiny kitchen utensils for easy accessibility – and admiration.

Below left. An old mattress given an 'instant' facelift. Here it is turned over the show how gay striped material, cut to size and taped on, can transform it into attractive seating.

Below right. Transformation scene! Mattresses have become chic modern seating, while the party trays were once supermarket packaging or perhaps moulding for household goods.

firmness and solidity to make good blinds (which use far less material than curtains), and blind-making kits are cheap. For curtains, or for a padded bedhead of the kind you hang from rings, ordinary wooden dowelling, painted or fabric-covered, is the cheapest sort of rod. Many stores have drawers full of odd rings and finials.

Soft furnishings

Chain stores sell cheap duvets, which in the long run save money otherwise spent on sheets and blankets—and immediately will save time, trouble, and possibly temper. They sell duvet covers, too—but it could be cheaper to make your own. It is only, really, a large pillowcase, with press-studs or tie-tapes at one end. With any duvet you will need a bottom sheet. About the cheapest way of getting a ready-made one is to scour the 'small ads' in your local newspaper. Chances are you will find someplace where odd single sheets, usually white, are sold off cheaply. Other bedding, like sheets, blankets, eiderdowns, duvets and towels come most cheaply at discount stores, many of which also sell by mail order. Look for the shops that sell 'seconds', or ends-of-lines; and once again, think of chain stores for cheap cushion pads, for foam rubber bundles that can be used as cushion fillings, and for velvety towels which can look very expensive.

Co-ordinated colour

Colour can play an enormous part in 'pulling together' or enhancing the cheapest decorative scheme. Some colours always look 'expensive', some look cheap in the wrong material or texture.

If in doubt, remember that black or white fits in almost everywhere. So do most of the creamy-beige colours, from the natural ivory shade of unbleached calico to the straw of rush baskets. Cheap lamps or china, which usually come in white, and a pale, neutral-coloured room make a good background.

If you do want an injection of brilliant colour, remember its impact is several times greater when used in group form. Why be

Right: *Belongings hanging from rails need not be scruffy eyesores. Here meat hooks are used as hangers, and the clothes match the bathroom colour scheme in brightness.*

content with just a scarlet cushion? Try a scarlet cotton cushion, a huge scarlet plastic ash tray on the nearby coffee table, and a bunch of scarlet, pink and orange paper flowers stuck in a mug beside.

'Bits and pieces'

Mirrors always look good, but tend to be expensive. Mirrorboard, on the other hand, is considerably cheaper. You can stick this self-adhesive board-backed mirror on to hardboard or walls, or cut it up into table mats, for a stunning effect, at a cost substantially less that that of real mirror.

For the living room, there are all sorts of decorations that can be made for next to nothing.

Patchwork cushions are mostly your own work—dressmaking remnants can be begged from friends, or even from dress manufacturers who would otherwise throw away these tiny scraps. Anyone with artistic talent can use the same bits and pieces, plus scraps of foil, felt, or sequins, to make collages.

All sorts of things look good as *objets trouves*. For example, a collection of stones, amassed from hillsides and beaches over the years, can look superb. (A handyman could mount these on acrylic sheet, for an even more arty look.) One exotic-looking wall sculpture, in glossy white, turned out to be simply the foam packing in which the vacuum cleaner had arrived, sprayed with white gloss paint! (Keep expanded polystyrene well away from heat, though, it is highly inflammable.) Grasses and flowers can be dried—even dunked in a bathful of dye. Beech leaves that have sucked up a mixture of glycerine and water will stay copper-bronze coloured for years. All these, once done, save on the expense of having fresh flowers.

Finally, perhaps the best money-saving tip of all is: learn how to cover . . . upholster . . . make lampshades . . . repair furniture. You will never know how skilful you can be, until you try.

The use of colour in the home

A good sense of colour is essential if your interior decor is to be a success. Apart from the technical skills involved in painting and paper hanging, you need to be able to combine colours and patterns for maximum appeal. With a little care you can choose a colour scheme that will add greatly to the beauty and comfort of your home.

Before starting to decorate your home, you should spend some time considering various colour schemes. When choosing colours that go well together there are no real hard and fast rules to bear in mind, and there is no such thing as a "good' or 'bad' colour. People's reactions to colour vary tremendously, and your feelings about a particular combination of colours might be quite different from someone else's.

The kind of colour scheme you choose will depend very much on the use to which a particular room is to be put. For instance, a good colour scheme for a study might be mainly brown—dark leather chairs with mahogany furniture and woodwork. The walls could be a cream or light chocolate colour, and the carpet a plum colour. Silver ware could be placed around on shelves, or in a glass fronted cupboard. With this sort of colour scheme the effect will be of solid and subdued comfort. This kind of colour scheme is ideal for a room like a study. In rooms where you relax for lengthy periods of time the emphasis should be on cheerful yet unobtrusive colours.

Try not to be too influenced by the latest fashion in colours. Many people have followed the latest trends slavishly—often with disastrous results. Your own tastes, combined with careful judgement, are far more important. When discussing colour schemes, the main concern is how to combine different colours successfully. It is here that you will benefit on how to get the most out of your personal preferences.

Colour properties

A very great deal has been written about the theory of colour. Before choosing a colour scheme for a particular room you should know about the basic properties of colour. These are hue, tonal value and chromatic intensity.

Hue is the quality which distinguishes one colour from another—red and blue for example. Black, neutral greys, and white have no hue.

There are three basic groups of colour—primary, secondary and tertiary. The colours in the primary group are red, yellow and blue. By mixing any two of these together you can get orange, green and purple. These are the secondary colours. Tertiary colours are mixtures of primary and secondary colours—adjacent to each other on the colour wheel. They are yellow green, blue green, blue violet, red violet, red orange and yellow orange. Altogether, twelve colours go to make the colour wheel, This will be of considerable help to you when working out possible colour combinations.

Tonal value refers to the lightness, or darkness, of a colour. For example, yellow is lighter than all but the palest of violets.

Light tones are more reflective than darker colours. This is why dark rooms are made brighter by the use of light coloured paints. On the other hand, rooms with large windows, with plenty of access to sunshine, will remain light and cheerful even with a very dark colour scheme.

A colour scheme made up of subtle tone changes will make a room seem larger and play down the appearance of awkward shaped furniture. Such a scheme will give a quiet overall effect. You should pick out something in an opposite shade to the general colour scheme. This will provide a point of interest and prevent the room becoming boring.

Strong tonal contrasts catch the eye. Your furniture will stand out where such a colour scheme is used. A contrast between the walls and curtains will make a room look much smaller. The reason for this is that the different surfaces will be 'cut up', or sepa-

Above and right: Two bedrooms are shown here—each with their own individual appeal. In one room a combination of blues is used to provide a dominant but restful colour scheme. Careful use of browns—highlighted with pink —gives the other room a character all of its own. A skilful choice of colour scheme can turn an ordinary room into something special.

Right. A living room will benefit from all
white decor. Areas of colour enliven the room.

rated. You'll find that the effect can be
pleasantly lively and stimulating.

An understanding of tone is one way of
making sure that you use colour attractively.
Two colours which do not seem to combine
satisfactorily may well do so when one of
them is lightened or darkened.

Chromatic intensity refers to the chromatic
brilliance of a colour. Adding grey to any
colour will lower its intensity. Of the primary
colours, red has the highest intensity,
followed by yellow, then blue.

The intensity of the colours you choose
will affect your colour scheme in a number of
ways. A room decorated in very intense
colours will be highly stimulating—reminis-
cent of the colours at a funfair. However,
you'll find such strong colours quite unsuitable for a living room and other leisure
areas of your house, where you spend a lot of
time. Only use intense colours in small doses.
Flowers, cushions and ornaments present
excellent opportunities for highly colourful
temporary displays. Remember that a room
decorated totally in low intensity colours can
be very dull. The stimulus of stronger colours
in small areas of the room is essential. Try
to create a balance between the two extremes.

For living areas, it's a good idea to concentrate on gradual colour changes for the
walls. For instance, you could start off with a
brilliant red and, by adding more and more
green, merge gradually into a rich brown. In

the same way, you can merge yellow into
cream, or blue into steel grey. By adding
white or black you can change a colour
totally. For example, red can be turned into
a restful pink by adding white.

The intensity of the colour you choose
should be related to the size and shape of the
surface to be covered. Warm colours like red,
orange and yellow are very dominant—
particularly in a small room. This can be

extremely tiring on the eye. Such colours are
best used for highlighting the colour of
objects like lampshades and ornaments.

Blues and greens are cool, retiring colours.
They are good when used as background
shades. Objects painted in these colours tend
to lose definition. This can be useful in
painting ugly—but essential—furniture.

You would be well advised to avoid the use
of contrasting full intensity colours—such as

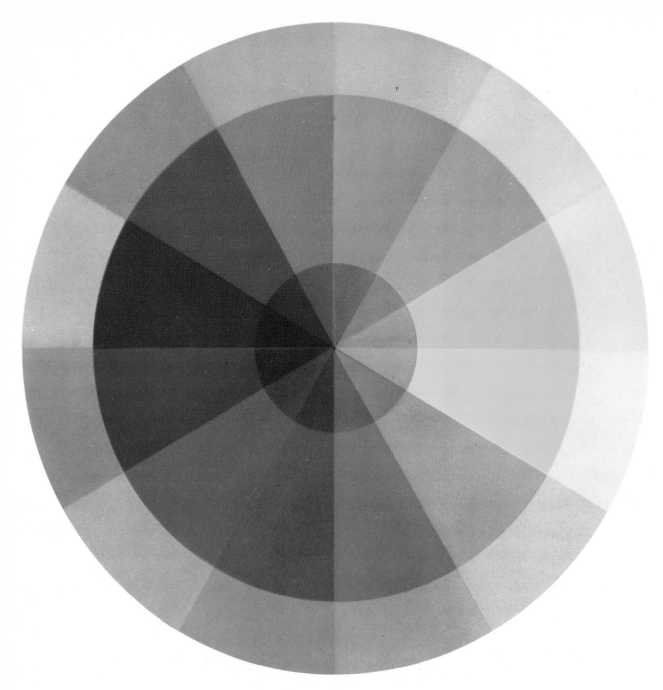

Above. A colour wheel, like the one shown here, is indispensable in the planning of colour schemes. Harmonizing or contrasting colours are easy to plan and choose.

red and green or orange and violet. They can provide initial excitement, but the long term effect will be tiring and dazzling.

Choosing the colour scheme

Before choosing your colour scheme there are several considerations to be taken in account. If you are fortunate enough to be decorating a large, well lit room, with a southerly aspect, you will be free to experiment with almost any colour scheme you may have in mind. On the other hand, if the room is on the small side the use of warm colours will make it look smaller still. The effect can be quite cosy—but also claustrophobic.

Aim at increasing the sense of space as much as possible. This involves using dull, cool colours on most of the larger surfaces like walls, ceilings and floors. The sense of space can be further increased if you incorporate the colours used in the small room into a larger, neighbouring room. This will prevent the small room from seeming to be cut off from the rest of your home. The pattern of the curtains in the small room might well be used for the wallpaper in the next room.

If you paint one wall in a darker colour than the others, it will have the effect of opening up the room. Don't choose a colour that contrasts too strongly with the others. The effect may be to diminish the room size.

A room may be dark either because the window is small or because it faces north. The use of dark colours over large areas of such a room will tend to accentuate the darkness. If the room is used mostly in the evening, find out if the colours you choose will look very different in the shop compared to your home. Shop lighting is deliberately chosen for display purposes, and is usually much brighter than domestic illumination. It is best to concentrate on light colours, as these will brighten the room considerably.

If your room is quite high, paint the ceiling in a dark shade. This will have the effect of lowering the ceiling. Don't use this method if your room is of an average height, as the result will be to 'lower' the room to an uncomfortable extent.

The right scheme for your home

When choosing a colour scheme it is often hard to know where to begin. Colours work best when they are related to their surroundings. For instance, the view from the window may suggest the dominant colour for a particular room. A picture, or the pattern in a set of curtains, may lead to a starting off point. Select a subordinate colour in the picture, or pattern, as the dominant colour in your scheme for the room.

Remember, there is no such thing as the 'right way' of choosing colours. If you intend to keep the existing carpets or curtains it is quite pointless selecting colours which clash with them. Always start with what you have, and build from there.

As far as possible, consider the walls and curtains first. These cover the major area in any room. Next, choose the colour or pattern of the carpet, and the colour of the ceiling. Having selected the colour scheme for the major areas of the room, you should consider the shade and patterns for any upholstery. Now you can think about the smaller objects in the room—like ornaments and small cushions. If your basic colour scheme is in light and restful shades, splashes of stronger colours will add interest to the room. Remember, any colours you consider must be seen in relation to the room you are decorating before a definite choice is made. Mistakes are difficult to avoid completely—but they can be kept to a minimum.

The final result of a successful colour scheme should be one of harmony, there should be some sort of theme. Try to establish a definite connection between living areas. This can be done by using the same dominant colour, or pattern, on walls or in curtaining. A living room, where you wish to relax and spend a lot of time, will benefit from subdued rather than pretty patterns. Also, there should be no strong contrasts in colour, or tone. Pretty patterns and strong contrasting colours are best used in rooms which are only used for brief periods—like bathrooms.

A sense of balance and proportion is all important. Colours and patterns should help to highlight the focal point in a room—be it a fireplace or a large table. Try to create a balance between patterned and plain surfaces. If you do this the eye will be neither over-stimulated or bored. Every room needs some light areas, no matter how dark the overall effect of the colour scheme is. Some surfaces, or objects, should be accentuated—even in the most subdued of rooms. A room decorated in warm colours needs a cold colour somewhere for visual relief.

Visual emphasis

Every room needs some sort of emphasis in the colour scheme to give point to the whole design. For instance, the table in a dining area could be emphasized with flowers. They will be shown off to better effect if the pattern of the wallpaper is not too strong. The visual emphasis in a room should relate to its function. In a dining area the main function is eating—which centres around the table. If too strong a colour or pattern is used here, the table will be subdued—where it needs to be highlighted.

Once you have learnt the basic rules of planning colour schemes you will be able to experiment more ambitiously. A well planned colour scheme will make your home much more attractive to the visitor—as well as a more comfortable place to live.

Below: A living room with a modern look—the key is the geometric pattern on the couches and abstract shapes in the painting.

An adventure in colour

Colour—the key to success in this modern home—is used boldly and imaginatively. The often seen whites and the neutral colours of natural surfaces have been eliminated. The cold and clinical impression, frequently associated with the 'modern' look, has been done away with because of the exciting and original colour treatment in this English country home.

Maroon is the dominant colour of the house and whether used all over, as in the dining room, or lightened to a colour wash of shocking pink, as in the main bedroom, it gives a feeling of warmth and friendliness.

The house is mainly on one level and built in a T-shape, surrounded by an attractive courtyard and garden. All the bedrooms, apart from the main suite and the spare room,

are on the ground floor. The feeling of space has been preserved through the use of glass and the closeness of the garden.

Lighting is totally up-to-date, with downlighters, spotlights and kinetic lights for effect. Dimmers have been used to give added adaptability to the lighting schemes. There are no standard lamps in the house and only one table light, on the study desk.

The totally modern feeling starts at the front door which is made of stainless steel. All the hall doors are faced in stainless steel with matching architraves, and white sand cement rendered walls and ceiling. The colour comes from a collection of bold avant-garde prints in stainless steel frames.

Entering into the sitting room, there is a feeling of openness and spaciousness. The huge windows link the interior to the garden outside. A generously cushioned seating pit in the centre of the room is closely carpeted with a white shaggy rug. The jumbo cushions are covered in linen with a geometric pattern of maroon, black and white.

At the far end of the seating pit is a rectangle of stainless steel, set into the floor. This is the lid to the hi-fi system, cleverly concealed underneath it. The system is piped throughout the house. The idea of building the hi-fi literally into the floor is a good one, because the records are easy to change from the nearby seats and the equipment does not clutter the room with extra furniture.

The outside perimeter of the room is covered with brindle-coloured quarry tiles. At the end of the room, in two arched recesses, are large fitted mahogany bookshelves with cupboards below. The arch on the left side is a concealed door. The whole unit can be swung open easily and it leads into the exciting garden room. The reason for a concealed door—besides being a good topic for conversation!—is that it makes the garden room into a private, quiet place. It also means the room can be effectively shut off in cold weather. The huge door is built on the same principle as a bank safe door. Being heavy, it is supported on three stainless steel strap hinges. The leading edge of the door is on a roller which runs on a stainless steel track.

The garden room is a kaleidoscope of colour with cheerful zig-zag stripes painted along two walls. The louvred doors conceal

Top: The original and bold colour treatment in the garden room leaves a decisive and unforgettable impression. A mini-kitchen and fitted cupboards are neatly concealed behind the louvred doors.

Left: *The kitchen-cum-dayroom. The vinyl floor and stainless steel surfaces make it a good room for children's play.*

Right: A dining room with a grotto-like effect. The perspex chairs and glass-topped table add to the sense of spaciousness. The bold pattern of the carpet constrasts smartly with the solid maroon walls.

fitted cupboards on one side and a Beekay mini-kitchen on the other. The kitchen is equipped with a small sink, fridge and boiling ring, making an ideal place for serving drinks, brewing coffee or heating snacks. One remaining wall has glass windows, and the other is covered with mirrors. At night, kinetic lights reflect off the white ceiling.

In contrast to the striking appearance of the garden room, is the open plan kitchen-cum-dayroom. The large stainless steel bar, echoed by the roomy bottle rack above, divides the cooking area from the eating and sitting area. A number of useful items have been built into the stainless steel counter top —two bowls for washing up, a circular pastry slab of marble, and an electric cooking hob. The raised oven and fridge have been fitted into a storage wall filled with cupboards and drawers, finished with a red laminated surface.

This kitchen unit is a superb example of the benefits of a well-planned layout. Although it is contained in a small space, the kitchen is efficient, easy to work in, and visually appealing. It is wise not to let a kitchen 'evolve' in a haphazard fashion—a great deal of thought should be given to the arrangement of storage units and appliances, ventilation, and plumbing.

The step down to the main part of the room is effectively set off by the touch of red laminated skirting. The centre of the room is used for family meals and as a play area for the children. The Provençal pattern floor is made of vinyl which is a time-saver when it comes to house keeping. In rooms where eating or children's play is going on, a vinyl floor is a boon to any housewife.

The dining room is yet another splash of colour with walls painted in maroon gloss. Instead of curtains, there are floor-to-ceiling shutters, also painted in maroon gloss, giving the room an almost grotto-like effect. Although the room is not a particularly large one, the choice of furniture gives a sense of spaciousness. The glass-topped table is on a stainless steel base. The transparent perspex chairs are visually unusual and also very practical because of their washable surfaces. The red-fronted cupboards are useful for serving and have the added attraction of inset stainless steel hot plates for keeping food warm.

If a house needs cheering up or you want to get a new look without spending a great deal of money, think carefully about changing the colour scheme.

Decorating with blinds

A blind is one of the most versatile of furnishing accessories. It can range from a cheap cotton roller that saves spending a fortune on curtains, to a sophisticated and more expensive Venetian blind that will last for years and cut out a dreary view.

Don't imagine that blinds can be used only for windows. There are many different ways of using them around the home for other purposes, like hiding a washing corner or making a room divider.

It is simple to make your own roller blinds and Roman shades, and there is also a huge selection to be found in the shops. These can be made to measure for your windows at very reasonable prices.

Choose anything from a plain holland that comes in a wide colour range, to all kinds of laminated fabrics in patterns and plains. The alternatives are rattan blinds (which are cheap) in a pleasant wood colour, or Venetian blinds (more expensive) in a good colour range from white to bright reds, yellows and greens. Look for concertina blinds in thick paper if you are working on a tight furnishing budget.

If you like adapting ideas, keep an eye on current trends in the pages of magazines, then use these ideas for blinds as a basis for making your own. The detail is the important point to watch—it's the final touches like braid and borders, or colour mixes, that will help you to make your own blinds with style.

Here are some ideas for using blinds around the house.

In the living room

One of the most basic uses for blinds in a living room, or any room for that matter, is to protect fine furniture from the sun during the daytime. Over a long period the sun fades dark and antique furniture, and many fabrics too.

Just plain white hollands, or roller blinds in a pale shade that tones with the colour scheme, can be fitted at the windows as well as curtains. When it's sunny, the blinds are pulled down to keep out the harsh rays, yet let in the light. In the evening the curtains are drawn as well. If you want to doll the blinds up a bit, use a band of the curtain material as a border along the foot of the blind.

If the windows are large, use fabric blinds instead of curtains. They will work out cheaper and give a much cleaner outline to the window. A full-length blind in a bright modern colour can look stunning. Used at a small window instead of curtains, a blind will let in more light during the daytime, because it will not encroach on the window space when it is rolled up.

305

Above: Blinds can be used to advantage out of doors as well as inside. Here two Roman blinds fitted to a simple framework act as a wind break on a balcony.

In a modern home you may find one or two large Venetian blinds make the ideal covering for a picture window overlooking a garden, particularly if the room catches the sun. The Venetian blinds can be kept rolled down in hot weather during the daytime, when they will let in light and air, yet keep out the heat.

Use a large blind to disguise an untidy study corner or shelves holding drinks in an alcove. Rattan blinds are a wise choice for this form of disguise. You could use a whole wall of blinds to screen off a fitted shelving unit. This is a smart idea if you prefer the neater finish of blinds to the more casual look of shelves crammed with an assortment of objects.

In a multi-purpose room

Blinds are a boon in a multi-purpose room or a bedsitter. They can be used so easily to screen eyesores, and as room dividers. In a bedsitter, use a blind to hide the washing arrangements.

You can do this by building light hardboard floor-to-ceiling 'walls' on either side

of the basin. Fit a gay blind at the front and you have an instant mini-washroom. If you are short of storage space, fit shelves above the basin and use the sides of the basin screen for hanging up towels, dressing gown, toothbrushes etc. Either build in the basin with a cupboard underneath it, or fit more shelves under to hold towels or shoes.

Also in a bedsitter, blinds can be used to hide the bed, which can be fitted away neatly in one corner of the room. Fix two rattan or bright cotton roller blinds to the ceiling, and during the daytime they can be pulled down to hide the bed.

Often, in a bedsitter, you may find you have to use 'make-do' furniture until you can afford what you really want. So the whole room can be made visually smarter if you hide a row of varied cupboards, and storage furniture, behind large cotton roller blinds.

Use a rattan or Venetian blind above a bar to emphasize the division between eating and sitting in a multi-purpose room. Also, use blinds instead of screens to help zone the different purposes of the room—for instance behind a sofa to enclose a seating corner or

Right: A blind made in the same fabric as the other furnishings in a room creates a total look, as in this hall, where the Roman blind matches the cover of the sofa.

divide it from a walk-through area, or to screen the stairs in a large room with an open staircase, or to hide a children's play corner.

In the kitchen

Blinds come into their own in the kitchen, because they are much more practical to use at windows than curtains. Laminated blinds are excellent, because they are so easy to keep clean. Venetian blinds are good for stuffy kitchens or those where you want to obscure the view, but they are more of a chore to keep clean than plain roller blinds.

Use blinds to pull down in front of a row of shelves, or to hide wall cupboards above a working surface. This is a particularly handy disguise in an open house or a combined kitchen/dining room. If the blinds are made to pull down just to the level of the flat surface, they will hide any unsightly mess left there from other parts of the room.

You could also use a long floor-to-ceiling blind to screen off a laundry area in the same way as for the washing arrangements in a bedsitter described above. You can keep washday gear on fitted shelves above the washing machine.

Below: Venetian blinds make practical screens, as they are washable. In this bedsitting room the alcove wash basin is concealed by the blind when it is not in use.

If the back door is glazed, use a blind. A light roller blind can be attached to the top of the door itself, so it won't get in the way if the door is opened when the blind is pulled down.

In the bathroom

Again, a blind is often the best answer for a window covering in a bathroom, particularly if you choose a laminated fabric, because it won't go limp in the steamy atmosphere.

If you want to divide up the room, try a tall, narrow Venetian blind to make a screen between the bath and lavatory. You could even use pvc roller blinds instead of shower curtains beside the bath. When the shower is in use, the blind is pulled down inside the bath to keep the splashes in.

In the bedroom

One of the most attractive ideas for a bedroom is to use a blind instead of a net curtain for privacy. A thick cotton lace makes a stylish fabric choice.

A good way of making more of a bedroom window is to have a roller blind or Roman shade in a fabric that matches the bedspread, then frame the window with semi-sheer curtains, caught back in loops, during the daytime. These could be made from the bedspread fabric again. Another idea is to have curtains in a plain fabric bordered and

There are many ways of brightening up plain blinds. Borders are particularly smart, and these can be either stuck or sewn on to a blind. Make a pop-art effect by appliqueing a bold geometric pattern or the shape of an apple to a plain blind—fun for a child's room.

The foot of a roller blind doesn't always have to be plain. It can be castellated, then bound, which is a good finish for a blind in a square pattern. Use fringes or bobbles, but remember that these will need washing if they are in a pale colour, so it is best to attach them with Velcro, so that they can be removed easily.

At difficult windows

Blinds can be great helpers if you want a covering for an oddly-shaped window. A good treatment for a small window in a curved dormer is to make a ruched blind which runs on curtain tracks fixed down each

Above: A canvas awning fitted outside a picture window or over a corner suntrap acts as an efficient sun blind, whose height can be regulated as necessary, according to the angle of the sun, to provide enough shade.

looped back with the patterned fabric.

Try making your own four-poster bed, and instead of curtains use blinds made of inexpensive ruched cotton. The blinds can be pulled down and kept firm in side tracks so the bed becomes almost like a cave.

Blinds can also hide a dressing corner, an unattractive old wardrobe, or a shoe rack.

In children's rooms

If light evenings or an early dawn keep the children awake, use a dark holland blind behind the curtains, and this will cut out the light. In fact a blind in any dark-coloured opaque fabric will do the trick.

Remember that blinds will flap on a windy night if the children are asleep with their door open. One way of stopping this is to make a pelmet and side frames so that the blind is held inside this and cannot flap about.

A box frame covering the sides and top of a window is simple to make and, for added interest, use a curved shape to give more effect. Paint the frame brightly or cover it with the same fabric as the blind. This is a

particularly smart idea which could be adapted for any room in the house.

For safety, cut off all long pulls on blinds and replace them with small rings, particularly in a room where the children are under six and like fiddling.

Using fabric

Be clever with the way you use fabric on blinds to make a more effective room scheme. Make wide scallops at the foot of a roller blind where you have used a bold curvy fabric—this will help to emphasize the movement of the pattern.

If you are using a row of fabric blinds as screens or at large windows, be sure that the fabric matches at the edges of each adjoining blind. This is particularly important with a geometric or regular pattern of any kind. A good match looks much more professional.

Instead of cupboard doors, you can use roller blinds made from a fabric that, for instance, matches the wallpaper. This is a smart idea for a bedroom, or a kitchen if the shelves are untidy.

Right: A blind is often the only solution to awkwardly shaped windows. Here a ruched blind fitted at the edges follows the shape of a dormer window neatly. When rolled up, a blind lets in the maximum amount of light.

side of the window. During the day the blind is pulled up above the window and covers the curved ceiling in the dormer attractively. At night it is pulled downwards to cover the window.

Blinds are by far the best way of dealing with sloping windows in attic rooms. Fix either roller blinds or folding Roman shades above the window, then construct tracks in the form of a right-angled 'box' on each side of the window so that when the blind is pulled down it will cling to the slope of the window.

Try vertical slatted blinds at a window with a top that slopes down at an odd angle. Use a blind rather than a curtain for a window in a narrow passage or small cloakroom, because it will take up less space and let in more light.

Other ideas

If you have a large garden-facing window that catches the sun, make it into more of a

Right: A roller blind made up in a semi sheer fabric will give French windows a softer appearance. When pulled down it gives privacy without keeping out too much light. When rolled up it does not impede the doors.

feature with a brightly coloured awning outside to bring in the effect of a shady patio. This will also prevent the living room from getting too hot in summer.

Besides conventional roller blinds, there are all sorts of other bright ideas for window decoration. Try covering a window with chains of basket-work hung vertically, or brightly coloured beads or flat pearlized plastic discs.

Even ribbons can look fun hanging at a breezy window. Make a heading of curtain tape or braid, then cut enough lengths of ribbon to hang vertically from the heading and cover the whole window. Each length of ribbon should overlap the next slightly. Use rainbow colours in a baby's window, and the ribbon blind will make fascinating mobiles for the baby to watch from his cot.

The modern look

When Formica purchased a turn-of-the-century terraced house in Richmond in 1972, it was in a dingy and dilapidated state—both inside and out. Formica undertook the job of a complete conversion and, after much careful and imaginative planning, there was a dramatic transformation, producing three separate, colourful and attractive flats.

The house consisted of three floors and a basement. Architect James Bath and his wife Valerie Bath, an interior designer, were called in to do the converting, decorating and furnishing. The architect's brief was to create three self-contained units, fully fitted and furnished, using Formica products wherever it was practical and sensible to do so.

The basement and ground floor became a roomy maisonette; the first floor a compact flat, designed for an older couple; and the top floor, a modern and streamlined flat which is featured here. Originally the top consisted of two rooms—one front, one back—and a central dividing corridor, with an access door at either end.

The architect decided on an open-plan scheme; from a space of only 140 square feet, he had to accommodate lounge and kitchen/dining areas, a bedroom and bathroom. By

removing hampering doors and partitioning walls wherever possible, he created fluidity of space which gives the top floor flat a feeling of being larger than it actually is. An illusion of space, emerging from clever visual treatment in a conversion, can be as important as the actual amount of space available.

The first step was to take away the wall by the staircase—the internal wall of the original back room—making the central corridor into an 'island' surrounded by oceans of space. Advantage was taken of the fact that the two corridor walls couldn't be removed because of the support they provided for the loft ceiling. Most of the old lath and plaster was removed from the studding so the new laminate cladding could have a secure foundation.

Both ends of the 'island' were then closed in with durable laminate-clad panels, postformed at the edges to avoid sharp corners and to create a streamlined effect—a feature of the interior design which is repeated throughout. A bathroom was then put into the 'island', maximising on the old corridor space. Special ventilation was then provided to meet the British Building Regulations.

The new, long and narrow bathroom has a

wc at one end, wash basin in the central area, and a shower unit at the other end. An outstanding feature of this room is the mock windows which help to eliminate a closed-in or confined feeling. The sky and floral scene which forms the mock window over the wc was incorporated in a panel of laminate by special 'artwork' processing during manufacture. The design is indestructible and makes for easy cleaning and care.

The areas on either side of the 'island' bathroom were then devised. On one side is the spacious lounge and the staircase and on the other, the cooking, eating and sleeping areas. In the latter section a useful prefabricated unit was designed to serve a dual purpose: firstly, it functions as a room divider between the sleeping area and the kitchen/dining area and, secondly, it incorporates a complete array of kitchen fitments on one side and a bedroom storage/hanging cupboard on the other.

This prefabricated unit is an ideal example of how one item can be used to best advantage through intelligent forethought. Some partitioning was needed between sleeping and

Above: The eye-catching living area, colour co-ordinated in fresh green and white. Clean, simple lines and bold, abstract design create a striking and streamlined look.

cooking areas as well as kitchen appliances and storage space for clothes. All these requirements were cunningly brought together in this well-organised unit. There is a fully-glazed door at either end of the wall unit which prevents heavy kitchen smells from getting into the bedroom, while also convey-

Right: *A cheerful kitchen, tailored for convenience in a modern age. The central unit provides all the necessary fitments—oven and hob unit, mini-fridge, sink and cupboards.*

Below: *Opposite side of the kitchen. The attractive dining table—with its graceful bench seat—adds an unusual touch, while the Formica woodgrain finish eliminates bothersome scuffs and stains. An adjoining cupboard/shelf unit makes for easy serving.*

ing freedom of movement, central to any open-plan scheme.

All the appliances are built in, including a handy eye-level wall oven, a modern hob and a small refrigerator. A waste disposal unit fitted into the sink overcomes problems of rubbish disposal. The practical laminate finish is designed with minimum cleaning and maximum visual appeal in mind.

Facing the kitchen unit is a dining table with a gracefully attached bench. The Formica wood-grain finish eliminates the need for a tablecloth—another labour-saving feature. In the alcove adjoining the block-up chimney breast, a useful cupboard unit, including a handy shelf, was built. No space could be wasted in designing this flat—every inch had to be utilised to the full.

On the bedroom side of the dividing wall unit are storage shelves and a built-in wardrobe which can be conveniently hidden by concertina-type doors when required. The low double bed here was made from block-board and designed, again, for a multi-purpose role. There are two large storage drawers in the base of the bed and, at the head, there is a cupboard with sliding doors.

As the structural changes were being made, Valerie Bath was concentrating on the decorative aspects. Her brief was to utilise Formica laminate surfaces wherever practical, making this flat superb for easy maintenance. Her first decision was a colour scheme which would be consistent throughout the flat, resulting in a feeling of co-ordination and integration from one part to the next. Her choice was a fresh green and white, with splashes of warm brown and cheerful yellow accessories.

In the lounge area, the theme is simple and striking. The generous white sofa, with its smooth curves and modern look, sets the pace. The blind behind adds an eye-catching note because of the boldly zigzagging, jumbo-sized stripes in green. The green is then repeated in two tones—on the side wall and in the stereo speakers, attached to the wall as both decorative and practical items.

The lines are clean and simple—no fussy details here. The low white-surfaced table is in keeping with the general tone which is

Left: *Making the most of a small bedroom area. The built-in bed is equipped with shallow cupboards and deep, roomy drawers. A shelf unit serves as a dressing table, set off by two mirrors framed in a cool green.*

Below: *Once a dingy corridor, now a compact bathroom. The mock window over the wc is livened up with a 'garden' design. Recessed shelves provide a useful storage area and a long mirror creates a feeling of space.*

carried through the dining/kitchen area into the bedroom where the brown and white duvet cover creates an unexpected accent in colour. The floor here and throughout the flat is a Finnish birch plywood with a clear polyurethane hard-wearing finish. No carpeting is required, just a scatter rug for the personal touch.

Formica has succeeded in producing a flat which is exceptional in two respects. Its interior design is unusual and unforgettable; and the materials used in construction and decoration are a great aid to the modern housewife who wants a home where housework and maintenance can be kept to a minimum.

50 handy hints

General

1. Before putting steel tools away, give them a thin smear of wax polish to keep them from rusting – this works better than vaseline.

2. You can make extra use of the shelves in your workshop by screwing the metal lids of screw-top glass jars to the underside. Then screw the jars to their lids to provide an ideal storage place for nails and screws.

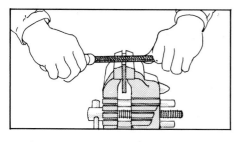

3. When filing metal, arrange the surface being filed as near the vice jaws as possible. This avoids 'chatter', or vibration, which blunts the teeth of the file.

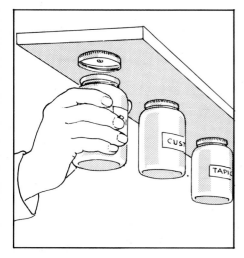

4. When marking a measurement from a ruler, make a V-shaped mark instead of a straight line for noticeability and greater accuracy.

5. Soak oilstones in a tray of light oil such as corn oil or sewing-machine oil before use, for best results. Worn or uneven oilstones can be resurfaced by grinding them on a sheet of glass covered in 80 grit silicon carbide powder mixed with water.

6. Loosen a door that sticks along the bottom edge by pinning a piece of coarse sandpaper to the floor and swinging the door back and forth over it.

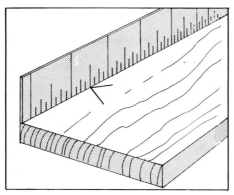

7. Cylinders can be held steady by sitting them in a V-grooved block – easy to make with a circular saw; otherwise use a tenon saw, keeping the cuts as straight as possible to stop the cylinder from rocking.

8. To insert a screw in a position you can't reach with your fingers, stick it to the tip of the screwdriver with thick grease or, in the case of heavy screws, adhesive tape.

9. When drilling horizontally into any surface with a twist or masonry bit, put a large washer halfway along the shank of the bit. If it moves towards you as you drill, lift the drill slightly; if it moves towards the surface, lower the drill. When it stays still, the drill is horizontal.

10. Always hang tools well out of children's reach, and keep them well away from the edge of benches. Even a screwdriver can cause injury if it falls from a height of only a few feet.

Carpentry

11. To avoid splitting wood when nailing it near the end, blunt the tip of the nail – but only slightly – by hitting it straight on with a hammer. (A tap is usually enough.)

12. To make it easier to drive a screw into hardwood, put a little wax polish or tallow on the point – but not vaseline or soap.

13. When setting a plane blade, rest the heel of the plane on a piece of white paper before sighting along the sole. This will make the blade easier to see.

14. When making a hole with a bradawl in any type of timber, set the chisel end of the bradawl across the grain, press it down and twist it back and forth. Do not turn it right round or let it lie along the grain.

15. Planes sometimes skid when used on hard or resinous woods. To prevent this, wipe a stick of tallow over the sole. If this doesn't work, the blade probably needs sharpening.

16. When trying to loosen a stubborn wood screw, first make sure that your screwdriver blade is exactly the right size for the slot in

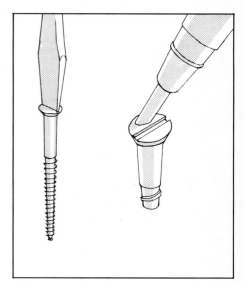

the head, or you will ruin the slot so that it no longer grips. If the wood screw appears stuck, try tightening it a little first, then turning it back. If this fails, put the blade of the screwdriver in the slot and tap the handle sharply a few times with a mallet. As a last resort, heat the screw head with a soldering iron.

17. G-cramps and sash cramps mark the surface of timber, but you can prevent this by putting a block of scrap wood on either

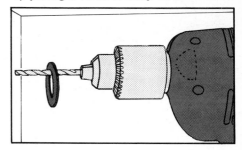

side of the work-piece under the jaws of the cramp. If you do bruise the surface of a piece of timber, with a misdirected hammer blow for example, put a piece of damp cloth over the affected part and apply a hot iron; the steam will make the wood swell back to shape.

18. Place a scrap wood block under the head of a claw hammer or a pair of pincers when using them to remove nails. This prevents you from damaging the wood. It improves the leverage as well. Draw the nail along the grain and towards the centre of the length of timber.

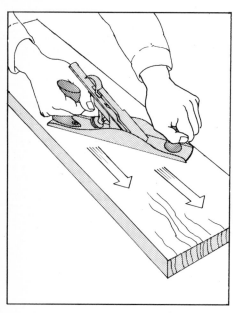

19. Curly-grained timber often chips during planing. To avoid this, set the blade very fine and plane along the evailing direction of the grain while holding the plane at 45° to the way you move it.
20. Second-hand or re-used timber is generally full of hidden nails and pieces of metal that will ruin a saw, chisel and plane blades. Go over the surface thoroughly with a disc sander fitted with coarse paper, or with a surform, to reveal most of them.

21. Large holes in timber are best filled with 'Dutch putty' – cellulose filler such as Polyfilla thinned with emulsion paint. This dries hard and much stronger than plain filler, and can easily be coloured with emulsion paint tinters.
22. When planing uneven timber, draw two or three pencil lines down the surface before you begin. These will then be planed off at the high spots first, revealing their location.
23. End grain planed without a shooting board tends to split. Avoid this by planing from the edges inwards; if you can't do this, bevel the edges all round first.
24. If you run out of G-cramps on a job, improvise with sections of car tyre inner tube used like giant rubber bands. Alternatively, use sash cord (but not nylon clothes line) with a piece of dowel passed through and turned to twist it tight.

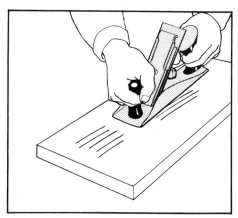

25. A simple way of fixing a batten to a wall so that nothing shows is to drive a screw into a plug in the wall leaving 12mm (½in) protruding. Drill a 12mm deep hole the width of the screw head in the back of the batten below the centre, and cut a slot the width of the screw shank upwards from this hole to the centre line. The batten can then be fitted and tapped down.
26. Wood bits designed for handbraces can be converted to excellent power tool bits by cutting off the square top of the shank,

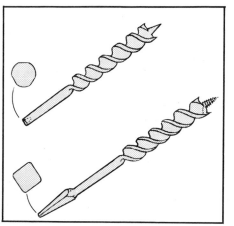

filing three small flats around it to accept the three jaws of the chuck, and filing the screw thread off the tip (this step is important).
27. Butt joints in timber can be strengthened by driving slightly over-length nails right through and clenching (bending over) the protruding points. This must be done along the grain, so that the point sinks right in, and with the head of the nail supported, so that it is not driven back out of the wood. This creates a much stronger joint than a straight-through nail.

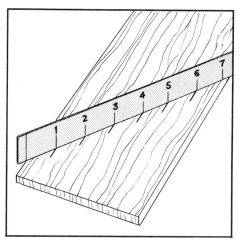

28. Always nail or screw through thin timber into thicker timber to give the fixings maximum holding power.
29. To divide a board into an equal number of widths (say seven), set a rule across the board at an angle so that the 0 mark touches one edge and the 7 mark the other. Then mark the positions of marks 1-6 on the board. To allow for the thickness of the saw blade, hang the 0 and 7 marks off the edge of the board by half the blade thickness on either side, and saw exactly down the middle of the marked lines.
30. To cut a very short piece off the end of a length of timber and across the grain (in this situation the piece being removed tends to break, causing the saw to slip out) clamp a piece of scrap wood alongside and saw through both.

Electricity
31. To stop terminal screws working loose, put a small spot of oil-based gloss paint on the threads. The stickier the paint the better; emulsion paint will not work.
32. Power tools are aged faster by neglect, dust and damp than by use, so when they are not being used, wrap them in absorbent material and store them in a dry cupboard.
33. When changing attachments on a power drill, always disconnect it from the power supply; however careful you are, there is always the chance of accidentally switching the drill on.

34. When working with power tools out of doors wear rubber boots to give some protection against accidental cutting of the power supply cable, failure of the tool insulation and so on.

Masonry

35. Cement mortar can be 'fattened up' – made more plastic and easier to lay – by adding a squirt of washing-up liquid to it. This must be a soap liquid, such as Fairy liquid, and not a synthetic detergent.

36. When checking that a course of brickwork or other work, is horizontal, ensure that there are no lumps of mortar sticking to the spirit level. Even a small piece would make it inaccurate enough to affect the job. To compensate for any inaccuracy in the level itself, use it once, then turn it end for end and use it again. Do not use a short level for checking a long run.

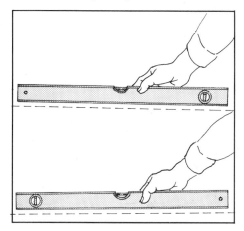

37. Never wash cement-covered tools in a plumbed-in sink: the cement will set in the pipe and block it. Wash them in a bucket and empty it where the dried cement won't show.

Decorating

38. To avoid bending the hairs of a brush when keeping it in a jar of water or spirit, drill a small hole through the handle near the bristles. This will allow you to hang it on a piece of stiff wire resting across the rim of the jar. This method of storage avoids stiffening.

39. As an excellent substitute for proprietary

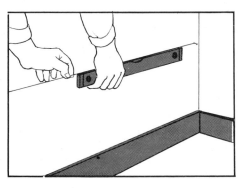

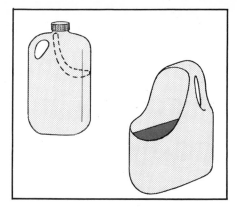

fibre wall plugs, dip cotton wool or old bandage in cellulose filler such as Polyfilla and pack it tightly into the hole. Let it dry before inserting the screw.

40. When drilling plaster, stick a small piece of transparent tape over the spot where you will drill. This will stop the drill slipping, and also keep the plaster from chipping.

41. Old polished furniture covered with dirt and a thick build-up of wax is best cleaned with an old fashioned brass polish such as Brasso. This is mildly abrasive, and will remove the wax without harming the varnish.

42. Measuring across the top of an alcove single-handed can be tricky. You can save trouble by cutting the ends of two battens to a point and laying them together so that they overlap with the points outwards. Hold this arrangement across the alcove and slide the battens apart until they touch the sides, then make a pencil mark across both battens. Take them down and rearrange them so that the pencil marks line up again, then measure across the battens from point to point. These 'pinch sticks' can also be used for measuring the inside diagonals of frames when checking them for square.

43. If you have to drill a lot of holes to the same depth, as you would for wall plugs, make a simple depth stop for your drill by cutting a piece of rubber or plastic tube to a suitable length and slipping it over the drill bit. You can also use dowel drilled down the middle.

44. Old well-stuck or waterproof wallpaper can be removed by scratching the surface thoroughly with coarse sandpaper or a wire brush (either can be mounted on a power drill to speed things up). Then brush on warm

water, preferably with a little vinegar or soda (but not both) added. When the paper begins to bubble up, scrape it off in the usual way. Water with washing-up liquid also helps.

45. Store paint tins upside down. This will stop air entering the tin and forming a crust on the paint.

46. Before cutting and hanging wallpaper, undo each roll and check for faults and colour matching. Even if the batch number stamped on the back of each roll is the same (which it should be) there may still be discrepancies. When batch numbers differ there can be marked differences.

47. When fixing shelves to a wall, don't rely on the skirting to indicate a horizontal line. For short shelves, use a spirit level. For

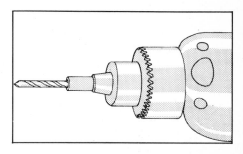

longer ones, temporarily pin (or get a helper to hold) one end of a chalked string to the wall. Stretch out the free end of the string taut and hold a spirit level underneath it, then move the string up and down until the level shows it is exactly horizontal. Hold the free end to the wall, then twang the string against the wall to mark the line. It is essential that the string is taut.

48. Paint of any type will cover corners better if the corners have been slightly rounded.

49. Large plastic washing-up liquid and floor polish containers with moulded-in handles can be cut to make useful paint containers that can be hung up when you are working on a ladder. But check that the type of paint you are using doesn't dissolve the plastic.

50. When painting around a window, allow the paint to flow slightly on to the glass; this gives a watertight seal.

Carpenter's basic tool kit

1. Tenon or back saw. These saws are available in blade lengths of between 203mm and 355mm (8in and 14in) with 13, 14, 15, 16 or 20 points per inch (ppi). This is used for jointing and cutting across the grain on small pieces. The back of the blade may be of brass or steel. The saw with 20 ppi is for cutting dovetails and it has a thin blade to give greater accuracy. The dovetail saw performs a ripping action, so cut along the grain on very hard wood.

2. Hand saw. This is used for cutting larger pieces of timber. There are three types of hand-saw. The one shown here is a panel saw. It is 508mm to 558mm (20in to 22in) long with 10 ppi. Its specialist purpose is for fine cross cut and jointing work and for cutting plywood, blockboard and hardboard. The other types of hand-saw (not

shown) are the rip saw and the cross cut saw. The rip saw is 661mm (26in) long with 5 ppi. Its specialist purpose is for cutting softwoods, working with the grain. The cross cut saw is 610mm to 661mm (24in to 26in) long with 6, 7 or 8 ppi and is specially used for cutting across the grain of hardwoods and softwoods and for working with the grain on very hard wood.

3. G cramps. These are used for a range of cramping purposes. These cramps are available in a 25mm to 457mm (1in to 18in) range of opening and between 25mm to 203mm (1in to 8in) depth of throat. When using G cramps always place a waste scrap of timber between the piece to be cramped and the shoes of the cramps. This prevents bruising of the piece.

4. Rachet brace. This has spring loaded

jaws in a screw tightened chuck. It is specially designed for holding wood auger bits (5). The brace is available with or without a reversible rachet in a sweep (the arc described by the turning handle of the brace) ranging from 148mm (5⅞in) to 355mm (14in).

5. Wood auger bits. These are used with 4.

6. Hand drill. This is used for holding wood and metal twist drill bits (7) and countersink or rose bits (8). The example shown here has a double pinion (cogged drive wheel).

7. Twist bits. These are commonly available in sizes ranging up to 13mm (½ in). The type of steel used depends on the use to which the bit is to be put.

8. Countersink or rose bit. This is used for countersinking drilled holes so that countersunk screw heads will fit flush with the surface of the piece you are working with.

9. Warrington pattern or cross pein hammer. This is used for general nailing and joinery and can be used for planishing and beating metal. Weights of these hammers range from 170g (6oz) to 450g (16oz).

10. Claw hammer. This is used for general purpose carpentry, in particular, for driving and removing nails. When taking out nails, make sure that the nail head is well into the claw of the hammer and, if it is necessary to protect the surface of the wood, place a scrap piece of timber between the claw and the wood. Exert even pressure to lever the nail out. Claw hammers are available in weights ranging from 450g (16oz) to 570g (24oz).

11. Carpenter's or joiner's mallet. This is used for general carpentry and cabinet work and is available in head lengths of between 100mm (4in) and 180mm (5½in).

12. Handyman's knife. This useful carpentry knife can be fitted with a variety of blades to suit specific purposes. The blades include angled concave, convex, linoleum and hooked blades. Wood and metal saw blades (12A and 12B) can also be fitted to this tool as can a blade for cutting plastic laminate.

13. Bench plane. There are various types of bench plane and they are available in a range of lengths and widths. The smooth plane (shown here) comes in lengths of between 241mm to 260mm (9½in and 10¼in) and widths of between 44mm to 60mm (1¾in and 2⅜in). The Jack plane (not shown) is available in lengths of between 356mm (14in) and 381mm (15in) and widths ranging from 50mm (2in) to 60mm (2⅜in). The Fore plane (not shown) is 457mm (18in) long and 60mm (2⅜in) wide. The Jointer or Try plane (not shown) is 561mm (22in) long and 60mm (2⅜in) wide. When working with resinuous or sticky woods, a plane with a longtitudinally corrugated sole makes the job of planing easier because friction between

the timber and the plane is reduced. If you do not have such a plane apply a spot of vegetable oil to the sole of your ordinary plane – this will perform much the same function.

14. Surform plane. This is one of a range of open rasp/planing tools, all of which are useful and versatile. They are primarily used for rough work but with care some reasonably fine craftmanship can be produced. Each tool in this range has replaceable blades.

15. Block plane. This small plane is particularly useful for fine cabinet work and for planing end grain. Available in lengths of between 152mm to 178mm (6in and 7in) and cutter widths of between 49mm (1 $\frac{15}{16}$ in) and 41mm (1 $\frac{5}{8}$ in).

16. Sliding bevel. This tool is used for setting out angles, or bevels. Available in blade sizes of 230mm (9in), 270mm (10½in) and 300mm (12in).

17. Bradawl. This is a chisel pointed boring tool used for marking screw positions and counterboring for small size screws.

18. Adjustable steel rule. The pocket size variety, when fully extended, range in length from 1.83m (6ft) to 3.66m (12ft). The larger varieties are available in either steel, glass-fibre or fabric in lengths of up to 30.5m (100ft).

19. Carpenter's square. This is used for setting out right angles and for testing edges when planing timber square. The tool has a sprung steel blade and the stock is protected by a thin strip of brass or other soft metal. Available in blade lengths of 115mm (4½in), 190mm (7½in), 230mm (9in) and 300mm (12in).

20. Marking gauge. This is used to mark one or more lines on a piece of timber, parallel to one edge of that timber. The type shown here is a mortise gauge which has a fixed point on one side and one fixed and one adjustable point on the other. Its

specific use is for marking out mortise and tenon joints but it can be used in the same way as an ordinary marking gauge.

21. Folding boxwood rule. This tool is also available in plastic. Primarily for joinery and carpentry use, it should be used narrow edge onto the timber for the most accurate marking. These rules are available in 600mm (2ft) and 1m (3ft) sizes.

22. Scriber marking knife. One end of this tool is ground to a chisel shaped cutting edge for marking timber. The other end is sharpened to a point and can be used for scribing metal.

23. Nail punch or set. This tool is used for tapping pin and nail heads below the surface of timber. A range of head sizes is available to suit pin and nail sizes.

24. Centre punch. This is used for spot marking metal to give a guide for drilling. The point is marked by tapping the wide end of the tool with a hammer. Automatic centre punches (not shown) are available. These are spring loaded so you do not have to tap the end of the tool.

25. Carpenter's pencil. This has an oblong shaped lead which is sharpened to a chisel edge so that it can be used to black in lines scribed on timber.

26. Pozidriv type screwdriver. This tip is designed for use with Pozidriv type screws which are increasingly replacing screws with the conventional blade head. The Pozidriv screw head allows for greater contact between the screwdriver tip and the screw head – providing of course that the correct size of screwdriver is used. This makes for greater torque (twisting power) and reduces the likelihood of tool slip and consequent damage to the work.

27. Cabinet screwdriver. This tool is available in blade lengths of between 75mm (3in) and 457mm (18in) and tip widths of between 4.8mm ($\frac{3}{16}$ in) to 13mm (½in). The screwdriver tip should fit the screw slot completely and the risk of tool slip will be further reduced if the screwdriver tip has been cross ground.

28. Carpenter's chisels. These are available in several shapes and sizes of both handles and blades. The firmer bevel edge chisels shown here are probably the most useful all round chisels to have in a basic tool kit. Chisel handles are either of ash, boxwood or plastic (shown here). Plastic handles are virtually unbreakable on quality chisels but timber handles should be treated with care and should only be hit with a wooden mallet. Blade widths vary from 3mm ($\frac{1}{8}$ in) to 50mm (2in).

29. Oilstones. These are used for sharpening the cutting edges of such tools as planes and chisels. There are two main kinds of oilstone, natural and artificial. Natural stone comes in several types. *Washita* gives a good finish

and cuts well. *Arkansas* is an expensive stone but it is of high quality and produces a very fine edge. These are the most commonly used natural oilstones. Artificial stones come in three grades – coarse, medium and fine – and have the advantage of maintaining their quality. They are available in a selection of sizes including 125mm x 50mm (5in x 2in), 150mm x 50mm (6in x 2in), 200mm x 50mm (8in x 2in), 250mm x 50mm (10in x 2in) and 200mm x 45mm (8in x 1 $\frac{3}{4}$ in).

30. Fine machine oil. This has many lubricating uses in the workshop and is a reasonable substitute for Neatsfoot oil when using an oilstone.

31. Honing gauge. This is a useful device for holding bladed tools at the correct angle for sharpening on an oilstone. The disadvantage of this tool is that it tends to cause wear in the centre of the oilstone rather than distributing the wear evenly over the whole stone.

32. Junior hacksaw. This is a general purpose saw for light metalworking jobs.

33. Shoulder pincers. These are used for pulling nails and pins from timber. If possible, always place a scrap of waste timber between the jaws of the pincers and the work piece to avoid bruising.

34. Slip joint pliers. This tool has a thin section so that the jaws can reach into tight places. It has two jaw opening positions and shear type of wire cutter.

Measuring and marking tools

Accurate and efficient measuring and marking is a must for nearly all DIY jobs – without this, articles of furniture or other things you make either won't fit together properly (if at all) or will look odd. This DATA SHEET lists the considerable variety of measuring and marking tools available, and tells you about their general and specific uses.

The procedure for marking off distances on timber and metal is straightforward, but a strict adherence to the basic requirements will make for accurate working – and save you time in the long run. When measuring and marking timber or metal you must work from a squared edge or line. To square a line across timber, you have to cut two edges of the timber – the face edge and the face side-square. Plane two edges square, checking for this periodically with a try square (24 in the DATA SHEET) and then mark them for later identification. Sight along the length of the edge being planed with a straightedge such as a steel rule (25).

If you wish to mark a line parallel to the long edge of a fairly narrow piece of timber, a marking gauge (9) will do the job. If the timber is wide – a man-made board, for example – measure the required width across the face side from the face edge at both ends of the board. Use a folding rule (28) laid on its edge for this. Mark the distance with a pencil and then join up the marks with a straightedge.

To square a line at right angles to the face edge lay the blade of a try square across the face side. Use a marking knife (one example is shown in 18) to score the timber, using the blade of the try square to guide the mark. Then fill in the scored lines with a carpenter's pencil (27), held against a steel rule (25) or try square.

If you wish to cut through the timber at this point, rather than simply measure from the squared line, continue the squared line around all four surfaces of the piece.

Marking and squaring off a required distance on metal is basically the same process though, of course, the metal edges have to be filed or ground rather than planed square. Use the engineer's square (23) and the steel rule (25) to check for this. To square lines across metal use a scriber (17 and 18) and an engineer's square. The marked lines will show up better if the metal is coated with

engineer's blue (5) before scribing.

1. Glazier's tee square and lath. These are used for direct scoring of glass with a cutter held against the tee square. These tools are also useful for marking out large man-made boards. Squares are available in 1m, 1.5m and 2m (36in, 60in, and 72in) sizes. Laths come in lengths of 1m, 1.5m, 2m and 3m (36in, 60in, 72in and 120in).

2. Chalk snap line and can of chalk. The chalk snap line is used for marking straight lines on both horizontal and vertical surfaces. The line is held at both ends and plucked in the middle – this leaves a chalk line on the surface. The snap line shown here can be filled with powdered chalk from a can (also shown). With other types, the line is rubbed with a solid piece of chalk.

3. Roofing square. This is a right angled steel square calibrated to allow all the angles necessary for roof construction to be easily marked. Instructions for using the tool are supplied by the manufacturer and once these are mastered the roofing square is invaluable in building carpentry. It can also be used for squaring up large carcasses such as wardrobe frames.

4. Plumb bob and line. This is used for testing verticals and it can also be used as a chalk snap line.

5. Engineer's blue. This is coated on metal to allow marked lines to show up more clearly. Available in either liquid form (shown here) or as a paste – the former is easier to use.

6. Builder's line and peg. This is used for checking the levels of brick courses. The pins are knocked into mortar course and a line level (21) hung on the string.

7. Boat level. This spirit level is used for checking horizontals and verticals on all small jobs.

8. Spirit level. This spirit level is used to check horizontals and vertical surfaces on larger pieces of work. Some levels have an adjustable glass for checking angles.

9. Mortise gauge. This is used to mark one or more lines on a piece of timber, parallel to one edge of that timber. Its specific use is for marking out for mortise and tenon joints but it can be used as an ordinary marking gauge (not shown).

10. Trammel heads. These are scribing points which are attached to a bar or batten between 19mm ($\frac{3}{4}$in) and 38mm ($1\frac{1}{2}$in) thick.

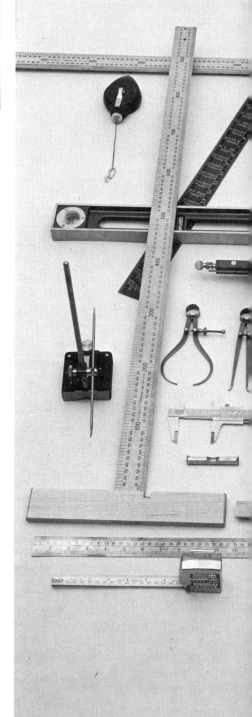

They are used for marking out large radii and curves.

11. Surface gauge. The marking part of this tool consists of a scriber with a hardened point that can be set at any position on the vertical spindle of the tool. The spindle, in turn, can be set at any angle you require. The scriber is used to mark a line on metal parallel to the base of the tool.

12. Outside calipers. These are used for measuring the external diameter of circular or irregularly shaped items. The range of sizes goes from a 50mm (2in) maximum opening to a 915mm (3ft) maximum opening.

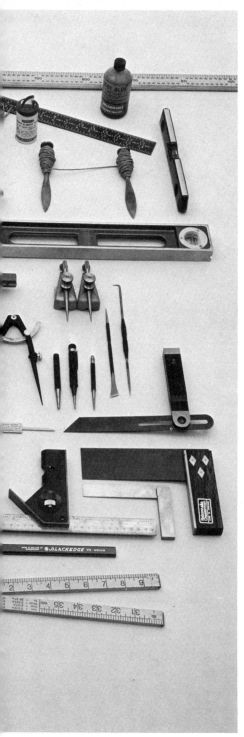

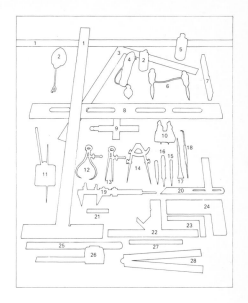

tapping the wide end of the tool with a hammer.

16. Automatic centre punch. This centre punch is spring loaded so you do not have to tap the end with a hammer. Spring pressure of the tool can be adjusted within the range of approximately 2.2kg (5lb) for light punching to about 13kg (30lb) for heavy punching.

17. Universal scriber and marking knife. One end of this tool is sharpened to a point for scribing metal and the other end is ground to a chisel shaped cutting edge for marking wood.

18. Engineer's scriber. This is used with a steel rule and square for marking metal.

19. Vernier caliper gauge. This is a very accurate calibrated gauge for measuring internal and external diameters.

20. Sliding bevel. This tool is used for setting out angles, or bevels. Available in blade sizes of 230mm or 9in, 270mm or 10½in and 300mm or 12in.

21. Line level. This is used with a builder's line (6). When using the tool the line must be as taut as possible. Not a particularly accurate tool, the line level is used mainly as a guide.

22. Combination try and mitre square. This is used for marking angles and mitres. The blade, along which the stock slides, is calibrated in either metric or imperial measurements, or both.

23. Engineer's square. This is used for marking right angles across metal. The stock is hardened steel – this is so that rough metal edges do not damage the tool.

24. Carpenter's square. This is used for setting out right angles and for testing edges when planing timber square. The blade of the tool is sprung steel and the stock is protected by a thin strip of brass or other soft metal. These squares are available with 115mm or 4½in, 150mm or 6in, 190mm or 7½in, 230mm or 9in and 300mm or 12in blades.

25. Steel rule. These range from 150mm or 6in to 900mm (3ft) lengths. They are accurately calibrated for fine work.

26. Adjustable steel tape. The pocket size variety, when fully extended, range in length from 1.83m (6ft) to 3.66m (12ft). The larger varieties are available in either steel, fabric or glassfibre in lengths up to 30.5m (100ft).

27. Carpenter's pencil. This has an oblong shaped lead which is sharpened to a chisel edge so that it can be used to black-in scribed lines.

28. Folding boxwood rule. This tool is also available in plastic. Primarily for joinery and carpentry use, it should be used narrow edge onto the timber for accurate marking. These rules are available in 600mm or 2ft and 1m or 3ft sizes.

The larger sizes are commonly used by sculptors and potters.

13. Inside calipers. These are used to measure internal diameters.

14. Dividers. This tool has hardened ground points and is used for stepping out odd measurements and scribing circles on metal. Sizes range from 125mm (5in) maximum opening to 300mm (12in) maximum opening.

15. Centre punches. A fine centre punch is shown towards the right of the photograph, a coarse centre punch towards the left. These are used for spot marking metal to give a guide for drilling. The point is marked by

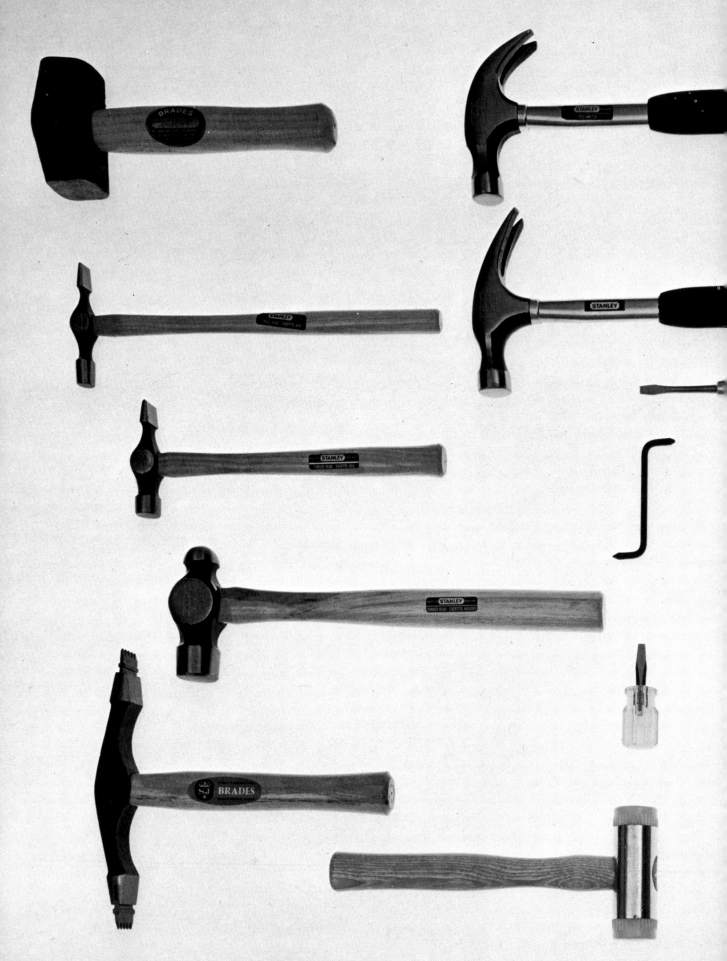

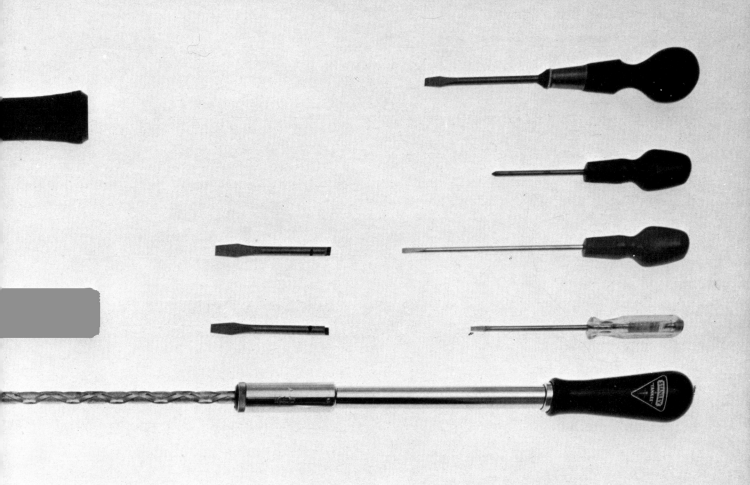

Hammers and screwdrivers

Fig. 1. Club hammer. 1130-1800g (2½-4lb). Used for general heavy hammering, particularly in building and demolition work. In conjunction with a bolster chisel it is used for cutting bricks, shaping paving stones, knocking through brickwork and so on.

Fig. 2. Pin or telephone hammer. 100-110g (3½-4oz). Used for tacks, panel pins, fine nailing and braddling. The wedge shaped end is used for starting small nails while holding them between your fingers.

Fig. 3. Warrington or cross pein hammer. 170g-450g (6-16oz). Used for general nailing, joinery and planishing or metal beating.

Fig. 4. Ball pein or engineer's hammer. 110-1360g (4oz-3lb). Used for metal working. The round end is used for starting rivets, for example. This is the hammer to use for *masonry nails* as its hardened steel face will not chip.

Fig. 5. Scutch or comb hammer. Used for trimming and shaping common or hard bricks which would damage a brick trowel. The combs can be replaced after wear.

Fig. 6. Soft-headed hammer. Used in metal beating and in general work where it is important not to damage a surface. The soft head also avoids the possibility of a spark setting off an explosion.

Fig. 7. Claw hammer. 450-570g (16-24oz). Used for general purpose carpentry, particularly for driving and removing nails. When taking out nails, make sure the nail head is well into the claw and lever evenly.

Fig. 8. Ripping claw hammer. Used similarly to the claw hammer in work where speed rather than care is essential.

Screwdrivers, too, have a range of functions and sizes. Match the screwdriver tip as closely as possible to the screw slot to prevent damage to either.

Fig. 9. Standard slotted screwdriver. Used for general screwdriving of single slotted screws.

Fig. 10. Crosshead screwdriver (Pozidriv or Philips). Used with cross slotted screws to provide greater purchase and positive location.

Fig. 11. Parallel tip screwdriver. Used in engineering, and otherwise, when the screw sits inside a recess of the same width.

Fig. 12. Electrical screwdriver. The insulated handle contains a neon indicator which lights when the blade is touched against a live source. You must ensure that the insulatation is safe for the voltages you intend to check.

Fig. 13. Archimedean (or Yankee) spiral ratchet screwdriver. Used for general purpose screwdriving. Pushing the handle home automatically drives or removes screws. When locked, at length or closed, the ratchet allows screws to be driven or removed without taking the blade from the slot.

Fig. 14. The chuck can take blades of different widths, and even drill bits.

Fig. 15. Double-ended cranked screw-driver. Used for driving awkwardly-placed screws.

Fig. 16. Stub screwdriver. Used in confined spaces. You can grip the square shank with a spanner to give greater purchase.

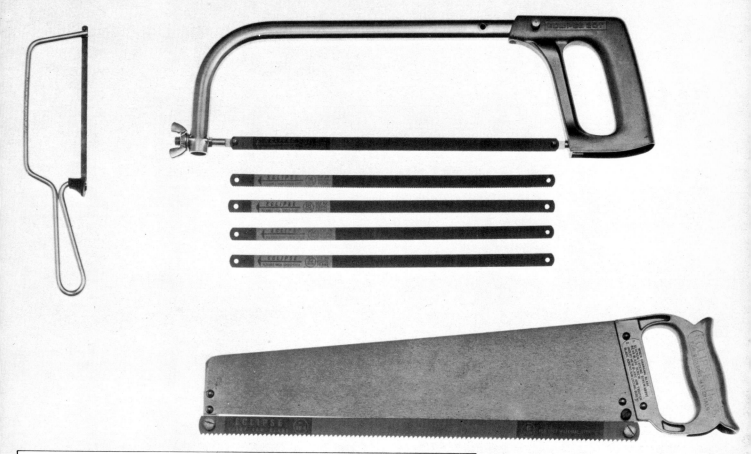

Saws

Knowledge of a few technical terms will help explain the DATA SHEET.

Points per inch (ppi) refers to the number of saw teeth to the inch along the saw blade. Woodworking saws with a small number of ppi are suitable for cutting softwoods and those with a larger number should be used for sawing hardwoods.

The kerf is the name given to the width of the saw cut.

The gullet is the distance between one saw tooth and the next. The gullet carries sawdust out of the kerf to make the task of sawing easier.

Fig. 1. Hand saw. There are 3 types of hand saw. **A. Rip saw.** 661mm (26in) long with 5 ppi. It is used for cutting softwoods working with the grain. The teeth are chisel edged to shave off the fibres of the grain. The large gullet carries the sawdust out of the kerf. **B. Cross cut saw.** 610mm to 661mm long (24in to 26in) with 6, 7 or 8 ppi. The saw is used to cut across the grain of hardwoods and softwoods and for working with the grain on very hard woods. The knife point shaped teeth gives the sharper cut needed when working across the grain. **C. Panel saw.** 508mm to 558mm long (20in to 22in) with 10 ppi. The panel saw is used for fine cross cut and jointing work and for cutting plywood, blockboard and hardboard. The teeth are a similar shape to those of a cross cut saw.

Fig. 2. Double sided saw for cutting greenwood. One side is fine toothed for cutting slender plants and the other has large open gullets to carry away sawdust when cutting larger timber.

Fig. 3. Tenon or back saw. 200-357mm long with 13, 14, 15, 16 or 20 ppi. It is used for jointing and for cutting across the grain on small pieces. The back may be brass or steel. The saw with 20 ppi is for cutting dovetails. Its blade is thin to give greater accuracy. All cuts made with a dovetail saw should be along the grain as it performs a ripping action.

Fig. 4. A. Saw knife or pad saw with a keyhole blade. **B. Metal keyhole saw blade.** Both are used for cutting small irregular shapes in the middle of a board.

Fig. 5. Flooring saw. 6 to 10 ppi. The rounded nose allows you to cut into floor boards without damaging adjacent boards.

Fig. 6. General purpose saw. The teeth are hardened and tempered. It is used for cutting wood laminates, plastic, mild steel, rubber, asbestos, etc. It is a handy odd job tool but is not recommended for first class, accurate work. The handle is adjustable to enable work in awkward places and positions.

Fig. 7. Coping saw. It has very fine teeth and is used for cutting tight curves. Tension is applied to the replaceable blade by tightening the handle.

Fig. 8. Fret or piercing saw. It is similar to coping saw but is deeper to allow work with larger boards. There are many types of blade available, the choice depending on what material you wish to cut.

Fig. 9. Junior hack saw. General purpose saw for light metal work.

Fig. 10. Adjustable frame hack saw. It can take 254mm to 305mm (10in to 12in) blades. Blades are available in range of ppi from 14 to 32.

Fig. 11. Sheet saw. This is available with 305mm (12in) blade with 14 to 32 ppi for cutting metal or 407mm (16in) blade with 6, 10 or 14 ppi for cutting thicker building material such as asbestos cement insulation slabs and metal covered plywood. It is more accurate for cutting straight lines than general purpose saw.

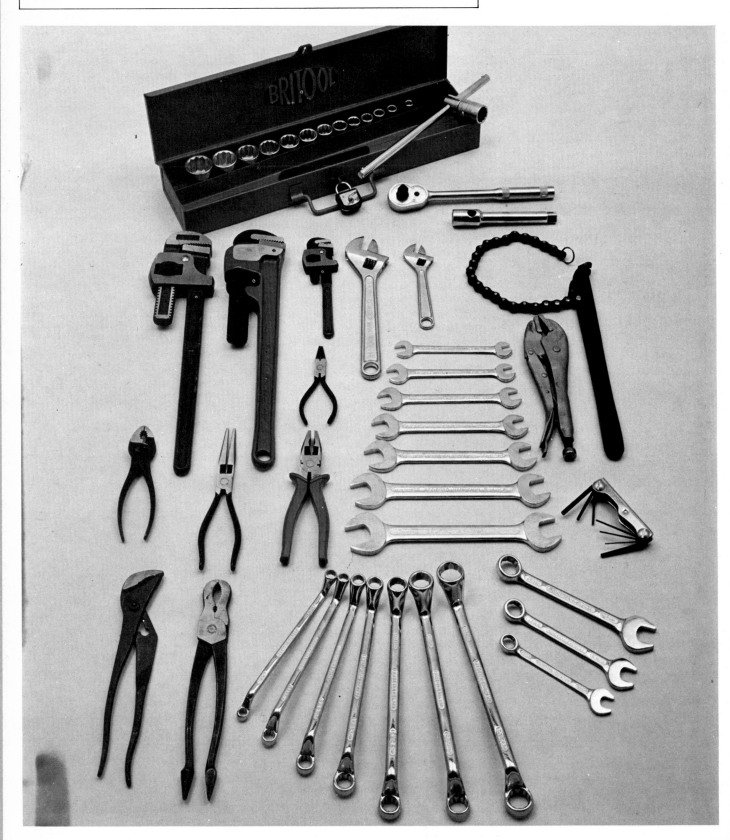

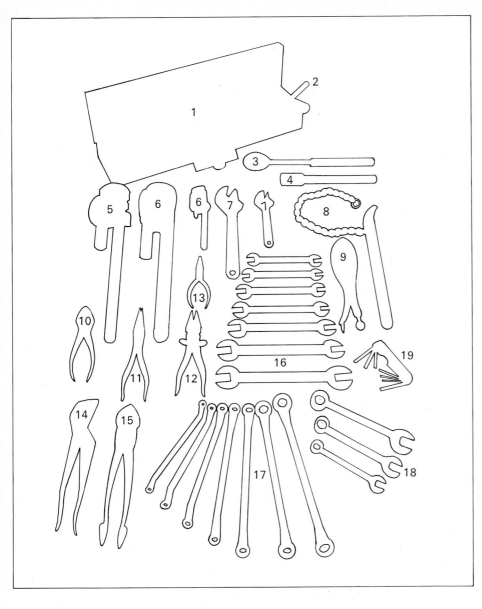

The jaws are too large for such nuts which can easily be damaged – and this could result in the loosening of these nuts and bolts and the creation of a potentially dangerous situation.

8. Chain wrench. This is an easily adjustable wrench for shifting heavily rusted or encrusted iron pipe joints. It is lighter to use though less effective than the heavy duty pipe wrench. Available in handle lengths of between 300mm (12in) and 450mm (18in).

9. Universal gripping and clamping tool. This tool has a variety of trade names including Mole and Grip-Lok. Available in a wide variety of shapes and sizes. An attachment is available which allows the tool to be used as a mini bench vice.

10. Slip joint pliers. This tool has a thin section to allow the nose to slip into tight places. It has two jaw opening positions and a shear type wire cutter.

11. Needle nosed side cutting pliers. These are used for fine wire work. Radio pliers are the same except that they have insulated handles.

12. Electrician's or combination square nosed pliers. These are heavy duty pliers with a square nose and serated hole – both of which can be used for holding small diameter tubing and nuts and bolts. Usually this tool has two types of wire cutter, a shear cutter and a side cutter. The handles are insulated but make sure when you buy this tool that the handles are guaranteed to withstand any voltage with which the pliers are likely to come into contact.

13. Round nosed pliers. These pliers do not have a great deal of domestic application but are useful for coiling or twisting wire.

14. Water pump pliers. These are adjustable pliers with up to six different jaw positions. They are general purpose pliers useful in plumbing.

15. Scotch gas pliers. These are general purpose pliers, used where a light but firm grip is needed.

16. Open ended spanners and wrenches. These are available in every nut and thread size encountered.

17. Ring spanners. It is perferable to use these spanners wherever possible as they are far less likely to slip than open ended spanners. You can also obtain greater torque with these spanners.

18. Combination spanners. These tools have an open spanner at one end and a ring spanner at the other. For a complete set you will obviously need twice as many spanners than for a full set of ring or open ended spanners.

19. Allen keys or hollow head wrenches. These are used with hexagonal hollow headed screws.

1. Socket set. Some of the accessories used with the socket set are the tee bar wrench (2), the rachet handle (3) and the extension bar (4). Sockets are available in the following thread styles:- American Fine (AF), British Standard Whitworth (BSW), Iso metric (M) and British Association (BA). Sockets for the last thread style are very small. These tools are used for loosening nuts and, providing you use the right size socket, the tool will not slip. There is, therefore, less chance of damaging the head of the nut than with a spanner. You can also achieve greater torque, or circular force, with these tools than with a spanner. Other accessories for the socket set (not shown) are speed braces and the universal joint. These allow the sockets to be used in awkward positions. A torque wrench (not shown) can be calibrated to allow nuts or bolts to be tightened to a specific pressure. Socket sets are fairly expensive to buy but, as with most of the tools shown here, they can usually be hired.

2. Tee bar wrench.
3. Rachet handle.
4. Extension bar.
5 and 6. Pipe wrenches. These types of pipe wrench are available in lengths ranging from 150mm (6in) to 1000mm (48in) and will cope with pipe sizes ranging from 13mm (½in) to 150mm (6in) diameter. These wrenches are mainly used for work on iron pipes – they can easily damage softer metals like copper and brass. The head is sprung loaded and this, together with the toothed jaws, enables a strong grip to be exerted on round pipe sections as opposed to hexagonal nut sections.

7. Adjustable wrench or spanner. This is a very useful tool, particularly for copper plumbing. They are available in a range of lengths from 100mm (4in) to 500mm (20in) with jaw opening of between 13mm (½in) to 163mm (2½in). Do not use this wrench on fine engineering nuts or bolts of the type used, for example, for automobile assembly.

Cramping and clamping tools

Accurate carpentry, especially the sawing or planing of timber, depends on holding the workpiece in a steady position. Also, one of the last stages in all carpentry projects, that of assembling the components, requires the application of sufficient pressure to push the pieces together. This DATA SHEET illustrates the common clamping tools – those that hold workpieces firmly – and cramping tools – those that force components together.

This brief guide to cramping techniques enables you to make a really efficient job of your projects.

1. Woodworker's vice. This can either be fixed permanently to a work bench (as in 14) or may be fitted with a simple cramping device to allow temporary fixing to a table. This model is shown here. Jaw widths vary from 100mm (4in) to 263mm (10½in).

2. Sash cramp. This is used for cramping large, regular-shaped objects such as doors and window frames. These cramps are available in the simple rectangle (shown here), light T-bar, and strong T-bar sections. Working lengths vary from 610mm (24in) to 2.1m (84in).

3. Lengthening bar for a sash cramp. This is used for extending the working length of a sash cramp. Available in lengths ranging from 610mm (24in) to 1.5m (61in).

4. Mechanic's vice. This sturdily built vice will withstand heavy hammering. Use fibre jaws with the vice when holding soft metals. This type of vice is also available with a swivel base and comes with jaw widths ranging between 63mm (2½in) and 200mm (8in).

5. Corner or mitre cramp. This is used for holding two mitred pieces of timber at right angles to each other while they are pinned or glued – particularly useful in the construction of pictures and other frames. Some mitre cramps have a device which guides a tenon or back saw cut to give a reasonably accurate 45° mitre.

6 and 6A. Heavy duty and medium duty G or C cramp. This is the most common portable holding tool. Available in jaw openings ranging from 50mm (2in) to 457mm (18in).

7. Deep throat G or C cramp. Available in jaw openings of between 50mm (2in) and 100mm (4in).

8. Bench holdfast. A very quick action holding device which drops into metal collars fixed into the bench surface at convenient points. Maximum openings range from 172mm (6⅞in) to 225mm (9in).

9. Quick action cramp. This is probably the most useful all-round cramp, but it is not as readily available from tool stores as the G cramp.

10. Cramp heads. These are used in conjunction with a length of hardwood batten with fixing holes drilled through it. This tool is a cheap, but less stable, alternative to the sash cramp.

11. Universal gripping and clamping wrench. This adjustable wrench can be set by means of a knurled adjusting screw to grip or lock at a pre-set jaw width. It is available under several trade names including Mole and Grip-Lok.

12. Edging cramp. This tool is particularly useful for fixing laminate or timber edging strip to narrow sections. Available in 50mm (2in), 63mm (2½in) and 75mm (3in) working openings.

13. Web clamp. This is a very versatile tool which can be used for cramping irregular-shaped pieces as well as regular-shaped items.

14. Carpenter's front vice. See 1.

15. Tail vice. This is used to hold any size of timber in conjunction with the metal bench dogs (15A). It enables a workpiece up to 7/8ths of the bench length to be firmly held.

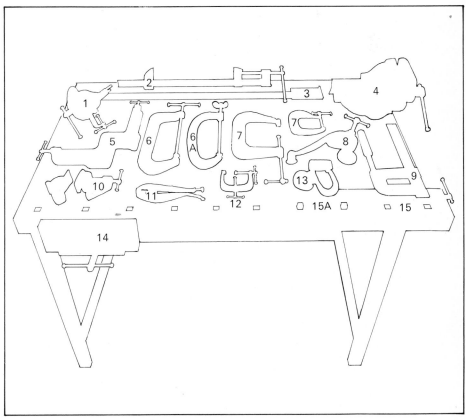

All about nails

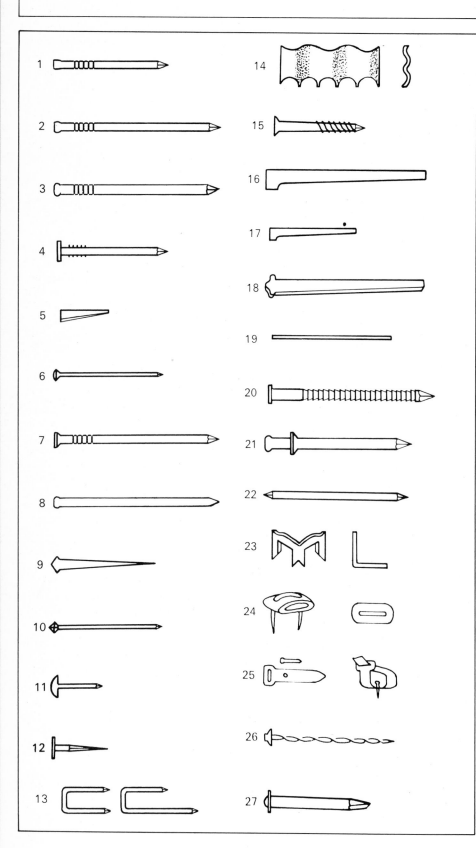

Commonly used nails:

1. Lost head nail. Head can be punched below surface for a neater finish in fine work.
2. Round wire nail. For work where strength is more important than a neat appearance.
3. Oval wire nail. Oval cross-section makes nail less likely to split wood.
4. Clout nail. Large-headed, for fixing roofing felt, etc., to wood.
5. Picture sprig. Headless, holds glass to picture frames; also for fixing down lino.
6. Panel pin. Small nail for securing light pieces of wood; used in conjunction with glue.
7. French nail. For rough carpentry work; large, ugly head ensures a firm grip.
8. Masonry pin. Hardened steel nail for fixing wood direct to masonry.
9. Wrought nail. Soft iron nail; point can be 'clenched' (turned over) for extra grip.
10. Hardboard pin. Unusual head shape countersinks itself in hardboard, can be filled over.
11. Chair nail. Decorative head for fixing leather, etc., in upholstery work.
12. Tack. Small nail with broad head, for fixing down carpets and fabrics.
13. Staple. For securing wire, upholstery springs, etc., to woodwork.

Special-purpose nails:

14. Corrugated fastener. For butt-jointing timber quickly and easily: not very strong.
15. Screw nail. For fastening sheet materials to wood. Great holding power.
16. Floor brad. Holds down floorboards. Great holding power, but now obsolete.
17. Joiner's brad. Small carpentry nail used where extra holding power is needed.
18. Cut clasp nail. Obsolete general-purpose nail superseded by oval wire nail.
19. Needle point. Steel pin for fixing small mouldings: head broken off flush.
20. Annular nail. Used like the screw nail (15), but larger and stronger.
21. Duplex head nail. For concrete formwork: double head permits easy removal.
22. Dowel nail. For end-to-end hidden joints in high-quality work.
23. Chevron. For joining corners of frames where strength and appearance are unimportant.
24. Insulated staple. For securing telephone and other low-voltage wiring.
25. Saddle tack. For wiring: first tacked down, then folded over and fastened.
26. Roofing nail. For securing corrugated iron or asbestos roofing to wooden rafters.
27. Chisel-headed nail. For fastening gutters, etc., direct to mortar.

All about screws, nuts and bolts

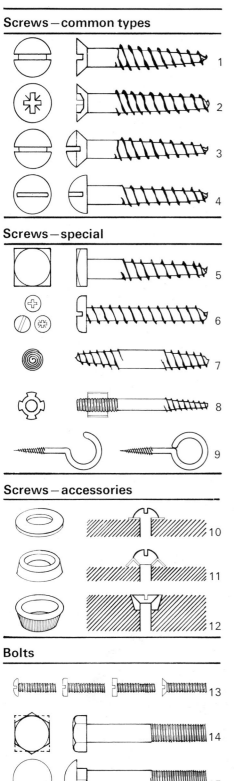

Screws—common types

1

2

3

4

Screws—special

5

6

7

8

9

Screws—accessories

10

11

12

Bolts

13

14

15

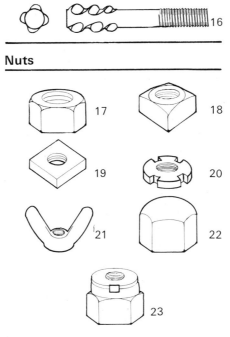

16

Nuts

17

18

19

20

21

22

23

Bolts—accessories

24

25

26

27

Screws and bolts provide enormous holding power, but are simple to fix. The types shown here are the ones you are likely to come across when fixing both wood and metal, together with the most commonly used accessories.

Screws / common types
1. Countersunk wood screw. For general use; head let in flush with wood surface.
2. Pozidriv head countersunk screw. Fixed with special non-slip screwdriver.
3. Raised head countersunk screw. For fixing door-handle plates, etc., to wood; decorative head designed to be seen.
4. Round head screw. For fixing hardware without countersunk holes to wood.

Screws / special
5. Coach screw. Extra-large wood screw with square head; tightened with spanner.
6. Self-tapping screw. For sheet metal; cuts its own thread as it is screwed in; has slot, Phillips (cross), or Pozidriv head.
7. Dowel screw. For invisible fixings; two pieces of wood twisted together to tighten.
8. Handrail screw. For 'pocket' screwing; head screwed on from side with screwdriver.
9. Cup hook and screw eye. Large number of shapes and sizes available.

Screws / accessories
10. Flat washer. For round head screws; spreads load to give a strong grip.
11. Screw cup-raised type. For countersunk or raised head countersunk screws; spreads load, improves appearance.
12. Screw cup-socket type. For countersunk screws; hammered into pre-drilled hole for a completely flush fixing.

Bolts
13. Machine screw. Not a screw, but a bolt. Small sizes only; available with (l to r) round, pan, cheese or countersunk heads.
14. Machine bolt. Large sizes only; available with hexagonal or square heads.
15. Coach bolt. Large bolt with a square collar under the head that stops it from turning when the nut is done up.
16. Rag bolt. For bolting wood or metal to concrete; jagged head is set in wet concrete and holds bolt firmly when concrete dries.

Nuts
17. Hexagonal nut. Commonest type, available in a wide range of sizes.
18. Square nut. This type available in large sizes only, e.g. for coach bolts.
19. Flat square nut. Small sizes only; thinner than 18 in proportion to width.
20. Handrail nut. Used on handrail screw (8) and in other places where nuts have to be tightened from the side in a small space.
21. Wing nut. Tightened by hand; for use where nuts must be undone quickly.
22. Domed nut. Decorative nut, generally chromium plated.
23. Locking nut. For places where vibration might make nuts undo; has fibre ring inside to make it hard to turn.

Bolts / accessories
24. Flat washer. Same as (10); used in same way; also makes nuts easier to turn.
25. Single coil washer. For metal fastening only; spring shape prevents bolts from undoing.
26. Internal and external tooth washers. Gripping teeth keep bolts from undoing.
27. Timber connector. Used between pieces of wood bolted together.

1. The butt joint is the simplest of all joints in carpentry. It may be made straight or right-angled, and needs nails, glue or screws to hold it together.

2. The dowelled joint is basically a butt joint reinforced with dowels—lengths of wooden rod. Both halves of the joint are drilled at once to make the holes line up.

3. The secret dowelled joint is better-looking, because the ends of the dowels do not show. The two rows of holes are drilled separately, so great accuracy is essential.

4. The mitred joint has a very neat appearance, because no end grain is visible. Unfortunately, it is a very weak type of joint unless it is reinforced in some way.

5. The halving joint is used at the corners of a rectangular frame. It is simple to make, has a reasonably neat appearance, and is quite strong if glued together.

6. The T halving joint is a variant of the usual L-shaped halving. It is used in conjunction with the previous type of halving in the construction of simple frameworks.

7. The X halving joint is the third member of this versatile family. It is used where two pieces of timber have to cross without increasing the thickness of the frame.

8. The dovetail halving joint is an extra-strong halving. Its angled sides make it impossible to pull apart in a straight line, though it still needs glue to hold it rigid.

9. The through housing joint is used for supporting the ends of shelves, because it resists a downward pull very well. It, too, must be reinforced with glue or screws.

10. The stopped housing joint has a neater appearance, but is harder to make because of the difficulty of cutting out the bottom of the rectangular slot neatly.

11. Tongued-and-grooved joints are most commonly found along the edge of ready-made boarding. But a right-angled version is also found, for example at corners of boxes.

12. The lapped joint has a rebate cut in one side to hide most of the end grain. It is often found in cheap cabinet work, because it is easy to make with power tools.

13. The mortise-and-tenon joint is a very strong joint used to form T shapes in frames. The mortise is the slot on the left; the tenon is the tongue on the right.

14. The through mortise-and-tenon joint is stronger than the simple type. It is generally locked with small hardwood wedges driven in beside, or into saw cuts in, the tenon.

15. The haunched mortise-and-tenon is used at the top of a frame. The top of the tenon is cut away so that the mortise can be closed at both ends, and so retain its strength.

Four more kinds of mortise-and-tenon joint:

16. The bare-faced tenon is offset, with a 'shoulder' on one side only. It is used for joining pieces of different thicknesses.

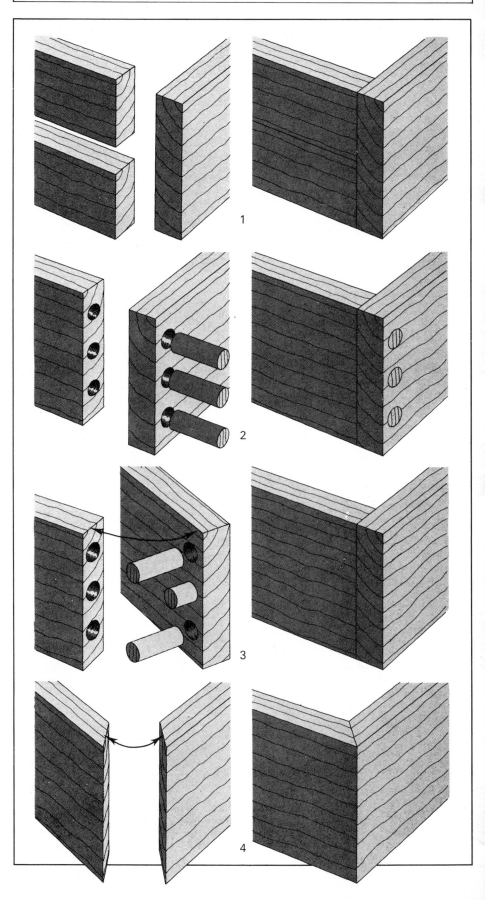

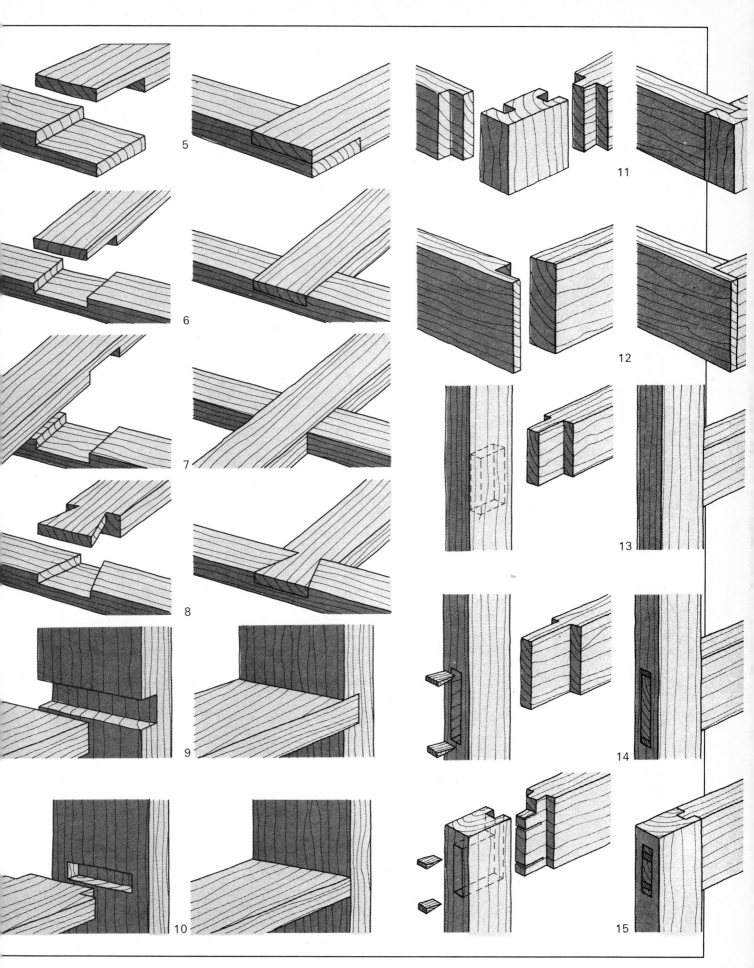

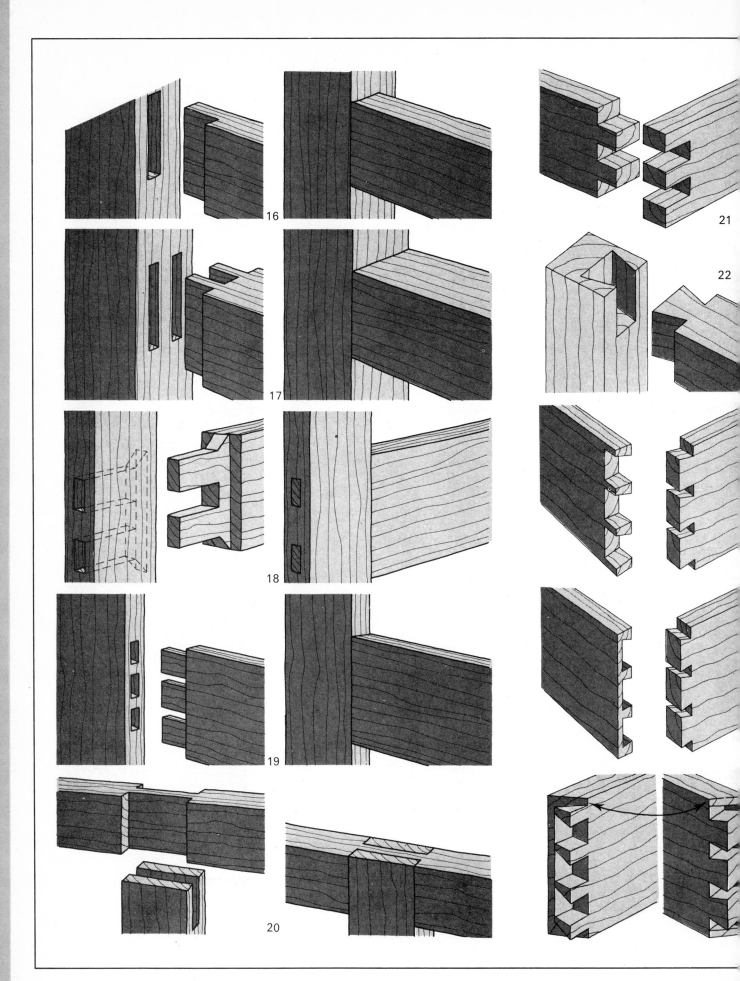

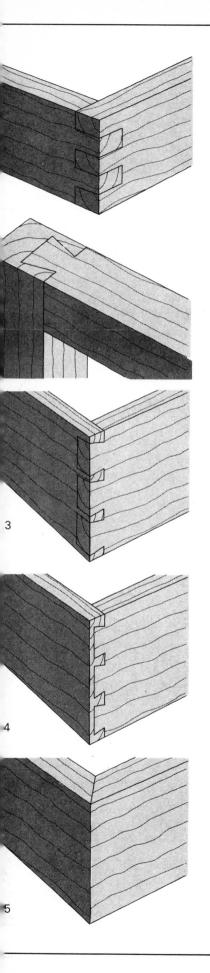

17. Twin tenons are used in very thick timber. They give the joint extra rigidity and do not weaken the wood as much as usual.

18. Forked tenons add rigidity to a deep, narrow joint. The angled edge of the tenon is sometimes found in a haunched m-&-t joint.

19. Stub tenons are used on even deeper joints, but are weaker and less rigid than the forked tenons shown above.

20. The bridle joint is used where a long horizontal piece has to be fitted into the tops of several vertical pieces.

21. The box joint is quite strong and has a decorative appearance. It is used for the corners of wide frames and boxes.

22. The single dovetail, like all dovetails, is extremely strong and hard to pull apart. It is used at the corners of heavy frames.

23. The through dovetail is used at the corners of boxes where great strength and a good appearance are required.

24. The lapped dovetail is nearly as strong, but also has one plain face. It is used in very high-quality cabinet work.

25. The mitred secret dovetail is also used in very high-quality work. It looks like a mitred joint, but grips like a dovetail.

26. The lapped secret dovetail looks like a lapped joint. It is slightly easier to make than a mitred secret dovetail.

27. The cogged joint is like a dovetail with the tails subdivided into smaller tails. It is extremely strong and rigid.

28. The scarfed joint is used for joining frame members end-to-end where only moderate strength is required.

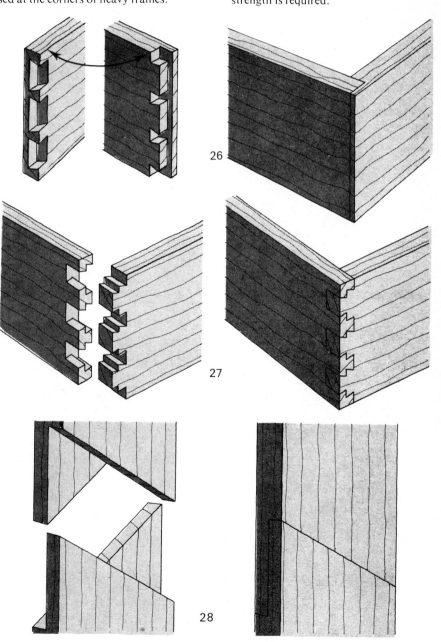

333

Index

If a page number in this index appears in bold type, an illustration accompanies the text on that page.

Pictures supplied by:

Bavaria Verlag: 55T, 61, 189, Peter Bell: 26TL&B, Robert Belton: 141TL, Ueli Berger A. Hablutzel: 197, John Bethell/Westinghouse: 74/5, 75, 234B, 247, Leonard Bezzola: 220, 253B, Hedrich Blessing/Architect Alden & Dow Associates: 51, 57, 134TL, Michael Boys: 28CR, 47, 98, 100, 101, 151T, 186, 190T, 250, 256BR, 276C&B, 279B, 306/7, Camera Press: 64, 129, Heidede Carstensen: 58, 72/3, 152, 196, 298T,BL, 306L, 308, Heidede Carstensen/Studio Die Wohnform: 34, 36/7, 55B&T, 60, 78/9, 155T, 177, 178, 178/9, 179, 229/230, 284T, 284C, 247B, 252, 256TL, 256CR, 307, 308/9, Heidede Carstensen/Studio Huelsta: 104, 106, Heidede Carstensen/Moebel: 150B, Heidede Carstensen/Studio 2000: 13, 69, 76, 77, 95, 96, 150T, 151B, 156, Heidede Carstensen/Studio Umstaetter: 149, 295L&R, 296T, BL&BR, 298BR, 299, Heidede Carstensen/Zuhause: 219, Cindy Cassidy/J. Vaughan: 234T, La Maison de Marie Claire: 126, Concord Lighting: 254, Conway Picture Library: 82/3, 88T&B, 153T, 180C, 233C, 277, Clive Corless: 303, 304T&B, 305, Crown Wallpaper & Paint: 9, DGW: 24, Dralon: 10/11, 18, Alan Duns: 191, 220(insert), 221(insert), 259, Brecht Einzig: 141BL, Richard Einzig: 14, 59, 250/1, 276T, Elle/Scoop/Transworld: 309, Features International: 97TL, Femina/ Conzette & Huber: 23, 233C, Fibre Glass Ltd.: 262, courtesy of Formica Ltd.: 310, 311T&B, 312T&B, Studio Geisler: 26/7, 27, 28T&BL, Rob Grant: 195T, 284B, 245, James Halstead Ltd.: 215, 217L&TR, Nelson Hargreaves: 38/9, 111, 112, 113, 116, 117, 118, 161, 162, 163, 165, 166/7, 210/11/12, 259, 267/68/69, 316/7, 318/9, 320/1, 322/3, 324/5, 326/7, John Hovell: 134TR&BR, courtesy of Laconite Ltd.: 200, Le-be: 195B, Jean Pierre Leloir: 80, Bill McLaughlin: 20, 97BR, Gordon McLeish: 214, 217BR, Nigel Messett: 101, 144, 145, 157, 158, 159, 160, 270, 282/3, Brian Morris: 180B, 234C, 247TL& TR, 255, Nairn Floors: 221, Grazia Neri: 43, J.C. Nicolas Pour Print: 81, Nilson/Anthony: 83, 97BL, PAF International: 108T&B, 288, Photo & Text: 232, Pilkington: 169, 170, 171, 173/74/75, Pinto: 97TR, Tim Street Porter/ Liz Whiting: 86, Paul Redman: 50, 65, 66, 222B, Ruth Rutter: 142, Sandersons Ltd.: 233T, Julian Seddon/David Essex: 180T, Mira Showers: 198R, Harry Smith: 134BL, Syndication International: 10, 11, 12, 135, 136, 281, Thorn Lighting: 253T, Transworld: 25, 79, 87, 187, 227, Tri-Art: 19, 21, Tubby: 279T, 204/5, 206, Elizabeth Whiting: 78B, 79T, 85, 153B, 155B, 188, 190T, 198L, 253C, 256TR, 297, Wicanders Ltd.: 222, Zefa: 301T.

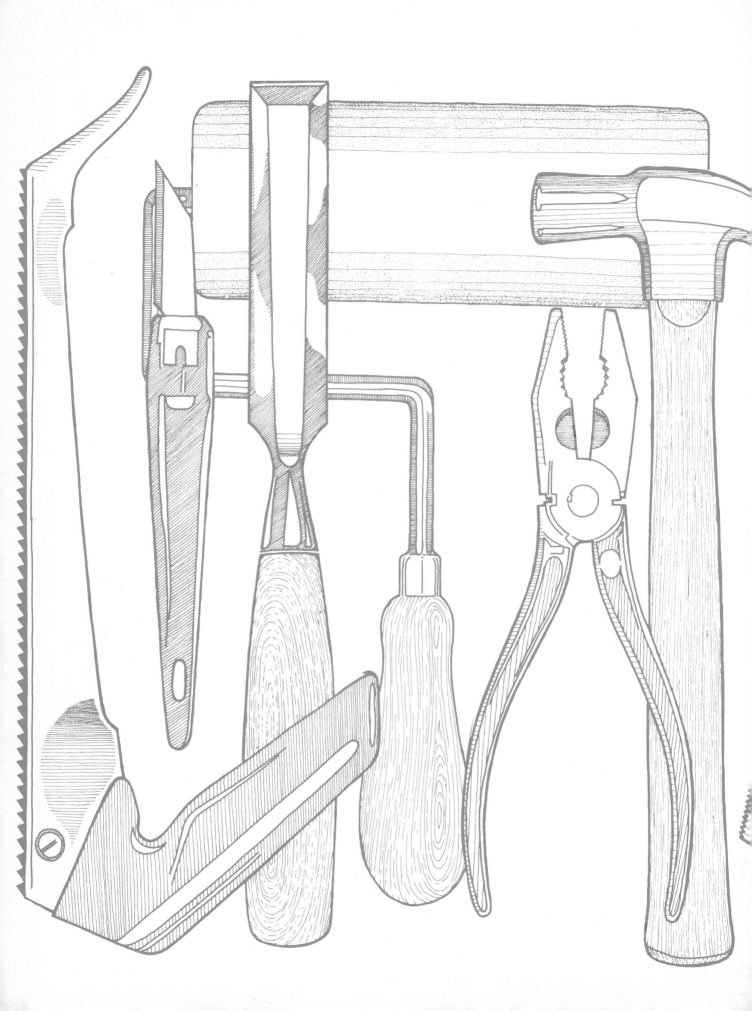